COMMUNITIES AND TECHNOLOGIES 2005

Communities and Technologies 2005

Proceedings of the Second Communities and
Technologies Conference, Milano 2005

Edited by

PETER VAN DEN BESSELAAR
University of Amsterdam The Netherlands

GIORGIO DE MICHELIS
University of Milano Bicocca, Italy

JENNY PREECE
University of Maryland, U.S.A.

and

CARLA SIMONE
University of Milano Bicocca, Italy

 Springer

ISBN-13 978-90-481-6904-7 (PB)
ISBN-13 978-1-4020-3591-3 (e-book)

Published by Springer,
P.O. Box 17, 3300 AA Dordrecht, The Netherlands.

Printed on acid-free paper

Table of Contents

PART 1: LOCAL COMMUNITIES

PART 2: VIRTUAL COMMUNITIES

PART 3: KNOWLEDGE & SCIENTIFIC COMMUNITIES

PART 4: EXPERIMENTS

PART 5: SYSTEMS

From the Conference Chairs

This volume consists of the papers presented at the second international conference on Communities and Technologies (C&T 2005). After a very successful first conference in 2003 in Amsterdam, the second one attracted about the same number of submissions and workshop proposals. This suggests that the scholarly interest in the relationships between communities and technologies is lasting, and that the C&T conference has become a major international forum for presenting and discussing this work.

Researchers have a growing interest in the effects information and communication technologies have on communities, because communities are increasingly recognized as one of the basic forms of social organization and coordination. The needs, interests, and practices of community members and the locality of the community influence how communities evolve and function. Communities provide the foundation for social practices, experience and social integration in the following ways.

Firstly, within a globalizing society, communities play a crucial role. Problems such as new forms of political participation and civic engagement, maintenance of cultural identities, or the integration of various social groups need to be tackled at the community level. Secondly, communities also reshape how we learn and share knowledge, both as individuals and in and between organizations. While earlier research and development focused on storing, classifying and retrieving explicit knowledge represented in documents and data bases, it is now generally accepted that communities are an important forum for sharing implicit (tacit) situated knowledge. Thirdly, knowledge sharing between communities is a prerequisite for innovation and social change. And finally, new types of communities, e.g., on-line communities, change relationships between producers and consumers, doctors and patients, teachers and students, and between citizens and politicians.

Advances in electronic networking technologies embody promise to enable and stimulate inter-community and inter-organizational cooperation and communication if managed appropriately. However, many of the ICT infrastructures and systems that are intended to do this fail because of lack of adequate understanding about the social dynamics of communities. In practice, information technologies may support or hinder community formation, or change the dynamics of existing communities for better or worse depending on how they are employed. A considerable research agenda needs to be addressed if society is to reap the benefits of social information technologies.

Understanding the relationships between communities and technologies requires multidisciplinary research efforts involving researchers from different fields of applied computer science and information science (Computer Supported

Cooperative Work, Computer Supported Collaborative Learning, Artificial Intelligence, Information Retrieval, Human Computer Interaction, Information Systems, Social Informatics) and social sciences (Anthropology, Communication Studies, Economics, Innovation Studies, Management and Organization Science, Psychology, Political Science, Sociology).

In this volume we are pleased to present research papers from a range of disciplines covering a variety of topics. These papers result from a selective reviewing process. We received more than 100 full paper submissions. We undertook an intensive peer review process in which each paper was assessed by at least three reviewers. This resulted in the selection of 23 papers that are included in this volume. Both the number of submissions, and the quality and diversity of accepted papers indicate the development of the research field and we are sure that you will enjoy reading them. The 23 papers have been written by some 60 authors, with an average of almost three authors per paper. And, in five cases the co-authors have different nationalities. This indicates that the C&T research field itself is also a connected community.

   The research papers in this volume are only one aspect of the C&T 2005 conference. In addition to the paper sessions, the conference offered thirteen challenging workshops, a panel, a highly demanded tutorial by Larry Prusak (IBM Consulting Group, Boston, USA), and stimulating keynote lectures by Marco Susani (Advanced Concept Group, Motorola, Cambridge, USA) and Noshir Contractor (University of Illinois, Urbana-Champaign, USA).

A conference like this one cannot take place without considerable enthusiasm, support and encouragement as well as hard work. In particular, we gratefully thank:

- All those who submitted a paper or workshop proposal to the conference. The standard was very high, which reflects well on the state of art in the field.
- All of those who contributed to the conference through organizing workshops, and through paper presentations.
- All of those who contributed to the organization of the conference. Setting up a major international conference is a complex endeavor and the efforts of many are needed to make it a success. Special thanks go to the workshops chair Fiorella De Cindio, the local organizing chairs Alessandra Agostini and Marcello Sarini, and to Silvia Calegari who worked hard to develop and maintain the conference www-site. Thanks for that!
- The members Program Committee and the other reviewers who worked diligently to ensure that the conference was of high technical quality.
- The sponsors of C&T 2005 for their contributions to the conference.

Many of these individuals to whom we owe thanks are listed elsewhere in this volume.

These proceedings are a contribution to the academic discourse on communities and technologies. Keep up the good work!

Peter Van den Besselaar   Giorgio De Michelis

Jenny Preece   Carla   Simone

C&T 2005 SPONSORS

Convivio, the Network for People-Centred Design of Interactive Systems

University of Milano Bicocca, Italy
- Department of Informatics, Systems and Communication (DISCo)
- Inter-disciplinary Doctorat on Quality of Information Society (QUA-SI)

University of Milano, Italy

CONFERENCE CHAIRS

Giorgio De Michelis	University of Milano Bicocca, Italy
Carla Simone	University of Milano Bicocca, Italy

PROGRAM CHAIRS

Jenny Preece	University of Maryland, USA
Peter Van den Besselaar	University of Amsterdam & Royal Netherlands Academy of Arts and Sciences – The Netherlands

WORKSHOP CHAIR

Fiorella De Cindio	University of Milano, Italy

LOCAL ORGANIZING CHAIRS

Alessandra Agostini	University of Milano, Italy
Marcello Sarini	University of Milano Bicocca, Italy

PROGRAM COMMITTEE

Mark Ackerman	University of Michigan, USA
Alessandra Agostini	University of Milano, Italy
Erik Andriessen	Delft Technical University, The Netherlands
Stefania Bandini	University of Milano Bicocca, Italy
Andreas Becks	Fraunhofer FIT, Germany
Ann Blandford	University College London, UK
Amy Bruckman	Gatech, USA
John Carroll	Virginia Tech, USA
Andrew Clement	University of Toronto, Canada
Elisabeth Davenport	Napier University, UK
Peter Day	University of Brighton, UK

Peter Van Baalen   Erasmus Universiteit, The Netherlands
Peter Van den Besselaar   University of Amsterdam & KNAW, Netherlands
Bart Van den Hooff   University of Amsterdam, The Netherlands
Barry Wellman   University of Toronto, Canada
Etienne Wenger   CPsquare, USA
Volker Wulf   University of Siegen & Fraunhofer-FIT, Germany

OTHER REVIEWERS

Matthias Baume   Technische Universität München, Germany
Miriam Daum   Technische Universität München, Germany
Aldo De Moor   Tilburg University, The Netherlands
Antonio Dini   University of Milano, Italy
Marco Durissini   Fraunhofer FIT, Germany
Magy Seif El-Nasr   Pennsylvania State University
Umer Farooq   Pennsylvania State University
Andrea Forte   Georgia Tech, USA
James M. Hudson   Georgia Tech, USA
David Kensche   RWTH Aachen, Germany
Markus Klann   Fraunhofer FIT, Germany
Ivan Longhi   University of Milano, Italy
Marco Loregian   University of Milano Bicocca, Italy
Sara Manzoni   University of Milano Bicocca, Italy
Selmar Meents   Free University, The Netherlands
Marco Prestipino   University of Zurich
Daniela Redolfi   University of Milano, Italy
Tim Reichling   University of Siegen, Germany
Laura Ripamonti   University of Milano, Italy
Mary Beth Rosson   Pennsylvania State University
Uwe Sandner   Technische Universität München, Germany
Wendy Schafer   Pennsylvania State University
Christian Seeling   Fraunhofer-FIT, Germany
Leonardo Sonnante   University of Milano, Italy
Gunnar Stevens   University of Siegen, Germany
Liisa Syrjänen   University of Oulu
Yuriy Taranovych   Technische Universität München, Germany
Michele Telaro   University of Milano Bicocca, Italy
Walter Thoen   Free University, The Netherlands
Eleftheria Vaseiliadou   University of Amsterdam, The Netherlands
Michael Veith   University of Siegen, Germany
Sven Walter   Technische Universität München, Germany
Lu Xiao   Pennsylvania State University

Does the Internet Enhance the Capacity of Community Associations?

Christopher Weare[+], William E. Loges[*], Nail Oztas[∘]

[+]University of Southern California, USA *Oregon State University, USA ∘Gazi University, Turkey
weare@usc.edu, bill.loges@oregonstate.edu, noztas@gazi.edu.tr

Abstract. We employ a social network approach to explore the Internet's impact on the capacity of community associations. We focus on how increased e-mail use affects the cohesion and democratic character of associations, and operationialize these concepts employing the standard social network measures of density and centralization. The analysis employs network data from 41 community associations that are comparable on a variety of factors, but which vary in their use of the Internet. It finds that the technological nature of e-mail as well as the background and interests of its users matter. Members of community associations do consider e-mail to be a distinctive communication mode and employ it differently from other modes such as phone and face-to-face communication. Increased use of e-mail is found to be associated with increased network density, a critical support for collective action. In contrast, increased e-mail use can either lead to increased or decreased network centralization, an indicator of the degree to which associational activities provide opportunities for the development of civic skills. In associations with relatively similar levels of e-mail use among members, the technology leads to more decentralized communication patterns, but in associations with disparate reliance on e-mail, e-mail use is associated with increased centralization.

Introduction

Small volunteer associations are an integral building block of robust communities. They provide venues for collective action, cultivate social capital, act as channels of information, and mediate between communities and state power (Chaskin, Brown, Venkatesh, and Vidal 2001; Granovetter 1973; Putnam 2000; Warren 2001). Voluntary associations, however, encounter imposing barriers to success. While the work of associations often yields substantial community benefits, the

P. van den Besselaar et al. (eds.), Communities and Technologies 2005, 1-18.
© 2005 Springer. Printed in the Netherlands.

specific benefits for individual volunteers are limited, giving rise to incentives to "free ride" off of the efforts of others. In addition associations face substantial coordination costs in organizing the efforts of several busy and geographically dispersed volunteers.

The means of communication available to community associations influences their success in overcoming these barriers. Recent research into the role of communication technology and community building has shown that the communication infrastructure in the communities in which people live influences their ability to use available technology effectively for purposes of enhancing the quality of community life (Ball-Rokeach, Kim, and Matei 2001). As the Internet becomes ubiquitous, its impact on the communication infrastructure available to communities is important to understand. DiMaggio, Hargittai, Neuman, and Robinson (2001) note, however, that there has been little systematic study of how community-level voluntary associations use the Internet and whether the Internet affects their structure and enhances their effectiveness. This gap in the literature is unfortunate because the communication capabilities offered by the Internet should be particularly useful to community associations (Weare 2002). Association members are geographically dispersed, do not share a common place of work, and must balance associational activities with other commitments. In this situation, the asynchronous character of e-mail and its ability to broadcast messages are especially useful for keeping members in contact. Given that there is significant evidence that communication between organizational members is a critical factor facilitating successful collective action, such structural changes are likely to have significant effects on associational performance (Heckathorn 1993; Macy 1991; Sell and Wilson 1991).

This research focuses on the cohesion and democratic character of small, voluntary associations. Cohesion (the relative frequency of contacts between the members of a group) is of interest because of its relation to the development of common norms and bonds of trust that promote associational capacity (Coleman 1990; Wasserman and Faust 1994). An organization's democratic character (the degree to which it enables members to participate in core decision-making functions) is important because more decentralized and democratic structures and processes are linked to the development of civic skills and civic virtues among associational members (Parsons 1971; Putnam 1993; Verba, Schlozman, and Brady 1995; Warren 2001). This paper focuses on the effects of increased use of e-mail on the cohesion and democratic character of voluntary associations, holding other variables constant. It employs a social network approach to define and operationalize measures of cohesion and democratic character. It then analyzes network data collected from 41 community-based associations that are comparable on a variety of factors known to influence network structure, but which vary in their use of the Internet.

Social Networks

Cohesion and democratic character are concepts that can be operationalized through network analysis. This analysis employs two frequently utilized concepts: *density* and *centralization*.

Density is the ratio of existing ties among group members to all possible ties in their network. Density is closely linked to the concept of cohesion because an increase in the number of ties increases the probability that people interact directly. Density, also, has been shown to affect the flow of information in networks (Burt 2000; Monge and Contractor 2003; Rogers 2003; Scott 2000). In a high-density network, actors are tied directly to most others in the network. Because information-sharing is key to the coordination of group behavior, the density of a network has much to do with the capacity of an association to function. Specifically, research has shown that it is possible to affect the degree of "free-riding" in voluntary associations by effectively communicating the contributions and expectations of others (Cason and Khan 1999; Heckathorn 1993; Sell and Wilson 1991).

The homophily of group members (i.e., their similarity to one another) is an important contingent factor. Because more homophilous groups tend to support denser networks of communication, homophily is in general associated with greater cohesion (Brass 1995; Monge and Contractor 2003; Rogers 2003). Nevertheless, heterogeneity has advantages too. Heckathorn (1993) has shown that early in the stages of group formation, heterogeneity can facilitate collective action because highly motivated actors, or those with high capacity to make material contributions, may voluntarily offer those resources without polarizing the group or demanding complete reciprocity from the other members. Over time, Heckathorn notes, these conditions change. If cliques of homophilous members form, for example, within-clique communications may increase the apparent density of communications for the group as a whole, but reduce valuable contacts and willingness to compromise between dissimilar members (Huckfeldt and Sprague 1987). These contingencies are important in the study of voluntary associations because a central argument concerning the importance of engagement in civil society is the beneficial effect of exposure to people with different backgrounds, interests, and goals (Lipset 1981; Mutz 2002; Weatherford 1982). Moreover, if it can be shown that communication technology facilitates certain kinds of communication and discourages others, associations can choose available technologies that enhance their ability to work together productively.

Centralization is the extent to which a group's communication tends to flow through a specific person or persons rather than being more evenly distributed throughout all of its members (Freeman 1979; Scott 2000; Wasserman and Faust 1994). At the individual level, an actor's centrality indicates the importance or prominence of an individual within a network. Networks with higher levels of group centralization are those in which there is a higher degree of variation in the centrality of individuals.

Among the many specific measures of centrality that have been identified, we focus on betweeness centrality because it (or more precisely its inverse) best captures the democratic character of associations. Betweeness centrality measures the extent to which a person serves as a link between two others seeking to communicate in a network. Specificially, person j's betweeness centrality is the proportion of all existing paths that connect all others in the network that include j. The group-level measure of centralization is derived from the sum of squared differences of each actor's centrality in comparison to the most central actor in that group. The analysis presented here focuses on the normalized centralization index, which expresses a group's centralization as a proportion of the maximum centralization of a group of that size.

The centrality of individuals in a network is related to power. Research has demonstrated that "actors who are the most important or the most prominent are usually located in strategic locations within the network" (Wasserman and Faust 1994, p. 169). These strategic locations were found to be central locations in a network, which provide extensive opportunities for involvement with others, more visibility, accessibility, control over resources, and brokerage of information (Ibarra 1993; Krackhardt and Brass 1994; Wasserman and Faust 1994). Organizations with low levels of centralization have a more democratic structure that distributes control over resources, maintenance of relationships, and information more evenly among their members. Verba, Schotzman, and Brady (1995) connect such decentralized structures with the acquisition of civic skills by their members. Also, Ajuha and Carley (1999) argue that decentralized organizations generally have more satisfied members, and that in "virtual organizations" (i.e., those that rely on electronic communication to accomplish their goals) "absence of prior structure allows the members to develop new structures through informal interaction in response to particular tasks" (1999, p. 745).

The Internet and Network Structure

The present study takes the approach de Sola Pool (1983) termed *soft technological determinism*—a concept that describes Castells' (2000) analysis as well. Castells highlights the Internet's ability to affect social networks by allowing people to search for and connect to individuals and organizations that otherwise would be impossible to find off-line, i.e. establishing more "weak ties" (Castells 2000; Granovetter 1973). Internet communication can reduce the costs of communication and change the character of mediated communication (e.g., Internet communication is asynchronous and low in social valence), and thus can change the structure and character of relationships.

In particular, the broadcast capabilities of electronic mail are significant. When children play "telephone" by whispering a message to one another, the fun of the game is the artificial constraints they place on their communication (e.g., artificially constraining centralization by forcing people in the same room to speak softly, and only directly to one other) and the consequences that ensue as the message deteriorates as it makes its way through the network. In fact, the Internet allows people to overcome that game's problem (and the limitations of organizational hierarchies) by "broadcasting" the same message to multiple recipients, usually with no extra marginal cost. While the term broadcasting accurately describes this ability, the Internet provides an additional capability that radio and television broadcasting do not: the ability for recipients of the message to respond quickly and to the entire network. One broadcast e-mail message can generate additional communication throughout the network, further increasing density, and perhaps decreasing centralization as the whole network is activated.

The Internet's technical characteristics are not, however, the only factor influencing individuals' communication patterns. Their goals, skills, and social context are co-determinants. People differ in terms of their ability and inclination to use the Internet (Jung, Qiu, and Kim 2001; Loges and Jung 2001; Wood and Smith 2001). People already connected to the Internet differ in their skill levels, their access from different places, and the importance they place on the Internet, a combination of objective and subjective dimensions that Jung, Qiu, & Kim (2000) call *Internet connectedness*.

The Internet and Group Cohesion

No matter how fond a person is of his or her colleagues in a voluntary association, practical obstacles to communicating with them can discourage communication that might otherwise build strong relationships between members (Burt 2000). The introduction of the Internet to an existing social network should increase that network's density by mitigating these constraints. For example, Internet communications enable individuals to establish "weak ties" with others with whom they might not otherwise connect (Castells 2000; Granovetter 1973; Sproull and Kiesler 1986; Sproull and Kiesler 1991). In addition, Sproull and Kiesler (1986, 1991) observe that e-mail increases network contacts by reducing communication inhibitions based on status. Sceptics have argued that Internet use may have the opposite effects, reducing social contacts by taking away from time previously employed for personal contacts (Nie, Hillygus, and Erbring 2002). Nevertheless, the preponderance of empirical work on the Internet's effects on sociability has found positive, if small effects (Shklovski In Press).

The effects of an e-mail broadcast on group density are particularly strong for small, low-density networks, which are common characteristics of informal, community-based associations. The overall impact of any observed increase in density, however, is mitigated by the manner in which the technology is employed. Mediating factors include the importance of the message, the status of the message sender, the information processing capabilities of individuals, and the presence of alternative media (Ahuja and Carley 1999; Sproull and Kiesler 1991). Homophily is another factor to consider as an intermediate cause of higher density and when interpreting the effects of changes in density, because people who are similar to one another are more inclined to communicate in any medium.

The Internet and Network Centralization

The Internet is also likely to affect patterns of centralization within networks, but in contrast to density, the direction of change is not clear *a priori*. The use of e-mail might increase centralization if one or a few members use e-mail to broadcast to most other members of the network. To the degree that Internet use correlates with attributes that make an actor central to networks, such as high status and strong technical and communication skills, previously central members would become more central to a network when the Internet becomes available (Rethemeyer 2002). Nevertheless, the Internet may decrease network centralization if decreased costs generate more widespread communication throughout the network. Bikson and Eveland (1990) note that when groups with otherwise-similar tasks differ in their access to e-mail, those with access share leadership roles more than those without. Overall, existing empirical results support both causal directions, finding cases in which Internet use has both increased and decreased centralization (Ahuja and Carley 1999; O'Mahony and Barley 1999).

As with the discussion of density above, however, changes in centralization are mediated by characteristics of the network's members, not merely the technical attributes of the Internet. Real power in associations is redistributed more slowly than communication patterns. For example, O'Mahony and Barley conclude that the literature shows an "equalizing effect" among e-mail users, but "there is little evidence that computer mediated communication broadens democratic participation in organizational life" (1999, p. 135). In addition to the mediating effects of power differentials, different levels of Internet connectedness (Jung, Qiu, and Kim 2001) affect the likelihood of network members engaging in broadcasting and responses to broadcast messages. An association populated by members who desire more decentralized communication structures may nonetheless show evidence of high centralization if a few members high in Internet connectedness generate most messages.

Since the research into the effects of the Internet on the structure of social networks has not produced consistent findings that allow for firm predictions about the relationship between Internet use and density and centralization, our analysis is guided by the following basic research questions:

RQ1: Does use of electronic mail produce new patterns of communication in intra-association networks, or does e-mail simply replace previous modes of communication?

RQ2: Does use of electronic mail increase the density of intra-association networks?

RQ3: Does use of electronic mail increase the centralization of intra-association networks?

Methods

Participants

We explore these research questions employing a unique data set that includes social network indicators for a group of board members of neighborhood councils (NCs). In 1999, Los Angeles voters ratified a new charter that included provisions to create a system of neighborhood councils. Although officially considered organs of Los Angeles city government, neighborhood councils share many of the characteristics of informal associations. Other than requirements that neighborhood councils represent all segments of their neighborhood and that they have an elected board, the charter ceded great discretion to the neighborhoods in the design and makeup of their councils. In particular, each neighborhood was free to define its boundaries and develop its bylaws.

The boards differ in many respects. They represent neighborhoods encompassing between about 11,000 to more than 85,000 residents with an average population of about 40,000. These neighborhoods vary significantly in terms of socio-economic and ethnic makeup, from very rich enclaves of primarily white homeowners to diverse mixes of poorer, less educated recent immigrants. The neighborhood council boards are composed of between 9 and 41 members, with an average of 20. The boards that had organized earliest had been certified by the city for 20 months at the time of our survey, while other boards had been certified for as little as seven months. In all cases, however, ad hoc committees had been working to organize neighborhood councils for many months prior to certification. Some bylaws have created highly formal decision-making structures while others are less structured, allowing more fluid and spontaneous participation by stakeholders. Most importantly, these boards contend with many of the prototypical problems of informal, community organizations: (1) they rely on a small cadre of highly committed volunteers to keep the board together, (2) all members need to balance their NC activities with other responsibilities, and (3) the involvement levels of other members are fluid. The survey focused on elected board members, though there were notable cases in which highly active NC members did not hold board positions.

At the time of our survey, 45 NC boards had been certified by the city of Los Angeles and had sitting elected boards. Because we were unable to get complete lists of board members for four boards, they are excluded from a number of analyses, though we use the individual level data from those boards when appropriate.

Members of this research team personally visited board meetings and invited members to take the survey either online or by telephone in the summer of 2003. The survey was available in Spanish and English. Out of 894 total board members, 587 respondents began the survey, for a response rate of 66%. Five hundred and eighty-two surveys yielded usable network data, and of these 541 respondents had initiated contact with at least one other board member. In total, there are 3,141 communication dyads, including responses from the four incomplete boards. While this survey was designed to gather responses from all members of each eligible board, the response rate may be sufficient to estimate network characteristics with some confidence. Costenbader and Valente (2003) have shown that the measures of centrality employed here are fairly robust when response rates are higher than 60% within a network.

Measures

The questionnaire item of most importance in this paper presented board members with a list of all other members of their NC board. They were then asked, "Thinking about the two weeks just before your most recent Neighborhood Council meeting, which board members were you in touch with during that time to discuss matters concerning politics, government, or neighborhood issues?" For those members with whom they had been in contact, respondents were asked whether they had been in contact by e-mail, face-to-face, or by telephone. Multiple communication modes were accepted. Finally, the respondents rated the importance of contact with the other board member for their work on the NC. In a small network (as most of the NCs are), density is most accurately measured when respondents are able to select others from a complete roster with no limit on their nominations, and to employ loose criteria for nominating someone (Costenbader and Valente 2003; Scott 2000).

Respondents also were asked which of the stakeholder groups the city wanted the NCs to represent they felt closest to (these included such groups as residents, employers, property owners and those with children in the neighborhood's schools). Other items in the questionnaire provided indicators of Internet connectedness. These included measures of the respondents' confidence that they could perform a variety of tasks online, use of the Internet to gather information, and questions regarding the places from which they regularly have Internet access (e.g., home, school, their workplace, and libraries). These indicators were combined into a single scale measuring overall Internet connectedness. Respondents also were asked to rate their political conservatism or liberalism on a five-point scale. Demographic variables included age, education, household income, ethnicity, and length of residence in their community.

Results

NC board members are not typical of the average resident in the neighborhoods they represent. Consistent with earlier findings about political participation, NC board members are more commonly white, wealthy, older, well educated, home owners, and long-time residents of their community (Verba, Schlozman, and Brady 1995) (Table 1). They expressed a much higher than average interest in politics, averaging 3.5 on a 4-point scale ranging from not at all interested to very interested. Their political ideology, however, did mirror the range of views of the entire city population, with most respondents expressing moderate views on a 5-point scale between very conservative and very liberal.

	N	Mean	Mode	Std. Dev.	Minimum	Maximum
Income in dollars	500	74,320	110,000	32,856	10,000	110,000
Education (years)	565	15.8	18.0	2.1	10	18
age (years)	558	51.1	49.5	12.6	16	68
Years lived in community	587	16.3	23.0	7.6	0.5	23
Interest in local politics	570	3.5	4	0.6	1	4
Political ideology	562	2.7	3	1.1	1	5
Uses Internet	563	93.1%				
Home Internet access	531	87.8%				

Table 1: Demographic Characteristics of Neighborhood Council Board Members

Board members operate in an environment in which e-mail is strongly promoted. The General Manager of the Department of Neighborhood Empowerment, the city department that manages the neighborhood council system, openly states that he is only able to communicate to individuals by e-mail due to the time pressures under which he works. Similarly, many intra- and inter-organizational conversations, activities, and notices are communicated over the Internet. Thus, NC members face pressures to adopt e-mail, and many of them have. Ninety-three percent accessed the Internet, and almost 88% had an Internet connection at home. Even on the least well connected board, 71% of its members were online and 67% had access at home. These results indicate a level of Internet connectedness higher than is usual in Los Angeles (Jung, Qiu, and Kim 2001; Loges and Jung 2001).

As is expected with informal organizations, the degree of individual involvement and group cohesion vary markedly. The average NC board member was in contact with about 38% of the other board members. The number of contacts, however, was skewed to the right by the small number of board members who were most heavily involved. Less than 5% of board members contacted more than 85% of their colleagues, and this group accounted for over 19% of all contacts. Normalized network centrality varied accordingly, with an average of 4.9, but a maximum of 80.36. Only about 10% of board members had a normalized centrality above 10. At the board level, the average density was 37.4% with a high of 64.9% and a low of 13.9%. Normalized centralization averaged 27.8% and ranged between 3.6% and 79.7%.

E-mail and Patterns of Communication

Our findings show that e-mail plays a central role in intra-group communication for these organizations. As seen in Table 2, 21.3% of contacts between board members are mediated solely by e-mail, and in over 58% of all dyads, e-mail is at least one of the communication modes employed. There is a distinct bimodal distribution in the degree to which individuals rely on e-mail. Over 14% of board members have no contacts with others by e-mail, while 16.3% have employed e-mail communication with everyone with whom they have been in contact. The remaining 69% are uniformly distributed between these two extremes.

Communication Mode	Frequency	Percent
E-mail Only	657	21.3%
Offline Only	1288	41.7%
Both E-mail and Offline	1145	37.1%
Total	3090	100%

Table 2: Mode of Communication for All Dyads

As expected, discussion pairs composed of social and economic elites tend to rely more on e-mail either exclusively or in addition to offline modes of communication. Of more interest, time appears to play a role in the choice of communication modes. Individuals that have been involved with the board for a longer time tend to rely proportionally less on communications solely by e-mail and have more frequent face-to-face contact (Figure 1). Similar results were obtained for boards that have been certified for a longer period of time, but these results do not reach standard levels of statistical significance.

For dyads homophily is strongly associated with the choice of communication media, in that similar individuals are more likely to communicate by e-mail. Respondents were asked which stakeholder group they represented on the board; consequently, they can be divided into dyads between individuals from the same stakeholder group and those from differing stakeholder groups. Of the discussion pairs composed of members of the same group, over 70% employed e-mail, while only 61% of discussion pairs composed of differing stakeholders did so. Similar results are obtained when one examines differences in political ideologies. Over 70% of the discussion pairs of individuals with identical ideological leanings are mediated by e-mail. In contrast, 68.4% of the discussions between individuals with the most extreme ideological differences occur solely offline.

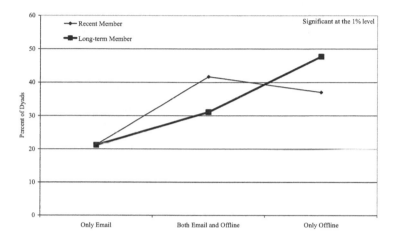

Figure 1. Choice of Communication Mode by Associational Tenure.

E-mail and Associational Density

Research question 2 involved the relationship between e-mail use and the network density of associations. Given that almost 22% of all contacts in our sample employ only e-mail communications, it is not surprising that e-mail appears to increase the density of NC board networks. If we assume that all e-mail-based communications constitute new contacts that would not have occurred in the absence of the availability of e-mail, the addition of e-mail to offline forms of communication increases the density for almost all boards. Of the 41 boards, 32 boards experience statistically significant (at the 5% level) increases in density ranging between .025 and .3. Another 4 boards experience smaller increases in density that are only statistically significant at the 10% level. The average increase is substantial. The average board in our sample has 20 members and an offline density of .3, indicating that 57 of the 190 possible pairs of organizational members are in contact with one another. When added, the e-mail network, on average, creates 13 new ties connecting a pair of board members.

To examine the extent to which e-mail communication really represents contact between members that would not have occurred in the absence of e-mail, we estimate a model of organizational density. For explanatory factors, we include characteristics of organizational members, the age of the organization, and the number of members with high levels of Internet connectedness. This particular model is supported by the notion that due to the broadcast capability of e-mail, only a few Internet savvy members are needed to tie the group together through e-mail. Table 3 presents two versions of the model, one of the basic model and a second that includes organizational size because density is known to be sensitive to organizational size. The two models generally support the notion that having a larger number of Internet savvy members on a board increases group density, though in the second model the coefficient is only marginally statistically significant.

Variable	Model 1	Model 2
Average age	-.055 (.730)	-.175 (.212)
Average education (years)	.254* (.066)	.119 (.323)
Months since NC officially recognized by city	.247* (.065)	.204* (.072)
Average number of organizational memberships	-.059 .(696)	-.023 (.859)
Average hours of volunteer work	.508*** (.001)	.431*** (.002)
# of board members with high Internet connectedness (top quintile)	.414*** (.008)	.225* (.100)
Board size		.472*** (.000)
Adjusted R^2	.479	.642

Dependent variable is mean degree
N = 41   *** Sig. at .01 Level   * Sig. at .10 Level
Reported coefficients are standardized betas. T-scores are reported in parentheses.

Table 3: Board Network Density as a Function of Internet Use

Moreover, the importance of the broadcast capability of e-mail to increasing organizational density is borne out by the pattern of e-mail communications. Among the council board members examined here, wide use of e-mail is relatively rare. Only 18 out of 522 board members (3.4%) contact 85% or more of their board through e-mail. E-mail, though, is clearly preferred when one wishes to communicate broadly. Only two members contacted 85% or more of their board by phone, and only six did so face-to-face. These individuals who employ e-mail broadly, moreover, are associated with those boards for which e-mail increased their density most. For the ten boards that had the largest increases in density associated with e-mail, eight had at least one member that contacted at least 85% percent of the board by e-mail. In contrast, of the other 31 boards only six included such an e-mail broadcaster.

Organizational Network Centralization and Actor Centrality

Research question 3 concerned the relationship between e-mail use and network centralization. As the empirical literature has found, the relationship between the use of Internet communications and group centralization is ambiguous. An important contingency factor is the distribution of Internet use. A single or only a few users who employ e-mail lists to broadcast messages can increase centralization. This effect is countered by the degree to which the lower communication costs associated with e-mail decrease the burden of maintaining redundant ties, leading to more dynamic communication exchanges between a larger proportion of organization members.

The importance of the distribution of Internet use and other intermediary factors is evident in these organizations. We calculated a measure of the change of centralization due to e-mail communications, equaling the betweeness centralization index for each board including all contacts minus the same index for only offline communications. The results vary widely. Forty-six percent of the boards saw centralization decrease with the addition of e-mail links, 46.3% saw centralization increase, and 7.3% saw no change.

To examine how both the intensity and distribution of e-mail use among organization members affect centralization, we regressed centralization on three variables: 1) the proportion of overall board communications that employ e-mail, 2) a dummy variable equal to 1 for boards with higher than average variance in e-mail use among its members and 0 otherwise, and 3) an interaction term between the first two variables. The results presented in Table 4 show that overall boards that rely more heavily on e-mail are not, on average, more or less centralized. Boards in which members vary more in their use of e-mail are, on average, less centralized, but centralization in these boards increases markedly as they rely more on e-mail communications. In sum, it is the combination of e-mail use and the distribution of its use that matters. Increased use of e-mail in an organization composed of members with similar levels of e-mail use decreases centralization, but in an organization composed of members with disparate e-mail use patterns, e-mail leads to increased centralization.

In contrast to these results on group centralization, e-mail use does not appear to have a significant effect on individuals' centrality within their neighborhood council boards. The correlation between individuals' centrality within networks of offline communications and their centrality within online communications is relatively low, only .31. This suggests that the advent of e-mail could be enabling some individuals to rise in centrality within associations. However, e-mail communication does little to alter the core of individuals who appear to control these neighborhood councils. In 17 of 41 boards, the five most central actors are also the five most central in the offline network, and in another 16 boards only one of the five most central actors was not in the top five in the offline network. In only one board was it the case that all five of the most central actors were not among the most central members in the offline network.

Variable	Model
Proportion of communication by e-mail in board	-.077 (-.451)
High variation in e-mail use	-1.13** (-2.33)
High Variation * Proportion of e-mail	1.47*** (2.87)
Adjusted R^2	.194

Dependent variable is mean degree
N = 41   ***Sig. At .01 Level ** Sig. at .05 Level
Reported coefficients are standardized betas. T-scores are reported in parentheses.

Table 4: Board Network Density as a Function of Internet Use

Discussion

Voluntary associations that seek to work together to strengthen their communities require conditions that encourage cohesion among their members and a structure that encourages participation. A large number of theorists have linked the development of large-scale organizations and other social structures to developments in information technology (Bell 1974; Beniger 1986; Castells 2000; Innis 1951; Pool 1977; Pool 1983). However, they often have little to say about the micro- or meso-level processes that must accompany the macro-level social changes they describe. Our results on the micro-level organizational impacts of information technology provide qualified support for claims about the social influence of information technology, but we find that the effects of the Internet do not necessarily lead to more democratic structures.

Use of the Internet provides organizations with some specific capabilities that can build cohesion and generate communication that might not otherwise occur. However, we find that e-mail contact is more common between people who are similar to one another in their political outlook and the interests they represent on their neighborhood council. The broadcast capability of the Internet may allow information to be shared throughout a group efficiently, and thus reassure members that they are on an equal footing where information-access is concerned. But the purpose of that equality is to allow people of diverse backgrounds and interests to work together for the common good. If e-mail becomes a medium that allows cliques to form more effectively, the cohesion of the association could be threatened.

We find that Internet use increases the density of associational communications. To the extent that increased density helps associations maintain contact, disseminate information quickly and efficiently, monitor the actions of members, and forge social bonds that prepare them for the give and take of neighborhood-level politics, new technology has the potential to mitigate a fundamental obstacle to group cohesion and collective action. This shift has the potential to strengthen and expand the role of associational activity in a wide range of social arenas such as urban governance and non-profit service provision.

Associations relying on the Internet do not appear to develop less centralized, more democratic structures than less-Internet connected groups. In fact, if members within an association differ widely in the extent of their Internet connectedness, the association may tend toward greater centralization in the communication within the group as one or two members become conduits through which more and more messages pass. This might encourage members to acquire more Internet skills, but it may also encourage free-riding as the association's members assume that the more highly Internet-connected among them will perform the lion's share of the group's communication work (such as distributing information internally and maintaining contacts outside the association).

Further research is required to identify the specific role that Internet communications play in organizational activity. We find, for example, that the propensity to use the Internet for associational communication decreases as tenure in the association grows longer. This tendency suggests that the Internet is more helpful for forming initial ties within the association than it is for maintaining these ties on an ongoing basis. Associations like neighborhood councils in Los Angeles begin with no routine tasks, no clear role definitions, and no specific times and places at which the group will meet. As the association matures, routines and roles stabilize. The Internet appears most helpful in the early, somewhat chaotic phase of association life –what population ecologists termed as the challenges associated with liability of newness– and less helpful as routines become established.

Our findings support the utility of employing a soft technological determinism perspective given that we find that individuals' goals, skills, and social context do influence the use and impacts of technology. The relationship between Internet use and associational centralization is the most obvious example. It is not the mere presence of the Internet that centralizes an association, but the distribution of people with various levels of skill and inclination to use the Internet that makes a difference in centralization. To the extent that democratization and decentralization are similar and reinforcing concepts, the findings indicate that the Internet will foster democratic associations only if the people in these associations have similar levels of Internet connectedness. In this way, Internet connectedness becomes akin to a civic skill. It also implies a digital divide problem—people with less Internet access (for whatever reasons) may be able to join a NC, but not as able to become a central player in the NC, thereby receiving information later and less reliably. Since Internet access is correlated with socioeconomic status, ethnicity, and age in Los Angeles (Jung, Qiu, and Kim 2001; Loges and Jung

2001), neighborhood councils in places with concentrations of low-connected people may consist of board members who are less representative of their neighbors than other boards.

The addition of the Internet to the toolkits of community organizations does not have totally predictable results. The motives and interests of the members of an association will be influential in determining the difference the Internet makes. Awareness of the potential benefits of the Internet and of the potential pitfalls can prepare an association to take steps to get the most out of this technology. Most of the impacts we report here, positive or negative, can be affected by decisions members of an association make deliberately, such as providing Internet training for less-skilled members. It is important that theories of the way the Internet affects human communication not be understood to make such effects inevitable, leading to blue-sky expectations or needless fears that keep people from realizing the advantages they and their associations might have enjoyed.

Acknowledgments

This research was supported by National Science Foundation Information Technology Research Grant #0112899. The authors would like to thank attendees of the University of California, Irvine Social Network seminar and the USC seminar series on civic enterprise for helpful comments. In addition, we thank Kyu-Nahm Jun, Mark Elliot, and the Los Angeles Department of Neighborhood Empowerment for their assistance. All errors are our own.

References

Ahuja, Manju K. and Kathleen M. Carley. 1999. Network Structure in Virtual Organizations." *Organization Science* 10:741-757.

Ball-Rokeach, S. J., Y. K. Kim, and S. Matei. 2001. "A communication infrastructure perspective on communication and society." vol. 2001: Annenberg Center for Communication, University of Southern California.

Bell, D. 1974. *The Coming of Post-Industrial Society: A Venture in Social Forecasting*. London, UK.: Heinemann.

Beniger, J.R. 1986. *The control revolution: Technological and economic origins of the information society*. Cambridge, MA: Harvard University Press.

Brass, D. J. 1995. "A Social Network Perspective on Human Resources Management." Pp. 39-79 in *Research in Personnel and Human Resources Management*, edited by G. Ferris. Greenwich, CT: JAI Press.

Burt, Donald S. 2000. "The Network Structure of Social Capital." in *Research in Organizational Behavior*, vol. 22, edited by R. I. S. a. B. M. Staw. Grenwich: JAI Press.

Cason, T. and F. Khan. 1999. "A laboratory study of voluntary public goods provision with imperfect monitoring and communication." *Journal of Development Economics* 58:533-552.

Castells, M. 2000. *The Rise of the Network Society*. Malden, MA: Blackwell.

Chaskin, Robert J., Prudence Brown, Sudhir Venkatesh, and Avis Vidal. 2001. *Building Community Capacity*. New York: Aldine de Gruyter.

Coleman, James S. 1990. *Foundations of Social Theory*: Harvard University Press.

Costenbader, Elizabeth and Thomas W. Valente. 2003. "The stability of centrality measures when networks are sampled." *Social Networks* 25:283-307.

Freeman, L.C. 1979. "Centrality in social networks: conceptual clarification." *Social Networks* 1:215-239.

Granovetter, Mark S. 1973. "The Strength of Weak Ties." *American Journal of Sociology* 78:1360-1380.

Heckathorn, Douglas D. 1993. "Collective action and group heterogeneity." *American Sociological Review* 58:329-350.

Huckfeldt, Robert and John Sprague. 1987. "Networks in Context: The Social Flow of Political Information." *American Political Science Review* 81.

Ibarra, H. 1993. "Network centrality, power, and innovation involvement: Determinants of technical and administrative roles." *Academy of Management Journal*:471-501.

Innis, Harold Adam. 1951. *The Bias of Communication*. Toronto: University of Toronto Press.

Jung, Joo-Young, Jack L. Qiu, and Yong-Chan Kim. 2001. "Internet connectedness and inequality: Beyond the "divide"." *Communication Research* 28:507-535.

Krackhardt, David. and D. J. Brass. 1994. "Intraorganizational Networks: The Micro Side." Pp. 207-229 in *Advances in Social Network Analysis: Research in the Social and Behavioral Sciences*, edited by S. Wasserman, Galaskiewicz, J. Thousand Oaks, CA: Sage Publications.

Lipset, Seymour Martin. 1981. *Political Man*. Balimore: Johns Hopkins Press.

Loges, William E. and Joo-Young Jung. 2001. "Exploring the digital divide: Internet connectedness and age." *Communication Research* 28:536-562.

Macy, M. W. 1991. "Chains of cooperation: Threshold effects in collective action." *American Sociological Review* 56:730-747.

Monge, Peter R. and N.S. Contractor. 2003. *Theories of Communication Networks*. New York: Oxford University Press.

Mutz, Diana C. 2002. "Cross-Cutting Social Networks: Testing Democratic Theory in Practice." *American Political Science Review* 96:111-126.

Nie, N., S. Hillygus, and L. Erbring. 2002. "Internet Use, Interpersonal Relations and Sociability: Findings from a Detailed Time Diary Study." in *The Internet in Everyday Life*, edited by B. Wellman and C. Haythornthwaite. Malden, CA: Blackwell.

O'Mahony, S. and S.R. Barley. 1999. "Do digital telecommunications affect work and organization? The state of our knowledge." *Research in Organizational Behavior* 21:125-161.

Parsons, Talcott. 1971. *The System of Modern Societies*. Englewood Cliffs, NJ: Prentice-Hall.

Pool, Ithiel de Sola. 1977. "The Social Impact of the Telephone." Pp. 502. Cambridge, Massachusetts: The MIT Press.

—. 1983. *Technologies of Freedom*. Cambridge, MA: The Belknap Press of Harvard University Press.

Putnam, Robert D. 1993. *Making Democracy Work: Civic Traditions in Modern Italy*. Princeton, NJ: Princeton University Press.

—. 2000. *Bowling Alone: The Collapse and Revival of American Community*. New York: Simon & Schuster.

Rethemeyer, Randy Karl. 2002. "Centralization or democratization: Assessing the Internet's impact on policy networks. A theoretical and empirical inquiry." Ph.D. Thesis, Public Administration, Harvard University.

Rogers, E.M. 2003. *Diffusion of innovations*. New York: Free Press.

Scott, J. 2000. *Social Network Analysis: A Handbook*. Thousand Oaks, CA: Sage.

Sell, J. and R. Wilson. 1991. "Levels of information and contributions to public goods." *Social Forces* 70:107-124.

Shklovski, I., Kiesler, S., Kraut, R. E.. In Press. "The Internet and Social Interaction: A Meta-analysis and Critique of Studies, 1995-2003." in *Domesticating Information Technology*, edited by R. Kraut, M. Brynin, and S. Kiesler. New York: Oxford University Press.

Sproull, L. and S. Kiesler. 1986. "Reducing social context cues: Electronic mail in organizational communication." *Management Science* 32:1492-1512.

—. 1991. *Connections: New ways of working in the networked organization*. Cambridge, MA: MIT Press.

Verba, Sidney, Kay Lehman Schlozman, and Henry E. Brady. 1995. *Voice and Equality: Civic Voluntarism in American Politics*. Cambridge, MA: Harvard University Press.

Warren, Mark E. 2001. *Democracy and Association*. Princeton, NJ: Princeton University Press.

Wasserman, Stanley and Katherine Faust. 1994. *Social Network Analysis: Methods and Applications*, Edited by M. Granovetter. New York: Cambridge University Press.

Weare, Christopher. 2002. "The Internet and Democracy: The Causal Links Between Technology and Politics." *International Journal of Public Administration* 25:659-692.

Weatherford, M.S. 1982. "Interpersonal Networks and Political Behavior." *American Journal of Political Science* 26.

Wood, A.F. and M.J. Smith. 2001. *Online communication: Linking technology, identity, & culture*. Mahwah, NJ: Laurence Erlbaum Associates.

Information Technology in Support of Public Deliberation

Andrea L. Kavanaugh[+], Philip L. Isenhour[+], Matthew Cooper[+], John M. Carroll*, Mary Beth Rosson*, Joseph Schmitz[•]

[+]Virginia Tech, USA, *Pennsylvania State University, USA, [•]Western Illinois University, USA

kavan, isenhour, macooper@vt.edu, jcarroll@ist.psu.edu, mrosson@psu.edu, J-Schmitz@wiu.edu

Abstract. Increased citizen-to-citizen discussion and deliberation is an important potential of digital government initiatives. This paper presents findings from a longitudinal study of such outcomes using household survey data, focus groups and one-on-one interviews from a mature community network - the Blacksburg Electronic Village (BEV) in Blacksburg, Virginia, and surrounding Montgomery County. It addresses the questions of who is using computer networking for civic participation, what impact the Internet has on their involvement with other people and local community, and the design problems that citizens experience with local e-government initiatives. A pattern of Internet use is emerging in which local formal and ad hoc groups of interested citizens distribute information on issues of interest among themselves and use online tools to raise awareness and educate, and under some circumstances to deliberate on public policy. Modified tools are suggested to facilitate deliberation and to integrate citizen feedback more effectively into local government decision-making.

Introduction

New interactive information and communication technology (ICT) can greatly spur equal access to information and foster vibrant participatory debate (Laudon, 1977; Barber 1984; Pool, 1984; Dutton et al., 1992; Etzioni, 1992; Guthrie and Dutton, 1992; O'Sullivan, 1995; Raab et al., 1996; Schuler, 1996; CSTB, 2000; OMB, 2002; Horrigan et al., 2004). Just now, they are beginning to meet this

P. van den Besselaar et al. (eds.), Communities and Technologies 2005, 19-40.

potential. The Internet is becoming an efficient and effective channel for government to "broadcast" civic information through web sites and listservs and exchange email with interested citizens (Patterson and Kavanaugh, 1994; Schmitz et. al., 1995; Carroll and Rosson, 1996; Cohill and Kavanaugh, 1997, 2000; Lin, 2000; Nie, 2001; Norris, 2001; Kavanaugh et al., 2002; Horrigan, 2001; Kirn, 2002; Larson and Associates, 2002a, b; Horrigan, et al., 2004). Background information on issues, ideas and developments has always been essential for citizens to become aware, weigh trade-offs, and form opinions on issues of common interest.

Most online government initiatives, however, starting with early interactive technology experiments such as QUBE (cable TV) and Santa Monica's Public Electronic Network (PEN), demonstrated that it is much easier to ask for citizen input than to make effective use of it. Since those early trials, government publishing of official records, forms and other information online as well as posting of email addresses for the public to contact government representatives has increased dramatically. But these government activities consist largely of broadcasting (government to citizens) and they offer limited interaction between government and a few individuals via email. While these broadcasting activities represent important stages in promoting democracy throughout the citizenry, as they make government more transparent, they should be only the first of several stages that facilitate increased citizen awareness, engagement, and participation.

Our project seeks to re-focus the digital government discussion around factors that make for an effective democracy rather than for efficient government. We focus on citizen participation in local governance - especially, local voluntary associations - and on better ways that technology can support and facilitate the involvement of individual citizens and groups from all strata of a community.

Civic Participation and Social Ties

Civic participation encompasses a broad range of basic rights, duties and responsibilities (e.g., Davis and Fernlund, 1991). Duties of citizens are not voluntary and include attending school, obeying laws and paying taxes. In contrast, basic rights and responsibilities are voluntary and include voting, holding elected office, influencing government, practicing one's own religion, expressing what one thinks in speech and in writing, attending public meetings, serving the community, and contributing to the common good (e.g., helping neighbors and fellow citizens). It is crucial that citizens read, write, and evaluate political arguments if they are to participate in democratic decision-making processes. The aspiration for an informed, engaged populace is one of the most constant elements of democracy in America (Dahl, 1989, and others). The requirements and consequences of public education with an attendant freeing of minds underlie the protections of free speech (Meikeljohn, 1948). Democratic theory typically envisions a system of government designed to foster deliberation just as much as it is to enhance participation (Schudson, 1992).

Deliberation differs from participation in that it involves more public discussion, negotiation, prioritizing, consensus building, and agenda setting (Barber, 1984; Coleman and Gotze, 2002; Coleman, 2003). It is a multifaceted group process, one that typically occurs in public spaces, such as voluntary associations and public meetings that transpire in what Oldenburg (1991) characterizes as "Great Good Places." For most people, citizenship is not this multifaceted and active (Pateman, 1970; Verba and Nie, 1972; Milbraith and Goel, 1982; White, 2001). Few citizens participate actively in political processes, as indicated by low voter turn out and other civic engagement indicators such as those itemized by Putnam (2000), and others. Classical political theory posits that our democratic system of government works despite ill-informed and inactive citizens. According to elite theories of democracy, this successful functioning derives from the active, well informed, participation of a minority of citizens - often referred to as political 'elites' (Lasswell, 1948; Fishkin, 1991; Bottomore; 1965; Bachrach and Baratz, 1962).

People who belong to multiple groups act as bridging ties across groups (Simmel [1908]; Wolf, 1950; Wellman, 1988) and contribute towards 'bridging' types of social capital (Putnam, 2000) - or what Granovetter (1973) calls weak social ties. Bridging (or weak) ties increase the pace and flow of information and ideas throughout a community. Citizen engagement tends to be higher in communities that have dense social networks, high levels of trust and both 'bridging' (across groups) and 'bonding' (within groups) types of social capital (or what Fischer (2001) and others refer to as 'in-bound social networks'. When people with bridging ties use communication media, such as the Internet, they enhance their capability to educate community members and organize for collective action. Communities with a rich organizational life (i.e., numerous voluntary associations) provide many opportunities for bridging social capital to develop and grow. Nie, Powell, and Prewitt (1969) found that along with social class (high SES), rich organizational life represents the economic development component that most strongly affects mass political participation. Groups educate members, both cognitively and experientially, and generate satisfaction (or spur opposition) to political action, especially in local politics (Newton, 1997).

Presently, the capability of Internet technology to facilitate deliberation is much less clear than its capability to facilitate participation - more private, passive, and individual activities. Keeping informed and participating take time, a scarce resource for the better educated, political elites and for the general populace. Much evidence suggests that the Internet can alleviate constraints of time by providing anytime/anywhere information and discussion. For these and other reasons, the Internet may serve as a medium with great potential to revive civic participation (Milbraith and Goel, 1977; Barber et al., 1997; Davis and Owen, 1998; Wilhelm, 2000; Norris, 2001; Horrigan, Garrett and Resnick, 2004).

IT and Civic Engagement

One of the earliest 'digital' government experiments used cable TV (the QUBE system) in Columbus, Ohio in the early 1980s. QUBE demonstrated that interactive information technology can facilitate direct citizen participation in political decision-making (Arterton, 1987). Although the QUBE experiment in tele-democracy seemed to improve citizen access to decision making and to broaden participation, Arterton concluded that two-thirds of citizens still did not participate, regardless of the potential utility of this information technology. Recently, many studies found that government agencies enthusiastically adopt the Internet to communicate with citizens (Brants, 1996; Horrigan, 2001; Cook et. al., 2002; Larson and Associates, 2002a, b; Bimber, 2003). Larson and Associates (2002a) found that 88% of local elected officials used email and the Internet during their official duties; a large majority of respondents reported that email with constituents helps them to understand public opinion. But the respondents agreed that email was 'not very effective' for engaging the public in debate.

Why would the Internet as a medium for participation differ from cable TV? The Internet is distinctive because it fills a unique 'media gap' for small group communication (Tomita, 1980; Neuman, 1991). It can augment public spaces and create qualitatively new "Great Good Places" (Oldenberg, 1991) that bring groups of citizens together, and foster genuine deliberation. Moreover, existant local groups can consolidate public interests and foster deliberation which group representatives can later convey back to local government agencies. These enhanced functions of local groups may strengthen their vitality in the community. Scholars have noted other Internet features that support deliberation, specifically: interaction, horizontal communication structure, lack of government censorship, and fairly low cost (Barber, et al., 1997; Tsagarousianou, et al., 1998).

Studies regarding the citizen side of participative processes find that civic exchange has increased - at least among interested citizens - with the aid of Internet applications such as the Web, email, and listservs (Kirn, 2000; National Research Council, 2000; Norris, 2000; Carroll and Rosson, 2001; Katz et. al., 2001; Kavanaugh and Patterson, 2001; Resnick, 2001; Kavanaugh et al., 2003; Horrigan et al., 2004). According to Bandura (2000, 2002), people engage in civic life and use the Internet for civic purposes when they feel that their participation and their computer mediated communication is both worthwhile and efficacious. Bandura's argument builds on his concept of self-efficacy (Bandura, 1997) and suggests that collective efficacy would be important, as well. Collective efficacy and social trust explain much of the form and the level of civic and political activity (Seligson, 1980; Wolfsfeld, 1986; Bandura, 2002; Carroll and Reese,

2003). Bandura (2001) noted that new electronic technologies provide "vast opportunities for people to bring their influence to bear" on "collective civic action" (p. 17); however, he warned that "perceived efficacy will shape how the internet changes the face of social activism" (Bandura, 2002, p. 11).

Blacksburg and Montgomery County demonstrate that with useful ICT support, interested citizens download government information from town and county websites or listservs and they keep up to date with local news and issues (Kavanaugh et al., 2000; Kavanaugh et al., 2003). Sometimes, serving as 'weak social ties' between diverse groups, leaders or members of two or more groups forward messages from one group listserv to another. To what extent and under which circumstances do citizens get beyond information distribution activities and engage in actual deliberation such as consensus building and negotiating? Several community groups have created web sites and use them to disseminate information. While different viewpoints are represented on the web to widely varying degrees, to what extent is *discussion* that might usefully be carried out electronically in public forums lost using these conventional ICT tools?

Technology support for online deliberation and civic participation must address several questions. First, how can a broad range of citizens best use these technologies to communicate ideas and opinions about local issues? Next, how can the government effectively use technology to efficiently disseminate information and effectively manage feedback? Additionally, how can these two parallel and often independent patterns of activity be better linked and thereby aid government efforts better to enable and inform online deliberation? Lastly, how can the results of these deliberations be made more accessible to decision-makers?

ICT tools to support online deliberation can evolve in many ways. In some cases, they may be provided as part of government initiatives, as in the case of discussion boards available on government web sites. They may also be independent of, but enabled by, government initiatives. For example, a personal weblog might be used for commentary and discussion of town council meeting minutes or a zoning plan that is posted on the government site. In still other cases, they may evolve in response to a *lack* of online government initiatives, or because of perceived inadequacies of such initiatives. While analysis of requirements for enhanced tools must look at how successful online deliberation tools have evolved and are used, it also must seek to discover why connected users do not take advantage of the opportunities that the network infrastructure already provides them. Are citizens simply unaware of suchtools, government-sponsored or otherwise, that are available to them? Online tools that allow users to reuse existing structures or encourage them create content in the context of existing activity ought to serve as possible remedies. For example, tools could allow citizens to create weblogs by copying and modifying templates, publish annotations to government content in their own virtual spaces, or create discussions, chat, or weblog entries with new consumer technologies such as wireless devices in public hotspots or with camera-enabled cell phones.

Are the systems that are available to support deliberation too complex for less computer-savvy citizens? Deliberation inherently requires the creation of content, something that users accustomed to merely consuming web content may feel is beyond their reach. Minimalist tools that allow users to initiate deliberation in a way that feels like a simple extension of web browsing, while at the same time providing scaffolding to support the creation of more advanced structures seem to represent workable solutions to these problems. Focusing on web accessibility for all tools can help ensure that the technical requirements for access are minimized, allowing users who may only have dial-up connections, older equipment, or access only through public terminals to participate.

Contemporary successful discussions, mailing lists, weblogs, and similar constructs can become unwieldy over time simply because of the volume of contributions. Techniques for managing scale, relevance, and accreditation of contributions to public forums have been explored in systems such as Slashdot (www.slashdot.org) and Kuro5hin (www.kuro5hin.org) and might be applicable to civic discussions (Benkler 2002; Fiore et al., 2002). Do users who know of these opportunities and have the skills to participate just fail to see the benefits, or perhaps do they overestimate the risks of contributing to public forums? Visible mechanisms that allow decision-makers to learn from and contribute to online deliberation efforts could provide additional motivation for citizens to participate.

Security and authentication may also represent important concerns for some users. Simple id and password mechanisms, authentication based on public key infrastructure, and smart cards are approaches that offer varying degrees of confidence in the sources of contributions to public forums. However, each of these strategies presents technical and usability barriers that may discourage broad participation (Ellison, 2000). In extending prior research, we investigate factors such as awareness, skill, and motivation using surveys, interviews, focus groups, workshops and our participant observation with government officials and with community members. We also build on experience with long-term participatory design (Carroll et al., 2000) to determine requirements for - and subsequently prototype - software tools that leverage existing online and offline deliberation practices while addressing the awareness, skill, and motivation of potential users. Participatory design is the inclusion of users or user representatives within a development team, such that they actively help in setting design goals and planning proptotypes (Carroll et al., 2000, p. 239). Our investigation of requirements for addressing the needs of underrepresented groups builds on prior work that examines the impacts of cultural differences in usability evaluations (Vatrapu and Pérez-Quiñones, 2003).

In prior research we also used path analysis to test a set of related hypotheses; we found the independent variables of education, extroversion, and age -

mediated by variables that represented 'bridging' or 'weak' social ties across community groups, collective efficacy (Carroll and Reese, 2003) and Internet use - explained the outcome variable of civic participation after respondents went online (Kavanaugh et al., 2005). That is, the path model showed, as with other studies, that higher education was an important predictor, along with extroverson and age, but it contributed mediating variables of Internet use for political and civic purposes and collective efficacy, and found them to signficantly predict higher levels of civic participation since getting on the Internet.

Local E-Governance

The Town of Blacksburg (population about 46,000 in 2004), Virginia Tech, and the local phone company (Bell Atlantic of Virginia, now Verizon) founded the Blacksburg Electronic Network (BEV) community network during 1993. For the past decade, the BEV has served as a site for extensive research on how to get a community network "right" and has provided a replicable model and benchmark for many subsequent community networks (Patterson and Kavanaugh, 1994; Carroll and Rosson, 1996; Patterson, 1997; Cohill and Kavanaugh, 1997, 2000; Silver, 1999, 2000; Kavanaugh, 2003; Carroll and Rosson, 2001; Kavanaugh and Patterson, 2001; Kavanaugh and Schmitz, 2004; Kavanaugh et al., 2003; Silver, 2004; BEV and VCE, 2004; Kavanaugh et al., 2005).

The Town of Blacksburg (TOB) lies within Montgomery County; it has jurisdiction within town limits and governs with an elected Town Council. Some services and responsibilities of the County Board of Supervisors overlap town territory, e.g., the public library and public school systems. Virginia Tech comprises the main economic base and the primary affiliation of town residents, with a student, faculty and staff population of about 27,000 in 2004. Internet penetration within Blacksburg was 91% of the population in 2002. Most of the remaining percentage has been identified as 'second-hand' users (others get information and/or email for them), (Dunlap, et al. 2003). In Montgomery county, Internet users comprised 78% of the population in 2002 and second-hand use was also common.

The Town of Blacksburg developed a website for government information and services with training and support from the staff of BEV, which has been hosting the town site since 1993. The TOB web site (http://www.blacksburg.gov) functions include: access to departments, updates about town events and emergencies (Blacksburg Alert), calendar of events, forms (e.g., dog license, special use permit), publications (Town Code, Town Charter, Comprehensive Plan), job opportunities, Geographic Information System (GIS), and Town Council meeting agendas, minutes, background documentation, and staff reports. Blacksburg Alert functions as a reverse 911 system; that is, the town government can quickly contact many subscribed citizens with special messages of interest or with emergency information (e.g., weather problems and unexpected school closings). Citizens may select from many topics that might interest them, and receive notification via email or phone.

The TOB also offers digital video streaming from its web site of recorded town councils meetings (broadcast earlier live). This archive of town council meetings can be very helpful for citizens who are not able to attend town meetings in person due to other demands on their time. Although it is well established that many more people are interested in civic affairs in a community than actually show up at public meetings – the TOB online video is not indexed in any way and thus finding relevant content (by agenda item, for example) is quite time consuming and frustrating.

The Montgomery County government also set up a web site in the early 1990s, first with help from the BEV staff and later from the school district which falls under its jurisdiction. County government contracts with several different local Internet Service Providers to provide email services for staff; this makes staff addresses inconsistent and harder to remember. As with the Town of Blacksburg, the County website (http://www.montva.com) includes: access to departments, calendar of events, forms and publications, FAQ to answer citizen questions online, Comprehensive Plan, and GIS. The County also provides a one-way listserv of updates on topics related to county government (budgets, meetings, transportation, etc.) and interested citizens can subscribe to any or all of these updates via email or they can view them on the county web site.

The County also has oversight of the Montgomery Floyd Regional Library (MFRL), (http://www.mfrl.org) which serves all of Montgomery and neighboring Floyd Counties. In addition to traditional library services, MFRL provides computer services which include free public Internet access through computer labs, beginner training on Internet use, and online education resources, (e.g., GED tutorials, GIS, online versions of local newspapers, and online encyclopedia).

Research Design

We are extending findings from prior research that uses findings derived from quantitative and qualitative data using a random survey sample of households in Blacksburg and Montgomery County, from interviews (focus groups and individual and small group) with local citizens, community groups, and town and county government representatives. We also draw from extensive long-term participant observation on the part of the authors. This paper focuses on findings from focus groups, semi-structured interviews with citizens and government, and our participant-observation that are part of a larger study supported by the National Science Foundation (IIS-0429274).

The primary purpose of the focus groups (conducted in December 2003) was to explore questions with community leaders and activists about their participation in local governance and their use of information and communication technology (ICT), including email with local government staff and elected officials and local government web content. We were also interested to learn about these engaged citizens' problems or their frustrations while using ICT for civic purposes. We also sought to learn about what ICT capabilities they would like to have in the future. We did not attempt to recruit non-activists at this point because we were not confident that non-activists were using ICT for civic purposes. Thus, we sought to understand some of the parameters framing the use of ICT by those who presently use it for civic participation. The question of why some people do not use ICT for civic participation will be addressed in a future paper as part of our larger study. We recruited participants for the four focus groups by contacting local civic organizations, business oriented groups, and ethnic groups and individuals who subscribed to local government issue listservs A total of 13 actually participated (7 dropped out, due to sickness, exams and no-shows).

Wc followed up on the focus groups in late Summer/Fall 2004 using additional in-depth interviews with several active individuals in citizens groups. One of these groups is a community wide grassroots organization, known as Citizens First for Blacksburg; another is a neighborhood organization called Miller SouthSide Alliance. While these two groups represent grassroots initiatives at varying levels (community versus neighborhood), both involve citizen-to-citizen interaction and deliberation on civic issues and employ a pervasive use of information technology that yields clear outcomes from their collective action.

We also conducted individual and small group interviews with local government staff (Montgomery County, Town of Blacksburg) over a three month period during Fall 2004. We recorded most of these interviews and supplemented them with our own collective notes for additional analysis and reflection. During these interviews, staff members described their current uses of ICT, common ways they interacted with citizens, and ways that they felt information technology could better support government interaction with citizens. More information about the citizens groups, government, and others interviewed, is available on the project website (http://java.cs.vt.edu/public/projects/digitalgov).

Results

The citizens and citizen groups that we interviewed are using ICT for different kinds of information seeking (e.g., from government sites or email), one-on-one email with government staff or officials, broadcasting information (to each other), and for some deliberation (e.g., discussion with each other on common issues). Government representatives are concerned generally with maintaining content that is easy to find and to use and helpful to both staff users and community users. We have made several suggestions for tools modifications that might enhance options for: 1) government interaction with citizens, and 2) citizens' interaction with each other. We summarize these recommendations below.

Citizens Groups

Community leaders: The community leaders who participated in the focus groups were well educated, activists, and experienced Internet users who were generally older, but not retired. They generally used both the Town and County websites to get information, and used email with government staff or elected officials. Several of them also acted as liaisons between government and their community group (e.g., attending public meetings and forwarding emails from "Blacksburg Alert"). Most of them served as moderators or owners of listservs for their organizations. For communication with local elected officials and government staff, the participants' first choice was generally face-to-face communication because its synchronous, immediate interaction allowed them to see the other's reactions. They generally concurred that their second choice was communication via telephone and their last choice was communication via email.

The participants usually went to the Town or County site for something specific (such as the GIS), not just for browsing. They also suggested that contact information, such as name, email or phone, be provided on web pages wherever feedback or questions are likely, and not just provided on one page within the site. This might make it easier for users to interact with appropriate staff, as needed.

Citizens First for Blacksburg: The grassroots group Citizens First (CF) led an awareness campaign regarding Town Council decisions about alternative sewer options for the Tom's Creek Basin (TCB) that eventually resulted in a landslide victory for several candidates in the 2004 Town Council elections. The controversial TCB gravity sewer option was seen by many as means to subvert the Town's Comprehensive Plan, a consensus-based document which had been developed with perhaps 2,000 citizens over several years. There was a sense among many town residents (expressed by the CF group) that the more expensive gravity sewer design would allow real estate developers to build more densely in the TCB area than the Comp Plan permitted. TOB also considered alternative designs.

After the then Town Council had only a 4-3 majority vote to incur $2 million in debt for the more expensive gravity sewer design, it decided to amend the 5-2 vote requirement in the Town Charter (intended to promote fiscal responsibility) to only require a 4-3 majority. It also proceeded to sign a contract for construction of the controversial sewer option. When CF emailed these changes to the Town Charter and the signed contract for the controversial sewer option out to hundreds of citizens on their list, a critical mass of concerned residents coalesced to oppose these changes to the Town Charter. Coincidentally, three council seats were open for town elections in the coming months; two challengers and one incumbent campaigned opposing the rush to decide the TCB sewer issue.

While preparing for the town elections, CF leaders regularly sent out emails with detailed information about organizing activities, such as from whose front porch (e.g., "with large, but friendly dog") to pick up and later to drop off yard signs, including phone numbers and email addresses to contact if help was needed to pick up signs. Over 200 residents asited in leafleting, phone calling, posting signs, hosting house parties, and forwarding email. As voting day approached, CF organizers sent out detailed information about specific voting locations based on residential area, the hours for voting, the types of ID required, and how to vote by absentee ballot.

The Blacksburg Town Council Elections featured a record turnout on May 4, 2004. Moreover, the proportions of votes were almost identical at both the Municipal Building (where TCB residents vote) and at the Recreation Center where residents from other town areas vote; this suggests that the city-wide CF campaign was effective. The voters elected the three candidates supported by CF who garnered a total of 80% of the vote. The following week, the new Town Council voted to terminate the contracts, funding, and easement proceedings for the TCB gravity sewer and opted to consider further the merits of the two design options and engage in more public debate to build consensus.

The Miller South Side Alliance: (MSA) formed as a grassroots neighborhood group that was concerned with potential traffic problems after the Town announced during Spring 2002 that a contract had been awarded for the nearby construction of a new office building and parking garage. The MSA grew within a few months into a formal non-profit organization (501-3C). Their initial concerns centered around traffic but later the group developed a neighborhood master plan that they submitted to the Town in Fall 2004 for approval and formal incorporation into the Town Comprehensive Plan.

The MSA secretary did not even know how to open email when MSA was formed, but she began to send email messages to neighbors using a one-to-many strategy, and checking the Town website for relevant information. She wanted to have a group discussion arrangement (listserv, forum or chat) even just with the executive committe, but she did not know how to use these ICTs. Email has served as a source of support *and* frustration during the grassroots organizing for MSA. At first the secretary sent long emails, and re-typed long passages of content from the Town website, not knowing how to cut and paste content. Some recipients complained about their length, or didn't seem to be reading them completely. She later learned how to attach documents to minimize length, but some people complained that they couldn't receive attachments. Eventually she learned how to type links to online content into her email messages which reduced length of emails and avoided problems with attachments.

There was much deliberation among neighbors in person, by phone, and online during the process of debating the potential traffic problems and the development of a master meighborhood plan. People did not always agree, but their views were conveyed to the secretary for the record and shared with others. Some neighbors argued that their taxes would be increased if neighbors sought new traffic controls. The neighborhood master plan and the traffic initiative were sometimes at odds with each other. There was concern among some neighbors that the neighborhood plan would divert the Town's attention from the traffic initiative.

The MSA secretary credits the Internet with sustaining the group over the two and half years since its inception. Without computing, it would have been impossible to keep track of who was doing what. Computing helped to galvanize neighbors and to educate them on grassroots issues and official procedures to address grievances. After more than a year of official and residential deliberation about traffic control, including innumerable emails among neighbors, surveys of residents, neighborhood meetings and public hearings, the MSA traffic control petition was denied by the Town because their survey lacked a required response rate of 67% in favor of the traffic control measures; the MSA survey had "only" a 64% favorable response rate for new controls. However, the MSA neighborhood master plan was completed and submitted to the Town in Fall 2004 for approval and integration into the Town Comprehensive Plan. Because the traffic safety concerns were incorporated into the neighborhood master plan, they are likely to become "blessed" by the Town Comprehensive Plan.

Government Groups

The Town of Blacksburg: TOB has enhanced and integrated some of its online content to allow interested citizens and groups to find and use information. While the TOB had been posting agendas of town council meetings for several years, in Summer 2004, it began linking background documentation from each related agenda item (e.g., an agenda item about a special use permit would be linked to the completed permit application under consideration). Thus, citizens could access the same documents that town council members had used for their meetings. The TOB Comprehensive Plan and the GIS system are also integrated online; this facilitates comparing these two records (e.g., current and planned land use, zoning, and ownership). The "Blacksburg Alert" service provides a useful mechanism for the TOB to broadcast information to citizens. Although it is a one-way medium, broadcasted information can stimulate public deliberation particularly when it goes to an interested group of stakeholders, such as neighborhood or homeowners associations, like the MSA. Alert information can also stimulate second-order communication efforts when a representative or liaison citizen subscribes and forwards the alerts to others in their group(s).

Montgomery County: Discussions with the County government revealed that the Planning Department stimulated important citizen-to-citizen deliberation when it began a two-year development process for the county-wide Comprehensive Plan for 2025. In this case, ICT played an important role in this process, by reinforcing face-to-face meetings and discussions printed in county newsletters. The government reported that information technology helped to attract broader citizen participation in the planning effort, including participation from members of underrepresented populations (i.e., lower education or income).

An initial series of face to face meetings convened by the county to develop this Comp Plan of 2025 began in 2000; these meetings were only attended by about ten individuals at each meeting. The county staff member responsible for this process decided that major communication strategy changes were essential to reach a broader and more diverse population, especially persons with less education or income. She changed the language and the style of the county newsletter to be much simpler (less jargon), more educational (explaining what county documents and input processes existed), and she used a more graphical format (to catch attention and convey complex information more effectively through pictures, tables and graphs).

The County staff worked closely with representatives from 88 local organizations (out of a total of 300 contacted) to boost citizen participation in the Comp Plan development. Group representatives received special training to facilitate face-to-face deliberation within their own organizations about the issues to include in the Comprehensive Plan and met in county work-groups throughout the Summer 2003 to do the actual writing. Throughout this intensely participative process, the Planning Department maintained a website that archived a record of feedback from citizens garnered from face-to-face meetings, emails, and telephone calls. The site also archived drafts and latest revisions of Comp Plan sections for further comments and feedback. Each background document, consultant's report, survey data finding, and even the raw data were posted on the County website. Staff even re-typed and posted citizen email messages (anonymously). Although not all county residents could access the Internet, especially persons with lower education or income, staff members were careful to keep online content accessible for those with slower access via dial-up connections. County staff received comments from some residents that their trust and confidence in the county's willingness to listen and respond to their feedback had increased because the web site reflected residents' input.

Preliminary Requirements Analysis

As citizens have come to expect a greater range of on-line government services, government agencies have, perhaps not surprisingly, grown somewhat more risk-averse in their information technology efforts. Among the factors fueling this trend are legal implications of allowing public creation of content on official systems, security concerns, the overhead of rigorously validating and subsequently maintaining each new tool deployed. Limited technology resources are focused on providing the kinds of basic information dissemenation and customer service that citizens increasingly expect. Even the most innovative government organizations are subject to these constraints. Given that it may be neither practical nor desirable to host systems that directly support citizen deliberation on government servers, our design efforts will follow two interdependent, but separate, paths: 1) analysis of design guidelines and patterns for government-provided information, and 2) prototyping of tools that citizens can use for deliberative activities.

For systems maintained by government agencies, we intend to focus primarily on issues of accessibility and complementarity with the tools that are likely to be employed by citizens, rather than proposing significant modifications to current infrastructure. Facets of complementarity include ensuring that content is published in open, accessible formats and is easily addressible. Citizens who wish to discuss a section of, for example, a comprehensive plan should be able to point their readers to the specific section. Conversely, users who wish to discover where deliberation of the plan is happening should have access to tools that track and aggregate citizen discussions. Such tools would likely be useful for both citizens and government officials, as they could help uncover proposals or events that were generating "buzz," identify synergies among community groups, and give greater exposure to "political entreprenuers" who bring new ideas into the conversation. Emerging standards such as "TrackBack" are designed specifically to support this type of bi-directional linking and aggregation (http://www.movabletype.org/trackback/). As the volume of government and citizen-created content grows, syndication mechanisms such as RSS (Really Simple Syndication), provide a flexible way to publish summaries of recent contributions and updates.

Several specific ideas for such technology enhancements have emerged from discussions with Town and County government personnel. For example, the meetings of both the Blacksburg Town Council and the Montgomery County Board of Supervisors are videotaped and televised on a community channel. Agendas, summaries, and digital video are posted to the web. (Blacksburg currently makes video available online, while the County plans to do this in the future.) The video captures details that may be missing from a summary, but, aside from the general unwieldiness of video, it is difficult to address and link to specific segments of a video stream. Technology that added this capability could make published summaries more useful, as citizens would be able to scan the meeting agenda for items relevant to their interests and click on a hyperlink that would take them directly to the video segment they wish to review. This would also allow citizens to post on weblogs or forums, to point readers to specific events in meetings, or to bookmark video segments.

In another example, the Montgomery/Floyd Regional Library (MFRL) serves as a source of authoritative information that is likely to be useful in deliberative activities. The MFRL recently begun to take a more active role in managing their web presence, but would still like to find easier ways to update web pages that change rapidly, such as news items and upcoming events, in ways that allow them to distribute this work across the library staff. Wiki-style tools could support these authoring tasks, while RSS could make new content more visible and accessible.

In designing tools specifically for use by citizens, our interest is to facilitate the entry of new participants and to support the discovery of new ways of combining components that support core dissemination and deliberation tasks. In our prototyping activities we use software infrastructure previously developed for the NSF-sponsored TeacherBridge (ROLE; REC-0106552) and Learning in Networked Communities (LiNC; REC-9554206) projects. In the LiNC project, we developed CORK (Content Object Replication Kit), a toolkit for transparently replicating Java objects, as a basis for tools that allowed synchronous and asynchronous collaboration (Isenhour, Rosson, and Carroll 2001). We subsequently extended this work by creating a system called BRIDGE (Basic Resources for Integrated Distributed Group Environments), which provides mechanisms for browsing and modifying structured collections of CORK-based objects from web browsers and interactive clients. In the TeacherBridge project, a number of local K-12 teachers are using BRIDGE-based tools to create content such as secure web-editable pages for course management; interactive chat rooms for literature discussions; threaded discussions for persuasive writing exercises; and synchronous workspaces for distributed group projects. These creations are web-accessible, interactive, shareable, reusable, and have been created or adapted by users with a wide range of computer skills.

Discussion

Public deliberation tends to occur, as prior studies have shown, among people with higher levels of education and extroversion, and at a middle life cycle stage. These are also strong predictors of multiple group memberships and of Internet use for civic and political purposes. The focus group participants, the MSA neighborhood association members, and Citizens First for Blacksburg organizers were all community leaders with multiple group affiliations who used the Internet for civic engagement. The unique feature of the Internet among information and communication technologies is precisely its multipoint-to-multipoint capability to support and facilitate group interaction. Group meetings and public places provide the 'great good spaces' where much deliberation occurs and social capital accumulates. Several studies show that Internet household penetration throughout the US has risen steadily (Horrigan, 2001; Horrigan, et al., 2004; Madden, 2003) and almost two-thirds (62%) of Americans report that the Internet had become part of their daily routine (Hoffman, et al., 2004). This means that the high Internet penetration rates in Blacksburg, Virginia and surrounding Montgomery County are no longer so unusual. Rather, Blacksburg and Montgomery County offer a view to the near future for other American small towns and their surrounding rural counties with similar socio-economic characteristics (i.e., predominantly middle class).

Bearing in mind Bandura's warning that perceived efficacy will shape how the Internet changes the face of social activism, we can expect that citizens with lower socioeconomic status (SES) will not be drawn into local governance simply because government information is available online. The collective and political efficacy of people with lower education or income will increase only as they learn hopefulness through, for example, demonstrated and persistent government interest in their concerns (as in the case of the County Comprehensive Plan development). Incentives to participate in discussion are also greater when other like-minded cohorts are present. As such, it is especially important for these underrepresented groups that ICTs are easy to use and that their design simplifies the effort to produce online content and to participate in online discussion. While there may be other ways that intrinsic motivation to participate in public deliberation can be generated, we focused on some of the most salient factors that have been identified in prior studies and our own research. It is important to explore motivations to participate further.

Online tools designed to facilitate deliberation require that they be web-accessible, interactive, shareable, reusable, and have been created or adapted by users with a wide range of computer skills. Hence, while new end-user tools will need to be designed as requirements for deliberation systems emerge, their development can proceed from a proven software infrastructure base.

Our experiences with TeacherBridge have served to validate a key assertion about the value of component-oriented systems for end-user authoring: Rather than attempting to design the "right" system, we should seek to provide components that allow useful constellations of tools to emerge. These will first be discovered by the more innovative users (or, perhaps, those with the greatest perceived needs), and can then be copied by the broader user community. To some degree this mirrors the evolution of tool use that has already occured in groups such as the MSA. We are building on the current set of BRIDGE components to provide easily configurable and composable threaded discussions, weblogs, wikis, polls, interactive chats, and other tools that can be used by citizens to augment mailing lists, static websites, and similar technologies already in use.

While the capability to construct new kinds of tools to meet specific needs will appeal to users who have appropriate combinations of innovativeness, motivation, technical savvy, and available time - inclusiveness demands simplicity. Ideally, users who are less comfortable with technology and, perhaps, only have network access in public places such as the library, must also be able to contribute. The goal of minimizing barriers to entry for new users has implications not only for usability of deliberative components, but also for security and authentication.

In our work on the TeacherBridge project, we have been able to provide a growing set of templates, collections of components that can be instantiated for a specific task and then customized if the user desires. For example, a template for a class home page might have a calendar for deadlines and events, standard pages for class descriptions, a contact page for parents, and a secure threaded discussion for class members. We envision similar templates emerging for organizations such as a neighborhod planning group, where the collection might contain pages for describing the organization and neighborhood to new residents, a secure wiki for drafts of planning docs, and a set of weblogs for neighborhood members. The ability to instantiate such a template via a simple user interface may encourage more organizations to become engaged in open deliberation.

Openness, in the sense of public visibility for deliberative contributions, is critical for building consensus across organizations and providing feedback to government agencies. However, the appropriate configuration of read- and write-access will vary from group to group and user to user. Systems should therefore support multiple models of ownership, membership, and editorship and they should represent systems that range from single-citizen weblogs with open comment sections, to members-only forums, or to edited neighborhood journals in which many may contribute but final publication is at the discretion of the owner.

Requirements analysis for prototyping efforts is still in an early stage. Our emphasis on flexible component-oriented systems allows us to explore a number of fundamental design questions in the context of deliberation. Given flexible components, what kinds of "deliberative structures" emerge? What are the implications of different discussion structures encouraged/enforced by tool selection and security policies? For example, there are ongoing debates as to the usefulness of comments in weblogs, with some arguing that referer tracking and Trackback is more useful: People are free to respond to an entry, at any length they choose, on their own weblog, in such a way that readers can find a link to the external comments. This approach eliminates the inherent problems of an open comment section, but requires considerably more effort on the part of the commenter. Examining questions such as this in the context of a live, diverse system also provides insights into the way credibility evolves in online communities whose members are likely to work together, attend the same church, see each other at the grocery store, or send their children to the same school.

Acknowledgments

We are grateful for support from the National Science Foundation Digital Government award (IIS-0429274) for the research described in this paper. We would like to acknowledge our research collaborators Manuel Pérez-Quiñones and Daniel Dunlap and our project partners the Town of Blacksburg and Montgomery County, as well as various citizens groups.

References

Arterton, F.C. 1987. *Teledemocracy: Can technology protect democracy?* Newbury Park, CA: Sage Library of Social Research.

Bachrach, P. and Baratz, M. 1962. Two Faces of Power. *American Political Science Review* 56: 947-52.

Bandura, A. 1997. *Self-efficacy: The exercise of control.* New York: Freeman.

Bandura, A. 2000. Exercise of human agency through collective agency. *Current directions in psychological science,* 9 (3), 75-78.

Bandura, A. 2001. Social cognitive theory: An agentic perspective. *Annual review of psychology,* 53, 1-26.

Bandura, A. 2002. Growing primacy of human agency in adaptation and change in the electronic era. *European Psychologist,* 7 (1), 2-16.

Barber, B. 1984. *Strong democracy.* Berkeley: University of California Press.

Barber, B., Mattson, K., and Peterson, J. 1997. *The state of 'electronically enhanced democracy:' A survey of the Internet.* New Brunswick, NJ: Walt Whitman Center of the Culture and Politics of Democracy.

Benkler, Y. 2002. Coase's Penguin, or, Linux and the Nature of the Firm. *Yale Law Journal,* 112 (3), 369 - 447.

Bimber, B. (2003). *Information and American democracy: Technology in the evolution of political power.* NY: Cambridge University Press.

Blacksburg Electronic Village and Virginia Cooperative Extension. 2004. Getting Rural Virginia Connected. *Final Grant Report* (51-60-01007), US Department of Commerce, TOP Program.

Bottomore, T.B. 1965. *Elites and Society.* New York: Basic Books.

Brants, K. 1996. An Exercise in Local Electronic Democracy. *Media, Culture and Society,* 18, 233-247.

Carroll, J.M. and Rosson, M.B. 1996. Developing the Blacksburg Electronic Village. *Communications of the ACM,* 39 (12), 69-74.

Carroll, J.M. and Rosson, M.B. 2001. Better home shopping or new-democracy: Evaluating community network outcomes. *Proceedings of CHI 2001: Conference on Human Factors of Computing Systems.* (Seattle, WA; March 31-April 5). NY: ACM, 372-379.

Carroll, J.M. and Reese, D. 2003. Community collective efficacy: Structure and consequences of perceived capacities in the Blacksburg Electronic Village. *Hawaii International Conference on System Sciences, HICSS-36* (January 6-9, Kona).

Carroll, J.M., Chin, G., Rosson, M.B., and Neale, D.C. 2000. The development of cooperation: Five years of participatory design in the Virtual School. *DIS 2000: Designing Interactive Systems.* New York, ACM, 239-251.

Cohill, A. and Kavanaugh, A. 1997, 2000 (revised edition). *Community Networks: Lessons from Blacksburg, Virginia.* Norwood, MA: Artech House.

Coleman, J. 1988. Social capital in the creation of human capital. *American Journal of Sociology,* 94: 95-120.

Coleman, S. 2003. *A Tale of Two Houses: The House of Commons, the Big Brother House and the people at home*. London: The Hansard Society.

Coleman, S. and Gotz, J. 2002. Bowling Together: Online public engagement in policy deliberation; http://bowlingtogether.net

Computer Science and Telecommunications Board (CSTB). 2000. *Information Technology Research for Federal Statistics*. Washington, DC: National Academy Press.

Cook, M. Lavigne, M. Pagano, C. Dawes, S. and Pardo, R. 2002. Making a Case for Local E-government. Center for Technology in Government, SUNY Albany.

Dahl, R. 1989. *Democracy and its critics*. New Haven, CT: Yale University Press.

Davis, J. and Fernlund, P. 1991. *Civics: Participating in our democracy*. New York: Addison-Wesley.

Davis, R. and Owen, D. 1998. *New media and American politics*. NY: Oxford University Press.

Dunlap, D., W. Schafer, J.M. Carroll and D.D. Reese. 2003. Delving deeper into access: Marginal Internet usage in a local community. Paper presented at HOIT (Home Oriented Informatics and Telematics), Irvine, CA.

Dutton, W., Wyer, J. and O'Connell, J. 1993. The Governmental Impacts of Information Technology: A case study of Santa Monica's Public Electronic Network. In R. Banker, R. Kauffman and M. Mahmood (eds.) *Strategic information technology management*. Harrisburg, PA: Idea Group.

Ellison, C. 2000. Naming and certificates. In *Proceedings of the Tenth Conference on Computers, Freedom, and Privacy*. pp. 213-217. ACM Press.

Etzioni, A. 1992. Teledemocracy: Ross Perot left the residue of a good idea behind him: The electronic town meeting. *Atlantic* (October), 34-39.

Fiore, A., Tiernan, S., Smith, A. 2002. Observed Behavior and Perceived Value of Authors in Usenet Newsgroups: Bridging the Gap. In *Proceedings of the SIGCHI Conference on Human Factors in Computing Systems*. pp. 323-330. ACM Press.

Fishkin, J.S. 1991. *Democracy and deliberation*. New Haven, CT: Yale University Press.

Granovetter, M. 1973. The Strength of Weak Ties. *American Journal of Sociology*, 78:1360-80.

Guthrie, K. and Dutton, W. 1992. The politics of citizen access technology: The development of public information utilities in four cities. *Policy Studies Journal*, 20, 574-597.

Hoffman, D., Novak, T. and Venkatesh, A. 2004. Has the Internet become Indispensable? *Communications of the ACM*, 47 (7), 37-42.

Horrigan, J. 2001. *Online communities: Networks that nurture long-distance relationships and local ties*. Pew Internet and American Life Project; http://www.pewinternet.org.

Horrigan, J., Garrett, K. and Resnick, P. 2004. The Internet and Democratic Debate. Pew Internet and American Life Project; http://www.pewinternet.org.

Isenhour, P.L., Rosson, M.B. and Carroll, J.M. 2001. Supporting Interactive Collaboration on the Web with CORK. *Interacting with Computers,* 13, Special Issue on Interfaces for the Active Web, pp. 655-676.

Katz, J., Rice, R. and Aspden, P. 2001. The Internet, 1995-2000: Access, civic involvement, and social interaction. *American Behavioral Scientist* 45 (3), 405-419.

Kavanaugh, A. 2003. When Everyone is Wired. In J. Turow and A. Kavanaugh (eds.) *The Wired Homestead: An MIT Press sourcebook on the family and the internet.* Cambridge, MA: MIT Press, pp. 423-437.

Kavanaugh, A., Cohill, A. and Patterson, S. 2000. The Use and Impact of the Blacksburg Electronic Village. In A. Cohill and A. Kavanaugh (Eds.), *Community Networks: Lessons from Blacksburg, Virginia.* Norwood, MA: Artech House, pp. 77-98.

Kavanaugh, A. and Patterson, S. 2001. The Impact of Community Computer Networks on Social Capital and Community Involvement. *American Behavioral Scientist,* 45 (3): 496-509.

Kavanaugh, A. Reese, D.D., Carroll, J.M., and Rosson, M.B. 2003. Weak Ties in Networked Communities. In M. Huysman, E. Wenger and V. Wulf (Eds.) *Communities and Technologies.* The Netherlands: Kluwer Academic Publishers, pp. 265-286.

Kavanaugh, A. and Schmitz, J. 2004. Talking in Lists: The consequences of computer mediated communication on communities. *Internet Research Annual, 1,* 250-259.

Kavanaugh, A., Carroll, J.M., Rosson, M. B., Reese, D. D. and Zin, T.T. 2005. Participating in Civil Society: The case of networked communities. *Interacting with Computers* 17, Special Issue on Designing for Civil Society, pp. 9-33.

Kirn, K. 2002. Building Social Capital on the Web: The case of Minnesota E-Democracy. In Turow, J (Ed.), Energizing Voters Online: Best Practices from Election 2000. Report no. 39, Annenberg Public Policy Center, University of Pennsylvania.

Larson, E., and Associates. 2002a. *Digital Town Hall: How local officials use the Internet and the civic benefits they cite from dealing with constituents online.* Pew Internet and American Life Project; http://www.pewinternet.org.

Larson, E., and Associates. 2002b. *The Rise of the E-citizen: How people use government agencies' web sites.* Pew Internet and American Life Project; http://www.pewinternet.org.

Lasswell, H.D. 1948. *The Analysis of Political Behavior: An empirical approach.* London: Routledge and Keagan Paul.

Laudon, K. 1977. *Communication Technology and Democratic Participation.* NY: Praeger.

Maddux, M. 2003. America's Online Pursuits: The changing picture of who's online and what they do. Pew Internet and American Life Project; http://www.pewinternet.org.

Meikeljohn, A. 1948. Political Freedom: The constitutional powers of the people. New York: Harper and Row.

Milbraith, L. and Goel, M. 1982. *Political participation: How and why do people get involved in politics?* 2nd edition. New York: University Press of America.

National Research Council. 2000. *Digital Democracy: Exploring the promise of information technology in promoting participation in the political process.* Washington, DC: The National Academies.

Neuman, R. 1991. *The Future of the Mass Audience.* New York: Cambridge University Press.

Newton, K. 1997. Social Capital and Democracy. *American Behavioral Scientist,* 40 (5), 575-586.

Nie, N. 2001. Sociability, interpersonal relations, and the Internet: Reconciling conflicting findings. *American Behavioral Scientist 45* (3), 420-435.

Nie, N., Powell, G., and Prewitt, K. 1969. Social structure and political paritcipation: Developmental relationships, Part I, II. *Amerian Political Science Review* 63: 361-378, 808-832.

Office of Management and Budget (OMB). 2002. *E-Government Strategy: Simplified delivery of services to citizens.* Washington, DC.

Oldenburg, R. 1991. *The great good place: Cafes, coffee shops, community centers, beauty parlors, general stores, bars, hangouts, and how they get you through the day.* New York: Paragon House.

O'Sullivan, P. 1995. Computer networks and political participation: Santa Monica's teledemocracy project. *Journal of Applied Communication Research 23,* (May), 93-107.

Pateman, C. 1970. *Participation and democratic theory.* Cambridge, UK: Cambridge University Press.

Patterson, S. 1997. Evaluating the Blacksburg Electronic Village. In A. Cohill and A. Kavanaugh (eds.) *Community Networks: Lessons from Blacksburg, Virginia.* Norwood, MA: Artech House, pp. 59-75.

Patterson, S. and Kavanaugh, A. 1994. Rural Users Expectations of the Information Superhighway, *Media Information Australia.* 74 (November), 57-61

Pool, I. de Sola. 1984. *Technologies of freedom.* Cambridge, MA: Harvard University Press.

Putnam, R. 2000. *Bowling Alone: The collapse and revival of American community.* NY: Simon and Schuster.

Raab, C., Bellamy, C. Taylor, J., Dutton, W., and Peltu, M. 1996. The Information polity: Electronic democracy, privacy, and surveillance. In W. Dutton (Ed.) *Information and communication technologies: Visions and realities.* New York: Oxford University Press.

Resnick, P. 2001. Beyond bowling together: Sociotechnical capital. In John M. Carroll (ed.) *Human Computer Interaction in the New Millenium.* Reading, MA: Addison-Wesley, pp. 647-672.

Schmitz, J., Rogers, E., Phillips, K., and Paschal, D. 1995. The Public Electronic Network (PEN) and homeless in Santa Monica. *Journal of Applied Communication Research 23,* (May) 26-43.

Schudson, M. 1992. The Limits of Teledemocracy. *The American Prospect.* Fall: 41-45.

Schuler, D. 1996. *New community networks: Wired for change.* New York, NY: ACM Press.

Seligson, M.A. 1980. Trust, efficacy and Modes of Political Participation: A study of Costa Rican peasants. *British Journal of Political Science,* 10, 75-98.

Silver, D. 1999. Localizing the global village: Lessons from the Blacksburg Electronic Village. In B. Browne and M. W. Fishwick (eds.) *The Global Village: Dead or Alive?* Bowling Green, OH: Popular Press, pp. 79-92.

Silver, D. 2000. Margins in the wires: Looking for race, gender, and sexuality in the BEV. In B. Kolko, L. Nakamura, and G. Rodman (Eds.) *Race in cyberspace.* London: Routledge, 133-150.

Silver, D. 2004. The Soil of cyberspace: Historical archaeologies of the Blacksburg Electronic Village and the Seattle Community Network. In D. Schuler and P. Day (eds.) *Shaping the Network Society.* Cambridge, MA: MIT Press, pp. 301-324.

Simmel, G. [1908] Group expansion and the development of individuality. In Donald Levine (ed.), *Georg Simmel on individuality and social forms.* Chicago: University of Chicago Press, 1971.

Sproull, L. and Kiesler, S. 1991. *Connections: News ways of working in networked organizations.* Cambridge, MA: MIT Press.

Tomita, T. 1980. *The Media Gap Model.* Tokyo: Japan Ministry of Communications.

Tsagarousianou, R., Tambini, D. and Bryan, C. (eds.) 1998. *Cyberdemocracy: Technology, cities and civic networks,* London: Routledge.

Vatrapu, R. and Pérez-Quiñones, M. 2003. *Culture and International Usability Testing: The effects of culture in structured interviews.* Virginia Tech MS Thesis of R. Vatrapu; http://scholar.lib.vt.edu/theses/available/etd-09132002-083026

Verba, S. and Nie, N. 1972. *Participation in America: Political democracy and social equality.* NY: Harper and Row.

Wellman, B. and Berkowitz, S.D. (Eds.) 1988. *Social Structures: A network approach.* New York: Cambridge University Press.

White, C. S. 1997. Citizen participation and the Internet: Prospects for civic deliberation in the information age. *The Social Studies,* January/February: 23-28.

Wilhelm, T. 2000. *Democracy in the Digital Age.* New York: Routledge.

Wolff, K. 1950. *The Sociology of Georg Simmel.* New York: The Free Press.

Wolfsfeld, G. 1986. Evaluational Origins of Political Action: The case of Israel. *Political Psychology,* 7, 767-788.

Local Communities: Relationships between 'real' and 'virtual' social capital

Sonia Liff

Warwick University, UK
Sonia.Liff@Warwlck.ac.uk

Abstract. The paper explores forms of 'real' and 'virtual' social capital within a geographical area of the UK comprising 65 'communities'. Measures of real social capital based on formal community organisations were compared with web-activity relating to the same communities. Three main types of websites were identified: first a local government scheme which created 'identikit' websites for each of the places which could then be taken up by local people; second a similar scheme operated by a private company and covering the whole of the UK; and third independent, bottom up sites created by social entrepreneurs or community groups. Numbers and forms of organisations and websites, and levels and forms of community web-based participation were measured for each community at two points in 2004. The analysis suggests no strong correlation between these measures of real and virtual social capital. The analysis further suggests that providing a ready made website rarely results in the creation of a developed community site – although it may provide outlets for more limited information exchanges. However bottom up sites which reflect the heterogeneity of real communities are also rare. Interviews with participants suggest the need to understand more about the social networks, practices and organisational forms that sustain community engagement with community websites.

Community-based ICT initiatives have often involved the establishment of place-based websites which provide a 'virtual' representation of that community to itself and the wider world, a site for discussions about community initiatives, a forum for projects such as local history groups and so on. Alongside community locations providing access to the internet and computer training such websites have been seen as having the potential to make an important contribution to community regeneration by promoting local issues, re-establishing a sense of

P. van den Besselaar et al. (eds.), Communities and Technologies 2005, 41-53.

identity and promoting communication. This is an approach which has been
described and endorsed by a range of practitioner and academic accounts (in the
US, examples include Schuler, 1996; Schon et al, 1999; Mele, 1999).

This paper explores the relationship between real communities and their virtual
representations within a diverse geographical area and highlights the extent to
which different kinds of community networks appear to be able to engage
community participation.

The Wider Relationship between Real and Virtual Social Capital

The successful examples of community engagement with ICTs highlighted above
can be seen as a useful antidote to earlier dystopian visions of the internet creating
an homogenised global culture and destroying people's engagement with their
local communities, neighbours, and even fellow household members. However
such cases are normally the result of intensive and sustained community capacity
building activities. For this reason the question of whether there is a more general
relationship between the health of local communities and the development of
local community networks (and if so of what type and in which direction) remains
contested.

One way of measuring the strength of communities is to assess their social
capital. Putnam (2000) defines this as the connections between individuals –
social networks and the norms of reciprocity and trustworthiness that arise from
them. Putnam further distinguishes between bonding and bridging social capital.
Bonding social capital refers to the strong, multi-layered, forms of connection
which are usually thought to be characteristic of kinship relationships and
traditional communities. Bridging social capital is characterised by looser
relation-ships, which might for, example, provide a link between distinctive social
groupings. Putnam uses a wide range of measures to judge the extent of social
capital, ranging from personal socialising through to membership of formal civic
organisations.

Putnam (2000) raised a number of concerns about the ways in which the
internet might be destructive to social capital. These included the consequences
of differential access ('the digital divide') for people's access to internet-based
social networks and the tendency of people to use the internet to engage with very
narrow communities of interest which might be destructive of bridging social
capital. He suggested that rather than community networks creating social capital,
the opposite might be true with local communities with strong social capital being
a necessary pre-requisite for effective community networks. However, Katz et al
(2001) and Wellman et al (2001) both find positive empirical associations
between internet use and various dimensions of social capital (although the

survey methodology they employ makes it difficult to be sure about the direction of these links).

These studies are based on internet use (or non-use) in general rather than specific involvement with local community networks. In relation to the latter, Kavanaugh & Patterson (2001) argue that even if Putnam is right about the initial need for effective communities, there is additional potential for a community network to build social capital locally by drawing in new participants. Interestingly their empirical work shows that the longer people have been on-line the more likely they are to use the network for social capital building activities. In a similar vein Jankowski et al (2001) argue that community integration can be seen as both a consequence and / or an antecedent of community media use.

Overall then the evidence seems to suggest that there is no necessary conflict between internet use and social capital and indeed that one might expect to their co-existence. Most of the empirical evidence (Kavanaugh & Patterson excepted) is based on data on individuals rather than communities. As such, while it can look at demographic variations between individuals it is not in a position to comment on outcomes in different kinds of community. Nor have the studies looked at whether outcomes can be related to the different kinds of community networks in which participants might engage.

The current study provides an opportunity to consider some of these issues by comparing outcomes in a variety of different types of community in relation to different types of web presences. It allows different types of questions to be asked. For example would we expect more atomised communities, such as those with a high proportion of residents who commute to work elsewhere, to engage less in community networks but perhaps use the internet in more instrumental ways (which might be characterised as bridging rather than bonding social capital) or would one expect to see examples of individually initiated websites, or none at all?

Of course whatever the strength of such dynamics one would not expect to see the relationship between real and virtual social capital existing in isolation from other variables. Both might be expected to be influenced by factors such as the size of the community and its demographic make up. Further, it seems at least possible that such structural variables will not fully explain the emergence of particular forms of social practice relevant to understanding the form of website / community network use that arise from, say, links between communities or the presence of individuals with a particular mix of skills.

Study of Local Websites in a District Authority Area

Research has been carried out within an area defined by a second level tier of local government (and English District Council) and which contains 65 settlements ('communities'). The area is largely rural, consisting mainly of small villages (with various levels of identity, clearly defined boundaries and separation from each other). There are also a small number of larger places. Public transport is poor and some settlements are defined as isolated on this measure. However the main road network provides quite good links to major regional settlements, for those with their own transport. In the 1980s and 1990s the area was subject to relatively high unemployment as a result of mining closures and this led to a range of regeneration measures (which have now largely ended).

A sense of the way these settlements vary can be gleaned from an assessment of the number and type of formal community organisations which exist. This has been assessed on the basis of a database (Infolinx) held by the County Council and covers organisations ranging from sports clubs, self help groups, and societies based on shared interests or around a particular event. This database is available via the websites discussed below but existed prior to their development and is maintained independently of them. It is of course likely that such a database, with which there is no particular incentive to register and which does not have the resources to seek out, or even validate, the information it is given is far from a perfect measure. In particular it is likely to over-represent formal organisations such as Guides or Scouts, Churches or sports activities linked into national leagues and under-represent the relatively informal interest based groups. However there seems no reason to assume that it will be differentially inaccurate between the communities studied here. Additional information on these communities comes from local knowledge.[1]

This data show that of the 65 settlements 39 had none or one registered community organisation. Some of these places are tiny and may see themselves primarily in relation to another settlement. As such this finding would not imply that the residents had no collective activities. However not all the cases can be explained in this way. At the other extreme 8 places had 20 or more organisations registered. These were all the larger settlements in the area. There does not appear to be any straightforward relationship between the affluence of the communities and this measure of social capital.

The District Authority area falls within that covered by a rural partnership body (this encompasses representatives from County and District authorities, police and other service providers, rural community council etc. and runs shared projects but is not a level of government as such). As part of its ICT strategy this body has established a website for every 'rural' settlement (in practice everywhere except the County town). These websites (which can be found via www.leicestershirevillages.com) are mainly based on generic information held by the contributing bodies, supplemented by a number of shared national links. The websites have a central area which contains an image of the place (invariably an

---

[1] My engagement with this study is both as an academic and as a participant observer. As a resident and an 'active citizen' I am able to draw on local knowledge that goes beyond the formal methods described.

image of the built environment) and an invitation to contribute local content and to become involved in the administration of the site (see figure 1 for an example).

Figure 1 An example of a village page on LeicestershireVillages

Individuals need to register before they can post their messages which then appear on an area originally called *Your Pages* and now re-titled *Local Pages*. Other than content contributed by residents the strongest element of 'local' content is the use of databases collected by various parts of local government for a variety of purposes which can be searched to 'find my nearest ...' in a variety of categories including accommodation and football teams.

These 65 websites were examined for evidence of any local content resulting from citizen engagement with the initiative. There are only certain places where local people can post on the website so the parts which formed a basis for this search was clear. However not all thing posted in these places originated with the community. For example under *Local Contacts* the community development officer for the area has posted her details for every village. Under *Local News* there were similar multiple posts from the library service. *Local Events* took one to a generic site with arts events – although in this case it was possible to post additional local ones. The Local Web Directory had a mixture of links to business, local authority and community sites but none appeared more local than the District Council level. These things may clearly be relevant to the local community – but they are not from the community. Where community-generated content did exist it was recorded and categorised, with one area of interest being whether it appeared to be evidence of some type of community engagement (e.g. postings from local groups, announcements of meetings, discussion of issues of local concern) or whether it seemed to be a more individual exchange of information (e.g. small ads, offers of business services). This analysis was repeated 7 months later to get a sense of the extent to which such participation was on-going, and to avoid the problems inherent in analyses carried out at one point in time.

These 65 settlement names were then used as the basis of a search on GOOGLE to find other web representations of these places. The top 50 hits relating to each place name were examined. Most of these could not be considered as village websites. Instead they were what could be called directory sites – usually relating to hotels, but also to pubs, churches and other establishments. These effectively use the search for a particular place to take one to a site which claims to be able to, for example, 'Find a hotel near X'. The quality of the information found varies, with many being very poor, but in any case they do not even claim to provide any wider information about the place and its community and so were excluded from further study.

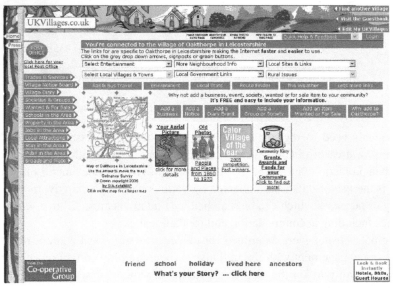

Figure 2 An example of a village page on UK Villages

UK VILLAGE sites appeared for a significant proportion of the places (www.ukvillages.co.uk). This is a national commercial site which claims it has created websites 31,000 'communities'. These again contain largely generic links (although of quite a high level of sophistication in terms of taking one to a part of the linked site relevant to the geographical area of interest, and avoiding the problems of searching only within postcodes that plague many such sites). As with LEICESTERSHIRE VILLAGES (and a number of other such sites) they encourage local content in the form of individual posts to places with labels like 'Village Notice Board'. Again such sites (see Figure 2 for an example), where they existed, were examined to see whether local use was being made of the site and if so in what form. This analysis was also repeated at a second point in time as described above.

A number of independent sites were also identified via the Google searches. These included sites which appeared to be established by local small businesses (usually offering commercial website creation or related ICT services) which said that they had been created for village use. Other sites appeared to be a spin off from some local heritage or related project, often funded with public sector grants. A small number were established by individuals or by independent community groups (see Figure 3 for an example). All these sites were explored for the breadth and depth of community engagement. All these investigations also provided an opportunity to assess more informally other aspects of social capital, in particular 'bounded solidarity' where Pigg & Crank (2004) argue that there have been no empirical studies. They identify five dimensions of social capital using the term bounded solidarity to mean 'a source of collective identity and a resource for action against threats from external sources' (4).

Figure 3. An example of an independent village website in the area

In addition to web-based research, face to face interviews were held with those responsible for the UK VILLAGES and LEICESTERSHIRE VILLAGES sites and with some of those running independent sites.[2] These interviews covered a range of issues relating to the origins of their website, why it had taken the particular form it had (structure, design, funding etc.), their interest in local participation and views on how it could be encouraged, and how they saw their positioning relative to other websites also intending to represent these local places.

Evidence of Virtual Social Capital

This study was not intended to explore the role of community networks in 'real' community life. It was rather intended to explore the circumstances under which such community networks might exist, including any association with the characteristics of the community in terms of levels of real social capital. It was also intended to explore whether the 'technical' characteristics or the ownership of sites appeared to be significant in encouraging (particular types of) participation. Such participation is taken as key for a web presence to be seen as a site of virtual social capital.

The study found a range of independent sites which varied in the breadth and depth of community information and participation. The original analysis found a local group of churches which had created sites for 6 places and had included some broader community information. Local heritage and environment projects were the basis for 2 sites and a further 2 were created by local regeneration projects. Social entrepreneurs and local community groups had created sites for 6 places and a further 2 sites were originated by individuals or families. Seven places were making some use of the LEICESTERSHIRE VILLAGES sites through the then 'your pages' facility. However in only one case was this a standalone, relatively rich community facility (in one case the site simply linked through to the independent community site, in other cases there were individual postings relating to business services or to single societies or events). No 'community' use was made of the UK VILLAGES sites, although there were a few individual postings of business services.

Taken together these findings appeared to indicate relatively high levels of virtual social capital. However this was primarily of the 'bridging' type involving individual instrumental participation around the exchange of goods and services. This was particularly (though not exclusively in either direction) the case in relation to the multiple web presences created as part of the UK VILLAGES and the LEICESTERSHIRE RURAL PARTNERSHIP. Sites with a wide range of community activities represented virtually were relatively rare (less than 10% of the places explored) and predominantly (although again not exclusively) relating to the

---

[2] The data reported here is work in progress and to date has only involved those at the 'producer' end of these websites. There will be further interviews with local residents which are needed to address the participation issues more fully.

larger, more affluent settlements. In some cases this appeared to be simply contacts for different groups making it was difficult to determine the range of actual community participation.   So in only a few cases were there any discussions of village issues, reports from community groups etc. There was no automatic mapping of the real onto the virtual with examples of places with apparently high real social capital but with little or no web presence and visa versa. In some cases these might be explained by a more detailed consideration of the characteristics of places and communities (including a richer measure of real social capital than the one used here) but it seems likely that the interventions of various regeneration bodies and the actions of individuals with distinctive skills are also intervening variables. The strongest cases did seem to involve the co-existence of rich and diverse real social capital with some more specific expertise in technical and design skills.

The second analysis, seven months later, acted as a check on any over-optimistic interpretation of the web-based analysis. In many cases descriptions of events remained in identical form despite the fact that they were now in the past. Similarly some sites, or elements within them, which had promised that they were in the process of development remained frozen in time. Nevertheless there were some developments, showing that a methodology which tracks changes over time can provide a better indication of live social capital (as opposed to both the institutionalised remnants of past activities, or a one-off initiative that never became fully embedded in community practice) than does one-off surveys.

Social Practices that sustain (virtual) Participation and Social Capital Building

Those running both the multiple sites discussed in this paper stressed that one of their objectives was local participation. For the local authority site this satisfied wider social objectives relating to community regeneration as well as more specific targets relating to internet access and participation in e-government transactions. The commercial organisation also saw themselves as providing a genuine resource for the community. However in addition such local information was a resource for their website, likely to increase its credibility as a provider of local information and increase visitor numbers. This in turn had proved useful for negotiating contracts with public sector bodies who wished to link into the data and / or have a presence on the site (a conscious decision had been made not to accept commercial advertising on the site since this was felt to detract from its community feel, but links with bodies such as the Post Office or Tourist Information were not seen to have this disadvantage).

Both bodies also stressed a range of advantages that they had over bottom up initiatives. These included their ability to appear early in search engine generated lists of sites and the economies of scale they could achieve, both by using resources from a number a projects and through the replication of information across a range of websites that made updating relatively more efficient. They both also felt that participation in their sites was much easier than it was on the typical community site. By this they meant that contributors did not need to know anything about web design or software such as Frontpage. Instead they made their contribution more in the style of an email. However it is worth noting that this is a very 'technical' definition of 'easy to use' in that it does not take account of the social skills and confidence needed for this form of participation, nor of the sense of being part of something that might make such participation meaningful. It is also incidentally based on a view of participation in a community site not shared by the community activists interviewed. In general they did not see those who simply brought in photographs or a handwritten notice that they wanted on the website as not being full participants. One commented "I try to get them to scan it in but often they don't want to know, it scares them to death ... but it's the result, they see it up there and say 'hey that's my picture'. That's full participation".

UK VILLAGES felt that they had achieved good levels of local participation and stressed the numbers of posts they received and specific local sites where there was a lot of activity (however the area under consideration here did not have any such sites or high levels of participation). LEICESTERSHIRE VILLAGES was keen to get higher levels of participation and recognised that this did require some engagement with local communities rather than just waiting for it to happen automatically. They had taken photographs of all the places and used these to give the websites at least some distinctive local feel. There was also concern to engage 'community champions' although they lacked any clear strategy for identifying and reaching them. Interestingly they had rejected a route that might have given them regular contributions on matters of local interest by people who at least on some definition might be considered 'community champions'. This occurred as a result of the decision to provide a parallel set of websites relating to each location's Parish Council (the lowest tier of local government). The reasoning was that the Parish Council as a formal body should not be associated with the type of informal and perhaps more critical commentary that could be expected on a village site (in contrast many bottom up local sites would see Parish Council activities as a central part of their coverage)..

On the basis of this analysis it would appear the multiple identikit community website model has limited ability to engage community participation. In some cases this is likely to be, at least in part, because the locations targeted had very little going on in the way of 'real' social capital. If people do not identify in a social sense with the place where they are living then they are unlikely to want to participate in a website that defines itself in this way. In other cases there did appear to be real community activity (as defined by the presence of community organisations) which did not 'translate' into virtual participation. In some cases it may be that the community's knowledge and use of the internet is insufficiently high for participation to occur without a much more developed community-based ICT project. However it may also be that this standardised model of local websites gives insufficient weight to the desire of communities to see themselves as distinctive from their neighbours and to choose their own way of representing their identity (the bounded solidarity aspect of social capital referred to earlier). This suggests a greater need to draw on concepts of community as a symbolic resource which Cohen (1985) argues is as much about articulating difference from one's neighbours as it is about articulating one's own shared values. This certainly seemed to be an issue from the perspective of one community activist who had introduced an interested group to the options of either having a site within the Leicestershire Villages format or designing their own. He was clear that the appeal of a website was that it incorporated their own design. More detailed, research would be needed to assess the balance between these explanations.

This is not to suggest that the bottom up initiatives were inevitably successful in translating 'real' social capital into a virtual presence or in creating a virtual presence in the absence of much evidence of social organisation. In a number of cases they too were unable to sustain any continuing or widespread community participation. In these cases it may well be the fact that those responsible for the sites were not themselves well integrated with the social networks of the place they were attempting to represent. In others it may just be the well established problems of sustaining initiatives for which there may well have been initial enthusiasm. Some local community sites which were well maintained were arguably stronger examples of communities of interest (for example in relation to environmental projects) than they were representations of the whole community. This is both a cautionary reminder of both the changing nature of communities (or as some would have it the myth of a form of community that has never really existed) and that any particular virtual representation of place is inevitably partial – and in a healthy real and virtual community contested!

The Wider Significance of Participation in Different types of Community Networks

It is important to relate such findings to an understanding of the terms of competition between the different types of sites identified and an analysis of its likely outcomes. Location based websites which have developed as the result of some bottom up initiative (either by someone resident in the place or by one or more community based organisation) are likely to have community participation and ownership as central operating principles. While top down sites owned by the Local Authority or commercial organisations may solicit local content and contributors their format and the content is not likely to be under the ultimate control of the community. As can be seen these differences and other factors do not completely determine the extent of locally generated content but in general there is a connection between the type of site and the type of participation (if any) in favour of the independent sites.

This is an important finding since a number of commentators (Kubicek & Wagner, 2002; Carroll & Rosson, 2003) suggest that that bottom up community initiatives may be incorporated, taken over, or stifled by larger scale developments such as the multiple sites discussed here. This relates in part to their economic and other advantages detailed earlier but may also involve more active intervention. For example in this case one local body had taken the view that, since websites had been created for all areas by the Rural Partnership, grants relating to community ICT initiatives should be used to encourage the take up of such sites rather than to create alternatives.

The relative rarity of even community run sites which do engage widespread, forms of participation suggests the need for better understandings of the social practices (Brown and Duguid, 2002) which influence how such social outcomes are achieved in a variety of contexts. It is clear that the assumption that the provision of a website and a relatively simply technical means to upload information will result in the creation of community sites which will in their turn support local communities is ill founded. While this is unlikely to come as a surprise to those with experience of other examples 'community development' imposed from above, it is important to demonstrate the distinctiveness and significance of a different model of community networks if they are to survive.

References

Brown, J.S. & Duguid, P. (2002) *The Social Life of Information*, Boston, Mass: Harvard Business School Press.

Carroll, J.M. & Rosson, M.B. (2003) 'A Trajectory for Community Networks', *The Information Society*, 19, 381-93.

Cohen, A. (1985) The Symbolic Construction of Community, Tavistock.

Jankowski, N., Van Selm, M. & Hollander, E. (2001) 'On crafting a study of digital community networks: theoretical and methodological considerations' in Keeble, L. & Loader, B. (eds) *Community Informatics: Shaping Computer-Mediated Social Relations*, Routledge.

Kubicek, H. & Wagner, R. (2002) 'Community Networks in a Generational Perspective: The change of an electronic medium within three decades', *Information, Communication & Society*, 5, 3, 291-319.

Katz, J.E., Rice, R.E. & Aspden, P. (2001) 'The Internet 1995-2000: Access, Civic Involvement and Social Interaction', *American Behavioural Scientist*, 45, 3, 405-19.

Kavanaugh, A.L. & Patterson, S. (2001) 'The Impact of Community Computer Networks on Social Capital and Community Involvement', *American Behavioral Scientist*, 45, 3, 496-509.

Mele, C. (1999) 'Cyberspace and disadvantaged communities: the Internet as a tool for collective action'. In: Smith, M. & Kollock, P. (eds.) *Communities in cyberspace*. London: Routledge.

Pigg, K.E. & Crank, L. D. (2004) 'Building Community Social Capital: The Potential and Promise of Information and Community Technologies', *The Journal of Community Informatics,* 1, 1. Available online from http://ci-journal.net.

Putnam, R.D. (2000) *Bowling Alone: The Collapse and Revival of American Community*, Simon & Schuster.

Schön, D., Sanyal, B. & Mitchell, W. (1999) *High Technology and Low-Income Communities: prospects for the positive use of advanced information technology*. Cambridge Mass: MIT press.

Schuler, D. (1996) *New Community Networks: Wired for Change*. Reading, Mass: Addison-Wesley Publishing.

Wellman, B., Quan-Haase, A., Whitte, J. & Hampton, K. (2001) 'Does the Internet increase, decrease or supplement social capital: Social networks, participation and community commitment', *American Behavioural Scientist*, 45, 3, 436-55.

Extending Social Constructivism with Institutional Theory: A Broadband Civic Networking Case

Murali Venkatesh[+], Dong Hee Shin*

[+]Syracuse University, USA, *Penn State University, USA
mvenkate@syr.edu, dxs75@psu.edu

Abstract. A longitudinal study of broadband civic network design is analyzed using social construction of technology (SCOT) approach and then through the lens of institutional theory. SCOT is useful to show *how* artifacts take on the forms they do; institutional theory, by locating (design) action in a cultural, historical and structural context can complement SCOT by explaining *why* they tend to assume certain forms. Broadband civic networking initiatives often have mixed goals: ensuring financial viability and realizing normative social aims. In the present case, this tension was resolved by fitting the network's technological and social form to a criterion of legitimacy prevailing among power centers in the broader field; this succeeded in eliciting necessary financial resources to sustain the network, but at the expense of the project's normative aims. Institutional approaches theorize the relation of cultural ideas and social structure, and that of structure and social action, to interrogate micro-politics of social constructions and the (intended/unintended) forms they assume. To engage the *Why* question, constructivists need to theorize action. Sociological institutional theory offers pointers.

This paper documents design of the Urban-net, a broadband civic network. The Urban-net project was funded by a New York state program. In 1995, as part of a settlement of a regulatory case, Telco (a telecommunications service provider) committed $50 million to develop and deploy advanced telecommunications infrastructure/services in economically poor and underserved areas. A program was set up to solicit proposals from consortia of public organizations (e.g., local government, schools), community-based organizations (CBOs), and small businesses via a competitive request for proposals (RFP) process.

P. van den Besselaar et al. (eds.), Communities and Technologies 2005, 55-74.

Network subscribers paid subsidized service charges and were eligible for additional funds for user training or customer premise equipment (CPE). Eighty per cent of the grant returned to Telco to fund development/deployment of network infrastructure and services. Grant funds could not be used toward technical staff or consultants or software development. To be eligible for the subsidy, subscribers were required to connect to the network backbone, which would inter-connect subscriber sites and the Internet.

A project steering committee (hereafter committee) with public organizations, CBOs and private citizens was formed to submit a proposal, which was subsequently granted $3.8 million. Small businesses were poorly represented and are left out of the analysis. Values espoused by the program were internalized by the committee via contact with selection committee members during proposal development; an aim of the project, accordingly, was to develop the Urban-net as a civic network delivering public information, social services and broadband technology access to residents. The larger aim was to improve quality of life in social and economic terms (access to information/services and job opportunities) for residents and cross-agency cooperation among service providers.

(De)Constructing the Urban-net

We trace the design of the Urban-net over thirteen design meetings using social construction of technology (SCOT) (Bijker, 1995). To show that artifacts are socially shaped, the analyst deconstructs the artifact on its meanings for relevant social groups (RSGs) and traces how some lose and others gain ground.

Groups participating in design -- the committee, public organizations, CBOs -- had previously shaped planning and proposal development as co-authors, respondents and research informants and endorsed the proposal's interpretation of the Urban-net as a civic network. The other participants – Telco designers, responsible for technical network design – came into the process espousing the program's aims, which matched this interpretation. Groups' interpretation of the Urban-net began to diverge when design got underway. These interpretations were not mutually exclusive: the realization of one would not have precluded the realization of the others. But one prevailed over the others to closure.

A technological frame provides actors with conceptual resources to interpret an artifact. It can organize actors by helping communicate their assumptions /expectations and recruit others to their interpretation (Bijker, 1995). The frame helps constitute the artifact and group(s) with reference to it; its effects are material as well as social. Bijker enumerates elements of such a frame. In Table 1, we use Bijker's operationalization to describe the committee's original framing of the Urban-net as a civic network. Securing subscription commitments was the committee's goal for the design process. Public organizations and CBOs would have to subscribe to the Urban-net for the project's social aims to be realized.

The Urban-net's technological infrastructure would comprise two parts: network backbone and the access network. Backbone refers to switching equipment at Telco central offices (switching centers) and to telecommunications links interconnecting central offices. The access network linked the central office to subscriber site. Telco designers had a two-fold design objective: specification of backbone capacity (the number of subscribers it would support and the speed at which it would support them) and access network end-points: what user sites would connect to the backbone using what services? Four access network services were eligible for subsidies at start of design: digital subscriber line (the slowest and cheapest broadband service and the only service CBOs could afford and were interested in) and asynchronous transfer mode/cell relay service (ATM/CRS) at three different speeds, all of them significantly faster and pricier than DSL. Later in the process, DSL was dropped for regulatory reasons and gigabit Ethernet service added to the list.

At meeting # 4, designers' focus shifted from the access network to the backbone in response to the frustrations they faced in estimating user demand (Table 2). CBOs needed information on the CPE relief amount, which was computed by program authorities and was not yet known. The Urban-net planning process had revealed just how poorly equipped CBOs were in their ICT and support infrastructure; CBOs saw in the project an opportunity to upgrade their ICT and Internet access capacity (Table 4), but whether they could afford the upgrades or not depended on the CPE relief amount.

Around meeting # 5, general managers who had represented public organizations on the committee from the project's outset began yielding their seat to their MIS managers. Most MIS managers appeared unaware of or did not share the project's social aims; they were concerned with cutting telecommunications costs via the project's subsidized services. ATM/CRS was new to them, and they were wary of it for that reason; they were concerned with the additional costs of upgrading CPE upgrades and help-desk support that subscription to ATM/CRS would entail. They were shopping for a backward-compatible service, and ATM/CRS did not fit. They were not interested in DSL.

The picture changed dramatically with the announcement, in meeting # 6, that gigabit Ethernet service was now eligible for program subsidies. The service was attractive to MIS managers. They knew the technology well: it was based on the Ethernet technology their office LANs used. Thanks to its "enormous" bandwidth, they could use the service as a cost-effective intra-organizational backbone to link their campuses over the Urban-net backbone (Table 3), replacing multiple T1 connections with a gigabit Ethernet connection at significant savings.

The decisive turn in closure process occurred in meeting # 8. The committee learned of a program ultimatum that grant funds would be reallocated if signed contracts were not in place by the first quarter of 2000 (all second round projects were subject to the condition). Private citizen committee elites argued that unless public organizations signed up for high-end services the grant was in jeopardy, and implied that even if CBOs signed up for a low-end service like DSL it would not avert revocation. This interpretation proved influential within the committee and resulted in self-enlistment of a majority of its private citizen members in the MIS managers' frame (Urban-net for intra-organizational connectivity). MIS managers' enthusiasm for gigabit Ethernet coupled with their financial resources assured the committee that the grant would be secure from revocation. Protecting the grant became the urgent new project aim, in light of which public organizations were cast as indispensable *early adopters*. The project's social aims could be addressed in the future, after the *crisis* (revocation risk) was averted; rhetorically, *early adopters* allowed for later adoption by the rest. As it turned out, DSL became ineligible for subsidies and the Urban-net was priced out of CBOs' reach. The committee had hoped a DSL substitute might be approved, but this did not occur.

Closure resulted from three transition points. The first was a transition from the social to the technical and differentiated the project's technological means (the backbone), projected as achievable in the near-term, from its social ends. Approval of gigabit Ethernet catalyzed the second: the shift from inter- to intra-organizational connectivity, a shift favored by MIS managers. In the third, the Urban-net's institutional entrepreneurs (DiMaggio 1988) – private citizen committee elites – appropriated the rationale of the first transition (designers' differentiation and temporal sequencing of the technological and the social) and fused it with an extant social organization (the committee) in support of the second, powering MIS managers' frame to closure.

Private citizen committee members opposed to the institutional entrepreneurs' interpretation of the ultimatum (hereafter referred to as dissidents) advocated fidelity to the project's original aims with a cross-subsidy proposal (meeting # 9):

> "Since the large players are getting such a good deal, could we require them to provide resources and services to the community and the smaller agencies? Large players have to see themselves as resource providers. This is part of their responsibility..."

The committee as a body never revisited this argument. The project's social aims were dormant at best at this time; "getting the network off the ground" and averting the "crisis" dominated committee discussions post-ultimatum.

Public organizations' readiness to commit to gigabit Ethernet refreshed debate in the committee over an omnibus service contract versus bilateral contracts. With the first, the committee would negotiate one contract with Telco covering all subscribers. With the second, subscribers would negotiate contracts bilaterally with Telco. From meeting # 7 on, dissidents were vocal in backing an omnibus contract. By aggregating demand and negotiating as a buying group, they believed volume discounts could be realized to cut subscription costs. The contract could be drafted to benefit future subscribers as well.

Late in the design process, the committee learned that services pricing would be subscriber-specific. The committee's assumption that charges would be lower if more sites signed on proved to be incorrect. Telco's clarification on subscriber-specific pricing strengthened the case for bilateral contracts made by MIS managers. They argued that an omnibus contract was infeasible and that it would jeopardize the grant by delaying the contracting process.

The sequence of turns leading to closure was not the product of conspiracy among these groups to bias organizational form. The first transition stemmed from an institutionalized response to challenges the designers faced in securing subscription commitments. They realized they had to actively sell the Urban-net services to prospective users, and this was not part of their regular job or project responsibilities. They reacted to their predicament by reverting to their habitual identity and modus operandi as technical professionals with well-defined, taken-for-granted work practices and jurisdictional boundaries. MIS managers reacted to gigabit Ethernet in line with their institutionalized organizational role. The habitual frames these actors fell back on in the situation were *assumptive* frames – institutionalized interpretive schemes that structure day-to-day meaning-making and "mediate the routine enactment of organizational life" (Ranson, Hinings & Greenwood, 1980). Assumptive frames remain taken-for-granted and unarticulated in the *routine of action* and may be entrained when conditions are ill-defined to structure action along reassuringly habitual lines. Designers' and MIS managers' actions were independent of one another but stemmed from similar motivations: enacting routines was their way of coping with situational indeterminacy and the lack of an unequivocal action script structured and legitimated by the project's social aims. Their organizational role came with institutionalized criteria for validating their own and others' situated behavior; their project role did not.

The institutional entrepreneurs' interpretation of the ultimatum was an instance of *strategic* framing – "conscious strategic efforts by groups of people to fashion shared understandings of the world and of themselves that legitimate and motivate collective action" (McAdam, 2003). While designers' and MIS managers' actions were structured by assumptive frames, the institutional entrepreneurs reframed the committee's collective identity and mission relative to the project's initial frame.

Theorizing organizational form and action

Closure entails a stabilization of social relations as well as a particular technological form and its cultural meaning(s). We use institutional theory to interpret closure as the emergence of "orderly, stable, socially integrating patterns" of order from unstable conditions (Selznick, 1949). Institutionalization refers to the process by which *institutions* – cultural abstractions like rules, shared meanings, logics – are fused with *social organization* to constitute repeated patterns of interaction (Fligstein, 1999). The SCOT idea of closure, per this view, is the process of institutionalization or stabilization of a social arrangement structured by, and structuring, the particular material form assumed by the artifact. Stress is on the word *repeated*: assuring ongoing reproduction of the constructed order via social interaction is a defining feature of institutionalization (Jepperson, 1991).

Institutionalization of new organizational form plays out in micro-interaction and in the broader relational field that embeds it. New institutionalists theorize relation of micro- to macro-social – individual-level action to social structure – by arguing that action is constrained (not determined) by actors' cultural and organizational affiliations. In using this view, we address gaps in current theorizing in the so-called "new" institutionalism. Institutionalization as a process (versus institution as achieved state) is a neglected area, as is the role of interests, power and opportunistic action in the process (Hirsch & Lounsbury, 1997). Rejecting the rational actor model of purposive behavior, new institutionalists view *order-affirming* action stemming from taken-for-granted worldviews that socialized actors reproduce without conscious thought; such behavior reproduces the existing order (DiMaggio & Powell, 1991). A concern with institutional persistence derives from new institutionalism's structuralist slant, but it cannot explain organizational change and emergence of new forms. To explain genesis and change, one must grant actors the ability to behave rationally and strategically in *order-challenging* ways. Even new institutionalists note limitation of a "theory that denies the reality of purposive, interest-driven" behavior (DiMaggio, 1988).

If new institutionalists have focalized persistence of order, "old" institutionalists like Selznick (1949) were concerned with the role of interests, power and agency in the genesis and transformation of organizational form. We need both old and new institutionalist perspectives to account fully for organizational dynamics. New forms emerge not in a social vacuum but in relation to an existing order. This order with its institutionalized power relations and opportunity spaces (Brint & Karabel, 1991) shapes emergent organizational form and constrains conduct of actors in it. As *constrained entrepreneurs* (Brint & Karabel), actors are capable of *acting new* orders into being; they are not condemned merely to reproduce or *enact* the existing order. Contending actors' relative power is a critical issue at such times. This paper catches the Urban-net's technology and social organization at a definitive moment of "institution-building", in the conflicted, inherently political process leading to technological and social stabilization.

Why did stabilization occur along certain lines? More generally,

> "Where new organizational forms come from is one of the central questions of organizational theory…(N)ovel social structures matter because they underpin organizational diversity" (Rao, 1998, p. 912).

Organizational diversity enhances society's capacity for social innovation. The Urban-net was proposed to institute new relational patterns across organizations and functional sectors, infusing structural diversity into the field. Despite this aim, the resulting form reproduced existing social arrangements; instead of catalyzing new relations, the Urban-net's technological and social configuration affirmed prevailing ones. The Why question – Why did the Urban-net take on the form it did? – is the empirical version of the question on formal origins and directs attention to the particular macro-structural and micro-contextual forces that patterned the Urban-net in a particular way.

Macro-structure

All organizations are "located within broader social structure that will constrain the forms they can develop" (Ranson et al., 1980). As artifacts develop in a particular social-historical milieu, dominant cultural logics and organizations directly or indirectly influence emergent form. Second, pre-existing structures and logics subsume a potentiality – causal *tendency* -- to reproduce themselves in the emergent form through, for instance, control over financial resources. As open systems, organizations depend on the environment for resources, and "external control of resources is one type of...constraint" on emergent form (Kimberly, 1975). Resource-holders will steer resources to where "their own interests would be respected", and organizational elites can successfully elicit resources to the extent they can provide such assurance. The nature and direction of such influence and consequences for emergent form are key analytic concerns. The analyst would identify macro-structural forces impinging on the micro-social setting where developmental work actually occurs and (a) evaluate whether or not their reproductive potential was realized in emergent form and (b) specify contextual contingencies activating/deactivating this potential en route to stabilization of a particular form (Tsoukas, 1989).

For realist sociologists, macro-structure is temporally prior to action (Archer, 1995). An actor confronts structure as an objectified "accretion of past practices and understandings" (Barley & Tolbert, 1997). Macro-structure is both product of and constraint on human action (Barley & Tolbert): it must be continually and necessarily *enacted* – instantiated in action – if it is to organize social life and have social consequences. The relation is structurational, mutually-constitutive. To the realist, the social world is differentiated and stratified (Tsoukas, 1989). Incumbents hold positions in macro-structure; positions pre-exist incumbents and pattern their access to resources and constrain their behavior. Relations between positions (not incumbents) describe macro-structure (Porpora, 1989). A firm manager has power to fire or promote a subordinate; the firm itself may be implicated in authority and dependency relations with other entities in its operating context. Causal powers (of control in this case) stem from the position and its incorporation "into a wider structure of relations of production" (Tsoukas).

We locate the Urban-net actors in a particular macro-structure or inter-organizational field – defined as social relations linking organizations "lacking formal authority over one another…(located) within a…limited geographical area" (Scott & Meyer, 1991). We bound the field to include all eligible organizations and Telco. This field historically pre-existed the project and implicated the players – public organizations, CBOs, the committee, Telco – in a web of constraints and opportunities. Actors representing these players were both constrained and enabled by the field, which aided realization of some interests and frustrated others. To prevail, actors need power over others: all contests occur within structures "that have not been created by the actors involved… (T)he first such structure is the existing distribution of power itself" (Munch & Smesler, 1987). Macro-power distribution typically is asymmetrical.

SCOT has been criticized for its inadequate conception of social structure (Winner, 1993). Bijker has since responded to his critics, viewing social structure as a "contingent set of heterogeneous relations" and directing analysts to model (action) *patterns* that arise when social groups are constituted and interact with one another in a range of different structural circumstances" (1995). However, he elides a key question: Why are certain patterns more likely to stabilize than others? Constructivists must explain why artifacts, and the social organization of consensus that develops around them, tend to assume particular forms (this is a question in new institutionalism as well, see Brint and Karabel, 1991).

In any field, some entities are more powerful than others due to their structural position and access to resources. Power centers can decisively shape the milieu within which actors act. Analyzing the re-positioning of community colleges as terminal vocational schools from academic feeder schools, Brint and Karabel (1991) note that power can result from contextual influence, as measured by an organization's centrality for the operating context of relevant others. Four-year colleges, who had been contextually influential as coveted targets of junior college transfers, yielded ground to business firms when job credentialing, not credentialing for transfer, become junior colleges' reformulated interest and mission. In the present case, public organizations were well-entrenched power centers. They were seats of administrative authority – city and county government agencies – and providers of necessary services -- public libraries, education, healthcare. Relative to CBOs, they were well-resourced, which rendered them contextually influential with businesses like Telco. Initially, their centrality to the project stemmed from their ownership of information others relied on. Some had statutory oversight authority (for example, the county administered Medicaid), which meant no services-related initiative could expect to succeed without them.

For Telco, public organizations' contextual influence stemmed from their buying power. They represented large business accounts to be courted ahead of the competition. They had always been valued clients due to their size, and now they represented a strategic opportunity field for high-end broadband services through the project. Telco was itself a power center, its historical significance as a major local employer was further enhanced by its designation as authorized provider of program-approved services. But public organizations could always threaten to take their custom elsewhere if they were not satisfied, as was demonstrated when, frustrated by design delays, MIS managers moved the committee to float a request for quotes to competitors for the service they wanted (gigabit Ethernet). The area featured aggressive smaller telecommunications firms and this strengthened their hand. This action put the committee on notice as well: MIS managers' tolerance for delay was limited. They could, if they chose, bypass the committee and deal directly with providers, as soon became evident.

The committee's dependency relation with public organizations and the latter's contextual influence with the committee were defined and amplified by the institutional entrepreneurs' interpretation of the ultimatum. They were deemed indispensable for the project; they were the only group that gained influence during the design process. Their centrality to the project now stemmed from their financial resources. CBOs' influence with the committee waned. Their interest in a DSL-like service was deemed insufficient to avert revocation. They were not as vital to the committee's operating context at this time.

The committee failed to emerge as a power center independent of the public organizations. The committee was a formally-constituted body, with legal powers to represent subscribers in contract negotiations. But it never developed an independent identity or managerial capacity to act cohesively. At meeting # 7, for instance, a legal professional consulted by the committee exhorted it to start "functioning as a committee". The comment was with reference to rumors that some public organizations, exploiting the competitive situation, had initiated contract discussions with service providers bypassing the committee. The consultant urged the committee to ensure that "no one (participates) in the project except through you". Instead, the reverse happened. The committee cast itself as a subsidiary actor to public organizations; it diminished to a nominally authoritative actor that legitimized MIS managers' interest by enlisting in their frame. By self-enlisting, the committee saved itself from irrelevance and legitimized its official role as the project's sole authorizer.

A structuralist would argue that actors' access to "power and resources determine(s) the degree to which...interests are realized" (Fligstein, 1999). Public organizations prevailed because of structural power, which stemmed from their control over resources -- resources that were necessary given the economics and technical complexity of broadband. But attributing formal variation to resource availability is incomplete and deterministic if it is assumed always that resources pre-exist in a given structure as "pools of free-floating assets" (Rao, 1998). Often actors must actively mobilize resources through social coalitions. Institutional entrepreneurs create opportunity in a field of constraints, in the process reframing meanings, interests, relations and self-identity. By negotiating strategic coalitions, actors can change social structure (albeit slowly and not easily).

With their cross-subsidy proposal, dissidents attempted to redistribute resources more equitably in the field. By leveraging the program subsidy, they sought to mobilize new resources from public organizations to assist CBOs get online. The dissidents invoked the progressive activist identity implicit in the civic networking frame, and their proposal resulted from allegiance to the Urban-net's original mission as a services delivery amenity: the greater the diversity of service providers, the greater the range of services and populations supported. Dissidents felt (as did program selection committee members) that CBOs, as grassroots operations, often had a better sense of neighborhood needs and served them more effectively than larger providers. Bringing CBOs online would expose their clientele, among the area's poorest, to broadband and the Internet and online information, helping bridge the digital and economic opportunity divide. As vital neighborhood access points for Urban-net resources – even if these were, to start with, restricted to information and Internet access pending development of other services -- CBOs would gain contextual influence with the committee, thus re-defining the relationship to their advantage.

Interests "are built into a … position by the relationship of that position to other positions" in social structure (Porpora, 1989) and supply incumbents with "presumptive motives for acting". The behavior of designers, MIS managers and CBOs is amenable to a structuralist reading. Designers entered the design process espousing two interests. The first stemmed from their position at Telco: to build the Urban-net infrastructure. The second stemmed from the project's social aims. The tension between these interests only became evident as the process unfolded. Designers' focus shift to the backbone resulted from preference for predictability and control that technical specification afforded (recall that they had to sell access network services, a task they were not used to). A preference for predictability is a universal interest structuring much social behavior (DiMaggio, 1988).

MIS managers' cost-cutting interest predated the project and was articulated in the frame they brought with them to the committee. The Urban-net's subsidized service charges were most appealing to them given the doing more with less environment they operated in. Despite differences in organizational size/function, financial/ICT resources and administrative structure, and despite never operating as a group, these actors all interpreted the project in the same way: as a cost-cutting opportunity. Roles/relations affiliates have with technology tend to influence their framing of it (Orlikowski & Gash, 1994). MIS managers saw low-cost technology/services as vital to the operating efficiencies their organizations demanded of MIS. They could readily use institutionalized, standardized criteria to evaluate such opportunities in technical and financial terms. Furthermore, their interpretation of the project reflected the way their organizational superiors likely evaluated their role performance (Orlikowski & Gash).

CBOs were attempting to systematize their fund-raising operations and smarten up their image over the period covered by this research. The Internet had emerged as an indispensable tool for fund-raising through broad solicitations and by facilitating access to information on grant opportunities. CBO representatives referred to exemplar CBOs that had used the Internet strategically to grow their organizations. They were under pressure -- from their boards and donors, and often from themselves, from their self-identity as service professionals – to emulate these success stories. CBOs did not see themselves as a group for the many differences – in size, function – that separated them. Rather it was the common challenges they faced – lack of resources, including ICTs, and crippling dependence on ever-diminishing state and federal monies (prompting a search for alternative sources) – that made for a remarkable uniformity of response to the Urban-net as an Internet access ramp.

Interests must also be viewed as products of cultural-political (re)construction by actors; interests are not immutable but can change. Organizational interests form in opportunity spaces in the inter-organizational field (Brint & Karabel, 1991). Post-ultimatum, the Urban-net's institutional entrepreneurs succeeded in eliciting resources from the environment by reformulating the committee's mission and collective interest to securing the grant (versus securing the project's social aims), with the change defended as the outcome of re-assessment prompted by the "crisis". MIS managers' willingness and ability to subscribe (versus CBOs' indecision) provided the opportunity and was used as justification for the change. Their interest was effective – interest backed by necessary resources -- and the committee's revised interest was shaped by that of the project's "rescuers": mobilizing effective interest was portrayed as the only viable response to the crisis. Crises provide classic institution-building leverage points (Fligstein, 1999).

An organization's environment can constrain its form through control over resources and by prescribing constitutive norms of legitimacy (Ranson et al., 1980). The two could be mutually-supportive: (re)framing the Urban-net to fit with MIS managers' notions of what was formally "desirable, proper (or) appropriate" was successful in attracting resources. Dissidents' cross-subsidy plan, and their proposal for an omnibus contract, on the other hand, fit poorly with cultural models available to resource-holders; MIS managers rejected them claiming there was no organizational precedence for such practices. The Urban-net's institutional entrepreneurs aligned themselves with MIS managers in respect to these proposals, but were careful to reassure dissidents that the project's social aims were merely being deferred. They were careful to justify their actions because one of the dissidents spoke unofficially for the Mayor.

How did elite actors manage to mobilize strategic coalitions for closure without losing key actors opposed to them? A key lies in cultural-political discourse. Micro-interaction analysis allows study of meanings, interests, identities and relations as actors construct and reconstruct them in discourse en route to forging strategic coalitions and stabilizing the social (and technological) order (Fligstein, 1999). It allows the analyst to link situations and interactions to embedding macro-structures, to analyze how these intersect and with what consequences for emergent form. A preliminary, micro-level discursive analysis of closure is summarized below, using the medium of technological frame.

Constructivists can learn from social movement research on the "dynamics of collective action at the intermediate meso level" (McAdam, 2003) – specifically, discourse mechanisms actors use – to analyze the macro-micro intersection. Social movement theory is concerned with conflictual politics of change and can illuminate "how collectives coordinate their efforts to challenge the existing order" (O'Mahony, 2002). The politics of institution-building have been characterized in social movement terms (Fligstein, 1999). Analyzing micro-level coalition formation is crucial to understanding the micro-construction of artifacts. Coalitions themselves are socially constructed, first in terms of social categories – race, class etc. Institutional entrepreneurs then (re)construct strategic coalitions by framing meanings, interests, identities and relations discursively to realize preferred aims. Bijker's (1995) micro-politics can be sharpened with insights on the *micro-construction* of frames and social coalitions.

Micro-politics

Technological frames guide group interaction by furnishing members cultural meanings, goals and "tools...for action" (Bijker, 1995). Invoking Giddens' notion of structuration, Bijker suggests that frames need to be "continuously sustained" by the actions that they both enable and constrain; they must be enacted. They help structure, and are structured by, the social dynamic that stabilizes both the artifact and the group: the "construction of the artifact, the forming of a relevant social group, and the emergence of a technological frame are linked processes" (Bijker). Bijker sees frames arising from social interaction. They are "not an individual's characteristic, nor a characteristic of systems or institutions; technological frames are located between actors, not in actors or above actors". We find Orlikowski and Gash (1994) more persuasive, who see frames more inclusively as products of socio-cognitive and institutional processes.

Socialization informs actors of their organization's institutionalized logics. Consequently, they will tend to frame new phenomena – including technology -- not naively but through their socialization. Such frames are assumptive in character. Strategic frames may draw on alternative assumptive logics or emphasize different elements of prevailing logics and arise from social interaction. Strategic framing may be seen in dialectical relation to assumptive frames, and often must resonate to a degree with the latter to be productive in mobilizing coalitions.

Assumptive frames are individually held, inter-subjectively formed aids for organizing/interpreting social reality. They derive from cultural (institutional) logics (Hirsch & Lounsbury, 1997) and are organizationally-structured. Logics constitute meanings, interests, identity(ies), and relational opportunities and make these available to the actor to elaborate (Friedland & Alford, 1991). Actors don't come empty-handed into situations but bring assumptive frames with them; these *priors* inform their evaluation of their own and others' actions on their situational meaning and appropriateness. Assumptive frames constitute an actor's social persona and are an "individual's characteristic". Without engaging the self, it is difficult to account for an actor's relation to strategic frames and, indeed, to other actors: Why are some frames /coalitions more compelling than others?

The notion of frame resonance (Snow & Benford, 1988) may hold a key. Tarrow (1992) elaborates that social movement organizers typically "attempt to relate their goals and programs directly to the existing values and predispositions of their target public...". Organizers "often must operate within the cognitive and evaluative universe that they find rather than create a new one". Committee members backing MIS managers' frame in the present case, for example, took pains to portray it as not inimical to the project's civic networking frame, and of members' dispositions linked to that frame, in an attempt to win converts.

Social movement analysts recognize the role of discourse in cultivating shared frames and social coalitions, both indispensable to mobilizing actors. Institutional entrepreneurs in the present case forged a strategic coalition by skillfully using specific discursive strategies -- identity qualifying and temporal cuing (Mische, 2003) – en route to closure on their terms.

Identity qualifying – indicating "which aspect of an actor's multiple identities and involvements are active right now" (Mische, 2003) – is a strategy actors use to align themselves with particular reference groups. The designers and later, the Urban-net's institutional entrepreneurs relied on such a cue to manage the tension between the project's technological means and social ends. Faced with the impasse over securing subscriber commitments, the designers compartmentalized their technical identity from the social but were careful to note that their technical focus on the backbone was only a temporary shuffling of design priorities. Their technical focus was presented as the necessary means to the project's social aims. This allowed them to segment their identity as technical professionals from the embattled one as facilitators of project's social ends, but without rejecting the latter. Identity qualifying went hand in hand with their temporally-sequenced re-construction of project timeline and a plausible justification of this new narrative intended for relevant key actors. The civic networking frame was a master frame within which they articulated a sub-frame. The two were similar in structure and content (sharing "common categories" and "similar values on… categories", Orlikowski & Gash, 1994), but the sub-frame featured a local, temporally-cued inflexion, a "necessary" technical design goal: backbone specification.

Their focus shift was a stylistic (rhetorical) shift as well, a shift from discourse on network uses, which was social in its aims, to technical discourse. The designers' discourse was technical in two senses: it was technical in its focus (the backbone). Further, it took on a decidedly technical tone in the way the backbone was characterized. The backbone's data switching capabilities were stressed over its function as an enabler of social inter-connectivity. By talking up the backbone, designers shifted discourse away from network's social applications, which MIS managers saw as expense items to be wary of. The backbone's projected performance was relevant to MIS managers: they were reassured they could save on telecommunications costs without compromising their networks' performance.

Purposively or unwittingly, actors used discourse to divide and differentiate but also to accommodate. The designers' technically-toned discourse disenrolled some actors (CBOs) and enrolled others (public organizations) and decontextualized design discourse from the project's social aims and recontextualized it in technical terms. MIS managers' cost-cutting concern discouraged discourse on network uses that would increase their costs. The cost criterion gave MIS managers an "objective" way to evaluate telecommunications services availed through the project versus the open market. By stripping the project's social agenda from their evaluation, these actors could, and did, publicly relate to the project merely as customers "shopping around for the best deal". This stance enhanced their contextual power with the committee after the revocation ultimatum. Here again, their discourse helped decontextualize the project from its historical /social bases and recontextualize it strictly in bottom-line terms.

Importantly, institutional entrepreneurs as well as dissidents were interested in looking for a new committee organizational form based on mutual accommodation of each group's preferences. The former reassured the latter that the project's normative aims were merely being deferred; a spokesperson said project by-laws could be reviewed after the "crisis" had safely passed to change the committee's orientation to collective benefits. Dissidents' cross-subsidy proposal recognized that the economics of broadband called for new social contractual models where resource-rich could be *required* to subsidize the resource-poor. Both were prepared to be pragmatic in their efforts to institutionalize their preferred arrangements via a revised committee structure and mission; both wished to avoid confrontation and were interested instead in how the present structure and mission could be expanded to *accommodate* a negotiated co-existence while *preserving* interests of each (O'Mahony, 2002).

Conclusion

Cultural ideas shape organizational form and endow it with value. The Urban-net's form as envisaged in the proposal, and the committee structure and mission (as well as its collective interest and identity) were shaped by civic networking ideals. The growing visibility in the U.S. of such ideals in the nineties informed the committee's thinking as well as the way selection committee members conceptualized program-funded networks and their societal benefits. Culture – "shared beliefs and understandings...of a group or society" (Zald, 1996) – penetrates everyday social life and social action that it helps organize via social structures. The political *process* by which cultural abstractions acquire organizational form and are stabilized in a social structure is a specific concern of institutional theory. Analysts have noted the value of relating social constructivist projects to broader culture (e.g., Winner, 1993). Institutional analysts theorize this crucial relation in culture-structure terms both as it plays out within the organization and exogenously – between the organization and its embedding milieu and attend to the dialectical tension between pressures for and against organizational change to explain social constructions and the forms they assume.

An organizational form persists from assumptive aspects of the organizational culture(s) that constrain socialized actors to *order-affirming* actions. The form reproduces itself through actors' taken-for-granted everyday enactments. Culture describes enduring shared elements of organizations, but it can also have a discursive and emergent character (Zald, 1996). Proponents of *order-challenging* action may appropriate culture contentiously as they re-frame shared interests, meanings, and identities and mobilize coalitions for change. Culture thus is implicated in organizational persistence as well as change. Social movement theorizing unpacks the intersection of culture and structure in micro-level framing activity. These insights combined with institutional theory can deepen constructivist analysis. We summarize below the value these add to SCOT ideas.

Social constructivists need to locate groups in structural terms and theorize action on that basis. An outline for such a theory suggested by the Urban-net case covers the following elements. Variation in organizational form is constrained by prevailing macro-structure, which subsumes the potential to reproduce itself in emergent form through, for example, control over resources. By unthinkingly enacting institutionalized role behaviors, socialized actors help reproduce prevailing macro-structure. Actors are also assumed capable of strategic action. They can mobilize new resources in a given structure as they pursue alternatives to the status quo, but whether they prevail or not would depend on their ability to mobilize social coalitions. Macro-structural influence on action is mediated by institutional conditions at the micro-level. Prevailing cultural logics can shape micro-social action. Any setting features multiple, possibly contradictory logics, some more institutionalized than others, and their interaction produces intended or unintended consequences for emergent form. Actors' role performance can vary with institutional conditions. An actor from a more institutionalized setting will tend to act in institutionalized ways in a new setting, unless the latter features comparably institutionalized logics. These would serve as a countervailing set of considerations to inform his contextual evaluation of what actions qualify as legitimate in it. Institutional conditions can be designed to increase the likelihood that actors will activate certain cultural logics and deactivate others.

As a social construction any artifact, arguably, bears the imprint of *some* RSG. Constructivist views run the risk of functionalist accounting of form: that a technology and its social organization take the form they do to enable designers realize their goals through them. How then would one explain unanticipated outcomes? Organizations do sometimes assume the form their designers intended. But outcomes often also do diverge from institutional designers' intention, as in the present case. This formal variability must be accounted for. It may be explained by analyzing the institutional conditions that warrant *actor-centered functionalist* versus non-functionalist explanation (Pierson, 2000). Conditions in the committee were less institutionalized than in the field and failed to effectively counter particular action patterns expressive of and isomorphic with, institutionalized interests and power in the field. The committee started out with a notion of legitimate organizational form but failed to elicit necessary resources from the field to institutionalize it. The resulting "interaction among intentions" (Goodin, 1996) has been resolved at least for now by fitting the Urban-net to opportunities available in the field. Had the committee instituted conditions consonant with its norm of legitimacy drawn from the civic networking ideal, the resulting form might have been quite different.

"Design" reflects intention and yet, organizational form often is unintended. *Indirect* design is possible: accidents do happen, but their "frequency and direction...can be...shaped by intentional interventions" (Goodin, 1996). Possible interventions designed to increase the likelihood of realizing the project's social aims include two: expanding the committee's managerial capacity and instituting social controls. The first develops from access to new resources and political techniques (Brint & Karabel, 1991). Aligning with cognate social movements with a history of framing issues and mobilizing collective action effectively might be one strategy. Social learning (Pierson, 2000) is another. The committee, for example, could learn from other program-funded projects in the region that managed to support social aims without compromising on project viability and institute similar provisions in the Urban-net project by-laws.

Social controls (incentives/disincentives) can shape what courses of action are pursued. Institutionalizing philanthropic (versus self-interested) behavior by Minneapolis corporations, Galaskiewicz (1991) reports, was helped by "peer pressure and selective incentives of the corporate philanthropic elite"; at the macro- (inter-organizational) level, corporate philanthropic behavior was rewarded with national publicity via the media. Controls may instantiate the publicity principle, requiring that "institutional action...be...publicly defensible" (Goodin, 1996). Actors are less likely to focalize selfish interests if they are held accountable to a different ethic (Pierson, 2000); this would depend on whether or not institutional actions can be monitored. Insofar as the Urban-net develops as an intra-organizational network (private amenity) tied to powerful stakeholders, monitoring the committee's actions itself would be a challenge. Invisibility, of course, raises the threshold for social control.

Like social movement organizers, institution-builders must mobilize actors sympathetic to their claims. Bijker's (1995) micropolitics centers on technological frames but is silent on coalition-building dynamically through framing. Frames that organize order-affirming conduct must be differentiated from order-challenging frames. The former are institutionalized fixtures of organizational reality and are assumptive in nature; taken-for-granted, everyday actions are shaped by the opportunities and constraints defined through them. The latter are purposive, emergent cultural-political resources dynamically constructed and defined to mobilize and legitimize contentious action. Strategic framing and strategic coalition-formation are linked. It is useful to differentiate groups defined more or less tightly with reference to social categories (such groups may be called *macro-constructions*) from strategic coalitions (*micro-constructions*). Institutional entrepreneurs in the present case micro-constructed a strategic coalition through discourse; they helped institutionalize the strategic frame by fusing it with the committee's organizational base to sustain repeated interaction patterns. Bijker's account of framing is thin both in its institutional (macro-social, assumptive) and discursive (micro-social, strategic) dimensions, and misses the dynamism of their intersection in coalition-building.

References

Archer, M.S. (1995). Realist social theory: The morphogenetic approach. Cambridge, UK: Cambridge University Press.

Barley, S.R., and Tolbert, P.S. (1997). Institutionalization and structuration: Studying the links between action and institution. Organization Studies, 18(1), 93-117.

Bijker, W. E. (1995). Of bicycles, Bakelites, and bulbs: Toward a theory of sociotechnical change. Cambridge, MA: The MIT Press.

Brint, S., and Karabel, J. (1991). Institutional origins and transformations: The case of American community colleges. In W.W. Powell & P.J. DiMaggio (Eds.), The new institutionalism in organizational analysis. Chicago, IL: University of Chicago Press.

DiMaggio, P. (1988). Interest and agency in institutional theory. In L.G. Zucker (Ed.), Institutional patterns and organizations: Culture and environment. Cambridge, MA: Ballinger.

DiMaggio, P.J., and Powell, W.W. (1991). Introduction. In W.W. Powell & P.J. DiMaggio (Eds.), The new institutionalism in organizational analysis. Chicago, IL: University of Chicago Press.

Fligstein, N. (1999). Social skill and the theory of fields. Unpublished mss. Department of Sociology, University of California, Berkeley.

Friedland, R., and Alford, R.A. (1991). Bringing society back in: Symbols, practices, and institutional contradictions. In W.W. Powell & P.J. DiMaggio (Eds.), The new institutionalism in organizational analysis. Chicago, IL: University of Chicago Press.

Galaskiewicz, J. (1991). Making corporate actors accountable: Institution-building in Minneapolis-St. Paul. In W.W. Powell & P.J. DiMaggio (Eds.), The new institutionalism in organizational analysis. Chicago, IL: University of Chicago Press.

Goodin, R. E. (1996). Institutions and their design. In R.E. Goodin (Ed.), The theory of institutional design. Cambridge, UK: Cambridge University Press.

Hirsch, P.M., and Lounsbury, M. (1997). Ending the family quarrel: Toward a reconciliation of "old" and "new" institutionalisms. American Behavioral Scientist, 40(4), 406-418.

Jepperson, R.L. (1991). Institutions, institutional effects, and institutionalism. In W.W. Powell & P.J. DiMaggio (Eds.), The new institutionalism in organizational analysis. Chicago, IL: University of Chicago Press.

Kimberly, J. R. (1975). Environmental constraints and organizational structure: A comparative analysis of rehabilitation organizations. Administrative Science Quarterly, 20, 1-9.

Mische, A. (2003). Cross-talk in movements: Reconceiving the culture-network link. In M. Diani & D. McAdam (Eds.), Social movements and networks: Relational approaches to collective action. Oxford, UK: Oxford University Press.

McAdam, D. (2003). Beyond structural analysis: Toward a more dynamic understanding of social movements. In M. Diani & D. McAdam (Eds.), Social movements and networks: Relational approaches to collective action. Oxford, UK: Oxford University Press.

Munch, R., and Smesler, N.J. (1987). Relating the micro and macro. In J.C Alexander, B. Giesen, R. Munch & N.J. Smesler (Eds.), The Micro-Macro Link. Berkeley, CA: University of California Press.

O'Mahony, S. C. (2002). The emergence of a new commercial actor: Community managed software projects. Unpublished doctoral dissertation. Stanford University.

Orlikowski, W., and Gash, D.C. (1994). Technological frames: Making sense of information technology in organizations. ACM Transactions on Information Systems, 12(2), 174-207.

Pierson, P. (2000). The limits of design: Explaining institutional origins and change. Governance: An Interdisciplinary Journal of Policy and Administration, 13(4), 475-499.

Porpora, D. V. (1989). Four concepts of social structure. Journal for the Theory of Social Behavior, 19(2), 195-211.

Powell, W.W. (1991). Expanding the scope of institutional analysis. In W.W. Powell & P.J. DiMaggio (Eds.), The new institutionalism in organizational analysis. Chicago, IL: University of Chicago Press.

Rao, H. (1998). Caveat Emptor: The construction of non-profit consumer watchdog organizations. American Journal of Sociology, 103(4), 912-961.

Ranson, S., Hinings, R., and Greenwood, R. (1980). The structuring of organizational structures. Administrative Science Quarterly, 43(3), 1-17.

Scott, R., and Meyer, J. W. (1991). The organization of societal sectors: Propositions and early evidence. In W.W. Powell & P.J. DiMaggio (Eds.), The new institutionalism in organizational analysis. Chicago, IL: University of Chicago Press.

Selznick. P. (1949). TVA and the grass roots. Berkeley, CA: University of California Press.

Snow, D.A., and Benford, R.D. (1988). Ideology, frame resonance and movement participation. In B. Klandermans, H. Kreisi, & S. Tarrow (Eds.), From structure to action. Greenwich, CT: JAI Press.

Tarrow, S. (1992). Mentalities, political cultures, and collective action frames: Constructing meanings through action. In A.D. Morris & C.M. Mueller (Eds.), Frontiers in social movement theory. New Haven, CT: Yale University Press.

Tsoukas, H. (1989). The validity of idiographic research explanations. Academy of Management Review, 14(4), 551-561.

Winner, L. (1993). Social constructivism: Opening the black box and finding it empty. Science as Culture, 3(16), 427-452.

Zald, M.N. (1996). Culture, ideology, and strategic framing. In D. McAdam, J.D. McCarthy & M.N. Zald (Eds.), Comparative perspectives on social movements: Political opportunities, mobilizing structures, and cultural framings. Cambridge, UK: Cambridge University Press.

Goals	cross-organizational network infrastructure promoting cross-sectoral connectivity and applications
Key problems	ascertaining who will connect to whom for what applications and resources; applications development-related issues; securing commitment from potential subscribers
Problem-solving strategies	publicizing exemplary uses of broadband; "show-how" demonstrations and trials
Requirements to be met by solution	Serve economically poor and underserved
Current theory	e-government; civic networking; community development approaches
Perceived substitution function	dial-up civic network
Exemplary artifact	operational broadband networks

Table 1. Steering committee's interpretation: Urban-net as a civic network

Goals	specification of network backbone
Key problems	estimating customer demand for access network service
Problem-solving strategies	backbone specification as near-term objective
Requirements to be met by solution	Adequate capacity to meet projected demand
Current theory	public data network design methods
Exemplary artifact	Operational projects

Table 2. Designers' interpretation: Urban-net as backbone

Goals	cost-effective cross-organizational network infrastructure
Key problems	site eligibility for program subsidies, total cost of subscription
Problem-solving strategies	survey, in-house estimates
Requirements to be met by solution	back-compatibility with CPE and on-site technical support staff skills; cost-effectiveness relative to existing services
Perceived substitution function	T carrier leased line services
Exemplary artifact	Gigabit Ethernet service

Table 3. MIS managers' interpretation: Urban-net as intra-organizational infrastructure

Goals	inexpensive high-speed Internet access; CPE upgrade
Key problems	ascertaining total cost of subscription; ascertaining what and how of connectivity; uncertainty over CPE relief amount
Problem-solving strategies	None
Requirements to be met by solution	competitive with Internet access over cable
Current theory	Exemplary use of Internet by CBOs
Perceived substitution function	dial-up connection to Internet
Exemplary artifact	Internet access over cable (DOCSIS)

Table 4. CBOs' interpretation: Urban-net as Internet access ramp

Minimalist Design for Informal Learning in Community Computing

Mary Beth Rosson, John M. Carroll

Center for Human-Computer Interaction, Pennsylvania State University

mrosson@psu.edu, jcarroll@ist.psu.edu

Abstract. We discuss the role and characteristics of informal learning in a community computing context. We argue that minimalist design can be adapted to the needs of community computing, and that its principles can be used to envision and develop community activities and technologies that promote active learning. We illustrate these ideas with several community computing projects that exemplify how to embed learning in meaningful activities, enable learners to make progress quickly, promote thinking and inference, evoke and leverage prior knowledge, and support error recognition and recovery. We conclude with a discussion of how minimalism might be used more broadly to guide the design of community computing systems and activities.

Informal Learning in Community Computing

Community computing refers to the use of networking, software, and activities to support community interactions. Classic examples include the Cleveland Free Net (facilitating dissemination of public health information; Beamish, 1995), and Montana's Big Sky Telegraph (improving teachers' access to library resources in rural Montana; Uncapher, 1999). Community computing is distinctive in that participants are neighbors in the traditional sense; they live in physical proximity and share physical, economic and social resources. In contrast to Internet communities, the information character of community computing is primarily local—description, news, and events pertaining to clubs and churches, public schools, municipal government, voluntary associations, retail businesses, regional economic development and social services.

P. van den Besselaar et al. (eds.), Communities and Technologies 2005, 75-94.

An important facet of community computing is *learning*. Learning may occur as an incidental outcome but is an inherent consequence of any creative human activity; people learn even when they "merely" pursue familiar interests and concerns in new ways. The Cleveland and Montana communities did not simply accomplish community goals more efficiently; they evolved a local Internet culture of new skills and practices. They learned how to use Internet technologies to accomplish new community functions. In Cleveland community health information dissemination evolved into community health discussions through which the hospital staff learned about the needs of their customers. In Montana, people accessed online libraries for existing information; the community created novel coding schemes to digitize Native American cultural artifacts, enabling cultural dissemination back *into* the libraries.

Communities support technology learning in many ways, including just-in-time training classes offered through adult learning centers, community colleges, and so on. In this paper we focus on *informal learning* (IL), working from McGiveney's (1998) broad characterization: informal learning occurs outside of intentional learning environments such as classrooms; arises through people's activities and interests; and even when provided in response to perceived needs is conveyed in a flexible and informal fashion. In the Cleveland and Montana examples, although there may have been an explicit effort to learn about community members' needs on the one hand, and coding schemes, on the other, the shared learning was emergent and entirely situated in the ongoing activities and goals of the community.

Community computing provides an especially rich—and challenging—context for analyzing and supporting informal learning processes (Figure 1). Community groups are often structured and managed in an *ad hoc* fashion. Goals and activities may vary dynamically as a function of membership, current leadership, and resources. Although this adds to the complexity of community group interaction, it also raises the opportunity for many different individuals to "step up" to the needs of their groups.

Within these dynamic group structures, people enact multiple roles, relating to other members as parents, business colleagues, volunteers, and so on. Community members who *bridge* multiple groups have the potential for great impact on the community, in that they tend to be highly educated and more involved in civic concerns (Kavanaugh et al., 2003; Kavanaugh et al., 2005). Cross-group membership also has implications for informal learning, as people are able to see and act on the possibilities for cross-fertilization of ideas, methods, and resources (Putnam, 2000).

The members of community groups vary tremendously in what they bring to shared efforts: in business settings, people collaborate because they have a "job" to do, but in the discretionary context of community efforts, motivation is often intrinsic but varies considerably across individuals. The diverse motivations interact with resource limitations such as time available, making it very difficult to develop and implement targeted learning opportunities. Also, because part of the shared capital in a community is a physical place, a variety of concrete experiential outcomes and rewards become more possible and common. Belonging to any community of practice implies a bond among members, but if we are managing the earth, this bond is inherently multifaceted and will lead to many levels and modes of interaction.

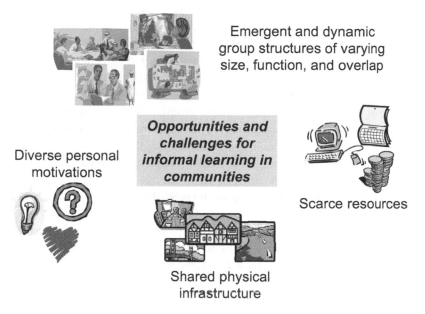

Figure 1. Opportunities and challenges for learning in community computing

The unpredictability and complexity—but also the richness of motivations, backgrounds, and roles—of community computing highlight a need for informal, contextualized learning processes that leverage community members' goals, skills, time, technology, and other resources *if* and *when* they are available. In the balance of this paper we argue that minimalist design provides a guiding framework for initiating and sustaining a broad-based learning culture that accommodates the just-in-time context of community computing. We first briefly review the principles of minimalism and suggest how they can be generalized to address community computing contexts. We illustrate our arguments by reflecting on several of our own community computing projects, concluding with ideas for future analysis and discussion.

Minimalism as a Model for Informal Learning

Minimalism is an instructional design framework intended to address the needs of computer users as *active learners* (Carroll, 1990). Minimalism was a response to empirical studies of novice and experienced computer users as they attempted new tasks. Active learners often reject the prescribed goals and activities of training materials, instead developing and pursuing their own goals. They explore features in pursuit of these goals, working from whatever prior knowledge they possess, whether it is useful or not. When they make mistakes, active users try to understand what has happened, often learning something in the process. A key insight behind minimalism is that learning resources and tools should not protect users from these active learning tendencies but rather should *design for* the tendencies, thereby anticipating and supporting learning by doing.

Minimalist design can be summarized through five basic principles, each emphasizing an important characteristic of active learning that can be encouraged and reinforced through appropriate instructional design:

- *Embed learning in meaningful activities.* People are motivated by real tasks in the real world, not by artificial exercises that introduce new content bit by bit. Designers should offer learning tasks that connect with learners' real world goals and concerns but still achievable by novices.
- *Allow learners to get started quickly.* Learners want to take action and enjoy evidence of progress from the start. Minimalist designs should make it possible for learners to take concrete actions right away, rather than expecting preliminary effort such as reading or planning. Minimalist designs should coordinate presentation of information with opportunities for action to every extent possible (van der Meij & Carroll, 1995).
- *Rely on learners to think and to improvise.* When instructions tell learners what to do step by step, active users often respond by skipping around, in essence forcing themselves to think and improvise, but often ending up in error tangles. Designers instead should construct open-ended materials requiring inference while also offering tips for successful action.
- *Evoke and support the use of prior knowledge.* Learners understand new material with respect to what they already know, using analogies and generalization to make sense of new concepts. Designers should analyze learners' prior knowledge, using metaphors to promote learning transfer.
- *Prevent, mitigate and leverage errors.* Nuisance errors (like mis-typing a URL) should be anticipated and prevented when possible. But many errors are an opportunity for further learning when active users are considering and testing solutions. Designers should provide feedback that makes it clear when users are in an error state and offer tips that guide recovery.

Minimalist instruction was developed in response to human tendencies toward active learning. Because it emphasizes learning by doing, minimalism addresses many of the characteristics of informal learning, for instance the connection of learning to real world activities and reliance on the learner to initiate and manage the reflection and learning process (Dewey, 1933) Minimalism views learners as motivated by intrinsic goals and learning as an ongoing process integrated with everyday experience. As such it is well suited to the needs of informal learning in community computing.

Minimalism in a Community Computing Context

Minimalism assumes that learners are situated in real world activities and that they use this real world context to make sense of new experiences with computing; however most work in minimalism has focused on sense-making by individuals (Carroll, 1998). To consider the role of minimalism for community computing, we must first consider how its principles can be extended or adapted to the problems of technology learning in a community context (Table 1).

Minimalist principle	Adaptation for community computing
Embed learning in meaningful activities	Embed learning in a rich and multi-faceted activity, supporting synthesis and compromise
Allow learners to get started quickly	Provide varied options for rapid results suitable for varied backgrounds, including social scaffolding
Rely on learners to think and to improvise	Design activities that require cooperation and have unpredictable emergent properties; provoke bridging, perspective-switching, and mutual adaptation
Evoke and support the use of prior knowledge	Encourage and support bridging among groups; make the highly distributed and evolving knowledge of the group visible and organized by familiar structures
Prevent, mitigate, and leverage errors	Make it safe and possible for members to monitor and contribute to others' work as well as their own; anticipate, support conflict recognition and resolution

Table 1. Adapting minimalism to a community computing context

One contrast between the body of work on minimalism and the context of community computing is that community learning is a shared and distributed process; it takes place at the level of groups rather than individuals. The learning that takes place is a collective achievement across a potentially diverse set of individuals with complementary or even competing personal motivations (Bertelsen & Bødker, 2003; Engeström, 1987). From a minimalist perspective, the important implication is that meaningfulness will be multi-faceted, with different stakeholders participating under different conceptions of what and how things are happening. Imagine an activity in which volunteers make home technology visits to house-bound elders: the volunteers understand the activity as technology outreach, but for the elders the meaning may lie in the social interaction. The meaningfulness of the overall activity lies in the mutual recognition and synthesis of individuals' goals and motivations (Kuuti & Arvonen, 1982).

With respect to helping learners make progress quickly, a community context again suggests a more expansive view. Minimalist designs rely on tools or instructions that reduce preliminaries, focus learners' attention on just the right information, and offer a protected path to a meaningful goal (Carroll & Carrithers, 1984; Carroll & Kay, 1985; Rosson, Carroll & Bellamy, 1990). Such training techniques would surely be useful in community computing, but because of members' diverse background designers must offer multiple entry points into an activity, enabling the most novice members to participate when time is available, yet allowing sophisticated members to make progress at more challenging levels. By leveraging the indigenous knowledge and social structure of a community, designers can create social scaffolding techniques—perhaps encouraging more expert group members to create learning models for the less expert.

An important element of minimalist design is to amplify learners' inquiry and sense-making. In a self-paced learning context, one way to do this is to initiate goal-oriented activities where procedural details are sketchy or absent (e.g., Carroll & Carrithers, 1984). At a group level, this might be accomplished by engaging members in distributed activities where no individual holds a complete understanding of how other participants are contributing (Hutchins, 1995). Technical support for inquiry in such a context could be a history system that not only logs members' activity streams but also their rationale. Alternatively one might recruit social mechanisms for provoking group inquiry and reflection, for instance organizing cross-generation or cross-cultural groups that must test and establish common ground in order to collaborate (Rosson & Carroll, 2003; Veinott et al., 1999).

Community knowledge is diverse, distributed, and evolving. The group can access, engage with, and benefit from their shared knowledge to the extent that it is available for application in the right place and at the right time. This implies a requirement for knowledge management—enabling the community to capture, organize and recruit members' knowledge, both tacit and explicit (Davenport & Prusak, 1997). Technical approaches to this might involve member profiles and history, perhaps including an explicit expertise database (Ackerman & Malone, 1990). An alternative is to collect a variety of information about the community's activities (e.g., online objects or files accessed, changes instrumented, messages posted) and offer visualizations or other tools to extract patterns from the data (Hill & Begole, 2003). A social technique might be to initiate and reinforce "pockets of expertise" in the community (Rosson, 2004).

Finally, the social structure of a community leads to an expanded view of problem recognition and recovery. As groups pursue shared goals, the members who are active will vary in the expertise, time, and other resources that they can contribute; the quality or accuracy of their contributions may vary accordingly. The community must be able to monitor, detect, and correct problems experienced by individuals or subgroups, with the result that the group and its activities evolve together. A designer can encourage social support of this sort by enabling flexible ownership and digital editing rights (e.g., the Wiki model; Cunningham & Leuf, 2001), or by providing for reputation or other expertise mechanisms that highlight sources of expertise (and accompanying responsibility; Kelly, Sung & Farnham, 2002).

Minimalist Design for Community Computing

Over the past decade we have studied a variety of issues and Internet technologies in community computing (Carroll, 2002; Carroll & Rosson, 2001; Carroll & Rosson, 1996). We have worked in several contexts, including K-12 education (Isenhour et al., 2000), senior citizens (Carroll et al., 1999) and inter-generational computing (Rosson & Carroll, 2003), civic groups (Carroll et al., in press; Kavanaugh et al., 2003) and non-profit organizations (Merkel et al., 2004). Although our community computing projects were not developed with minimalism as an explicit design goal, together they illustrate features that begin to define a minimalist design space for such efforts.

Figure 2 offers an overview of four projects that we highlight in the current discussion. BLACKSBURG NOSTALGIA was an early Internet application built in collaboration with the town's senior citizens (Carroll et al., 1999). It used interactive forms to collect stories of what it was like to live in this town in the 1950's and 1960's; these stories were often prompted by photographs taken during that era, and were elaborated, refined, and sometimes even corrected through other residents' comments and annotations.

TEACHER BRIDGE is an ongoing participatory design project in which public school teachers build online artifacts and activities in a collaborative space that allows them to share, reuse and build their teaching practices together (Kim et al., 2003). COMMUNITYSIMS was an exploration of cross-generational learning and collaboration in which middle school students worked with senior citizens to raise and discuss community issues using visual simulations (Rosson et al., 2002; Rosson & Carroll, 2003). CIVIC NEXUS is a relatively new project in which we are working with non-profit community groups to help them understand their needs and goals for information technology, as well as how to acquire and sustain the skills for meeting these needs (Farooq et al., 2005; Merkel et al., 2004).

Although each of these projects was motivated by different community computing research goals, they share the fundamental belief that the learning and use of community computing skills should occur in an informal manner that is contextualized by the needs and resources of the group. In this section we reflect on characteristics of the projects that illustrate how the five minimalist design principles might be applied within a community computing context.

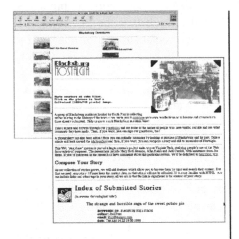

Blacksburg Nostalgia: memories of town's senior citizens evoked by photos, enhanced collaboratively

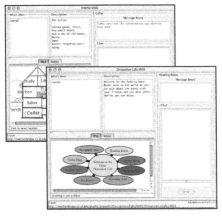

TeacherBridge: learning activities designed, shared, reused within an online teacher community

CommunitySims: community issues explored through cross-generation development of visual simulations

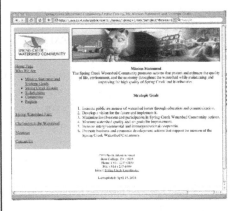

Civic Nexus: non-profit community organizations learn how to advance their own IT skills to meet their goals

Figure 2. Overview of four community computing projects used as examples.

Embed Learning in Meaningful Activities

In two of our projects, informal learning opportunities developed out of existing activities. This has the advantage of fitting the new computing services into an established set of goal structures and methods. For example, NOSTALGIA was conceived as a web-based enhancement to a story-collection process that was already underway using email and listservs. The meaning of this activity was tied to residents' shared history of interactions and events in a familiar set of places that had evolved over time. TEACHER BRIDGE offers teachers a suite of tools (web editors, shared data tables, electronic whiteboards, etc.) within a collaborative authoring environment. But rather than enrolling teachers in a "collaborative authoring" activity from the start, we tapped their strong existing motivation to create teaching materials. Our strategy was to engage teachers by supporting well-established pedagogical goals, while at the same time enabling a new framework for sharing and collaboration among teachers (Carroll et al., 2003). In this sense, the informal learning about one another's efforts emerged as a by-product of the familiar activity of classroom lesson development.

In contrast, the COMMUNITYSIMS and the CIVIC NEXUS projects illustrate the *discovery* of meaningful activities as an integral part of informal learning. In COMMUNITYSIMS our vision was of cross-generation construction and discussion of simulations that address community issues (e.g., noisy neighborhoods, smoking at school). But we predicted from the start that middle school students and elderly citizens would have differing reactions to this goal; one of our research tasks was to investigate these reactions and find a way to synthesize them into a shared effort. We discovered that the elders understood the project as community education and the students as game-playing; this led us to reconceive the project as a role-playing activity in which elders designed community simulations that were implemented by the students. The synthesized activity was multi-faceted, enabling the rather different participants to at once respect their complementary strengths and to find a comfortable framework for their interactions. The students learned about community issues and the elders learned about the design and implementation of interactive graphical simulations.

In CIVIC NEXUS we have been helping community groups reflect on and understand their own goals with respect to computing (Merkel et al., 2004). For instance in one case a watershed conservancy group had initiated a website development activity by hiring an outside expert. They found that this activity was more complex than they had imagined—the expert built a perfectly lovely website but one that did not convey the group's image of itself. With our help the group has reconceptualized the activity as conveying their mission to the public and is now working on their own version of a website. We showed the group how to use scenarios to better understand their computing goals, for example taking an abstract concept like "mission" and exploring it through a concrete usage episode.

Allow Learners to Get Started Quickly

Our community computing projects exemplify two complementary techniques for helping groups to make progress quickly. One of these is based on the recognition that group members will vary in their starting point and so will need differing options for participation. The second recognizes that because some members of the group are better prepared for the new technology, the activity should enable them to take the lead so that the group as a whole makes rapid progress.

In our TEACHERBRIDGE project, we recognized that teachers vary considerably in their technology background, but we wanted any motivated teacher to be able to quickly get up to speed in the collaborative environment. Our approach was to provide simple web-based editing tools (building from the wiki paradigm) that operate in parallel with fully interactive Java-based tools for creating and editing web pages, discussions, calendars and so on. Teachers who are comfortable authoring web pages can use the simpler tools to work *on the same objects* as those created by other teachers using the more sophisticated tool suite.

From a group activity perspective, an early measure of progress is the speed with which pre-existing activities can be reconstituted in a new community computing system. For instance, most of the non-profit groups in the CIVIC NEXUS project already have some web presence and they do not want to start over using new tools. Thus we have emphasized the process of reusing existing content (e.g., importing a series of HTML pages into a content management tool). In this way a group can quickly have a rough prototype (one that is also familiar) and focus on editing and enhancement rather than building new content from scratch.

The NOSTALGIA project is simple in its technology but illustrates an important social technique for making progress quickly. We identified senior citizens who had significant Internet expertise and recruited them as our "lead users", ensuring that a critical mass of town memories were contributed and discussed in the first weeks of system use. At the same time, we serves as intermediaries for elders who wanted to contribute but were not ready to use the web interactive system— if they sent a story or annotation to our research team, we would post it on their behalf. We are using a similar strategy in CIVIC NEXUS: in one activity involving courseware construction by high school students, we quickly identified those who had network expertise and oriented them toward installation of server software, while others just as quickly began developing courseware content (web pages).

The COMMUNITYSIMS project also used a form of social scaffolding to move the activity along quickly. Because participants were assigned a role (elders were simulation designers, students were programmers), they had less need to negotiate common ground with their young or elderly partner; the complementary responsibilities made it clear who should do what. Stereotypes are often seen as limiting and potentially damaging to interpersonal behavior, but in this situation they seemed to streamline the cross-generation interaction, providing a sort of "bootstrapping" for collaborative exchange.

From an informal learning perspective, the COMMUNITYSIMS project faced the risk that the visual simulation programming process would slow down the activity, frustrating participants and sapping their intrinsic motivation. The simulations were built using STAGECAST CREATOR, a visual language that uses visual before-after rules and programming by demonstration to build simulations that play out as a series of connected animations (Smith & Cypher, 1999). We addressed this issue by providing a number of canonical simulations that could be played and quickly enhanced, enabling early progress and reward. During the more extended simulation and construction process, we encouraged design teams to employ a very lightweight "tool" for quick results—paper and pencil for sketching characters and action. One way to see the sketching process is as a low-fidelity prototype that can be developed in a participatory fashion regardless of the partners' technology expertise (Erickson, 1995; Muller, 199?).

Rely on Learners to Think and to Improvise

A fundamental goal of minimalist design is to provoke the learner into an active learning process of inference and problem-solving rather than one of rote learning, procedure following, and repetition. In group activities, this contrast is often discussed by comparing collective behavior that is situated and emergent versus behavior that is pre-defined and regulated (cf. Suchman's [1987] situated action versus Winograd's [1987] action workflow approach).

Our community computing projects are all open-ended in nature. The most prescribed is NOSTALGIA, where we were clearly requesting a certain type of entry (town memories). However even in this case, the tool did not enforce any content or format restrictions, and in fact we observed that contributors learned to use the tool for unexpected purposes (e.g., online greetings). In the COMMUNITYSIMS workshops we provided examples of the sorts of simulations we thought were suitable, but the ideas generated and implemented by the participants were more broad-ranging and creative than our starting set. The younger students were quite content to build characters and actions that had some aspect of fantasy, while the older participants proposed and encouraged "real world" connections to actual places and events taking place in the town. The resulting simulations illustrated an interesting combination of fantasy intermixed with familiar names, buildings, and other details (Rosson & Carroll, 2003).

Some of our community computing tools have features that were explicitly designed to provoke inference and engagement. For instance TEACHERBRIDGE includes "awareness" mechanisms that convey the current status of group efforts.

One of these is a timeline that visualizes whether and how often a project component has received attention, including deadlines that might be looming. Group members can make inferences about activity needs and decide whether and how they should take steps to meet these needs. Similarly, teachers can find, view and test work products created by other teachers, but if a teacher wishes to create a similar artifact she must discover how it was constructed—the system facilitates this by storing information about the object's creator.

In the CIVIC NEXUS project we are exploring a minimalist form of participatory design in which we refrain from co-designing technology solutions. Instead we present multiple possibilities and highlight the tradeoffs associated with each. The goal is to provide enough assistance that the group can actively discuss and choose among options, learning more about their needs, values, and resources in the process (Merkel et al., 2004). At a conceptual level this is analogous to the early work on minimal manuals, where the instructional designer uses open-ended instructions or queries to make learners think about how to solve a problem rather than tell them directly what to do (Carroll & Carrithers, 1984). The method can be conveyed by the metaphor of a *bard*: an actor who stands at the periphery but who tells stories that enhance the group's self-understanding (Carroll & Rosson, in press).

Evoke and Leverage Learners' Prior Knowledge

The knowledge of a group is distributed and evolving, so one objective of minimalist design is to make the group's collective knowledge more apparent and accessible. A good example can be seen in TEACHERBRIDGE: the system records everything that happens, every object that is created or browsed, every change that is made, emails or chat messages sent. For instance, suppose that an interactive discussion room is created by one teacher for her class, reused by a second teacher for a related discussion, and used by a third as a model for a class debate. The knowledge about how to create these educational activities and the consequences of using them for different purposes is distributed across the three teachers. But because the system records all of these interactions and transformations, an interested teacher can access this knowledge. For example she might view a social network of an object's authors and users, and may choose to contact them directly or to explore other class activities they have created.

The stories that residents contributed to NOSTALGIA were a natural mechanism for evoking, elaborating and refining the local history knowledge distributed among community residents (see also Palaver tree paper). We further reminded the senior citizens of their shared knowledge by acquiring, digitizing, and presenting historical photos of buildings and other familiar sites in the town. This is analogous to the evocative role of *sacred places* in community discussions (Erickson, 2000).

As with other minimalist design principles, a designer may use social techniques to engage a group's prior knowledge. In the COMMUNITYSIMS project we knew that the knowledge bases of our cross-generation community members would be diverse—middle school students are familiar with the social and material concerns of 12-14 year olds, whereas elderly residents are familiar with civic concerns, policy tradeoffs, and so on. To ensure that we offered content that would connect with both groups, we carried out a preliminary workshop in which we worked with middle school teachers and elderly citizens to brainstorm simulation topics that would be age-appropriate. For example, the teachers directed us to student-relevant topics like flirting and sexual harrassment, while the older users proposed topics like voter education and neighborhood watch. Because this project was aimed at integrating two segments of the community with rather different knowledge bases, we were careful to provide initial examples that would make contact with each subgroup.

Prevent, Mitigate, and Leverage Errors

Minimalist design research has provided many examples of scaffolding intended to prevent or minimize the damaging consequences of errors—for example *training wheels* that inactivate system function choices known to cause confusion and frustration (Carroll & Carrithers, 1984). Such a technique enables the learner to make a mistake, and to discover that it is an inappropriate step to take, but without suffering any other consequence. In the context of community computing an analogous approach leverages the group's social structure and shared goals to create a social form of scaffolding; other members of the community would be able to help a member having difficulty, even to the extent of correcting an error directly.

The TEACHERBRIDGE environment was designed with this sort of social scaffolding in mind. When a teacher creates a new object, she can decide what other members of her community should be able to view it and who if at all should be able to edit it. If she makes it editable by others, not only can they explore her creations, they can enhance them with their own edits, whether minor fixes like formatting or spelling problems, or more significant enhancements like new embedded objects. Because the system also has extensive support for object histories and versions, these friendly amendments are made with low risk; the original author can always choose to reinstall an earlier version. These mechanisms are descendents of Ward Cunningham's wiki concept (Cunningham & Leuf, 2001) and are designed to create a community culture of shared responsibility, a sort of good citizenship directed at ensuring high quality.

A related example can be seen in the simulation-specific commenting facility in COMMUNITYSIMS. When a simulation is posted for sharing, it is allotted its own mini-discussion thread, a place for other users (or even the author) to post reactions and suggestions. We discovered that many of the comments posted were aimed at perceived problems or complaints about the simulations, for example suggesting places where the action needs to be smoothed out, or where the message does not come across. In this case it is up to the author to address the problem, but other members of the community assist with problem recognition and possible solutions.

In the CIVIC NEXUS project, problem recognition and recovery is subsumed under the more general concern of technology capacity management. A high level objective in all of our non-profit partnerships is *sustainability*: when the research project is over, the group must be able to maintain (and even further develop) the technology it needs to achieve its goals. Sustainability includes the recognition and recovery from problematic situations (e.g., the server software becomes outdated) but goes beyond this to include management of technology skills and plans. In CIVIC NEXUS we are designing for sustainability by understanding our research objective to be initiation of an ongoing learning *process* rather than development of a *product* or solution.

Discussion

We have used the minimalist design framework to reflect on several of our projects in community computing, illustrating how these projects contain a number of features designed to promote informal learning. We posited that the context of community computing engenders a mix of opportunities and challenges for informal learning; for instance the diversity of the groups and their members' motivation creates opportunities for cross-fertilization and mutual learning, but at the same time makes the learning process relatively unpredictable and distributed across time, people, and locations. The general lack of resources leads to an important requirement for flexible, just-in-time learning mechanisms. The minimalist techniques discussed in this paper and summarized in Table 2 are offered as guidance to designers seeking to support informal learning in a community computing context.

For example, we noted that informal learning must be motivated by and grounded in meaningful behavior. Within a community computing context, we argued that designers' focus should be on *activities* rather than on system functions, and that these activities should have a shared meaning in the community that is multi-faceted and emergent. Designers can promote a shared understanding among community members by helping them to recognize contrasting or complementary views and to synthesize them into a reconceptualization of the group's activity. Designers might facilitate a synthetic process such as this by providing group members with lightweight tools for externalizing and combining one another's differing views.

Design principle	Example minimalist strategies
Meaningful activities	*Social*: Discussion and synthesis of contrasting or complementary goals *Technical*: Lightweight tools (e.g. sketching) for developing a shared understanding
Get started quickly	*Social*: Stereotypical role definitions *Technical*: Multiple levels of commitment; importing content from existing activities
Think and improvise	*Social*: Discussion of tradeoffs and design rationale; teams with diverse membership *Technical*: Pervasive activity awareness
Prior knowledge	*Social*: Content customized to different subgroups and knowledge bases *Technical*: Data about members' creations, usage, and transformations; tools for mining these data
Error recovery	*Social*: Designing for technology capacity management *Technical*: Collaborative editing with versioning; object-specific commentary or annotations

Table 2. Social and technical approaches to minimalist design

The diversity of community groups might seem like a deterrent to rapid progress in a learning situation, but we showed how we were able to leverage the diversity in a team by setting up a role-playing situation in which different members had clear but complementary responsibilities. Similarly we argued that encountering different or even competing viewpoints and capacities in a group can be the inspiration for thinking and improvisation.

We suggested that if designers provide pervasive support for access rights and versioning within a community, they may encourage a culture of shared responsibility in which members help to monitor and correct one another's work. We also argued for a broader view of problem detection and correction, where it is subsumed by the more general concern of technology capacity management.

Note that the strategies summarized in Table 3 have been classified as primarily social or technical in nature. These labels are not intended to be mutually exclusive—a tool used to mine group members' online interaction data is a technical innovation but it clearly is working with information that is social in character. However the contrasting labels do help to express the complementary contributions of technical and social design elements in community computing. This is an important general lesson to draw from our discussion: community computing should be analyzed as a socio-technical system, and the minimalist design strategies should incorporate both social and technical approaches.

Another general observation about the community computing projects we have reviewed is that all have relied extensively on participatory design methods (Carroll & Rosson, in press). Meaning and intrinsic motivation are an essential ingredient of informal learning and designers will not be able to appreciate community member's concepts and concerns unless they work with them, probe their views, present options, and listen to reactions.

Indeed, our current work in the CIVIC NEXUS project is leading us to a new view of participatory techniques that are appropriate for community computing. The lack of stable governing structures and resources makes the sustainability of any community computing intervention a first order concern (Merkel et al., 2004). If a research project enhances the technological support for a group's activity, what happens when the project is over? Will the group be able to maintain its new technology and activities? Can the group learn and evolve as the technology evolves? If the goal of the participatory engagement is seen as the development of a community computing "system" (or even an activity), chances are that the intervention will not be sustainable in the longer term, for instance as the non-profit group's membership evolves, and its resources come and go. Instead we are coming to believe that a more appropriate design goal is to initiate a *technology learning practice*. A socio-cultural change of this sort may not lead to specific designed artifacts, but it may be resilient to changes in membership, the departure of the research group, and so on.

As designers, we find it difficult to resist a solution-oriented exchange with our community partners—we hear their needs; we have great ideas about how to solve their problems; we want to help! But if instead we carefully listen and reflect back to them what we have heard, we may be able to do even better: we may be able to help them help themselves.

Not surprisingly, our emerging view of participatory design is minimalist itself. We try to identify modest problems that a group can tackle immediately, so that they can see themselves making progress. We encourage them to build from their own knowledge by telling them stories about what we have heard them say, so that they can better understand what they do or do not already know. We avoid giving them detailed instructions for new activities, instead presenting options and tradeoffs for them to consider. When we identify sources of energy (even when they are in the form of a conflict) we reflect these back into the process to inspire thinking and improvisation. Finally we try to guide them toward more effective intra-group communication (e.g., using scenarios) so that they can monitor their own understanding and progress toward goals.

Community computing presents a challenging and rewarding context for design. If our goal is to integrate community members' informal learning about technology into their real world activities, then the sustainability of the learning process must become a high-priority requirement in our work. Ultimately this may cause us to shift our attention from the design of community computing *systems* to the evolution of community computing *practices.*

Acknowledgments

We thank the members of the Computer-Supported Collaboration and Learning Lab at the School of Information Sciences and Technology, The Pennsylvania State University, as well as members of the Center for Human-Computer Interaction at Virginia Tech. Several of the projects mentioned in this paper were supported by grants from The National Science Foundation (REC-9554206, ITR-0081102, ITR-0353075, REC-0353101, and IIS-0342547).

References

Ackerman, M.S. & Malone, T.W. 1990. Answer Garden: A tool for growing organizational memory. In *Proceedings of the Conference on Office Systems* (pp. 31-39). New York: ACM.

Beamish, A. 1995. *Communities On-Line: Community-Based Computer Networks.* Masters Thesis, Department of Urban Studies and Planning, MIT.

Bertelsen, O.W. & Bødker, S. 2003. Activity Theory. In J.M. Carroll (Ed.), *HCI Models, Theories, and Frameworks: Toward a Multidisciplinary Science* (pp. 291-324). San Francisco: Morgan Kaufmann.

Carroll, J.M. 1990. *The Nurnberg Funnel: Designing Minimalist Instruction for Practical Computer Skill.* Cambridge, MA: MIT Press.

Carroll, J.M. (Editor) 1998. *Minimalism beyond "The Nurnberg Funnel".* Cambridge, MA: M.I.T. Press.

Carroll, J.M. & Carrithers, C. 1984. Blocking learner errors in a training wheels system. *Human Factors, 26(4),* 377-389.

Carroll, J.M. & Kay, D.S. 1985. Prompting, feedback, and error correction in the design of a scenario machine. In B. Curtis & L. Borman (Eds.), *Proceedings of Human Factors in Computing Systems: CHI '85* (pp. 149-154). New York: ACM.

Carroll, J.M., Choo, C.W., Dunlap, D.R., Isenhour, P.L., Kerr, S.T., MacLean, A., & Rosson, M.B. 2003. Knowledge management support for teachers. *Educational Technology Research and Development,* 51(4), 42-64.

Carroll, J. M., & Rosson, M. B. 1987. The paradox of the active user. In J.M. Carroll (Ed.), *Interfacing Thought: Cognitive Aspects of Human-Computer Interaction.* Cambridge, Mass: MIT Press (pp. 80-111).

Carroll, J. M. & Rosson, M. B. 1991. Deliberated evolution: Stalking the View Matcher in design space. *Human-Computer Interaction, 6*(3&4), 281-318.

Carroll, J.M. and Rosson, M.B. 1996. Developing the Blacksburg Electronic Village. *Communications of the ACM,* 39 (12), 69-74.

Carroll, J.M. & Rosson, M.B. 2000. School's Out: Supporting authentic learning in a community network. *IFIP Conference on Information Technology at Home* (Wolverhampton, United Kingdom, June 28-30).

Carroll, J.M. and Rosson, M.B. 2001. Better home shopping or new-democracy: Evaluating community network outcomes. *Proceedings of CHI 2001: Conference on Human Factors of Computing Systems.* (Seattle, WA; March 31-April 5). NY: ACM, 372-379.

Carroll, J.M. & Rosson, M.B. 2003. A trajectory for community networks. *The Information Society*, 19(5), 381-393.

Carroll, J.M. & Rosson, M.B. (in press). Participatory design of information systems. To appear in *Human-Computer Interaction in Information Systems Design.*

Carroll, J.M., Rosson, M.B., Isenhour, P.L., Ganoe, C.H., Dunlap, D., Fogarty, J., Schafer, W., & Van Metre, C. 2001. Designing our town: MOOsburg. *International Journal of Human-Computer Studies*, 54, 725-751.

Carroll, J.M., Rosson, M.B., VanMetre, C.A., Kengeri, R., & Darshani, M. 1999. Blacksburg Nostalgia: A Community History Archive. In M.A. Sasse & C. Johnson (Eds.), *Proceedings of Seventh IFIP Conference on Human-Computer Interaction INTERACT 99* (Edinburgh, August 30 - September 3). Amsterdam: IOS Press/International Federation for Information Processing (IFIP), pages 637-647.

Cunningham, W., & Leuf, B. 2001. *The Wiki Way: Collaboration and Sharing on the Internet.* Reading, MA: Addison-Wesley.

Davenport, T.H. & Prusak, L. 1997. *Working Knowledge: How Organizations Manage What They Know.* Cambridge, MA: Harvard Business School Press.

Dewey, J. 1933. *How We Think: A Restatement of the Relation of Reflective Thinking to the Educative Process.* Boston: D.C. Heath.

Engeström, Y. 1987. *Learning by Expanding.* Helsinki: Orienta-Konsultit.

Erickson, T. 1995. Notes on design practice: Stories and prototypes as catalysts for communication. In J.M. Carroll (Ed.), *Scenario-Based Design: Envisioning Work and Technology in System Development* (pp. 37-58). New York: John Wiley & Sons.

Erickson, T. 2000. Lingua Francas for design: Sacred places and pattern languages. *Proceedings of DIS 2000* (pp. 357-368). New York: ACM.

Farooq, U., Merkel, C., Nash, H., Rosson, M.B., Carroll, J.M. & Xiao, M. 2005. Participatory design as apprenticeship: Sustainable watershed management as a community computing application. *Hawaii International Conference On System Sciences: HICSS 38.* Kona, HI, January 2005.

Granovetter, M. 1973. The strength of weak ties. *American Journal of Sociology,* 78:1360-80.

Isenhour, P., Carroll, J.M., Neale, D., Rosson, M.B., & Dunlap, D. 2000. The Virtual School: An integrated collaborative environment for the classroom. *Educational Technology & Society*, 3(3), 74-86.

Hill, R. & Begole, J. Activity rhythm detection and modeling. In *CHI 2003 Extended Abstracts.* New York: ACM.

Hutchins, E. 1995. *Cognition in the Wild,* Bradford: MIT Press.

Kavanaugh, A. Reese, D.D., Carroll, J.M., & Rosson, M.B. 2003. Weak ties in networked communities. In M. Huysman, E. Wenger and V. Wulf (Eds.) *Communities and Technologies 2003* (pp. 265-286). Amsterdam: Kluwer Academic Publishers.

Kavanaugh, A., Carroll, J.M., Rosson, M. B., Reese, D. D. & Zin, T.T. 2005. Participating in civil society: The case of networked communities. *Interacting with Computers* (in press).

Kelly, S.U., Sung, C., & Farnham, S. 2002. Designing for improved social responsibility, user participation and content in online communities. In *Proceedings of CHI 2002* (pp. 391-398). New York: ACM.

Kim, K., Isenhour, P.L., Carroll, J.M., Rosson, M.B., & Dunlap, D.R. 2003. Teacher Bridge: Knowledge management in community networks. *Home and Office Information Technology: HOIT3.* April 2003, Irvine, California.

Kuutti, K. & Arvonen, T. 1992. Identifying potential CSCW applications by means of Activity Theory concepts: A case example. *Proceedings of CSCW 1992* (pp. 233-240). New York: ACM.

McGiveney, V. 1999. *Informal Learning in the Community. A Trigger for Change and Development.* Leicester: NIACE.

Meij, H. van der & Carroll, J.M. 1995. Principles and heuristics for designing minimalist instruction. *Technical Communication, 42,* 243-261.

Merkel, C.B., Clitherow, M., Carroll, J., & Rosson, M. 2004. *Sustaining computer use and learning in community computing contexts: Making technology part of "Who They are and What They Do".* Paper presented at CIRN 2004: Sustainability and Community Technology, 9/29-10/01, 2004. Monash University, Prato, Tuscany, Italy.

Merkel, C. B., Xiao, L., Farooq, U., Ganoe, C. H., Lee, R., Carroll, J. M., & Rosson, M.B. 2004. Participatory design in community computing contexts: Tales from the field . *Proceedings of PDC 2004* (pp.1-10). New York: ACM Press.

Muller, M.J., Wildman, D.M., & White, E.A. 1993. 'Equal opportunity' PD using PICTIVE. *Communications of the ACM,* 36(4), 54-66.

Putnam, R. 2000. *Bowling Alone: The Collapse and Revival of American Community.* New York: Simon and Schuster.

Rosson, M.B. 2004. Computer-supported cooperative work: Vignette. In *Berkshire Encyclopedia of Human-Computer Interaction.*

Rosson, M. B. & Carroll, J. M. 1996. Scaffolded examples for learning object-oriented design. *Communications of the ACM,* 39(4), 46-47.

Rosson, M.B. and Carroll, J.M. 2003. Learning and collaboration across generations in a community. In M. Huysman, E. Wenger & V. Wulf (eds.), *Communities and Technologies 2003* (pp. 205-225), The Netherlands: Kluwer Academic Publishers. (Amsterdam, September 2003).

Rosson, M. B., Carroll, J. M., & Bellamy, R. K. E. 1990. Smalltalk scaffolding: A case study in Minimalist instruction. In J. C. Chew & J. Whiteside (Eds.,) *Proceedings of Human Factors in Computing Systems, CHI'90 Conference* (pp. 423-430). New York: ACM.

Rosson, M.B., Carroll, J.M., Seals, C., & Lewis, T. 2002. Community design of community simulations. *Proceedings of Designing Interactive Systems: DIS 2002* (pp. 74-83). New York: ACM.

Rosson, M. B., Carroll, J. M., & Sweeney, C. 1991. A View Matcher for reusing Smalltalk classes. In S. P. Robertson, G. M. Olson, & J. S. Olson (Eds.), *Proceedings of Human Factors in Computing Systems, CHI'91 Conference* (pp. 277-284). New York: ACM.

Rosson, M.B. & Seals, C. 2001. Teachers as simulation programmers: Minimalist learning and reuse. In *Proceedings of CHI 2001* (31 March - 4 April, Seattle, WA), pp. 237-244.

Smith, D.C. & Cypher. A. 1999. Making programming easier for children. In Druin A., ed. *The Design of Children's Technology,* Morgan Kaufmann, San Francisco, 1999, pp. 201-222.

Suchman, L. 1987. *Plans and Situated Action: The Problem of Human-Machine Communication.* Cambridge, UK: Cambridge University Press.

Uncapher, W. 1999. New communities/new communication: Big Sky Telegraph and its community. In M. Smith & P. Kollock, eds., *Communities in Cyberspace.* Routledge.

Veinott, E.S., Olson, J., Olson, G.M., & Fu, X. 1999. Video helps remote work: Speakers who need to negotiate common ground benefit from seeing each other. *Proceedings of CHI 1999* (pp. 302-209). New York: ACM.

Vygotsky, L.S. 1962. *Thought and Language.* Cambridge, MA: MIT Press.

Winograd, R. 1987. A language/action perspective on the design of cooperative work. *Human-Computer Interaction*, 3(1), 3-30.

Virtual Community Management as Socialization and Learning

Daniel Pargman

Royal Institute of Technology, Sweden

pargman@nada.kth.se

Abstract. How does a (virtual) community thrive and survive over time? From having studied a thirteen-year old Swedish-language adventure mud, I here suggest that our understanding of the answer has to be built on a social theory of learning that takes into account that learning has to do with community, practice, meaning and identity. Making a "career" in a community of practice can be regarded as a movement from the periphery to the core, a movement from being a novice to becoming an expert in the activities that are central to the community. On that journey, the individual is over time "configured" into learning how to act, reason and think about the community in the right way.

Introduction

Most MUDs - text-based social virtual environments - are either young or dead. Multi-User Dungeons (MUDs) are the descendants of single-player text-based adventure games such as *Adventure* and *Zork*. The first MUD[1] was created in 1978-1980 at Essex University by Roy Trubshaw and Richard Bartle (Bartle 2003). Although the focus of research during the 1990's has been on studying muds that are used for purely social or for instrumental purposes (e.g. distance education, language learning), the prevalent usage of such systems is and has always been gaming. And modern-day descendants of mud systems are not used for work or "serious" purposes but rather "just" for fun – running so-called

---

[1] The term MUD will be written with lower-case letters (mud) in this text for reasons of legibility (cf. radar instead of RADAR – *radio detecting and ranging*).

P. van den Besselaar et al. (eds.), Communities and Technologies 2005, 95-110.

Massively Multiplayer Online Games (MMOGs) such as *Everquest* and *Star Wars Galaxies* are quickly becoming big business. But apart from such huge and commercially successful online computer games, most muds are usually not run as commercial enterprises. The code bases for a variety of "strands" of different mud systems are free to download on the Internet. The threshold for starting up and running a mud is consequently low – almost but not quite within the reach of an individual, but surely within reach of said individual and a few friends of his or hers. As examples of digital grass-roots initiatives, the question of sustainability of such systems therefore becomes interesting. Some muds survive and become long-lived while most quickly wither and die. What makes a virtual community hold together, thrive and develop over time? Turning the question around, how does a virtual community die?

If we exclude *force majeure* reasons *(e.g. "acts of God")* such as the computer hosting the community unexpectedly "dying"[2], what remains are two different ways that a mud can die. The first is that the players desert it (or the player base is usurped by newer games etc.). The second is that the developers (managers/ administrators) desert it (or fall out due to conflicts with each other etc.). I am here interested in how developer attrition is countered in a mud by holding on to and fostering new generations of developers. I find that question at least as important for the longevity of the mud/virtual communities as any other question and claim that reproduction of the developer base is the key to survival. It doesn't even matter if developer attrition is high as long as enough new developers can be recruited, instructed and socialized. If that process is successful, the mud and the collective of developers can withstand more serious challenges which in turn increase longevity.

Questions of survival and reproduction become especially interesting in a virtual community that constitutes a bottom-up grass-roots initiative and where all work is voluntary and unpaid and all usage is free. Adventure (gaming) muds are usually such organizations. Numerous articles have by now been written about muds. A minority of them has dealt with adventure muds (most instead deal with muds used for social or instrumental purposes such as education, collaboration between researchers etc.). With few exceptions (for example Bartle 1996, Bartle 2003), what has been written about adventure muds has been based on material collected inside the muds and from the perspective of the players rather than the perspective of the developers who maintain and are in charge of the mud. Here, the focus is however on "the work to make it work"; the work behind the scenes to make an adventure mud continue to run and the principles that structure that work.

The virtual community this research is based on, SvenskMud, is a Swedish-language adventure mud - an Internet-accessible multi-player on-line game – and

---

[2] It could be that such reasons constitute the majority of failures, but, such failures are quite straight-forward and not of interest here.

it is one of few non-English muds on the Internet[3]. SvenskMud ("SwedishMud") was started in July 1991 by a student a Swedish University and it is the oldest non-English-language mud in the world. It has been developed in a way that shares many characteristics of how Linux and other open-source programs are developed[4] (Raymond 1999, Moody 2001, Torvalds and Diamond 2001, Feller and Fitzgerald 2002). Since the start thirteen years ago, more than 100 developers have contributed to SvenskMud's 3+ million lines of "code" (not everything is computer code in a more strict sense).

SvenskMud is a *community of practice* (Lave and Wenger 1991, Wenger 1998) that is founded on computing. After describing what a community of practice is and why SvenskMud is one, I will in this paper:

(1)   Describe how a player makes a "career" in SvenskMud by moving from the periphery to the core of the community as he or she[5] moves from being a novice to an expert in the activities of the community.

(2)   Describe how the community "configures" its members and how such a configuration socializes players and developers from solitary disparate individuals into full members of the community.

(3)   Describe how the configuration process in point 2 itself is reconfigured over time.

(4)   Analyze SvenskMud in terms of Turner's (1969/1995) *communitas*.

Method

I have studied SvenskMud over a period of three and a half years using a "convergent methodologies" approach (Schiano 1997). The assumption is that a combination of methods makes it possible to discern patterns and draw conclusions that could be difficult to support or even notice with a more narrow approach.

I have - with due permission - collected three different types of data; naturally occurring non-elicited data, elicited data and data from two different sorts of participant observation studies. The collected materials span:

• *Non-elicited data*: information from the SvenskMud homepages, public discussions on bulletin boards within SvenskMud and different sorts of on-line documentation including rules for the developers, programming manuals and the computer code itself that constitutes the game.

---

[3] In the mid- to end-90's the proportion on non-English muds were between 1-2%. As of today (2004), the number of non-English muds listed on a popular listings service (<http://www.mudconnector.com>) is between 3-4%.

[4] See Pargman (2000b) for an explicit comparison between development of muds and open source software.

[5] Most players are male rather than female and I will therefore primarily use male pronouns in this text.

- *Elicited data*: data from three surveys, interviews and informal conversations with active developers on- and off-line as well as a forum I initiated for discussing different aspects of playing and running SvenskMud.
- *Participant observation* data: observations from using/playing SvenskMud over a period of two years and data from participating in five real-world weekend-long design meetings – or mini-conferences – that the SvenskMud developers organized over a period of five years.

The full results are developed in Pargman 2000b. I have translated all quotes from original Swedish material.

Communities of practice

Communities of practice (Lave and Wenger 1991, Wenger 1998) are inexorably tied to a social theory of learning. Such a theory takes as points of departure that:
- Learning is social, learning is part of human nature, and, we are quite good at it.
- Learning is not confined to a certain place or situation and thus has no beginning or end.
- Learning instead happens best when it is a side product of, or part of other activities.
- Learning is not necessarily the effect of teaching. And when we are being taught, we learn many other things than the subject at hand.

According to this type of social learning theory, learning has to do with *community* (learning as belonging), *practice* (learning as doing), *meaning* (learning as experience) and *identity* (learning as becoming) (Wenger 1998).

A community of practice consists of people undertaking a collective endeavor such that newcomers learn the ins and outs from older hands and that a (formal or informal) system of apprenticeship is in place. SvenskMud, and, many if not most professions or workplaces are communities of practice. Becoming a member of such a community of practice is a matter or learning how to act, reason and think in the *right* way, learning how to handle common or unusual, simple or difficult situations. It is a matter of learning everything that needs to be known beyond the technically specified necessary skills and pre-defined written-down instructions and of moving from the periphery to the core as one moves from being a novice to an expert in the relevant activities.

A movement from the periphery to the core can be described and discussed in terms of a "career"[6] of an individual. He or she moves from 1) wanting, trying,

---

[6] The term career does not imply that the activities in questions must be work-related. It instead has to do with fulfilling the expectations on a social role and "learning the ropes" of something – whatever that something is (see for example Goffman 1959).

pretending to be to 2) becoming identified and *identifying with*, and finally to 3) *becoming* an expert programmer, nurse, policeman, mental patient or inmate. It is a movement from being a legitimate peripheral participant to becoming a full member of the community of practice.

SvenskMud as a community of practice

A SvenskMud career corresponds to a movement from being a novice player to becoming an intermediate and later an expert player, then becoming a developer (called "magician" in SvenskMud[7]) and finally becoming a Senior magician and perhaps even an Arch magician (see figure 1).

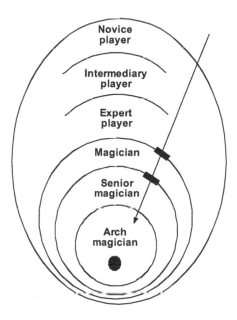

Figure 1. A "career" in SvenskMud as a movement from periphery to core and from novice to SvenskMud expert. A player can stop or opt out of the "career path" at any step in the process. Stronger resistance is encountered before a player can become a magician (developer) and again before becoming a Senior magician. The black dot represents SvenskMud's creator and formal owner, Linus.

The transition from player to magician is the most important and significant in the career of a SvenskMud player. That movement is deeply significant within SvenskMud and is accompanied by so many requirements and procedures that it

---

[7] The terms "developer" and "magician" will be used interchangeably in the text from hereon.

is reminiscent of a fully-fledged initiation rite/rite of passage (van Gennep 1909/1960). I have observed that many magicians remember the exact date when they became magicians, much like other persons remember a wedding day or the birthday of a child[8]. The movement from novice player to magician can take one or several years in SvenskMud. In one extreme case, a person who started to play SvenskMud in 1991 almost became a magician 1994 but started to work instead. He returned to SvenskMud 1997 and finally became a magician three years later and altogether nine years after he started to play SvenskMud – at a time in his life when he was the joint owner of a small computer consulting company.

The transition from "ordinary" magician to Senior magician makes demands on the magician in question, demands that he (or she) is perceived to be "a sensible person, can [...] produce code and that he has some sense of responsibility" (interview with Joorin, Arch magician, 981013). SvenskMud is a community based on computing and this is the point when those who can not or do not want to learn to program stop from moving further towards the core.

How then do players become "magician material"? And how are players who are "magician material" or newly minted magicians recruited, instructed and socialized so as to become fully-fledged and productive members of the SvenskMud development team? And furthermore – as is necessary for survival and longevity – how does SvenskMud itself adapt and change over time? I suggest that it is done through a three-tiered process of configuring the player, of configuring the magician and of configuring SvenskMud itself. To "configure" a player or a magician is here equivalent to the process of socializing that player/magician.

Configuring the player

SvenskMud can easily be perceived as a "blooming buzzing confusion" for a new player. Not everyone feels inclined to take up the challenge to make sense of a world where you have to learn everything anew, up to and including the commands for how to walk and how to talk.

To become part of the community of SvenskMud players is inexorably connected to learning to become knowledgeable in the activities of that community, i.e. of playing SvenskMud. A player who wants to program in SvenskMud (thereby altering the fabric of the virtual world) will acquire many of the relevant concepts before actually becoming a magician, just by playing and exploring the game. Understanding the "affordances" (dramaturgical cues) offered by the virtual world serves to socialize a player long before that player has the option of becoming a developer.

---

[8] The same was true for the mud British Legends (Richard Bartle, personal communication). People who became wizards on the same day there were "twins".

The handbook for SvenskMud magicians states three different normative purposes behind the many quests that players have to solve before they can become magicians

"1. They should stimulate the players' joy of discovery and encourage mental activity.

2. They should prevent playing from becoming mechanical [...].

3. They should force the players to explore a very large part of the world before they become magicians so they know what there is to be found and create a [mental] image of the world."

Even if the SvenskMud developers succeed in their goal of always hiding the computer code from the player – for example by camouflaging error messages – the whole SvenskMud world still constitutes a reflection of that underlying computer code. An implicit understanding of the code is developed through extended use of SvenskMud. The relationship between the SvenskMud world and the underlying computer code is in this sense analogous to the relationship between the lived-in world and the rules of physics that govern the world, a theme that is further developed in Pargman (2000a). By playing SvenskMud, a player will get accustomed to many of the concepts that govern the SvenskMud world and will come to understand many of the SvenskMud goals, symbols and values. SvenskMud players without any previous knowledge of (the workings of) muds or computers thus "subconsciously" prepare themselves for possible future careers as SvenskMud magicians.

This process bears many similarities to the "primary socialization" of a child into a member of society, a socialization that "make appear as necessity what is in fact a bundle of contingencies" (Berger and Luckmann 1966, p.155). This is the *purpose* of configuring the player and it is intimately connected to the regrowth of SvenskMud magicians and SvenskMud's survival over time. I illustrate this through a description of how a career in SvenskMud can start off:

A SvenskMud player would absorb the essence of mudding practice simply in the process of playing they game. A Swedish boy who eventually becomes a SvenskMud magician most likely has access to a computer with an Internet connection at home, since magicianhood nowadays primarily is mediated through Internet Service Providers and telephone lines9. Boys in such families, without being identified as apprentice SvenskMud magicians, absorb the essence of SvenskMud practices (of both players and magicians) as well as specific knowledge about many procedures, simply in the process of playing SvenskMud. They know what the life of a magician is like (for example, that he needs to deal with quarrelsome troublemakers at all hours of the day or night), what kind of stories the women and men who have explored the mud far and wide tell, what kind of treasures and other artifacts need to be collected, and the like. As novice

---

9 It is also possible (but increasingly unlikely) that he only has access to computers and the Internet at his public school or a library.

players, they might not make a lot of noise in the mud, but they would hear stories of difficult cases, of miraculous outcomes, and the like. As they become more experienced and grow older, they may be solving quests, killing monsters, getting needed experience points. A novice player might be present when a magician stops for a visit and a conversation at the daily visit to the mud10.

Configuring the magician

Where primary socialization is the original unconscious socialization of a child into a member of society, the secondary socialization is the conscious training into a specific role or position in the social order (Berger and Luckmann 1966). In SvenskMud, secondary socialization corresponds to the training to become a good SvenskMud magician. Let us illustrate this by describing how the hypothetical career above could continue:

Later, the learning is less "accidental", less peripheral and more conscious. Eventually, after he has become a magician himself, he might look at some of the computer code behind the game, perhaps just out of curiosity and to find out exactly how a specific object in the game worked. At some point, he may decide that he actually wants to write this kind of code. He then pays more attention and joins a project under the supervision of a Senior magician. The Senior magician might see his association primarily as one that is of some use to her. ("darik already knows how to fix such a bug, so I can ask him as I am too busy.") As time goes on, the apprentice takes over more and more of the work load, starting with the routine and tedious parts, and ending with what is in SvenskMud the culturally most significant, the birth of a new area or a guild in the SvenskMud world. In the words of one magician:

"What makes SvenskMud a good mud for the magicians? The fact that there are other magicians who are willing to train new magicians, up to and including novices of programming"

Where rules for the SvenskMud players are more or less non-existent (the general rule is that everything that is possible is allowed), the activities for SvenskMud magicians are more tightly surrounded by rules. Learning to become a SvenskMud magician consists partly of learning to program LPC - a mud-specific variant of the C programming language - and partly of learning (to share) the SvenskMud values etc. as well as developing a sense of commitment and responsibility to the community.

Much of the technical advice to developers on how to program in SvenskMud as well as guidelines for the content are at the same time advice on the proper behavior of a SvenskMud magician. As such they represent lessons regarding the

---

10 Do note the not-so-incidental similarities between this description of growing up to become a SvenskMud magician and Jordan's (1989) description of growing up to become a Yucatec Mayan midwife in Mexico!

specific values, practices and goals that represent "the SvenskMud way" of solving problems, of debugging code, of relating to players, of relating to other magicians etc. From an important document, *RULES*, a magician for example learns that it is an ideal in SvenskMud to:

"Cooperate!

Always use objects that already exist to do different things. A suitable way to do that is with the instruction "inherit". LPC is an object-oriented programming language with multiple inheritance.

If there are no ready objects [that do exactly what you want to do] then talk to a magician who has already created [a similar] object so that you both will use the same object (it saves time and energy!)."

Another advice for magicians was posted to one of the bulletin boards that is available exclusively to SvenskMud magicians:

"[...] But I would also like to point out something for those who code (most often new magicians). Players are idiots ;-) and one should code idiot-safe. What I mean is, don't think "I won't bother to code that because no-one will figure out that you can do a thing like that anyway", believe me, they do. If there is some way the code can bug out they will find it sooner or later ;-) So, it is better to stop most of the ways code can bug directly even if that means more code in the end... it will be worthwhile."

An "underlying principle" that always should direct the actions of all magicians, states that magicians should:

"Never affect the situation of the players directly in the game, neither positively nor negatively.

Your only influence on the players should be exhorted via what you have created [programmed], not in any other way."

The SvenskMud rules for magicians are divided into laws and recommendations and they regulate four different spheres:

(1) *Rules that pertain to "SvenskMud – the game"*. How magicians should role-play when interacting with SvenskMud players and advice on a general level for how to design appropriate SvenskMud content. Examples of this is a law that states that a magician never should hurt a player and a recommendation that states that a magicians should not create weapons that are "too good" for the players.

(2) *Rules that pertain to "SvenskMud – the computer program"*. Advice on how a magicians should go about when they program in SvenskMud. An example of this is a recommendation that states that magicians should adapt the price of healing to what is stated in the file /doc/build and that the lowest price shall be 5 öre/point healed.

(3) *Rules that pertain to "SvenskMud – the hobby"*. Advice that aims at making SvenskMud an enjoyable environment for every *person* sitting in front of a computer (both players and magicians). An example of this is a

law that states that magicians should be polite towards other players and that magicians should not spread rumors about players or other magicians.

(3)   *Rules that pertain to SvenskMud in relation to the surrounding Swedish society.* Advice on how magicians should behave so as to reduce the possibility of creating a conflict for example between SvenskMud and Swedish laws. An example of this is a recommendation that states that real persons never should be portrayed in SvenskMud. The argument behind the recommendation states that:

"Satire is difficult. It has to be done in the right way not to become slander. With the present interest of the Internet (that started 1994 and 1996 still is high) and my (Linus) experience of the level of ambition that those journalists who have an interest in the Internet usually has, I suspect it would be totally impossible to use satire without being misunderstood. Don't do it! (Or wait until the 21st century[11] so the journalists get some time to mature)."

The SvenskMud rules are not the only way to learn "the SvenskMud way" of solving problems, of debugging code, of relating to players and to other magicians etc. Another important document is the 50 pages long *Handbook for SvenskMud magicians – an aid for the builders in SvenskMud.* The handbook among other things documents the early history of SvenskMud, its goals and a wealth of specific information on how to program in LPC.

The handbook also contains 10 spoof commandments of which one states that "Thou shalt steal". The explanation states that "if you don't know how to do certain things, then try to recall where you have seen something similar and check out how it is done there. The best way to learn is to see how others do things". This commandment is complemented by no less than two more commandments that say just about the same thing. One states that "Thou shalt covet thy neighbor's house and his rooms" and the explanation states: "run around in other areas, check out what they build, send a lot of bug reports and then do better yourself".

This obviously points at something that is considered to be important in SvenskMud. It is also interesting to note that such advice has to do with both "hard" issues pertaining to technology, code, programming etc. and with "soft" issues pertaining to shared values and what is considered to be a desirable attitude to have as a SvenskMud magician.

Perhaps SvenskMud (and open source projects) are some of the few programming environments where the developers both are recommended and actually *do* spend considerable time reading the code of others for no other reason than to learn? The habit of reviewing the programming code of others and of having your own code reviewed is an excellent but sadly neglected practice to

---

[11] It is the 21st century but satire is still discouraged in SvenskMud.

improve the code itself and the abilities of programmers and software engineers (Weinberg 1971/1999).

One magician who didn't know how to program before he came in contact with SvenskMud intimately ties together social concerns and technical practices when he describes how he works. Do also take notice of the implicit commitment and responsibility to the community in his statement:

"I read what the other person [I have a project together with] has programmed and correct it and he corrects what I have done. We toss everything back and forth between us all the time. You learn incredibly much by doing so, he sees what I do and I see what he does and then you get acquainted with the code and you correct it. And it's impossible to correct the code if you don't understand what it does.

It becomes totally different here. If a magician creates something that is really bad, that affects the views of the players on the other magicians too[12]. It casts a shadow over all magicians.

If a player comes and reports a bug in someone's area you look into and read through the code that bugs and then you learn the other [magician's] ways of coding and in the end you know that if something bugs in his files, he has probably made such-and-such error."

Configuring SvenskMud

Configuring new members (players and magicians) is a necessary survival strategy for SvenskMud and every other community of practice. It is through these activities that individuals learn "the SvenskMud way" and that SvenskMud reproduces itself over time, survives and becomes long-lived. One question related to survival remains to be answered here though and that is how the system for configuring players and magicians itself changes over time. If configuration is learning, how then does "SvenskMud - the organization" itself learn and change over time? How does SvenskMud question whether its operating norms are appropriate? Where is the "second loop" of learning (Argyris and Schön 1978) that characterizes flexible organizations in changing environments?

The answer is that the SvenskMud real-world design meetings constitute the second loop of learning. Since Sweden is a relatively small country, the active SvenskMud magicians have taken to meeting regularly once or twice per year. Beyond solving current problems in SvenskMud, these meetings simultaneously serve two other important functions. *The first* is to keep a discussion of SvenskMud's future and possible changes in direction alive. Question of SvenskMud's values, goals and practices are thus consciously externalized and discussed at these meetings. *The second* function is to pull the community of

---

[12] Not the least because SvenskMud players have no way of knowing which magician has created what in the game.

magicians together, in effect reinforcing common values, goals and practices. These values are thus internalized which in its turn leads to increased commitment and responsibility of individual magicians. By discussing current problems face-to-face, by eating out and programming together, these meetings serve to closely unite the most active magicians. One of the leading Arch magicians, "Magnus", has taken upon himself to call together and supervise the SvenskMud meetings:

> "Far back in time, Linus decided most things himself, but he had a lot of opposition and he had difficulties getting anywhere. Me, when I became Arch magician effectuated that we should meet physically, IRL [In Real Life], to discuss the difficult questions. [...] If three Arch magicians have different opinions, then the wrong persons are Arch magicians. The Arch magicians [and Linus] have met now [...]. When it has been about bigger issues, the Arch magicians have together made the decisions, even though Linus formally decides. I have wanted greater changes more quickly, [another Arch magician] has been more objective and wants to do things slower"

All the important policy changes during SvenskMud's hectic and turbulent years in the end of the 1990's were the outcome of such meetings. A recurring aspect of these meetings was the display of certain "cult" artifacts; the computer punch card with the first sketch of SvenskMud's original outline on the back, the huge master map covering all the 6000+ distinct location in the SvenskMud world etc. The display of these intensely meaningful and highly significant artifacts has a high symbolic value and represents yet another force that serves to socially construct a common history and a common future (vision) of SvenskMud to unite the magicians. Such rituals (as all rituals) pull the group together and lay a foundation for understanding – *feeling* – what SvenskMud means and what it means to be a leading SvenskMud magician. It allows ordinary persons – most whom are in their teens or 20's - to be part of a living tradition and of history in the making and to do one's share to pass that tradition on to future generations of SvenskMud players and magicians.

Part of what it means to be a leading magician in SvenskMud is to have been at a SvenskMud meeting, to seen those cult artifacts, to have met the other leading SvenskMud magicians and to have been inspired by or having programmed with Linus sitting at your side.

SvenskMud as Communitas

Turner (1969/1995) describes how life-crisis rites, or rites of passage (van Gennep 1909/1960) mark the transition from one phase of life to another in tribal (pre-modern) societies. These life-crisis rites typically occur around events such as birth, death, marriage and status elevation. Such events are still celebrated in the western world but their significance has been waning, e.g. the significance of marriage decreases when it can be done at the spur of the moment, when half of all marriages end with divorce and when it becomes common to marry for a second or third time.

Traditional initiation rites (rites of passage) usually unfold over a longer (but limited) period of time. During that period of time, the person is betwixt and between, in a "liminal", threshold state outside normal societal structures. These temporary ritual transitions have at times expanded to become permanent conditions in modern societies with a complex division of labor. The most obvious examples are religious movements, sects and orders that position themselves outside of the normal social order. Perhaps less obvious examples are counter-movements that place themselves outside the bounds of the ordinary structured hierarchical society such as the hippies, green or utopian communes and Hell's Angels. Turner calls these counter-movements *communitas*.

What all such movements have in common is that they offer (the promise of) community, comradeship, homogeneity and equality. "But the spontaneity and immediacy of communitas can seldom be maintained for very long. [...] and it is the fate of all spontaneous communitas in history to undergo what most people see as a "decline and fall" into structure and law." (Turner 1969/1995, p.132).

Something these movements have in common then is that as they grow and mature, they decline and fall into structure and law and in this process create elaborate power structures within their midst. Their initial "anti-structure" is thus transformed into structure once again - albeit an alternative structure compared to that of mainstream, surrounding society. It is among these systems of simultaneous structure and anti-structure - of egalitarian values amidst hierarchical structures that sometimes can be spectacularly elaborated - that I place SvenskMud.

SvenskMud simultaneously nurtures an ethos of equality and a level playing field (every player starts his life anew in SvenskMud with two empty hands) as well as a fiercely hierarchical and meritocratic power structure. This might seem like an elaborate contradiction, but what is characteristic about SvenskMud is that its hierarchies have nothing to do with the position that an individual has in the surrounding society and that every person - no matter his or her position in the ordinary society - enters SvenskMud on the same conditions and with the same possibilities. This is true at least in theory but much can of course differ SvenskMud users from each other in terms of their programming, language and other skills, equipment, time and knowledge etc.

There is no official SvenskMud discourse surrounding the issue but both the equality and the hierarchies are so to say built into the system, decreed and implemented through computer code (Lessig 1999). As in other counter-movements, SvenskMud allows those who are powerful in the ordinary structured and hierarchical society the opportunity to be fully and unconditionally accepted as equals (instead of the nagging suspicion that they are only accepted because of how they have *performed* instead of what they *are*). SvenskMud at the same time allows those who are powerless in the ordinary society (in SvenskMud most significantly youths) a chance at power and fame:

> "In a small circle, I was for a while someone everyone looked up to, had great respect of, asked for help with programming from, admired…"

Conclusions

A community offers the individual a chance of being part of a collective enterprise, of being part of something that is greater than the individual. I claim that an important factor as to what makes a mud survive and become long-lived lies in succeeding in making it into a *community* based on shared values, goals, practices, symbols (etc.) and by succeeding in fostering a sense of mutual commitment and responsibility among its members (further developed in Pargman 2000b). In SvenskMud, this is more specifically done through configuring the player, configuring the magician and configuring SvenskMud itself. That SvenskMud is a successful community is evident in a variety of ways, not the least because it has managed to attain the venerable age of thirteen years – an eternity on the Internet. I again quote a SvenskMud magician to illustrate this claim of success:

> "There is a good spirit of unity in SvenskMud. You can trust a SvenskMud magician. Sometimes you sleep over at each others' place and lend out the keys to your apartment to someone you in fact don't know the name of in real life."

An important characteristic that has been demonstrated several times in this paper is that in *virtual* communities, social concerns become difficult to separate from technical practices that relate to the "material" substrate these communities are based on – computer code and programming practices for manipulating digital discreet discontinuous silicon-based units of logic. Social and technical issues interact and co-evolve in a virtual community in such an intimate way that they often merge (O'Day et. al. 1996). A mud in use is at the same time a technical system *and* a social system (Bruckman 1992) and if one changes significantly, so will also the other.

As to the all-importance of shared values, concerns and goals in building - or *growing* - communities, it is pertinent to finish the paper by once more stressing the significance of what one of the leading SvenskMud Arch magicians [senior developers] quite incidentally remarked: "if three Arch magicians have different opinions, then the wrong persons are Arch magicians".

Acknowledgments

I thank Lars-Christer Hydén, Tessy Cerratto and Richard Bartle for comments on drafts of this paper.

References

Argyris, C. and D. Schön. *Organizational learning: A theory of action perspective*. Reading, MA: Addison-Wesley, 1978.

Bartle, Richard. "Hearts, clubs, diamonds, spades: Players who suit muds". *Jrn. of Mud Research* 1, (1996) 1 <http://www.mud.co.uk/richard/hcds.htm>.

Bartle, Richard. *Designing virtual worlds*. Indianapolis, Indiana: New Riders Publishing, 2003.

Berger, P. and T. Luckmann. *The social construction of reality: A treatise in the sociology of knowledge*. London: Penguin books, 1966.

Bruckman, Amy. *Identity workshop: Emergent social and psychological phenomena in text-based virtual reality*. Unpubl. manuscript, 1992. <ftp://ftp.cc.gatech.edu/pub/people/asb/papers/identity-workshop.ps>.

Feller, J. and B. Fitzgerald. *Understanding Open Source Software Development*. Edinburgh, England: Pearson Education Limited, 2002.

van Gennep, Arnold. *The rites of passage*. London: Routledge & Kegan Paul, 1909/1960.

Goffman, Erving. "The moral career of the mental patient". *Psychiatry: Journal for the Study of Interpersonal Processes* 22, no 2 (1959).

Jordan, B. Cosmopolitan obstetrics: Some insights from the training of traditional midwives. *Social Science and Medicine* 28, pp.925-944 (1989).

Lave, J. and E. Wenger. *Situated learning: Legitimate peripheral participation*. Cambridge: Cambridge University Press, 1991.

Lessig, L. *Code and other laws of cyberspace*. New York: Basic Books, 1999.

Moody, G. *Rebel Code: Linux and the Open Source Revolution*. London, England: Penguin books, 2001.

O'Day, V. , D. Bobrow and M. Shirley. "The social-technical design cycle". *Proceedings of Computer-Supported Cooperative Work (CSCW'96)*. Cambridge, MA, 1996.

Pargman, Daniel. "The fabric of virtual reality: Courage, rewards and death in an adventure mud". *M/C - A Journal of Media and Culture* (special issue on "games") 3, No. 5 (2000a). <www.media-culture.org.au/0010/mud.html>

Pargman, Daniel. *Code begets Community: On social and technical aspects of managing a virtual community*. Ph.D. Dissertation. Dept. of Communication Studies, Linköping University, Sweden, 2000b.

Raymond, Eric. *The Cathedral and the Bazaar: Musings on Linux and Open Source by an Accidental Revolutionary*. Sebastopol, CA: O'Reilley & Associates, 1999.

Schiano, Diane. "Convergent methodologies in cyber-psychology: A case study" *Behavior Research Methods, Instruments, & Computers* 29, No. 2 (1997): 270-273.

Torvalds, L. and Diamond, D. *Just for Fun: The Story of an Accidental Revolutionary.* New York, NY: Texere, 2001.

Turner, Victor. *The ritual process: Structure and anti-structure.* New York: Aldine de Gruyter, 1969/1995.

Weinberg, Gerald. *The psychology of computer programming.* New York: Dorset house, 1971/1998.

Wenger, Etienne. *Communities of practice: Learning, meaning and identity.* Cambridge, UK: Cambridge University Press, 1998.

File-Sharing Relationships – conflicts of interest in online gift-giving

Jörgen Skågeby⁺, Daniel Pargman*

⁺Linköping University, Sweden, *Royal Institute of Technology, Stockholm, Sweden
jorgen.skageby@ida.liu.s, pargman@nada.kth.se

Abstract. This paper suggests a relationship model for describing, analyzing and foreseeing conflicts of interest in file-sharing networks. The model includes levels of relationship ranging from the individual (ego), to the small group of close peers (micro), to a larger network of acquaintances (meso) to the anonymous larger network (macro). It is argued that an important focal point for analysis of cooperation and conflict is situated in the relations between these levels. Three examples of conflicts from a studied file-sharing network are presented. Finally, the relationship model is discussed in terms of applicability to other domains, recreational as well as professional.

Introduction and Background

File-sharing applications, services, communities and networks have become increasingly popular during the past few years. Using digital media, computer networking, and computer-mediated communication to transfer digital goods is now an important part of many peoples' lives. File-sharing is a contended practice and powerful actors (e.g. record companies etc.) are doing their best to suppress it. General attention has been directed towards the dubious nature of sharing services and user behavior (free-riding, copyright infringement et c). Our position here is however that there is little doubt that many users find the act of *sharing* fulfilling in itself. While certain ideologically motivated activities that are part of the current file-sharing culture (Giesler & Pohlmann, 2002) – such as "making stuff generally available" – violates current laws and various rights of ownership and redistribution it's hardly the main motivation for most users. This suggests an

P. van den Besselaar et al. (eds.), Communities and Technologies 2005, 111-127.

opportunity for exploring file-sharing networks on a level which is not directed towards "overthrowing the existing market system", but rather as the base for services and applications with general social utility and suitable for non-recreational contexts. For us, the interest is in the aspects of sharing where it seems viable that we can develop technologies that meet both consumer and commercial concerns.

The public image of online file-sharing is almost always framed as if it is a way for people to get access to goods and download free material. The corresponding assumption for many is that the only thing that motivates users of file-sharing applications is the act of getting or receiving digital goods. Thus, the focus of much commercial development of file-sharing technologies is on finding ways to make access to digital media legal, easy and economically viable. In other words, technical development circles around improving downloading (or "getting") aspects of file-sharing technologies. However, to accentuate another – and to certain extent opposing view – we start by providing a definition of the verb "share" (from Wordnet 2.0):

1: have in common
2: use jointly or in common
3: have, give, or receive a share of
4: give out as one's portion or share
5: communicate

Even though the definition of sharing above suggests an important "giving"-dimension, much scholarly work has been directed only towards the needs and structures of "getting" or downloading. However, within the online file-sharing networks there are of course also users who *provide* material – in fact, the activity of *giving* is a fundamental aspect of file-sharing networks. Some studies (Adar & Huberman, 2000; Golle et al., 2001) show that a small percentage of the population of a file-sharing network provide a major part of the available digital goods. More recent studies claim that this is not necessarily the case (Parker, 2004). Whether the average user is a provider of files or not, there is no question that much digital goods is uploaded, or given away, in file-sharing networks. We therefore suggest, unlike many other researchers (Feldman et al., 2004; Golle et al., 2001), that focus should not exclusively be put on trying to solve potential problems that stem from "getting" behavior, but also in attempting to understand, facilitate and encourage "giving" behavior. More specifically, the task should in terms of file-sharing not only be one of preventing "free-riding" and "leeching" behavior, but also in trying to thoroughly examine and understand what makes gifting worthwhile for the, sometimes few and seemingly altruistic individuals who constitute the backbone of a file-sharing network. After having gained a better understanding of the motivation of such individuals, the next logical step would be to develop "gifting technologies" (McGee & Skågeby, 2004) by describing suitable norms or design principles of robust file-sharing networks, or, features that could be incorporated directly into software that would encourage and simplify "giving" behavior in file-sharing networks. We are of course not suggesting that self-interest is not part of file-sharing behavior, but current interpretations almost exclusively emphasize self-interest at the detriment of all other types of motivation where we feel that the development of software features which leverages "gifting" is a necessary complement to features solely directed towards limiting or stopping "getting".

We naturally take into account that there are users who do not give at all, or who give only in order to receive. We also have to take into account that there are other users who grant access but do not even know that they are doing so or what they are granting access to. Still, there are also users knowingly and willingly give/grant access and whose behavior cannot easily be explained in terms of exchange or trade. A profound questions is: what is it that motivates and makes people give (i.e. produce public goods) in the context of file-sharing instead of succumbing to the temptation of over-use and deplete limited public goods, i.c. the well-know "tragedy of the commons" (Hardin, 1968). It is clear that these users act on *other* motivations than pure self-interest, motivations we know surprisingly little about.

There are many different aspects to file-sharing; technical, legal and social are the most apparent and they have all received much public and academic attention (see (Iamnitchi et al., 2004; Lui & Kwok, 2002; Premkumar, 2003) for examples). Social studies of file-sharing have looked at a range of phenomena at a number of different levels – from individual experiences to groups and entire file-sharing networks. The choice of a suitable unit of analysis is of course a methodological necessity. However, as individuals we act on different levels simultaneously, e.g. both as individuals and as members of various groups (small or large). This can create tensions between needs and concerns of the individual and needs and concerns of the individual-as-part-of-a-group. Such tensions between the individual rationality (acting in self-interest) and the collective rationality (acting in the interest of the group) are generally referred to as social dilemmas (Kollock, 1998; Orbell & Dawes, 1981). For an individual with "gifting needs", self-interest is by definition something that falls out of the frame of the gift (Kolm, 2000). Still, to merely explain the needs, concerns and motivations of digital gifters as "collective interest" seems be too much of a reduction. Our suggestion here is to refine and differentiate between three different "levels" – micro, meso and macro – of collective interest. It is in the relationship between different levels that we can identify important social patterns of conflict and cooperation. This more nuanced view of the otherwise monolithical concept "the collective interest" accordingly gives us the possibility to better represent and analyze the behavior of gifting users. As part of an ongoing study of giving behavior in file-sharing networks, we develop a model in this paper that better explains many nuances in patterns of behavior in the relationship between gifting individuals and the larger networks they are part of.

The paper is structured as follows: we start by providing a short background on online gift-giving and social dilemmas. This is followed by a proposal for a refined model for analyzing social dilemmas in file-sharing networks. We end the paper by discussing the potential usefulness of the model in areas other than file-sharing.

Online gift-giving and Social Dilemmas

The question of what constitutes a gift or gift-giving has a long history surrounding it (see (Osteen, 2003) for an overview). There is quite a controversy about the existence or non-existence of "pure" altruistic gifts depending on how you choose to define it. It is not our intention to here participate in that philosophical debate. Rather, this research has a more pragmatic and exploratory approach in which we look for behavior that resembles altruistic gift-giving or at least behavior that is not purely self-centered.

Kolm (2000) considers the difference between self-interest and 'other' motivations in a general model of economic transfers (of which gift-giving is a part).

Coercion (taking)	Exchange	Reciprocity	Pure gift- giving
Self-centered motivation		Other oriented motivation	

Table 1. Four modes of economic transfer (Kolm 2000).

By contrasting these different modes of transfer, we can get a clearer picture of what gifting can be. Kolm explains the modes by stating that taking and exchange have selfish or nontruist (acting selfishly towards one agent while acting altruistically towards another) motivations while reciprocity and gift-giving are based on other-oriented motivations. One explanation lies in a general incentive structure Kolm calls the rationality of equality. The rationality of equality includes a sense of justice as well as a sense of recognition or empathy towards others.

How are the modes of transfer realized in online file-sharing networks? Someone who takes and takes but never gives is called a leech (or leecher). A leech only downloads and never uploads digital goods. Needless to say, leeches are not looked upon favorably in file-sharing networks. It is not possible to compare leeching to the mode of *coercion* (e.g. stealing or acquiring something by force) as the goods offered in file-sharing networks are offered voluntary, but it is still clear that this sort of behavior is strongly reproachable based on the reactions it triggers. A fair amount of *exchange* takes place in file-sharing networks, that is, users who tit-for-tat trade files with each other on a "you get this if I get that" basis. These are users who are interested in keeping a strict and explicit balance between what they give and what they get. Likewise, in reciprocal gifting the obligation to give back can be strict, and so to speak form an exacting balance. However, reciprocity is about returning *gifts* and thereby has a larger degree of freedom, ambiguousness and uncertainty. In a reciprocal return of a gift there is no explicit or precise agreement. It's concerned with treating others as you have been or wish to be treated yourself. There are certain social-psychological effects which show that people tend to give when they have been given to, even if the people who gave to them and the people they give to are not the same. Similar to that, people are more inclined to give to other givers, even if they do not give to oneself. This is often referred to as generalized reciprocity (Putnam, 1993, 2000) – meaning that we have a relation of gifting in which two transfers of gifts affects one agent but not necessarily the same other participants. In contrary to exchange, reciprocity is implicit, flexible and uncertain and it more often than not focuses on social relationships. The reciprocal system is often kept hidden. In fact, the more explicit the rules of reciprocation, the less the will to reciprocate (Godbout & Caillé, 1992). As a gifter and receiver of gifts you want to keep as far from a contractual agreement as possible, because the contractual agreement strengthens market value and diminishes the social bonding value of the gift. In fact, to revert to monetary terms in something that started out as gift-giving often hints at frustration or disillusionment. There are of course selfish forms of reciprocity and gifting, in which the giving to others is aimed at obtaining beneficial by-products (this is referred to in the biological literature as pseudo-reciprocities or pseudo-gifting since it more clearly imitates the exchange mode (Connor, 1986)). *Pure gift-giving* refers to the disinterested gift, the gift you give without an expectation of a return. In terms of research, gift-giving has mainly focused on the open-source movement and recreational file-sharing. Research on open source communities as gift economies has found motivations such as feelings of creativity, improvement of programming skills, monetary reward, community obligingness (Lakhani & Wolf, 2003) reputation as code-writer and as reassuring the quality of the code (Bergquist & Ljungberg, 2001). Some of these motivations are clearly self-centered (money, skills, reputation), while others are harder to categorize (community obligingness, assuring quality of code). Interestingly, work in the area of open source has also identified groupings of kinship as a structure visible in larger sharing networks (Zeitlyn, 2003). As for file-sharing, it has been described as a "parasitic gift economy" (Giesler & Pohlmann, 2002), referring mainly to combination of the modes of coercion, exchange and, to some extent, reciprocity. Other studies have tried to explain the flaws in current understandings of motivations in online gift-giving (Levine, 2001), suggesting that it needs further research.   Kollock (Kollock, 1999) adds two incentive structures which address the 'other' end of the motivational spectrum: because others have a need for [the gifted goods] and because "the good of the group enters one's utility equation". The latter is furthermore described as the merging of individual and collective interests. While this presents a case where the controversial existence (or not) of pure altruistic gifts becomes highlighted, a merger of interests is not always possible, and if possible can be preceded by a process fraught with conflict.

As previously noted, the tension between the interests of an individual and the interests of the group, which that very same individual belongs to, is called a social dilemma. Social dilemmas were described in terms of the tension between the individual rationality (acting in self-interest) and the collective rationality (acting in the interest of the group). The recognition of this conflict has been argued to be part of making community studies include symbolic, and not only geographical co-locational, dimensions, for example to include online venues (Fernback, 1999). The temptation to act in a self-centered fashion is often very strong for the individual since the benefits are often more or less immediate and, estimated to be larger in the short term. Nonetheless, if a large number of individuals put their self-interest first, the group as a whole gets a smaller benefit (or no benefit at all) compared to if most or all individuals acted primarily with the interests of the whole group in mind. Hence, social dilemmas can be described as a conflict between different levels of rationality and where the individual experiences it as a conflict between the short-term, selfish interests (the individual rationality) and the long-term, altruistic/group interests (the collective rationality).

In an online situation, how do gifting individuals balance trade-offs between their own benefits, the benefits of other individuals and the "greater good"? This is a fundamental question for understanding needs and behaviors of both individuals and groups, in file-sharing networks. The gift-giving perspective becomes more visible once the question is transformed into a dilemma of balancing the giving of public and private (digital) goods. The overall dilemma for a user of a file-sharing network lies in the temptation to exclusively take, or download, from others and not give anything in return. However, if no one engaged in gift-giving behavior, there would be no digital goods available for downloading and the network cease to function as a "gateway" between giving and receiving. Digital goods are being given away online in groups with various "social densities". Such groups can range from small "cabals" where real-world ties are strong to tightly-knit online communities, semi-anonymous groups and large networks of complete strangers. An individual user can often be part of such groups at several different "levels" at the same time. Correspondingly, for a user with *gifting* interests (i.e. other than self-interest), the dilemma is how to consider the trade-offs between different levels of receivers. Indeed, it is common for different kinds of gifters to practice different gifting behaviors based on their estimation of the relative trade-offs between the individual good and the greater good. While the terms individual and collective rationality represent a profound notion within sociology and social psychology (and many other disciplines), they do not seem to fine-grained enough to describe the gift-giving behavior exercised by many individuals in file-sharing networks. To understand such networks, we suggest that it is necessary to consider trade-offs between egoistic (e.g. *personal*) interests, interests of a small group (or several groups) of well-known individuals (e.g. *friends*), of small networks (e.g. *acquaintances*) and of large networks (e.g. *strangers*). Notably, since the paper's focus is on online gift-giving, we will here only consider the tensions where (obvious) self-interest is not a part of the equation.

Model of Relationships

The notions of micro, meso and macro generally relate to levels of reality entailing our entire social world. It is not our intention to suggest that a file-sharing network constitutes a self-contained world. Such networks are of course influenced and controlled by external factors of "reality" (such as laws for example). However, the network is at the same time a file-sharing space containing its own practices, norms, values and structures. Likewise, different types of peer interaction will be an important part of understanding and describing the social dynamics of file-sharing (Ebare, 2004). Although there is no consensus as to whether virtual communities could be considered "real" communities, it is beyond doubt that virtual venues – including file-sharing networks – include many structural and cultural patterns. One pattern is the various levels at which interaction occurs in such networks.

The interaction in file-sharing networks happens between the individual, small groups (with strong ties (Granovetter, 1973) between members), networks (with weak ties between member) and large networks (with very weak or no ties between members). These levels relate to the general notions here of ego (the individual), micro (group of close peers), meso (small networks) and macro (large networks) (see Table 2, next page).

The term 'relationship' refers both to the prototypical relationship between actors at each level of the model (that of being friends, acquaintances and strangers) and also to the relationships between different levels in terms of patterns of conflict and cooperation (described below). That is, the *typical* relationship at the micro level is one of being friends; the *typical* relationship at the meso level is one of being acquaintances and the *typical* relationship at the macro level is one of being strangers. That does not mean that *every* relationship at (for example) the meso level always has to be one of being acquaintances. Such a hard definition would not allow for a certain necessary degree of flexibility in for example accounting for a movement over time from being strangers to being acquaintances to being friends. Also, at a specific point in time, someone can be included into a network of peers that I belong to without me (yet) having made the acquaintance of that person.

Level of Relation	Group Structures	Common Incentive structures
Ego	Me, myself and I	Self-interest, maximizing own benefit
Micro	Small group of close peers, well-known *friends*	Social, reciprocity
Meso	Small networks of peers, recognized *acquaintances*	Social, individual and general reciprocity
Macro	Large networks of file-sharing users, anonymous *strangers*	Ideology, Rationality of Equality

Table 2. Model of Relationships

When moving from ego to macro, each new level contains more individuals/nodes. In parallel, the requirements for inclusion (barriers to entry) diminish when moving from ego to macro. What these requirements technically consist of and how they are met differ in different communities/networks but a general observation is that requirements become more rigid when moving from macro to ego. Another dimension is that of public and private goods. In terms of giving goods, moving from ego to macro increases the number of potential receivers, or in other words, the more we move from ego to macro, the more we move from gifting of private goods towards gifting public goods.

At the **macro-level**, the structures addressed are large networks. Inclusion requirements at this level are low, often only requiring that a file-sharing application is installed and used. To the individual, these networks are pseudonymous and ubiquitous. They can be for example the network (all users constituting nodes on a particular network), the application "community" (the entire group of people who use a specific application) or even the entire universe of file-sharing activities at large.

At the **meso-level** we find smaller networks, which carry more requirements for inclusion. In a file-sharing network they might relate to interests or types and quality of potentially giftable goods. Inclusion can be based on reciprocity (balancing the amount of goods given versus taken) and responsivity (responding to a social request of inclusion or to an instrumental request of a certain item). These networks are still pseudonymous and social ties are generally weak (but still strong enough to motivate a different behavior than at the macro level). There might also be temporal aspects to these networks, as a certain network might exist only for a short period of time. The reason for this being that they might be considered as passage of trust or a level of consideration before moving towards a closer (or a more distant) relationship.

On the **micro-level** the social relations and motives are stronger. They might still be based on reciprocity, but the goods are often transferred with a larger *bonding value* (Godbout & Caillé, 1992) encoded. These can refer to online friendships developed over time, often grounded in similar taste in shared goods. Another option is that there do exist offline social ties, i.e. the group is embedded in social relationships that exist also outside of the Internet.

The **ego-level** refers to the single individual and his or her position in the networks.

These levels are of course interdependent and they co-influence and co-evolve over time. The model supports a hermeneutic way of considering the parts and the whole. As we stated earlier, it is in the relations between levels that interesting tensions can be found. The model allows the identification of six simple types of relations, *ego-micro, ego-meso, ego-macro, micro-meso, micro-macro* and *meso-macro*. We choose to not make a difference between ego-micro and micro-ego and we will not consider complex relations between more than two levels in the model here.

In this paper we will only analyze three types of relations, *micro-meso, micro-macro* and *meso-macro*. As apart from *ego-micro, ego-meso* and *ego-macro* relations, these three relations do not involve a conflict between the individual and the collective rationality. They are more interesting to look at here as they all represent different kinds of tensions and conflicts of interest *within* what has previously just been labeled "collective rationality". These relations have therefore been especially difficult to perceive and analyze before. Also, they all represent situations where self-interest is not obvious. Understandably, it can be hard to completely distinguish ego-level motivations from other levels, but we will give examples below where it is not very obvious what the individual's gain consist of in choosing between different alternatives. In terms of Kolm's modes of economic transfer, all choices represent different alternatives that at the same time are all based on other-oriented/non-self centered motivations.

Examples of conflicts of interest in file-sharing networks

Users of file-sharing networks are very innovative in using available technological features to differentiate between various other users. We will therefore start by describing some generic technical features of file-sharing applications to provide the necessary vocabulary for understanding the rationale of users. These features were all present in the studied application and are, in some form or another, present in most of today's file-sharing applications.

Capping mechanisms limit the upload or download speed by specifying a maximum value (the speed is "capped"). The ability to "cap" the speed provides an incentive scheme for people to gift or reciprocate – and to "punish" those who don't. In a way, *capping* is a milder variation of banning. For example, instead of banning a certain receiver, the gifter might decide to "only" cap their download speed. In reverse, the receiver can, by upholding social bonds or reciprocating in another desirable way increase or remove the cap.

Banning is a mechanism used to stop computers or users (depending on what criteria for banning is used, ip-number or user name, for example) from uploading or downloading. The feature is typically used for anti-gifting purpose and *not* using such mechanisms can be a sign of gifting. (Note that this is a complicated issue. Users may not be aware of such banning possibilities, so the fact that they do not ban is not necessarily evidence of deliberate gifting.)

Download slots regulate (decrease or increase) the number of possible simultaneous downloads.

Queue bumping the queue is the number of persons waiting for an available download slot. By bumping a queuing user up or down in the queue, the gifter can increase or decrease the waiting users' queue number. It is also possible to remove someone from the queue completely.

Buddy lists are lists of friends and acquaintances and they are usually integrated with different messaging features. Buddy lists have been integrated with banning and capping features in file-sharing applications and can be used to target people who will get "VIP treatment." The integration of buddy-lists with file-sharing features has generated much controversy as many feel that it strongly violates the very spirit of file-sharing.

Despite the fact that all of the technical features listed above concerns different ways of *restricting* access, the foremost feeling with the individuals who made use of them was that open file-sharing (i.e. sharing without restrictions and to anybody) was the ideal state. This in itself represents an interesting tension and gives support to the weight put on the *gifting* side of file-sharing. As we shall see below, the restrictive features can be used both offensively and defensively to distribute and optimize gifting according to individual preferences.

Data Collection

Although we see the need of more quantitative studies, it is our belief that, at this point, the most rewarding perspective into online gift-giving behaviors and 'other' motivations is taken by qualitative studies. Qualitative studies intended to inform the design of technology have for a long time been part of the CSCW (Computer-Supported Cooperative Work) field. The use of ethnography as a design informant has also been suggested to expand out of the constrained and focused area of work into other domains (Hughes et al., 1994). We believe that the studies of the vivid, recreational file-sharing (and in particular file-gifting) we see online today, has not only the ability to inform the design of recreational systems, but also be applicable in other, more utility-focused domains as well.

For this research we used a range of methods most accurately described as virtual ethnography (Hine, 2000) or netnography (Kozinets, 2002). In simple terms netnography is "ethnography adapted to the study of online communities". The study was conducted over a period of six months. During this period we combined participatory observation in the application itself, as well as in the corresponding web forums. Continuous field notes were taken during the interaction through the application. However, the most gratifying source turned out to be the web discussion groups (or bulletin boards) associated with the sharing application in question. From the forum we collected 580 relevant messages at various length. These messages were coded with regard to the motivation for gifting and technical feature used. From the data a pattern of different types of collective interests emerged. This pattern consequently formed the basis for the developed relationship model. As an additional way of verifying the results from the discussion-group and application observation, ten brief interviews with users were conducted through the applications communication features. These users were randomly selected.

Micro-Meso tensions (friends vs. acquaintances)

These tensions concerned the trade-offs between a smaller group of close friends and a larger group of acquaintances (trusted or considered peers). For example, users would keep buddy lists to which acquaintances would be invited. However, within this buddy list, they would also keep a queue to allow friends to skip ahead if necessary. In this way they used the available features of the application to distinguish between friends and acquaintances. In this case the buddy-list represented acquaintances while the queue bumping targeted specific friends. The motivation for this behavior was often social. Allowing someone to skip the queue symbolized a wish to keep or strengthen a social bond to "someone special". The outcome was often in favor of friends, but there were also examples of the reverse as some users who did *not* allow friends to skip ahead in queue. In the words of one user: "They'll have to wait like the rest in my list". The rationale for this was that keeping a queue where everyone on the buddy list is equal was more important than keeping social ties with specific individuals. There was a strong element of politeness present here. *Even though* the queue as such was ubiquitous to the users in line (it was possible to request a notification of your queue number, but it was not automatically updated), the moderator of the queue (i.e. the gifter) felt it impolite to go against the sequence of the queue.

Micro-Macro tensions (friends vs. strangers)

The micro-macro tensions were the most prevalent in the study. There were users who for social and technical reasons favored sharing with close friends. However, there were also users who strongly disagreed with the use of *any* restrictive features. One user states: "To me, only sharing with your friends is the same as sharing nothing". This user represented a group of users who favored the rationality of equality over any other motivation. The most important concern was to gift to anybody interested, regardless of him or her being a friend or not. To these users the notion of sharing had a strong aspect of fairness and was often dichotomized as "[…] either you're sharing files or you're not". The discussions between users who favored friends over strangers and users who favored strangers over friends also revealed a general social tension. Closely connected to this clash of social and ideological motivations was a tension concerning the use of communicative features in the application. This was a tension between what we may call *communicators* and *instrumentalists*, or between the desire to be friendly or anonymous.

The communicators saw the purpose of file-sharing as a way of making friends. They emphasized the communicative and "have in common"-aspects of file-sharing. They felt that this emphasis also benefited the community spirit and created stronger social ties between the members of the network. Somewhat counter-intuitively, the way of generating the communicative environment was through (the restrictive feature) buddy-lists. This generated a setting in which the communicator's desire was to get strangers to communicate before receiving any goods (i.e. setting up a requirement for inclusion).

The instrumentalists on the other hand saw personal communication (and making friends) as a nuisance and an unnecessary hindrance for the most important function of the network: to give and receive goods without restrictions. One user tellingly explained: "I don't think it's very efficient to strike up a friendship with someone every time you want to download a file." By "having" to communicate with others, the transaction costs rise and to them decreases the overall utility of the file-sharing network. Instrumentalists have thus coined the term "burdens of sharing" to refer to the will of giving away goods but to remain "undisturbed" by questions, further recommendations and social small-talk. In terms of levels of relationships, this tension can be seen as a will to move in one of two different directions – either towards the micro-level of interaction (communicators) or towards the macro-level (instrumentalists).

Meso-Macro tensions (acquaintances vs. strangers)

A situation where users would opt for the relations with strangers over acquaintances was the indirect discovery of potentially interesting material. In the words of a user: "At first, I was sharing with just people in my user [buddy] list

[...] BUT it appears that browsing files of people who download from me is very interesting to find rare pieces". Though the incentive could be argued to be self-centered in this case, the relation is imbalanced (mostly in favor of the other party) and open-ended (it requires a deliberate repeated action of "browsing" by the gifter to "pay off"), thus more similar to gift reciprocity. To further accentuate the gifting aspects, this behavior was also used to attract other users to one's own goods. Users shared popular material in order to interest potential receivers in other gifted goods. Another tension on this level was with users who experienced that they had limited technical resources, but still wanted to gift as effectively as possible. For that purpose they used buddy lists to regulate to who and when they were able to provide goods. In the words of one user: "i don't have a fast pc like other people...what's the point of sharing when i transfer a file at 1.2kb/s...when i had 'share with everybody' the line [queue] was so long people just got tired of it and didn't bother waiting...at least if i regulate who d/ls [downloads] from me...they'll get some satisfaction that there file will be done quickly". In this case the usage of restrictive features was motivated by being able to gift files at a "reasonable" speed and to users who seemed interested enough. In other words, users concerns with gifting efficiently made them favor certain strangers by turning them into acquaintances (through buddy lists and communicative establishment of level of interest). Instead of giving to anyone interested (macro-level strangers) certain application features allowed the user to coordinate and optimize gifting by moving recipients to a closer level of relationship (meso-level acquaintances).

Notably, with all relations concerning the macro-level there was a strong ideological preference for keeping file-sharing open and available to anyone. That is, the ideological motive of keeping the spirit of gifting (as opposed to strict exchange) prevailing was favored over ties to both friends and acquaintances. As one user puts it in a discussion on the topic "Sharing ain't trading": "When you share something you do it with no expectation of anything in return. ... When you expect something in return that's trading."

Discussion

Our studies spurred a need to refine the notion of individual and collective rationality when considering social dilemmas. The relationship model developed in this paper has two main functions. *First*, it is suitable to describe findings from our empirical studies in actual file-sharing networks. As such, the model has explanatory value as it has helped us to understand tensions and conflicts that were difficult to perceive and identify before. *Second*, it is a useful tool for inferring potential (not-yet-identified) conflicts between the different levels (ego, friends, acquaintances, strangers). As a model it can however be used in two more ways; as a methodological tool in stating perspectives, i.e. from which level's view you're comparing relations to other levels; and also as a way of describing the entities existing in a file-sharing network. It has been a modeling of general types of peer interaction somewhat in line with what Ebare (Ebare, 2004) suggests.

The application of the model to file-sharing networks is this far promising. We have in this paper given a few brief examples of how the model can be used to describe and capture conflicts of interest with gifters in file-sharing networks. Future work will go into further detail with these conflicts as well as test the model's applicability to other types of tensions in file-sharing networks (the relations between ego and the other levels). As far as conflicts are concerned, the dimensions of gifting openness and restrictiveness and the tension between communicators and instrumentalists, seem like promising analytical targets for the relationship model. Previous studies has also suggested dimensions of active, passive, pro-active and responsive gifting (McGee & Skågeby, 2004), dimensions that could be related to relationships. Many other studies indicate that online gift-giving is an undirected action, aimed at a large audience and no particular individual. For example: "Gifts are often not given to anyone in particular. They are made public [...]" (Bergquist & Ljungberg, 2001) and "[...] actions and contributions in a virtual community are usually not of a directed nature" (Balasubramanian & Mahajan, 2001). Contrary to these findings, our studies suggest that many users actually did perform active and directed gifting. After the data collection for this paper was finished one file-sharing application also incorporated features for directed gifting. The nature and motivations of active and directed online gifting will probably generate different relationships and our future work will surely incorporate this phenomenon.

Concurrently with deepening the understanding of gifting motivations within recreational file-sharing networks, it is also important to try to generalize the findings and relate to broader scopes of interest. Thus, it is important to note that even though we mainly address *conflicts* and *tensions* in this paper, the relationship model is not limited to such types of interaction. It might as well be used to describe and identify patterns and structures of *cooperation*. It is possible to say that we have started our investigation by asking "where are there differences in opinion about suitable behavior in file-sharing networks" and "what do people quarrel about in file-sharing networks?" It should be pointed out that an equally valid starting point would have been to ask "how come, and in what ways do people cooperate in file-sharing networks?"

It also seems as a representation with a more differentiated approach towards analyzing "collective rationality" could fruitfully be used to look also at other phenomena than file-sharing networks. One such phenomenon could for example be tensions and conflicts of interest in so-called Massively Multiplayer Online Games (MMOG). These Internet-based games can have many thousands of simultaneous users connected and some examples of the more well-known games are called Everquest, Dark Age of Camelot, Star Wars Galaxies and Lineage. Social interaction within these complex games can easily be analyzed from the perspectives presented here. The different levels of analysis would again correspond to self (ego), friends (exclusive buddy lists or small group of close peers), acquaintances (network of recognized peers – typically called "guilds" or "alliances" within these games) and strangers (the mass of anonymous players that constitutes the whole virtual world/society). Another domain, which could be further analyzed with help of the relationship model, is open source software development. We have already seen quite an interest for this movement in terms of gift-giving. We believe the broadened analysis of levels of relationships could add valuable insights to the understandings of this phenomenon.

Another important goal is to draw design conclusions from these types of studies. From this point of view, an interesting observation from this study is that gifting users combine rather simple features to create sets of functions to pinpoint and address specific needs or generate desirable outcomes. Perhaps more importantly, these features are, at first glance, directed towards restricting access and as measures designed for hindering gifting. Indeed, the use of restrictions was often grounded in an estimated limitation of, mostly technical, capabilities, and as such the features were considered "necessary evils". Even so, users actively combined features to optimize or coordinate their gifting to acknowledge the relations considered most appropriate. As one user, addressing macro-level relations, summarizes it: "I only have rules because of my consideration for everyone and my desire to share as much as possible. It sounds ironic and contradictory, but it works [...]". Consequently, we can argue that design to make selfishness generate positive externalities can still be a part of leveraging gifting behavior (although the user might not be aware of it, which adds an element of ethical consideration). We further argue that there are viable reasons to examine digital gifting in combination with the design of technology. The relationship model and the types of peer interaction plus the patterns of conflict and cooperation it describes can provide an important tool of analysis and prediction in this process. Expanding the center of attention from "getting" problems to include the needs of gifters will draw a more complete picture of file-sharing. This picture would likely benefit from the responding development of potent, wide-ranging, useful, and economically viable services for, not only *obtaining* digital goods, but also *gifting* them.

We have in this study focused on gift-giving behaviors in file-sharing networks and for this purpose developed the relationship model as a more nuanced view on social dilemmas in these settings. Conclusively, we see the relationship model as having the ability to frame many other types of social activities and relationships in both recreational and professional domains.

References

Adar, E., & Huberman, B. A., 2000. "Free Riding on Gnutella", First Monday, 5, number 10.

Balasubramanian, S., & Mahajan, V., 2001. "The Economic Leverage of The Virtual Community", International Journal of Electronic Commerce, 5, number 3, pp. 103-138.

Bergquist, M., & Ljungberg, J., 2001. "The Power of Gifts: organizing social relationships in open source communities", Information Systems Journal, 22, number 305-320.

Connor, R. C., 1986. "Pseudo-reciprocity: Investing in Mutualism", Animal Behavior, number 34, pp. 1562-1584.

Ebare, S., 2004. "Digital music and subculture: Sharing files, sharing styles", First Monday, 9, number 2.

Feldman, M., Lai, K., Stoica, I., & Chuang, J., 2004. "Robust Incentive Techniques for Peer-to-Peer Networks", Proceedings of the EC'04, New York, USA, ACM.

Fernback, J., 1999. There is a There There: Notes Toward a Definition of Cybercommunity. In S. Jones (Ed.), Doing Internet Research: Critical Issues and Methods for Examining the Net,London: Sage,

Giesler, M., & Pohlmann, M., 2002. "The Anthropology of File Sharing: Consuming Napster as a Gift", Proceedings of the ACR Conference'02, Atlanta, Georgia, USA.

Godbout, J., & Caillé, A., 1992. The World of the Gift (D. Winkler, Trans.). Quebéc: McGill-Queen's University Press.

Golle, P., Leyton-Brown, K., & Mironov, I., 2001. "Incentives for Sharing in Peer-to-Peer Networks", Proceedings of the 3rd ACM Conference on Electronic Commerce, Tampa, Florida, USA, ACM, pp. 264-267.

Granovetter, M., 1973. "The Strength of Weak Ties", American journal of Sociology, 78, number 6, pp. 1360-1380.

Hardin, G., 1968. "The Tragedy of the Commons", Science, New Series, 162, number 3859, pp. 1243-1248.

Hine, C., 2000. Virtual Ethnography. London: Sage.

Hughes, J., King, V., Rodden, T., & Andersen, H., 1994. "Moving Out from the Control Room: Ethnography in System Design", Proceedings of the ACM Conference on CSCW, Chapel Hill, USA, ACM, pp. 429-439.

Iamnitchi, A., Ripeanu, M., & Foster, I., 2004. "Small-World File-Sharing Communities", Proceedings of the The 23rd Conference of the IEEE Communications Society, Hong Kong.

Kollock, P., 1998. Social Dilemmas: The Anatomy of Cooperation. In Annual Review of Sociology, pp. 183-214.

Kollock, P., 1999. The Economies of Online Cooperation: Gifts and Public Goods in Cyberspace. In M. A. Smith & P. Kollock (Eds.), Communities in Cyberspace,London: Routledge,

Kolm, S.-C., 2000. Introduction: The Economics of Reciprocity, Giving and Altruism. In L.-A. Gérard-Varet, S.-C. Kolm & J. M. Ythier (Eds.), The Economics of Reciprocity, Giving and Altruism,London: MacMillan Press Ltd., pp. 1-44.

Kozinets, R. V., 2002. "The Field Behind the Screen: Using Netnography for Marketing Research in Online Communities", Journal of Marketing Research, 39, number 1, pp. 61-72.

Lakhani, K. R., & Wolf, R. G. (2003). Why Hackers Do What They Do: Understanding Motivation Effort in Free/Open Source Software Projects (No. Working Paper 4425-03): MIT Sloan School of Management.

Levine, S. S., 2001. "Kindness in Cyberspace? The Sharing of Valuable Goods On-line", Proceedings of the 10th Annual EICAR Conference, pp. 86-112.

Lui, S. M., & Kwok, S. H., 2002. "Interoperability of Peer-To-Peer File Sharing Protocols", ACM SIGecom Exchanges, 3, number 3, pp. 25-33.

McGee, K., & Skågeby, J., 2004. "Gifting Technologies", First Monday, 9, number 12.

Orbell, J., & Dawes, R., 1981. Social Dilemmas. In G. M. Stephenson & J. M. Davis (Eds.), Progress in Applied Psychology, pp. 37-65.

Osteen, M., 2003. Questions of the Gift. In M. Osteen (Ed.), The Question of the Gift,London: Routledge,

Parker, A. (2004). The True Picture of Peer-to-Peer Filesharing: CacheLogic.

Premkumar, G. P., 2003. "Alternate Distribution Strategies for Digital Music", Communications of the ACM, 46, number 9, pp. 89-95.

Putnam, R. D. (1993, March 21). The Prosperous Community - Social Capital and Public Life. The American Prospect, 4.

Putnam, R. D., 2000. Bowling Alone: The Collapse and Revival of American Community. New York: Simon & Schuster.

Zeitlyn, D., 2003. "Gift economies in the development of open source software", Research Policy, 32, number 7, pp. 1287-1291.

Acceptance and Utility of a Systematically Designed Virtual Community for Cancer Patients

Jan Marco Leimeister, Helmut Krcmar

Technische Universität München, Germany

{leimeister; krcmar}@in.tum.de

Abstract. Virtual Communities (VCs) offer ubiquitous access to information and exchange possibilities for people in similar circumstances. This is especially valuable for patients with chronic / life-threatening diseases as they exhibit strong needs for information and interaction. Grounded on the preceding findings of the analysis on the user-centric construction of the VC *krebsgemeinschaft.de*, this article describes the evaluation of the underlying design elements and success factors by assessing the user's acceptance and usage of the site. The results obtained empirically substantiated insights into the systematic development and operation of VCs in general and for a sub-group of cancer patients in the German healthcare system in particular.

General conditions for cancer patients and potentials of Virtual Communities

Cancer is the second most frequent cause of death in Germany with approximately 338000 newly diagnosed people yearly (Deutsche Krebshilfe 2003). It is astonishing that until 2001 few information or interactive sites for cancer patients could be found on the German-speaking internet (Daum et al. 2001). With this background, the COSMOS[1] -research project developed, introduced, and operated a Virtual Community (VC) for cancer affected persons.

---

[1] The research project COSMOS (Community Online Services and Mobile Solutions) is a joint project

P. van den Besselaar et al. (eds.), Communities and Technologies 2005, 129-148.

This article focuses on the evaluation of acceptance and usage of the site by intended users. The basis for this project was preliminary work on the systematic and user-orientated design of the Virtual Community *krebsgemeinschaft.de* (Arnold/Leimeister/Krcmar 2003; Leimeister 2004; Leimeister/Daum/Krcmar 2002). After a brief description of the situation of patients, we outline the potentials of a VC for this user group. We then summarise the central design elements as well as the specific characteristics of these elements for the case of krebsgemeinschaft.de. Further, the acceptance and utility of the site are evaluated and discussed. The paper concludes with an analysis of the implications of the findings.

The situation of cancer patients

Most people react to a diagnosis of cancer with shock and disbelief. Not only the diagnosis but the ensuing treatment as well cause disturbances in daily routines and devastate plans for the future. Provoked by a life-threatening diagnosis, the patient often falls into a psychological crisis. This crisis causes a strong demand for sense-making processes concerning the new situation (Madara 1997).

A desire to seek and attain information on cancer and its treatment is one method used by cancer patients to assist them and those close to them to make sense and therefore cope with a devastating situation. The search for information is only one aspect of the coping-process: patients also seek emotional support from similarly affected persons. Hence, the desire for interaction can emerge.

Information needs

Cancer patients often exhibit a high demand for information after diagnosis or during therapy (Bilodeau/Degner 1996; Brockopp et al. 1989; Derdiarian 1987; Hinds/Streater/Mood 1995; McCaughan/Thompson 1995; Mills/Sullivan 1999). This demand can result from the asymmetric distribution of information between physician and patient.

The type of requested information has been shown by recent research on the characteristics of the demands of cancer patients. Kaminski et al. (2001), for example, identified strong interest in obtaining information pertaining to various areas including the effects of cancer on life, work, family or sexuality (for similar findings see (Bilodeau/Degner 1996; Leydon et al. 2000; McCaughan/Thompson 1995; Shuyler/Knight 2003)). The attending physician is often overstrained by the patient's drive for information. Survey research on patients and self-help groups as well as analyses of patients requests to medical service providers (Bahrs/Klingenberg 1995; Hiller 2001; Ruprecht 1998) have shown that patients are not only interested in medical competence in the classical sense, but to a great

of the Technische Universität München and O2 (Germany) GmbH & Co. OHG. The project is supported by the Ministry of Education and Research FKZ 01 HW 0107 –0110. Further information can be found under http://www.cosmos-community.org

extent in the physicians' ability to communicate and relay human interest in dealing with the unique problems of the individual patient (Hiller 2001). Mutual acceptance, emotional care, empathy, a holistic treatment as well as higher quality and better cooperation between all parties involved in the treatment process are mentioned as potential fields for improvement.

Demand for interaction

One can often sense patient's inner wish for empathy and interpersonal interaction. Interaction with others with similar backgrounds and disease plays an important role for patients (Forbiger 2001). Their demands are not necessarily restricted to scientific facts, but also to sharing first hand experiences that are derived from personal symptoms and interpreted for the individual situation (c.f. (Ferber 1987; Mills/Sullivan 1999; Moeller 1996; SEKIS 2000)). In order to cope with the new situation or to discuss treatment possibilities, the affected person needs one or more interlocutors. There exists an intense interest in similar cases and the experiences of others (Bilodeau/Degner 1996; Lieberman et al. 2003; Manaszewicz/Williamson/McKemmish 2002).

Cancer patients do not always search for partners as sources of information or interaction. But those who do actively cope with their situation through interaction and information seeking are reported as experiencing less depression, fear, and complaining behaviour, are better socially integrated and often make better progress in their healing process (McPherson/Higginson/Hearn 2001; Zemore/Shepel 1987)).

Legal framework for internet-based medical services in Germany

The public health system in Germany is a highly regulated sector. Laws and rules of professional conduct regulate how health care workers act. Medical information services on the internet are subject to the general legislation of internet services. It is well known, however, that there are few rules and guidelines that regulate the content of medically-oriented web sites (Dierks/Nitz/Grau 2003, p. 95).

Although general, the following concepts provide a rough legal framework for web-based medical information services: legal liability is assumed for the content of external websites linked to other parties' content, consideration of limits and boundaries placed on the medical profession's limits and boundaries in terms of the differentiation between information and advice, aspects of data security in the context of telematic services as well as specifics for the circulation of scientific information to laypersons. This legal framework influences patient internet-services in Germany as it requires for user- and usage-agreements as well as disclaimers. Furthermore, computer-mediated individual medical advisory services are illegal. Only physicians are allowed to offer this service after a face-to-face consultation has taken place. Therefore, general information services are the only type of patient information sites that are legally permitted by German law.

Potentials of Virtual Communities for patients

Patient services are commonly bound to specific opening hours. Centers or offices that are potential sources of information have specified times of operation and require that the patient or family member physically present him- or herself to obtain the desired information. Similarly, conventional support-groups meet at scheduled times and places (mostly in city centres) and interaction with members is dependent on physical presence. Internet services have advantages in that they are always available and easily accessible.

Up-to-datedness, anonymity and needs-based coverage of patient information

The timely relevance of information in the internet is often far better than in other media forms. Considering the possible importance of health-related information on a subjective or an objective professional level, this medium can bare a crucial advantage. New research findings and developments are available much faster through the internet. Due to the higher perceived anonymity of the internet (c.f. Döring 2003), one will probably find users to be more open with their comments, especially concerning difficult topics such as life-threatening diseases or traditionally taboo topics. A quote from Anja Forbringer, a cancer survivor, illustrates this point: "*It is not easy for me to speak [fact to face] about the »problem cancer«. The more anonymous internet is a great help*".
Web-based information provides patients or information seekers with the opportunity to pick and choose which information they need and when. But due to the different usage of the provided information depending on the media used, different requirements arise for online texts than for paper-based ones, a challenge for Virtual Communities that want to provide edited and quality-assured informations for members.

Interactivity, empathy and empowering patients

The internet with its different services offers multi-lateral interaction possibilities. It integrates a feedback channel and provides collaborative mass communication: users can simultaneously be senders and receivers of information (Döring 2003, p. 41f.; Rafaeli/LaRose 1993).

Interaction within Virtual Communities often allows the development of empathy between members (Preece 1999; 2000; 2001) as well as emotional integration into a community of peers. Empathy can be characterized by three criteria (Levenson/Ruef 1992, p. 234): a) *knowing* how the other person feels, b) *feeling* what another person feels and c) *answering/acting according to this feeling* for the misery/woe of the other person. A sense of community is considered a fundamental ingredient of a working VC (Blanchard/Markus 2002) and it is often based on the existence of empathy among the members.

Interaction between members of a VC generates an information pool of credibility as members contribute their often extensive knowledge and experience to the pool (Schubert 1999, p. 100), (Peppers/Rogers 1997, p. 244). The existence of such VCs can lead to an information asymmetry in favour of the members and contribute to the empowerment of patients. The members of a VC might reach a higher market potential and simultaneously a higher market power (Lechner/Schmid 2001) (Schubert 1999, p. 99) for patients.

Central design elements of a VC for patients – the case of *krebsgemeinschaft.de*

Important design elements for a VC for patients are the presentation of content (information services), the functionalities, the usability and the accessibility of the system as well as the use of trust building components (Leimeister 2004).
In the following we summarize the design elements and their characteristics for the VC *krebsgemeinschaft.de*, a VC for breast cancer patients in the German-speaking internet.

Information services

The major challenge in the area of information services lies in the amount of editorial and quality-assured content on the topic breast cancer for this VC. There were two major challenges: the transformation of medical terminology to an understandable language and the implementation of a structure for this complex subject. As a result of iterative development and several rounds of discussions with experts (for background information see also (Arnold/Leimeister/Krcmar 2003)) the following categorisation of the content was developed and ranked according to the expected relevance for the users:

a) *cancer treatment* (therapy, managing treatment side effects); b) *identifying cancer* (early recognition, diagnostic methods) c) *cancer research* (study results, facts and figures) d) *living with cancer* (sports, nutrition, family, sexuality) and e) *experiences with cancer* (reports of affected persons).

The division into main- and sub-categories was intended to help the user to understand the provided information in a structured way, to support cognitive processing and to minimize the cognitive load.

Functionalities

The functionalities section offers a discussion forum / bulletin board, a "ask the expert" section, a contact search for members, and chat modules. Further services provided on member's personalized start page include: individual interaction services such as an internal mailing-system, a guestbook, buddy-lists and awareness-functions such as "friends online", "users chatting" or "number of members of the krebsgemeinschaft.de" (see Fig 1).

The discussion forum/bulletin board enables an asynchronic exchange between members. It not only supports communication, but also supports the process of members getting to know one other. This, then, supports the creation and the cultivation of a sense of a community (Blanchard/Markus 2002).

The service *"ask an expert"* is a modified form of a discussion forum where users post their questions and designated experts in that area provide answers. The service is organized in periodic cycles; each cycle has a featured focus or theme and a prominent expert. This system reduces the work-load for the experts and the service is easier to organize. Users of this service can easily make inquiries without time pressures.

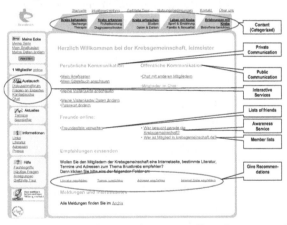

Figure 1: Information and interaction services as well as the personalized starting page for members on krebsgemeinschaft.de (Source: (Leimeister 2004, p. 201)).

The *contact search* aims at supporting the members in finding people in similar situations and/or with similar interests. The service is designed to offer an easy possibility for contacting other members. This service also fosters direct interaction between members and enhances a sense of community.

The *chat* offers the possibility to get in contact with other members simultaneously. It is a synchronic real-time communication which requires at least two participants. To increase the probability of meeting other users in the chat room, fixed chat hours were established.

Usability

Potential users of services on the internet decide within seconds whether or not they want to use services; thus, the usability of services and sites is of major importance to potential users. Aspects such as layout, colour, graphics, and scripts play an important role. These aspects are often subsumed under the term usability. Usability is always context- and usage-specific. That is the reason why there are no generally valid rules for creating usability. Usability and the overall impression have a strong influence on whether websites appear trustworthy and credible (Fogg et al. 2002). From the various usability-principles (compare e.g. (Mannhartsperger/Linder/Zellhofer 2003, p. 17ff)), one can derive the following meta-principles:

Adequacy of a task: a dialogue with a system is adequate if it is supporting the execution of the task of the user without burdening him with unnecessary details (e.g. from the dialogue system).

Conformity with expectations: a system's behaviour conforms to the expectations if each element or each part if the system represents that part of the design and content that the user expects.

Consistency: a uniform appearance of a system within one context is named "consistency". Consistency is crucial for usability because the user can rely on already learned patterns und does not have to adapt to new systems. Consistency is one of the most important usability principles (Mayhew 1992) and leads to usability (Spolsky 2001),(Nielsen 2002).

Visibility: Well designed human-machine-interfaces have easily visible control elements. Each control element (knob, button, etc.) controls optimally only one function (Norman 1988, 1992).

Accessibility

As the internet ensures the transmission of information in form of text, it can contribute to overcome physical defects of users. The usage of one sense organ can be replaced by the usage of another (WEBforALL 2004a). This issue is especially important for target groups such as cancer patients whose often treatment-induced physical restrictions limit mobility.

Different kind of barriers can exist on websites. They are created by the use of specific configurations and designs and might restrict handicapped people from using the services.

Since May 1ˢᵗ 2002, German government web sites as well as all graphical user interfaces provided by them must be designed to allow persons with handicaps to use them unrestrictedly. A barrier free internet site is easily read and navigated with tools available for handicapped users. To achieve this, providers have developed design guidelines for barrier free internet sites (e.g. (WEBforALL 2004b)).

Trust supporting components

In addition to user friendly interfaces and useful services, trustworthiness is an important success factor for a VC. A set of trust-supporting components consists of a transparent provider concept (who is providing the service and what is his motivation to do so), an adequate access right concept and reasonable role models (which tasks and roles exist within the VC, who is responsible for them and which set of authorization does each actor have), an anonymity concept (each user should be able to determine independently how much of his private data he wants to share with other users), and the usage of trust-seals. For this last component, the trust seal promoted by the German Federal Health Ministry *afgis* (Health Information System Action Forum, http://www.afgis.de/index.php?lang =e) is used for *krebsgemeinschaft.de*. For further information concerning the development and design of the trust supporting components see (Ebner /Leimeister/Krcmar 2004; Leimeister/Ebner/Krcmar 2005, Leimeister 2004).

Acceptance and usage of *krebsgemeinschaft.de*

Evaluation criteria and methods

To evaluate the efficacy of the design components used during the development of *krebsgemeinschaft.de* it was necessary to identify criteria for the success of each single component and the sum of all components. Measuring success and consequently identifying a cause-effect chain for single components is difficult as the effect of each individual component on the user cannot be easily isolated. Frequently, only the sum of all actions and influences is assessable. Figure 1 illustrates the previously mentioned design components and their cumulative effect on the acceptance and usage of *krebsgemeinschaft.de*.

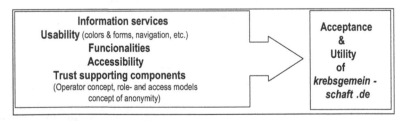

Figure 1: Intended cause-effect chain between design components and usage and utility of *krebsgemeinschaft.de*

Specific indicators for the success of VCs can be found on different levels of abstraction, although one has to state a lack of systematic approaches and operational suggestions for measuring the success of VCs. We will consequently apply evaluation techniques from both classical social research and online research, especially log file analyses, online surveys, document analysis and observations. These techniques will be applied to the case of the VC *krebsgemeinschaft.de*. All data refer to the period from 19.08.02 to 22.05.03 unless otherwise specified. We begin with the quantitative analysis of the server log files, and then we will analyze the conducted online member surveys. Finally several archive analyses will be conducted and observations will be analysed.

Empirical findings

Performance measures for the evaluation of interactive elements within the community

The core of a VC is the interaction of the members which mainly occurs in chat rooms or discussion forums/bulletin boards. The following criteria were used to measure "member-to-member interaction" (adapted from Cothrel 2000, p. 18):

Key figures for the assessment of the number of visitors (average values per *week*)	
(1) Total number of visits per week	899
(2) Total number of page impressions per week	4627
Criteria for the discussion forum (averages per *month*)	
Number of users in discussion forum per month	275
1. Number of active users (writing messages) per month	22
2. Number of passive users (read only) per month	253
(1) Number of articles	
a. Number of articles – posted per month	11,6
b. Number of articles – read per month	Ca. 550
c. Number of replies posted per month	25,3
Criteria for the chat (average values per *month*)	
(1) Number of users in chat	190 (different IPs per month)
a. Number of active users (writing messages)	190
b. Number of passive users (read only)	n.n.
(2) Number of messages	n.n.
(3) Number of users connected	n.n.

Table 1: Key data for the usage of *krebsgemeinschaft.de* during the period 08/2002-05/2003.

Log-file-analyses and their purely quantitative values are insufficient to evaluate a VC. A small number of active users (like the one which has evolved in *krebsgemeinschaft.de*) contribute more to the "life" of a community than a greater number of passive users, so called "lurkers" (Nonnecke/Preece 2000). For that reason we used qualitative analyses in form of member surveys, observations and archive analyses. All empirical findings are to be compared and triangulated.

Usage of services

We focused on the usage of the different components of *krebsgemeinschaft.de*. We started with analyses of the usage of both the edited and quality assured content. After that we analysed the users' behaviour concerning the interaction services (chat, forum, ask experts, contact search).

Usage of the edited content – content categories (top level): The graphical presentation and positioning of the content on the website is presented in figure 1. The content categories and their arrangement were chosen in correspondence with their expected importance as found in other media and services for cancer patients. The top-level content categories (designed as index-cards) with the categories *cancer treatment, identifying cancer, cancer research, living with cancer* and *experiences with cancer* were arranged in seceding order from left to right.

For all content categories (index cards) a similar development of the user numbers could be observed. The user numbers declined after the first weeks followed by a ground-building process on a more or less stable level. Relatively high values could be seen in the last month of observation in the categories *"cancer treatment"* and *"living with cancer"* (contradicting the assumption that living with cancer would be ranked 4 in interest). Accordingly, these topics seemed to be of exceptional interest for the users of *krebsgemeinschaft.de*. As the editorial content had not changed for a longer period of time, it could be assumed that frequent visitors had saturated their demand for information on the pages and omitted them during later visits. Only a few "new" members registered in the VC in the analysed period. This could provide an explanation for the declining user numbers in this section. The total decline could be a first hint for the existence of an individual member life-cycle that correlates with an individual information-demand-curve, which could depend e.g. on the phase of illness or the time elapsed since diagnosis.

Interaction services: The analysis of the development of the single interaction services showed clearly that the contact search was rarely used. The reason for this might be that following the launch of the platform, a group building process among new members had started. In consequence, many users did not have the problem of finding others since they were already integrated into a newly emerging group. On the other hand, a reason could be the poor implementation of the service. Within the framework of the surveys it was mentioned by several users that the contact search was not working as it should or more precisely it functioned too slowly.

Discussion forum/bulletin board: The discussion forum was a frequently used service of *krebsgemeinschaft.de*. In total, 367 entries were posted during the evaluation period. Of these, 114 were new threads and 253 were replies to these threads. This means, that there were more than an average of two replies per request whereas the number of answers varied between 0 (often no answer was expected) and 9. Most answers were directly connected to the question. Rarely did a discussion emerge that was unrelated to the initial posting. To evaluate which issues were discussed in the discussion forum, a content analysis of the threads and replies was conducted. Two main thematic blocs could be identified: 1) postings that stated a rather factual demand for information, and 2) emotional postings seeking emotional support from other members and demonstrated a wish for emotional integration into a community as well as for empathy. Often the two categories could not be separated as some of the requests for information were posed in an emotional context. Examples were questions about hair loss after chemotherapy or breast reconstruction following mastectomy.

All in all, the discussion forum was mainly used to share individual experiences with others and to learn from others' experiences. When applying this categorisation the major part of the threads has to be assigned to the "factual" category, but a high percentage of these postings also bared the already mentioned emotional aspects. Of interest, very intimate and personal postings were made in the forum. Members spoke honestly and openly about their feelings and personal experiences. However, the content generated during the first month after the launch was made by only a few members who were very intensively engaged in *krebsgemeinschaft.de*.

Nicpages and guestbooks: The anonymity concept of *krebsgemeinschaft.de* offered the members the possibility to decide on their own which personal data they wanted to reveal to the other members of the community by means of their personal nicpage (non-registered users/visitors do not see any member data). The members have four choices of anonymity levels: *Show nothing* (other members will see the note: "The member does not want to show his/her data."), *anonymized* (displayed: user name, state, status, kind of relationship to the illness, date of diagnosis, type of cancer, stage of the disease, form of therapy, hobbies, interests), *anonymized but show all to friends* (members of a users buddy list can see all available user data, other members see the data available on the anonymized level), and finally the level *show all* (displayinged: all available user data). The nicpage is situated above the guestbook of the member and can be accessed by clicking on the user name at any place within the VC.

In May 2003 there were 634 active guestbooks in *krebsgemeinschaft.de*. 273 (43.1%) chose "show nothing", 272 (42.9%) "anonymized", 9 (1.4%) "generally anonymized and all to friends", and 80 (12,6%) displayed all data to all members of the VC. A strong correlation between the degree of anonymity and the number of entries in the guestbook could be identified: While 273 owners of a guestbook with the anonymity level "show nothing" only received 30 entries; the 272 guestbooks with the nicpage configuration "anonymized" received 217 entries. The 80 guestbooks in the "show all"category made up for a total of 383 entries and the 9 guestbooks with the level "anonymized but show all to friends" had 3 entries.

These data seems to indicate that openness could be a major precondition for the functioning of the VC. The more data other members can see, the more entries they themselves post. If members show openness and trust by revealing their identity, they will be rewarded by receiving more postings in their guestbooks. This is supported by the construct of "reciprocity" (Preece 1999, 2000; Preece/Maloney-Krichmar 2003). According to this principle, the provision of information to the community is a catalyst for receiving information and reaction from the community or more precisely from other members.

It is important to annotate that the distribution of the guestbook entries was asymmetric. On the one hand a large part of the guestbook did not get any entries and on the other hand some very active members in *krebsgemeinschaft.de* had more than 40 entries.

This situation, as well as the fact that many of the entries in the discussion forum were posted by few members, indicates that a small and very active community of members had emerged. This group contributed very much to the life within the community and *krebsgemeinschaft.de* seemed to play a vital role in their real lives.

The relationships of these active members to each other seemed to be very close and the interaction between them exceeded the limits of the VC and reached into their everyday "real" lives. These members cared very much about the situation and the problems of other active members and tried to support each other.

Member surveys: Acceptance and utility of *krebsgemeinschaft.de*

From quantitative analyses one can not easily derive conclusions about the individual usage and usability of the platform. It is even more difficult to gain insights into the utility for users created by their usage of a single specific service within *krebsgemeinschaft.de*. For the purpose of this article, we define usage as the frequency of usage of specific services as declared by the respondent. Following the design components of the VC, the usage behaviour was analysed for both information and interaction services. Both spheres were addressed with closed- and open-ended questions. We define utility as the subjective impression of the respondents concerning advantages they received from using *krebsgemeinschaft.de*. This aspect was also addressed in member surveys using open- and closed-ended questions.

Overall evaluation: All in all the participants in the survey assessed the design of *krebsgemeinschaft.de* as positive (figure 2). This is not surprising when considering the fact that most respondents were using the service intensely. A frequent usage itself can be seen as a positive assessment of the service.

On average, the users agreed that the site was clearly structured, easily readable, and that desired content could be found easily. Especially the coloured design was perceived as positive. Users were always aware of the author of the content. The loading time and the technical performance of the platform were rated less favourably.

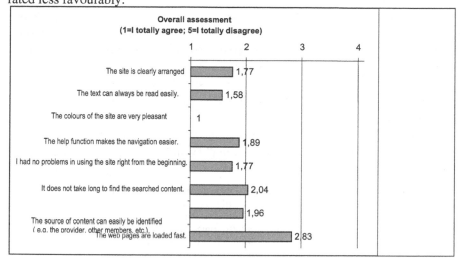

Overall assessment
(1=I totally agree; 5=I totally disagree)

The site is clearly arranged — 1,77

The text can always be read easily. — 1,58

The colours of the site are very pleasant — 1

The help function makes the navigation easier. — 1,89

I had no problems in using the site right from the beginning. — 1,77

It does not take long to find the searched content. — 2,04

— 1,96

The source of content can easily be identified
(e.a. the provider. other members. etc.).
The web pages are loaded fast. — 2,83

Figure 2: Overall evaluation of *krebsgemeinschaft.de* (n=27)

Correlation between usage of different services and duration of membership in *krebsgemeinschaft.de*: The data shows a relation between the lentgth of membership and usage behaviour concerning the usage of information services. 55.5% of the people who were members for less than six month were using the information services „each time" they visited the VC. In comparison, only 40% of those persons with memberships older than 6 months used these pages this frequently. A conclusion could be that the subjective importance of the information service declines with increasing length of membership.

An even clearer correlation exists between the „duration of membership" and the usage of interactive services. The usage of these services increased significantly during membership. 38.5% of those who were members for more than 6 months used them "each time" whereas none of the users with less than 6 months membership chose that answer.

The findings are indicators for an individual membership life cycle, which becomes manifest in different usage levels of the system. It can be assumed that those new members were faced with a high demand for "hard facts" as their diagnosis was more recent than that of older members. As time elapsed the users often developed far reaching knowledge and therefore the need to use the information services became less important. The usage of the interactive services shows an inverse development. The longer the person was a member, the more intense the community feeling was and the more intense the usage of the interactive services became.

Utility: The analysis of the direct question about the felt utility of *krebsgemeinschaft.de* revealed two major reasons for using the VC: On the one hand the site offered professional knowledge about cancer and on the other, a perhaps more important aspect, users established contact to other persons in similar situations. Respondents declared that social relationships and empathy could easily develop. These findings are similar to the results of the analysis of the forum postings. Furthermore the members said they could easily integrate emotionally in a community and support one another. The establishment of "real-life" meetings reinforces this point.

The following answer to the question "how has the membership in krebsgemeinschaft.de changed your situation" exemplifies the importance of the service:

> "The interchange with others is very beneficial for me. Especially right after the diagnosis friends and family assume that life goes on as before. That's wrong!! Of course you don't want to speak all the time about your (bad) mood and your medical status and somehow no one wants to hear it all the time. Therefore the interchange with other patients is important: You get the mental support you need and it is good to know you're not the only person struggling with such a situation. And it is very impressing and supportive to read how other women can cope with the situation. That resurrects your own will to fight and helps you to cope with the healing process or medical set-backs."

Trust-Support: During the conception and implementation of *krebsgemein-schaft.de,* trust supporting elements were designed and implemented in the VC (Leimeister/Ebner/Krcmar 2005). The process of trust building should be supported by these components in order to contribute to the establishment of a community. To evaluate the effect of trust-supporting components, an online-survey, guided by the following research questions, was conducted among the members:

(1) Do the members of krebsgemeinschaft.de assign a positive perceived competence and a positive perceived goodwill to the operators?

(2) Do the members of krebsgemeinschaft.de trust the operators of the community and their provided content?

(3) Do the members of krebsgemeinschaft.de assign a positive perceived competence and a positive perceived goodwill to the other members?

(4) Do the members of krebsgemeinschaft.de trust the other members and the user-generated content?

The results (for further details on the survey, results, thresholds, etc. see Leimeister/Ebner/Krcmar 2005) seem to confirm the effect of these trust building components. Members were asked about both the trust in the providers of *krebsgemeinschaft.de* (especially in their expertise) and the trust in the other members (especially in their benevolence) seemed both to be high.

The behaviour of the questioned members fits well to this finding: They were prepared to use information provided by the community as well as to provide their own knowledge and experiences to other members. Therewith they stated clearly that they trusted that their data was being handled in a secure manner and that the provided information was of high quality. Furthermore it could be proved that a large proportion of the questioned members were acting according to statements made in the surveys (for further details see (Leimeister 2004).

Discussion and Conclusion

The evaluation of *krebsgemeinschaft.de* revealed various findings. First of all, *krebsgemeinschaft.de* can be rated as a successful VC. The registration numbers have increased; there was a stable highly active core community and an extended community with passive members (lurkers). Inside the core community the reciprocity-principle was working very vividly in terms of the exchange of information, empathy and support. The communication was characterized by a high degree of empathy and trust towards both the provider and the other members. The conception of trust supporting components seemed to have lead to the desired outcome.

The number of violations against the rules of the community or incidents that could be categorized as rude or impolite was very low. The active members were very content with the social interaction within the VC. The fact that most members who were involved in the VC from day one still actively participated in the community after 24 months advocated for strong loyalty ties to *krebsgemeinschaft.de*.

Concerning the demand-coverage of the community-platform, most members seemed to be satisfied, though different functions were rated quite differently. Furthermore it could be seen that the design (e.g. the GUI and the design of functionalities) was generally assessed as user-friendly. However, the surveys showed as well, that some of the VCs characteristics were not known and therefore not used by members (e.g. the anonymity concept or the contact search), additionally these features were not working satisfactorily during the period of analysis. Moreover results revealed that the technical reliability of the platform was more important to the members than sophisticated services or functionalities. The technical equipment was not the limiting factor but the conception of a service was much more important for its success. This became obvious through the very different usage of the service "ask experts": By means of shorter reply times, high quality and easily understood answers, the usefulness and frequency of usage of the service was increased immensely. This conclusion was derived from user feedack (approx. 100 emails) to the community management.

The user feedback in the board and in the mails to the community management also showed the central role of qualitative valuable content as an asset for attracting potential users. Another critical success factor in building this VC was the role of the community management which ensured activity and attractiveness until the critical mass of users had been reached.

The evaluation showed furthermore that there was a shift in the information and interaction demands depending on membership duration. The desire for interaction and the appreciation of this feature seemed to increase correspondingly with length of membership.

Consequences for further research – First of all, the findings of this explorative research should be compared with research findings from other types of VCs in order to improve the capacity of the results. A quantitative research model could be developed on the basis of these research findings and used to expand the theoretical foundations for Virtual Communities.

Additionally there are several chances and challenges for VCs created by new technical possibilities. Ubiquitous accesses to VCs through mobile digital devices as well as new (mobile or rather context sensitive) services for VCs are potentially very rewarding (e.g. an emergency system for cancer patients with a locating service or a mobile pill reminder). The relevance of these innovations for VCs cannot yet be assessed.

Furthermore, there is a need for research on the role and tasks of community management. There is a lack of substantial work on administration tools (especially if a community manager acts as administrator for several communities) that efficiently and effectively support management.

The analysis of social interactions within VCs and the effects on the social network of the members have yet to be fully investigated. Research on the exact utility of healthcare-oriented VCs seems to be especially promising when focussing on the measurement of the VC's influences on the perceived quality of life and the costs of treatment.

Recapitulating, the results of this article demonstrate empirical proof that the chosen approaches for user-centric development, implementation and operation of a VC for cancer patients within the German healthcare system lead to a success as demonstrated by high ratings given to the VC by users. Results convey a rich understanding of multi-dependent influences on Virtual Communities in general and contribute to a better understanding of community building for patients.

References

Arnold, Y.; Leimeister, J. M.; Krcmar, H. (2003): COPEP: A Development Process Model for a Community Platform for Cancer Patients. In: Proceedings of the XIth European Conference on Information Systems (ECIS), Naples.

Bahrs, O.; Klingenberg, A. (1995): Die Beurteilung ärztlicher Arbeit durch Teilnehmer von Selbsthilfegruppen. In: Stand und Zukunft der Qualitätssicherung in der Allgemeinmedizin. Eds.: Szecsenyi, J.; Gerlach, F., Hippokrates, Stuttgart 1995.

Bilodeau, B. A.; Degner, L. F. (1996): Information needs, sources of information, and decisional roles in women with breast cancer. In: Oncology Nursing Forum, Vol. 23 (1996), Nr. 4, S. 691-696.

Blanchard, A. L.; Markus, M. L. (2002): Sense of Virtual Communtiy-- Maintaining the Sense of Belonging-. In: Proceedings of the 35th Hawai'i International Conference on System Sciences (HICSS 36), January 2002, Hawai'i.

Brockopp, D. Y.; Hayko, D.; Davenport, W.; Winscott, R. N. (1989): Personal control and needs for hope and information among adults diagnosed with cancer. In: Cancer Nursing, Vol. 12 (1989), Nr. 2, S. 112-116.

Daum, M.; Klein, A.; Leimeister, J. M.; Krcmar, H. (2001): Webbasierte Informations- und Interaktionsangebote für Onkologiepatienten - Ein Überblick. Arbeitspapier Nr. 109. Universität Hohenheim, Lehrstuhl für Wirtschaftsinformatik, Hohenheim 2001.

Derdiarian, A. (1987): Informational needs of recently diagnosed cancer patients. A theoretical framework. Part 1. In: Cancer Nursing, Vol. 10 (1987), Nr. 2, S. 107-115.

Deutsche_Krebshilfe (2003): Krebs: Zahlen, Daten, Fakten. In: http://www.krebshilfe.de/neu/medieninfos/zahlen_daten_fakten.htm, zugegriffen am 29.10.2004

Dierks, C.; Nitz, G.; Grau, U. (2003): Gesundheitstelematik und Recht. Frankfurter Schriften, MedizinRecht.de-Verlag, Frankfurt a. M. 2003.

Döring, N. (2003): Sozialpsychologie des Internet : die Bedeutung des Internet für Kommunikationsprozesse, Identitäten, soziale Beziehungen und Gruppen. 2. Auflage, Internet und Psychologie, Hogrefe, Göttingen 2003.

Ebner, W.; Leimeister, J. M.; Krcmar, H. (2004): Trust In Virtual Healthcare Communities: Design And Implementation Of Trust-Enabling Functionalities. In: Proceedings of the 37th Hawai'i International Conference on System Sciences (HICSS 37), January 2004, Hawai'i.

Ferber, C. v. (Eds.) (1987): Gesundheitsselbsthilfe und professionelle Dienstleistungen: Soziologische Grundlagen einer bürgerorientierten Gesundheitspolitik Springer, Berlin 1987.

Fogg, B. J.; Soohoo, C.; Danielson, D.; Marable, L.; Stanford, J.; Tauber, E. R. (2002): How Do People Evaluate a Web Site's Credibility? Results from a Large Study. In: http://www.consumerwebwatch.org/news/report3 _credibilityresearch/stanfordPTL.pdf, zugegriffen am 10.11.2004, Stanford University, Consumer WebWatch, Sliced Bread Design, LLC.

Forbiger, A. (2001): Leben ist, wenn man trotzdem lacht. Heyne, München 2001.

Hiller, B. (2001): Unkonventionelle Verfahren in der Onkologie : der Informationsbedarf der Anrufer beim Krebsinformationsdienst im Deutschen Krebsforschungszentrum zu Methoden mit bisher unbewiesener Wirksamkeit, PHD-thesis, Universität Heidelberg.

Hinds, C.; Streater, A.; Mood, D. (1995): Functions and preferred methods of receiving information related to radiotherapy: perceptions of patients with cancer. In: Cancer Nursing, (1995), Nr. 18, S. 374-384.

Kaminski, E.; Thomas, R. J.; Charnley, S.; Mackay, J. (2001): Measuring patients response to received information. In: European Journal of Cancer, Vol. 37 (2001), Supplement 6, p. 387.

Lechner, U.; Schmid, B. F. (2001): Communities - Business Models and System Architectures: The Blueprint of MP3.com, Napster and Gnutella Revisited. In: Proceedings of the Hawaiian International Conference on System Sciences (HICSS), Hawaii.

Leimeister, J. M. (2004): Pilotierung virtueller Communities im Gesundheitsbereich - Bedarfsgerechte Entwicklung, Einführung und Betrieb. PHD-thesis, Hohenheim University.

Leimeister, J. M.; Ebner, W.; Krcmar, H. (2005): Design, Implementation and Evaluation of Trust-supporting Components in Virtual Communities for Patients. In: Journal of Management Information Systems, Vol. 22 (2005).

Leimeister, J. M.; Daum, M.; Krcmar, H. (2002): Mobile Virtual Healthcare Communities: An Approach To Community Engineering For Cancer Patients. In: Proceedings of the Xth European Conference on Information Systems (ECIS), pp. 1626-1637, Gdansk.

Levenson, R. W.; Ruef, A. W. (1992): Empathy: A psychological substrate. In: Journal of Personality and Social Psychology, Vol. 63 (1992), No. 2, pp. 234-246.

Leydon, G. M.et al (2000): Cancer patients' information needs and information seeking behaviour: in depth interview study. In: British Medical Journal, Vol. 320 (2000), No. 7239, pp. 909-913.

Lieberman, M.et al (2003): Electronic support groups for breast carcinoma: a clinical trial of effectiveness. In: Cancer, Vol. 4 (2003), Nr. 97, pp. 920-925.

Madara, E. J. (1997): The mutual-aid self-help online revolution. In: Social Policy, Vol. 27 (1997), No. 3, pp. 20-27.

Manaszewicz, R.; Williamson, K.; McKemmish, S. (2002): Breast Cancer Knowledge Online: Towards Meeting the Diverse Information Needs of the Breast Cancer Community. In: Proceedings of the Electronic Networking - Building Community.

Mannhartsperger, M.; Linder, J.; Zellhofer, N. (2003): Ergebnisbericht „Usability von Gesundheitsinformationen im Internet". Interface Consult, Vienna 2003.

Mayhew, D. J. (1992): Principles and guidelines in software user interface design. Prentice Hall, Englewood Cliffs 1992.

McCaughan, E. M.; Thompson, K. A. (1995): Issues in patient care: information needs of cancer patients receiving chemotherapy at a day-case unit in Northern Ireland. In: Cancer Nursing, Vol. 18 (1995), No. 5, pp. 374-384.

McPherson, C. J.; Higginson, I. J.; Hearn, J. (2001): Effective methods of giving information in cancer: a systematic literature review of randomized controlled trials. In: Journal of Public Health Medicine, Vol. 23 (2001), pp. 227-234.

Mills, M. E.; Sullivan, K. (1999): The importance of information giving for patients newly diagnosed with cancer: a review of the literature. In: Journal of Clinical Nursing, Vol. 8 (1999), No. 6, pp. 631-642.

Boston where they presented the ideas of the group to world leaders and the international press. At no point was more than one adult participating in each online group, and those adult moderators were trained to keep their participation to the minimum. Some of the participants dropped out after two months when they discovered that they had not been elected as delegates, and some dropped out after three months, after the in-person summit in Boston. Many, however, stayed on for an additional 9 months, and some are still participating – for example, writing an online newspaper that has survived for 6 years (Cassell 2002).

It is the email messages sent to the forum prior to announcements of the election results that is the focus of this article. These messages, numbering almost twenty thousand, allow us to explore the various linguistic strategies, conscious or not, that participants used to express themselves and win influence among their peers.

Latin America & Caribbean	Argentina	21	Europe	Croatia	11
	Bolivia	9		France	27
	Brazil	38		Greece	32
	Colombia	23		Lithuania	9
	Costa Rica	17		Romania	11
	Honduras	10		Ukraine	6
	Jamaica	20		United Kingdom	14
	Mexico	15			
	Uruguay	19	South Asia	Bangladesh	8
				India	19
North America	Canada	36		Indonesia	5
	United States	67		Malaysia	6
				Nepal	8
Africa	Cameroon	10		Pakistan	20
	Kenya	10		Philippines	6
	Namibia	9		Thailand	15
	Senegal	12			
	South Africa	30	Pacific Islands	Australia	22
	Uganda	8		New Zealand	17
	Zimbabwe	9			
			East Asia	China	58
Middle East	Israel	10		Hong Kong	8
	Lebanon	23		Singapore	14
	Morocco	2		South Korea	8
	United Arab Emirates	17		Taiwan	13

Table 1. The JUNIOR SUMMIT participants: Countries and number of children.

Literature Review

Early claims about the Internet promised a power-leveling democratic environment that would be blind to race, gender and physical traits. Yet research on computer-mediated communication (CMC) demonstrates that gender- and status-based power relationships have been reproduced in online environments, either by choice or by socialization (Herring 1993). In short, gender and nationality are not necessarily invisible online (Herring 1993). In what follows, we examine the relationships between gender, power, leadership and language use before turning to the scant literature on leadership online.

Leadership involves the ability to influence individuals to adopt collective or group goals over personal ones—in essence, leadership involves persuasion rather than domination (Hogan, Curphy et al. 1994). Many studies suggest that men tend to be perceived and elected as leaders more often than women (Bass 1990). In terms of their leadership language style, men are generally considered to use more authoritative or assertive speech, while women are considered to use a more personal and facilitative style (Bass 1990). Interestingly, studies show that language that fuses both styles, assertive and supportive, has the most influence in group management (Bass 1990).

Language is social action; and language can be used to assert power over the listener (Holtgraves 2002). For example, even the simplest speech act, such as saying hello to a passerby, can be an act of power or dominance over a listener, as it requires of that passerby to acknowledge the speaker (Hart 1987). Expressing an opinion, teaching or preaching are also powerful uses of language, especially in comparison to asking for advice or asking for directions (Hart 1987). A distinction between powerful and powerless language remains an important consideration in social interaction, especially the effects of powerful or powerless language as a persuasive device.

Features of language that have been described as powerless include *hesitations* such as "umm," *hedge* phrases such as "I kinda feel," or *tag questions* such as "…right?" (Lakoff 1975, 2004 2004; Gibbons, Bush et al. 1991; Holtgraves and Lasky 1999). Speakers who use this kind of language are often perceived as less assertive, credible or even competent than people who use more powerful speech (Holtgraves and Lasky 1999). Speakers who use these tentative linguistic devices are also perceived less favorably than powerful speakers (Holtgraves and Lasky 1999), producing negative perceptions of a speaker's sociability and competence (Gibbons, Bush et al. 1991). While early interpretations of these results focused on the tentativeness and uncertainty of the speaker, more recent work has demonstrated that this kind of "powerless" language may in fact be used to exhibit respect to the listener, rather than deference (Eckert and McConnell-Ginet 2003).

For example, research has found that women were considered more persuasive than men when using a "powerless" style (Carli 1990). Speakers independently judged as 'powerful' talk more, but also use language that involves direct and specific features, as well interrogation or injection rather than hedges or indirection. (Brownlow, Rosamond et al. 2003). Bass (1990) characterized men's language in organizational settings as competitive and aggressive, using interjections, slang or informal speech, and third person reference. By contrast, the language of women in these settings is characterized by passive agreement, tag questions, intensifiers and the relating of personal experiences (Bass 1990). Research shows that, despite stereotypes about gossiping, men actually talk more than women, especially in institutional settings, and what they say is often better received in these settings (Eckert and McConnell-Ginet 2003). And, *contra* myths of women's self-effacing language, Pennebaker (2003) and his colleagues find that women use more first person singular pronouns in both spontaneous speech and writing (Pennebaker, Mehl et al. 2003).

Emergent leadership involves the study of perceptions of leadership among otherwise leaderless groups (Hogan, Curphy et al. 1994), an area of special interest within the study of online communities, where leaders may emerge through their language or behavior. A very early study in emergent leadership found that sociability, responsibility, confidence, cooperation but also dominance were factors in how leaders were perceived in a group (Hogan, Curphy et al. 1994). Similarly, a more recent study suggests that the ability to recognize different cultural values, performance, trust, and communication ability explain how leaders emerge during the initial stages of a project (Sarker, Grewel et al. 2002). Interestingly Bass (1990) found that authoritarian-style personalities aren't likely to emerge as leaders in a leaderless group.

Other studies have continued to adduce evidence for what is sometimes called the "babble theory hypothesis" (Sarker, Grewel et al. 2002); that is, the sheer *amount* of communication can predict leadership in an online community. Misiolek & Heckman (2005), for instance, find that leaders in virtual teams initiated communication more often than non-leaders, and received more responses from other group members. Furthermore, perceived leaders play a more active part in initiating tasks and processes (Misiolek and Heckman 2005). Similarly, Yoo & Alavi (2002, 2004) find that emergent leaders sent more emails, longer emails, and more task-oriented emails than other members. Interestingly, demographic factors such as age or experience did not affect emergent leadership (Yoo and Alavi 2002; Yoo and Alavi 2004).

In sum, while gender differences may exist in language use or communicative styles, these differences do not determine leadership skills. For instance, a fusion of both assertive and supportive language may have the strongest influence on a group (Bass 1990). Furthermore, leadership can be defined as an ability to persuade a group (Hogan, Curphy et al. 1994), yet both powerful and powerless speech impact persuasiveness. While Hart (1997) is convinced that dominant language can provide the winning ticket in an election, other factors such as personality, cognitive ability, cooperation and sociability may have as strong an impact on perceptions of leadership (Hogan, Curphy et al. 1994).

Finally, predictors of emergent leadership in online communities vary. While some scholars claim that sociability, achievement, responsibility, cultural values, performance and trust are indicative of perceived and elected leaders online (Bass 1990; Sarker, Grewel et al. 2002), others have found the mere amount of communication, in terms of messages and message lengths, to be the most powerful factor (Yoo and Alavi 2002; Yoo and Alavi 2004; Misiolek and Heckman 2005).

The Present Studies

This chapter examines the discursive and linguistic features of an online community in order to find predictors of leadership online. In particular, we investigate the use of talk about the self and talk about others, informative and interactional talk, powerful and powerless language (such as the use of hedges or tag questions), as well as the amount of communication that took place. We pursue this investigation through data from the online interactions of JUNIOR SUMMIT participants during the first six weeks of a two-month period, which culminated with an online election. Based on the study of this multinational, online democracy of young people, we pose the following questions:

Do children who were elected present themselves differently than those who were not? Can we predict who was elected by looking at children's online conversation? In the absence of access to face-to-face cues, what characteristics of language correlate with leadership positions? Are the online voices of boys and girls distinguishable? Do they follow the gender lines suggested by literature on men and women's communicative styles? Are girls and boys elected for the same criteria?

Given that assertive speech styles lead listeners both to like speakers and to accept their arguments, we can hypothesize that those elected to attend the in-person Summit employed powerful language in their email messages. In general, it would be easy to hypothesize that those who were elected to the in-person conference would speak with certainty, avoiding tentative language and hedges. We might also guess that they would issue directives with greater frequency and post longer messages and more messages than their peers who were not elected.

As for content, it seems likely that delegates would offer more ideas to the forum than the average participant. Given the low-context nature of computer-mediated communication and the fact that candidates must be known by their constituents, we can hypothesize that elected delegates may have provided relatively more biographic information and personal narratives about themselves than their peers.

Finally, we would expect girls to use different language than boys online, along the lines of the literature reviewed, such that girls would write less, but use more hedges and more personal pronouns. And, we would expect fewer girls than boys to be elected leaders, since gender has been found to mitigate perceived leadership potential.

Method

The data sets that comprise the JUNIOR SUMMIT are of three types: (1) the 48,000 messages posted to the online forum for the period September 1998-September 2003; (2) in-depth interviews about the effects of the JUNIOR SUMMIT conducted with 78 participants from 20 countries 5 years after the Summit began; (3) questionnaires on socio-psychological variables (primarily self-efficacy, meaningful instrumental activity, social networks) filled out by the same subset of 78 of the children 5 years after the summit began. In this chapter, we discuss results from analyses carried out on a subset of this huge data set. We present our data as two separate studies of the Junior Summit. In the first study, we analyze word frequencies for one sample of participants (n = 274), who posted 7755 messages in the first 6 weeks of the JUNIOR SUMMIT. In the second study, we examine in greater detail, using both word frequencies and hand-coding of content, 2369 messages posted by a second sample of Summit participants (n = 33) during the same six-week period.

The subjects whose messages are analyzed in these studies represent a subset of the entire JUNIOR SUMMIT population; in particular, we only examine messages posted by children who participated independently (as opposed to as a part of a team or group of children) and who chose English as the language which they would use during the Junior Summit (although by no means were all of these children native English speakers).

Study 1

Participants

The first study includes data from 274 participants (54% female, 46% male) between the ages of 9 and 16 (mean age = 13.83, sd = 1.77), representing 84 countries. Again, this set of participants represents children who participated as individuals (not groups), and who chose English as their language of participation.

Procedure

For the first study, we examined the total number of words, total number of messages, and average message length for each participant, as well as a word frequency analysis. As discussed by Pennebaker, Mehl & Niederhoffer, (2003), word frequency can be a powerful tool in understanding the psychological and sociological profiles of individuals and communities.   We employed a computational word frequency analysis software package, *Linguistic Inquiry Word Count* (LIWC) (Pennebaker, Mehl & Niederhoffer 2003), to analyze a number of categories including first person singular and plural pronouns, negations, assent, positive emotion, family, reference to the future tense. We also added some categories of our own (such as hedges, "WH" questions, apologies and JUNIOR SUMMIT-related language).   A complete description of LIWC's functionality, dictionaries and external validity are available at http://homepage.psy.utexas.edu/homepage/faculty/Pennebaker/Reprints/LIWC2001.pdf

We took several steps to prepare the data. To adhere to the assumptions for our statistical analysis (i.e., a normal distribution of data that is representative of our population), we removed outliers and standardized our data using z-scores.

Because subjects wrote messages of various lengths, we converted the word counts to percentages, by dividing each word count by the number of total words written by each participant. Participants who wrote *longer messages*, might have *more instances* of each word, which would skew the results, and this conversion ensures that we avoid such erroneous results.

Study 2

Participants

The second study includes 33 participants (67% female, 33% male) between the ages of 9 and 16 (mean age = 13.53, sd = 1.77), representing 14 countries. This set of participants was randomly selected to represent the Junior Summit participants as a whole (including a range of countries, urban vs. rural contexts, high- vs. low-SES, delegates vs. non-delegates).

Procedure

The second study further examined the kinds of language use found in Study 1. In addition to examining the total number of words, total number of messages, average message length, and to carrying out word frequency analyses on this data set, we also conducted a detailed hand-coded analysis of the content of participant messages. No previous work captured the detail we hoped to achieve with our analysis, and thus after looking at work by Bales (1951); Herring, (1996); Rafaeli and Sudweeks (1997); Rourke, Anderson, Garrison and Archer (2001), we ultimately developed our own codebook.   In addition, because we hoped to capture the ways in which the participants themselves chose to constitute community through language, we did not start off with an *a priori* list of content categories to search for. Instead, using a Grounded Theory–inspired methodology (Strauss and Corbin 1994), in which codes are inductively and iteratively derived from the study of the phenomenon represented, we developed a 34-feature codebook to capture the ways in which participants express ideas, give feedback to peers, and present themselves online. Each message could have more than one instance of each code; for example, a single message might have multiple requests for feedback.

The 34 codes we developed divide into: (1) "informative"-- meaning that the utterance conveys information, and is able to stand on its own; and (2) "interactive" or "interpersonal" -- meaning that the utterance is in some way a response to the contribution of another (Rafaeli and Sudweeks 1997). Thus "share personal narrative" is an *informative* code, while "agree and add ideas" is *interactive*. Examples of codes within the informative category are "presenting opinions," "proposing concrete solutions," and "delegating work". Examples of codes within the interpersonal category are "agreement," "requesting feedback," and "greetings".

Inter-rater reliability on content coding was assessed for the team of three coders, and Cohen's kappa scores were calculated for each code. The kappa score of the individual codes (for example 'biographic information' or 'personal narrative') ranged from 0.22 to 1.0 with a mean and mode of 0.66. Codes that had low inter-rater reliability, or were very infrequent, were omitted from analysis. Only five out of the 32 codes had kappa scores below 0.5; none of those are discussed here.

Again, we took several steps to prepare the data for analysis. We removed outliers and standardized our scores. As previously described, we converted word count scores into percentages, to control for total words. Additionally, and for the same reasons, we converted each category in the content analysis to represent instances of each code for every 100 words. We chose 100 words rather than total words or even one word in order to create workable values (in most cases, we have as little as zero and as many as 25 instances of a code).

Results

For each study, we ran ANOVAs to compare mean differences between groups. Our interest was in the features that predicted election to delegate status, and so we looked at a comparison between the groups of delegates versus non-delegates. But, we are also interested in gender, and the intersection between gender and leadership. For this reason we also look at features that differentiate boys and girls in the forum, girl delegates from girls not elected as delegates, boy delegates from boys not elected as delegates; and, finally, girl delegates versus boy delegates.

Study 1: Word Use Features (n = 270)

We hypothesized that delegates would post longer messages and more messages than their peers who were not elected. In fact, "campaigning" by sending out frequent and lengthy messages may have had some effect. At the most rudimentary level, in actual numbers, delegates wrote longer messages and more overall messages than non-delegates. They wrote, in fact, more than twice as many messages, averaging 11.45 messages per week while non-delegates averaged 4.11. For the first six week, prior to the announcement of elections, in the sample of 274 children, 7,755 messages were written. 5,090 came from 231 non-delegates and 2,665 came from 43 delegates.

Interestingly, however, these figures hold true both for the six weeks prior to elections and the six weeks following elections, suggesting that delegates were not simply bulk mailing in order to be elected. Likewise, in actual untransformed means, delegates' messages were longer both during the first two weeks of the forum, and over the entire three month period before the in-person summit.

Features of Language: Delegates vs. Non-Delegates

Our next hypothesis was that those elected would employ more powerful language in their messages. For instance, we predicted that delegates would speak with certainty, avoiding tentative language and hedges. We also believed that delegates would issue directives with greater frequency, and offer more ideas than the average participant. However, contrary to prediction, there were no differences in these specific features between delegates and non-delegates.

Instead, as depicted in Table 2, delegates use more language about cognitive processes in their messages, a category that represents insightfulness, pointing out discrepancies and evaluating certainty. Delegates also include more words concerning social processes in their posts. This category represents talk about the process of communication and frequent references to "friends", "family" and other humans. Delegates also use more "we" words than non-delegates (including "we," "us," "ours"), and ask more WH-questions (Who, What, When, Where). suggesting perhaps a greater or earlier feeling of group identity. The use of 'we' words is of particular interest because it can be seen as an index of community building and thus, on an individual level, a signifier of allegiance to a group. In this same population, the use of "we" increased over the first three months of the forum for all participants while "I" decreased (Cassell and Tversky 2005). In addition to demonstrating individual versus group identity (i.e, "I" vs. "we"), pronouns are also thought to be indicative of a person's level of focus or involvement with others (Pennebaker, Mehl et al. 2003). This means that, instead of asserting beliefs and formulating ideas, delegates are concentrating on interpersonal processes.

Feature	Delegates: Mean (sd)	non-Delegates: Mean (sd)	ANOVA
Total Words	9,603 (6,599)	3,169 (4,503)	$F(1,270) = 60.94, p<.001$
No. of Messages	61.98 (40.01)	22.03 (26.26)	$F(1,270) = 68.11, p<.001$
Cognitive Processes[a]	.089 (.015)	.083 (.019)	$F(1,270) = 3.95, p<.05$
Insight[a]	.025 (.007)	.022 (.008)	$F(1,270) = 5.84, p<.02$
Social Processes[a]	.249 (.025)	.238 (.033)	$F(1,270) = 4.50, p<.04$
We[a]	.050 (.008)	.045 (.014)	$F(1,270) = 4.80, p<.03$
WH Questions[a]	.012 (.004)	.010 (.005)	$F(1,270) = 6.71, p<.01$

Note: a. LIWC results presented as percentage of total words.

Table 2. Delegates and non-Delegates

Features of Language: Girls vs. Boys

In terms of gender, we predicted that fewer girls than boys would be elected leaders, since gender has been found to mitigate leadership in the face-to-face world. However, more girls (23) were elected than boys (20). We also hypothesized that girls would use different language than boys, along the lines of the literature reviewed, such that girls would write less, but use more hedges and more personal pronouns. Contrary to prediction, there were no overall gender differences found in the word frequency counts of Study 1.

However, an examination of girl delegates and girl non-delegates does reveal some differences. For example, girl delegates average more messages and more words than girl non-delegates. As depicted in Table 3, girl delegates also employ more social processes in their messages than girl non-delegates.

Feature	Girl Delegates: Mean (sd)	Girl Non-Delega-tes: Mean (sd)	ANOVA
Total Words	10,773 (7,028)	3,124 (4,654)	$F(1, 147) = 44.09, p<.001$
No. of Messages	68.17 (41.58)	22.87 (28.03)	$F(1, 147) = 43.07, p<.001$
Social[a]	.250 (.030)	.240 (.036)	$F(1, 147) = 4.06, p<.05$

Note: a. LIWC results presented as percentage of total words.

Table 3. Girl Delegates and non-Delegates

Similarly, boy delegates average more messages and total words than boy non-delegates. As depicted in Table 4, boy delegates also refer to work and jobs to be done more often. Boy delegates also ask more WH-Questions than their non-elected counterparts. This demonstrates that the boy delegates are concentrating on tasks, but also on interpersonal processes, more often than boy non-delegates.

Feature	Boy Delegates: Mean (sd)	Boy Non-Delega-tes: Mean (sd)	ANOVA
Total Words	8,257 (5,958)	3,222 (4,337)	$F (1, 123) = 19.91, p<.001$
No. of Messages	54.85 (37.91)	21.04 (24.04)	$F (1, 123) = 27.02, p<.001$
Job[a]	.0086 (.0034)	.0088 (.0068)	$F (1, 123) = 6.06, p<.02$
WH-Questions[a]	.011 (.004)	.010 (.005)	$F (1, 123) = 7.37, p<.007$

Note: a. LIWC results presented as percentage of total words.

Table 4. Boy Delegates and non-Delegates

Study 2: Word Use Features and Additional Content Analysis (n = 30)

Our second study adds considerably more detail to what we know about the JUNIOR SUMMIT participants. The LIWC is capable of capturing many aspects of an individual's writing style, but only those that can be explored through the frequency of particular lexical items or groups of words. Thus, in addition to word frequency analyses, in this second study we also present results from a methodology that allowed us to concentrate on the content of the participants' messages. For example, categories such as "giving feedback on an idea" cannot be captured through analyses of single words, but are an important index of involvement with others. Our content analyses, therefore addressed questions such as how the children proposed new ideas, whether they gave feedback to one another, and the nature of their feedback. For each table below, the items listed in **BOLD** represents hand-coded content analysis features.

In the most general terms, for this sample as well we predicted fewer girls than boys to be elected leaders, since gender has been found to mitigate leadership. However, in Study 2, more girls (13) were elected than boys (9).

We wondered whether content analysis would reveal more powerful language, and once again, our first hypothesis was that delegates would employ more powerful language in their messages. For instance, we predicted that delegates would offer advice, make counter-arguments, and so forth. We also believed that delegates would issue directives with greater frequency, and offer more ideas than the average participant. Because delegates would be engaged in this kind of task talk, we believed that they would share less information about themselves.

Results indicated that delegates did indeed share less biographical information about themselves, and were less likely to engage in social niceties, or to agree without adding further information. Thus their language concentrates more on the work of the JUNIOR SUMMIT, and less on externalities or superficialities. However, our other hypotheses were proven resoundingly wrong...once again.

As depicted in Table 5, delegates offer advice less often than non-delegates, and less often offer a counterpoint to an idea or topic. Delegates, on the other hand, did synthesize the ideas of the group or another individual more often than non-delegates. They also referred to themselves more often. Remember that these analyses were all conducted on frequency data: the number of these features found per one hundred words. Thus, our analyses are not skewed by the fact that delegates produced a sheer quantity of messages greater than non-delegates.

Feature	Delegates: Mean (sd)	non-Delegates: Mean (sd)	ANOVA
Total Words	12,964 (7793)	6,665 (5430)	$F(1,29) = 6.27$, $p<.02$
Words Per Message	173.62 (67.83)	112.53 (37.87)	$F(1,29) = 5.15$, $p<.03$
Amplifiers[a]	.006 (.002)	.009 (.003)	$F(1,29) = 8.58$, $p<.007$
Certainty[a]	.022 (.005)	.026 (.004)	$F(1,29) = 5.56$, $p<.03$
Fillers[a]	.0027 (.0010)	.0031 (.0016)	$F(1,29) = 4.29$, $p<.05$
Self-Reference[a]	.413 (.026)	.390 (.026)	$F(1,29) = 8.02$, $p<.008$
Offer Advice[b]	.006 (.012)	.014 (.019)	$F(1,29) = 5.61$, $p<.03$
Agree[b]	.068 (.069)	.116 (.063)	$F(1,29) = 4.42$, $p<.04$
Ask for Information[b]	.108 (.073)	.204 (.165)	$F(1,29) = 6.97$, $p<.01$
Share Biographical info[b]	.241 (.161)	.459 (.205)	$F(1,29) = 7.07$, $p<.01$
Counterpoint[b]	.037 (.039)	.079 (.046)	$F(1,29) = 9.91$, $p<.004$
Niceties[b]	.279 (.185)	.407 (.191)	$F(1,29) = 4.71$, $p<.04$
Synthesize Ideas[b]	.021 (.025)	.009 (.012)	$F(1,29) = 5.39$, $p<.03$

Note: a. LIWC results presented as percentage of total words. b. Content analysis results presented as number of occurrences per 100 words.

Table 5. Delegates and non-Delegates

Feature	Boys: Mean (sd)	Girls: Mean (sd)	ANOVA
Fillers[a]	.0032 (.0015)	.0027 (.0010)	$F(1,29) = 5.30, p<.03$
Hedges[a]	.007 (.002)	.006 (.002)	$F(1,29) = 5.01, p<.03$
Junior Summit Reference[a]	.007 (.004)	.004 (.002)	$F(1,29) = 5.31, p<.03$
Offer Advice[b]	.014 (.018)	.006 (.012)	$F(1,29) = 5.70, p<.02$
Apologize[b]	.029 (.023)	.080 (.058)	$F(1,29) = 4.49, p<.04$

Note: a. LIWC results presented as percentage of total words. b. Content analysis results presented as number of occurrences per 100 words.

Table 6. Boys and Girls

Features of Language: Girls vs. Boys

We also hypothesized that the content analysis would reveal that girls used different language than boys online, along the lines of the literature reviewed, such that girls would use more hedges or tentative language. In fact, while it was true that girls apologized more often than boys, results indicated that boys used more fillers, such as "You know?" or "I mean". They also used more hedges, such as "sort of", "kinda", "perhaps", or "almost" than girls. On the other hand, boys also offer advice more often, and make more JUNIOR SUMMIT-related references. See Table 6.

Gender and Leadership: Girl Delegates and Boy Delegates

Within the group of delegates, we expected to find similar differences in language use, along the lines of the literature reviewed, such that girl delegates would use more tentative language than boy delegates, but also speak in ways that promote group cohesiveness. As shown in Table 7, girl delegates did indeed apologize more often, agree while adding ideas to the group, and contribute social niceties more often than their male counterparts, while boy delegates referred to themselves more often, as well as synthesizing the ideas of the group or another individual more often than girl delegates.

Feature	Boy Delegates: Mean (sd)	Girl Delegates: Mean (sd)	ANOVA
Apology[a]	.0003 (.0002)	.0008 (.0005)	$F(1,20) = 6.88, p<.02$
Self-Reference[a]	.426 (.023)	.404 (.024)	$F(1,20) = 4.54, p<.05$
Agree & Add Ideas[b]	.039 (.036)	.101 (.068)	$F(1,20) = 6.24, p<.02$
Niceties[b]	.173 (.107)	.352 (.195)	$F(1,20) = 4.57, p<.02$
Synthesize Ideas[b]	.039 (.028)	.009 (.011)	$F(1,20) = 12.06, p<002$
Note: a. LIWC results presented as percentage of total words. b. Content analysis results presented as number of occurrences per 100 words.			

Table 7. Girl Delegates vs. Boy Delegates

We limit our discussion here to the differences over the first six weeks in order to observe the effect of gender on voting, which took place at the six-week mark. However, looking at the longer time interval, all previously reported differences also held true for the longer duration of the forum. The persistence of the trends over time suggest that these are personal attributes due to character or socialization of the individual participants, and not merely a function of their environment or what is happening during that day or week in the online forum.

Features of Language: Girl Delegates vs. Non-Delegates and Boy Delegates vs. Non-Delegates

We've described the sets of features that distinguished girl delegates from boy delegates. But what kinds of girls were elected from the pool of girls – did girl delegates, for example, more resemble the general boy population? Importantly, as we will see, many of the features of language that distinguished girl delegates from the general girl population, and boy leaders from the general boy population, were the same features that, in this particular community, distinguish boys and girls. That is, as will see (and with some notable exceptions), girls were elected when they were the most girl-like, and boys were elected for being the most boy-like, according to the language-use standards of this community.

As depicted in Table 8, girl delegates did utilize more words in each message than girl non-delegates. Girl delegates – just like the group of delegates as a whole -- also share less biographical information, and offer fewer counterpoints to ideas or topics found within the group messages.

Feature	Girl Delegates: Mean (sd)	Girl Non-Delegates: Mean (sd)	ANOVA
Words Per Message	162.26 (60.97)	111.33 (34.20)	$F(1,20) = 5.11, p<.04$
Number[a]	.015 (.003)	.018 (.004)	$F(1,20) = 4.46, p<.05$
Share Biographical Info[b]	.293 (.181)	.473 (.214)	$F(1,20) = 4.52, p<.05$
Counterpoint[b]	.037 (.038)	.070 (.029)	$F(1,20) = 4.67, p<.04$
Note: a. LIWC results presented as percentage of total words. b. Content analysis results presented as number of occurrences per 100 words.			

Table 8. Girl Delegates and Girl non-Delegates

As depicted in Table 9, there are a considerable number of differences between boy delegates and boy non-delegates. Again, in line with our hypothesis and our first study, boy delegates average more words per message than non-Delegates.

We also hypothesized that boy delegates would use more powerful language than boy non-delegates. Here, our results are mixed. We find that boy delegates use more tentative speech, such as "maybe" or "perhaps", but they also use more causation features in their language, which includes words such as "because", "effect", "hence". Boy delegates also use "I" more often, as well as general self-reference such as "me" and "we".

By comparison, boy non-delegates use more amplifiers ("really" "incredibly") as well as mild or hedged opinions. They also use more social niceties, and agree with ideas more often. On the other hand, boy non-delegates also present concrete solutions more often than their counterparts. As with the general population of delegates, boy non-delegates share more biographical information, as well as references to their homes. Thus, while boy delegates are indeed focusing on the work of the summit more than non-delegates (producing fewer social niceties, for example), their language is not more powerful than the non-delegates.

Feature	Boy Delegates: Mean (sd)	Boy Non-Delegates: Mean (sd)	ANOVA
Words per Message	190.04 (77.37)	117.94 (70.09)	$F(1,9) = 7.27, p<.03$
Amplifiers[a]	.006 (.0018)	.010 (.0001)	$F(1,9) = 13.41, p<.005$
Causation[a]	.010 (.002)	.007 (.003)	$F(1,9) = 5.55, p<.04$
Death[a]	.001 (.0005)	.000 (.0000)	$F(1,9) = 14.48, p<.004$
Home[a]	.009 (.002)	.005 (.003)	$F(1,9) = 7.20, p<.03$
I[a]	.375 (.017)	.328 (.024)	$F(1,9) = 11.17, p<.009$
Self-Reference[a]	.426 (.023)	.374 (.030)	$F(1,9) = 7.75, p<.02$
Tentative[a]	.065 (.00532)	.049 (.00004)	$F(1,9) = 16.01, p<.003$
Agree[b]	.055 (.046)	.152 (.021)	$F(1,9) = 7.77, p<.02$
Share Biographical Info[b]	.166 (.090)	.398 (.206)	$F(1,9) = 7.34, p<.02$
Niceties[b]	.173 (.107)	.475 (.140)	$F(1,9) = 12.15, p<.007$
Mild Opinion[b]	.064 (.055)	.255 (.230)	$F(1,9) = 6.99, p<.03$
Present Concrete Solution[b]	.039 (.024)	.162 (.067)	$F(1,9) = 25.15, p<.001$

Note: a. LIWC results presented as percentage of total words. b. Content analysis results presented as number of occurrences per 100 words.

Table 9. Boy Delegates and Boy non-Delegates

Strategies that Work for Both Genders or Only for One

As evident from the results presented above, the features that predict which participants of the JUNIOR SUMMIT were elected delegates to the in-person symposium in Boston were not a unitary set of features – nor a set of features motivated by previous research on leadership. Breaking down the results by gender, however, does reveal an interesting set of differences between what aspects of linguistic style characterize girl delegates vs. boy delegates, and girl and boy delegates vs. the population of boys and girls that they come from.

In this section we address what appears to be the crux of the matter: what is the interaction between gender and delegates status? What features predict being elected for both boys and girls, and what features are good for girls and bad for boys, and vice versa?

The first interaction illustrated in Figure 1 demonstrates that emphatic language is used in equal amounts by boy and girl delegates. However, in order for this to be the case, boys delegates must use more emphatic language than the general boy population, and girls must reduce the amount in which they use emphatic language. Emphatic language indicates emphasis, and includes words such as "a lot", "really" "more" or "such a". In general writings about gender, girls are thought to use more of these emphatic terms than boys. However, the use of emphatic language is not successful for girls. Thus, in this instance, we are seeing boys and girls converge on a strategy for leadership language, which is somewhere in between the usual use of this language by the general population of boys and girls.

The next interaction between gender and delegate status, illustrated below in Figure 2, involves *tentative* language, and also illustrates convergence in language style between boys and girls who are elected delegates. The general boy population uses virtually no tentative language. In order to be elected a delegate, however, boys' use of tentative language skyrockets. Girl delegates, on the other hand, reduce their level of tentative language from the general girl population – ending up using less tentative language than boy delegates.

The final interaction shown below in Figure 3 demonstrates the most indicative of the interpersonal language traits, and that is synthesizing ideas that have been brought up by others. Boy non-delegates engage in virtually none of this kind of behavior. Those boys who are elected delegates, however, are even more synthetic in their posts than girl delegates.

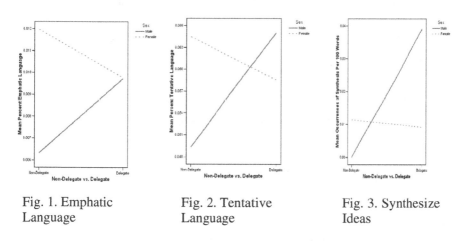

Fig. 1. Emphatic
Language

Fig. 2. Tentative
Language

Fig. 3. Synthesize
Ideas

Note: Girls are represented by the dotted line; boys are represented by the solid line. The left-side represents non-delegates; the right-side represents delegates.

Conclusion

The results presented above examine the discursive and linguistic features of the JUNIOR SUMMIT, an online community of over 3,000 children from 139 different countries, in an effort to find predictors of how leaders are elected, and to explore potential gender differences among leaders. In particular, we explore the indexes of powerful and powerless language (Hart 1984; Gibbons, Bush et al. 1991; Holtgraves and Lasky 1999; Holtgraves 2002), as well as the amount of communication that took place during the first six weeks of the JUNIOR SUMMIT, in which the election took place.

Getting elected to delegate status was a highly coveted outcome. Delegates won an all-expenses paid trip to Boston where they spent a week working with faculty and students at MIT, and meeting ministers of technology and of education from around the world. JUNIOR SUMMIT participants also knew that delegates would be extensively interviewed by the international press, and would come home covered in a kind of glory rare for a ten- to sixteen-year old child. Finally, participants were told that delegates would have a chance to get the JUNIOR SUMMIT's ideas implemented at a global level. The desirable nature of this prize meant that many of the participants were intent on proving themselves worthy delegates of their group, and some were even intent on being elected at all costs. Thus, some campaigning was obvious from the very beginning of the online forum. For example, one group sent out daily missives, including the one in Figure 4 below.

This group of children, however, was not elected to delegate status. Instead, our results illustrate that delegate status seems to be predicted by an ensemble of linguistic style traits that merge presenting ideas with doing interpersonal work.

WORLD GOVERNMENT

SOME HARD TO BELEIVE BUT TRUE FACTS
*INDIA'S EXPENDITURE ON MILITARY IS RS. 35,620 CRORES.
*MILITARIES ARE INCAPABLE OF RESOLVING DISPUTES.
*THEREFORE, THIS MONEY GOES WASTE.

WE ALL WANT
*A SELF RELIANT AND SATISFIED WORLD.

HOW CAN IT BE DONE
*BY ESTABLISHING A WORLD GOVERNMENT.
*BY REMOVING MILITARIES OF ALL COUNTRIES SIMULTANEOUSLY.
*THE MONEY USED FOR MILITARY CAN BE USED FOR THE BETERMENT OF THE WORLD.

ONLY THING WE HAVE TO DO IS SPREAD THIS MSG
* FOR DETAILS CONTACT FANTASTIC 4, HOME11

Figure 4. A Sample Campaigning Post

Our first hypothesis was that delegates would post longer messages and more messages than their peers who were not elected. Results indicate that mere quantity of posts does in fact correlate with elected leadership, as those young people who posted more often, and posted longer messages, were more likely to be elected delegates, similar to recent findings on emergent leadership in other virtual communities (Yoo and Alavi 2004; Misiolek and Heckman 2005).

Our next hypothesis was that those elected would employ powerful language in their email messages. For instance, we predicted that delegates would speak with certainty, avoiding tentative language and hedges. We also believed that delegates would issue directives with greater frequency, and offer more ideas than the average participant. This turned out not to be the case, as delegates did offer ideas, but also synthesized the ideas of others. This result conflicts with some studies on leadership (Bass 1990), but resonates with others that suggest a combination of powerful and supportive language has a strong influence on groups (Hogan, Curphy et al. 1994).

We also expected elected girls to use different language than elected boys online, along the lines of the literature reviewed, such that girls would write less, but use more hedges and more personal pronouns (Schieffelin 1990; Brownlow, Rosamond et al. 2003; Eckert and McConnell-Ginet 2003). Contrary to prediction, we found no gender differences between the amount of messages or the length of messages. We expected fewer girls than boys to be elected leaders, since gender has been found to mitigate perceived leadership potential (Bass 1990). This also was not the case, since more girls than boys were elected by their peers.

A number of findings, however, differentiated girl delegates from the general girl population and boy delegates from the boy population in such a way that for many of these features the "most girl" girls and "most boy" boys were elected. More interestingly, however a number of features were predictive of election for boys and not for girls, and vice-versa. And not all of these features fall into the classical understanding of men and women's language. In particular, whereas the language of girl delegates was quite stereotypically female, the language of boy delegates illustrated a mixture of linguistic style features, whereby some (such as the absence of social niceties or apologies) have been documented as successful for boy leaders. Others, however, are quite unexpected for male leaders. Thus, boys were very likely to synthesize the contributions of others, and to hedge their statements, and modify them with tentative language.

How do we understand these results? To our mind, it is clear that even if the online world reproduces gender and power (Herring 2001), there are ways in which the online world may allow gender and leadership to be pulled apart. In particular, as other results on emergent leadership have demonstrated, collaboration, sociability and persuasiveness may play more of a role in the absence of face-to-face features such as height (Bass 1990; Sarker, Grewel et al. 2002). In addition, as has been described for physical organizations, persuasiveness may be instantiated in different kinds of linguistic skills. These aspects of leadership may in fact give girls an advantage, as demonstrated in the higher numbers of girls elected as delegates. This means, in sum, that both advancing claims **and** listening skills may both play a primordial role in a world election where talking and listening are the only options.

Acknowledgements

Thanks to Modupe Adeleye, Hangyul Chung and Megan Tucker for insightful and painstaking coding and analysis, to Jenya Kaganova, Bill Revelle and Jelani Mandara for brilliant statistical consultation, and to Diana Owen for invaluable suggestions on the manuscript. We are indebted to the Kellogg Foundation for gracious and generous funding, and to the 3062 Junior Summit participants who have illuminated our vision of what it means to be a child, and a citizen of the world, and have made our lives immeasurably richer.

References

Bales, R. F. (1951). Interaction Process Analysis. Cambridge, Addison Wesley.
Bass, B. M. (1990). Handbook of Leadership. New York, The Free Press.
Brownlow, S., J. A. Rosamond, et al. (2003). "Gender-linked linguistic behavior in television interviews." Sex Roles: A Journal of Research **49**(3-4): 121-133.
Carli, L. (1990). "Gender, Language and Influence." Journal of Personality and Social Psychology **59**: 941-951.
Cassell, J. (2002). "We Have these Rules Inside": The Effects of Exercising Voice in a Children's Online Forum. Children in the Digital Age. S. Calvert, R. Cocking and A. Jordan. New York, Praeger Press: 123-144.
Cassell, J. and D. Tversky (2005). "The Language of Online Intercultural Community Formation." Journal of Computer-Mediated Communication.
Eckert, P. and S. McConnell-Ginet (2003). Gender and Language. Cambridge, Cambridge University Press.
Gibbons, P., J. Bush, et al. (1991). "Powerful versus powerless language: Consequences for persuasion, impression formation, and cognitive response." Journal of Language and Social Psychology **10**: 115-133.
Hart, R. P. (1984). Verbal Style and the Presidency: A Computer-based Analysis. New York, Academic Press.
Hart, R. P. (1987). The Sound of Leadership: Presidential Communication in the Modern Age. Chicago, University of Chicago Press.
Herring, S. C. (1993). "Gender and democracy in computer-mediated communication." Electronic Journal of Communication **3**(2).
Herring, S. C. (1996). Two variants of an electronic message schema. Computer-Mediated Communication: Linguistic, Social and Cross-Cultural Perspectives. S. C. Herring. Amsterdam, John Benjamins: 81-108.
Herring, S. C. (2001). Gender and Power in Online Communication. Bloomington, Center for Social Informatics Working Papers.

Hogan, R., G. J. Curphy, et al. (1994). "What We Know About Leadership." American Psychologist **49**(6): 493-504.

Holtgraves, T. M. (2002). Language as Social Action: Social Psychology and Language Use. Mahwah, New Jersey, Lawrence Erlbaum Associates.

Holtgraves, T. M. and B. Lasky (1999). "Linguistic power and persuasion." Journal of Language and Social Psychology **18**(2): 196-205.

Lakoff, R. T. (1975, 2004). Language and Woman's Place: Text and Commentaries. New York, Oxford University Press.

Misiolek, N. L. and R. Heckman (2005). Patterns of emergent leadership in virtual teams. 2005 Hawaii International Conference on System Sciences (HICSS-38), Waikoloa, HI.

Pennebaker, J. W., M. R. Mehl, et al. (2003). "Psychological aspects of natural language use: Our words, our selves." Annual Review of Psychology **54**: 547-577.

Postman, N. (1985). Amusing Ourselves to Death: Public Discourse in the Age of Show Business. New York, Penguin Books.

Rafaeli, S. and F. Sudweeks (1997). "Networked Interactivity." Journal of Computer Mediated Communication **2**(4).

Rosenberg, S. W., S. Kahn, et al. (1991). "Creating a Political Image: Shaping Appearance and Manipulating the Vote." Political Behavior **13**(4): 345-367.

Rourke, L., T. Anderson, et al. (2001). "Methodological issues in the content analysis of computer conference transcripts." International Journal of Artificial Intelligence in Education **12**.

Sacks, H., E. A. Schegloff, et al. (1974). "A Simplest Systematics for the Organization of Turn-Taking for Conversation." Language **50**: 696-735.

Sarker, S., R. Grewel, et al. (2002). Emergence of leaders in virtual teams: what matters? 35th Annual Hawaii International Conference on System Sciences, Maui.

Schieffelin, B. B. (1990). The Give and Take of Everyday Life: Language Socialization of Kaluli Children. Cambridge, Cambridge University Press.

Strauss, A. L. and J. Corbin (1994). Grounded Theory Methodology - An Overview. Handbook of Qualitative Research. N. K. Denzin and Y. S. Lincoln. Thousand Oaks, Sage Publications: 273-285.

Sullivan, D. G. and R. D. Masters (1988). ""Happy Warriors": Leaders' Facial Displays, Viewers' Emotions, and Political Support." American Journal of Political Science **32**(2): 345-368.

Yoo, Y. and M. Alavi (2002). "Electronic Mail Usage Pattern of Emergent Leaders in Distributed Teams." Sprouts: Working Papers on Information Environments. Systems and Organizations **2**.

Yoo, Y. and M. Alavi (2004). "Emergent leadership in virtual teams: what do emergent leaders do?" Information and Organization **14**(1): 27-58.

A Bosom Buddy Afar Brings a Distant Land Near: Are Bloggers a Global Community?

Norman Makoto Su, Yang Wang, Gloria Mark, Tosin Aiyelokun, Tadashi Nakano

University of California, Irvine
{normsu, yangwang, gmark, oaiyelok, tnakano}@ics.uci.edu

Abstract. Information communication technologies on the Internet such as Usenet, Internet relay chats and multi-user dungeons have been used to enable virtual communities. However, a new form of technology, the weblog, or "blog", has quickly risen as a means for self-expression and sharing knowledge for people across geographic distance. Though studies have focused on blogs in Western countries, our study targets the global blogging community. Inspired by previous studies that show significant differences in technology practices across cultures, we conducted a survey to investigate the influence of regional culture on a blogging community. We asked the research question of whether bloggers are more influenced by their local cultures with respect to their sense of community, or rather whether a "universal" Internet culture is a stronger influence of community feeling. Our results, based on a multilingual worldwide blogging survey of 1232 participants from four continents show that while smaller differences could be found between Eastern and Western cultures, overall the global blogging community is indeed dominated by an Internet culture that shows no profound differences across cultures. However, one significant exception was found in Japanese bloggers and their concealment of identity.

Introduction

Never before have [people] been able to maintain intimate and continuing contact with others across thousands of miles; never has intimacy been so independent of spatial propinquity...And never before has it seemed economically feasible for the nodally cohesive spatial form that

P. van den Besselaar et al. (eds.), Communities and Technologies 2005, 171-190.

marks the contemporary large settlement to be replaced by drastically different forms, while the pattern of internal centering itself changes or, perhaps, dissolves.

Order in Diversity: Community without Propinquity (Webber, 1963)

Written over four decades ago, Melvin M. Webber prophesied a new sort of urban city not confined in locality, and whose community would thrive through advanced communication technologies. No doubt, Webber did not envision the Internet as this new technology; however, since its inception, the Internet has proved to be fertile ground for growing communities without propinquity, or what are commonly called *virtual communities*.

A virtual community is defined as a geographically disperse group connected through information technology ("Virtual," 2005). Our title is adapted from Bo Wang's famous poem *Seeing Du Shaofu off to His Post in Shu Zhou,* written in the Chinese Tang dynasty. This poem expresses how community can be experienced despite geographic separation, foreshadowing the advent of virtual communities.

A new kind of virtual community has recently emerged: blogs. Blogs, short for weblogs, are webpages whose content are periodic, reverse chronologically ordered posts. The meteoric rise in blogging has been due to several factors. Whereas previously blogs were relegated to the technically savvy, the proliferation of specialized hosting sites and user friendly online publishing tools dedicated to blogging has greatly increased the accessibility of blogging. Blogging has also entered the mainstream consciousness through popular media coverage. For example, bloggers played a major role in fundraising for the recent Howard Dean 2004 U.S. democratic primary campaign (Manjoo, 2003).

Blogs differ from most Internet communication technologies in two ways:

(1) *Blogging is writer-centric.* The blog writer has full control over content; they may modify comments or restrict access. With the prevalence of free blogging services providing low learning curve tools such as WYSIWYG editing of blog entries in browsers, blog writing is very easy. Thus, as opposed to technologies such as chat rooms which enable reciprocal expression, the blog is primarily the writer's vehicle of expression to which readers respond.

(2) *Blogs are link-heavy.* They contain both in and out-bound links. Depending on the genre, blogs can average up to 1.89 out-bound links per entry (Herring et al., 2004). *Blogrolls,* usually a side-list of links on the writer's homepage, serve as a sort of hit parade of blogs the writer recommends. Blogs directly facilitate in-bound linking to a writer's entries by providing a stable *permalink* to any specific entry. *Trackback* links allow writers and readers of a blog's entry to see what other bloggers are also discussing with respect to that same issue.

Thus, blogs support the formation and maintenance of a social network of both writers and readers. A blog is an open system for communication as new information outside of the direct reader/writer contributions are easily accessed to integrate into the discussion. Herring et al. (2004) consider blogs a new Internet genre that fuses multimedia with conventional text-based communication tools.

While there has been a spate of research on blogs, most studies to date have only targeted the English speaking community, or more specifically, U.S. blogs. However, blogging exists globally. For example, the largest Japanese language blogging service, Hatena Diary, as of January 2004, has just more than two million bloggers registered (Nielsen, 2004). Though accurate estimates are lacking, Chinese blogs in 2004 number from 100,000 to over 400,000 (Mao, 2004; Zhao, 2003). In Taiwan, *Cheers* magazine quotes an estimate of 100,000 bloggers for 2004 ("Living," 2004). Though we could not find a tally of European blogs, LiveJournal's statistics indicate a total of about 340,000 bloggers in the United Kingdom, Netherlands and Finland (LiveJournal, 2004). From this sample of the world, we can see that blogging has truly become a global phenomenon. Though it has not reached the mainstream consciousness to the same extent as in the U.S. (e.g., a survey of 7765 Japanese Internet users revealed that a scant 6.4% have ever heard of the word blog (CatRep, 2004)), there is no doubt a sizable population of non-U.S. bloggers.

Though now a global phenomenon, blogging in non-American cultures has been relatively ignored by researchers. In a study investigating culture and virtual communities, Becker and Mark (1999) asked whether community characteristics of social binding and social coherence could develop across geographically disperse groups. This question arises again as we look at blogs. If we consider a blog as a community consisting of the writer(s), contributors and readers, then do blogs in different geographic regions have similar community characteristics? On the one hand, we might expect significant differences between blogging communities of different world cultures, and, on the other extreme, we might expect the Internet to have "erased" any such distinctions—instead, a blogging culture that is relatively homogeneous may exist globally. In this paper we ask the research question: Do nationality and geographic region affect how bloggers experience community, or rather do bloggers worldwide experience the same sense of community irrespective of the country or region where they live? Does an Internet culture exist for bloggers that influences a uniform sense of community? Rather than focus on whether blogs are international (different languages in blogs, especially in Asia, limit international participation), our interest is instead whether blog writers around the world have similar community characteristics. We conducted an international study of bloggers to investigate this question.

Related Work

Due to their recent fame, attention has been given to research on blogs. Herring et al. (2004) describe a study of 203 blogs from blog.gs where most blog authors were found to be young adult males located in the U.S. who create personal style journals updated almost daily. An average of 0.65 links and 0.3 comments were found per post. Bar-Ilan's more focused analysis of 15 "professional" topic-oriented blogs discovered that the majority of posts describe or quoted embedded links that led to a variety of targets such as other blogs, news items and content sites (Bar-Ilan, 2004). In-depth studies of blogs using ethnographic techniques by Schiano et al. (2004) have shown blogs to have a cornucopia of functions—from diaries of personal expression to travelogue progress reports. A further elaboration by Nardi et al. (2004a) provides an activity theory analysis framework for understanding blogging. Krishnamurthy's work follows the burst of blog activity after 9/11; he creates a taxonomy of blogs, splitting them into four quadrants with two axes: personal vs. topical and individual vs. community (Krishnamurthy, 2002).

To the best of our knowledge, no research has dealt specifically with cultural differences in blogs; however, a number of studies have analyzed the complex interplay between culture/gender and technologies. Teng et al. (1999) compared Eastern (Korea and Singapore) to Western (United Kingdom and United States) IT practices. One of their findings was that Eastern cultures had a more favorable perception of the intensity in decision communications in IT compared with Western cultures. Simon's research on web sites found significant differences across cultures and genders in certain web site perceptions (Simon, 2001). Furthermore, work by Chau et al. (2002) suggests that web site design for Asia should give attention to social communication whereas for the U.S. it should be rather information search. Fogg et al. (2001) show significant differences between Finns and Americans, and for gender, in perceiving web credibility. Researchers have also advocated the careful consideration of culture in computer technologies. Olson and Olson (2003) argue that as distributed collaboration becomes more multicultural, software engineers need to gain a deeper understanding of the cultural norms of their colleagues. Khaslavsky (1998) recommends incorporating cultural models into design practices of consumer products.

Much of the hypotheses conjectured in these papers are based on Hofstede's well-known work, *Culture and Organizations* (1991). Though written nearly a decade ago, it remains the de-facto standard for characterizing cultures. While not dealing specifically with technology per se, Hofstede's book details a large-scale quantitative study at IBM that revealed ten dimensions where cultures differ.

Some research has shown significant differences between subgroups of a virtual community. Roberts (1998) showed that people had a sense of belonging to newsgroups (Usenet), and that the dimensions of community differed along gender lines, with experiences best predicted for women by reading habits and for men by the presence of other females. Kretchmer and Carveth (2001) discuss whether "*cyberspace removes race from human interaction.*" Racial identity is also analyzed by Burkhalter (1998). Donath (1998) discussed that despite the mask of anonymity in cyberspace, people find ways to assert their own identities (either directly or indirectly) to differentiate themselves from other members.

The Global Blogging Community Methodology

Though culture has been defined in a multitude of ways (over 150 definitions of the word "culture" exist (Kroeber and Kluckhohn, 1952)), we use *nationality* as the primary criterion in determining cultural identity. Indeed, while shared contexts can form in cultures in a variety of ways, e.g. through a common language found in print, such as newspapers (Anderson, 1991), Hofstede (1991) makes a compelling argument in the use of nationality as a criterion for culture:

> ...the concept of common culture applies strictly speaking, more to societies than to nations. Nevertheless, many nations do form historically developed wholes even if they consist of clearly different groups and even if they contain less integrated minorities...there are strong forces towards further integration: (usually) one dominant language, common mass media, a national education system, a national army, a national political system, national representation in sports events with a strong symbolic and emotional appeal, a national market for certain skills, products and services.

Though not perfect, this division allows us to group people by common language, proximate geographic region, and/or other common traditions. Though the concept of community has many different aspects, in this paper we have chosen to focus on examining in blogs several dimensions of a community that according to Preece and Maloney-Krichmar (2003) are particularly relevant: activism, reputation, social connectedness and identity. We discuss these facets in the following sections.

Activism

In the popular media, blogging is perhaps most recognized as an enabler for collective action (Klam, 2004):

> Back in 2002, Marshall helped stoke the fires licking at Trent Lott's feet, digging up old interviews that suggest his support for Strom Thurmond's racial policies went way back; Marshall's scoops found their way onto The Associated Press wire and the Op-Ed page of The New York Times...a platoon of right-wing bloggers launched a coordinated assault against CBS News and its memos claiming that President Bush got special treatment in the National Guard; within 24 hours, the bloggers' obsessive study...migrated onto Drudge, then onto Fox News...

Thus, some bloggers seek to influence events in the world through blogs. Nardi et al. (2004a) noted that bloggers often wrote exhortations that unequivocally expressed a set of steps they wanted their readers to take. Numerous examples of activism can be found during the recent 2004 U.S. presidential campaign. Many blogs sprung into existence as organizing mechanisms, e.g. for boycotting broadcasting sponsors (Davis, 2004). Bloggers will often encourage others to blog:

"blogging and readers together beget the social activity of blogging" (Nardi et al. 2004a). We are interested in seeing how activism differs across culture.

Reputation

In this dimension of community, we ask: how *accountable* are bloggers for their content, and how important is their blog's reputation to them? Indeed, for some, blogging is mainly for themselves. Nardi et al. (2004b) note that:

> Most bloggers are acutely aware of audience...calibrating what they will and will not reveal. Many bloggers explained that they have a kind of personal code of ethics that dictates what goes into their blogs, such as never criticizing friends or pressing political opinions that are openly inflammatory. Not that bloggers eschew controversy...but they typically express themselves in light of their audience.

How does accountability and reputation compare in blogs that are based in different world regions? Do the culture and values of a region influence how accountable people feel for their blog content? Or rather, is accountability of content a value that is commonly shared among Internet bloggers irrespective of their local culture?

Social Connectedness

Many bloggers feel a sense of community and belonging with other bloggers. As mentioned earlier, blogrolls, trackback links and comments reveal a blogger's connections. In fact, such social-network links are often used by blog ranking services such as the Blogdex aggregator to determine popularity. Nardi et al.'s interviews reveal that people often blog to seek others' opinions and feedback, as well as updating others' on their current status (Nardi et al., 2004a). The particular blog lists or blog rings that a blog belongs to are also indicative of their social circle. For example, specialized forums and listings for Asian-American bloggers such as Rice Bowl Journals exist and blog rings such as University of California Irvine's LiveJournal community cater to students at that university.

In our exploration of blog communities, we are interested in how well connected people feel to others through blogging. How has blogging fostered friendship? How connected are people to other blogs via links and comments? We compare social connectedness across bloggers in different geographic regions.

Identity

Herring et al. (2004) state that:

> ...many bloggers include explicit personal information on the first page of their blogs...a full name (31.4%), a first name (36.2%), or a pseudonym (28.7%). More than half (54%) provide some other explicit information (e.g., age, occupation, geographic location)...the identity of the author is apparent to some extent in most blogs.

Donath (1998) describes how in virtual community interactions, the medium provides an affordance to either conceal or reveal identity. Blog writers (and readers) have full control over how to reveal their identity. Blog services will often provide a "profile" page for bloggers to provide information about themselves. Pseudonyms provide an identity while maintaining privacy. Aliases are used not only by bloggers, but also in entry references. Blogs allow one to freely assert their own identity without social stigmatism, e.g. Iranian women use blogs as an outlet for expression in a traditionally conservative society (Hermida, 2002). We compare how blog writers and readers from different cultures reveal identity.

Methodology

Data for our study was gathered via a web-deployed survey that was targeted for blog *writers*. Participation in the survey was strictly voluntary and all respondents were informed that their responses would be anonymous. Demographic survey questions were adapted from the *GVU Center's WWW Surveys* (2005). Questions related to community dimensions were gleaned from observations of current blogs, conversations with bloggers and research papers (e.g. Nardi et al., 2004b). Our English survey version had 51 questions. Native speakers of (traditional and simplified) Chinese, Japanese and Korean translated the English survey. Afterwards, reverse translation was used to verify that the questions were equivalent to their respective English counterparts. We hosted a website that provided a FAQ, explanation of our research goals and contact information to field inquiries regarding our blog survey. The English language survey was deployed in early summer of 2004, and the Asian language survey was deployed in late summer of 2004. Both were active for a six month period.

To gain an appropriate sample of blog authors, we used several methods to advertise our survey: 1) The first author advertised the survey on a blog, blogsurvey.blogspot.com, with trackback features, 2) We registered our survey blog in major blog search databases, 3) Really Simple Syndication (RSS) feeds were augmented to allow readers to be notified of changes (RSS is an XML communication standard that allows a web developer to easily publish updated content in a format easily understood by a number of RSS aggregators), 4) We added blogs who advertised our survey to our blogroll, 5) We sent email asking bloggers to fill out the survey and to also post an entry encouraging readers to fill out (and further propagate a link to the survey in their own blogs), 6) We posted information on blogging forums and IRC chats and 7) word-of-mouth.

During the deployment, we received many insightful comments and criticisms from bloggers. Some pointed out minor mistakes in spelling, while others had high level questions regarding our research. Even some of the more popular "monster" bloggers took time to personally respond and advertise our survey.

An Overview of International Blogs

From a total of 1404 respondents, we extracted 1232 respondents who were grouped into distinct regions or countries. Over 200 respondents were excluded from our analysis because they did not form a critical mass of respondents that we felt could be classified into a "common" regional culture. Those classified in the Japanese, Chinese and Taiwan groups were only those who lived in these locations and spoke the official language. We did not apply this requirement to respondents of Southeast Asian countries, where English is often fluently spoken. Fig. 1 summarizes the groups used in our analysis. North America consists of U.S. and Canada. Western Europe consists of Denmark, Finland, France, Germany, Iceland, Italy, Ireland, Netherlands, Spain, Sweden, Switzerland and the U.K. Southeast Asia consists of Indonesia, Malaysia, Philippines, Singapore, Thailand and Vietnam. Our response rates could be related to our recruiting efforts in regions. For example, we lacked resources to actively recruit Korean participants and received only 13 responses from Korea.

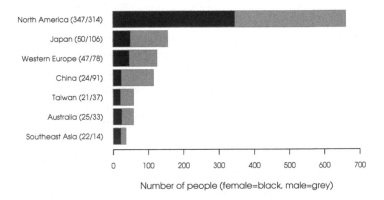

Fig. 1: The regions where valid participants were living at the time they filled out the survey.

Fig. 2a shows bloggers' reports of the primary content of their web page. Interestingly, Japanese blogs were dominated by hobby and recreational blogs (40%), whereas personal blogs dominated for the other cultures. Australia had a large proportion of political blogs (36%). There was a notable lack of religious blogs across Asian cultures—only Japan had any religious blogs (0.01%). China had a larger proportion of professional/academic blogs (21%) comparatively. Though over half of North American blogs are personal, a large percentage were categorized as political, hobby and religious blogs.

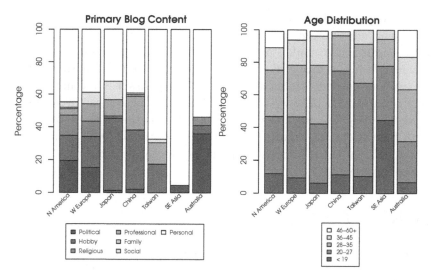

Fig. 2a: The primary content of blogs.

Fig. 2b: Age distribution of bloggers (excluding non-responses).

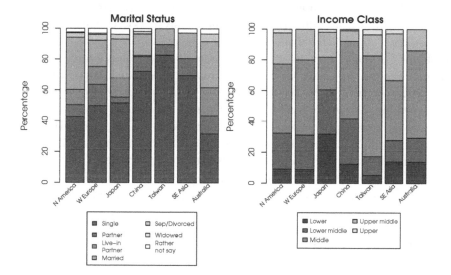

Fig. 3a: The marital status of bloggers.

Fig. 3b: The income class of bloggers.

Consistent with previous studies (Herring et al., 2004), most bloggers are young, single (Fig. 2b and 3a) and male. China, Southeast Asia and Taiwan—presumably countries where blogging and the Internet itself is still a budding technology—seem to have a larger proportion of younger bloggers versus Western Europe, North America, Japan and Australia. We combined countries into two groups based on length of Internet usage: the first included Southeast Asian, China and Taiwan, and the second included Western Europe, North America, Japan and Australia. An ANOVA between these two groups revealed significant differences in age: $F(1,1230) = -7.63$, $p < 0.001$. As illustrated in Fig. 3b, Japanese respondents reported being significantly lower in income compared to other countries: $F(1,1229) = -14.52$, $p < 0.001$. All cultures had over 50% who reported that they had previously written a diary: Japan–54%, Australia–57%, Western Europe–57%, Southeast Asia–64%, North America–65%. China (70%) and Taiwan (73%) had the highest proportion of respondents reporting keeping a diary prior to blogging.

Analysis of Community

Questions were grouped according to the dimensions of community described earlier: activism, reputation, social connectedness and identity. Cronbach's alpha was used to measure the internal consistency of questions in each category. This is the total proportion of a scale's total variance that can be attributed to a common source (DeVellis, 2003). Questions whose addition to the category brought alpha below 0.60 were dropped. Question scores were then linearly combined, with their weights determined by principal component's analysis (PCA), which calculates the best linear combination that accounts for the most variance in the items. Thus, we obtained a single score from a combination of survey question scores related together. See the Appendix for question groupings. Statistical significance was determined via the ANOVA and Kruskal-Wallis (nonparametric) tests, the latter used when the data was not normally distributed. Posthoc tests were conducted via pairwise t-tests and Mann-Whitney (nonparametric) tests with Hommel's correction for post-hoc tests. Hommel's method is an extension of the Bonferroni adjustment which assumes independence between tests (Hommel, 1988). Table 1 lists each principal component and their statistics. The R statistical programming language was used. Next we describe our results for each community dimension.

Dimension	Cronbach's	% Total Variance Explained	Eigenvalues
Reputation	0.64	52.02	5.28
Activism	0.84	85.96	5.10
Social Connectedness	0.79	39.38	8.58
Identity	0.61	77.57	8.58

Table 1: Principle Component Values

Activism

A Kruskal-Wallis rank sum test revealed significant differences ($H(6,1218)$ = 23.5, $p < 0.001$) across all groups in the activism dimension. Fig. 4a shows only the significant results found in post-hoc tests with the principal component scores. Post-hoc tests (Fig. 4a) showed significant differences between Japan and Taiwan, China, North America and Western Europe.

Fig. 4b depicts a box plot diagram. The horizontal line represents the median, and the diamond represents the mean. The bottom and top of the box represent the first and third quartile, respectively. Points that lie outside of the whiskers (the end points of the lines) are not within the 1.5 interquartile range. Each box plot corresponds to the principal component scores for a particular country.

Most groups were close to the midpoint of the activism score. However, Japan was significantly different compared to all other regions. The results suggest that Japanese bloggers have less concern with activism compared to other cultures.

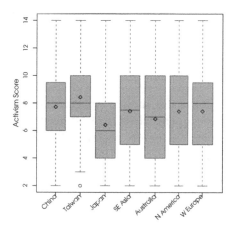

Significant Contrasts	p-value
Japan–Taiwan	***
Japan–China	***
Japan–N America	**
Japan–W Europe	*

***: $p < 0.001$, **: $p < 0.01$, *: $p < 0.05$

Fig. 4a: Significant contrasts on activism.

Fig. 4b: Box plots of activism. High values indicate more concern with activism.

Reputation

All cultures differed significantly in the reputation dimension, ($F(6,1191)$ = 8.40, $p < 0.001$). Post-hoc tests (Fig. 5a) with pairwise t-tests found statistical significance between China and North America, Western Europe, Australia and Japan. Taiwan was significantly different from North America, Japan, Australia and Western Europe. Though most of the countries had similar comparable medians in the reputation score (Fig. 5b), China and Taiwan reported placing more value on their blog's reputation compared to other countries.

Significant Contrasts	p-value
China–N America	***
Japan–China	***
Taiwan–N America	**
Taiwan–Japan	**
China–W Europe	**
China–Australia	**
Taiwan–Australia	**
Taiwan–W Europe	*

***: $p < 0.001$, **: $p < 0.01$, *: $p < 0.05$

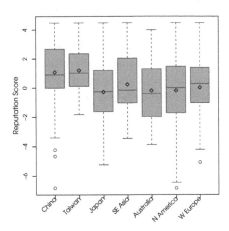

Fig. 5a: Significant contrasts on reputation.

Fig. 5b: Box plots of reputation. High values indicate more concern with reputation.

Social Connectedness

All cultures also showed significant differences ($F(6,1191) = 18.94$, $p < 0.001$) in their social connectedness. Post-hoc tests (Fig. 6a) showed Japan was significantly different than North America, Western Europe, Australia and Southeast Asia.

Significant Contrasts	p-value
Japan–N America	***
Japan–W Europe	***
Japan–Australia	***
China–N America	***
Taiwan–W Europe	***
China–W Europe	***
Japan–SE Asia	***
Taiwan–Australia	**
China–Australia	**
Taiwan–SE Asia	*
China–SE Asia	*

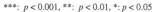

***: $p < 0.001$, **: $p < 0.01$, *: $p < 0.05$

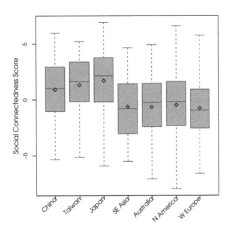

Fig. 6a: Significant contrasts on social connectedness.

Fig. 6b: Box plots of social connectedness. High values indicate lower social connections.

China had statistically significant differences with the same countries as Japan. Taiwan, while similar to China in showing significant differences with Europe, Australia and Southeast Asia, was not significantly different than North America. Fig. 6b shows that Japan, China and Taiwan (East Asian regions) appear to be less socially connected to others through their blogs compared to Western Europe, Southeast Asia and Australia.

Identity

A Kruskal-Wallis rank sum test revealed significant differences ($H(6,1215)$ = 221.15, $p < 0.001$) in identity across all groups. Post-hoc tests (Fig. 7a) showed significant differences between Japan and all other regions. China and Taiwan showed significant differences with North America. Fig. 7b shows most countries were on the negative side of the scale, indicating that they were not likely to hide their identities and/or personalities. In stark contrast, Japan had significant differences with all other countries and is high on the positive side, indicating a strong preference for privacy and possibly for the use of alternative identities in blogs. The non-overlapping box plots show high confidence in this difference.

Significant Contrasts	p-value
Japan–China	***
Japan–N America	***
Japan–W Europe	***
Japan–Australia	***
Japan–SE Asia	***
Japan–Taiwan	***
China–N America	**
Taiwan–N America	**

***: $p < 0.001$, **: $p < 0.01$, *: $p < 0.05$

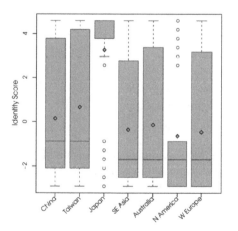

Fig. 7a: Significant contrasts on identity.

Fig. 7b: Box plots of identity. High values indicate one who reveals less of his or her identity.

Other Analyses Relating to Community

In addition to the four community dimensions, we also examined how different cultures viewed blogging as an outlet for private expression. Fig. 8a depicts answers to the survey question: *I would express things in my blog that I would not express to my closest companion(s).* From hereon, we refer to this question as depicting *entrustment*. A Kruskal-Wallis rank sum test revealed significant differences ($H(6,1217) = 208.39$, $p < 0.001$) across all groups. Post-hoc tests (Fig. 8b) showed significant differences between Taiwan, Japan and China with North America, Western Europe and Australia. Southeast Asia had significant differences with North America and Western Europe. We see here a noticeable divide between East and West, with East Asian countries (including Southeast Asia) reporting that they were more willing to express things on their blog than to their closest associates.

Finally, we also ran a two-way ANOVA on culture and a blog's primary content category (Fig. 2a). There were *no* significant effects from the interaction between culture and blog content on any of the aforementioned dimenions or questions.

Significant Contrasts	p-value
Japan–N America	***
China–N America	***
Japan–W Europe	***
Taiwan–N America	***
China–W Europe	***
Taiwan–W Europe	***
SE Asia–N America	***
Japan–Australia	***
SE Asia–W Europe	***
China–Australia	*
Taiwan–Australia	*

***: $p < 0.001$, **: $p < 0.01$, *: $p < 0.05$

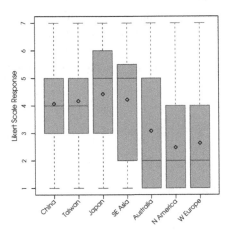

Fig. 8a: Significant contrasts on "I would express things in my blog that I would not express to my closest companion(s)."

Fig. 8b: Box plots of the statement in the caption of Fig. 8a. High values indicate more agreement with this statement.

Discussion

In this study, we asked whether bloggers in different world regions might be more influenced by local culture or by a "universal" Internet culture in how they experience community. Our results suggest that 1) overall, bloggers around the world share quite a bit in common in how they experience community through their blogs and 2) some differences do exist, possibly related to local cultural influences. We first discuss the latter point.

Our data showed that "Western" cultures often grouped together, as did "Eastern" cultures. This trend was noticed by Hofstede (1991) in his culture dimensions such as power distance (PDI) and his long-term orientation index (LTO). For example, Asian cultures tended to have a higher power distance; in other words, they expected and accepted unequal power distributions in society. On the other hand, the U.S., Great Britain and some European countries were on the lower end of the PDI spectrum. This same grouping repeats itself in our study, albeit with some variations, in the social connectedness and entrustment dimension. For all dimensions, North America, Western Europe and Australia showed no statistically significant differences between each other. It is possible that Australia's long history of British administration may in part give its culture a European flavor.

Southeast Asia also shares a history of British influence and colonialism since the 1800's. Even today, primary schools in these countries still teach British English. On the other hand, due to three mass migrations from China to Southeast Asia ("Indonesian," 2005), a sizable community of Chinese live side by side with their indigenous neighbors in Southeast Asia. This unique mix may explain why on some of our dimensions, Southeast Asians tended to group with Eastern cultures (e.g., entrustment), whereas on other dimensions, they grouped with Western cultures (e.g., social connectedness).

Recent articles (Honan, 2004) have dealt with how the political environment in China has shaped and affected bloggers' practices. On the outside, its communist based government seems to be diametrically in contrast with Taiwan's democratic government. However, despite this cultural-historical backdrop, we found not one significant difference between bloggers from China and Taiwan across our dimensions. In fact, in looking at their response distributions, it is remarkable how similar they are. We can offer several plausible explanations. First, blog content in Taiwanese and Chinese blogs were dominated by personal blogs. In China, the perception of blogging as a personal outlet may have been influenced by the large media coverage of a blogger named Zimei Mu. Mu wrote nonchalantly about her sexual encounters, thus inciting controversy, and at the same time, gaining a massive readership of 20 million users (Honan, 2004). This was how many Chinese first learned of the word "blog." This personal side of blogging is further evidenced by the large number of Chinese bloggers who were diarists. Second, the majority of the Chinese and Taiwanese populations are of the Han ethnicity. Both the traditional and simplified Chinese languages stem from a single unique creation of the Han ethnicity that unifies these diverse groups. Third, deep-rooted traditional Chinese values associated with Confucianism, art (paintings and calligraphy), holidays and architectural styles are pervasive throughout every facet of life in both Chinese and Taiwanese cultures. For example, Chinese culture places a great deal of importance on the concept of face (Hofstede, 1991); losing face is humiliating, often in a public context. This may help explain why Taiwanese and Chinese bloggers indicated a high value for reputation. Finally, our demographics show a preponderance of young, middle class writers in the both the Taiwanese and Chinese blogging community. Far from the previous stance of self-imposed isolation imposed by the Chinese government, the late economic success of Taiwan has necessitated the redefinition of Chinese culture as not only transferring from China to Taiwan but also from Taiwan to China. Tu (1994) writes that *huaren* (people of Chinese origin), as opposed to *Zhongguoren* (citizens of the Chinese state) for Chinese intellectuals best describes the modern "cultural China"—one with no geopolitical emphasis. An example of this intellectual unity is that both Chinese and Taiwanese, with the commonality of *huaren*, worked together in the 1970s in the Diaoyutai Movement to protest Japanese encroachments on disputed islands (Tu, 1994).

In many of our comparisons, Japanese bloggers were exceptions. In activism, Japan was the only country that was significantly different than the other countries. Japanese tended to care less whether their blog would influence others. We noticed a slight lack of importance placed on reputation and on the degree of social connectedness in Japanese blogs. The dominance of hobby/recreational oriented blogs may explain a Japanese perception of blogging as entertainment. Though purely speculative, news articles (Watanabe, 2004) have reported that Japanese blogs are fancier and geared towards entertainment.

Perhaps the most striking difference between Japan and the other world regions was in their view of identity. Compared to other cultures, the Japanese score was highly skewed towards not revealing identities, even with the use of aliases. Similarly, Japanese blog writers noted that they used blogs, rather than their closest friends, to express themselves (Fig. 8a and 8b). This presents a paradox in that, on the one hand, Japanese view blogs as an entertainment medium, whereas on the other hand, Japanese express personal matters and are extremely private. We can resolve this by viewing blogs as a tool for anonymous entertainment and expression. One such place does in fact exist for Japanese, 2ch.net, a very loosely organized online forum where anonymity is the norm. Onishi (2004) states: "*In a society in which subtlety is prized above all, face-to-face confrontation is avoided, insults can be leveled with verbal nuances and hidden meanings are found everywhere, there is one place where the Japanese go to bare their souls and engage in verbal combat: Channel 2 [2ch.net]*". Perhaps blogs provide this same sort of medium for Japanese to assert their identity in a traditionally collectivist culture (Hofstede, 1991), while allowing a more controlled way for organizing and controlling their content.

Despite these differences, however, the crux of our paper's findings is that while statistically significant differences and groupings did occur, the *magnitude* of difference in data distributions of the dimensions across cultures was more often than not small. Moreover, the wide range of different blog content categories themselves had no significant effects on our dimensions across culture (see the previous section).

Limitations of our Study

Results from our survey can potentially suffer from self-selection bias. We did not randomly sample our respondents by demographic region. As a result, systematic bias can be introduced, and thus we can only say that our sample represents those blog writers motivated to fill out our survey. While we cannot say these results are wholly representative of blog authors in general, we believe that our data is, nevertheless, a good contribution to a deeper understanding of the international blogging community. Another limitation is that our classifications of countries may have been at the wrong granularity (e.g., by not separating Southeast Asia into individual countries). We feel, however, that the cultural similarity within the groups that we created was far higher than similarity across our groups.

Conclusions

We envision that blogging will only increase in popularity and we hope that our study will open up a new research direction examining the international blogging trend. Certainly, geographically defined cultures do play a role in technology—Indonesian cell phone users pointing their phones to Mecca to pray is but one case (Goto, 2004). However, as our study suggests, a distinct culture of media practice that connects distributed cultural regions does emerge. How does such a culture develop in the blogging community? In addition, it is unclear whether cultural-historical explanations can adequately account for the few differences we did find. Addressing these concerns can lead the designer to decide what local cultural aspects, if any, should be taken into account. Indeed, preconceived notions of the effects of culture on IT practices may too easily sway the designer to make unnecessary commitments.

Our results indicate that bloggers on the whole perceive a shared sense of community in the blogosphere. Notwithstanding the social, political, and economic differences between the regional cultures of our participants, bloggers painted a remarkable picture of congruity in their experiences with activism, reputation, social connectedness and identity. Thus, we can posit that bloggers themselves represent a unique culture that permeates through regional boundaries. Though we did find trends that *may* be explained by cultural differences, these differences were overshadowed by the overall consonance of the data. It is indeed heartening to see that despite the large seas that separate our lands, the global blogger, our "bosom buddy", nevertheless brings these distant lands near.

Acknowledgments

Much of the work in developing the survey was due to Jon Froehlich, Brandon Herdrick, Xuefei Fan, Kelly H. Kim and Louise Barkhuus. We are grateful to danah boyd, Li-Te Cheng, Paul Dourish, Xiangdong Fang, Mengjuei Hsieh, Kevin Huang, Mardi Klein, Kotori, Isaac Mao, moondial, Bonnie Nardi, Robert Newcomb, Fusako Su and Haifeng Yan for their advice and assistance. This research was supported by the National Science Foundation under grant no. 0093496.

References

Anderson, B. (1991). *Imagined Communities: Reflections On the Origin And Spread Of Nationalism.* London: Verso.

Bar-Ilan, J. (2004). An Outsider's View on "Topic-oriented" Blogging. *Proc. of the Alt. Papers Track of the 13th Int. WWW Conf.*, 28-34.

Becker, B., & Mark, G. (1999). Constructing Social Systems through Computer-Mediated Communication. *Virtual Reality*, 4, 60-73.

Burkhalter, B. (1998). Reading race online: discovering racial identity in Usenet discussions. M. A. Smith & P. Kollock (Eds.), *Communities in Cyberspace* (60-75). New York: Routledge.

CatRep. (2004, Feb.). Recent trends and perspective in Blog 2004. Retrieved Jan. 28, 2005, from http://shop.ns-research.jp/p-blg01.shtml

Chau, P. Y. K., Cole, M., Massey, A. P., Montoya-Weiss, M., & O'Keefe, R. M. (2002). Cultural Differences in the Online Behavior of Consumers. *CACM'02*, 45(10), 138-143.

Davis, N. (2004). Boycott Sinclair Broadcast Group. Retrieved Jan. 28, 2005, from http://www.boycottsbg.com/default.htm

DeVellis, R. F. (2003). *Scale Development* (Vol. 26). Thousand Oaks: SAGE Publications, Inc.

Donath, J. S. (1998). Identity and deception in the virtual community. M. A. Smith & P. Kollock (Eds.), *Communities in Cyberspace* (29-59). New York: Routledge.

Fogg, B. J., Marshall, J., Laraki, O., Ospiovich, A., Varma, C., Fang, N., et al. (2001). What Makes Web Sites Credible? *Proc. of CHI'01*, 61-68.

Goto, K., & Subramanian, S. (2004, Nov.). Culture Matters: An Interview with Genevieve Bell. Retrieved Jan. 29, 2005, from http://www.gotomedia.com/gotoreport/news_1104_bell.html

GVU Center's WWW User Surveys. Retrieved Jan. 28, 2005, from http://www.cc.gatech.edu/gvu/user_surveys

Hermida, A. (2002, Jun. 17). Web gives a voice to Iranian women. Retrieved Jan. 28, 2005, from http://news.bbc.co.uk/2/hi/science/nature/ 2044802.stm

Herring, S. C., Scheidt, L. A., Bonus, S., & Wright, E. (2004). Bridging the Gap: A Genre Analysis of Weblogs. *HICSS-37*, 40101b.

Hofstede, G. (1991). *Cultures and Organizations: Software of the Mind.* New York: McGraw-Hill.

Hommel, G. (1988). A stagewise rejective multiple test procedure on a modified Boneferroni test. *Biometrika*, 75, 800-802.

Honan, M. (2004, Jun. 4). Little red blogs. Retrieved Jan. 28, 2005, from http://www.salon.com/tech/feature/2004/06/04/china_blogs/

Indonesian Chinese. (2005, Jan. 28). Wikipedia: The Free Encyclopedia. Retrieved Jan. 28, 2005, from http://en.wikipedia.org

Khaslavsky, J. (1998). Integrating Culture Into Interface Design. *Proc. of CHI'98*, 365-366.

Klam, M. (2004, Sept. 26). Fear & Laptops on the Campaign Trail. *NYT Mag.*

Kretchmer, S. B., & Carveth, R. (2001). The Color of the Net: African Americans, Race and Cyberspace. *Computers & Society*, 31(3), 9-14.

Krishnamurthy, S. (2002). *The Multidimensionality of Blog Conversations: The Virtual Enactment of Sept. 11*. Internet Research 3.0, Maastricht, NL.

Kroeber, A. L., & Kluckhohn, C. (1952). Culture: A Critical Review of Concepts and Definitions *Papers of the Peabody Museum of Harvard Archaeology & Ethnology* 42(1). Cambridge: Museum Press.

LiveJournal. (2004, Nov. 15). LiveJournal.com Statistics. Retrieved Nov. 15, 2004, from http://www.livejournal.com/stats.bml

Living in the Digital Age. (2004, Nov.). *Cheers Magazine.*

Manjoo, F. (2003, Jul. 3). Blogland's man of the people. Retrieved Jan 28., 2005, from http://www.salon.com/tech/feature/2003/07/03/dean_web/

Mao, I. (2004, Jul. 14). Slowing down, Chinese blogosphere. Retrieved Jan. 28, 2005, from http://www.isaacmao.com/meta/2004/07/slowing-down-chinese-blog-from-recent.html

Nardi, B., Schiano, D. J., & Gumbrecht, M. (2004a). Blogging As Social Activity, or, Would You Let 900 Million People Read Your Diary? *Proc. of CSCW'04*, 222-231.

Nardi, B. A., Schiano, D. J., Gumbrecht, M., & Swartz, L. (2004b). Why We Blog. *CACM'04*, 47, 41-46.

Nielsen//NetRatings. (2004, Feb. 27). Hatena Diary is #1. Retrieved Feb. 1, 2005, from http://csp.netratings.co.jp/nnr/PDF/227_2004release_j_final.pdf

Olson, J. S., & Olson, G. M. (2003-2004). Culture Surprises in Remote Software Development Teams. *QUEUE*, 1, 52-59.

Onishi, N. (2004, May 9). Japanese Find a Forum to Vent Most-Secret Feelings. The New York Times.

Preece, J., & Maloney-Krichmar, D. (2003). Online Communities. J. Jacko & A. Sears (Eds.), *Handbook of Human-Computer Interaction* (596-620). Mahwah: Lawrence Erlbaum Associated Inc. Publishers.

Roberts, T. L. (1998). Are Newsgroups Virtual Communities? *Proc. of CHI'98*, 360-367.

Schiano, D. J., Nardi, B. A., Gumbrecht, M., & Swartz, L. (2004). Blogging by the Rest of Us. *Ext. Abstracts of CHI'04*, 1143-1146.

Simon, S. J. (2001). The Impact of Culture & Gender on Web Sites: An Empirical Study. *The DATABASE for Advances in Info. Sys.*, 32(1), 18-37.

Teng, J. T. C., Calhoun, K. J., Cheon, M. J., Raeburn, S., & Wong, W. (1999). Is the East Really Different from the West: A Cross-Cultural Study on Information Technology and Decision Making. *Proc. of ICIS'99*, 40-46.

Tu, W.-m. (1994). Cultural China: The Periphery as the Center. W.-m. Tu (Ed.), *The Living Tree: The Changing Meaning of Being Chinese Today* (1-34). Stanford: Stanford Univ. Press.

Virtual Community. (2005, Jan. 23). Wikipedia: The Free Encyclopedia. Retrieved Jan. 28, 2005, from http://en.wikipedia.org/

Watanabe, S. (2004, Jun. 17). Blogger Unification. Retrieved Jan. 28, 2005, from http://blog.japan.cnet.com/watanabe/archives/001321.html

Webber, M. M. (1963). Order In Diversity: Community Without Propinquity. J. Lowdon Wingo (Ed.), *Cities and Spaces*. Baltimore: John Hopkins Press.

Zhao, L. (2003, Dec. 4). The Private and Public Space Behind Blogging. Retrieved Jan. 28, 2005, from http://www.wenxuebao.com.cn/wxpd/ss/lxsd/t20031204_1177.htm

Appendix: Dimensions of Community

Reputation
- The reputation of my blog is important to me.
- It is important to me that my friends/colleagues/acquaintances offline know of my blogs' reputation.
- It is important to me that I regularly create meaningful blog entries.
- The appearance of my blog is important to me. (e.g. no typos, consistent format, color scheme, easy to browse).

Activism
- It is important to me that I influence others through the opinions stated on my blog.
- It is important to me that my blog can influence events in the world.

Social Connectedness
- About how many blogs do you directly link to from your main blog page (i.e., not including blog entries and comments)?
- How often do you currently comment on other blogs?
- How many people do you think read your blog per day (your best estimate)?
- How often do you receive comments on your blog?
- How often do you get e-mails regarding your blog?
- Since starting a blog, I have become more connected with people like me.
- How long have you been reading blogs (your best estimate)?
- How long have you been writing your blog (your best estimate)?
- How many different blogs do you regularly read during a week?

Identity
- As a blog writer, do you actively try to conceal your real-world identity (maintain anonymity)?
- How often do you use aliases (nicknames) instead of real names in your blog entries (e.g. when you refer to other people)?

Archetypes of Knowledge Communities

J.H.Erik Andriessen

Delft University of Technology, the Netherlands

erika@tbm.tudelft.nl

Abstract. Knowledge sharing communities can be found in many organizations, but their forms and functions appear to be quite diverse. This implies that questions concerning the *functioning of communities, (*how do they work) and questions concerning *success conditions* (how to organize and facilitate them) cannot be answered in a general way. The purpose of this article is to develop the theory in this area by discovering basic dimensions along which communities differ, and by identifying basic types of knowledge communities, underlying the diversity of knowledge sharing groups. Through an analysis of the literature and of a series of communities in large organizations, two basic dimensions and five archetypes of knowledge communities are identified.

Introduction

The discussion concerning knowledge sharing communities takes place in two widely divergent frameworks, i.e. social learning theory and knowledge management theory (see below). Within the two frameworks the concept of knowledge sharing community has quite different connotations and different aspects of this phenomenon appear to be central. The framework of *social learning theory* focuses particularly on knowledge sharing and apprenticeship in informal communities of more or less co-located professionals (Lave and Wenger, 1991).

The idea of communities as breeding grounds for sharing experiences and solving problems has, however, found an open ear and eye in modern companies, looking for systematic ways of strengthening its most important asset, the know-

P. van den Besselaar et al. (eds.), Communities and Technologies 2005, 191-213.

ledge embedded in their employees. Knowledge managers that previously focused
on the development of digital information systems to capture and distribute
valuable knowledge have discovered the value of 'communities of practice'.

The various needs for knowledge sharing in organizations resulted in the
growth of a wide variety of channels and forms, many of which differ quite
substantially from the original concept of Lave and Wenger (1991). Theoretically,
however, this has resulted in a confusing situation. Some authors do not
differentiate between various forms and discuss Communities of Practice as if
they are all basically the same. Moreover, they provide principles and guidelines
as if success conditions for all communities are more or less identical. Other
scholars try to take account of the differences by distinguishing between two or
three (sub) types, but their typologies are not identical. Since everyone prefers to
have his or her own concepts, many new terms are invented, such as community
of interest, community of commitment, interest group, network, network of
practice, knowledge network, knowledge community, internal community,
expanded community, formal network and epistemic community. The final effect
appears to be that different names are applied to the same phenomenon and the
same name appears to refer to different phenomena. The theory about knowledge
sharing in organizational communities is in need of an overview of the basic types
of structures, their processes and success conditions.

The purpose of this article is to analyze the processes and structures, aspects
and dimensions in which these communities differ and to identify the variety of
groups described. This is done by both studying the literature and by analyzing a
series of concrete communities. The objective is to develop a classification model
and to identify a small number of archetypes. In that way unjustifiable
generalizations concerning learning and interaction in, or cooperation and
facilitation of communities may be avoided.

The discussion is limited to communities of employees and workers. This may
include inter-organizational communities and of course communities of
governmental or university employees. But Internet communities, open networks
like Yahoo groups, customer service sites, citizen action groups or neighborhood
communities are outside the scope of this discussion. Not because these groups
are not dealing with knowledge exchange, but because the context is not
organization oriented and the dynamics in these communities may therefore have
quite different characteristics.

Two Perspectives

Social learning theory

About fifteen years ago the idea of Communities of Practice was developed in the
framework of social learning theory applied to organizational apprenticeship

(Lave and Wenger 1991). Studies of what were called 'communities' of tailors and meat cutters, of midwifes and copier machine maintenance men, were undertaken (Lave and Wenger 1991; Orr 1990; Brown and Duguid 1991). They confirmed the principle that professional learning is 'situated learning', where groups of co-located workers are the framework both for transferring knowledge, particularly from experienced workers to apprentices, and for developing new solutions and innovative ideas. The rationale behind the concept of situational learning is the fact that knowledge is different from simple information. It is information that is experienced and interpreted by a person, it is related to an actual situation and it makes sense to that person. Knowledge is often very implicit, not consciously articulated, i.e. it is tacit.

Like Lave and Wenger (1991), Brown and Duguid (1991) also emphasized the situated aspect of social learning in co-located groups. Their focus however was the contrast between formal and informal organizing. Formal descriptions of work (e.g., 'office procedures') and of learning courses are often abstracted from actual practice. As a result education, training and technology design tend to focus on abstract representations of work processes, to the damage actual practice. Management often assumes that complex tasks can be successfully mapped onto a set of simple Tayloristic, formalized steps that can be followed without need of significant understanding or insight (and thus without need of significant investment in training or skilled technicians). By relying on formal descriptions, managers develop a conceptual view that does not take into account the importance of non-formal practices. In their case studies Brown and Duguid discovered how the burden of linking formal descriptions to actual practice rests with communities of employees. By bridging this gap they protect the organization from its own shortsightedness. If the employees adhere to the formal approach, their company's services will be in chaos. The employees therefore develop sophisticated non-formal practices.

Summing up, central in all these ideas is the concept of 'practices', around which groups share, acquire, and create their knowledge. It is knowledge related to a common professional discipline, a skill or a topic. The focus in this perspective is on more or less collocated groups of professionals who develop a shared repertoire and resources such as routines, vocabulary, stories, symbols, artifacts, and heroes that embody the accumulated knowledge of that group. This shared repertoire serves as a foundation for future learning.

Knowledge management theory

Meanwhile management in knowledge intensive companies was looking for ways in which experiences of their employees can be shared, valuable skills can be kept in the company when employees leave, and the creation of new solutions and innovative concepts can be stimulated. In the eighties and the beginning of the nineties all knowledge processes, i.e. acquiring, developing, storing, exchanging and applying knowledge, was regarded to benefit enormously from investing millions of dollars in 'knowledge technologies'. Procedures to elicit knowledge from employees, to convert it into a systematized form and to store it in company wide repositories were, and often still are, very popular.

This codification approach (Hansen et al., 1999) has seen many failures (Huysman and de Wit 2002), an important reason being that people find it difficult to explicitly describe their experiences and the insights they have found. Moreover, there is psychological resistance against providing and using knowledge that is separated from its owner i.e. that is made *impersonal*. Exchanging knowledge with others may provide status and is trustworthy for the receiver. Putting knowledge in a system is cumbersome, removes it from its context and rarely provides personal rewards.

Companies therefore developed new strategies with a focus on people meeting each other, on interpersonal knowledge sharing, on master-apprenticeship relations, on knowledge intermediaries ('knowledge brokers') and on knowledge networks and communities. These networks may consist of people from different and geographically distributed units of the organization. The concept of 'communities of practice' thus became related to groups of professionals from different organizational units who have a common interest in certain work related topics and share there knowledge on a regular basis.

Certain scholars and consultants in this area defined these communities of practice in a way that also included the above mentioned co-located groups of professionals. Wenger (2000) defines CoPs as follows: "*The term 'community of practice has been used for over a decade to describe social communities or groups that have cultural practices reflecting their collective learning*". Botkin (1999, 241) defines CoPs as "*highly informal groups of people that develop a shared way of working together to accomplish some activity. Usually such communities include people with varying roles and experience*".

However, other definitions accounted for the fact that the various types of communities growing up in the era of knowledge management, were most often organizationally and geographically dispersed, depended on 'mediated communication', i.e. ICT tools, to interact, and had sometimes ample management backing. Gongla and Rizzuto (2001, 843), discussing IBM's "knowledge networks," referred to these communities as "*institutionalized, informal networks of professionals managing domains of knowledge*". They define the common characteristics of these knowledge networks as follows:

- They are global in scope, connecting practitioners worldwide and fostering a sense of community.
- They are responsible for a domain of knowledge. This responsibility includes gathering, evaluating, structuring, and disseminating

knowledge that is shared among community peers and across customer projects and seeing to its evolution.

- They adopt a small set of common roles for managing knowledge
- They provide opportunities for sharing tacit knowledge among community members
- They use the common enterprise-wide Lotus Notes and Domino application
- They are sponsored by a business unit and fostered where the business sees a need for managing knowledge for its core competencies or to meet customer or market demands.
- They are neither organization units nor teams.

This type of knowledge sharing group is clearly different from the more or less co-located groups of old-timer and new-coming practitioners as described by Lave and Wenger (1991) or Brown and Duguid (1991).

Research methodology

Should one conclude from the discussion above that we are talking about two completely different phenomena? On the one hand local, informal groups of experienced but traditional workers, and on the other hand, globally distributed groups of expert knowledge professionals? This would be a wrong conclusion for two reasons. Firstly in both cases the groups are supposed to focus on learning in an informal context of knowledge-eager employees. And secondly, because in actual practice one can find types of knowledge communities, that appear to combine characteristics of both (see below). Some scholars in this field have distinguished two or three types of communities, but the categorizations of these scholars are not similar. Others have identified aspects in which communities can differ, implying that those aspects can be used to differentiate between certain types of communities.

In this article I will try to answer the question whether there are perhaps some basic forms, let us say archetypes, of knowledge sharing communities. To find these archetypes I have tried to discover whether a small set of e.g. to or three basic dimensions can be found that underlie the major aspects in which knowledge sharing communities appear to differ. When such basic dimensions can be found, concrete examples of communities can then be plotted in the (two or three dimensional) space that is defined by these dimensions. Inspection of the way these communities are clustered can then result in the identification of certain (arche-) types of communities.

The identification of dimensions has been done by analyzing the literature in a qualitative way, and by analyzing the characterization of a number of communities in a quantitative way. This approach consists of the following steps:

- *Step 1. Identifying key characteristics.* Through a study of major publications on communities, the various aspects are identified that are used by these scholars to describe and differentiate between communities.
- *Step 2. Scoring knowledge communities.* Nine case studies in organizations have been performed, in which a variety of knowledge sharing communities were studied. These communities will be characterized ('scored') in terms of the key characteristics found in step 1.
- *Step 3. Extracting basic dimensions.* The relationships between these 'scores' are analyzed to discover underlying basic dimensions that differentiate the communities studied.
- *Step 4. Identifying ideal types.* Both the case study communities and the types of communities found in the literature will be plotted in the dimensional space. The result will be analyzed to discover basic types of communities.

Identifying key characteristics

In this section major publications concerning knowledge sharing communities are studied, to discover which aspects of communities are considered important. All authors have come to their views on the basis of practical experiences with knowledge communities. The phenomenon of organizational knowledge communities, and particularly the systematic study of them, is quite young, and therefore also well-grounded publications. The publications will be presented in chronological order.

Wenger (1998) does not give much attention to differences between various types of knowledge communities. However, he stresses that communities of practice consist of members who are informally bound by what they do together – from engaging in lunchtime discussions to solving difficult problems – and by what they have learned through their mutual engagement in these activities. Their basic purpose is to develop members' capabilities. A community of practice is thus different from a community of interest (or informal networks) that does not imply a *shared practice and interactions*, but serves only to exchange (business) information.

McDermott (1999b) uses a comparable approach. He takes the *degree of connection and identity* among members as the key dimension to distinguish between three types of networks:
- *user groups,* i.e. individuals who are all interested in certain types of information, but with hardly any interaction and a weak identity,
- *networks,* groups of people who share a common interest, exchange questions and solutions, but have limited sense of common identity and rarely meet as a network

- *communities of practice*, groups who share a common identity, history, and purpose, which is often directed at developing best practices.

Collison (1999) describes the two types of communities distinguished within the BP-Amoco Company, i.e. Communities of Practice and Communities of Commitment. The difference between the two is explained in terms of *contract value*, i.e. the degree to which the community has to deliver concrete results. CoPs have limited contract value, while Communities of Commitment have high contract value. According to Collison communities of practice are sometimes given resources by the business, often to the extent of funding a network coordinator, but do not collectively contract to deliver value to the organization. There is often no defined membership, and no fixed program of meetings, the network preferring to meet continuously but virtually. Communities of Commitment resemble to quite an extent project teams, because they were sponsored and resourced by the company, often held performance contracts or expectations, had defined membership, and a formal program of meetings with objectives and deliverables. An example was the maintenance managers' network; a network of refinery managers committed to reducing the maintenance cost to a target level fixed by the organization. From these descriptions it becomes clear that the two types of communities not only differ in contract value but also in aspects of *formalization* such as defined *composition* (only experts or experts plus newcomers) and formal agenda's.

The aspect of formalization is also taken up by Botkin (1999), stressing the aspect of visibility. He distinguishes between 'communities of practice' and 'knowledge communities'. A major characteristic of communities of practice is their informal structure, spontaneous origin, and therefore their (in)*visibility*. Knowledge communities are *"purposely formed - some like those at AT&T even have formal membership lists - and their purpose is to shape future circumstances. They are highly visible to every businessperson in the organization"*. Both types of communities contain members with a common passion to create, share, and use new knowledge; in both cases participation gives a sense of identity. CoPs however are informal groups, with open *boundary*, while the knowledge communities have sometimes closed boundary.

Allee (2000) refines the above-mentioned distinctions between two types of communities, by distinguishing 'internal and extended communities of practice' and knowledge and business networks'. She makes these differentiations on the basis of two related dimensions, i.e. *'relationships'*, from simple to complex; and *'connectivity'*, from tight to loose (see figure 1).

On the one end of the continuum are work groups and project teams, who have clear membership and connectivity. At the other end are informal knowledge networks and business networks where relationships are always shifting and changing. The knowledge and business networks serve primarily to pass along information. They are not held together by a joint purpose, so they are very loose and informal.

Work Groups	Project teams	Internal CoPs	Extended CoPs	Knowledge Networks	Business Networks
Tight		*Connectivity*			Loose
Simple		*Relationships*			Complex

Figure 1. Different types of communities and networks (after Allee, 2000)

Brown and Duguid (2001) show that effective knowledge sharing and creation also can take place in large loosely coupled groups. This happens where large groups have a common practice, such as in scientific associations. *'Where practice is common, communication can be global'*, and so scientists from all over the world can share knowledge, even without knowing each other. But Brown and Duguid prefer to call these groups 'Networks of Practice' (NoPs), since most members will never interact or know each other. NoPs consist of members from various organizations and have a much larger *size*, but with less *'reciprocity'*, than CoPs that are internally focused, tight-knit groups who work together on the same or similar tasks. Thus people know each other, which results in high reciprocity. NoPs work on a similar domain, but may never meet, don't take action and produce little (creative) knowledge.

Where Brown and Duguid point at inter-organizational membership as an important determinant of reciprocity and identity, various authors (e.g. Kimble, C., Hildreth, P., and Wright, P. 2000; Ruuska and Vartiainen, 2003; Andriessen et al. 2004) regard *geographical distribution* and *mode of interaction* as a major determining factor concerning interaction and identity building. Some communities consist of members working relatively close together and have mainly face to face meetings. Other communities however are geographically widely distributed and interact mainly electronically or combine the two modes of interaction.

Finally, developmental stages of communities may in some cases be considered as separate types. In the literature two types of stage models are to be found, i.e. life cycle models (from birth to death) and evolution models (from low to high level of maturity). Wenger (2000) and McDermott (1999a) present a life cycle model with stages such as planning, start-up, active, sustain/renew, and close. Gongla and Rizzuto (2001), however, present an evolution model of stages, based on their experience in IBM. The model describes how communities transform themselves, becoming more capable at each stage.

The first two stages are for developing and defining its existence. During these stages and the 'engaged stage' access to one another as community members and individual learning are key functions. At the 'active stage' members are working together to solve business problems and to exploit business opportunities. They make the community's shared knowledge available to external groups. At the adaptive stage, a community has moved to a level where it senses and responds to external conditions. At this stage, the community innovates and generates, creating significant new business objects—new solutions, new offerings, new methods and new processes. In their view communities can mature and dissolve at any one of these stages beyond the initial formation level. It does not appear to be fruitful to regard the stages in a life cycle model as separate types of communities, but certain stages in evolutionary models may be considered as such because the *purposes* of the community change radically.

	Potential	Building	Engaged	Active	Adaptive
Definition	A community is forming	The community defines itself and formalizes its operating principles.	The community executes and improves its processes.	The community demonstrates benefits from knowledge management and the collective work of the community.	The community and its supporting organization(s) are using knowledge for competitive advantage.
Fundamental Functions	Connection	Memory and context creation	Access and learning	Collaboration	Innovation and generation

Table 1: Stages in the evolution of communities (Gongla and Rizzuto, 2001)

The issue of purpose is further differentiated by Andriessen et al. (2004). On the basis of various case studies they came to the conclusion that all communities exist for knowledge sharing, but that this knowledge sharing appears to serve several functions. These functions can be arranged on a dimension of individual versus organization orientation:

1. solving immediate individual problems, e.g. through sending of and responding to 'who can help me on this problem'-emails in networks of professional
2. exchanging experiences, individual learning and building a wider perspective on the practice the group is working in
3. developing best practices, manuals, guidelines for the organization
4. developing innovative solutions for the organization.

Apart from what Collison (see above) called the informal 'communities of practice' and the formal and strategic 'communities of commitment', Andriessen et al. identified two other types of communities, i.e. '*daily practice communities*' and '*problem solving communities*'. The first type consists of employees from different organizational units, in near physical proximity, coming together regularly and face to face to discuss issues of common interest (see AtosOrigin's Expertise Groups, next section). These groups resemble to some extent the original craft based communities of practice described by e.g. Lave and Wenger

(1991) and Orr (1991), in the sense that they are working in relatively close proximity, include experts and new comers, and meet mainly face to face. The 'problem solving community' consists generally of a large number of geographically and organizationally dispersed employees of the same discipline, such as all 500 Oracle employees in Europe and Africa working with ERP systems (see next section). Through the ICT network they exchange questions and answers concerning the solution of certain practical problems.

Table 2 summarizes the key characteristics of knowledge communities that were identified by the various authors.

- *Contract value*: degree to which the community has to deliver concrete results (Collison 1999).
- *Purpose*: Having a common mission versus only exchanging information (Allee), or also: having an organizational orientation, i.e. developing best practices or even innovative solutions, versus an individual orientation, i.e. exchanging information for solving personal problems and learning (Gongla and Rizzuto 2001; Andriessen et al. 2004).
- *Defined membership*: whether the community is closed or open for new members (Collison 1999; Brown and Duguid 2001), having fixed or shifting relationships and membership (Allee 2000).
- *Degree of formalization*: having more or less formal meetings and an appointed coordinator (Collison 1999); formally set-up by management and clearly visible to management (Botkin 1999)
- *Composition*: only experts or both experts and newcomers (Collison 1999).
- *Reciprocity* (connectivity): degree to which members interact mutually and know each other (Brown and Duguid 2001; Allee 2004)
- *Identity*: Feelings of cohesion, trust and belongingness (McDermott 1999a; Botkin 1999);
- *Intra- or inter-organizational* (Brown and Duguid 2001)
- *Geographical dispersion* (Kimble et al. 2000; Ruuska and Vartiainen, 2003)
- *Size* (Brown and Duguid 2001)
- *Type of interaction*: face to face and/or via ICT (Kimble et al. 2000; Ruuska and Vartiainen, 2003).

Table 2. Key aspects of knowledge sharing communities

This list of aspects will be used to characterize a series of communities that were studied by our group in recent years (Andriessen et al. 2004). The relations between the characterizations of the various communities will then be used as the basis for discovering basic dimensions.

Case studies

In this section case studies concerning a variety of communities will be presented. In the next section they will be characterized in terms of the aspects that were identified in the previous section.

Unilever

Unilever is a multinational company specializing in consumer products in the areas of food, cosmetics and detergents. The company has subsidiaries in approximately 90 countries worldwide. A corporate level unit has started initiatives such as 'Knowledge Workshops' to enhance knowledge sharing and to improve innovative processes. The first knowledge workshop was organized when the company faced problems in the processing of tomatoes, and gave birth to a community of experts. Setting up communities at Unilever now proceeds quite formally. A high level management 'champion' is committed and together with him ten to twenty organizationally and geographically distributed employees are selected carefully and then asked to join the community. The experts are brought together for a workshop of about a week, to exchange information, to organize the group and care for teambuilding. A facilitator coordinates the group activities. A handbook for facilitators has been developed. The communities are globally dispersed, but certainly in the beginning ICT was hardly used for their communication. One reason appeared to be the incompatibility of the ICT platforms used in the various companies. Moreover, because of their strategic nature many communities are able to have face-to-face meetings once or twice a year.

AtosOrigin

AtosOrigin provides ICT services including consultancy, implementation and system integration. These services are provided world wide, with a total of 28,000 staff. Six thousand staff are based in the Netherlands in various geographical locations. Within AtosOrigin in the Netherlands, there are three types of communities, i.e. (local) 'Expertise Groups', (national) Networks of Performance and (national) Performer Groups.

Expertise Groups are initiatives within (Dutch) regional sections of the AtosOrigin company. They consist of consultants working in that section, who exchange experiences concerning a work related topic. Examples of CoPs are those focusing on Oracle Databases, on Microsoft software, or on Java programming, but also one concerning Project Management. They come together face to face about once a month. The meetings consist of presentations, talks about projects, sharing literature or new ideas learned in courses attended. They have a formally appointed leader. Most groups have also social events to support the process of building group identity and trust. Each consultant in that section of the company has to be member of at least one Expertise Group and – in some regions - can be a secondary member of one or two others. The use of ICT is very limited since the main interactions take place during the monthly meetings.

Networks of Professionals (NoPs) are bottom up growing networks of company employees, distributed nation-wide. The goal of NoPs is not only to exchange but also to create new knowledge. The topics of the NoPs are to some extent parallel to those of the expertise groups. NoPs have to have at least five members in order to be granted official status and be given company backing and support. There are no rules relating to membership or functioning of the community. Individuals are free to join a NOP and may be member of more than one such group. The members interact through various ICT tools, but some also organize now and then a face-to-face meeting.

Performer Groups (PGs) are particularly focused on developing and storing best practices and guidelines for project management in certain domains. The storage is done in a dedicated software tool called Performer. The groups cannot be established without management approval, and employees wishing to join a Performer group must formally request membership via the group moderator. Anyone who is a member of a performer group can add information to the shared database, although the moderator has the final decision on whether items added to the database should be altered or removed. Staff that make requests for information contained in the Performer database may be granted access, although they will not become formal members.

Delft Cluster

Delft Cluster (DC) is a consortium of five organizations in the Netherlands specializing in the area of sustainable river-delta development. The consortium consists of research institutes and companies. This network of organizations was formally established in 1999 and is sponsored by the Dutch government. DC has defined seven themes of expertise and each of these themes has defined several projects in which interested sector organizations can participate. The projects contribute to the overall DC goal to strengthen its knowledge and position in the field of sustainable river-delta development. The five organizations have a common goal of developing and sharing knowledge about river-delta development, but at the same time they can be competitors when trying to acquire commercial or scientific projects. Members of the organizations meet each other in knowledge sharing communities but also in various kinds of other interactions such as research programs, projects or advisory boards. The DC cases give therefore many examples of 'overlapping memberships'.

The communities have varying practices concerning interactions: formal meetings, informal gatherings connected to other meetings such as committees or conferences. The role of ICT is rather limited. Most people involved have there own email facilities, but the communities as such are hardly supported by proprietary systems. DC has tried to introduce a groupware tool for all communities to use, in order to overcome incompatibility of systems used.

Oracle

Oracle Corporation is the world's second largest independent software company. The company offers its services in more than 145 countries around the world. Oracle's Europe and Middle East Africa (EMEA) division has over 12,000 employees and is host to over half of Oracle's subsidiaries. Communities of practice (or 'Professional Communities' as they are widely known in Oracle) existed for many years as informal networks of experts with common interests who regularly shared 'tricks of the trade'. However, since the year 2000 there has been a concentrated effort in EMEA to formalize some of these communities. This effort focused on building structured communities of practice that have a specific business purpose and reason for being. On the other hand 'communities of interest' which have no formal structure or sponsorship still play a role in peer-to-peer communication and collaboration.

Currently about 3,500 employees in EMEA (around 30%) are members of one or more communities, such as on systems for ERP, for Customer Relations Management or on Java development. There are over 80 CoPs, with sizes ranging between 17 members to about 500. The main goals of the CoPs are to spread and increase member knowledge, to develop professional skills, to help members to resolve problems quickly, and to help recruit and retain talent within the corporation. The problem solving function appears to dominate in many CoPs.

In all CoPs membership is open to anyone who wishes to join or is interested in the area. Oracle employees must be member of one community, although the employee can choose which PC to join. Each community is led by a formally recognized 'Community Leader' who is usually a well-respected subject matter expert with good leadership skills. The majority of these leaders have this role in addition to their primary role within a country organization and not as a full time job. In many of the most active communities the leaders are supported by a group of core members who drive the community with their active participation. A Professional Community Leader Bonus Award Program is in operation and this provides some assessment of the functioning of the Oracle communities.

Habiforum

Habiforum is the Dutch expert network for multiple space use, established to initiate and stimulate innovations in this area. To reach that goal Habiforum has set up approximately ten Communities of Practice. Every community within Habiforum is initiated by contracting a so-called core-team, which then attracts other members. All the communities within Habiforum are supported by a website for sharing documents and finding information on the topic and the members of the community. This website is sparsely used by the community, but face-to-face meetings and excursions are successful. We had the opportunity to study two of these communities in-depth, the communities MultiSpace and

Transferia (fictitious names). The core-team of MultiSpace unites five persons of four different companies and institutions active in this field: three consultants, an architect and a researcher. It focuses on multiple space use in industrial estates. To find more members for the community the core-team relied on their networks of clients and colleagues. In the community mainly local authorities are represented, but also real estate developers and researchers. These institutions had to pay a fee to become a member. Membership of the community includes free access to all activities for at least two of their employees and free access to the closed part of the website of the community. One type of meeting that is organized to stimulate knowledge sharing is the so-called Pressure Cooker, a 24-hour meeting combining social activities with intensive brainstorm sessions.

The community Transferia (pseudonym) consists of a group of top-level managers of various organizations associated with the issue of developing transport connection points, so-called transferia. This closed group meets about 4 times a year to discuss the possibility of finding *integrated* solutions for the design of such transferia, instead of the traditional way of having one-to-one meetings between project developer and each of the related organizations. These top managers meet to exchange their experiences and viewpoints but also to make deals with their colleagues in an informal setting. Apart from having meetings, the top managers also have excursions to existing transferia, where they interview people at the spot. In this way they can bridge the distance between their high-level office position and the reality of the design and functioning of transferia.

Our group studied all the above-mentioned communities personally. Information about one other knowledge sharing communities could be derived from direct communications with expert informants, i.e. the community of Shell drillers.

Shell

Shell is an oil company of Dutch - British origin. The organization is divided among the three basic businesses of oil, chemicals, and exploration and production (E&P). The 'division' of E&P has ca. 30,000 employees, of which about 70% is member of some kind of network. In 1998 Shell contained many small communities of 20 to 300 members. The groups were mostly informal in origin, with hardly any structure or facilitation. In 1999, the small groups were combined into global networks called communities of practice. In E&P communities can be found on the issues such as sub-surface processes, of surface processes and of wells. Such CoPs may have 1500 to 2000 members. Smaller communities are dealing with issues of e.g. competitive intelligence or of Human Relations. The communities have so-called 'hub-coordinators' for facilitation. The role of most communities is limited to daily problem solving. They serve mainly as a source of information for those members who have a problem in their work and seek the expertise of colleagues to solve this problem. Embryonic subgroups may form for a short time, discussing a specific issue. Members do not meet face-to-face, but send their questions and reactions via a simple email discussion list facility. A department responsible for working standards regularly analyses the email messages to find elements that may be turned into standards. In this way shared knowledge is turned into organizational knowledge.

Basic dimensions and archetypes

The communities discussed above were characterized in terms of a low, middle or high position on each of the identified aspects. The scores for each community can be found in the Appendix (Appendix, Table I). The analysis of the data in Table I of the appendix proceeded in two steps. First the scores of the nine communities on the eleven aspects were visually compared. Through inspection it was clear that the scoring on some aspects were completely identical. For the rest correlation coefficients (spearman rho) were computed. On first sight the set of communities presented seems to be a very small sample and too limited to calculate correlations. However, one has to take into account that some of these communities stand in fact for a series of 'sister-communities'. We studied in detail only one Unilever community, but several other Unilever communities have about the same characteristics. Of the AtosOrigin communities we studied in fact four expertise groups, while in the Oracle Company we studied six communities.

It appeared that certain patterns of scores were highly related, resulting in the identification of two clusters of aspects, which can be considered to be two basic dimensions for differentiating knowledge communities. It must be noted that the identification of clusters of related aspects does NOT imply that all the aspects in one cluster are basically identical. Aspects are placed in the same cluster because they tend to go together in the communities studied. Nevertheless, the discussion below will highlight that there are good reasons to speak of two underlying dimensions.

The first cluster: Institutionalization. The patterns of scores on the first five aspects in table 4, were either the same (contract value, composition and boundary) or correlated higher than rho=.80, p<.01[1] which each other, while correlating low with other aspects. These relations imply that the purpose of having organizational knowledge development as objective goes together with having strong accessibility rules and institutionalized coordination, in short: high formality. On the other hand, a focus on individual learning and problem solving is found in communities, which are open for new members and have relatively

---

[1] This is a spearman correlation, significant at the .01 level. Since the number of observations is small and the number of aspects relatively large, these correlation coefficients have to be interpreted with care.

low formalization. This dimension is called '**institutionalization**'. Size appears to be quite strongly negatively related (rho= -89, p=.001) to the aspects in this cluster, particularly to formalization. It indicates that the highly institutionalized communities are obviously quite small, compared with the less institutionalized ones.

The second cluster: Connectivity. Also the pattern of the community scores on the Reciprocity (level of interaction between members) and Identity (having feelings of cohesion and belongingness) dimensions were almost completely identical. This dimension is called '**connectivity**'. Interestingly, size is also related to this cluster, i.e. rho= -.62 (p=.04) with reciprocity and rho= -.71, (p=.016) with identity. This suggests that the smaller the communities, the higher the connectivity.

The three last aspects, i.e. being intra- or inter- organizational, geographical dispersion and mode of interaction, were also expected to form a cluster. This was based on the idea that organizational dispersion would imply geographical dispersion, and that dispersed group members would communicate by electronic means. However, neither substantial relations amongst these three aspects, nor with the other aspects were found. As far as we can conclude on the basis of this set of communities, it appears that intra-organizational communities can be as widely dispersed geographically as inter-organizational communities. Formulated in this way, this is quite plausible, given the multinational character of many of these companies. More remarkable however is that some highly dispersed communities, such as the globally dispersed Unilever community, are not communicating more in mediated ways than less dispersed communities. It supports the notion that face to face meetings are deemed to be of high importance, even for community members working at a great distance from each other.

The two dimensions are represented in figure 2 and the eleven knowledge sharing groups presented above are plotted into this two dimensional space (bold), on the basis of their factor scores. Added are also the types of knowledge communities described by the authors presented in section 5. These communities are not specific concrete communities, such as the bold ones, but generalized types. However, they are derived from experience with real knowledge communities in companies and described in sufficient detail in the literature to be positioned quite well in figure 2. The patterns in figure 2, and also the discussion in section 5, suggest that knowledge communities cluster in four, or perhaps five, types:

1. Informal communities: Groups of employees with a common area of interest, often closely related to their work (practice), with substantial interaction, a common history and 'culture' (shared concepts, ideas, stories etc). Their main purpose is to learn from each other; transfer of this common knowledge to the company is of less importance. However, some organizations recognize the potential gap between individual learning and organizational learning and nominate specialists who have to analyze what is discussed in these communities and who may turn this harvest into new ideas, concepts and guidelines for the organization.

These communities are generally not very formalized, although some may receive support when they have proven their value. These groups are to some extent similar to the original Lave and Wenger (1991) communities of practice (although geographically and organizationally much more dispersed), which may be the reason that most of them are called 'Community of Practice', while most other knowledge sharing communities receive other names. These communities grow spontaneously, are either small altogether or have a small core and a larger circle of peripheral members. Two success conditions are probably found in a very active coordinator or core group and adequate ICT support.

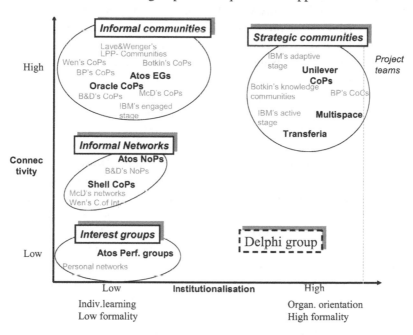

Figure 2. A classification of knowledge sharing groups in three dimensional space
B&D=Brown and Duguid; BP=British Petrol; McD=McDermott; Wen=Wenger

2. Informal Networks. Between the Informal Communities and the next (third) type, i.e. the Interest Groups, many scholars identify a group with intermediate interaction and identity. Brown and Duguid (1991) speak of Network of Professionals, who consist of members from various organizations and are much larger than what they call CoPs. The members of NoPs work on a similar domain and communicate, but may never meet and don't take common action. McDermott (1996b) speaks of networks of people who share a common interest, exchange questions and solutions, but have little sense of common identity and never or rarely meet as a network. Andriessen et al. (2004) identify the Problem Solving Community, consisting of employees of the same discipline, exchanging questions and answers concerning the solution of certain practical problems. Although the size may be quite large they still display some form of group identity, based on commonality in function and organization. Informal Networks have limited purposes and seem to thrive without many success conditions, except minimal commitment and good email connections.

3. *Interest groups*, i.e. groups of people who have no other interest than to hear and learn individually about a certain topic. These groups have very low formality, members come in and leave easily, there are no clear boundaries and also limited interaction and identity. Most members do not interact or know each other and the main knowledge exchanging activity is often that individual members all interact bilaterally with the same information source. These groups are often very large. Some are the totality of all employees who consult the same company intranet and have as common identity only the fact that they are all member of the same company. All these groups have a high virtuality, i.e. communication in this type of community is through electronic means. Actually the existence of Intranets and other electronic means have given rise to this type of networks. The quality of Interest Groups is a.o. dependent on the quality of the information provided and the accessibility of the website.

4. *Strategic communities* i.e. groups of experts having the same sense of common culture and identity as Informal communities. However activities are more oriented towards *organizational learning*. They are highly supported with resources and have a strong 'contract value' i.e. they are expected (implicitly or explicitly) to perform for the company; develop best practices or even innovative solutions. They often consist mainly of a limited number of experts, without any periphery of 'lurkers', since membership is not open. In some cases (like BP's Communities of Commitment), these groups resemble project teams and sometimes cross the border between knowledge communities (learning oriented) and workgroups or task forces (product oriented). Like most knowledge communities in large companies, many of these strategic communities are organizationally and geographically distributed and communicate therefore electronically. Some of them however do limit their interaction mainly to face-to-face meetings. Strategic communities require intensive preparation, member selection, support and coordination to be effective.

5. *The Delphi community?* The existence of a fourth but empty quadrant in figure 2 raises the question whether there exists a fifth type of community. This would imply a network of professionals, with high organization (and innovation) orientation and with high formality, but with low interaction and common identity. A social structure with these characteristics seems at first sight to be quite a strange phenomenon. High formality, such as reflected in a selective recruitment of members, having rules and roles, such as a coordinator, seems to

be difficult to combine with lack of interaction and group feeling. Nevertheless it is possible to imagine theoretically such a phenomenon (although it would probably not be called a 'community'). It would consist of a number of selected experts, who do not interact reciprocally and have no cohesion whatsoever. However, a coordinator would deal bilaterally with these experts, and he could 'extract' innovative ideas for the company through a kind of Delphi methodology. This methodology implies that the experts provide opinions and ideas and react upon the suggestions of the other experts. This is a kind of knowledge sharing. Although I do not know of the existence of such a group, it may serve the purpose of exchanging knowledge for the sake of both personal learning and organizational innovation. It would therefore belong to the 'family' of knowledge sharing groups.

Discussion

The analysis in this article has resulted in the identification of five archetypes of knowledge sharing communities, of which one, the Delphi community, has not been found yet in community research, but is at least theoretically possible. The Strategic Community is characterized by high interaction and identity and also high formalization, existing only of a 'core' of members. The Informal Community has high interaction and identity, but low formalization. It often consists of a core of active members and a large periphery (and possibly 'cliques'). Informal Networks have medium interaction and low formality. Generally there is no core – periphery differentiation. Interest Groups have both low interaction and low formalization and may be said to exist only of peripheral members. The Delphi Community finally has low interaction and identity but high institutionalization. There is no core and no periphery, but only a process of 'extraction' of information by a coordinator. Of course these are ideal types, which means that in actual practice communities may be found that have characteristics of more than one type or oscillate between types.

Having identified four or perhaps five basic types implies that one should be very careful with *terminology*. Different terms have been used such as community of practice, community of interest, community of commitment, interest group, network, network of practice, knowledge network, knowledge community, internal community, expanded community, formal network and epistemic community. Some terms denote the same phenomenon, while for instance the same term of 'community of practice' has been applied to different types of communities, that is, to strategic communities, to informal communities and to informal networks (seldom to interest groups). I make a plea for indeed employing a wide definition for the term 'community of practice', in such a way that it covers each of the three archetypes.

Dispersion or technology. Two dimensions appear to be sufficient to describe the main differences between communities and to identify the five archetypes.

The expectation concerning the existence of a third dimension, i.e. 'dispersion', including mode of interaction, was not supported. Our studies, however, suggest that differences between *business unit* communities, *organization communities* and *inter-organizational communities* appear to be quite strong. The differences between intra-organizational communities (level 1 and 2) and inter-organizational communities (level 3) are rather strong and essential. Identification, and particularly formalization is quite different in nature for these two 'levels', which may imply that we should distinguish in all five archetypes *an A-type (intrA-organizational) and a B-type (Between-organizational)*.

Dynamic changes. The concept of 'archetype' should not be associated with stability and clarity of boundaries. On the contrary, communities are generally quite loosely institutionalized, with shifting membership and also shifting purposes. Particularly a shift of purpose over time is quite common. Actually, communities are not static but dynamic. Classification may help in the identification of certain characteristics and in developing support, but communities often change in nature. In a previous section the difference between life cycle dynamics and evolutionary dynamics was expounded.

A third type of dynamics may be called *subgrouping*. In our experience communities thrive and change also through the emergence of subgroups. The purpose of these subgroups may be to prepare a special meeting, to develop a certain plan, which is afterwards again discussed in the whole community, or just to communicate about a special issue that may not (yet) be interesting for the whole community. An example is what happened in the Oracle community of the AtosOrigin company, where a subgroup of members developed a plan to transfer their experience in the newest Oracle database design methods to the rest of the company.

Research agenda: The central dimensions and the archetypes have been identified on the basis of an in-depth analysis of literature and case study material. Together they can be viewed as a theory about the variety of knowledge sharing groups. Empirical research is needed however to confirm or specify this theory. This implies particular attention to the following questions:

- Do the various aspects in actual practice indeed correlate as stated, and are institutionalization and connectivity indeed basic dimensions for mapping knowledge sharing groups?
- Do the first four archetypes indeed crystallize at the indicated places in the 2- dimensional space, or are they to be found 'all over the place' i.e. can they have all combinations of the two dimensions?
- Are the A-type (intra-organizational) and B-type (between-organizational) to be found in each archetype and are the differences in each archetype comparable?
- Is the Delphi community a viable knowledge sharing community? Does it exist already?

- What are the success conditions for the various archetypes?

To achieve answers to these questions it is necessary to compare systematically the characteristics of many diverse knowledge-sharing communities. Towards this end a research program and standardized assessment tools have been developed (Andriessen and Verburg 2004).

References

Allee, Verna (2000). *Knowledge Networks and Communities of Practice.* http://www.odnetwork.org/odponline/vol32n4/knowledgenets.htmldecember

Andriessen, J. H. Erik, Mirjam Huis in 't Veld and Maura Soekijad (2004). Communities of Practice for Knowledge Sharing. In J. H. Erik and Andriessen and Babette Fahlbruch (Eds.), *How to manage experience sharing: From organizational surprises to organizational knowledge.* p173-194. Oxford, UK: Elsevier.

Botkin, James,W (1999). *Smart business: how knowledge communities can revolutionize your company.* New York: The Free Press.

Brown, John Seeley and Paul Duguid (1991). Organizational Learning and Communities-of-Practice. Towards a Unified View of Working, Learning, and Innovation. *Organization Science 2/1*: 40-57

Brown, John Seeley and Paul Duguid (2001). Knowledge and Organization; A Social-practice Perspective. *Organization Science 12/2*: 198-213.

Collison, Chris (1999). Connecting the new organization. How BP Amoco encourages post-merger collaboration. *Knowledge Management Review 7/2*: 12-15.

Gongla, Patricia and Christine R. Rizzuto (2001). Evolving communities of practice: IBM Global Service experience. *IBM Systems Journal,* 40/4: 842-862.

Hansen, Morton T., Nitin Nohria and Thomas Tierney (2000) What's your strategy for managing knowledge? *Harvard Business Review,* 77/2: 106-116.

Huysman, Marleen, and Dirk de Wit (2002) *Knowledge sharing in practice.* Dordrecht: The Netherlands: Kluwer.

Kimble, Chris, Paul Hildreth and Peter Wright (2000). Communities of Practice: Going Virtual. In Yogesh. Malhotra (Ed.) *Knowledge Management and Business Model Innovation,* 220-234. Hersey, London: Idea Group Publishing.

Lave, Jean and Etienne Wenger (1991). *Situated Learning. Legitimate Peripheral Participation.* Cambridge: University Press.

McDermott, Richard (1999a). Learning across Teams: The Role of Communities of Practice in Team Organizations. *Knowledge Management Review,* 7/3.

McDermott, Richard (1999b). Nurturing Three Dimensional Communities of Practice: How to make the most out of human networks. *Knowledge Management Review,* fall .

Orr, Julian E. (1990). Sharing knowledge, celebrating identity: Community memory in a service culture. In P. Middleton and D. Edwards (Eds.) *Collective remembering: memory in society.*, p167-189. London: Sage Publications.

Prusak, Laurence and Don Cohen (2001). How to invest in Social Capital. *Harvard Business Review,* 79/3, 86-93.

Ruuska, I., and M. Vartiainen (2003). Communities and other social structures for knowledge sharing - A case study in an Internet consultancy company. In M. Huysman, E. Wenger, and V. Wulf (Eds.), *Communities and Technologies*: Dordrecht, Kluwer Academic Pub.

Wenger, E. (1998). *Communities of Practice; Learning, Meaning, and Identity.* Cambridge, University Press.

Wenger, Etienne (2000). Communities of Practice and Social Learning Systems. *Organization,* 7/2: 225-247

Wenger, Etienne and Snyder, W. M. (2000). Communities of Practice: The Organizational Frontier. *Harvard Business Review,* 78/1: 139-145.

Appendix

- Purpose: 1=individual organization; 2= both; 3=organizational orientation (ORGORI)
- Contract value: 1=low; 2= medium; 3=high (CONTRAC)
- Formalisation: 1=no appointed leader, few rules and procedures; 2=appointed leader; 3=appointed leader, several rules and procedures (FORMAL)
- Composition: 1=all kinds of members; 3=only experts; (no score 2) (EXPERTS)
- Boundary: 1=access for anyone; 2=limited membership access; 3=closed membership (CLOSED)
- Reciprocity: 1=low level of interaction; 2=medium; 3=high level (RECIPROC)
- Identity: 1=low level of shared feeling of group identity; 2=medium; 3=high level (IDENTITY)
- Size: 1=10-40; 2=41-150; 3= >150 members (SIZE)
- Intra-organizational: 1=Interorganizational; 2=Intra-organizational but from different business units in very large companies; 3=Intra-organizational in relatively small companies (INTRA-ORGAN)
- Geographical dispersion: 1=local; 2=national; 3=international (DISPERSE)
- Mode of interaction: 1=mainly face to face communication; 2=both; 3=mainly ICT based communication (ICTUSE)

Table A. Meaning of scores for each key aspect.

	Uni-lever	Atos EG	Atos NoP	Atos PG	Transferia.	Oracle	Multi space	Shell Drill	User Grp
Purpose	3	1	2	3	2	1	2	1	1
Contract Value	3	1	1	3	3	1	3	1	1
Formalization	3	2	1	3	3	2	3	1	1
Composition	3	1	1	3	3	1	3	1	1
Boundary	3	1	1	3	3	1	2	1	1
Reciprocity	2	3	2	3	2	2	2	2	1
Identity	3	3	2	3	2	2	2	2	1
Size	1	1	2	1	1	2	1	3	3
Intra-organ.	2	3	3	3	1	2	1	2	1
Geogr. Dispersion	3	1	2	2	2	3	2	3	3
Mode of interaction	2	1	3	3	1	3	1	3	3

Table B. Scoring of the communities on the key aspects

	Orgori	Contrac	Formal	Experts	Closed	Reciproc	Identity	Size	Intraorg	Disperse	Ictuse
ORGORI	1,000	**,833**	*,705*	**,833**	**,857**	,272	,508	*-,646*	-,129	,186	-,159
CONTRACT	**,833**	1,000	**,926**	1,000	**,968**	,207	,387	**-,767**	-,509	,139	-,484
FORMAL	*,705*	**,926**	1,000	**,926**	**,896**	,394	,538	**-,892**	-,505	,133	-,598
EXPERTS	**,833**	1,000	**,926**	1,000	**,968**	,207	,387	**-,767**	-,509	,139	-,484
CLOSED	**,857**	**,968**	**,896**	**,968**	1,000	,245	,458	*-,742*	-,408	,169	-,396
RECIPROC	,272	,207	,394	,207	,245	1,000	**,846**	*-,623*	,240	-,080	-,245
IDENTITY	,508	,387	,538	,387	,458	**,846**	1,000	*-,711*	,169	,129	-,292
SIZE	*-,646*	**-,767**	**-,892**	**-,767**	-,742	*-,623*	-,711	1,000	,266	,118	*,742*
INTRAORG	-,129	-,509	-,505	-,509	-,408	,240	,169	,266	1,000	-,486	,508
DISPERSE	,186	,139	,133	,139	,169	-,080	,129	,118	-,486	1,000	,269
ICTUSE	-,159	-,484	*-,598*	-,484	-,396	-,245	-,292	,742	,508	,269	1,000

Bold: Correlation is significant at the .01 level (1-tailed).
Italic: Correlation is significant at the .05 level (1-tailed).

Table C. Spearman Rho correlations between the key aspects of knowledge communities. On the number of observations, see the discussion in section 7.

Local Virtuality in an Organization: Implications for Community of Practice

Anabel Quan-Haase[+], Barry Wellman[*]
[+]University of Western Ontario, Canada; [*]University of Toronto, Canada
aquan@uwo.ca, wellman@chass.utoronto.ca

Abstract. We focus on two phenomena in our case study of a high-tech firm. *Local virtuality*: The pervasive use of computer mediated communication for interaction with physical proximate people, even when located near-by. *Hyperconnectivity*: The instant availability of people for communication anywhere and anytime. We show that computer mediated communication has gone beyond long-distance media to be the predominant mode of communication. The result is a high level of trust and community, especially in a department with high interdependence and a common goal.

A Computer Mediated Organization

Even as computer mediated communication (CMC) – the internet and all that – permeates most organizations, there is more assertion than evidence about how CMC is actually affecting them. How does CMC affect communication, community and trust in organizations? The routinized, normalized use of CMC is especially evident in high-tech companies of knowledge workers whose employees are technologically savvy. Hence, we use a case study of communication in such a high-tech firm to address this question. We focus especially on two phenomena in the firm. (1) *Local virtuality*: The pervasive use of computer mediated communication for interaction with physical proximate people, even when located near-by. (2) *Hyperconnectivity*: The instant availability of people for communication anywhere and anytime.

P. van den Besselaar et al. (eds.), Communities and Technologies 2005, 215-238.

We argue that CMC facilitates collaboration, but only when it works within the norms and structure of collaborative community. We suggest that computer-supported social networks flourish in organizations where information represents a key asset, informal networks have supplemented traditional hierarchies, the flow of information has become critical for success, and communication often crosses work group and organizational boundaries. We ask if collaboration in such a community is based on an interdependent, organic solidarity where people feel a sense of reciprocity toward other members of the community and make their information freely available? Are relations principally peer-to-peer or hierarchical? We wonder if employees are bridging group and physical boundaries as the information and communication technologies (ICT)-networked organization contends? Is communication across boundaries occurring at the expense of local, within-group communication?[1]

The debate about the effects of technology on organizational communities is a continuation of a 150-year-long tradition in the social sciences to see if community is declining or flourishing since the Industrial Revolution. Our research calls into question two beliefs: One, that CMC destroys community or at least is ineffective because it is disconnected from community; the other that CMC enables enormous increase in cooperation by allowing far-flung people to interact. The first of these sees only traditional community as valid; the second ignores the need for community and trust entirely. Our argument is a third one: that CMC enables wider collaboration but only when it works within the norms of collaborative community.[2]

Rather than analytically isolating CMC, we study it in the real world context of how it is embedded in a variety of ways in which workers actually communicate, including FTF and telephone communication. We show how CMC has become routinized and integrated in an organization, creating hyperconnected local virtualities of ubiquitous, multiple communication. We analyze how the different characteristics of specific CMCs afford somewhat different communication possibilities. For example, the store and forward nature of email supports asynchronous exchanges where sender and receiver do not have to be online simultaneously. By contrast, instant messaging (IM) demands simultaneous presence for successful communication.[3]

---

[1] Émile Durkheim's seminal discussion of organic solidarity, *The Division of Labor in Society*, was published in French in 1893 and translated into English in 1933.

[2] The debate about the internet and community is collated and summarized in Wellman and Haythornthwaite (2002), Walther (1997), and Spears and Lea (1992).

[3] Asynchronous communication is also starting to become more popular on IM as teenagers and adolescents leave each other messages when not online.

KME: A Case Study

We use a case study of a high-tech, CMC-pervaded organization to illuminate the situation. Knowledge Media Enterprises ("KME", a pseudonym) is an 80-employee high-tech corporation located in a major North American city. KME was founded in 1997 and expanded during the technology boom. Its involvement in knowledge-intensive activity and its high reliance on CMC make it a good place to study collaborative community in a networked organization. KME is a post-industrial firm that offers knowledge-based services and software to clients for whom it hosts and facilitates online communities of practice. As a high-tech firm, KME has the latest communication equipment, and all employees are technologically savvy. This makes KME a good place to investigate how CMC support collaborative community.

Data collection took place in 2002 through surveys, interviews, and observations: 27 out of 28 departmental employees responded to the survey: 11 in the software development department and 16 in the client services department. The lengthy self-administered survey gathered information about communication at each of three social/locational distances: within the department, with other colleagues in the organization, and with people outside the organization. [4] In addition, participants reported about how often they seek information from and socialize with colleagues in both the software development and client services departments. This allowed us to examine employees' social networks.

Ten survey participants were interviewed by Quan-Haase in December 2002, with each interview lasting approximately 45 minutes. Five employees were recruited from each department, coming from a range of positions and roles. The interviews focused on the employees' use of information sources, social contact, communication patterns, problem solving techniques and use of media.

There were four women in the sub-sample; this ratio is approximately representative of the gender distribution in the complete sample. Participation in the interviews and observations was voluntary.

This chapter is based on questions in the interviews about the use of media. The purpose of these questions was to understand participants' personal media use and unique media profiles, including what media participants believe are appropriate for communicating with different types of communication partners and for communicating different types of messages. In this way, the social context of media use also could be examined.

Specifically, participants were asked what type of media they use on a daily basis to communicate with colleagues inside and outside of KME. They were also

---

[4] For more information about the use of information sources and working relationships in KME, see Quan-Haase and Cothrel (2003), Quan-Haase (2004), Quan-Haase and Wellman (2004, 2005). The scale for the instrumental, social and media networks was: 1="never"; 2="a few times a year;" 3="1/month;" 4="1/week;" 5="several times a week"; 6="1/day"; 7="several times a day."

asked about each medium's relevance for their work in terms of frequency of use and types of tasks performed. To obtain more detailed information on media use, participants were also asked about what aspects of each medium they perceived as most useful – and why. In addition, participants were asked to report what type of medium they thought of as optimum for specific kinds of communication and information search and to discuss the characteristics of the medium that they felt made it the best choice. Participants were also asked to report specific instances that were representative of their use of various media.

The interviews were tape-recorded, transcribed, and imported into NVIVO software that is specifically designed for the analysis of interviews. We followed Anselm Strauss' grounded theory when using NVIVO to code the interviews, developing themes through coding. We discuss here only on the themes that relate to media use, the maintenance of community.

Quan-Haase also observed full-day work practices to help understanding of how people handled CMC, and how they fit CMC into their relationships and communication. She observed the everyday work practices of a sub-sample of 10 KME employees for two weeks: each department was observed for one week. One-on-one observations were conducted during employee's workdays because otherwise interactions taking place online would have been missed.

The analytic framework employed for the observations was a combination of grounded theory and social network analysis. Notes were taken on a daily basis and behaviors were recorded in a time diary. The notes were then coded and themes were developed in the same grounded theory manner as with interviews. Social network analysis guided the observations by focusing our attention on social relationships and their influence on the choice and use of media.

The one-on-one observations started at 9.00 AM and finished when the employee left the office (at approximately 4.30 PM). Through one-on-one observations of a workday, all FTF and online interactions could be observed and recorded, including email, instant messaging, FTF and phone exchanges. The start and end time, duration, and content of interaction were recorded.

The Software Development and Client Services Departments at KME

We compare work roles and communication patterns in two main KME departments: *software development* and *client services*. While tasks are somewhat similar within each department, they are different across the two departments. The *software development* department had existed for 2.5 years and consists of 12 employees.[5] Its main task is to create software packages that are largely used by the client services department. The *client services* department had existed as a functional department for 4.0 years and consists of 16 employees. The client

[5] At the time of data collection, one employee from the software development department was on holidays and did not participate in the study.

services department supports communities of practice for other organizations that operate online to exchange knowledge.[6] Some of their clients are units of large, world-famous organizations. The department works hard and skillfully to create *virtual localities:* online "spaces" where participants would sign on, come to know their electronic neighbors, and share best practices.

The software development department is expected to develop and implement new functionalities quickly. As the industry is under intensive scrutiny, software must be innovative and high quality. By contrast, the client services department is expected to work closely with clients and provide them with high-quality services. The client services department does not operate to the same extent under the time and innovation pressures of the software development department. The software development department is isolated from the rest of the company, a separation that developers regard as advantageously allowing them to concentrate on their work without being distracted by noise and interruptions from other departments. Software developers work in a large open space, with a washroom and a small kitchen next to the meeting room,

The work culture of the two departments is very different. The KME software development department consists of a highly qualified team of programmers that were formerly employed by companies such as Microsoft. The work culture of the software development department is characterized by the highly individualistic work habits of programmers.[7] Often, there is no predetermined work schedule. In the lead up to a release date, employees often work at least 50 to 60 hours per week. The software development department also frequently socializes by going out for lunch or coffee. Many of the meetings are impromptu, taking place in a small meeting room in the middle of the office. A high level of communication and exchange between members of the software development department is necessary because of the interdependence of all components of the project.[8] Moreover, consultation on design issues is also required because they affect the operability of the code. The software development department functions as a cohesive, horizontal team. Although three managers (1 upper manager and 2 middle managers) oversee the development cycle and ensure compatibility of the software components, individual department members work independently. Furthermore, all members of the department are involved in decision-making for

---

[6] A good discussion of what communities of practice are and their relevance to knowledge sharing in organizations can be found in Wenger (1998, 2000) as well as Wenger, McDermott, and Snyder (2002).

[7] In accord with Carmel and Sawyer (1998), the work of software developers reflects many attributes of the entrepreneurial legend: long hours, grit and determination, and high risk. See also Boorsook (2000), and Taylor (1999).

[8] Brooks (1974) in his investigation of how IBM developed the Systems 360 operating system documented how team behavior was the driver of software development. While this is also the case at KME, where employees work on a single software that requires high levels of integration, it is important to note that not all software development depends on highly interrelated tasks.

the development cycle. This is essential because individual components must be successfully integrated.

By contrast, the client services department works more independently. Community managers are not required to coordinate their activities because their work consists of interacting with individual clients. As such, community managers communicate primarily with clients and their respective managers. They work in cubicles. Their structure and culture is individualistic. Each online community has a dedicated community manager assigned to oversee the needs of the client and the users. This reporting structure means it is unnecessary for community managers to collaborate or communicate frequently with other community managers.

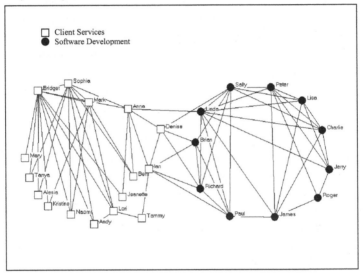

Figure 1. Information Network- Weekly Exchanges

Work Networks

We had not expected differences in communication to be extensive between the two departments. In practice, connectivity within the two departments has quite distinct patterns.[9] The software development department is a densely knit network that resembles a core team. Pairs of people in the software development department communicate more often on a daily and weekly basis. Moreover, people in the software development department communicate with a higher percentage of fellow department members than do those in the client services department. The software development department was relatively egalitarian, with managers and developers having similar communication patterns. This suggests that all individuals are sought for information regardless of their

---

[9] To investigate the instrumental networks of the two departments, we examined weekly exchanges of information among department members and between departments.

hierarchical position. By contrast, the client services department is sparsely connected. Most information exchanges occur between department members and managers, or among managers. There is little communication among department members. Figure 1 shows how middle and upper managers are clearly the most central persons in this department. Thus, managers in the client services department are more likely to be the harbingers of information in comparison to the software development department, where department members are as likely to control the flow of information as managers.

Socializing Networks

We asked KME employees how often they meet colleagues from their own department or from the client services department for lunch, coffee, dinner, and/or a drink. Like the work network, Figure 2 shows that the socializing network of the software development department is more densely-knit than the network of the client services department. Moreover, in the software development department, there is no difference between hierarchical positions in terms of socializing.

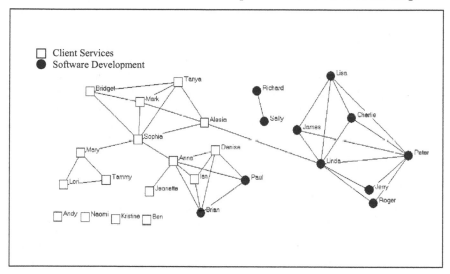

Figure 2. Social Network –Annual Interactions

By contrast, upper managers in the client services department are linked to each other, but in the socializing network they are not linked to other department members as they are in the work network. In the software development department, two department members are isolated from the rest of the department and only socialized with each other. In the client services department, there are more isolates – a total of four department members. In addition, the department is divided into three clusters linked by a single person: Sophia.

In short, work exchanges on a weekly basis occur primarily within the boundaries of the departments, with few bridging ties. Information exchanges follow the hierarchical structure of communication of the organization in the client services department, but not in the software development department, where department members exchange information among themselves. In the client services department, managers are central for the flow of information. Overall, socializing occurs less frequently than information exchange in both departments. Again, the software development department has denser socializing networks than the client services department. While socializing also primarily occurs within the boundaries of the departments, two members of the software development department are part of the socializing network of the client services department. Thus, important work and social linkages exist between the two departments.

High-Tech Collaborative Community at KME

Hyperconnectivity

KME people communicate a lot: informing, coordinating and collaborating. Collaboration in this technology-intensive firm takes place both face-to-face (FTF) and via CMC. Most communication is within the department. Employees report a mean of 285 days per year of within-department communication.[10] Although lower in frequency, CMC is also the predominant means of communication between departments, with a mean usage of 213 days per year for email and 215 for IM. Employees also communicate a mean of 178 days per year with people elsewhere in KME. The ratio of communication with colleagues elsewhere in the organization to within-department communication is 0.62.

When they communicate, employees share best practices and jointly address problems. Local virtuality – the use of CMC for local communication – is endemic.[11] Employees use CMC regularly as a convenient means of collaborative communication, creating a dense virtual network of exchange. Their frequent communications online have taught them whom they can trust – to respond, produce, provide reliable and valid information, and to keep confidences and commitments.

---

[10] The original 7-point scale has been transformed into days per year: "never" = 0; "a few times a year" = 5; 1/month = 12; "1/week" = 52; "several times a week" = 130; "1/day and several times a day" = 365. Much social network research has shown that while specific metrics of communication frequency tend to be unreliable, comparative metrics tend to be valid The ratios have been obtained by calculating the proportion of communication between distances. For example, the ratio "Colleagues Inside Organization/Work Group" is 178/285=0.62. In this example, the mean days per year communication with colleagues elsewhere in the organization is divided by the mean days per year communication within the work group.

[11] See Quan-Haase and Cothrel (2003) for a discussion of the emergence of local virtualities at KME.

Most are hyperconnected,[12] although the degree of hyperconnectivity is not only a result of the technology-intensive nature of KME. Task complexity and task interdependency are key factors in determining group structure and CMC use. Hyperconnectivity is more pronounced in the software development department, where tasks are interdependent, than it is in the client services department, where tasks are independent.

Collaborative Community

Formal Meetings and Informal Exchanges

Collaboration at KME operates through both formal meetings and informal exchanges. Formal meetings occur frequently in both departments. They are scheduled routinely in advance or on an *ad hoc* basis to deal with emergencies. They are held in the two departments' meeting rooms equipped with speakerphones and audiovisual equipment.

All employees in the software development department are customarily present during formal meetings. Ad hoc meetings are more common in the software development department because decisions made about the software can influence various components and it is considered important that all members are aware of these changes. Developers need to be up-to-date with changes, decisions or problems occurring with the software. Their expertise is valued, and their input is considered relevant. This emphasis on participation is a key aspect of the way the software development department works as a collaborative community.[13]

Formal meetings also occur frequently in the client services department. However, not all department members attend all meetings. The only ones who attend routinely scheduled meetings are those working on a specific account and the managers and middle managers. *Ad hoc* meetings typically take place between two or three employees. The client services department's large size makes it difficult to schedule meetings for the entire department. The lack of common meetings creates fragmentary understanding of other employees' challenges and problems in their accounts. This has lead to lower levels of understanding among employees and to a collaborative community that is less tightly knit.[14]

---

[12] A search on Google provided a number of hits for the term "hyperconnected." The way the term hyperconnected is used varies considerably among the sites. The term is usually not defined. Some links referred to a usage of the term hyperconnected in the context of mathematics. In general, in the context of technology, hyperconnected is used to refer to the connections between web sites. Biz Stone (2004) uses the term hyperconnected to refer to the linkages between weblogs. Wired Magazine used the term to describe children who are born in the digital age (Wired Magazine, 2002). None of the uses that we are aware of have applied the term to refer to physical work settings are workers are always on, available for communication anywhere and anytime.

[13] The high degree of collaboration among the software development department reflects previous arguments that the most important factor in software development is team interaction, which has been referred to as "peopleware" (DeMarco and Lister (1987) and Constantine (1995)).

[14] Cohen and Prusak (2002) see the creation of shared understandings among coworkers as a key

While formal meetings are important and provide an opportunity to share knowledge, communication, coordination and collaboration is usually informal. Most informal collaborations take place one-on-one rather than in groups, with people contacting someone to discuss their needs. The most common communication is asking questions to obtain clarification or work lore about a specific matter. However, there was frequent communication devoted to in-depth problem solving, where one person would help another make sense of a problem and think through various strategies to find a solution. A third type of communication occurred when the person originally contacted referred the questioner to others better equipped to help.

Commitment to Community

Commitment at KME is interpersonal, departmental, and organizational. FTF meetings and encounters provide a broad bandwidth of communication, enabling employees to assess voice tone, body language, and physical presentation of self. Frequent CMC has bred *interpersonal* awareness, understanding, and trust. But, while CMC does not allow people to smell each other, its highly frequent use provides a ubiquitous, backcloth of communication. The combination of CMC, FTF and phone communication enables people to understand the concrete interests and identities of others in collaborative relationships, and to provide the communication auspices for creating and maintaining trust.[15]

As a *department*, software development is more committed to collective community than client services. Software development's small size and focus on a single goal fosters group cohesion. The developers feel ownership of the software and commit much time and effort to improving it. By contrast, "community managers" in client services often work on different accounts. While most employees do similar work, their work does not contribute to a single effort: the success of one account is independent of others. Thus, department members do not share a common goal and do not feel part of a team in the same way as software developers do. Nonetheless, frequent email and IM – hyperconnectivity – in client services support a sense of collaborative community where people advise and help each other, making all easily reachable.

Employees in both departments are invested in the success of the *organization*. They have chosen to work in KME because it is a high-tech firm, and they believe that its products can lead to large revenues. Many of the employees identify with the firm and see their own personal success closely linked to it. The ethic of contribution to the collective value is spurred by the involvement often found in startup firms that struggle to find a niche in the market place and require the support of employees to be successful. Many KME employees had given up

---

organizational process. They see shared understandings as a prerequisite for the development of trust. Unless people can develop shared understandings, it will be difficult for them to trust each other.

[15] See also Heckscher and Adler (2005).

stable jobs in established companies with the hope that the startup will be successful and they will directly benefit from earnings They believe they have better chances for advancement than in established organizations, and often have potentially-lucrative stock or options as part of their compensation packages. Their contribution to the collective value consists of high-performance, long hours of work, and high commitment to the firm's goals. Thus, the ethic of contribution occurs through increasing the collective value as well as contributing to the success of others.

Media for Collaborative Community

Communication at KME has moved from the physical space to the virtual realm, where conversations consist of typed words. Clearly, local virtualities flourish in this high-tech organization,[16] where employees' work stations each have a computer terminal allowing them to easily send and receive messages via CMC. The physical setting is small, and people work in a crowded workspace. Moreover, people need to work with multiple others. Email – and especially IM – exchanges take less time than oral conversations allowing for a greater number of exchanges. Under these conditions, CMC is both more effective and less disruptive than oral communication – either FTF or telephonic.[17] This heavy reliance on CMC has not weakened workers' sense of collaborative community.

Some scholars have argued that CMC's limited capability in transmitting social cues about communication partners – such as voice tone, facial expressions, and body gestures – diminishes people's sense of connectivity. They consider CMC to be an inappropriate form of communication to promote collaborative community.[18] However, KME is permeated with strong social relationships, interpersonal trust, and vibrant networks of information exchange and coordination. Employees constantly help each other as they each have expertise in different areas and can pool together their knowledge toward joint problem solving.

CMC has not substituted for other forms of communication. Even though workers use CMC extensively to exchange messages and keep in touch with

---

[16] The term virtual localities is not new and has been used before in the study of rural communities, where it is defined as the use of email as a communication tool among non-anonymous parties and contrasted with global virtuality which refers to exchanges among anonymous parties (Koskikallio, 2002). We use the term here differently to describe local work settings where people are physically near each other and use CMC to exchange information, share best practices, and socialize (see Quan-Haase and Cothrel (2003) for a more detailed description).

[17] CMC is usually thought of as an alternative way of communication for long distance, boundary spanning exchanges (see Sproull and Kiesler (1991). Among the few studies of IM at work are Nardi, Whittaker and Bradner (2000). At KME, CMC is used for local exchanges as a result of a crowded work space and ease of use.

[18] These ideas about the lack of social cues in CMC compared to FTF are discussed in Rice (1993), Fish, Kraut, Root, & Rice (1992).

colleagues, they continue to value FTF meetings and phone conversations. Employees make an effort to use the phone or to walk over to their colleagues' desks to ask them a question. They see in these FTF meetings an important occasion to chat and to connect on a more personal level, which CMC does not provide in the same manner. Furthermore, people often arrange to meet via IM to get a coffee at a nearby Starbucks or go out for lunch.

Exchanges with a social purpose occur frequently between coworkers, and they create a sense of belonging to the organization, provide social support, and create meaningful work relationships. People build relationships, and their exchanges provide them with friendship, humor, and advice. Even though CMC currently does not have the capacity to transmit certain voice, visual, olfactory or touch cues, it allows for coworkers to remain in contact and to exchange social messages.[19]

Trust is in part a precursor for these vibrant networks. People interact more easily with those who they trust and feel close. Cohen and Prusak contend that trusting relationships among coworkers are the basis for knowledge sharing and joint problem solving.[20] They see the ties that link coworkers as the key factor leading to the success of a firm as they facilitate the flow of resources. Strong, trusting relationships are particularly relevant in the context of CMC because CMC can interrupt people's work. Interruption is in particular evident with IM interactions, where the message automatically pop-up on the screen. Nevertheless, when a close relationship links two people, then they do not perceive the interruption as intrusive. Trust plays an important role because employees need to trust that others will use the various media in appropriate ways, so that they don't interrupt others' work processes.

To some extent, CMC provides high-tech employees with an easier and more convenient form of communication because it allows for fast and continuous exchanges.[21] At KME, communication occurs almost simultaneously over multiple media, and not just sequentially. Employees often answer an IM and glance at their email while having a FTF conversation. IM takes priority over email, FTF, and the phone in this fast-paced environment, where people often must fulfill IM requests immediately. Thus, employees do not switch between media and people for communication, but rather use various media almost simultaneously to interact with different people.

---

[19] Although not used at KME, internet phones provide voice contact that mimic traditional telephones. They may develop additional capacity at a later time. Desktop videoconferencing systems have been around since the early 1990s (see, for example, Mantei, et al., 1991; Herbsleb & Olson, 2004). There have even been prototypes of remote transmission of smell and touch (Strong and Gaver 1996).

[20] Cohen and Prusak (2002) refer to the sum of relationships among coworkers that facilitate the flow of resources (information, knowledge, social support, etc.) in a firm as social capital. Social capital constitutes the key factor for success in a knowledge economy.

[21] See Kiesler and Sproull (1991) for first-order effects of technology. First-order effects of technology refer to increases in speed and efficiency related to the use of CMC in organizational communication.

In this local virtuality, fingers flying over keyboards appear to be easier than walking to another cubicle or picking up a phone. In light of media-message fit theories, the predominance of CMC is unexpected.[22] Yet, employees are already at their computers and staring at their screens. The time spent writing an email or an IM generally is shorter than the time it takes to lead a FTF or telephone conversation. As a consequence workers can communicate with each of their communication partners more frequently and they can communicate with more partners. In this way, IM and email combine to create hyperconnectivity.

CMC does not function as an independent communication system. Email and IM frequently leads to FTF encounters among colleagues. Often, employees would greet one another over IM and arrange to meet for lunch or coffee.

Thus, email, IM, FTF, and the phone serve different communication purposes, often working in synergy and not in competition with one another. FTF and the phone are used for dealing with complex problems that require extensive discussion. CMC is not disruptive of work processes in the same way that FTF and the telephone are. The physical setting at KME is small, and people work in a crowded workspace. Under these conditions, CMC provides an alternative and less disruptive means for communication. In addition, CMC provides unique features that are not available in FTF or phone exchanges. Email provides a medium to articulate complex issues and obtain responses that people can archive and refer to later. By contrast, IM serves as a meta-communication medium that affords informal talk about work, email exchanges, and other current organizational developments and concerns.

Computer Mediated Communication for Collaborative Community

CMC is not a single homogeneous medium.[23] Employees use email and IM in different ways.[24] Together, they help shape work community and trust at KME. Propelled through CMC, employees are to a large extent connected in real time opening the opportunity for a stream of constant exchanges. CMC has not only changed the speed of communication, but also its nature. Most obviously, both email and IM allow communication with spatially or temporally distant others, with email providing the additional ability to converse while not simultaneously logged on to the communication system. Employees can juggle multiple

---

[22] Message-media fit theory contends that the characteristics of media lead to different media choices (Daft & Lengel, 1986; Daft, Lengel, & Trevino, 1987). Messages that are complex or equivocal are transmitted via rich media, such as FTF and the phone because lean media, such as email, are not adequate.

[23] The fact that people use various media for different purposes suggests that a single dimension ranging from lean to rich is not sufficient to describe and predict media choice and adequacy, as message-media fit theory has attempted (Daft & Lengel, 1986; Daft, Lengel, & Trevino, 1987). Various media serve different purposes in different social context. Thus, while message-media fit theory is not refuted by the observations at KME, it needs to be expanded to include other relevant dimensions.

[24] In many organizations employees are now collaborating via IM, either as a complement to email or a replacement (Handel & Herbsleb, 2002; Herbsleb, Atkins, Boyer, Handel, & Finholt, 2002; Poe, 2001).

relationships, sometimes in small groups and sometimes in almost simultaneous one-to-one conversations. At KME, each person would have multiple IM windows open at the same time. Moving between IM windows – and thus conversations – is common practice. IM also partially solves the availability problem by providing information about who is logged on to the communication system, usually in their cubicle.[25] KME employees perceive sending an IM as a polite way of asking a question: the IM appears on the communication partners' screen alerting them of an incoming request, but unlike a phone call or FTF visit, the IM message does not force them to respond immediately.

KME has a strongly-emphasized culture of using IM. This is not only a matter of individual discretion, but also part of the norms of the organization. Employees rely on IM because of its speed and its real-time (synchronous) nature. Although employees could in principle ignore IM messages, in practice there is a norm of trying to reply within two minutes. This allows the senders of IMs to receive immediate feedback, at the cost of potentially interrupting the recipients. IM's ability to identify who is potentially available for contact promotes impromptu chats, requests for information, and clarification.

IM contributes to hyperconnectivity and facilitates collaborative community. Knowing whether other department members are connected or not and thus potentially available for communication creates a feeling of closeness and a sense of community. This is especially important in an environment were most employees spend the majority of their time sitting in cubicles in front of a desktop computer. IM provide the basis for routine exchanges that maintain a community of work. As IMs are not saved or archived, they represent a more transient, casual form of exchange. People often use IM for short social exchanges providing an opportunity to greet others or to share jokes. This promotes closeness among department members and integrates them into a web of online exchanges – both work and social. However, those with strong ties make more frequent use of IM than those with weaker ties. This strong-weak disparity is greater in IM than in email, phone or FTF contact.

People use email differently than IM. They would be more likely to send somebody they do not have a close, trusting relationship with an email because it is not synchronous and thus would not interrupt colleagues in their work. Furthermore, email is less often dashed off or used socially. Email leaves a record; it can be stored, checked at a later point in time and forwarded to other people in the department or organization. Email represents a more serious and instrumental form of communication. While people primarily use IM for one-on-one exchange of messages, email goes to a wider range of employees within the department and elsewhere in the organization.

---

[25] Nardi, Whittaker and Bradner (2000) conducted the first study to our knowledge about the use of IM in the workplace as a tool to identify other communication partners.

To a great extent, communication with other employees is the work of KME employees. They must obtain information; they must coordinate. Although hyperconnectivity creates new opportunities for exchange and collaboration leading to more dense networks, it also creates challenges. At times, IM-driven hyperconnectivity has negative effects on work processes. Each employee must deal with a larger number of requests that add up on a day-to-day basis. The social norms necessitate that employees be available for CMC, yet, KME employees frequently feel overloaded and at times overwhelmed by the number of incoming requests for information and coordination. Hypercommunication stops them from getting their "own work" done. Their densely knit, hyperconnected networks leads to interruptions while completing tasks. Employees are constantly multitasking, dealing simultaneously either with their own work demands and others' requests for information. Employees say they do not mind being available to answer others information requests, but the problem is that they often are not able to control when these interruptions occur. Clearly, the ease of sending CMC adds to the volume of communication.[26]

IM is the most disruptive, in part because the availability list allows people to know who else is around to communicate with.[27] It can have negative effects on work processes when employees feel overloaded with requests and cannot get their work done. Moreover, because people knew who else is around, they have expectations for how quickly they will get a response. When the expectations of rapid response are not met, conflict sometimes develops.

High-Tech Networking and Hierarchy

When we began studying KME we expected to find a networked, post-bureaucratic organization where people worked in shifting teams with multiple others, with little structured departmentalization and hierarchy. Instead, we have found KME to be a hybrid type of organization resembling an enabling bureaucracy, where rules about work and vertical and horizontal divisions of labor exist along with high levels of trust and community cohesion. [28]

KME has an explicit hierarchy that relates people and functions. The hierarchy provides a way of organizing individuals around work tasks as well as coordination and communication. Decision-making takes place at the top of the hierarchy and are communicated to the bottom. The impression from the decision-

---

[26] These findings are similar to those of a study of interruptions and availability in managerial jobs which found that managers want to be accessible to others, while at the same time maintaining control over these interruptions (Hudson, Christensen, Kellogg, and Erickson, 2002). See also the experiment done by Dabbish & Kraut (2004) showing that frequent monitoring of availability displays seriously affects attention.

[27] Kellogg and Erickson (2000) describe how information about a user that is transmitted by a communication system can be used for making social inferences about the status of the communication partner, including inferences about awareness, availability, and accountability.

[28] See Adler and Borys (1996).

making process is that KME continues to be a hierarchical organization. The roles and statuses of people at KME are clearly formalized. People know what their role is, to whom they report, and what the adequate type of engagement is.

On the other hand, KME is an enabling bureaucracy where rules about work and vertical and horizontal divisions of labor co-exist along with high levels of trust and community cohesion. Employees enjoy sufficient freedom to perform their job without needing to report constantly to their boss and asking for permission. Their meta-awareness of the reporting structure – combined with hyperconnectivity, trust, expertise, and experience – allows employees to work largely independently while connected to a larger departmental and organizational enterprise.

Bureaucracy and collaborative community worked side by side in both departments. Nonetheless, there were differences between departments in regard to the extent to which hierarchy determined communication. The client services department had a more pronounced hierarchy than the software development department as shown in Figure 1. In the client services department, departmental members occupy similar positions in the information and social networks suggesting that employees trust each other and information flows regardless of hierarchical position. The managers – Sally, Peter, and Charlie – have as many information exchanges as departmental members. By contrast, in the client services department, managers – Sophia, Bridget, Anna, Mark, and Ben – receive many more information requests than departmental members. This suggests that communication follows the hierarchical structure of the department with managers occupying central roles in the flow of information.

Although hierarchy and collaborative community can exist side by side, one consequence is an imbalance of expertise between management and the department members. In the case of KME, this imbalance refers to the knowledge required to manage online communities, and to design and develop the new software. While management has expertise with regards to the market, the sales, and the clients, they don't have a full understanding of the day-to-day tasks and problems of department members. The downside of this imbalance in expertise is that management cannot provide sufficient guidance in the execution of tasks; employees need to develop the expertise themselves. This places large responsibility on department members. Management trusts that they have the expertise to develop their own plan of action.

What is the role of CMC in this interplay between hierarchy and collaborative community? CMC supports communication among all employees providing an effective way to overcome status barriers. As discussed above, this is particularly the case in the software development department where department members need to be in close contact and constantly exchange expertise. Although in this department, the hierarchy is explicit, employees communicate via email and IM with those colleagues who have the expertise they need regardless of their hierarchical status. However, employees continue to be aware of status differences. While this is not reflected in their interactions within the department – where people knew each other and have established relationships of high trust – it clearly affects their interactions with the organization's management. CMC supports communication with all employees within the department, but does not remove hierarchical barriers outside the department.

In the client services department, hierarchical position influences to a greater extent who talks to whom than it does in the software development department (see Figure 1). The role of hierarchy also influences interactions via CMC. One form of accountability that is inherent in relationships with status differences is that employees feel compelled to reply to messages because receivers of messages knew that senders are aware that they have received the message. Thus, the awareness of others' availability leads to expectations in the sender about how long it should take the recipient to reply. A person's status within the hierarchy of the organization plays a key role in how they are replied to.

Conclusions

KME is a *local virtuality*. Most communication is via CMC, both email and IM. The high reliance on CMC is particularly interesting in light of the physical proximity of all employees. They are going online to exchange email and IM with colleagues who are sitting right next to them. The high volume of CMC use, within the department and beyond it, strongly suggests that CMC does not weaken trust in this organization. It is the social structure and ethic of contribution of the organization that is important to the formation of collaborative community; not the communication media alone. The KME way of working collaboratively involves the simultaneous independence of jobs combined with interdependencies. Although KME is not a thoroughly networked organization, people often have multiple work networks. They work simultaneously and sequentially with different members of their department.

KME is *hyperconnected*. The adding on of CMC to FTF and phone contact has created hyperconnectivity where community members – at work or elsewhere – are always connected to CMC and always available for communication. Employees can easily send an email or instant message (IM) to any other member of the organization regardless of status or formal role.[29] Hyperconnectivity has led to new forms of collaboration, in particular the constant monitoring of IMs.

KME is *glocalized*. Its members not only communicate via CMC locally, but CMC is even more their predominant means of communication with clients

---

[29] CMC can also lead to changes in organizational structure; in particular as leading to flatter hierarchies and horizontal forms of communication (Sproull and Kiesler (1991). At KME, CMC permeated the organization from the beginning.

elsewhere. Rather than the utopian dream of CMC making community independent of distance, CMC has become the way to communicate in this high-tech organization, both locally and globally.

CMC at KME affords *trust*. Our research shows that colleagues do not have to be in FTF contact to trust one another. There are frequent shorthand IM conversations, so much so that we marveled at their apparent intrusiveness. There are equally as frequent more structured emails that leave more time for thought, allow attaching documents, and provide an archive and paper trail. CMC intertwines with FTF encounters: both formal meetings and casual conversations. Our findings suggest that it is a fallacy that FTF contact is the only trustworthy form of communication. In a milieu with much individual networking and little direct supervision, it is hyperactive CMC that fosters collaborative community and trust within and between departments.

CMC at KME is *personalized and individuated*. Media choice theorists originally thought that people would choose between personal, individuated FTF communication and de-individuated CMC. That is clearly not the case at KME, where CMC use is personally tailored to specific relationships of work and friendship, and where CMC communication is inextricably entangled with FTF communication. These are not two separate worlds. Rather, they are multi-media ways of communicating and informing within formal and informal relationships.

Despite the formal hierarchical bureaucratic structuring of KME's departments, the departments – and KME itself -- are also networked. Of course, organizations have always had informal networks, but hyperconnectivity at KME allows more fluid and more active use of networked relationships, what Barry Wellman has called *networked individualism* and we have relabeled *individualized networks*. More people have the possibility to have links to people outside the workgroup and organization. These links serve as interconnectors between multiple networks, providing access to new information and possibly more creative problem solving.

While on an organizational level communication among employees was strongly influenced by hierarchy, we observed that there were differences between departments with regards to the extent to which hierarchy determined communication. In the client services department, hierarchy influenced who talked to whom, over what medium, and about what much more than in the software development department. Employees in the client services department were more aware of the hierarchical structure and behaved accordingly. By contrast, in the software development department hierarchy was less important for communication. Here the nature of the information needed and the expertise of colleagues determine communication.

The evidence provides a view that is more routinized and stable than a "networked organization" but more flexible and hyperconnected than a traditional bureaucratic organization. Employees are organized into departments. These departments significantly structure their work practices, and they are where most communication occurs - online as well as offline. Yet, KME is also a hyperconnected local virtuality. Within the stable framework of departments, its employees are communicating frequently and widely. There is no need to go to meetings; there is no need to get up from their cubicles. CMC provides them the flexibility and access to gain the information and coordination they need immediately – across and within departments. In short, while KME is not a networked organization, it is highly networked – with CMC networks providing the means for social networking.

Acknowledgements

Support for our research has been provided by BMO (the Bank of Montreal), Communication and Information Technology Ontario, the Institute of Knowledge Management (IBM), Mitel Networks, and the Social Science and Humanities Research Council of Canada. The first author acknowledges assistance from the Alumni Research Awards Program, Faculty of Social Science, the University of Western Ontario. We thank Paul Adler, Manuel Castells, Joseph Cothrel, Rob Cross, Charles Heckscher, Lynne Howarth, Richard Livesley, and Larry Prusak for their advice, and Alexis Kane Speer for her assistance. We especially want to thank all those employees at KME who completed the survey, and even more so, those who gave generously of their time with interviews and observations. A longer version of this chapter will appear in *Collaborative Community in Business and Society*, edited by Charles Heckscher and Paul Adler. New York: Oxford University Press, 2005. Used here by permission.

References

Adler, P.S. (2005). Beyond hacker idiocy. In C. Heckscher and P. Adler (eds.). *Collaborative Community in Business and Society*. New York: Oxford University Press (forthcoming).

Adler, P. S., & Borys, B. (1996). Two types of bureaucracy: Enabling and coercive. *Administrative Science Quarterly, 41*(1), 61-89.

Ahuja, M., & Carley, K. (1999). Network structure in virtual organizations. *Organization Science, 10*(6), 741-757.

Barlow, J. P., Birkets, S., Kelly, K., and Slouka, M. 1995. "What are we Doing On-Line." *Harper's,* August, pp. 35-46.

Bimber, B. A. (2003). *Information and American democracy: Technology in the evolution of political power*. Cambridge: Cambridge University Press.

Borsook, P. (2000). *Cyberselfish: A critical romp through the terribly libertarian culture of high tech*. NY: Public Affairs.

Bradner, E. (2001). *Social factors in the design and use of computer-mediated communication technology*. Unpublished doctoral dissertation, University of California, Irvine, CA.

Bradner, E., Kellogg, W. A., & Erickson, T. (1998). Babble: Supporting conversation in the workplace. *SIGGROUP Bulletin, 19*(3), 8-10.

Bradner, E., Kellogg, W. A., & Erickson, T. (1999). Social affordances of Babble: A field study of chat in the workplace. Paper presented at the ECSCW'99, the Sixth European Conference on Computer Supported Cooperative Work, Copenhagen, Denmark, 12-16 September.

Brooks, F. P. (1974). *The mythical man-month*. Reading, MA: Addison-Wesley.

Carmel, E. (1995). Cycle-time in packaged software firms. *Journal of Product Innovation Management, 12*(2), 110-123.

Carmel, E., & Sawyer, S. (1998). Packaged software development teams: What makes them different? *Information, Technology & People, 11*(1), 7-19.

Castells, M. (1996). *The rise of the network society*. Cambridge, MA: Blackwell.

Castells, M. (2000). *The Rise of the Network Society*. 2d. ed. Oxford: Blackwell.

Choo, C. W. (1998). *The knowing organization: How organizations use information to construct meaning, create knowledge, and make decisions*. New York: Oxford University Press.

Cohen, D., & Prusak, L. (2001). *In good company: How social capital makes organizations work*. Boston: Harvard Business School Press.

Constantine, L. L. (1995). *Constantine on peopleware*. Englewood Cliffs, NJ: Prentice Hall/Yourdon Press.

Culnan, M. J., & Markus, M. L. (1987). Information technologies. In F. M. Jablin, L. L. Putnam, K. H. Roberts, & L. W. Porter (Eds.), *Handbook of organizational communication: An interdisciplinary perspective* (pp. 420-443). Beverly Hills: CA: Sage.

Dabbish, L., & Kraut, R. (2004). Controlling interruptions: awareness displays and social motivation for coordination. *Proceedings of CSCW2004 conference,* Chicago, Nov (pp. 182-91).

Daft, R. L., & Lengel, R. H. (1986). Organizational information requirements, media richness and structural design. *Management Science, 32*(5), 554-571.

Daft, R. L., Lengel, R. H., & Trevino, L. K. (1987). Message equivocality, media selection and manager performance: Implications for information systems. *MIS Quarterly*.

Davenport, T. H., & Prusak, L. (1997). *Information ecology: Mastering the information and knowledge environment*. New York: Oxford University Press.

Davenport, T. H., & Prusak, L. (2000). *Working knowledge: How organizations manage what they know* (2nd ed.). Boston: Harvard Business School Press.

Davenport, T. O. (1999). *Human capital: What it is and why people invest in it* (1st ed.). San Francisco: Jossey-Bass.

DeMarco, T., & Lister, T. (1987). *Peopleware: Productive projects and teams*. NY: Dorsett House.

DiMaggio, P., Hargittai, E., Neuman, W. R., & Robinson, J. P. (2001). Social implications of the internet. *Annual Review of Sociology, 27*, 307-336.

Dubé, L. (1998). Teams in packaged software development: The software corp. Experience. *Information, Technology & People, 11*(1), 36-61.

Durkheim, E. (1960). *The division of labor in society* (2nd ed.). Glencoe, IL: Free Press.

Erickson, T., & Kellogg, W. A. (2000). Social translucence: An approach to designing systems that support social processes. *ACM Transactions on Computer-Human Interaction, 7*(1), 59-83.

Fischer, C. S. (1982). *To dwell among friends.* Berkeley, CA: University of California Press.

Fish, R., Kraut, R., Root, R., & Rice, R. (1992). Video as a technology for informal communication. *Communications of the ACM, 36*(1), 48-61.

Fox, R. 1995. "Newstrack." *Communications of the ACM* 38 (8): 11-12.

Hampton, K., & Wellman, B. (2003). Neighboring in Netville: How the Internet supports community and social capital in a wired suburb. *City & Community, 2*(4), 277-311.

Handel, M., & Herbsleb, J. D. (2002). What is chat doing in the workplace? Paper presented at the CSCW 2000, New Orleans, Louisiana, November 16-20.

Heckscher, C., & Adler, P. (2005). Introduction. In Charles Heckscher and Paul Adler (eds.), *Collaborative Community in Business and Society.* New York: Oxford University Press (forthcoming).

Heckscher, C., & Donnellon, A. (Eds.). (1994). *The post-bureaucratic organization: New perspectives on organizational change.* London: Sage

Herbsleb, J.D. & Olson, G. (Eds.) 2004. *Computer Supported Cooperative Work Conference Proceedings.* Chicago, November. New York: ACM Publications.

Herbsleb, J. D., Atkins, D. L., Boyer, D. G., Handel, M., & Finholt, T. A. (2002). Introducing instant messaging and chat in the workplace. Paper presented at the SIGCHI conference on Human factors in computing systems, Minneapolis, Minnesota, April 20-25.

Heydebrand, W. V. (1989). New organizational forms. *Work and Occupations, 16*, 323-357.

Hudson, J. M., Christensen, J., Kellogg, W. A., & Erickson, T. (2002). "I'd be overwhelmed, but it's just one more thing to do": Availability and interruption in research management. *Proceedings of the SIGCHI Conference on Human factors in computing systems*, Minneapolis, April 20-25, ACM Press, (pp. 97-104).

Jarvenpaa, S. L., & Ives, B. (1994). The global network organization of the future: Information management opportunities and challenges. *Journal of Management Information Systems, 10*(4), 25-57.

Katz, J. E., & Rice, R. E. (2002). Syntopia: Access, civic involvement, and social interaction on the net. In B. Wellman & C. Haythornthwaite (Eds.), *The Internet in everyday life.* Oxford: Blackwell.

Keil, M., & Carmel, E. (1995). Customer-developer links in software development. *Communications of the ACM, 38*(5), 33-44.

Kling, R. and Gerson, E. 1978. "The Social Dynamics of Technical Innovation in the Computing World." *Symbolic Interaction* 1: 133-46.

Koskikallio, I. (2002). Empowering rural communities (by ICT). Paper presented at the International Workshop, Helsinki, November 22-23.

Krishnan, M. S. (1998). The role of team factors in software cost and quality: An empirical analysis. *Information, Technology & People, 11*(1), 20 - 35.

Mantei, M, Baecker, B., Sellen, A., Buxton, W., Milligan, T. and Wellman, B. 1991. "Experiences in the Use of a Media Space. Reaching Through Technology." Pp. 203-208 in *Proceedings of the CHI '91 Conference*, Reading, MA: Addison-Wesley.

Miles, R. E., & Snow, C. C. (1986). Organizations: New concepts for new forms. *California Management Review, 28*(Summer), 62-73.

Monge, P. R., & Contractor, N. S. (1997). Emergence of communication networks. In F. M. Jablin & L. L. Putnam (Eds.), *Handbook of organizational communication* (2nd ed.). Thousand Oaks, CA: Sage.

Monge, P. R., & Contractor, N. S. (2003). *Theories of communication networks.* Oxford: Oxford University Press.

Nardi, B. A., Whittaker, S., & Bradner, E. (2000). Interaction and outeraction: Instant messaging in action. *Proceedings of Conference on Computer Supported Cooperative Work (CSCW)*, Philadelphia, Pennsylvania, December 2-6, ACM, Inc, (pp. 79-88).

Nohria, N., & Eccles, R. (1994). *Networks and organizations.* Boston, MA: Harvard Business School Press.

Orlikowski, W. J. (1996). Learning from Notes: Organizational issues in groupware implementation. In R. Kling (Ed.), *Computerization and controversy: Value conflicts and social choices* (2nd ed., pp. 173-189). San Diego: CA: Academic Press.

Poe, R. (2001). Instant messaging goes to work. *Business 2.0*, http://www.business2.com.

Quan-Haase, A. (2004). *Information brokering and technology use: A case study of a high-tech firm.* Unpublished Doctoral Thesis, Faculty of Information Studies, University of Toronto, Toronto.

Quan-Haase, A., & Cothrel, J. (2003). Uses of information sources in an Internet-era firm: Online and offline. In M. Huysman, E. Wenger, & V. Wulf (Eds.), *Communities and technologies* (pp. 143-162). Deventer, NL: Kluwer.

Quan-Haase, A., & Wellman, B. (2004). Networks of distance and media: A case study of a high-tech firm. *Analyse und Kritik, 28.*

Quan-Haase, A., Wellman, B., Witte, J., & Hampton, K. (2002). Capitalizing on the Internet: Social contact, civic engagement, and sense of community. In B. Wellman & C. Haythornthwaite (Eds.), *Internet and everyday life* (pp. 291-324). London, UK: Blackwell.

Rheingold, H. (2000). *The virtual community: Homesteading on the electronic frontier* (Rev. ed.). Cambridge, MA: MIT Press.

Spears, R., & Lea, M. (1994). Panacea or panopticon? The hidden power of computer-mediated communication. *British Journal of Communication, 21*, 427-459.

Sproull, L. S., & Kiesler, S. B. (1991). *Connections: New ways of working in the networked organization.* Cambridge, MA: MIT Press.

Stone, B. (2004). *Who let the blogs out? A hyperconnected peek at the world of weblogs*: St. Martin's Griffin.

Strong, R and Bill G. 1996. "Feather, Scent, and Shaker: Supporting Simple Intimacy." Presented at CSCW '96 Workshop on CSCW and Organizational Learning, Cambridge, MA,

Taylor, P. (1999). *Hackers.* New York: Routledge.

Van Alstyne, M. (1997). The state of network organization. *Journal of Organizing Computing and Electronic Commerce, 7*(3), 83-151.

Ward, R., Wamsley, G., Schroeder, A., & Robins, D. B. (2000). Networked organizational development in the public sector: A case study of the federal emergency management administration (FEMA). *Journal of the American Society for Information Science, 51*(11), 1018-1032.

Walther, J.B. (1997). Group and interpersonal effects in international computer-mediated communication. *Human Computer Research, 23,* 342-369.

Wellman, B (ed.). (1999). *Networks in the Global Village.* Boulder, CO: Westview Press.

Wellman, B. (2001a). The Persistence and Transformation of Community: From Neighbourhood Groups to Social Networks. Report to the Law Commission of Canada. October.

Wellman, B. (2001b). "Physical Place and Cyberspace: The Rise of Personalized Networks." *International Urban and Regional Research* 25 (2): 227-252.

Wellman, B. (2002). Designing the Internet for a networked society. *Communications of the ACM, 45*(5), 91-96.

Wellman, B., & Gulia, M. (1999). Net surfers don't ride alone. In B. Wellman (Ed.), *Networks in the global village* (pp. 331-366). Boulder, CO: Westview Press.

Wellman, B., & Haythornthwaite, C. (Eds.). (2002). *The Internet in everyday life.* Oxford: Blackwell Publishers.

Wellman, B. & Hogan, B. (2004). The Immanent Internet. Pp. 54-80 in *Netting Citizens: Exploring Citizenship in a Digital Age,* edited by Johnston McKay. Edinburgh: St. Andrew Press.

Wellman, B, Salaff, J., Dimitrova, D., Garton, L., Gulia, M. & Haythornthwaite, C. (1996). Computer Networks as Social Networks: Virtual Community, Computer Supported Cooperative Work and Telework. *Annual Review of Sociology* 22: 213-238.

Wenger, E. (1998). *Communities of practice: Learning, meaning, and identity.* Cambridge, UK: Cambridge University Press.

Wenger, E. (2000). Communities of practice: The key to knowledge strategy. In E. L. Lesser, M. A. Fontaine, & J. A. Slusher (Eds.), *Knowledge and communities: Resources for the knowledge-based economy* (pp. 3-20). Woburn, MA: Butterworth-Heinemann.

Wenger, E., McDermott, R. A., & Snyder, W. (2002). *Cultivating communities of practice: A guide to managing knowledge.* Boston: Harvard Business School Press.

Wired. (2002, September 10). *Born digital: Children of the revolution.* Retrieved October 16, 2004, from the World Wide Web: http://www.wired.com/wired/archive/10.09/borndigital.html.

Zachary, G. P. (1998). Armed truce: Software in an age of teams. *Information, Technology & People, 11*(1), 62-65.

Taking a Differentiated View of Intra-organizational Distributed Networks of Practice:

A Case Study Exploring Knowledge Activities, Diversity, and Communication Media Use

Eli Hustad[+], Robin Teigland*

[+]Agder University College, *Norway Stockholm School of Economics, Sweden
eli.hustad@hia.no, robin.teigland@hhs.se

Abstract: This study examines distributed networks of practice in a multinational organization in the energy and marine insurance industry. By taking a differentiated view of intra-organizational networks of practice, we identified three main categories of intra-organizational distributed networks of practice in terms of their primary knowledge activities - knowledge sharing, incremental knowledge creation, and radical knowledge creation. We then compared the networks along two dimensions: 1) the degree of diversity among network participants and 2) the communication media used by the network participants. Findings suggest that a higher degree of diversity is related to a higher degree of knowledge creation activities, but too much diversity may be restrictive when the primary activity is radical innovation. In addition, media use findings indicated an unexpected reverse relationship in which networks of practice with high task equivocality used leaner media than networks with less task equivocality. The results also indicate that the degree of diversity of a network's members may influence media use. Finally, support is found for second level media effects of media choice within the networks of practice, such as the degree to which individuals in the core of the network of practice may protect their domain.

239
P. van den Besselaar et al. (eds.), Communities and Technologies 2005, 239-261.

Knowledge Creation and Networks of Practice in Multinationals

To achieve competitive advantage, multinational organizations must continuously create knowledge at a rapid pace while simultaneously transferring and exploiting it throughout their global operations (Bartlett & Ghoshal 1989). According to the knowledge-based view of the firm the challenge of a multinational is not to divide a given task into activities to be performed efficiently by different subsidiaries but to position the company so that "separate knowledge pieces" from across the organization may be combined to initiate new tasks (Hedlund 1994). The ability to create a sustainable competitive advantage is then based on a firm's combinative capability, or the ability to generate new applications through the combination and recombination of existing knowledge (Kogut & Zander, 1992). However, as many multinationals continue to expand their operations and thereby increase the number of geographically dispersed locations, employees, functions, and external partners, the task of effectively making use of knowledge within the firm becomes more difficult. Both the complexity of the multi-unit organizational structure and the differences in language and local culture may lead to significant challenges. More recent research on multinationals is finding indications that *relationships of a more informal nature* are playing an increasingly significant role in the above knowledge activities (Hansen 1996, Tsai 2002), and this research provides tentative support for a positive relationship between participation in informal intra-organizational knowledge sharing and organizational performance (Hansen 1996).

One body of literature that has been paying increasing attention to the informal knowledge processes of firms is that of networks of practice (e.g., Brown & Duguid 1991, 2000, Wenger 1998). The concept of networks of practice and the subset of communities of practice (Brown & Duguid 2000, 2001) describe the informal social networks that facilitate learning and knowledge sharing between individuals conducting practice-related tasks. In contrast to the use of formal controls to support knowledge exchange, such as contractual obligation, organizational hierarchies, monetary incentives, or mandated rules, networks of practice promote knowledge flows along lines of practice through informal social networks (Brown & Duguid 2000, 2001). Thus, they are to be distinguished from dispersed teams that are formally mandated and goal-oriented.[1]

---

1 While network of practice relationships may emerge, that is not to say that the formal organization has no effect on their creation. For example, the formal organization may bring together individuals from across the organization. However, once the team is disbanded, individuals may continue to interact based on their own discretion due to the building of affective bonds. While this relationship originally is a formal one, it no longer falls under the "formal" category. As individuals form relationships based on biases and preferences for others, the creation of affective relationships may lead them to continue to interact regardless of formally defined structures (Stevenson & Gilly 1993). As a result, the position on networks of practice in this article falls between that of the formal organization entirely dictating interactions and that of relationships being truly emergent since the formal structure is argued

Within an organization, networks of practice typically consist of weaker ties linking individuals who are dispersed across an organization yet who are working on similar tasks using a similar base of knowledge. To date, there is a considerable number of empirical studies on communities of practice, a subset of networks of practice (e.g., Gherardi & Nicolini 2002, Lave & Wenger 1991, Wenger 1998) as well as a growing number of studies on electronic networks of practice (e.g. Nonnecke & Preece 2000, Wasko & Faraj 2000, 2004, Wasko, Faraj & Teigland, 2004), yet with the exception of a few studies (e.g., Hildreth, Kimble & Wright 2000, Lesser & Storck 2001), there is little research focuses specifically on the knowledge sharing and creation activities of *networks of practice whose members are distributed across an organization.*

With the above research gaps in mind, we performed an explorative case study in a small multinational firm operating in the marine and energy industry. Through a series of seventeen open-ended interviews in three European locations, we were able to build a rich picture of the firm's efforts to promote knowledge sharing and creation through intra-organizational distributed networks of practice. The study examines intra-organizational distributed networks of practice by investigating their *primary knowledge activities*, the degree of *diversity* of network participants, and the *communication media used* by the participants.

Such inquiry makes two important contributions.   First, this research empirically takes a differentiated view of networks of practice rather than a unitary one, resulting in identification of three categories of intra-organizational distributed networks of practice; 1) those whose primary activity is to *share critical knowledge* to support problem-solving in daily ongoing business activities, and those whose primary activity is to *create new strategic knowledge* through 2) incremental innovation or 3) radical innovation. Second, this research contributes to the literature on media choice and use since interesting findings indicate an unexpected reverse relationship between *the primary activity* of the networks of practice and the networks' *communication media use.*

The paper is organized as follows. In the following section, we briefly review the relevant knowledge-based view of the firm and intra-organizational network of practice and ICT literatures. These literatures provide the foundation for the development of two research questions. Section three describes the research methodology and provides a description of the research site. Section four reports the results of the empirical study while the last section provides a discussion of the results and the implications of this research for theory and practice as well as suggestions for future research.

---

to bias the shapes of networks of practice (Teigland 2003).

Theoretical Background and Development of the Research Questions

The knowledge-based view of the firm places considerable emphasis on taking a micro view of the organization with a particular focus on the individual (e.g., Nonaka 1994), and according to Grant (1996a, 1996b), competitive advantage results from how effective firms are in integrating the specialized knowledge of their members. Turning to multinational firms, one of the key issues underlying the knowledge-based view is to understand how knowledge is integrated across geographically dispersed units to create organizational capability (Hansen 1996).

Grant's theory of knowledge integration, however, represents a paradox: a focus on the efficiency of knowledge integration may hinder flexibility and the ability to create new knowledge and innovations. Network of practice and community of practice interactions may provide little additional knowledge over what an individual already knows. This may impede the ability to develop new and creative ideas (Granovetter 1973, 1983), thus resulting in core rigidities and competency traps – inappropriate knowledge sets that preserve the status quo and limit new insights. In addition, the knowledge in a tightly knit community of practice may be largely redundant. For example, Granovetter (1973, 1983) argues that closely-knit clusters in which individuals are well-acquainted and interact often are characterized by knowledge that is redundant. However, weak ties characterized by a relatively low involvement of time, emotional intensity, intimacy, and reciprocity, are instrumental to the diffusion of new knowledge.

Networks of Practice

Within the network of practice concept, Brown & Duguid incorporate Lave & Wenger's (1991) original work on communities of practice, describing this particular network of practice as consisting of "relatively tight-knit groups of people who know each other and work together directly...typically face to face communities that continually negotiate with, communicate with, and coordinate with each other directly in the course of their work" (Brown & Duguid 2000: 143). A central debate in the network of practice literature revolves around the knowledge sharing and creation activities performed by the various networks of practice. In some of the first literature, communities of practice have been positively linked to the creation of new knowledge through incremental improvements in local work practices in response to new problems (Brown & Duguid 1991). However, recent work has also noted that while communities of practice encourage knowledge sharing and incremental knowledge creation within communities, they may limit knowledge flows across communities and as such may place constraints on more radical knowledge creation and innovation in the wider organization (Brown & Duguid 2001, Swan, Scarbrough & Robertson

2002). For example, some researchers argue that more radical innovation occurs at the interstices between established groups and work activities since these interstices disrupt or fundamentally alter current work practices (Blackler 1995).

Boland and Tenkasi (1995) discuss innovation in their work on communities of knowing, which are similar to communities of practice, yet are found in knowledge-intensive firms. They argue that it is through dynamic interactions between communities that new configurations of knowledge really emerge. Organizations such as Ericsson, the telecommunications multinational, are trying to incorporate networks of practice and communities of knowing in their knowledge strategies (Hustad 2004, Hustad & Munkvold 2005), and are even focusing on promoting interaction between distinct communities, e.g., developing boundary practices (Carlile 2002, Wenger 1998) and hosting cross-community communication forums (Boland and Tensaki 1995).

Individuals who participate to a high degree in intra-organizational distributed networks of practice generally serve as brokers (Wenger 1998). These individuals act as bridges between local communities of practice and serve to transfer and translate knowledge between them. Due to the physically distributed nature of networks of practice, members are generally linked together through weak ties. Intra-organizational distributed networks of practice will have less redundant knowledge due to the weaker nature of the ties in these networks and thus may facilitate a higher degree of new knowledge creation.

Research Question 1. Knowledge Activities and Diversity

Knowledge sharing is not sufficient for creating a sustainable competitive advantage; firms must focus on knowledge creation through knowledge integration and the combination and recombination of firm-specific knowledge that is physically dispersed across the organization. Intra-organizational distributed networks of practice have a more extensive network of both internal and external contacts than local communities of practice. Individuals in other organizational units are more likely than co-located coworkers to have important knowledge that is non-redundant, generating access to sources of new ideas and innovations located across intra-firm boundaries (Granovetter 1973). Previous research has provided tentative support for the above since individuals participating in intra-organizational electronic networks of practice to a higher degree rated themselves as more creative compared to individuals participating to a higher degree in local communities of practice (Teigland & Wasko 2003).

Yet the limited previous research on intra-organizational distributed networks of practice has tended to focus on the dynamics of knowledge sharing as opposed to knowledge creation, thus leaving us with only a partial understanding of these important knowledge activities. One reason for this focus may be that most communities and networks of practice under study tend to be comprised of homogeneous as opposed to diverse members. This is no surprise since previous research in various fields such as social psychology, network theory, and diversity theory has found support for the principle of homophily, or the phenomenon that people develop relations with similar others (Homans 1950), thus suggesting that intra-organizational networks of practice emerge between like-minded individuals. However, networks of practice consisting of more homogeneous members are argued to be less likely to engage in knowledge creation and innovative activities (Justesen 2004).

Building on the above, for our first research question, we are interested in investigating the different knowledge activities within intra-organizational distributed networks of practice as well as whether there is a relationship between the kind of knowledge activity and the degree of diversity within the network of practice. Thus, our first research question is two-pronged and becomes the following:

Research Question 1: *What kinds of knowledge activities, e.g., knowledge sharing vs. knowledge creation, do intra-organizational distributed networks of practice conduct and what is the relationship between these knowledge activities and the degree of diversity of the network of practice's members?*

Information and Communication Technologies

Members of intra-organizational distributed networks of practice are highly reliant on information and communication technologies (ICT) such as intranets and groupware to communicate due to their dispersed nature (Vaast 2004). Ellis, Gibbs, and Rein (1991) define groupware as "computer-based systems that support groups of people engaged in a common task (or goal) and that provide an interface to a shared environment" (p. 40). There is a growing body of research in the IS literature that investigates dispersed teams and knowledge creation and sharing within them, e.g., the use of information technology to enable group processes in the context of virtual organizations and virtual teams (e.g. Orlikowski, 1992, Sproull & Kiesler 1991, Munkvold 2003). These synchronous (e.g., video and telephone conferences) and asynchronous (e.g., e-mail) technologies facilitate the interaction and knowledge activities between network members across geographical sites in a multinational with the company intranet as a common organizational junction and entrance to different types of collaboration technologies (Munkvold 2003).

Within the field of communication research, researchers have paid considerable attention to the choice and use of communication media by individuals. One of the most widely known and used theories is media richness theory. Media richness theory argues that communication media vary in their level of richness, or the ability of a medium to facilitate shared meaning or convey information and to reduce equivocality (Daft & Lengel 1986), i.e., the existence of multiple and conflicting interpretations (Weick 1979).[2] The original

---

[2] It should be noted that equivocality is not the same as uncertainty. Equivocality means not knowing which

media richness studies found that the managers observed based their choice of communication media on the equivocality of their managerial tasks at hand (Daft et al. 1987). Media richness theory suggests that individuals will be more efficient and effective when richer media are used for more equivocal tasks while leaner media are used for less equivocal tasks (Kahai & Cooper 2003).

However, the theory pays no attention to the social context of individuals making media choices since it assumes that media have fixed properties (or that individuals have the same perceptions of media richness), individuals make choices independently of the people around them, and choice-making is purely cognitive (Fulk, Schmitz & Steinfield 1990). As a result, a broad range of alternative explanations has been developed, including critical mass theory (Markus 1990), the social influence model (Fulk, Schmitz & Steinfield 1990, Lee 1994), the emergent network perspective (Contractor & Eisenberg 1990), the genre theory (Yates & Orlikowski 1992), interactivity (Zack 1993), channel expansion theory (Carlson & Zmud 1994), and critical social theory (Ngwenyama & Lee 1997). While these theories all take a somewhat different perspective, they do share the same underlying assumption that communication richness is not an intrinsic, objective property of the communication medium alone. Rather, the same medium could support rich communication among some users in some organizational contexts, while only supporting lean communication among other users in other contexts. Along these lines then, the best medium for communication is not the decision of a single person since it emerges from the organizational context and from the interactions among people in the context using the medium over time (Lee 1994).

Research Question 2. Knowledge Activities and Communication Media Use

Based on the seminal work of Wenger (1998), organizational co-location is a significant factor in the development of communities of practice (Sole & Edmondson 2002), and these networks have been found to reduce equivocality through patterns of exchange and communication through the rich communication medium of face-to-face interactions (Schenkel 2002). The primary processes of communities of practice involve mutual engagement, collaboration, and narration, not merely the performance of the same kinds of task (Brown & Duguid 1991). These are the processes that lead to a shared repertoire and as such, they depend on frequent interaction in which members share experiences and recount stories often in unexpected encounters or informal situations. With respect to intra-organizational distributed networks of practice, we would expect that based on media richness theory, this type of network of practice would tend to use richer media over leaner media since they are involved in knowledge activities with a high degree of equivocality similar to those of communities of practice.

---

questions to ask while uncertainty means not having the data required to answer a particular question. It has often been argued that people in lower organizational levels are more often faced with situations of uncertainty while upper managers are faced with equivocal situations (Rudy 1996).

Within a distributed network of practice, the geographical dispersion of individuals is likely to hinder the ability of individuals to spontaneously and frequently interact (Kiesler & Cummings 2002) and thus the ability to develop to the same degree a body of communal knowledge. The development of a sense of mutual accountability to the group may also be hindered since the dispersed nature may affect the group's ability to develop the necessary degree of trust, commitment, and respect (Orlikowski 2002). Finally, research on the problem-solving ability of communities of practice has found that when the use of richer media such as face-to-face and telephone negatively was impeded, the community of practice's ability to reduce equivocality and solve problems was negatively affected (Schenkel 2002).

Thus, the choice and use of communication media are particularly important for the ability of intra-organizational distributed networks of practice to reduce equivocality in their knowledge activities, and we would expect that they would tend to use richer media over leaner media to communicate. Additionally, knowledge activities that are more focused on knowledge creation than knowledge sharing involve a higher degree of equivocality, and the emergence of trust is necessary for knowledge creation and innovation to emerge (Fonseca 2002). Thus, we would further expect that networks of practice involved to a higher degree in knowledge creation activities would communicate to a higher degree through richer media than networks of practice involved in knowledge sharing activities. This leads us to our second research question:

Research Question 2: What is the relationship between the primary knowledge activities, e.g., knowledge sharing vs. creation, and the use of communication media by intra-organizational distributed networks of practice?

Research Site and Methods

In order to investigate the two research questions above, we chose to undertake this research in a single firm, Insure (pseudonym). While the objective in the future is to broaden the investigation to other firms, it makes sense to begin in a single case and then to re-evaluate on the basis of the findings from that study. We chose a case study because of the importance of studying network of practice knowledge activities in their real-life context (Yin 1989). This approach was particularly important given our emphasis on studying what *actual* intra-organizational distributed networks of practice existed, rather than the ones that top management assumed existed. A second reason for choosing a case study approach was that we felt the existing body of literature did not adequately describe the phenomenon under investigation (Eisenhardt 1989). Finally, a case study provides a more comprehensive in-depth study in one organization in which all the specificities that are unique for the organization are investigated more carefully.

The selection criteria were based on a number of factors: 1) globally dispersed operations, 2) participating in a highly knowledge intensive, fast-paced industry, 3) a networked organization with a high degree of two-way communication both vertically between headquarters and subsidiaries as well as laterally between subsidiaries, and 4) an explicit and active knowledge management strategy focusing on the transfer and utilization of organizational knowledge across functionalities and geographical locations. Finally, due to practical reasons, we were interested in choosing an organization with the majority of its operations located in Europe. Thus, for this study we chose a marine insurance multinational headquartered in Northern Europe.

Company Description

Insure is a multinational firm in the marine insurance and underwriting industry. The firm dates back to 1907 when a mutual protection and indemnity (P&I) association division was formed in Norway to provide marine liability insurance for regional sailing ships. Today Insure has three different product divisions (Protection & Indemnity, Marine, and Energy) and business areas comprising claims handling and underwriting activities. Insure has a 12% global market share and around two-thirds of the firm's members are domiciled in European and Nordic countries while the balance represents major industrial shipping interests in Asia and the Americas. In addition to insuring marine vessels of all types, Insure provides insurance in the oil and gas industry as well as conducts underwriting activities in the hull and machinery market. It is important to note that Insure is well known in the industry due to its ability to develop innovative insurance covers. With offices in nine different locations worldwide, Insure has approximately 330 employees comprising 27 nationalities and a number of knowledge disciplines, e.g., lawyers, maritime experts, experienced mariners, engineers and financial experts.

Data Collection and Analysis

We chose three organizational sites - Norway, England, and Finland, and collected data through interviews and secondary material. We chose interviewees to cover a range of hierarchical levels (from operational to top management), business operations, functions, and knowledge disciplines (lawyers with different legal competencies, mariners, engineers, financial experts, ICT, and knowledge management). We conducted seventeen interviews, each lasting approximately two hours. The structure of the interviews went from completely open-ended in the start to a more structured format. The interviews were taped and transcribed verbatim. The main source of secondary material was the Insure intranet, and this included internal reports, publications, presentation materials, workshop reports, and meeting agendas and minutes. This provided important contextual information of the company's knowledge management strategies, their day-to-day events, policies, and practices. Additionally, we were provided access to the email discussions in one of the identified networks of practice. This gave us a broader understanding of the complex knowledge activities performed and the participants' behavior in the interaction and knowledge activities within a particular network. The process of data collection and analysis proceeded iteratively, allowing themes to emerge and then to be examined more deeply as relevant.

Findings

Through our investigation, we found that Insure consisted of numerous distributed networks of practice 'spun' throughout the organization, and in particular we identified eleven intra-organizational networks of practice in our data. We identified these based on our definition of networks of practice, i.e., self-organizing and emergent, self-selecting and not defined by the organization's hierarchical structure, and responsible for establishing their own agendas and leadership (Wenger & Snyder 2000).[3] Members of these networks of practice were from different types of divisions, functional areas, product lines, professional specialties, and project teams. Thus, these networks of practice interwove and interacted with each other across various boundaries, and members often participated in several networks of practice. The following quotations illustrate some of these typical characteristics in networks of practice in Insure.

> People can start to be proactive themselves, to show initiative, ask questions about things, come with ideas, and in that way show that here is a person who we really need [in the network] .. So everyone is the master of his own fate...(Senior underwriter)

> People decide themselves, on a voluntary basis, they know when they don't make contributions any longer ...(Senior vice president)

Research Question 1: Knowledge Activities and Diversity

We investigated the eleven identified networks of practice on the two dimensions discussed above: primary knowledge activity and diversity (table 1). We first analyzed the networks of practice according to their primary knowledge activity. While we found a natural divide - knowledge sharing and knowledge creation, further investigation revealed that the knowledge creation networks of practice could be divided further into more incremental innovation and more radical innovation. We discuss this in more detail below. The next step was to investigate the diversity of the members in each of these networks, and the

---

[3] Additional networks of practice are likely to exist since our investigation covered only three out of nine
   locations.

following diversity categories emerged from the data: geographic location, nationality, business division and area, and knowledge discipline.

Network of Practice	Number of Locations, Participants, Nationalities	Business Divisions and Areas	Knowledge disciplines	Primary Knowledge Activities	Primary Communication Channel
1. Contract consultancy	4, 8-10, 6	P & I, Marine, Energy, claims, underwriting, defense	Lawyers with different legal expertise	Knowledge sharing Complex contracts questions from clients, requests from underwriters to legal expert group, problem solving, discussion, training and learning	e-mail Intranet - documents
1. Marine underwriting	6, 13-15, 4	Marine, underwriting	Underwriters	Knowledge sharing Underwriting guidelines, world market rumors and trends, fresh updates on market dynamics, updating new clients, discussions, assessing risk acceptance, news, administration information	Videoconferencing e-mail
1. P & I underwriting	2, 12-14, 3	P & I, underwriting	Lawyers, underwriters	Knowledge sharing Same as above	Videoconferencing e-mail
1. Defense claims network	3, 5, 4	Defense, claims	Lawyers	Knowledge sharing Sharing information regarding complex claims	Videoconferencing e-mail
2. P & I claims management network	6, 6, 4	P & I, claims	Managers	Knowledge creation Plans for new business establishments, discussion of complex and new claims, loss prevention-, cover- and underwriting issues, and exchange of legal experiences and expertise with the goal of creating improvements	Telephone conference e-mail Intranet - documents
2. Underwriting network	4, 6-10, 4	P & I, Marine, Energy, claims, underwriting	Managers, underwriters, lawyers, specialists, different professional backgrounds	Knowledge creation Plans for new business establishments, discussion of underwriting structures and quality management guidelines with the goal of creating improvements	Telephone conference e-mail Intranet - documents
2. Finance, underwriting network	4, 5-10, 4	P & I, Marine, Energy, claims, underwriting	Managers, lawyers, financial specialists, economists, different professional backgrounds	Knowledge creation Brainstorming and discussion of how to improve underwriting control systems, management decisions methods across business divisions, strategic discussions, management styles and philosophies	Telephone conference e-mail Intranet - documents
3. Working group 1	2, 7, 4	P & I, defense, underwriting	Lawyers	Knowledge creation Development of new products, refinements and further development of existing products,	Workshops e-mail Intranet - documents
3. Working group 2	2, 8, 4	P & I, claim, underwriting, defense	Marine biologist, lawyers, mariners, underwriters	Knowledge creation Same as above	Same as above
3. Working group 3	2, 7, 3	P & I, claim	Lawyers, ex mariners	Knowledge creation Same as above	Same as above
3. Working group 4	2, 8, 4	P & I, claim, underwriting, defense	Lawyers, managers, ex mariners	Knowledge creation Same as above	Same as above

Table 1. Intra-organizational Distributed Networks of Practice in Insure.

Our next step was to create a 'picture' of the identified networks of practice in Insure. We plotted their primary knowledge activity - to share knowledge or to create knowledge (the x-axis) against the degree of network member diversity (the y-axis) (figure 1). The figure shows the total diversity for each network based on the characteristics of the network's members: locations, nationalities, business divisions/areas, and knowledge disciplines. In order to ensure a consistent comparison between the networks of practice, we performed a relative comparison of them by weighting them according to the number of members within each. For example, to compare a network with five participants in three locations with another network with ten participants in the same number of locations, we divided the number of locations with the number of participants to get a relative comparable distribution of diversity parameters. Results indicate clearly that the middle group in figure 1 representing incremental innovation has the highest degree of diversity.

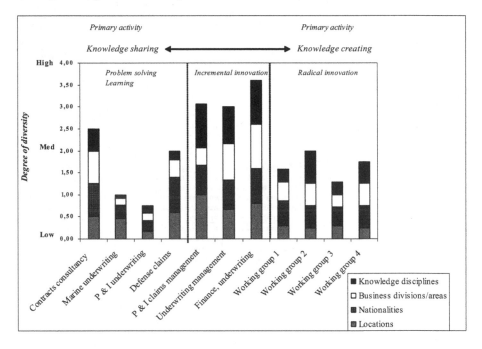

Figure 1. Knowledge Activity and Diversity in Insure's Intra-organizational Networks of Practice.

The first category of networks (left on x-axis in figure 1) whose primary activity is knowledge sharing and daily problem solving between locations has a low to medium degree of diversity. Two networks in this category have members belonging to the same business division and knowledge discipline (see also table 1); the other two networks in this category have a medium degree of diversity, where the network of contract consultancy has a slightly higher diversity than the network of defense claims.

The category of knowledge creation – radical innovation (right on the x-axis, figure 1) has a medium degree of diversity, and these networks have a nearly even degree of total diversity. Below are results for each of the three knowledge activity groups.

1. Knowledge Sharing: Problem-Solving and Learning

Four networks conducting knowledge sharing activities were identified: Contract consultancy, Marine underwriting, P&I underwriting, and Defense claims. The function of these networks is mainly to *share knowledge* and expertise with other employees but also to get feedback and support to deal with complex business questions from Insure's clients. The members also discuss environmental changes such as new market trends and internal questions like working procedures, methods, and guidelines. One of the interviewees emphasized the importance of daily discussions with his colleagues in the following quotation:

> We discuss all kinds of daily things…but we hold a fixed agenda about what is actually going on, let's say global marine info. When my colleagues are presenting to their clients in America or Asia, they are dealing with the same thing all the time - how the competitors are reacting, what the market is feeling, how prices are rising. So daily, I think that we are the best team in the whole world. We know exactly what is going on in the marine underwriting in the world, and it's the real info, it's not one month old or one week old, it's daily. (Senior underwriter).

We found that the identified knowledge sharing networks are more homogenous than the knowledge creation networks since in the former, members often belong to the same business division (e.g. Marine underwriting network, category 1). However, they do have a high degree of nationality and location diversity. The members of the networks in this category were more stable than the incremental innovation network in terms of participation and long-time membership.

2. Knowledge Creation: Incremental Innovation

In this group, we identified three networks, and the primary activity of these was incremental innovation, e.g., improving business and quality management processes as well as particular management styles and strategies. These networks have a higher degree of diversity in all categories. We also found that some core members participated over a longer period of time while other more volatile members participated only for a certain amount of time depending on the topics of interest. For example, when a shift occurred in a topic focus, new participants replaced old ones, depending on the participant's expertise. However, consistent with the community of practice concept (Wenger 1998), changing status from a core member to a more peripheral member or an 'outsider', or non-participant, was jointly determined, since it was the result of both voluntary action by the member as well as actions by existing members, e.g., being asked to join based on expertise. The following quotation illustrates the diversity in knowledge disciplines among the members:

> In the underwriting business, for example, one colleague and I have arranged a group that crosses departments [areas] and business divisions, we see who the relevant participants are and who will contribute to discussions around underwriting structures. We have made an email list and we meet every week in telephone conferences. (Senior vice president).

3. Knowledge Creation: Radical Innovation

We identified four networks involved in knowledge creation with a more radical innovation focus. (These networks of practice had labeled themselves 'working groups'.) These differed from the above incremental innovation networks since their primary activity was to develop a new type of insurance product as opposed to improving a process. Additionally, they transferred the knowledge and competence related to the new products they developed across the organization through such means as workshops and the distribution of electronic documents and product concepts on the intranet. These networks of practice exhibited diversity across all the categories; however, their degree of diversity was lower than that of the incremental innovation networks, particularly in terms of knowledge disciplines and geographical locations. This need for diversity in these networks was described in the following manner:

> We always try to get someone from each side, so it is a goal to try to have the three product areas represented; another goal is to try to get more distribution across the offices. (Senior underwriter)

> By having different people participate, for instance, someone who is participating on the cargos cover also deals with pollution claims [in the network] and gets something out of that...because otherwise it is a bit of a problem that people are becoming increasingly specialized, the expertise is becoming more and more narrow. (Lawyer)

Interestingly, we also found that these networks have been through a development process, moving from being completely informal, unstructured networks with ad hoc meetings to more formalized, structured, established networks with more fixed meetings and allocated resources and time to participate from management. In all the networks, the same two participants were co-located in the head office and were responsible for the coordination and administration of the networks as well as acted as catalysts to ensure continuous discussion and interaction between participants. Thus, these two individuals had core participant status while other members in other locations participated on a less frequent basis and thus had a more peripheral participant status. A core participant of one of these networks described one of these networks in the following manner:

> You see the purpose is to investigate new areas where we need to either expand an existing cover or to develop a new [insurance] cover...And first it was very informal, and individual claims handlers could either discuss it within, you know, their own working area, with other claim handlers or with their supervisor....But now, with this working group structure, at least if a claims handler wants to take up something in a proper forum, it exists...so instead of

having two people dealing with a cover question locally, now we are 5 or 6 people who could deal with this. (Lawyer).

Research Question 2: Knowledge Activities and Communication Media

The communication media used in the identified networks of practice are listed in table 1. We find that while all the networks used email to a very high degree for more daily, informal interactions, the three categories of networks of practice did vary in terms of the primary means of synchronous interaction. With respect to media richness theory, we expected that the radical innovation network would use regular synchronous interaction through face-to-face meetings or videoconferencing due to the high degree of equivocality in their knowledge activities. However, the leaner medium of e-mail was used in these networks, and face-to-face interactions where both core and peripheral members participated occurred only a couple of times each year. Neither was it expected that the knowledge sharing networks of practice would primarily use videoconferencing and the incremental innovation networks would primarily use telephone conferencing. Thus, there does not seem to be a direct relationship between knowledge activity and media use as predicted by media richness theory.

We then explored the relationship between diversity and communication media and found some interesting results. We expected that the most diverse network would use the richest medium of face-to-face interactions since communication might be impeded due to differences in languages, cultural behaviors, etc. However, we found that that the most diverse networks - incremental innovation networks, used the leaner medium of telephone conferencing over video and face-to-face. Additionally, we found that the most diverse network within the knowledge sharing networks - the Contract consultancy network, used the leaner media of email and document exchange as opposed to any form of synchronous media, be it face-to-face, video, or telephone, despite the more complex nature of the problems solved. Interviews revealed that this network was formed in order to increase the *efficiency* in handling difficult contract questions as well as to distribute complex questions that required a high degree of knowledge expertise and that were time consuming to handle. A second reason was related to learning: especially new, inexperienced lawyers could be trained while participating in this network. Members indicated that the reason they used email over richer media was due to efficiency considerations, e.g., to perform telephone or video conference meetings would require a lot preparation from the participants beforehand.

In the category of knowledge creation – incremental innovation, the participants preferred telephone conferences over video conferences, and one interviewee emphasized the 'any time anywhere' argument in favor of the telephone.

I don't really see the big value-added with video conferencing…you're more dependent on having a meeting room in each office that has the necessary video equipment so you have to have that room booked. There usually is a little bit of technology "clutter", you usually lose 15 minutes in the beginning each time…And there are also so many of us who travel a lot. So, for example if I book a video meeting in two weeks, then I have to be there right at that time. But if I have a telephone meeting, then I could just as well be here, at home, at an airport, anywhere.   Also, a lot of the underwriters travel a lot, so if you need to use the videoconference, does that mean that you can't participate? In the groups that I work with, the culture is that if you are out traveling then this is not an excuse to not participate. You participate no matter where one is. (Senior vice president)

As mentioned above, the identified radical innovation networks used mostly e-mail discussions to communicate. Interestingly, no synchronous communication media were used to discuss with the peripheral members from the branch offices (only email discussions) despite the availability of video conferencing equipment in all the locations and the members' ability to use the equipment.   One interviewee described this in the following quotation:

We have videoconferencing in two of our meeting rooms, so of course it is there. We have been thinking of using it, but so far we have not. It is easy to talk 'in the corner' on a more ad hoc basis…the problem could be to motivate the participants from the branch offices… they could feel kind of isolated…but they do participate by email, and when they participate, their contributions are of high quality. (Lawyer)

Discussion

Knowledge has difficulty crossing boundaries of practice even within an organization (Wenger, McDermott & Snyder 2002); however, interacting in intra-organizational distributed networks of practice enables individuals to take a fresh look at their own assumptions while facilitating knowledge recombination and integration.   According to Boland & Tenkasi (1995) it is through dynamic interactions between communities that new configurations of knowledge really emerge.   In Insure, we took a differentiated view of intra-organizational distributed networks of practice and found not only two, but three categories of networks of practice based on their primary knowledge activity: knowledge sharing, incremental knowledge creation, and radical knowledge creation. This finding could be expected when we consider the innovation literature that commonly makes the distinction between incremental and radical innovation (Dewar & Dutton 1986, Pennings 1988).

However, a surprising finding is that the incremental innovation networks have a relatively *higher degree* of diversity than the radical innovation networks. This is in contrast to former empirical studies on networks where high diversity is important to ensure radical innovation. Having ties to diverse parts of a broader social context will yield non-redundant information to a given node (Granovetter 1973), and networks of practice that have a diverse composition can utilize a broader external contact area. Why then are the radical innovation networks not more diverse than the incremental innovation networks? One explanation could be that the complexity of problems to be solved is very high in the radical innovation networks, and introducing a high degree of diversity in knowledge disciplines and cultural differences further complicates the innovation process. For example, Carlile (2002) proposes that knowledge is localized, embedded, and invested in practice and has observed that knowledge is both a barrier as well as a source of innovation in a product development setting. Additionally, former empirical findings have suggested that activities of a more radical innovative nature require a relatively lower degree of diversity than those of a more incremental nature (Justesen 2004, Katz & Lazer 2004).

When we investigated media usage by the various networks of practice, we found a reverse relationship rather than support for media richness theory, i.e., the knowledge sharing networks used a richer medium (videoconferencing) than the incremental and radical innovation networks, which used telephone and e-mail respectively. In addition, it was quite unexpected that we would find that the diversity of network members appears to have a relationship with the media used - the most diverse networks used leaner communication media, and the radical innovation networks that were less diverse, but with the highest degree of task equivocality, used the leanest medium. However, equivocality arises not only due to the nature of the task, but also because people attach meanings to situations and these meanings are not objective and singular, rather they are subjective, socially constructed, and multiple (Berger & Luckman 1966, Weick 1979). Communities of practice reduce equivocality through a series of iterative cycles in which members communicate around the problem at large, improving their communal understanding with each iteration (Schenkel 2002). Thus, it would be expected that *ceteris paribus* the more diverse a network is, the higher the level of equivocality since individuals come with a more diverse set of meanings and understandings to attach to situations. Our findings, however, tentatively suggest that leaner media are better at reducing equivocality arising from member diversity. One explanation may be that leaner media, such as email, are more flexible because the information processed, transferred, and shared is not required to be formalized (Hanseth & Braa 2000). With email, individuals may spend more time to understand the meanings attached by others to situations since they may reflect and reread messages. Additionally, telephone conferencing may be used over video conferencing due to its flexibility as described above by one interviewee. Another explanation may be that individuals may concentrate more on the content of the message as opposed to being distracted by body language. These findings further support alternative theories to media richness theory as well.

Our findings also have relevance for research on media effects, i.e., what effects different media have once they have been selected for a message. Sproull

& Kiesler (1991) have suggested that media effects (of computer-mediated communication) can be divided into first and second level effects. First level effects are efficiency related and relatively easy to foresee, such as information overload, while second level effects are more difficult to foresee since they are concerned with the social impacts on groups and organizations, e.g., equalization and social presence. Our research provides tentative support that the choice and use of technology has a second level effect on participation in the network of practice. For example, videoconferencing as it is used by the knowledge sharing networks requires members to be located in an office with video conferencing equipment and of course to be physically available at the arranged meeting. By using this type of technology, a network's core members may exclude participants who are not in one of the organization's offices most of their time, thus restricting their ability to move from the periphery to the core of the network.

In addition to the above, our findings also have implications for management. One issue is the degree of formality that is appropriate for the various networks of practice. At Insure, it is interesting to note that some of the networks of practice have become more formalized over time; however, this has not been an explicit intention or strategy by management, rather it has been quite a discrete and careful process. One of the initiators of the increased formalization of the radical innovation networks explained the rationale in the following manner:

> Of course it is very risky to be dependent on only one or two people [to drive the network], so after a while we realized that we needed to make things a bit more formal. It's not that things didn't work on an informal basis before, but we realized that this was a bottleneck... (Senior underwriter)

However, this formalization process has not always been that successful as seen in the following quotation:

> And we have tried other types of [networks of practice], which have not worked, and I think it was because we tried to formalize them, and it worked better when they were these unstructured, informal networks... (Lawyer)

The above is reflected in the Daphne dilemma as discussed by Van Aken & Weggeman (2000) that deals with the problem of finding the right balance between intent and spontaneity when approaching an elusive phenomenon. Striving for more exploitation of an informal innovation network may improve productivity while too much effort may destroy the informal character and so undermine the potential of a network of practice.

A second issue is achieving the right degree of diversity in networks of practice. While our findings suggest that diversity is related to both radical and incremental innovation in networks of practice, this diversity may be difficult to obtain since intra-organizational distributed networks of practice tend to emerge as 'similar' employees within the same interest field and knowledge discipline practice make 'homophilous ties' spanning multiple networks (Ibarra 1992). At the same time, our findings tentatively suggest that the type of network diversity is related to the primary activity of the network, thus creating an additional issue, i.e., will a high degree of diversity along knowledge disciplines or cultural differences increase the complexity in the context of the networks itself and thus inhibit creativity?

Conclusions, Limitations, and Future Research

In conclusion, we have investigated intra-organizational distributed networks of practice along two dimensions: primary knowledge activity and member diversity. Thus, these findings further support taking a *differentiated* view of networks of practice over a unitary one (Teigland 2003). Imposing one view on networks of practice masks possible heterogeneity that may be more important in explaining outcomes than a unitary one. Furthermore, we find tentative support that a higher degree of diversity is related to a higher degree of knowledge creation activities; however, too much diversity may be restrictive when the primary activity is radical innovation. Additionally, we find that the diversity of network members may influence media use by the intra-organizational distributed network of practice, but media richness theory is less supported in this study. Furthermore, tentative support is found for second level media effects within the networks of practice, such as the degree to which individuals may participate in a network.

Our research was exploratory and as such clearly has a number of limitations, thus providing for possibilities for future research. First, we have only looked at a limited number of intra-organizational distributed networks of practice within one firm. It would be interesting to see if our findings are generalizable to other firms as well as what the differences are between intra-organizational and *inter-*organizational networks of practice. Second, we have not explored any relationship between diversity, media usage, and the performance of the network of practice. Another interesting area for research is to further investigate the differences between the different kinds of networks of practice. For example, intra-organizational distributed network of practice members are not physically in the presence of each other, thus the nature of their interactions sharply contrasts with the ephemeral, typically private conversations between a limited numbers of individuals that occur in face-to-face communication in communities of practice. As a result, norms are not likely to be as dominating in intra-organizational distributed networks of practice as in communities of practice, allowing for more individual freedom in action (Squire & Johnson 2000).

A fourth area regards the knowledge itself that is shared within these different networks. As described by Wenger (1998), much of the learning and acquisition of knowledge by individuals in communities of practice occurs through an implicit mode. This is in line with Reber (1993) who argues that the acquisition of tacit knowledge occurs largely independently of conscious attempts to learn and largely in the absence of explicit knowledge about what was acquired. The acquisition by an individual of a community of practice's tacit knowledge implies frequent interaction through word of mouth and everyday "looking and seeing" (Gherardi & Nicolini 2002), thus making it difficult to achieve in the non-face-to-face settings that are typical of intra-organizational distributed networks of practice. Finally, one area of research could investigate the ability of networks of practice to be constructed and managed by firm management, a challenge reflected in the Daphne dilemma (Van Aken & Weggeman 2000) - striving for more exploitation of an informal innovation network may improve productivity while too much effort may destroy the informal character and so undermine potential.

References

Bartlett, C.A. & Ghoshal, S. 1989. Managing Across Borders: The Transnational Solution. Cambridge: Harvard Business School Press.

Berger, P.L. & Luckman, T. 1966. The Social Construction of Reality. London: Penguin Books.

Blackler, F. 1995. Knowledge, knowledge work and organizations: An overview and interpretation. Organization Studies, 16, 6: 1021-1046.

Boland, R. J., Jr. & Tenkasi, R. V. 1995. Perspective making and perspective taking in communities of knowing. Organization Science, 6, 4: 350-372.

Brown, J.S. & Duguid, P. 1991. Organizational learning and communities of practice. Organization Science, 2, 1: 40-57.

Brown, J.S. & Duguid, P. 2000. The Social Life of Information. Boston: Harvard Business School Press.

Brown, J.S. & Duguid, B. 2001. Knowledge and organization: A social-practice perspective. Organization Science, 12, 2: 198-213.

Carlile, P.R. 2002. A pragmatic view of knowledge and boundaries: Boundary objects in new product development. Organization Science, 13, 4: 442-455.

Carlson, J.R. & Zmud, R.W. 1994. Channel expansion theory: A dynamic view of media and information richness perceptions. Academy of Management Best Papers: 280-284.

Contractor, N.S. & Eisenberg, E.M. 1990. "Communication networks and new media in organizations." In J. Fulk & C. Steinfield (eds.), Organizations and Communication Technology. London: Sage.

Daft, R.L. & Lengel, R. H. 1986. Organizational information requirements, media richness and structural design. Management Science, 32, 5: 554-571.

Daft, R.L., Lengel, R.H. & Trevino, L.K. 1987. Message equivocality, media selection, and manager performance: Implication for information systems. MIS Quarterly, 11: 354-366.

Dewar, R.D. & Dutton, J.E. 1986. The adoption of radical and incremental changes: An empirical analysis. Management Science, 32, 11: 1422-1433.

Eisenhardt, K. M. 1989. Building theories from case study research. Academy of Management Review, 14, 4: 532-550.

Ellis, C.A., Gibbs, S.J., & Rein, G.L. 1991. Groupware: Some issues and experiences. Communications of the ACM, 34, 1: 39-58.

Fonseca, J. 2002. Complexity and Innovation in Organizations. London: Routledge.

Fulk, J., J. Schmitz, and C.W. Steinfield, 1990, "A social influence model of technology use." In J. Fulk and C.W. Steinfield (eds.), Organizations and Communication Technology, London: Sage: 117-140.

Gherardi, I.S. & Nicolini, D. 2002. Learning the trade: A culture of safety in practice. Organization, 9, 2: 191-223.

Granovetter, M. S. 1973. The strength of weak ties. American Journal of Sociology, 78, 6: 1360-1380.

Granovetter, M. S. 1983. The strength of weak ties: A network theory revisited. Sociological Theory, 1: 201-233.

Grant, R.M. 1996a. Prospering in dynamically-competitive environments: Organizational capability as knowledge integration. Organization Science, 7, 4: 375-387.

Grant, R. M. 1996b. Toward a knowledge-based theory of the firm. Strategic Management Journal, 17 (Special Issue): 109-122.

Hansen, M. 1996. Knowledge Integration in Organizations. Ph.D. Dissertation, Graduate School of Business, Stanford University.

Hanseth, O. & Braa, K. 2000. "Globalization and risk society." In C. U. Ciborra (ed.), From Control to Drift. The Dynamics of Corporate Information Infrastructures. United Kingdom: Oxford University Press: 41-55.

Hedlund, G. 1994. A model of knowledge management and the N-form corporation. Strategic Management Journal, 15: 73-90.

Hildreth, P., Kimble, C., & Wright, P. 2000. Communities of practice in the distributed international environment. Journal of Knowledge Management, 4, 1: 27-38.

Homans, G.C. 1950. The Human Group. New York: Harcourt Brace.

Hustad, E. 2004. Knowledge Networking in Global Organizations: The Transfer of Knowledge. Proceedings of the ACM SIGMIS CPR Conference, Tucson, Arizona: 55-64

Hustad, E., Munkvold, B.E. 2005 (forthcoming). IT-Supported Competence Management: A Case Study at Ericsson. Journal of Information Systems Management, 22, 2: 78-88.

Ibarra, H. 1992. Homophily and differential returns: Sex differences in network structure and access in an advertising firm. Administrative Science Quarterly, 37: 422-447.

Justesen, S. 2004. Innoversity in Communities of Practice. In P. Hildreth. & C. Kimble (eds.), Knowledge Networks: Innovation through Communities of Practice. Hershey: Idea Group Publishing.

Kahai, S.S. & Cooper, R.B. 2003. Exploring the core concepts of media richness theory: The impact of cue multiplicity and feedback immediacy on decision quality. Journal of Management Information Systems, 20, 1: 263-299.

Katz, N. & Lazer, D. 2001. Building effective intra-organizational networks: The role of teams. (Working Paper). Kennedy School of Business.

Kiesler, S. & Cummings, J. 2002. "What do we know about proximity in work groups? A legacy of research on physical distance." In P. Hinds & S. Kiesler (eds.) Distributed Work. Cambridge: MIT Press.

Kogut, B. & Zander, U. 1992. Knowledge of the firm, combinative capabilities and the replication of technology. Organization Science, 3, 3: 383-397.

Lave, J. & Wenger, E. 1991. Situated Learning: Legitimate Peripheral Participation. Cambridge: Cambridge University Press.

Lee, A.S. 1994. Electronic mail as a medium for rich communication: An empirical investigation using hermeneutic interpretation. MIS Quarterly, 18, 2: 143-157.

Lesser, E. & Storck, J. 2001. Communities of practice and organizational performance. IBM System Journal, 40: 831-841.

Markus, M. 1990. Toward a critical mass theory of interactive media. In J. Fulk and C.W. Steinfield (eds.) Organization and Communication Technology, London: Sage.

Munkvold, B.E. 2003. Implementing Collaboration Technologies in Industry: Case Examples and Lessons Learned, London: Springer-Verlag.

Ngwenyama, O.K. & Lee, A.S. 1997. Communication richness and electronic mail: Critical social theory and the contextuality of meaning. MIS Quarterly, 21, 2: 145-167.

Nonaka, I. 1994. A dynamic theory of organizational knowledge creation. Organization Science, 5, 1: 14-37.

Nonnecke, B. & Preece, J. 2000. Lurker demographics: Counting the silent. Proceedings of CHI'2000. Hague, The Netherlands: 73-80.

Orlikowski, W.J. 1992. Learning from Notes: Organizational Issues in Groupware Implementation. Proceedings of CSCW' 92, Toronto, Canada: 362-369.

Orlikowski, W.J. 2002. Knowing in practice: Enacting a collective capability in distributed organizing. Organization Science, 13, 3: 249-273.

Pennings, J. 1988. Information technology in production organizations. International Studies of Management and Organization, 17, 4: 68-89.

Reber, A.S. 1993. Implicit Learning and Tacit Knowledge, New York: Oxford University Press.

Schenkel, A. 2002. Communities of Practice or Communities of Discipline: Managing Deviations at the Öresund Bridge. Published Ph.D. dissertation. Stockholm School of Economics.

Sole, D. & Edmondson, A. 2002. Situated knowledge and learning in dispersed teams. British Journal of Management, 13: 17-34.

Sproull, L. S. & Kiesler, S. B. 1991. Connections: New Ways of Working in the Networked Organization. Cambridge, MA: MIT Press.

Squire, K.D. & Johnson, C.B. 2000. Supporting distributed communities of practice with interactive television. Educational Technology Research and Development, 48, 1: 22-43.

Swan, J., Scarbrough, H. & Robertson, M. 2002. The construction of 'communities of practice' in the management of innovation. Management Learning, 33, 4: 477-496.

Teigland, Robin. 2003. Knowledge Networking: Structure and Performance in Networks of Practice. Published Doctoral Dissertation. Stockholm: Stockholm School of Economics.

Teigland, R. & Wasko, M.M. 2003. Integrating Knowledge through Information Trading: Examining the Relationship between Boundary Spanning Communication and Individual Performance. Decision Sciences, 34 (2: Special Issue on Knowledge Management), 261-286.

Tsai, W. 2002. Social structure of "Coopetition" within a multiunit organization: Coordination, competition, and intraorganizational knowledge sharing. Organization Science, 13, 2: 179-190.

Vaast, E. 2004. The use of intranets: The missing link between communities of practice and networks of practice? In P. Hildreth & C. Kimble (eds.), Knowledge Networks: Innovation through Communities of Practice. Hershey: Idea Group Publishing.

Van Aken, J.E. & Weggeman, M.P. 2000. Managing learning in informal innovation networks: Overcoming the Daphne-dilemma. R&D Management, 30, 2: 139-149.

Wasko, M. & Faraj, S. 2000. It is what one does: Why people participate and help others in electronic communities of practice. Journal of Strategic Information Systems, 9, 2-3: 155-173.

Wasko, M. & Faraj, S. 2004 (forthcoming). Why Should I Share? Examining Knowledge Contribution in Networks of Practice. MIS Quarterly.

Wasko, M.M., Faraj, S., & Teigland, R. 2004 (forthcoming). Collective Action and Knowledge Contribution in Electronic Networks of Practice. Journal of the Association for Information Systems (JAIS)), Special JAIS Issue on Theory Development.

Weick, K. 1979. The Social Psychology of Organizing. Menlo Park: Addison-Wesley.

Wenger, E. 1998. Communities of Practice: Learning, Meaning, and Identity, Cambridge: Cambridge University Press.

Wenger, E. & Snyder, W.M. 2000. Communities of Practice: The Organizational Frontier. Harvard Business Review, January-February: 139-145.

Wenger, E. McDermott, R, & Snyder, W.M. 2002. Cultivating Communities of Practice. Boston: Harvard Business School Press.

Yates, J, & Orlikowski, W.J. 1992. Genres of organizational communication: A structurational approach to studying communication and media. Academy of Management Review, 17: 299-326.

Yin, R.K. 1989. Case Study Research: Design and Methods. London: Sage Publications.

Zack, M.H. 1993. Interactivity and communication mode choice in ongoing management groups. Information Systems Research, 4, 3: 207-239.

Structuring of Genre Repertoire in a Virtual Research Team

Roberto Dandi, Caterina Muzzi
Luiss Guido Carli University, Italy
rdandi@luiss.it, cmuzzi@luiss.it

Abstract. Genres are considered "as socially recognized types of communicative actions that are habitually enacted by members of a community to realize particular social purposes" (Orlikowski and Yates, 1994, p. 542). This paper studies the evolution of an e-mail-based genre repertoire and examines whether it is related to the degree of complexity associated to different tasks and to the phases of group development. The analysis focuses on the case of an international research team involved in a European project that uses mainly e-mail and other CMC technologies in order to execute different kinds of tasks.

Introduction

The analysis of communication genres within organizations may shed light upon the processes through which tasks are performed in virtual communities (Yates and Orlikowski, 1992). The introduction and use of Computer-Mediated Communication (CMC) influences the variety and variability of organizational genres since these may be created, reproduced or abandoned (Crowston and Williams, 1997; Davidson, 2000). Genre repertoire evolves over time and is deeply attached to the idiosyncrasies that characterize the community in which it is generated.

The paper investigates the evolution of an e-mail-based genre repertoire and asks whether it is related to the degree of complexity associated to different tasks and to the stages of group development. The analysis has studied the case of an

P. van den Besselaar et al. (eds.), Communities and Technologies 2005, 263-282.
© 2005 *Springer. Printed in the Netherlands.*

international research team involved in a European-funded project that uses e-mail and other CMC technologies to accomplish different kinds of tasks.

Brief literature review

«Drawing its origin from the sphere of classification developed in classical philosophy, a genre is commonly understood as a particular class, category, type, kind, style of a communicative practice, which is described, classified and recognized to belong to a group in accordance with some characteristic and distinctive features of its form, content or employed technique in its development» (Boudorides, 2001)

According to structuration theory, genres are considered "as socially recognized types of communicative actions that are habitually enacted by members of a community to realize particular social purposes" (Orlikowski and Yates, 1994, p. 542). A genre may be identified by its socially recognized purpose and shared characteristics of form.

Rather than serving an individual's own communicative intentions, a genre is constructed and recognized to serve the purpose of a relevant organizational community, whether small or large.

Its form refers to the observable aspects of communication, such as communication medium, structural features and linguistic ones.

Orlikowski and Yates (1994) and Yates, Orlikowski and Okamura (1999) used a coding scheme of genres in e-mails based on the two dimensions constituting the definition of genres (Tab. 1).

The structuration of genres over time occurs through a self-reinforcing mechanism in which different combinations of purpose and form are created and institutionalized through interactions among actors.

Genres emerge within a particular social-historical context and are reinforced over time as a situation recurs. Orlikowski and Yates (1994) believe that genres and genre repertoires are by-products of a history of negotiations between social actors that results in shared classifications, which gradually acquire the moral and ontological status of taken-for-granted events.

By using different genres in everyday life communication, actors generate the genre repertoire of their organization or community. Therefore, genre repertoire is "the set of genres enacted by groups, organizations, or communities to accomplish and express their work" (Orlikowski and Yates, 1994, p. 1).

When alterations to recognized genres or to established repertoires are performed enough to become widely accepted within a group, genre variants or new genres are formed and new repertoires are created. Therefore people produce, reproduce and change genres through a structuring process.

Genre repertoires vary in two ways:

(1) New conjunctions of purpose and form may arise and old genres can be abandoned. Therefore the composition of the repertoire varies.

(2)   There are shifts in repertoire use (e.g. in the frequency of genre use). In this case the intensity of use of certain genres varies.

These variations spring from several causes: "Over time, changes in task constraints, institutional procedures, media capabilities, and contextual factors may trigger changes in the genres that members choose to enact, producing variations in existing genres or even introducing new genres into the repertoire" (Yates, Orlikowski and Okamura, 1999).

Examples of purpose of e-mails:	Examples of form of e-mails:
• Non-work-related	• Opening/greeting
• Work-related	• Aside to an individual (personal)
• Technical	• Completed subject line
• Administrative	• Embedded message
• Question	• Embedded files (codes etc.)
• Response	• Graphical elements (emoticons)
• Solicitation	• Headings and subheadings
• Proposal	• Word/phrase emphasis
• Meta-comment	• List/specifications
• Apology	• Set-apart information
• Report	• Ellipsis (…)
• Announcement	• Signature
• Recreational	• P.S.
	• Informal/colloquial
	• Language/dialect used

Tab. 1 – Purposes and Forms of genres

Among the above mentioned causes we studied task changes, as we consider them the most probable influential factor in the evolution of repertoires. in other words, variety and variability in genre repertoire depend mostly on the variety and variability of the tasks performed by the actors. This argument is supports Ashby's law of requisite variety (1956): "the variety in the control system must be equal to or larger than the variety of the perturbations in order to maintain stability". In our context, communication patterns (the behavior of the control system) should be complex enough to execute effectively (maintain stability in) the performed tasks (the internal environment of the organization).

The composition of a genre repertoire varies according to the perceived variety of tasks that actors need to perform. If new tasks have to be accomplished, or different agents have different perceptions of the same task, new genres may arise in order to deal with this changed task complexity. In other words the variability of tasks allows for the emergence of new socially shared genres.

Task complexity has been defined in several ways (Campbell, 1988). For the purposes of this study we use interdependence as a proxy for complexity. According to Thompson (1966) there are three types of task interdependence:

• Pooled interdependence is the lowest form of interdependence among organizational actors. In this form, work does not flow between actors. Each actor contributes to the common good of the organization, but does his or her work independently.

• Sequential interdependence exists when the outputs of one actor become the inputs of another in serial form. This is a higher level of interdependence than pooled interdependence. The preceding actor must thoroughly complete his or her tasks to allow the subsequent actor to successfully perform his or her own. It therefore creates a higher need for horizontal integration mechanisms.

• Reciprocal interdependence is the highest level of interdependence. It occurs when the output of one actor serves as the input for a second actor, and the output of the second actor serves as the input for the first actor.

Each of these interdependences is associated with coordination mechanisms so that actors can perform their tasks effectively.

When a task requires pooled interdependence there should be a mediating technology that allows organization members to work independently but consenting to add up all the actors' performance outputs. The most common mediating technology for this is supervision: a boss distributes work among subordinates and then adds up all the reports coming from them. Actors share little interdependence because they are only connected through the mediating role of the boss.

In sequential interdependence among actors, the most efficient way to coordinate the efforts is to establish uniform procedures to complete the work units and design a specified serial order to perform them. Standardization is therefore the prominent mechanism for coordinating sequential interdependence. Actors have a medium degree of interdependence among them.

Finally with reciprocal interdependence, reciprocally interdependent actors work together closely and must be directly coordinated. This is the highest degree of interdependence that can occur among actors. Coordination is achieved only through mutual interaction, and participatory and horizontal structures are appropriate.

Both supervision and standardization can be considered hierarchical means of coordination because they present two properties (Biggiero, 2004): (i) asymmetry of authority (the boss decides subordinate behavior, not the contrary, and the standard cannot be changed by subordinates) and (ii) imposition of authority (the boss and the standard are imposed in a top-down logic, that is they are not chosen by people of lower hierarchical ranks).

Contrarily, mutual interaction and adjustment are democratic ways of coordinating people, as everyone may express opinions in the decision making process.

Burns and Stalker's model (1961), and other contingency models, theorize that "mechanic" systems (those with low interdependence and hierarchical coordination mechanisms) show hierarchical communication patterns, while "organic" systems (those with tasks with higher interdependence and higher mutual interaction mechanisms) need more participatory communication patterns. Less deterministically, constructivist perspectives (Weick, 1979; Salancick and Pfeffer, 1978) argue that task features are not objective but enacted, selected by the individuals' interactions and social perceptions. The higher the perceived complexity (or ambiguity and uncertainty) of tasks, the stronger is the need for collective sensemaking and therefore communication and interaction.

The model in Tuckman (1965) and Tuckman and Jensen (1977) describes the evolution of face-to-face groups over time and we will test whether this model is adapt to explain repertoire's evolution or not. Current research suggests that there are significant differences in group evolution patterns between online and face-to-face teams (Armstrong and Cole, 1995; O'Hara-Devereaux et al., 1994; Bordia, 1997; Goodman et al., 1987). However Furst et al. (1999) highlight the need for further research dealing with virtual teams in order to establish what aspects of face-to-face team and group development are generalisable to virtual team development.

According to Tuckman and Jensen (1977) groups undergo five phases of development:

(1) Forming: in this orientation phase group members find out about each others' attitudes, competencies and task responsibilities.

(2) Storming: in this phase individuals reveal their personal goals and interpersonal conflict becomes more likely.

(3) Norming: in this cohesion phase members establish working rules and role allocations.

(4) Performing: by this stage, the group has developed an effective structure, and everyone is committed to the group's objective, jobs are well defined and collaboration occurs more likely.

(5) Adjourning: in this final phase the group may disband, either because the objective has been accomplished or because members have left.

During the first phases (forming and storming), it is reasonable to expect genres of communication with few formal features and oriented to questioning and debating the ways to accomplish group objectives. In organizational terms, task complexity in these phases is high, as there is high interdependence between actors. In contrast, during the final phases of group development (norming and performing), it is more likely to find genres with higher formalization because routines have been established, and more operational genres such as reports and memo (Yates et al. 1999). Task complexity decreases and coordination mechanisms tend to be more hierarchical (more standardization and supervision).

Classification of organizational genres: proposal and hypotheses

We hypothesize that whenever perceived task complexity is low or medium (that is there is pooled or sequential interdependence among actors) emergent genres are those with command-and-control purposes such as directions on what others should do, reporting on what has been done, and deadline reminders. We also think that with low and medium perceived task complexity formalization is more likely to occur in terms of opening and closing greetings, the structure of the message, and the presence of a signature.

These assumptions derive from the above mentioned classification of coordination mechanisms. Hierarchical and formal genres are communication patterns that fit with pooled and sequential interdependences, as they require hierarchical coordination mechanisms to be dealt with.

In contrast, when task complexity is higher and actors are forced to mutual adjustment, under conditions of reciprocal interdependence, we hypothesise that genres showing participatory and interaction purposes (ballots, dialogues, proposals, requests of explications) are more likely to occur. Formalization associated to these genres is likely to be low (lack of structure, lack of formal greetings, emoticons and quick replies). This derives from the assumption that higher interdependence results in a more participatory coordination mechanism.

Drawing on Tuckman and Jensen's (1977) model of group development we hypothesise that during the early stages of the project (forming and storming phases) people use more participatory and informal genres of communications, while afterwards they rely more upon hierarchical and formalized genres of communication.

In the light of the two dimensions outlined (formalization – in the form - and degree of hierarchy – in the purpose) we obtain four classes of genres (Tab. 2).

- *Mechanic genres*: these are the genres of communication associated to bureaucratic and hierarchical coordination, where standardization of tasks and command-and-control are prevalent.
- *Task-oriented genres*: these genres have the same purpose of the previous ones but present less formalization. Actors tend to use command-and-control forms of coordination (information requests for example) but prefer to use an informal style of communication.
- *Organic genres*: these genres are associated to participatory mechanisms of coordination. Interaction is no longer based on asymmetry but occurs at the same level of authority. Formalization is low as tasks require more easy and fast communication. These genres are associated to complex tasks.
- *Formal participation genres*: these genres are as participatory as the previous ones but more formalized. This means that tasks are highly interdependent but some degree of style standardization is present.

FORM

		Low formalization	High formalization
Purpose	Command-and-control	2. Task-oriented genres	1. Mechanic genres
	Participatory interaction	3. Organic genres	4. Formal Participation genres

Tab. 2 – Classes of genres

In this study we test four hypotheses concerning classes 1 and 3:

- (H1) *The higher the interdependence in performing a task, the more likely is the occurrence of genres based on purposes of participatory interaction and on low formalization* (organic genres)
- (H2) *The lower the interdependence in performing a task, the more likely is the occurrence of genres based on purposes of command-and-control relations and on high formalization* (mechanic genres)
- (H3) *During the early stages of group development the occurrence of organic genres is more likely than that of mechanic genres.*
- (H4) *During the subsequent stages of the group development the occurrence of mechanic genres is more likely than that of organic genres.*

In this study we do not test hypotheses on the other types of genres we individuated in Table 2 because they are beyond the scope of this paper.

The case study

The case study is an international research team to which we belonged, involved in a European Commission-funded project called ORGMAIL (fictional acronym), aimed to understanding the organizational consequences of e-mail. Seven research centers from four European Countries participated in ORGMAIL: Italy, Greece, United Kingdom and The Netherlands. They came together by answering to a call for partners through a mailing list and had competences in different disciplines (social-psychology, management, organization theory, computer-mediated communication). The project started on May 1st 2001 and ended on October 31st 2003. During this period the team was composed of 19 members (8 senior researchers and 11 junior researchers) who relied on the mailing list for most of the communications (see frequencies of media use in ORGMAIL, Tab. 3). Other computer-mediated communication technologies were used far more than traditional means of communication (phone, fax and letter) with the only exception of face to face communication. We could therefore define ORGMAIL as a virtual community.

	For retrieving information	For allocating information
Mailing list (ML)	3.87	3.67
E-mails one-to-one	2.93	2.67
BlackBoard	2.87	2.33
E-mails one-to-many	2.53	2.53
Web-site	2.47	2.20
Face-to-face	2.40	2.53
Management ML	2.07	2.00
Phone	1.80	1.73
Chat	1.53	1.60
Fax	1.40	1.20
Letter	1.27	1.20

Tab. 3 – Average frequencies (1=never, 5=very often) in media use for retrieving and allocating information. Source: ML statistics for ORGMAIL's internal use

For the purposes of this study, we decided to analyze just the genres developed through the mailing list, which presents the highest frequency of use both in retrieving and allocating information. In any case a 100% coverage of the communication patterns is impossible, as one-to-one and one-to-many e-mails are not easily accessible, have been deleted or are missing, and face-to-face communication has been only partially tracked through the meeting minutes.

The project officially started in May 2001 and we covered eight months of interactions, up to December 2001. During this period the team was involved in the following tasks:

Task 1 Reporting to the European Commission: administrative/clerical activities such as creating and submitting management reports.

Task 2 Project coordination activities: project management activity.

Task 3 Literature review and identification of key issues.

Task 4 Identification of approaches and detailing research design.

Task 5 Sampling for standardized approach: searching for case studies to be analyzed in a standard way by all partners in all Countries (we call this level of analysis, "level one" or L1).

Task 6 Sampling for differentiated approaches: each partner searching for a case study to be analyzed without standardization or strong coordination with other partners (we call this level of analysis "level two" or L2).

Task 7 Selection of research tools. Development of research methods (survey, interviews structure etc).

Task 8 Scouting of the policy issues: analysis of European policies for the project issues.

Task 9 Policy implications of the field research. In this task ORGMAIL members produced a report to the EC in which they indicated how to address European policies towards better use of e-mail in organizations.

Task 10 Monitoring and self-observation. This task was devoted to an analysis of the ORGMAIL functioning and performance. It was managed and carried out by ORGMAIL members.

Task 11 Dissemination/exploitation: management and design of seminars and of the final workshop.

Task 12 Preparation of the project's brochure.

Task 13 Project web-site design and management.

This list reflects the formal list of tasks of ORGMAIL project as in official documents (project proposal, management reports) with the exception of task 12 (brochure preparation) which was part of task 11 (dissemination) and tasks 5 (sampling the standardized case study) and 6 (sampling the differentiated case studies) which formally were part of a single task (sampling). The necessity for this differentiation from the formal list became evident at the moment of assessing perceived task complexity. Dissemination and sampling, actually, were composed by different activities with different degree of complexity, and we decided to split them just for this reason.

The methodology

The sample is composed of 583 e-mail messages that were posted within the ORGMAIL mailing list from May to December 2001. Our research strategy may be summarized by the following steps:

(1) Operationalization of task complexity
(2) Codification of purpose and form for each e-mail message.
(3) Identification of emerging genres through a Principal Components Analysis.
(4) Correlation between emerging genres and task complexity.
(5) Analysis of such correlation over time.

Task complexity operationalization

Fig. 1 shows the schedule of these tasks and the ranking according to their complexity. We assigned a score of 3 to indicate maximum complexity (high interdependence), 2 to indicate medium complexity (sequential interdependence) and 1 to indicate low complexity (pooled interdependence). This ranking has been produced by four ORGMAIL members, who are scholars in organizational design and behavior. Most of the messages (62,5%) present task complexity 3, while 37% of them concern task complexity 1. Very few (0,5%) correspond to task complexity 2.

		m1	m2	m3	m4	m5	m6	m7	m8	Task complx
Task 1	Reporting to the EC									1
Task 2	Project Management									3
Task 3	Literature review/identification of key issues									1
Task 4	Ident. of approaches/Detailing research design									3
Task 5	Sampling L1									3
Task 6	Sampling L2									1
Task 7	Selection of research tools									3
Task 8	Scouting of the policies									1
Task 9	Policy issues for empirical research									1
Task 10	Monitoring and self-observation									2
Task 11	Peer Review									1
Task 12	Dissemination and exploitation actions									1
Task 13	Brochure									3
Task 14	Web site implementation									3

Fig. 1 – Task schedule and ranking of task complexity

Coding of the e-mail messages

We selected 6 items for the form and 9 items for the purpose (Tab. 4), following Orlikowski and Yates (1994) and Ducheneaut (2002): only "management" is an original item and refers to communication aimed to directing people and planning activities (top-down communication).

Purpose items:	Form items:
–Question	–Closing formula
–Answer	–Emoticons
–Ballots	–Reply with embedded message
–Management	–Lack of text structure
–Disagreement	–Openings and greetings
–Internal report	–Signature
–Meta communication	
–Technical support	
–Proposal	

Tab. 4 – Coded items for genres analysis

We coded all the messages according to these categories and to the task they belonged to (by investigating which task the content of the message referred to).

Then we added the variable "trimester" 1, 2 and 3 (and coded the messages according to the date they were sent) so as to be able to analyze the evolution of the repertoire over time (although "trimester" 3 is composed of two months: November and December 2001). All the variables related to the purpose and form were coded as continuous, and the task complexity and the trimester as nominal. Thus we considered our data "as if" they were quantitative, in order to simplify the graphical representation of the factorial axes.

Data analysis

As other authors have done in similar studies (Ducheneaut, 2002; Di Franco, 2003), we analyzed the data through a multivariate statistical method, namely Principal Component Analysis (PCA) and then we made a hierarchical clustering using the SPAD 4.5 software (Cisia-Ceresta, 1999).

We analyzed separately continuous and nominal variables because of their different scales, but then we juxtaposed the different couples of graphical representations in order to integrate the different kinds of variables.

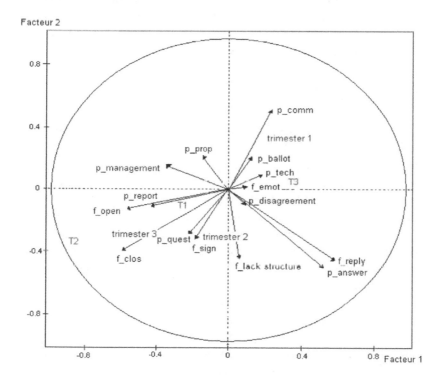

Fig. 2 – Circle of correlation, Factors 1 and 2

The aim of the PCA is to show the proximity of some variables to each other and to the axes (or factors). The position of the variables in the circle of correlation (Fig. 2) and their distance from the two axes indicate the importance of each variable with respect to the factors represented by the axes. When using

PCA, the researcher focuses on trying to interpret the meaning of the axes and thus of the position of the arrows in the two-dimensional space.

As shown in Fig. 2, in the circle of correlations all the variables of purpose and form are represented by arrows. The length of the arrow (that is the distance from the centre) represents the importance of the considered variable with respect to the axes. The cosine of the angle between two variables corresponds to the correlation between the two variables.

When two arrows are collinear but in opposite quadrants, it means that they are negatively correlated to each another.

After the PCA, we did a hierarchical clustering to better identify the emerging genres. We decided to cut the dendogram (the tree) at the fifth class and we included in this way 90% of all the messages. For each class, the software provided us with the list of variables according to which the class itself was above and below the mean of the sample. In other words, for each class we had the list of the most and least characteristic variables. According to the results of the cluster analysis, i.e. the genres that have emerged, we created a new variable in our dataset expressing the different genres being studied.

Results and discussion

Through the graphical representation obtained from the PCA analysis, we have interpreted Factor 1 and 2 as follows:

- Factor 1 (horizontal axis in Fig. 2): the degree of hierarchy in e-mail communication. On the right side of the circle, we find informal characteristics (embedded messages in the e-mails, emoticons) and participative items (ballots and disagreements). We have thus participatory interactions. On the left side of the circle we find formal characteristics (signature, openings and greetings, closing formulae) and hierarchical items (management e-mails and internal reports where collaborators report to their bosses) that is formal command-and-control communication.
- Factor 2 (vertical axis in Fig. 2): the task orientation of e-mail exchange. On the top side of the circle, we find planning or strategic messages (management, meta-communication, ballots and proposals), aimed to decide the "frameworks" for communication and work. In the down part we find more "operational" items like questions, answers, reply messages and lack of structure, that is the day-by-day activities.

The cluster analysis indicates there are five genres of e-mail communication in ORGMAIL mailing list (Tab. 5). As shown in that table, not all items of purpose and form appear in the description of classes. The statistical software indeed shows only those variables that characterize each class in a statistically significant way (test value >2).

Genre 1 represents the expression of disagreement on a given issue. This is usually a reply message that contains the original message. There are no indications about the degree of formalization. Genre 1 can be ascribed to the class of organic genres since disagreement is a form of participation. Just 2% of the messages belong to this genre. Disagreement was mostly expressed in task 12 (brochure preparation): more than one third of messages belonging to this genre concern the brochure preparation. This task was considered highly critical, as it concerned the project's presentation to external organizations (especially those that ORGMAIL wanted to analyze). In order to be effective, the research team concentrated many efforts and interactions in a task that otherwise and elsewhere would have been considered trivial. Some disagreement was therefore likely to occur. Task 2 (project management) presented also some disagreement (almost one third of the messages belonging to Genre 1). The expression of different points of view is, however, self-explaining: budget issues and decisions concerning the division of work are often potential sources of conflicts.

Genre 2 is related to technical and meta-communication issues. About 35% of the messages belong to this genre. These messages are very informal (no opening or closing greetings) and embed the original message, so that we could define them as answers to technical questions. They are composed of explanations about how to use communication media (web-site, blackboard) and suggestions/thoughts about how to behave when using such media (meta-communication). It is worthy to remember that ORGMAIL is a research project aimed to study computer-mediated communication: the team is encouraged to practice self-observation and this study is part of such strategy. Half of the messages in this genre involved communicating information concerning task 2 (project management), while 13% of them concerned task 12 (brochure preparation). These tasks have been coded as complex because they required high levels of interaction. Meta-communication can be viewed as a means for reducing ambiguity and uncertainty as it frames the situations (Weick, 1979).

Genre 3 is encompasses the messages aimed to sponsor interaction and participation: ballots and proposals. About 15% of the messages belong to this genre. We do not have information about the form of such messages, so we can say they are close to the other messages' mean under this issue. One fourth of the messages belonging to Genre 3 occurred when communicating information regarding task 2 (project management), while about 16% of them concern messages regarding task 3 (literature review and key issues), 15% regarding 11 (dissemination/exploitation activities) and 16% regarding task 12 (brochure preparation).

Genre 4 represents quick operational questions, without formality and aimed to obtain fast exchange of information. About 17% of the messages belong to this genre. We can ascribe this genre to the class of task-oriented genres. Genre 4 occurred mostly in messages concerning again task 2 (project management, 20%

of messages in Genre 4), task 5 (sampling level one, 15%) and task 6 (sampling level two, 15%).

	Genre 1 (N=14)	Genre 2 (N=211)	Genre 3 (N=89)	Genre 4 (N=101)	Genre 5 (N=109)
Presence of	P_disagreement F_reply_message	p_meta_comm p_technical f_reply_message p_answer	p_ballot p_proposal	p_question f_opening_greetin	p_internal_report p_management f_lack_structure f_closing_greetin f_opening_greetin
lack of		p_ballot p_management p_disagreement f_opening_greetin f_emoticons p_internal_report p_question f_closing_greetin f_signature	p_management p_technical p_internal_report p_answer p_question f_lack_structure	p_proposal p_ballot p_meta_comm p_management p_answer	p_proposal p_ballot p_meta_comm p_question p_answer f_reply_message

Tab. 5 – Genres from cluster analysis

Genre 5 is the opposite of Genre 4. It concerns messages aimed at supervising people (management) or reporting to others. Formality is manifested through opening and closing greetings. However this genre is associated with a lack of structure, therefore this is a moderately strong form of mechanic genre. About 19% of the total amount of messages belongs to this genre. Almost 30% of messages included in this genre concern task 3 (literature review and key issues), while task 6 (sampling level one) and task 2 (project management) are also highly represented in this genre (about 16% of messages in Genre 5, each). This can be explained by the fact that task 3 is the perfect example of pooled interdependence (members wrote separately their literature reviews by topic), while task 6 has a high presence of report messages (people reported the improvements in approaching multinational companies to the mailing list in order to gain access to the same organization throughout all the Countries involved in the project).

To put together these results we matched each genre to each category of our classification (Tab. 6):

		FORM	
		Low formalization	High formalization
Purpose	Command-and-control	2. Task-oriented genres: Genre 4	1. Mechanic genres: Genre 5
	Participatory interaction	3. Organic genres: Genre 1, 2 and Genre 3	Formal participation genres:

Tab. 6 – Classification of the ORGMAIL mailing list's genres

The ORGMAIL mailing list's genres can be traced in the PCA analysis as in Fig. 3. Along factor 1, we find genres 4 and 5 placed on the command-and-control side, and at the opposite, genres 1, 2 and 3, on the participatory communication side. Along the factor 2, we find genres 1, and 4 placed on the operational side, and at the opposite genres 2 and 3 and 5 on the strategic/planning side. These findings are consistent with our hypotheses because:

(H1) Mechanic genres (Genre 5) result associated with the lowest degree of task complexity T1 (task complexity 1) and T2 (task complexity 2)

(H2) Organic genres (Genres 2 and 3) are closer to the maximum degree of complexity T3 (task complexity 3)

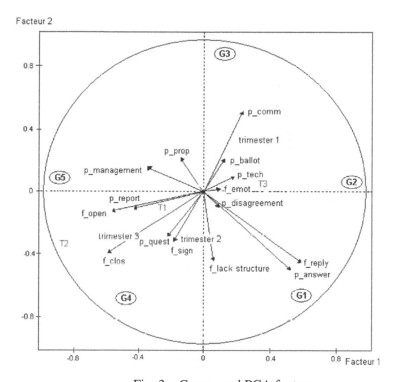

Fig. 3 – Genres and PCA factors

Finally, we ranked the five genres according to two criteria (based on the factor analysis): degree of participation (5=participation, 1=hierarchy) and degree of strategic orientation (5=strategic decision, 1=operational interaction). Then we averaged the two criteria in order to obtain a single hierarchy of genres, according to what we called the degree of genres complexity (maximum complexity reached with maximum participation and maximum strategic orientation). The correlation among task complexity and genres complexity resulted significantly positive (Spearman =0,134, p<0,01).

In Figure 3, we also have the graphical representation of the nominal variables (task complexity and trimesters). It emerges that during the first trimester of the project the consortium had to deal with complex tasks (the variable T3 is on the right side of the circle close to "trimester 1") more than with simple tasks. During the second and the third trimesters instead, the consortium dealt with less complex tasks (see the down left side quadrant). This finding confirms our hypotheses in evolutionary terms too: as shown in Fig. 4, organic genres (2 and 3) score the maximum absolute frequencies during the first trimester and decrease as time goes on. The mechanic genre 5, at the opposite, reaches the maximum during the last months, while it shows the minimum score during the first trimester when task interdependence was highest.

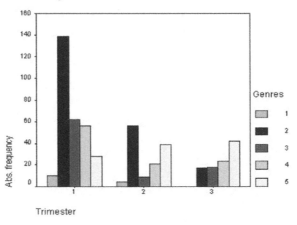

Fig. 4 – Frequencies of genres over time

These findings confirm also the hypotheses based on the model of group development:

(H3) Organic genres occurred more in the initial phase of the project (forming and storming). In particular, during the first trimester, messages with purposes such as disagreement (genre 1), meta-communication (genre 2), ballots, proposals (genre 3) occurred more than during subsequent periods. Formality in these messages is lacking.

(H4) Mechanic genres occurred more during the subsequent phases (norming and performing). In particular, during the second trimester, messages with question as purpose occurred more (genre 4); during the third trimester, messages with the purpose of reporting and management were predominant (genre 5). Formality increased, compared to the first trimester, as opening and closing greetings, and signature were more likely to occur.

Status	Trimester		Genre type					Totals
			1	2	3	4	5	
junior	Trimester 1	# of emails	3	37	18	18	12	88
		% of Total	0.6	7.1	3.4	3.4	2.3	16,8
	Trimester 2	# of emails	0	21	2	9	23	55
		% of Total	0.0	4.0	0.4	1.7	4.4	10,5
	Trimester 3	# of emails	0	10	5	10	25	50
		% of Total	0.0	1.9	1.0	1.9	4.8	9,5
	Total junior	# of emails	3	68	25	37	60	193
		% of Total	0.6	13.0	4.8	7.1	11.5	36,8
senior	Trimester 1	# of emails	7	102	44	38	16	207
		% of Total	1.3	19.5	8.4	7.3	3.1	39,5
	Trimester 2	# of emails	4	34	7	12	16	73
		% of Total	0.8	6.5	1.3	2.3	3.1	13,9
	Trimester 3	# of emails	0	7	13	14	17	51
		% of Total	0.0	1.3	2.5	2.7	3.2	9,7
	Total senior	# of emails	11	143	64	64	49	331
		% of Total	2.1	27.3	12.2	12.2	9.4	63,2
TOTAL		# of emails	14	211	89	101	109	524
		% of Total	2.7	40.3	17.0	19.3	20.8	100.0

Tab. 7 – Frequencies of emails by time, by status of the sender and by genre type

An explanation of these phenomena derives from the status of the senders of the email messages. As showed in Table 7, senior researchers (research unit heads) of ORGMAIL participated more in group discussion than junior researchers, especially during the early stage of the project. Furthermore, messages from senior researchers using organic genres (1, 2 and 3) and genre 4 outnumber messages from junior researchers with the same genres. At the opposite junior researchers use genre 5 (a mechanic genre) more than senior researchers.

This means that during the early stages of the project (forming and storming) senior researchers adopted organic genre messages to propose new ideas and identify group goals and task responsibilities, while during the subsequent stages (norming and performing) senior researchers limited their participation for management activities and junior researchers increased their participation for report activities

Conclusions

Through this study we found that ORGMAIL mailing list repertoire is composed of 5 genres. The repertoire evolved according to the evolution of the set of tasks performed, and to their complexity.

Genre repertoire changed over time in two ways: (i) in the composition, since during the last months there is no more trace of genre 1 (disagreement in reply messages). (ii) in the intensity of use of each genre, as frequencies in Fig. 4 easily show: organic genres prevail in the first months while the mechanic genre prevails in the last ones.

These findings confirm Orlikowski and Yates' (1994) frame; which describes genres as an output of social structuring, and confirm that the evolution of genre repertoire is correlated to the perception of task evolution and complexity.

Genres varied over time according also to Tuckman and Jensen's (1977) model on group development. In initial phases, when organization and task assignments are unclear, more participatory and informal genres occurred, while in later phases (last two months) mechanic genres became predominant.

Another contribution of this study is that it adds some clues for framing the genre phenomenon through a tentative classification of genres. This classification (Tab. 2) was obtained crossing the dimensions of the hierarchy/participation degree and the formalization degree.

From a theoretical point of view our findings can be placed in the systemic perspective flow. We applied Ashby's law to demonstrate that there should be an association between task complexity and genre repertoire. Furthermore, we tried to integrate organization theory with communication theory of genres by linking genre types with coordination mechanisms, and genres types with phases of group development. Finally, we integrated computer-mediate communication theory with organization theory

From the point of view of computer-mediated communication theory our findings confirm that e-mail, far from being a medium intrinsically democratic (for a review on this issue see Mantovani, 1994), can be used both for participatory/peer and autocratic/vertical relations. This result is coherent with the Emergent Approach (Markus and Robey, 1988) which claims that e-mail use is flexibly dependent on the group's appropriation of the medium, and is not pre-determined by the technology features.

This study has some limitations. Firstly, the study analyses social and organizational communication in a mailing list but does not include any assessment of social context: mutual acknowledgement, prior collaboration, identification in the group, trust among the actors. These social relationships may shed light upon the evolution of genres over time, too. Secondly, we analyzed just the electronic genres emerging through the mailing list. Even if this medium scores the highest frequencies of use (Tab. 3), we recognize that an analysis of the genres developed through all available other media would be more complete and interesting. Last but not least, our findings need to be validated by further investigations in order to be generalized to other contexts.

References

Armstrong D.L.., & Cole, P. (1995). Managing distances and differences in geographically distributed work groups. In S. Jackson & M. Ruderman (Eds.), Diversity in Work Teams: Research Paradigms for a Changing Workplace , Washington, D.C.: American Psychological Association: 187-215.

Ashby, R.W. (1956) An Introduction to Cybernetics, London: Chapman & Hall

Biggiero, L. (2004), Organizzazione e Trasformazioni d'Impresa, in Pilotti L. (editor) Strategie Innovative e Impresa della Conoscenza nella Competizione Globale, Roma: Carocci.

Bordia, P. (1997). Face-to-face versus computer-mediated-communication: A synthesis of the experimental literature. The Journal of Business Communication, 34(1): 99-120.

Boudourides M. (2001) Introduction to Genres. ORGMAIL Internal Report

Burns, T. and GM Stalker (1961). The Management of Innovation. Oxford: Oxford University Press.

Campbell D.J. (1988) Task complexity: A Review and Analysis. Academy of Management Review, 13: 40-52

Cisia-Ceresta (1999) SPAD 4.5, Montreuil

Crowston K., Williams M. (1997) Reproduced and emergent genres of communication on the World-Wide Web, Proceedings of the XIII Annual Hawaii International Conference on Systems Sciences, Wailea, HI, available at http://florin.syr.edu/~crowston/papers/webgenres.html

Davidson E. J. (2000) Analyzing genre of organizational communication in clinical information systems Information technology and people 13 (3): 196-209

Di Franco G. (2003) L'analisi multivariata nelle scienze sociali: Modelli log-lineari e variabili categoriali, Roma: Carocci

Ducheneaut, N. (2002). The social impacts of electronic mail in organizations: a case study of electronic power games using communication genres. Information, Communication, and Society, 5(2): 153-188.

Furst, S., Blackburn, R., & Rosen, B. (1999). Virtual team effectiveness: A proposed research agenda. Information Systems Journal, 9: 249-269.

Goodman, P. S., Ravlin, E., & Schminke, M. (1987). Understanding groups in organizations. In L. Cummings & B. Staw (Eds.), Research in Organizational Behavior ,Greenwich, CT: JAI Press, 9: 121-173.

Mantovani G. (1994) Is Computer-Mediated-Communication Intrinsically Apt to Enhance Democracy in Organizations? Human Relations, 47(1): 45-62

Markus M. L. and Robey D. (1988) Information Technology and Organizational Change: Causal Structuring Theory and Research. Management Science, 34(5): 583-598

O'Hara-Devereaux, M., & Johansen, R. (1994). Global Work: Bridging Distance, Culture, and Time. San Fransisco: Jossey-Bass Publishers.

Orlikowski, W., and Yates, J. (1994). Genre repertoire: Structuring of communicative practices in organizations. Administrative Science Quarterly, 39: 541-574.

Salancik G. R. and Pfeffer J. (1978) A Social Information Processing Approach to Job Attitudes and Task Design. Administrative Science Quarterly, 23: 224-253

Thompson, J. (1966) Organizations in Action, McGraw Hill

Tuckman, B.W. (1965) Developmental Sequence in Small Groups, Psychological Bulletin, 63: 384-399.

Tuckman B.W. and Jensen M.A. (1977) Stages of small group development revisited, Group and Organizational Studies, 2: 419-427

Weick, K.E. (1979) The Social Psychology of Organizing, Addison-Wesley, Reading, MA

Yates, J., and Orlikowski, W. (1992). Genres of organizational communication: A structurational approach to studying communication and media. Academy of Management Review, 17 (2): 299-326.

Yates, J., Orlikowski, W., and Okamura, K. (1999). Explicit and implicit structuring of genres: Electronic communication in a Japanese R&D organization. Available at: http://ccs.mit.edu/papers/CCSWP188.html

Principles for Cultivating Scientific Communities of Practice

Andrea Kienle[+], Martin Wessner*

[+]University of Dortmund, Germany, * Fraunhofer IPSI, Darmstadt, Germany

andrea.kienle@uni-dortmund.de, martin.wessner@ipsi.fraunhofer.de

Abstract. Scientific communities can be seen as a specific type of Communities of Practice (CoP). In this paper we analyze scientific communities from the CoP point of view. We show how models and design principles from CoP can be interpreted and adapted for scientific communities. Taking the CSCL (Computer-Supported Collaborative Learning) community as an example, we instantiate the adapted design principles and trace the development of this community based on an analysis of its first decade of existence (1995-2005). This analysis includes an analysis of CSCL conference proceedings and an analysis of the lists of participants and program committee members of CSCL conferences.

Introduction

The term *"Communities of Practice (CoP)"*, coined by Lave and Wenger (1991), has been further developed over recent years and is now widely accepted. It has been defined as *"groups of people who share a concern, a set of problems, or a passion about a topic, and who deepen their knowledge and expertise in this area by interacting on an ongoing basis"* (Wenger et al. 2002: 4).

A number of design principles have been proposed to cultivate CoPs (Wenger et al. 2002). These principles don't aim to design in the sense of specification and implementation of a process, but reveal the thinking behind a design. A design based on these principles and taking into consideration the current situation in the CoP is able to foster the liveliness of the CoP. While there exists substantial re-

P. van den Besselaar et al. (eds.), Communities and Technologies 2005, 283-299.

search to discuss the CoP approach in various domains (e.g. Allatta 2003 for the corporate context), discussing scientific communities as CoPs is less advanced.

The goal of this paper is to analyze scientific communities from the CoP point of view. Are scientific communities also CoPs? If so, then they can be cultivated as well, i.e. designed in order to foster their liveliness. Models and design principles for CoPs can be interpreted from the scientific community point of view and adapted to the specific characteristics of scientific communities.

The structure of this paper is as follows. After this introduction, we describe the characteristics of scientific communities and how practice in scientific communities changed in recent years (section 2). As an example of a scientific community we selected the international and multidisciplinary CSCL (Computer-Supported Collaborative Learning) community, which is characterized in section 3. We describe the CSCL community using an analysis of CSCL conference proceedings and an analysis of the lists of participants and program committee members of the CSCL conferences. Based on this we are able to discuss and adapt basic CoP models to describe scientific communities (section 4). Similarly, design principles for cultivating scientific communities are derived from generic CoP design principles and explained using data and observations from the CSCL community (section 5). Finally, we conclude the paper and point to some open research questions.

The Nature of Scientific Communities

A scientific community consists of people, usually working in groups of knowledge workers. Each group member is working on a particular aspect of the same overall problem or topic belonging to one or more research fields. In comparison to communities in the corporate context, scientific communities are more heterogeneous and the groups operate relatively independently (Doerry et al. 1997). A scientific community consists of various researchers who have different specialties. Also in each group members have various backgrounds and participate in various scientific communities. These characteristics indicate that scientific communities are Communities of Practice (CoP) in the sense of Wenger's definition mentioned in the introduction section above.

Given the heterogeneous nature of scientific communities in general as well as on the group level, deepening of knowledge and expertise (=learning) doesn't happen as participating in one specific scientific community only, e.g. as a straight path from a novice to an expert. Rather learning involves participating in different communities and switching the role of novice and expert depending on the current situation.

The groups building a scientific community are distributed over a certain region, nation or even world-wide depending on the nature of their research field. For interaction between the community members there are face-to-face meetings (especially conferences and workshops), research findings are distributed in printed form (e.g., as books and journals), and they engage in virtual activities like discussion forums, databases, websites, and mailinglists in order to communicate, cooperate or distribute findings in the community. The definition of the term "practice" for CoPs according to Wenger et al. (2002) focuses on these communal resources that form the basis of communication within a community: "*It (practice) denotes a set of socially defined ways of doing things in a specific domain: a set of common approaches and shared standards that create a basis for action, communication, problem solving, performance and accountability. [...]The practice includes the books, articles, knowledge bases, websites, and other repositories that members share*" (Wenger et al 2002: 38).

In addition to the geographical distribution, community members belong to different organizations and cultures; have a different native language etc. This complicates meetings as well as the distribution of findings. On the other hand, the existence of advanced technical communication and cooperation infrastructures allows increasingly global involvement of institutions and researchers in scientific communities (Birnholtz & Bietz 2003). This is visible in the composition of editorial boards, in the attendance at conferences and workshops, in multinational projects and joint publications.

An important change in the nature of scientific communities is caused by rethinking the traditional distinction between basic and applied research, between theory and practice (Stokes 1997). There is an emerging paradigm of what Stokes called use-inspired research, which combines the goals of understanding and use, insight and creation. This points to an additional heterogeneity which characterizes (at least some) scientific communities.

To sum up, a scientific community is a community of practice with

- members working in a common field of research,
- members being distributed across disciplines, organizations, cultures and geographical regions,
- methods from a variety of disciplines and scientific cultures,
- members using a combination of face-to-face interaction and increasingly technology-mediated interaction, and
- at least for some disciplines – members following or even combining practice of basic and applied research.

The CSCL Community as an Example - Data, Analysis, Methods

One example for a scientific community like described in the previous section is the CSCL community. Since a first workshop in 1989 a growing number of researchers participate in this community. An international conference series started in 1995, which includes six passed and one upcoming conference in 2005. Because of the growing interest on the work of this community an international journal of CSCL (ijCSCL) in printed and online (www.ijCSCL.org) form was founded in 2004.[1]

The common research interest of this community is the design and evaluation of computer support for collaborative learning. This interest attracts and builds on the expertise of participants from various disciplines (e.g. computer science, psychology, education science, cognitive science) which also come from different countries and continents (mostly North America, Europe and Asia).

In a retrospect on the first decade of this scientific community our aim here is to analyse the development of a scientific community in order to derive design principles for cultivating scientific communities. For the analysis of the CSCL community we combine several analysis methods.

In order to analyse the international distribution of authors, their continuity and their relationships we used a citation analysis of the CSCL conference proceedings. *"Citation analysis is the formal quantitative analysis of the literature produced by a field and the relationships among people as evidenced by whom they cite in their published articles. Especially in academic disciplines where the importance of publication and citation are high, the bibliographic references used in research documents can be an important mirror of how people in a field construe it. Citation analysis can be used for many purposes. For instance, it is used as a tool for journal evaluation (Garfield, 1972), identification of subgroups or invisible colleges (Crane, 1972; Sachs, 1984), identifying the shared knowledge of a community (Small & Greenlee, 1980), or characterizing disciplines or communities (Chubin, Porter, & Rossini, 1984)."* (Kirby et al., in press).

Citation analysis is used here as a social network approach. Social network approaches (Scott 1991) to scientific communities are based on the members of a community and focus on networks of people linked for example by co-authorship. It utilizes measures such as connectedness, diameter, centralization and density of a community. This has been applied to a number of research fields, too (see Newmann 2004 for an overview). Social network analysis has been applied also in the CSCL community in order to measure the cohesion in collaborative learning teams (Nurmela et al., 1999; Woodruff, 1999; Cho et al., 2002; Nurmela et al., 2003; Reffay & Chanier, 2003).

Furthermore we included the lists of participants and program committee members concerning their international distribution and continuity in order to get a closer look at different groups, each on different degrees of participation , of the CSCL community. Thereby we also analysed the relations between the lists of authors, participants and program committee members.

Data for our citation analysis was mainly gathered by analysing the proceedings of the six CSCL conferences in 1995 1997 1999, 2001, 2002 and 2003

---

[1] CSCL = Computer Support for Collaborative Learning

(Schnase et al. 1995; Hall et al. 1997; Hoadley & Roschelle 1999; Dillenbourg et al. 2001; Stahl 2002; Wasson et al. 2003). Additionally all available participants' lists were analyzed (CSCL 1999, 2001, 2002 and 2003). All together we included 692 artifacts (e.g. poster, papers), 125 program committee members (PCM), 1187 authors and 1462 conference participants (575 active and 887 passive participants) in our analysis.

For all persons involved in the community we recorded the following data

- **Name**
- **Country and continent**. This data enables us to analyze the distribution of the community.
- **Discipline**. This data enables us to analyze the multidisciplinary character of the community.
- **Conference** in which she/he participated as member of the program committee, as author, or as conference participant. On basis of this data we analyzed the continuity of the community and transitions between the different degrees of participation.

For a further analysis of the active participants – authors –we recorded for each author:

- **Co-authors** for the analysis of (strong) interaction between the participants of the community
- **Referenced authors** for the analysis of (weak) interaction between the participants. From the citations of each artifact we picked those people who participated at least once at an author.

Scientific communities can be analyzed in a number of ways and wrt. different aspects. In this paper we focus on the continuity in order to analyze how stable the CSCL community is and international distribution of the CSCL community members in order to explore how global the community is. An extensive analysis of the development of the CSCL community is ongoing work (see also Kienle & Wessner 2005) and should include for example the interdisciplinarity of the community.

Modeling the Participation in Scientific Communities

Wenger et al. (2002) promote a model for CoPs which classifies community members according to their degree of participation in the community. They differentiate between a core group (including a coordinator), active and peripheral participants and outsiders. Similar degrees of participation also exist in scientific communities. Here, we differentiate between the following groups: organizers, mostly program committee members (= core group), authors of papers (= active participants) and passive participants of conferences (= peripheral participants). Outsiders are people who are somewhat interested in CSCL, e.g. read single papers in conference proceedings, communicate with authors etc. but who are not members of the community.

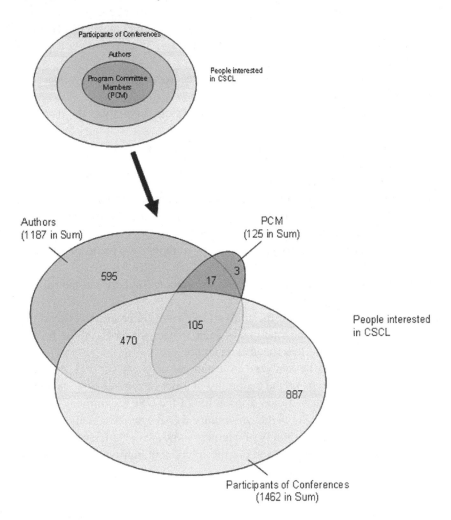

Different degrees of participation

However, by analyzing the data we found that these groups are not in a "part of" relation like the figure of Wenger et al. suggests and what is shown in the adapted figure 1 at the top. In the CSCL community these groups overlap only partly, e.g. the groups of authors and participants overlap only by 50%. To give consideration to this finding, we rearranged the figure (see fig. 1 at the bottom). This can be explained by a number of reasons. Many institutions enable their researchers only to participate in conferences where they have an accepted paper; and in some cases only one member of the group of co-authors is allowed to go there. Also budget restrictions and teaching load influence the ability to attend international conferences, especially if they are abroad. Further (qualitative) analysis is needed to explain and assess this finding.

In the various groups identified above we found also different degrees of participation. The groups of program committee members, authors and participants are quite heterogeneous wrt. the number of conferences they were involved. For example, from 1462 participants in the last four CSCL conferences 1216 (83.5%) attended only one conference (see table 1 for more details).

No. of confer- ences	No. of participants (data available only for 4 out of 6 con- ferences)	No. of authors (data for all 6 con- ferences)	No. of PCM (data includes the upcoming 7th con- ference)
1	1221 (83.5%)	949 (79.9%)	65 (52.0%)
2	183 (12.5%)	150 (12.6%)	32 (25.6%)
3	43 (2.9%))	61 (5.1%)	15 (12.0%)
4	15 (1.0%)	19 (1.6%)	5 (4.0%)
5		5 (0.4%)	5 (4.0%)
6		3 (0.3%)	1 (0.8%)
7			2 (1.6%)
Sum	1462 (100%)	1187 (100%)	125 (100%)

Table 1: Distribution of participation in three groups

For a further analysis of the group of authors, we divided them into two subgroups according to the intensity of authorship: authors who published at three (half of all) or more conferences vs. authors who published at one or two conferences (see table 2). First, it can be observed that the group of authors at three or more conferences, which denotes the more or less continuous active members of the community, is relatively small (7.4% of all authors). Nevertheless this small group has a great influence on the community. The analysis of the group of authors who are referenced by other authors in the community shows that 18.6% of referenced authors are those who published at 3 ore more conferences. This means that 93.2% of these group members are referenced. The large group of authors who contributed only to one or two conferences (92.6%) has a much lower impact on the community wrt. citations. Roughly one third (32.8%) of these authors are referenced by other authors in the community.

A model to characterize global CoPs is proposed by McDermott & Jackson (presented in Wenger et al. 2002: 127). In this model, various local or regional groups are connected via local coordinators to each other and a global coordinator. In scientific communities program committee members, principal researcher and

other engaged locally or regionally in the community's field of research take a
role similar to local coordinators.

	Authors at 1 or 2 conferences	Authors at 3 and more conferences	Sum
All	1099	88	1187
	92.6%	**7.4%**	100%
Referenced authors	360	82	442
	81.4%	**18.6%**	100%
Quotient Referenced/All	32.8%	**93.2%**	

Table 2: Authors in detail

International connections

To characterize the latest development in the CSCL community towards an internationally connected community, figure 2a and 2b show the international connections based on the references between different countries for the last two conferences, CSCL 2002 and 2003. For simplicity, only relations greater than 20 are
shown and countries having less than 20 incoming or outgoing references are not
included. The upper row denotes the origin of references (nationality of the referencing authors), the lower row the target of references (nationality of the referenced author). The thickness of the lines corresponds to the number of references.
From these coarse-grained representations one can already see that the international connections grow; e.g. in 2003 Norway is also connected to Finland and the
relation between Germany and USA gets stronger from 2002 to 2003. However,
any new or increasing relations from 2002 to 2003 are not visible in these figures
as they are below the threshold of 20 references.

A more detailed analysis (not presented here) identifies the individual persons
with the highest impact inside local groups (Kienle & Wessner 2005). To determine the impact of a person we looked at the number of references from papers of
local group members to a specific person as well as the number of co-authorships
with a specific person. Persons with the highest impact may be regarded as a kind
of local coordinators in the sense of CoP.

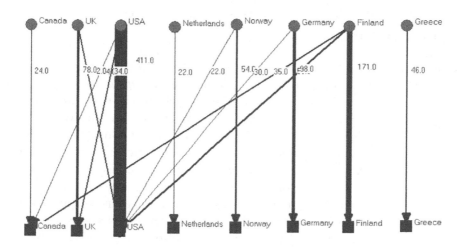

Figure 2a: References in the CSCL 2002 proceedings grouped by country

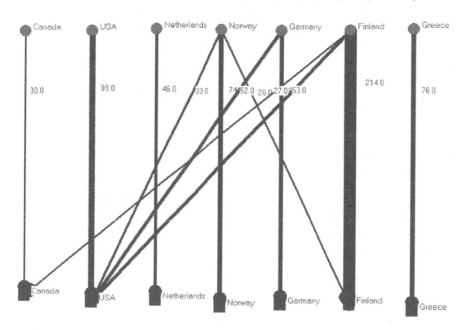

Figure 2b: References in the CSCL 2003 proceedings grouped by country

Design Principles for Cultivating Scientific Communities

Cultivating of a CoP can be achieved by *"valuing the learning they do, making time and other resources available for their work, encouraging participation, and removing barriers"* (Wenger et al 2002: 13). To make this more concrete a list of design principles to cultivate CoPs has been proposed (Wenger et al 2002).

In the following we look at one of these possibilities to cultivate a CoP, at encouraging participation. Especially, we focus on encouraging participation from different countries in scientific communities in order to increase the connectivity of the community members. For this we build on the models of scientific communities in the previous section. Design principles which aim at encouraging international participation are adapted to the specific characteristics of scientific communities. Using and presenting data and observations from our extensive analysis of the CSCL community (Kienle & Wessner 2005) which are relevant for this paper we trace these principles in this particular community.

These principles include smooth transitions between different degrees of participation (1), networking of local coordinators (2), rotation of meeting locations (3) and international program committees (4). Our principles are derived from Wenger et al.`s principles for cultivating distributed communities (see Wenger et al. (2002), pp. 119-137). More concretely, the first two of our principles are related to Wenger et al.`s second principle (for building up a structure), our third and forth principles to the third principle of Wenger et al. (for building a rhythm).

Smooth transitions between different levels of participation: horizontal and vertical paths

Wenger et al. (2002) point out that a *"good community architecture invites many different levels of participation"* (p. 55). These different levels allow a lively and also continuous community: new people with new ideas should be able to join the community as easy as possible; already existing members should be able to participate over a period of time and on different levels.

In scientific communities new people can join the community e.g. by a passive or active participation in conferences. In our data we analyse in which way people change between different levels of participation. While participation probably can be seen as a continuum, we can coarsely differentiate between the three levels participation at conferences, authorship and PC-membership (see the model of participation in scientific communities above). We compared for example the years of the first authorship or PC-membership (PCM; see table 3).

	Authors at 1 or 2 conferences (1099)	Authors at 3 and more conferences (88)	Sum (1187)
1. Only author	1017	52	1069
	92.6%	59.1%	90.1%
2. First author, then PCM	39	24	63
	3.5%	27.3%	5.3%
3. Same start: PCM and author	20	11	31
	1.8%	12.5%	2.6 %
4. First PCM, then author	23	1	24
	2.1%	1.1%	2.0%
5. Only PCM	--	--	97

Table 3: Different degrees of participation (transitions are in bold face)

Although the majority of authors are authors only and do not become PCMs, the data brought evidence for the existence of transitions between different degrees of participation:

- Most of the transitions occur from author to PCM (5.3% of all authors). This means that authors at one conference became PCM in subsequent years. As described above, we split up the group of authors in two groups according to the intensity of authorship. In the group of authors who contributed to three or more conferences (which are 88 authors; the "Top-88") the number of transitions is significantly higher. 27.3% of the "Top-88" authors became PCM in subsequent years. This transition may be seen as what Lave & Wenger (1991) call the way "from peripheral to full participation". We name this way **vertical path through a scientific community**: the participants do actively contribute to the community and are invited afterwards to join the core group.

- Other people start as author and PCM in the same year (2.6% of all). We assume that these people, after being asked for serving as a PCM, feel a high commitment for self contributing with an artifact.

- A third group started as PCM (2% of all PCMs became also author). Most of these PCMs are already experts in other scientific communities. They follow the **horizontal path into the community**: they do not start with the less active part as conference participant or author. This possibility offers new people to join the community in the most active role. This means that new ideas from and connections to other scientific communities are brought to this community on a high level.

As we have seen above there are new people joining the community each conference and existing members which participate over a period of time in the community. This combined with the existence of all possible transitions between different levels of participation is expected to lead to a lively and also continuous CSCL-Community. We sum up with the first principle. *Principle 1: Provide smooth transitions between different degrees of participation, e.g. vertical and horizontal paths*

Networking of Local Coordinators

As Wenger et al. (2002) point out, it is important to connect people in the community, especially to connect the local coordinators (p. 126). As mentioned above, in scientific communities such a role is taken by principle researchers or others engaged locally or regionally in this research field. These local coordinators influence by their publications, lectures and advice what other work is perceived by their fellows. In order to make available what has been done world-wide in the community and thereby to increase the internationality and advance the scientific progress, local coordinators play an important role. Fellows are likely to follow the model of the local coordinators.

Our analysis of the CSCL community shows the increasing international perception in the increasing degree of international references as well as in the increasing (but still low) amount of international co-authorships. It can be seen that the Top-88 authors (contributing to three or more conferences) are indeed more connected than the authors contributing to only one or two conferences. We expect from a further detailed analysis to be able to show also that newcomers are increasingly referencing international authors following the model of their local coordinators.

From this we derive the following principle. *Principle 2: In order to increase international participation in a scientific community the local coordinators should be connected among each other.*

Rotation of meeting locations

This principle is based on the Wenger et al.´s hint: "Rotate the location of face-to-face meetings" (Wenger et al. 2002, p. 131). While for Wenger et al. this aims to get members a better feeling for other members' particular issues and situations, in scientific communities this plays a different role. It provides a low barrier for new people living near the meeting (conference, workshop) location to enter the community. Data for the CSCL community clearly shows that for example the majority of authors at a CSCL conference come from the continent where the conference takes place.

The conferences 1995, 1997, 1999 and 2002 took place in North America; the conferences 2001 and 2003 took place in Europe. In figure 3 we see the composition of authors at the six CSCL conferences. Participation of European authors was strongest in those years where the conference took place in Europe; participation of North American authors was strongest in the other years where the conference took place in North America. But following the first conference in Europe (2001) the share of European authors increased also in the following conference (2002) in North America. From an analysis of the lists of participants and authors we see that a small but substantial percentage of the authors not only enter the community when the conference is located nearby but stay (at least for a while) in the community, i.e. continue to participate in following conferences.

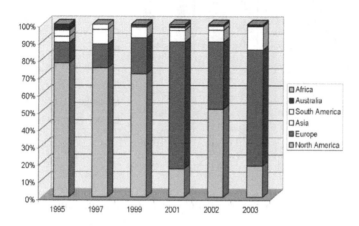

Figure 3: Distribution of authors by continents

From these findings we derive the following principle. *Principle 3: In order to increase international participation in a scientific community the conference location should rotate between different continents.*

International Program Committees

Wenger et al. (2002) recommend not only the mix of locations for face-to-face meetings, but also mixed preparation teams: *"Form meeting design teams of members from different locations"*. (Wenger et al. 2002: 131). For a scientific community this topic is related to the program (and organizing) committee: its members can be seen as multipliers who distribute information about the conference locally and encourage people from their local network to submit papers or posters to the conference. Therefore we expect that an international formation of the program committee leads to an international group of authors.

This correlation can indeed be seen in our data. Figure 4 shows the geographical distribution of the program committee members which is quite similar to the distribution of authors in figure 3. A citation analysis concerning the International Conference of the Learning Sciences (ICLS) showed the same relation in a different direction: a program committee of members from one country only corresponds with a low degree of internationality in the group of authors (Kirby et al., in press).

From these findings we derive the following principle. *Principle 4: In order to increase international participation in a scientific community the program committees should be composed internationally.*

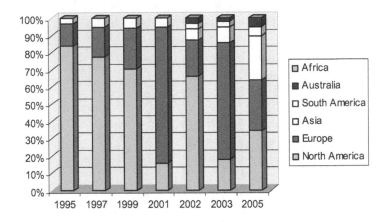

Figure 4: Distribution of PC members by continents

Conclusions and Further Work

This paper seeks to contribute to the understanding of scientific communities as Communities of Practice (CoP). Scientific communities can be seen as CoPs as they share a set of problems and a passion about a research field and aim to deepen their knowledge by interacting on an ongoing basis. On the other hand, models developed to characterize CoPs don't exactly match the situation in scientific communities. This was shown with the model of different degrees of community participation (Wenger et al. 2002).

We adapted the design principles for cultivating CoPs as introduced by Wenger et al. (2002) to the characteristics of scientific communities. It was shown how smooth transitions between different degrees of participation, networking of local coordinators, rotation of meeting locations, and international program committees help to cultivate the community wrt. its internationality.

As an example of a scientific community we characterized the international and multidisciplinary CSCL (Computer Supported Collaborative Learning) community. Based on data and observations from the CSCL community in its first decade of existence (1995-2005), basic models and adapted design principles have been instantiated.

There are a number of directions for extending the research presented in this paper. First of all, the quantitative approach taken so far should be complemented with a qualitative analysis. Thus important aspects like motivation and norms can be taken into account in order to further explain the effects described here. It seems promising to develop similar design principles for cultivating a scientific community which aim at other aspects of scientific communities like multidisciplinary or intercultural composition. The principles should be discussed also using data from other scientific communities in order to demonstrate their general applicability. Further research is needed to tackle other problems of (distributed) scientific communities, for example how to cultivate scientific communities depending on their current size. It has been argued that a community cannot grow infinitely (Shirky 2002). Above a certain threshold, an engaged community might turn into a passive audience, a group of people who mostly receive information rather than interact with each other.

Acknowledgments

The authors thank Marjo Krebbeks, Roy Pea, Jeremy Roschelle, Gerry Stahl and Barbara Wasson for providing participants lists of CSCL conferences. Thanks also to Isa Jahnke for valuable hints on communities and the anonymous reviewers for their very helpful comments.

References

Allatta, J. L. (2003). Structural analysis of communities of practice: an investigation of job title, location, and management intention. In M. Huysman, E. Wenger, V. Wulf (Eds.), Communities and technologies. Dordrecht: Kluwer, pp. 23-42.

Birnholtz, J.P., Bietz, M.J. (2003). Data at work: supporting sharing in science and engineering. Proceedings of the ACM Group 2003, pp. 339-347.

Cho, H., Stefanone, Mi., and Gay, G. (2002): Social Information Sharing in a CSCL Community. In G. Stahl (Ed.), Proceedings of the International Conference on Computer Support for Collaborative Learning 2002. Lawrence Erlbaum Associates (LEA), Mahwah, pp. 43-50.

Dillenbourg, P.; Eurelings, A.; Hakkarainen, K. (2001). European Perspectives on Computer-Supported Collaborative Learning. Proceedings of the First European Conference on Computer Support for Collaborative Learning (EuroCSCL 2001), Mc Luhan Institute, Maastricht

Doerry, E., Douglas, S.A., Kirkpatrick, A.E., Westerfield, M. (1997). Participatory Design for Widely-Distributed Scientific Communities. Proc. of the Third Conference on Human Factors and the Web, Denver, CO, 1997. Online: http://zfin.org/zf_info/dbase/PAPERS/Web97/web97-final.html [Last access: Jan 29, 2005]

Hall, R., Miyake, N., Enyedy, N. (Eds.)(1997). Proceedings of CSCL '97: The Second International Conference On Computer Support For Collaborative Learning. Lawrence Erlbaum Associates (LEA), Mahwah.

Hoadley, C.M., Roschelle, J. (Eds.) (1999). Proceedings of the Computer Support for Collaborative Learning (CSCL) 1999 Conference. Lawrence Erlbaum Associates (LEA), Mahwah.

Kienle, A., Wessner, M. (2005). Our way to Taipei: the first ten years of the CSCL community. Accepted for CSCL 2005.

Kirby, J., Hoadley, C. & Carr-Chellman, A. (in press). Instructional design and the learning sciences: A citation analysis. Educational Technology Research and Development.

Lave J., Wenger E. (1991). Situated learning: legitimate peripheral participation. Cambridge, University Press.

Newman, M.E.J. (2004). Coauthorship networks and patterns of scientific collaboration. Proc. Natl. Acad. Sci. USA, 101(Suppl 1): 5200 5205.URL: http://www.pubmedcentral.nih.gov/tocrender.fcgi? action=cited&artid=387296 [Last access: Jan 29, 2005]

Nurmela, K., Lehtinen, E., and Palonen, T. (1999). Evaluating CSCL log files by social network analysis. In C.M. Hoadley, and J. Roschelle (Eds.) Proceedings of the Computer Support for Collaborative Learning (CSCL) 1999 Conference. Lawrence Erlbaum Associates (LEA), Mahwah, pp. 434-444.

Nurmela, K., Palonen, T., Lehtinen, E., and Hakkarainen, K. (2003). Developing tools for analyzing cscl process. In B. Wasson, S. Ludvigsen, and U. Hoppe (Eds.). Designing for change in networked learning environments. Proceedings of the International Conference on Computer Support for Collaborative Learning 2003. Kluwer, Dordrecht, pp. 333-342.

Reffay, C., and Chanier, T. (2003) How social network analysis can help to measure cohesion in collaborative distance learning. In B. Wasson, S. Ludvigsen, and U. Hoppe (Eds.). Designing for change in networked learning environments. Proceedings of the International Conference on Computer Support for Collaborative Learning 2003. Kluwer, Dordrecht, pp. 343-352.

Schnase, J.L., Cunnius, E.L. (Eds.) (1995). Proceedings of the First International Conference on Computer Support for Collaborative Learning (CSCL '95). Lawrence Erlbaum Associates (LEA), Mahwah.

Scott, J. (1991). Social Network Analysis: A Handbook. London: SAGE Publications.

Shirky, C. (2002). Communities, Audiences, and Scale. Online: http://shirky.com/writings/community_scale.html [Last access: Nov 12, 2004]

Shumar, W., Renninger, A. (Eds.) (2002). Building virtual communities: learning and change in cyberspace. Cambridge University Press, Cambridge.

Stahl, G. (Ed.) (2002). Computer Support for Collaborative Learning. Foundations for a CSCL Community. Proceedings of the International Conference on Computer Support for Collaborative Learning 2002. Lawrence Erlbaum Associates (LEA), Mahwah.

Stokes, D.E. (1997). Pasteur's quadrant: basic science and technological innovation. Washington: Brookings Institution Press.

Wasson, B., Ludvigsen, S., Hoppe, U. (Eds.) (2003). Designing for change in networked learning environments. Proceedings of the International Conference on Computer Support for Collaborative Learning 2003. Kluwer, Dordrecht.

Wenger, E. (1998). Communities of Practice: learning, meaning and identity, Cambridge University Press, Cambridge.

Wenger, E., McDermott, R., Snyder, W.M. (2002). Cultivating Communities of Practice: A Guide to Managing Knowledge, Harvard Business School Press, Cambridge.

Woodruff, E. (1999). Concerning the cohesive nature of CSCL communities. In C.M. Hoadley, and J. Roschelle (Eds.) Proceedings of the Computer Support for Collaborative Learning (CSCL) 1999 Conference. Lawrence Erlbaum Associates (LEA), Mahwah, pp. 677-680.

A Study of Online Discussions in an Open-Source Software Community:

Reconstructing thematic coherence and argumentation from quotation practices

Flore Barcellini[+], Françoise Détienne[+], Jean-Marie Burkhardt[+,*], Warren Sack[#]

[+]INRIA-CNAM Eiffel Group, France, *Université Paris 5, France, #University of California, Santa Cruz, USA

Flore.Barcellini@inria.fr, Francoise.Detienne@inria.fr, Jean-Marie.Burkhardt@univ-paris5.fr, wsack@ucsc.edu

Abstract. This paper presents an analysis of online discussions in Open Source Software (OSS) design. The objective of our work is twofold. First, our research aims to understand and model the dynamics of OSS design that take place in mailing list exchanges. Second, our more long term objective is to develop tools to assist OSS developers to extract and reconstruct design relevant information from previous discussions. We show how quotation practices can be used to locate design relevant data in discussion archives. OSS developers use quotation as a mechanism to maintain the discursive context. To retrace thematic coherence in the online discussions of a major OSS project, Python, we follow how messages are linked through quotation practices. We compare our quotation-based analysis with a more conventional, thread-based analysis of the (reply-to) links between messages. The advantages of a quotation-based analysis over a thread-based analysis are outlined. Our approach provides a means to analyze argumentation and design rationales and promises a novel means to discover design relevant information in the archives of online discussions. Our analysis reveals also the links between the social structure and elements in the discussion space and how it shapes influence in the design process.

301

P. van den Besselaar et al. (eds.), Communities and Technologies 2005, 301-320.

Introduction

This paper presents an analysis of online discussions in Open Source Software (OSS) design. In OSS design, the Internet plays a very important role (Raymond, in DiBona et al., 1999). As Mockus, Fielding and Herbsleb (2000) state: "co-designers work in arbitrary locations, rarely or never meet face-to-face and coordinate their activity almost exclusively by means of e-mail and bulletin boards. One consequence of this is that virtually all information of an OSS project is recorded in electronic form." OSS design is distributed and mostly asynchronous. It takes place in three activity spaces (Sack et al, 2004): (1) the implementation space constituted by code archives and the mechanisms of versioning systems (e.g., CVS); (2) the documentation space predominantly authored, stored and distributed as web pages; and, (3) the discussion space in which messages and comments are exchanged in newsgroups, mailing lists, weblogs, and chat environments.

Our research aims to understand and model the dynamics of OSS design that take place in mailing list exchanges; i.e., within a specific area of the discussion space. Our second, long-term objective is to develop tools to assist OSS developers in the extraction and reconstruction of design-relevant information from previous discussions. A large part of the OSS design process takes place in the discussion space and is archived in the documentation space. Developers new to an OSS project are encouraged to study what has already been tried and accomplished. Considering the huge quantity of data generated and archived, proposing methods and tools to extract relevant data, especially design rationales, from the design discussions addresses a real need.

We show how quotation practices can be used to locate design relevant data in online discussion archives. Until now the dominant model used to represent conversation has been a based on the "reply-to" links, the threading, between messages. Our approach is based on quotation rather than threading. We understand quotation to be a context-preserving mechanism used in online discussions (cf., Eklundh and MacDonald 1994). In synchronous, e.g., face-to-face, discussions, participants take "turns." Frequently, a turn is a reply to the previous turn. For example, when one participant raises a question, in the next turn someone might answer the question. Thus, conversation analysis frequently entails finding adjacency pairs like question-answer or greeting-greeting, etc.. Within newsgroup or email-based discussions, quotation supports adjacency by maintaining two turns within a single message. In other words, by quoting the text of the previous message, one's message can incorporate both a question and an answer, or any number of other such adjacency pairs.

Our working hypothesis is that quotation-based representations are better than threading-based representations for the reconstruction of thematic coherence and for identifying and highlighting design activity that takes place within online discussions. We also hypothesize that quotation practices are linked to the social structure of an OSS project, specifically to the roles and differences of influence performed by project participants.

From among a wide variety of ongoing Open Source Software (OSS) projects, we have chosen to investigate the design processes of a major OSS project devoted to the development of a programming language called Python.

In the following sections we first review some prior studies of software design activities and the role of argumentation in the articulation and communication of design rationales. We then review prior work in thematic coherence analysis and in the analysis of quotation in online discussions. Finally, we present our quotation-based methodology and discuss our results.

Argumentation, collaboration and software design

Many previous studies of software design have analysed collaborative activities that take place in face-to-face meetings; e.g., brainstorming and technical review activities (D'Astous et al, 2001; 2004; Herbsleb et al. 1995; Olson et al. 1992). Researchers have identified various types of collaborative design activities.

One set of collaborative activities is related to the objects of design. These activities concern the evolution of the design problem and solution; e.g., elaboration of the problem and the enhancement or identification of alternative solutions. Evaluative activities – e.g., the evaluation of solutions or the articulation of alternative solutions – are also of this kind.

Another type of activity concerns the construction of common references, or common ground, by a group of co-designers. For example, clarification or cognitive synchronization activities take place when a group negotiates or constructs a shared representation of the current state of the solution.

Group management activities are a third kind of design activity. These activities are frequently related to issues of process. Project management activities that concern the coordination of people and resources - e.g., the allocation and planning of tasks – are of this kind. Meeting management activities – e.g., the ordering and postponing of topics of discussion – are another example of this kind of activity.

Co-designers accomplish design and evaluation activities by arguing with each other. These arguments have a very specific form and can be characterized as a sequence of "moves" or "turns."

For example, D'Astous et al. (2004) analyzed the argumentative moves in software technical review meetings. They found, for instance, that the elaboration of a solution can be followed immediately by either its evaluation alone or its evaluation and development of an alternative solution. Such review activities may, or may not, be preceded by a cognitive synchronization exchange. A cognitive synchronization exchange allows designers to articulate a shared representation of a design before it is evaluated. This argumentative move is referred to as a proposition-opinion. The review of a solution, in particular a negative review, leads participants to develop alternative solutions. An alternative solution may be a justification for the negative review or an answer to the weaknesses identified in the negative review. D'Astous et al. called this move opinion-arguments.

Argumentation makes explicit the design rationale; i.e., the reasoning behind the design of an artefact. By making their rationales explicit, designers have the means to keep track of past decisions and communicate these rationales to others outside the design team (Buckingham Shum and Hammond, 1994; Concklin and Burgess, 1991; Moran and Carroll, 1996). Different methodologies have been proposed to keep track of design rationales in design meetings. Unfortunately, designers often see these methodologies as imposing extra work on them; work that does not yield any immediate benefits for them. Our long term aim is to avoiding this objection by building tools capable of automatically extracting design-related information from archives of online discussions.

Open source software design

Open-source software design is a particular case of asynchronous, distributed, collaborative design (DCD). Descriptions of OSS design (DiBona et al, 1999; Elliott and Scacchi, 2004; Mockus et al. 2000; Raymond, 1999; Stallman, 2002) often highlight the following points:

- OSS systems are frequently built by large numbers of volunteers;
- work is not assigned; people undertake the work they choose;
- there is no explicit, system-level design;
- there is no project plan, schedule, or list of deliverables;
- work is done almost exclusively at a distance.

Empirical studies of the social organization and the dynamics of design processes of specific OSS projects have shown that these points constitute an idealized picture of OSS design. Specific OSS projects diverge from the idealized picture in a number of different ways.

For example, some OSS communities have a strict, hierarchical organization that stratifies developers into levels (Gacek and Arief, 2004; Mahendran, 2002). Centralized power structures of this sort are at odds with the flat, merit-based structure idealized by many OSS communities. The community we focus on, Python, has a very centralized organization. See Mahendran (2002) for an ethnographic study of the Python project and description of its hiearchicalized organization. The Python core developers (referred to as "administrators") have more power than ordinary co-developers in making executive decisions and modifying the code.

OSS design processes are not always as open-ended as the idealization might imply. Certain projects have prescribed means for controlling task assignment and for setting project plans and schedules. For example, the designers of Python engage in a specific design process called Python Enhancement Proposals (PEPs). PEPs are the main means for proposing new features, for collecting community input on an issue, and for documenting chosen design decisions. Some PEP documents describe new features of Python. Others specify more general information about the processes or organization of the Python community. When a PEP is written to describe a new language feature, it is suppose to provide a concise technical specification of the feature, a rationale for the feature, and a reference implementation.

The process of writing, reviewing and implementing PEPs is quite similar to two design processes used in conventional software projects: Request For Comments (RFCs) and technical review meetings. RFCs have been practiced for decades to define standards for the Internet (especially by the Internet Engineering Task Force, IETF). Technical Review Meetings (D'Astous et al., 2004) have been practiced in many corporate and governmental settings.

In Sack et al (2004) we have analyzed the PEP design process as a set of activities that take place in three different spaces: the discussion space, the documentation space, and the implementation space. Figure 1 shows an overview of the PEP process with links to these three activity spaces. Once a rough-draft PEP is accepted, the author of the PEP, called the champion, is responsible for posting the PEP to the community forums where the PEP is discussed. Archives of discussion, decisions regarding the PEP, and the different versions of a PEP are kept in the documentation space. Information about and the status of a PEP is, therefore, distributed between these two spaces. After a PEP has been accepted, it is given a final review by the leader of the Python project. Finally, if a consensus reached, a new piece of code is written to implement the PEP. This code is integrated into the project's code archive: the implementation space.

Previous studies of OSS design projects have focused on different activity spaces. Mahendran's (2002) ethnographic work illustrates how power is distributed across the three activity spaces - the discussion, implementation and documentation spaces. Ducheneaut's (2003) work investigated the evolution of links between people in two activity spaces – the discussion and implementation spaces – and showed how newcomers can be (but sometimes are not) progressively integrated into the social and the technical structure of the Python project. Sandusky et al. (2004) focused their analysis on the documentation space of the Bugzilla project. Mockus et al. (2000) focused their analysis on the implementation space. In this paper, we examine the dynamics of the discussion space and examine the influence of the social structure of the Python project on the discussion space.

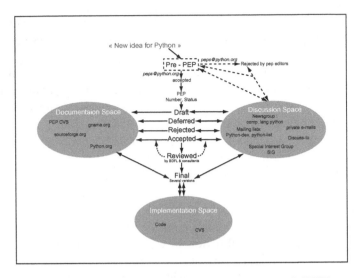

Figure 1: Overview of the Python Enhancement Proposal (PEP) process

Thematic coherence and quotation practices in online discussions

A large part of OSS design takes place in a discussion space where messages are exchanged between participants. Thematic coherence concerns how a message connects to previous messages of an exchange. In face-to-face conversation, coherence concerns how a turn connects to previous turns in a dialogue. Coherence in face-to-face conversation can be seen as actively constructed by participants across turn taking. In contrast to the face-to-face situation, in online conversations, a message can be separated both in time and place from the message it responds to. So, some form of explicit (or inferable) link between messages is usually required to understand the thematic coherence of an online discussion.

Current work on online discussions (e.g., Venolia and Neustaedter, 2003; Popolov et al. 2000) frequently assumes that the conversational structure is determined by "threading." I.e., the assumption is that the thematic coherence is determined by the "reply-to" links established between messages when participants reply to already posted messages. When a participant composes a reply to another message, the message-ID of the original message is placed in an "In reply-to" header on the reply message. The use of these message-to-message reply links and the outline-style presentation of message threads is practically universal among all known popular email software.

The threading approach is the main basis of tools for organizing and visualizing online discussions; e.g., Threaded Chat (Smith et al., 2000); Chat

Circles, Loom (Donath et al., 1999); and, Netscan (Smith et al., 2001). These tools suffer from several limitations. Some of them work with existing e-mail or newsgroup discussions, hence requiring no change in practice, but yield relatively little conversational structure (only basic threading). Others build rich conversational structures, but require a large change in practice: participants cannot use their usual desktop applications to post and read messages; they need, instead, to use the prototype tools developed by researchers.

The threading model is useful for analyzing conversational roles and for mapping the centrality of participants in a social network (see, for instance, Viégas and Smith, 2004). However, the threading model has some important limitations. Herring (1999) outlines how, in the threading model of online conversations, turn adjacency is disrupted; i.e., relevant responses do not occur temporally adjacent to initiating turns; e.g., an answer to a question might not arrive until long after the question is posted. This is a violation of sequential coherence (pragmatic principles of adjacency and relevance). Thus, this model provides an overview of the conversation but it is cannot correctly characterize its referential coherence.

To avoid this limitation, we propose to use quotations as the links to extract coherence in online conversations. Eklundh and Macdonald (1994) showed that quoting a message -- i.e., including it in a comment or reply -- was a widely used technique in e-mail dialogues. Quoting is seen as a context-preserving mechanism but the majority of responders use it selectively. Eklundh and Macdonald results showed that conversational participants perceived the use of quoting as contributing to the sense of the conversation when communicating in e-mail. Quoting is seen as a linguistic strategy (Eklundh and Rodriguez, 2004) used by participants to connect a comment to previous contributions to the conversation. Quoting creates the functionality of adjacency (Herring, 1999): it incorporates portions of two turns within a single message. It maintains context (i.e., portions of previous messages) and so can be use to retrace the history of a conversation.

As far as we know, there have been only two attempts to develop tools to automatically identify quotations and to represent online conversations based on quotation links between messages: Conversation Map (Sack, 2000) and a prototype inspired by Conversation Map called Zest (Yee, 2002). Our study expands on this work by analyzing quotation practices and participants' conversation roles within the context of a design activity, the design of OSS.

Study of online discussions in the Python OSS project

Corpus

Our message corpus was drawn from one of the major elements of the discussion space of the Python community: the python-dev mailing list hosts discussions pertinent to design decisions. We selected one conversation regarding a specific PEP (PEP 279). The corpus contains a total of about 3800 lines of text. The entire conversation is archived on the web and is public

PEP 279 proposes three different enhancements to Python: (1) a new index function; (2) a way to facilitate generator comprehension; and, (3) a means for generator exception passing. The corpus analyzed is composed of two discussions: part one (73 messages posted by 21 authors between March 28th and April 8th 2002) and part two (58 messages posted by 29 authors between April 24th and April 27th 2002).

Method

Our objective is to determine if correlations can be found between a participant's status and the patterns of quotation employed in a participant's posted messages. Our method is structured around the analysis of three aspects of online discussions:

(1)   quotation practices and message structure;
(2)   characterization of participation within the discussions and the declared status of participants in the project;
(3)   message content and activities analysis.

In the following, each message will be characterized according to these three aspects.

Quotation practices and message structure

We have observed that quoting is a general strategy employed by participants in the PEP 279 discussion:

- 84% of messages in part one of the corpus and 90% in part two contained at least one quote;
- 24% of message lines in part one and 34% of the lines in messages from part two are quoted lines;
- Half of the authors accounted for at least 16% (median) of the lines quoted.

Looking at the messages and the ways they were (or were not) quoted, we observed a similar set of results in both part one and part two of the corpus:

- 41% (in part one) and 47% (in part two) were not quoted at all;
- 29% (in part one) and 19% (in part two) were quoted once;
- 30% (in part one) and 35% (in part two) were quoted by between two and six different messages.

We categorized messages according to the alternation of blocks of quoted material and blocks of commentary (new text) in a message:

- A text-only message (TO), is a message that does not contain any quotations;
- A one-quote message (1q) is a message with one block of quotations followed by a comment. We distinguish two kinds of 1q messages:

- One quote-one source messages (1q-1s): these messages contain one quotation from one source message;
- One quote-multiple source messages (1q-Ms): these messages contain one block of quotations, but the quotations includes text from two or more source messages followed by one block of commentary;
- A multiple-quotes message is a message containing alternating quotes and comments (Mq). We distinguish three kinds of Mq message:
  - Multiple quotes-one source (Mq-1s) messages: several quotes of the same source message;
  - Multiple quotes-multiple sources (Mq-Ms) messages: embedding of quotations from several source messages;
  - Multiple quotes-multiple sources "composed" (Mq-MsC) messages: composition of quotations from several source messages.

Using these definitions, each message is categorized according to its structure and the source message(s) that is (are) quoted by the message. Aggregating part one and part of our corpus of messages we found that message structures are distributed as following:

- 9% text-only messages;
- 70% one-quote messages;
- 21% multiple-quotes messages.

Comparing discussion participation with participants' declared status in the Python project

Two major variables that might affect quotation practices include the level of participation exhibited by project members within the discussion list (python-dev) and a member's declared status within the Python project (as declared outside of the discussion list; e.g., the project administrators are declared on the project website: http://sourceforge.net/projects/python/).

As Mahendran (2002) pointed out the Python project has a centralized social structure. One can identify four important, declared roles:

- The project leader sometimes referred to (semi)-ironically as the BDFL (Benevolent Dictator For Life);
- The champion of the PEP: the one who proposes and writes the PEP. In our example discussion (concerning PEP 279) the champion is a project developer.
- The core team or administrators: nine people (at the time of our analysis) who are co-located with the project leader in a corporation called Zope. Their role is to maintain the code base, the documentation, and the PEP process.
- The developers: Only the project leader can accept a new developer into the list. To be accepted, new developers need to have demonstrated proficiency in Python. They are geographically distributed throughout the world.

To distinguish levels of participation in the online discussion, we have divided the population into two groups according to the median number of messages posted:

- HP-A/Dev: Administrators (including the project leader) and developers (including the champion) who sent more than two messages are High Participant Administrators (HP-A) or High Participant Developers (HP-Dev);
- LP-A/Dev: Those who posted fewer than two messages are termed Low Participant Administrators (LP-A) or Low-Participant Developers (LP-Dev).

Message content and activity analysis

Our message content analysis is a more fine-grain analysis based on a method developed in the field of cognitive ergonomics of design. Blocks of quotation or commentary contained in a message are categorized according to a coding scheme developed in our previous work (D'Astous et al. 2004; Détienne et al, 2003; Détienne et al. in press).

We identified the themes addressed by messages and found five themes corresponding to technical design problems:

(1)   P1: this theme concerns the issue of what functions, to be built into the Python language, are to be named; twenty-three alternative names were proposed;

(2)   P2: different possible syntaxes for the functions were discussed; eight such syntactic alternatives were articulated by the discussants;

(3)   P3: concerned the syntax, semantics and history of a technical issue concerning generator comprehension;

(4)   P4: concerned the technical issue of generator exception passing;

(5)   P5: concerned an orthogonal problem of name binding and the status of name spaces (i.e., two other technical issues).

We also characterized the message content with respect to the following categories of design activity (or the rhetorical function of the message):

- proposal of an (alternative) solution;
- evaluation: agreement/disagreement;
- group coordination;
- synthesis;
- clarification;
- explicit decision;
- other activities.

These categories were used to label the quotations and the comments in the messages. The analysis was done manually by the first co-author of this paper and validated iteratively with the second and third co-authors.

Results

Quotation practices, message structure, and thematic coherence

Our analysis of quotation practices allows us to compare a representation of online discussion based on quotation-based links between messages with a representation based on threading or "reply-to" links between messages. Figures 2a and 2b illustrate these two different ways of representing the PEP 279 discussion. In the figures, the circles represent email messages (labelled with an arbitrary number). Arrows joining the circles symbolize either a "is-a-reply-to" or a "is-quoted-by" link between two messages. The circles are colored to represent the different themes (i.e., the different design problems, P1-P5, enumerated above) addressed by the messages.

Figure 2a is an analysis of the discussion based on the threading, or reply-to, links between messages. Using the reply-to links to partition the messages, it appears to be the case that the conversation is fragmented into three different threads. This analysis by threads also corresponds to the way in which the discussion is archived on the web (at the URLs cited above).

Figure 2b, an analysis of the discussion based on quotation-based links between messages, reveals a distinctly different organization of the messages. In this analysis all of the messages are connected together, rather than the three distinct threads shown in figure 2a. In this analysis almost every message is linked to another message and the thematic coherence of the discussion is preserved. There are only three text-only messages that needed to be linked to the others using a reply to relationship.

In Figure 2b, four areas can be discerned: at the beginning of the conversation, the four themes (P1, P2, P3 and P4) are treated simultaneously in the messages (black circle) except for two messages that discuss only P2. Immediately thereafter two themes, P1 (blue circles) and P4 (pink circles), are the foci of discussion. Finally, an orthogonal problem, P5, emerges (orange circles).

The thematic coherence of the discussion, especially regarding P1, is better represented by the quotation-based links of Figure 2b than by the reply-to links of Figure 2a. Moreover, closer examination of the message contents reveals that the messages that are unlinked in Figure 2a are pivotal to the overall discussion. For example, message 68 initiates a discussion and constitutes a set of "opening remarks" crucial to the rest of the discussion. Message 4 generated several diverging branches of discussion. By comparing the position of messages 4 and 68 in figure 2a with their positions in figure 2b, one can see that the reply-to representation does a poor job of positioning them where they should be. Figure 2a shows messages 4 and 68 in detached and peripheral positions. In contrast, Figure 2b, constructed from the quotation-based links between messages, positions them as they should be, namely, in the "thick" of discussion. These results are consistent with our working hypothesis that a quotation-based representation is better than threading for reconstructing the thematic coherence of design-related online discussions.

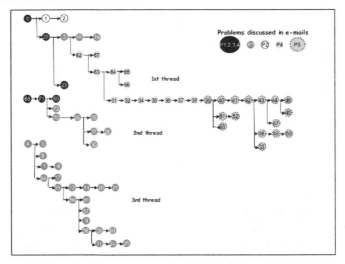

Figure 2a: Threading based representation of the links between messages

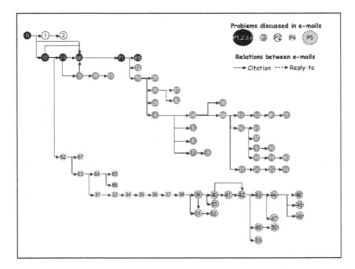

Figure 2b: Quotation-based representation of the links between messages

Finally, comparison of figures 2a and 2b shows that the set of messages that reply to a particular source message is a proper subset of the set of messages that quote the source (PEP 279 discussion). This suggests that quotation-based links contain more information that reply-to links.

In figure 3 we have layered another set of annotations on top of the graph shown in figure 2b (i.e., the graph constructed from quotation-based links between messages). The additional annotations in figure 3 outline groups of messages (with a dotted line) that all contain quotations from a given message. Figure 3 illustrates, what we will call, the "depth of quotation." Quotations of depth 1 are contained in messages immediately linked to the quoted message. Quotations of depth 2 are contained in messages that are linked to messages with quotations of depth 1; etc..

Figure 3 shows that the average depth of quotation is rather small. This result suggests that sub-thematic coherence could be constructed by partitioning messages into groups as was done for figure 3. More analyses would need to be done to determine if these message subsets based on the quotation of the same source correspond to a sub-thematic organisation.

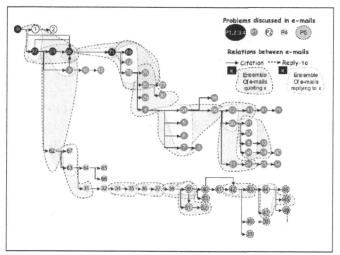

Figure 3: Sets of messages that quote particular source-messages and sets of messages that reply to the same source-messages

Quotation practices and degree of synchronicity

We also analyzed the flow of messages according to their posting time and the posting time of the messages in which they were quoted. Our objective was to obtain an overview of the degree of synchronicity of the PEP discussion. The geographically-distributed nature of the project makes this an important issue to study. The results are as follows:

- 50% of the messages quoted were quoted for the first time within an hour following their posting; 75% were quoted within five hours;
- 50% of the messages quoted a second time were quoted a second time within an hour following their posting; 75% of the second quotations occurred within seven hours of the message's posting;
- 50% of the third and 50% of the fourth quotations occurred within twenty-four hours of the posting of the message; 75% within 48 hours.

According to these results, it seems that there is a large degree of synchronicity; or, stated otherwise, sub-discussions organised around the same design topics have a weak degree of asynchronicity. In fact, late citations are often posted by co-designers who are far away from the USA (where most participants are) and their messages then arrive after design decisions have been taken.

Discussion participation and assigned roles in the Python project

Figure 4 represents the same discussion but messages are labelled with the project roles of their posters. The figure shows that the patterns of quotation -- sequential versus branch structure -- tend to correspond with the social position of the poster in the Python project: (1) a branching structure (when multiple messages quote from a single message) is generally initiated by a message posted by either the project leader or the PEP's champion; (2) High-participant Administrators are usually the ones to post messages that close a line of discussion; (3) sequential structures tend to alternate between messages posted by administrators and messages posted by developers. However, in the thematic drift away into P5 this is not observed. Here, the project leader and the PEP's champion stop participating until, finally, the project leader ends the discussion (with message 50). This analysis shows a relationship between the social structure of the Python project and participation in the online discussion. The social structure influences the design process as it unfolds in the discussion space.

Figure 5 shows that the depth of quotation achieved by a message is related to the message poster's status in the project. The project leader and the champion do not only initiate branching structures; their messages are also quoted much more deeply (i.e., repeatedly in subsequent messages) than the messages posted by the other participants. These results are consistent with the fact that this project has a very centralized social organisation and they show that key participants have a greater influence than others on the conversation.

Message content and design activity analysis

Analyzing the content of the quotations, we found that the most prevalent design activities quoted are Syntheses (N=49; i.e., 28%) and Disagreements (N=48; i.e., 28%) followed by Proposals (N=31; i.e., 18%) and Agreements (N=20; i.e., 12%). The PEP champion was the source of the largest number of quotations (N=40; i.e., 23%) followed closely by HP-Devs (N=37; i.e., 21%), HP-As (N=37; i.e.. 21%) and the project leader (N=36; i.e., 21%). Unsurprisingly, we found a small ler number of quotations from LP-Dev participants (N=20; i.e., 12%) and LP-As (N=3; i.e., 2%).

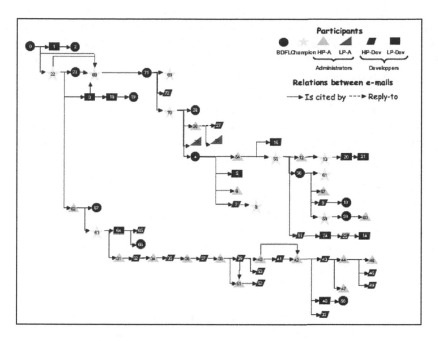

Figure 4: Status and position in the discussion

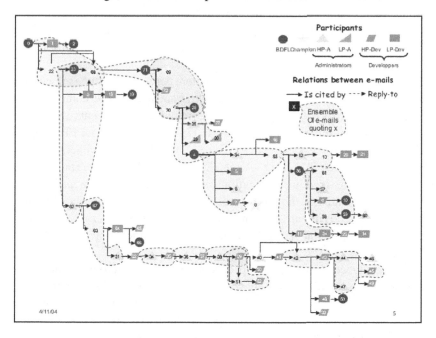

Figure 5: Depth of quotation and status of participant

Interestingly, there is a relationship of intermediate strength between the status of the quoting participant and the nature of activity contained in the quotation (V2 Cramer = 0.07). V2 Cramer is an indication of the strength of the relationship between two nominal variables. The relationship is considered to be weak when V2 < 0.4; intermediate when 0.4 < V2 < 0.16; and, strong when V2 > 0.16. Our statistical analysis indicates the following strong links between the status of the participants and the content they quoted:

- The PEP champion mostly quoted Decisions; other activity; and, to a slightly lesser degree, Agreements. Conversely, he did not quote Syntheses. This is easily explained since he was the author of most of the synthesizing messages and he does not quote himself.
- The project leader quotes Syntheses and Proposals. Conversely, he tends not to quote Agreements or Disagreements.
- HP-As mostly quoted Disagreements, Agreements, and Coordination messages. Conversely, they tend not to quote Proposals.
- LP-As quoted Proposals and tended not to quote Disagreements.
- HP-Devs mostly quoted Clarifications and Disagreements. They tended not to quote other activities and Agreements.

We also categorized the subsequent comments according to design activity. The most frequent activities that appeared in comments were Agreements (N=66) and Disagreements (N=58). Hence, 57% of the comments correspond to an evaluation activity, meaning that evaluation is the main activity related to the usage of quotation. We found lower frequencies for activities such as Clarification (N=28; i.e., 13%) and Proposals (N=26; i.e., 12%). Finally, we observed very few Decisions (N=14; i.e., 6%), Syntheses (N=11; i.e., 5%), or comments of Coordination (N=6; i.e., 3%).

Additionally, we investigated the correlation between the type of comment posted and the status of its author. Overall, about half of the comments were authored by HP-As (N=103; i.e., 47%). The remaining comments were mostly distributed between the project leader (N=37; i.e., 17%), the PEP champion (N=32; i.e., 15%) and HP-Devs (N=29; i.e., 13%). Very few comments were due to LP-Devs (N=15; i.e., 7%) or LP-As (N=2; i.e., 1%). Descriptive statistics show that, globally, there is a weak relationship between the design activity of a comment and the status of the participant (V2 = 0.03). Therefore, in general, the various types of activity are, roughly, equally distributed across all types of participants. However, it is remarkable that only the project leader posts Decisions.

We also analyzed the relationship between the set of activities quoted by a participant and the participant's subsequent commenting activity. Note that, in some cases, comments are preceded by a quotation that incorporates more than one design activity. Consequently, to perform the following analysis, we added the category "multiple activities" to our list of activity categories. We found a strong relationship between the type of activity in the quote and the nature of the activity in the associated comment ($V2 = 0.23$). In particular, we observed the following strong associations between activities contained in the quotation and in the subsequent comment:

- An Agreement is usually followed by a Proposal;
- A Disagreement is usually followed by a Disagreement comment. Conversely, Disagreements are not usually followed by Agreements;
- An Agreement is usually followed by a Synthesis;
- A quotation of a Coordination comment is usually followed a Coordination comment;
- Clarifications are usually followed by Syntheses or a previous clarification quotation;
- Other activities are associated with quotations presenting other activities.

Some of these associations may be interpreted in terms of argumentative moves as in D'Astous et al. (2004). Agreement-Proposal can be interpreted as an implicit disagreement justified by an alternative proposal. Conversely Agreement-Synthesis can be interpreted as an implicit agreement with a reinforcement of the consensus by a synthesis activity. Disagreement patterns (Disagreement-Disagreement) display diverging moves among participants. Finally, some patterns show an ongoing discussion of coordination (Coordination-Coordination) or are indicative of a co-construction of common knowledge (Clarification-Clarification and Clarification-Synthesis).

Furthermore, we found strong associations involving the Decision activity:

- A Proposal or Synthesis is usually followed by a Decision comment;
- A Decision is usually followed by either a Proposal or a Coordination comment.

Decision-Proposal pairs can be explained by the fact that some proposals are posted by geographically distant participants after a decision has already been made. Note that the strength of this result is probably exaggerated by the low number of explicit decisions in the corpus. Decision-Coordination pairs are apparent when a decision is made and then corresponding tasks are allocated to particular participants.

Discussion

Our study shows that a quotation-based analysis is a promising approach for identifying thematic coherence and design-relevant information in the archives of online discussions. A quotation-based analysis of thematic coherence was shown to be better than a thread-based analysis. The thread-based analysis incorrectly divided some theme-related messages into different threads and, furthermore, categorized as peripheral certain messages that were central contributions to the discussion. A quotation-based analysis did not exhibit these weaknesses.

Our content analysis of the messages revealed several interesting relationships between quotations and the comments that follow the quotations. We found that quotations are largely correlated with evaluative design activities. The relationships and correlations we have uncovered, between quotations and commentary, should aid us in the development of tools for archiving and visualizing online discussions. We intend to build on the quotation analysis procedures currently incorporated in the Conversation Map system (Sack, 2000) and, thereby, to provide some automated means to foster knowledge sharing in distributed collective practices.

Our analysis also revealed links between the organized social structure of the Python project and the shape of the discussion space. A participant's assigned role in the project organization affected whom the participant responded to in the online discussion and, therefore, influenced the unfolding of the design process within the discussion space. Two participants led the discussion we studied: the project leader and the champion of the PEP. This OSS community closely resembled the hierarchical organization of more traditional software design projects. This result can be opposed to the idealistic vision of OSS design.

Our study is an analysis of only one PEP discussion. PEP discussions can vary according to the status of the champion, according to whether the PEP has been accepted or rejected, and according to their (loose versus tight) coupling with other Python design tasks (Olson and Olson, 2000). In future work, we plan to replicate the analysis on a variety of other PEP discussions. In order to further extend our analysis to a wider sample of corpora, we plan to automate some parts of the structure and content processing. Currently under development is software to automatically identify quotation links between messages. We also hope to construct software to automatically analyse themes of discussion computing (Sack, 2000); and, to analyze patterns of argumentation, an admittedly much more difficult task akin to rhetorical structure parsing (Marcu, 1997).

Acknowledgments

This study was supported by the France-Berkeley Fund; the French TCAN-CNRS program; and, the National Science Foundation, Directorate for Computer and Information Science and Engineering, Division of Information and Intelligent Systems, Digital Society and Technologies Program, Award 0416353.

References

Buckingham Shum, S., and Hammond, N. (1994) Argumentation-based design rationale: what use at what cost? International Journal of Human-Computer Studies, 40, 603-652.

Concklin, E. J., and Burgess, K. C. (1991) A Process-Oriented Approach to Design Rationale. Human-computer Interaction, 6, 357-391.

D'Astous, P., Détienne, F., Robillard, P. N., and Visser, W. (2001) Quantitative measurements of the influence of participants roles during peer review meetings. Empirical Software Engineering, 6, 143-159.

D'Astous, P., Détienne, F., Visser, W., and Robillard, P. N. (2004) Changing our view on design evaluation meetings methodology: a study of software technical evaluation meetings. Design Studies, 25, 625-655.

Détienne, F., Burkhardt, J-M., and Visser, W. (2003) Cognitive effort in collective software design: methodological perspectives in cognitive ergonomics. Proceedings of the 2nd Workshop in the Workshop Series on Empirical Software Engineering, pages 17-25, Monte Porzio Catone (Rome, Italy), 29 September, 2003.

Détienne, F., Martin, G., and Lavigne, E. (in press) Viewpoints in co-design: a field study in concurrent engineering. Design Studies.

DiBona, C., Ockman, S. and Stone, M. (1999) Open Sources: Voices from the Open Source Revolution, O'Reilly and Associates Inc., Sebastol, CA.

Donath, J., Karahalios, K., and Viegas, F. (1999) Visualizing Conversations. Proceedings of HICSS 32, Jan 1999.

Ducheneaut, N. (2003). "The reproduction of Open Source software programming communities." Unpublished Ph.D. thesis, U.C. Berkeley.

Eklundh, K.S, and Macdonald, C. (1994) The use of quoting to preserve context in electronic mail dialogues. IEEE Transactions on Professional communication, vol.37, n°4, December 1994.

Eklundh, K. S., and Rodriguez, H. (2004) Coherence and interactivity in text-based group discussions around web documents. Proceedings of the 37th Hawaii international conference on Systems Sciences, 2004

Elliott, M., and Scacchi,W. (in press) Mobilization of Software Developers: The Free Software Movement. Information, Technology and People.

Gacek, C., and Arief, B. (2004) The Many Meanings of Open Source. IEEE Software, 21(1), 34-40, January/February 2004.

Herbsleb, J. D., Klein, H., Olson, G. M., Brunner, H., Olson, J. S., and Harding, J. (1995) Object-oriented analysis and design in software project teams. Human-Computer Interaction, 10, 2 and 3, pp 249-292.

Herring, S. (1999) Interactional Coherence in CMC. Proceedings of the 32nd Hawaii Conference on system sciences.

Mahendran, D. (2002) Serpents and Primitives: An ethnographic excursion into an Open Source community. Master's Thesis, School of Information Management and Systems, UC Berkeley, May 2002.

Marcu, Daniel (1997) The Rhetorical Parsing, Summarization, and Generation of Natural Language Texts. Ph.D. Dissertation, Department of Computer Science, University of Toronto, Toronto, Canada, December 1997.

Mockus, A., Fielding, R.T., and Herbsleb, J. (2000) A Case Study of Open Source Software Development: The Apache Server. In proceedings, International Conference on Software Engineering, pages 263-272, Limerick Ireland, June 5-7.

Moran, T. P., and Carroll, J. M. (1996) Design rationale: concepts, techniques and uses, Erlbaum, Mahwah, NJ.

Olson, G.M., Olson, J.S., (2000) Distance matters. Human-Computer Interaction, 15, 139-178.

Olson, G.M., Olson, J.S., Carter, M. R. and Storrosten, M. (1992) Small Group Design Meetings: An Analysis of Collaboration. Human-Computer Interaction, 7, 347-374.

Popolov, D., Callaghan, M., and Luker, P. (2000) Conversation space: visualizing multi-threaded conversation. AVI 2000, Palermo, Italy.

Raymond, E. S. (1999) The cathedral and the bazaar. Available at http://www.tuxedo.org/esr/writings/cathedral-bazaar/

Sack, W. (2000) Conversation Map: A content-based Usenet newsgroup browser. In Proc IUI 2000, ACM Press, 233-240.

Sack, W, Détienne F, Burkhardt, J.M., Barcellini F, Ducheneaut, N, Mahendran D. (2004) A Methodological Framework for Socio-Cognitive Analyses of Collaborative Design of Open Source Software. Distributed Collective Practices workshop in CSCW'04 conference. November 6-10, Chicago, US.

Sandusky, R.J, Gasser, L., and Ripoche G. (2004) Information practices as an object of DCP research, Distributed Collective Practices workshop, CSCW'04 conference, November 6-10, Chicago, US.

Stallman, R. M. (2002), Free Software, Free Society: Selected Essays of Richard M. Stallman, GNU Press.

Smith, M., Cadiz, J. J., and Burkhalter, B. (2000) Conversation Trees and Threaded Chat. Proc. of CSCW 2000, p. 97–105.

Smith, M., and Fiore, A.T. (2001) Visualization Components for Persistent Conversations. Proc. of CHI 2001, 136–143.

Venolia, G., and Neustaedter, C. (2003) Understanding sequence and reply relationships within email conversations : a mixed-model visualization. CHI 2003, April 5-10, Florida, USA.

Viégas, Fernanda B., Marc Smith. (2004) "Newsgroup Crowds and AuthorLines: Visualizing the Activity of Individuals in Conversational Cyberspaces," Proceedings of the 37th Hawaii Conference on system sciences.

Yee, K-P. (2002) Zest: discussion mapping for mailing lists. CSCW 2002 (demo).

Citizen Participation through E-Forum: a Case of Wastewater Issues

Vatcharaporn Esichaikul, Valailak Komolrit

Asian Institute of Technology, Thailand

vatchara@ait.ac.th

Abstract. To promote democracy, governments have encouraged citizens to voice their opinions on a number of issues. In this paper, the Government-to-Citizen (G2C) aspect of electronic governement, focuses on Citizen Relationship Management (CzRM). The highest stage of evolution in CzRM is participative democracy. One channel to promote participative democracy is through e-forums, which can enable a government to become "citizen-centric" to reflect the concept of good governance. In Thailand, e-forums have never been used as a formal consultative channel with citizens. The government has yet to organize a formal e-forum to consult citizens as it has done in off-line public hearings. In this research, a prototype of government e-forum was developed and evaluated. The application of the e-forum is to conduct an online hearing on wastewater issues.

Introduction

E-government can be defined as the application of information and communication technology (ICT) to bring about efficiency, effectiveness, transparency, and accountability of informational and transactional exchanges within government, between governments and government agencies at federal, municipal, and local levels, citizens and businesses; and to empower citizens through access and use of information [Boukis et al., 2003]. Citizen Relationship Management (CzRM) is concerned about how government can become "citizen-centric" in providing effective services to citizens through the use of IT tools. CzRM is embedded in the phases at different level of technology and need

P. van den Besselaar et al. (eds.), Communities and Technologies 2005, 321-339.
© 2005 *Springer. Printed in the Netherlands.*

sophistication. The highest technology and need sophistication stage is participative democracy. E-participation can deepen public involvement in the political process by increasing the frequency and enriching the content of dialogue between citizens and government.

E-participation can be conducted through an e-forum that involves citizens in discussion with officials and/or representatives. It may focus on a particular issue or be more general. In Thailand, e-forums for the purpose of engaging citizens in decision and policy making process have never been organized. However, citizens can post their message on websites. E-forums for the purpose of posting messages and expressing oneself are held at several websites, such as www.thaigov.net/webboard/, www.khonthai.com/webboard, www.ecitizen.go.th/ webboard, www.thaitambon.com, www.parliament.go.th, www.eldi.or.th, www.bma.go.th, www.thaijustice.com. E-participation, conducted through e-forums is still at its infancy, because much development is needed so that citizens can use the Internet to participate in the decision- and policy-making of the government. There are various kinds of features involved to promote e-s for the purpose of engaging citizens in decision- and policy-making processes in foreign countries. These features can be adapted to suit the Thai environment to promote e-forums. An application for the e-forum is to conduct a citizen hearing on wastewater issues. At present, an e-forum on wastewater issues has never been conducted, and only off-line public s are conducted, which are time consuming, require a lot of manpower, and involve high cost. Through an e-forum as an additional channel, more input from citizens can be collected to help the government establish policies relating to wastewater.

Background on Citizen Relationship Management

While e-government is concerned with the use of IT for efficient functioning of government department, Citizen Relationship Management (CzRM) is concerned about becoming "citizen-centric" in providing effective services to citizens [Xavier, 2002]. The private sector Customer Relationship Management (CRM) focuses on building relationship with clients to gain brand loyalty, sales, and profit, whereas CzRM focuses on providing services to constituents who must do business with the government. Eventhough citizens cannot "shop" with another government, they can vote [Miles, 2002]. Thus, CzRM can help government satisfy citizens' needs and wants, as well as gain popularity.

The Evolution of CzRM

Most government websites start off as providing basic information only, in which automation was used for cost minimization, effective governance, and efficient administration. The increase in demand for quality services as well as the advance in technology will force governments to be more citizen-centric. In the citizen-centric stage, the governments typically use multiple channels to deliver their services and to develop networking capabilities with different departments to provide seamless services to their citizens. The next level involves sophisticated data-mining tools to analyze and proactively anticipate the needs of citizens, customized to individual needs. Citizens will also participate in the setting of public policies and regulations. The evolution of CzRM is depicted in Figure 1.

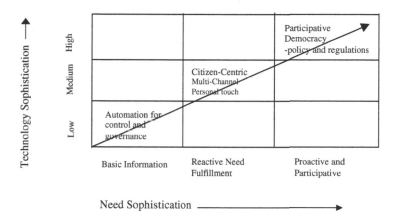

Figure 1: Evolution of CzRM (Xavier, 2002)

Participation in Decision-Making

Participative democracy has the highest technology and need sophistication in the CzRM evolution chart in Figure 1. E-democracy involves the use of ICT in support of citizen-centered democratic processes [Bend et al., 2002]. Citizens may choose from one of the following seven levels in e-participation [Mcdonough, 1999]:

- Access the information held by the government.
- On-line interaction with the government on service programs available to the public.
- On-line discussion of the issues with other citizens.
- On-line discussion of the issues with subject matter experts.
- On-line discussion of the issues with government officials.
- Contribution of ideas relative to the issues undertaken by the government.
- Voting on the issues.

Local community websites provide invaluable sources of information and a channel for people to express their opinions on local needs and priorities. Further links can be made to the local council and national government, in which global issues like sustainable development can be discussed at the grassroot level or from the bottom-up approach. The Internet can facilitate the communication among Members of Parliament, citizens, legislators, and executives, so that policies drawn reflect the needs of the people. It is now possible for large-scale participation in policy-making. The Internet enables communities of common interest and location to exchange ideas and share interests on issues affecting their livelihood.

E-democracy also enables political parties and pressure group to provide information through the Internet. Technology acts as a catalyst to bring forth a more democratic world by facilitating communication and making information available regardless of space and time. Public services can be provided to citizens on an individual basis, and opinions and needs can be collected, acknowledged, and responded to. Facilitators can help filter and structure submission to the website enabling comparison and also help summarize the discussion and responses to participants.

The following four requirements are needed for a meaningful and quality e-consultation and e-participation: numbers, accessibility, interactivity, and effect [Acland, 2003]:

- Numbers, in this context, does not necessarily mean involving large number of people. It means involving a properly represented cross-section of the population. Quality in e-participation can also be attained by involving named individuals and allowing sufficient time period for participation, surveys, and responses to take place.
- People should have easy access to the technology, which will provide equal opportunity for them to participate. It also means integrating different technologies for those who want to participate through letters, fax, or phones. It also means providing access opportunity for people with different abilities and language by breaking down barriers. People should be able to access background information, view the comments of others, and decide on their own.
- Interactivity pertains to participants getting feedback within 1-2 weeks of a process ending. The database needs to be sophisticated to allow the organizing, referencing, and analysis of large volumes of data in responding to participants. Moreover, participants should be allowed to set agendas, make reponses, and defend their stance.
- Quality will also be determined by the perceived effect. Any form of participation must be clearly defined with specific purposes. People can track government thinking and decision-making through a consultation process, which will bring about real transparency and accountability. The process needs to be evaluated in terms of who participated, why they participated, how they felt, the effectiveness of their participation, and the outcome, to keep a record and to make improvements.

Government E-Forum in Thailand

In Thailand, Prime Minister Thaksin Shinawatra is known for his support and vision in using ICT in the government. There are several government websites where citizens can post their comments, ideas, and problems. The government websites can be categorized into three levels: national, provincial, and local.

The following are examples of e-forums held at the national government websites:

At www.thaigov.net/webboard/, the e-forum is divided into three sections:
- General public section
- Member-only zone, with the following sub-sections:
  - Comments on government services
  - Public relations and announcement
  - Comments on ThaiGov.net
- Special corner (clubs and associations)

The general public section is the only section where registration is not required. The purpose of this section is to contact administrators, announce additional legal terms and conditions, inform problems and doubts in usage. However, the posting were not sub-categorized, thus there are a variety of topics ranging from advertising, comments on abortion, to government organization asking questions. In member-only zone, under the comments on government services sub-section, members can voice their opinion on government services in all agencies, areas for improvements or give examples of government agencies that have performed well. In the public relations and announcement sub-section, members can announce activities, seminars, employment news, change of address, telephone, or website. In the Comments on ThaiGov.net sub-section, members can comments on ThaiGov.net to improve its services to satisfy citizens even more. In the Special Corner, only privileged members belonging to that particular association can gain access.

At www.khonthai.com/webboard, there are two forums, one is for discussion on political parties, and the other is a general discussion on one's topic of interest. The political party discussion forum has a total of over 420 postings; however, citizens post on any issue from advertising to arms control to education. It would be more effective if forums were classified under topics, not by date posted. There should be a moderator to censor some of irrelevant postings. Citizens may post without giving any personal information. There is no search engine.

At www.ecitizen.go.th/webboard, the purpose is mainly to allow citizens to air their views on government business and services. Most of the postings are unanswered, and the postings are categorized alphabetically. It would be more effective to categorize by topics. There are over 200 postings, and citizens do not have to register or give any personal information when posting. There is a search engine to help locate topics.

At www.parliament.go.th, the purpose of the forum is to exchange ideas about politics and democracy. No membership is needed, and postings are ordered by most recently posted. There is no search engine, and it is not categorized.

www.eldi.or.th/forumMain.jsp, or the Thai Law Reform Commission website, provides a forum for citizens to post questions, opinions and views related to legislation. No membership is needed, and topics are ordered by date posted. There is no search engine.

www.thaijustice.com has the purpose of building an understanding between citizens and the law. Postings are ordered by date posted and a search engine helps to locate postings under a specific topic. No membership is needed. It is a very active site with many responses.

Some examples of government websites at the provincial level are as follows:

www.bma.go.th, or the Bangkok Metropolitan Administration website, allows citizens to post on any topic relating to Bangkok and the government. There is no search engine, and topics are ordered by date posted. No membership is needed.

www.phuket.go.th is a provincial website that offers two e-forums. One forum is titled as Phuket Governmental Computer Club and the other is Phuketandaman webboard. The purpose of the Phuket Governmental Computer Club forum is to discuss issues relating to computer and Information Technology such as zoning for Internet cafés, negative effects of computer games, etc. No membership is needed, but username and e-mail address are required. On Phuketandaman webboard, citizens can post topics relating to the sustainable development of the province. From observation, citizens post very useful comments but they go unanswered. Citizens are allowed to post harsh comments which a moderator should be able to edit. Only username and e-mail address are required. There is no search engine.

www.chonburi.go.th is another provincial website that offers an e-forum. From our observation, it is a pity to see that the e-forum has turned into an advertising board. This is because the purpose of the e-forum is not clearly stated except that it is a forum for citizens to exchange ideas and viewpoints. This forum definitely needs a moderator to screen some of the postings. It would be useful to have categories to post into. Questions to the e-forum are never answered and citizens will lose interest in the long run. No membership is required, and there is no search engine.

Some examples of government websites at the local level are as follows:

At www.thaitambon.com, the main purpose is to reach people at the tambon (district) level, especially concerning commercial activities and the well-being of the tambon. It is categorized according to the following topics: General Information, Recommendations and Comments; Products Wanted; Products for Sale; Tourism; Public Announcements; Tambon Administration; One Tambon, One Product; Internet News; Complaints; Products; E-commerce; Village Funds; and Progress/Developments. However, in each category it needs sub-forums.

No membership or personal information is needed when posting. There is a search engine, but it is not functioning properly.

At www.chiangmaicity.org, or the Municipality of Chiangmai, there is a survey form under Public Hearing, and an e-forum in which citizens can post on any topic. Therefore, the e-forum has too many slimming advertisements, and it needs a moderator to screen the postings. The main problem is that the purpose of the e-forum is not clearly stated, so there are too many topics. They should be categorized. No registration nor any personal information is required.

Development of an E-Forum on Wastewater Issue

Survey on E-Forum Features

In order to determine the features of the prototype e-forum, a survey of 100 subjects was conducted. They are students from four universities who have basic knowledge of ICT and Internet. Based on the survey, 72% of the respondents have visited an e-forum and 60% of those who have visited an e-forum have participated by posting or voting in the e-forum. The major reason for their participation are to hear the viewpoints of others, and to start a discussion. The third reason is that participation can be done in a calm and anonymous atmosphere. The major reason they like e-forums is that the topics are interesting to them, and that they can set the topic for discussion. Other reasons are that they do not have to join as members and that postings are anonymous. The main point they do not like about e-forums is that they have to sign up as members to participate. Of those who have visited an e-forum, 40% of them only observed the e-forum. The main reason is that they only wanted to read what others have to say. For those who have never participated in e-forum, topics they feel strongly about will motivate them to participate. The second and third motivating forces are that the e-forum has easy-to-use features with good design, and that participants do not have to join as members, respectively.

Interestingly, there are more respondents who agree that one should register as a member to participate in a government e-forum. However, only about 38% are willing to sign up as a member. The main reason they are not willing to sign up is that they are not interested. The second reason is that they do not think the government will listen to what they say. Sixty percent of those who are not willing to sign up will be encouraged to do so if their information is kept confidential and not shown to the public. The second feature that would encourage them to register is that there is an issuance of good citizen recognition certificates for those who have contributed meaningfully to the e-forum. Over 50% of the respondents are willing to reveal their full name and e-mail address. There were slightly more respondents who disagree that there should be a limit to the number of postings per topic per day. About 50% say there should be no limit to the number of postings.

Also, an interview was conducted with the officers of the Wastewater Management Authority (WMA) to assess the feasibility of conducting an e-forum. From the interview, it can be concluded that an e-forum is an economical mode of communication and can be used as an additional channel where citizens can express their viewpoints. Most agreed that e-forums can help in decision-making and policy of WMA, because viewpoints can be collected to predict trends. It can be used as an additional channel to the existing channel, but cannot be used to replace it, because most locals still do not have access to the Internet. At present, due to lack of funds, there is no plan to conduct an off-line public hearing. The main purpose for conducting an off-line public hearing is to promote understanding with the public, to listen to viewpoints, opinions and ideas of citizens, in order to reduce resistance to a project by involving the public in the decision-making stage. It is also conducted to assess the feasibility of launching a wastewater fee collection tariff, and the willingness and ability to pay.

The major problems faced in past public hearings were a lack of participation and cooperation, and getting answers and questions that were not focused on the issues but related to past failed projects of the government. There is also resistance from the public and problems of strong emotion from opinion leaders who won't listen to moderators.

Recommended topics for e-forums include willingness and ability to pay for wastewater fee, wastewater tariff, awareness of wastewater problems and solutions, opinion on WMA to operating all plants in Thailand, location of waste treatment plant and public opinion on environmental impact caused by wastewater treatment plants. Other interesting topics include penalties for non-payment of wastewater treatment service tariff, project acceptance level of citizens, and the citizen's satisfaction level on the wastewater treatment service provided by WMA.

The main problem is how to motivate people to participate. If membership registration is used, one can expect very few participants as evident in some government e-forums. Those that are active sites do not require registration but only username and e-mail address, which users are not required to reveal. Therefore, based on this survey, registration should not be required, and the participant does not have to submit his/her name or e-mail address in the prototype e-forum. However, if registration is required in an e-forum, a participant should be given the option of whether he/she wants to reveal his/her full name and e-mail address to the public. Also, the moderator should be able to send warnings and remove participants who have violated the rules. Since registration is not required in the prototype e-forum, it is difficult for the moderator to send warnings or remove a participant. So the moderator will delete postings that are offensive, indecent, abusive, hateful, harassing, libelous, unlawful, or not related to the topic under discussion. If the participant's email is available, a warning will be sent to him/her. The moderator will also publicly announce in the prototype e-forum that the posting has been deleted and provided reasons. There will be no limit to the number of postings per day. The moderator will also summarize the discussion. Participants can report any derogatory postings to the moderator. A search engine will help locate topics and postings will be labeled to reflect the writer's point of view.

System Functions

The e-forum features are selected from the results of the survey. These features help to design the system functions. There are two key players: the participants and the moderator. Figure 2 depicts the functions that can be performed by the participant and the moderator in the prototype e-forum.

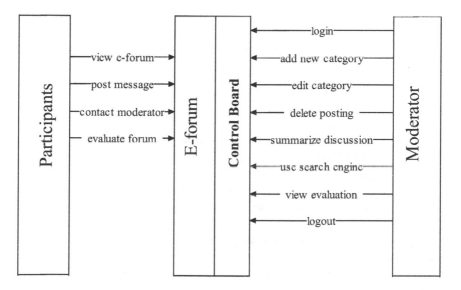

Figure 2: System Functions of E-forum Prototype

Function Hierarchy Diagram for Control Board

Moderator can perform the following main functions (see Figure 3):
- Login/logout
  The moderator can access the control board via login using username and password. The moderator can also log out of the system.
- Add new e-forum category
  The moderator can add a new category and enter background information and summary.

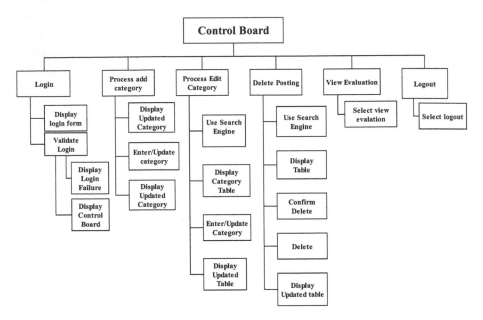

Figure 3: Function Hierarchy Diagram of Control Board

- Edit category
  The moderator can edit a category using the search engine. Category name, background, and summary can be edited.
- Delete posting
  The moderator can delete a posting. The moderator will select from among the four type of postings, which are category, question, idea, and argument. The search engine can be used to help locate the posting. A confirmation is needed to make a deletion from the database.
- View evaluation
  Evaluations made by the participants can be viewed by the moderator. The evaluation will calculate total votes and percentage of votes.

Function Hierarchy Diagram of E-forum

Participants can perform the following main functions (see Figure 4):
- View rules
  Rules and regulations including purpose and objective, are stated on this page.
- View and post a message

Function Hierarchy Diagram of E-forum

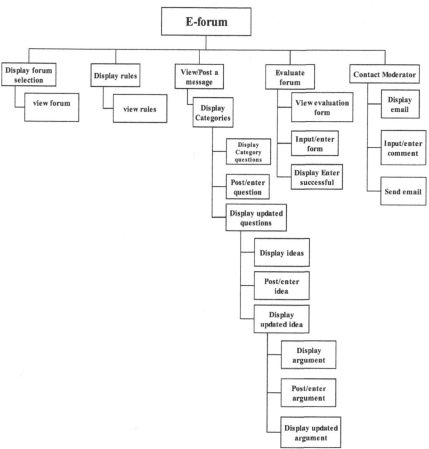

Figure 4: Function Hierarchy Diagram of E-forum

Message posting is categorized according to type. Participants can make three types of posting which are question, idea, and argument. A question is denoted by a light blue box; an idea is denoted by a yellow box; a pro argument is denoted by a green box; and a con argument is denoted by a red box. The participant will type the message in the text box. Name and e-mail address are not required to make a posting.

- Contact moderator
  If a posting is a threat to the safety or security of other participants, or if it contains derogatory remarks or uses excessive profanity, the user can report the posting to the moderator.

- Evaluate e-forum
  Participants can evaluate the e-forum and submit their opinions to the
  moderator via the Internet.

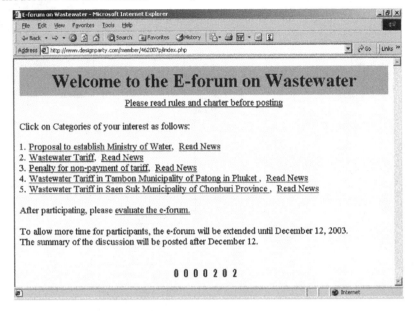

Figure 5: Home Page of the E-forum Prototype

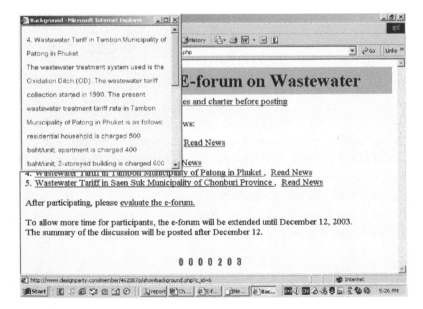

Figure 6: Popup of Read News

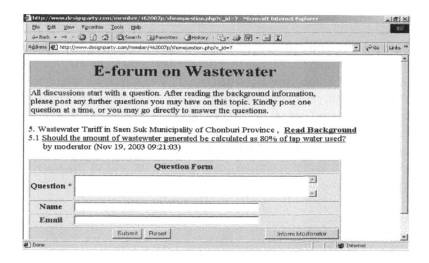

Figure 7: Question page using category id.

E-Forum Prototype

The prototype of the proposed e-forum is implemented to show the main functions. Some sample screens are shown above. Figure 5 shows the home page of the e-forum. Participants can read rules and click on the categories of their interest. The counter shows how many times this page has been accessed.

Participants can click on "Read News" on the home page to get an understanding of the topic category. "Read News" will appear as a popup screen.

If participant clicks on a category in the Homepage, the category questions will appear as in Figure 7. Participant can go back to read the background, and ask further questions. Participant can also click on the question, to go to idea page.

Prototype Evaluation

The content of the e-forum or the application used to assess the e-forum is on wastewater issues.   There are two topics for participants to select in which background information is obtained from newspapers and officially recognized sources. After the e-forum was conducted, a summary was prepared and posted on the website. For the evaluation of the e-forum prototype, 30 participants filled out the on-line evaluation form after they had participated in the e-forum. Participants were graduate students who had extensive experience using Internet.

Contents of the Forum

The topic categories under discussion in the e-forum are: 1) Proposal to Establish the Water Ministry, and 2) Wastewater Tariff. The topics chosen are current issues in the news relating to wastewater issues. The topics are interesting and debatable, and are currently being discussed by the government. The background on each topic is translated from newspapers and obtained from officially recognized sources. The aim of the background information is to give the participants a general understanding of the topic under discussion, in which participants can post further questions or ideas. At the end of the session, the summary of the discussion is posted on the website.

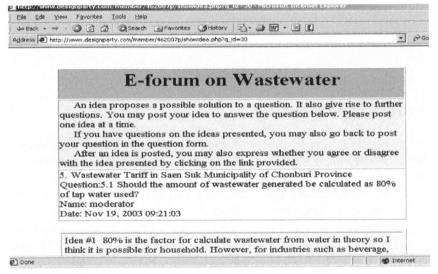

Figure 8: Idea Page

Proposal to Establish the Water Ministry

The background information on this topic is as follows:

„Mr. Samart Chokkanapitark, Director General of the Royal Irrigation Department, proposes that the government should establish the Ministry of Water to create unity by merging departments from the Ministry of Natural Resources and Environment (MNRE) and the Ministry of Agriculture and Cooperatives. At present, the problems of drought, floodings, and wastewater are handled by different ministries. If the Ministry of Water were established, the Royal Irrigation Department will act as the administrative body, and the Department of Water Resources, the Department of Groundwater Resources, and the Wastewater Management Authority will be merged together. A current issue is how the irrigation project to lay the pipelines system for the country has come to a stall for three months, because two ministries have conducted the same surveys, but obtained conflicting results. Thus, by establishing the

Ministry of Water, unity will be created, which can save time and funds." (translated from Krungthep Turakit, 13 Sept. 2003)

After conducting the e-forum, the summary is as follows:

The idea of establishing the Ministry of Water came about because the government can allot the budget for water management in a more coordinated manner. It will prevent different agencies under different ministries seeking funds for water management in overlapping projects. With the establishment of the Ministry of Water, the vision and objectives will move in the same direction, and the fixing of problems can be carried out with better efficiency and with more coordination. Depending on the merging departments and vested authority, the new integrated agency might be the Ministry of Water or Water Affairs, under the MNRE.

More ideas in the forum support the strategic reorganization of existing agencies that handle water management. Many support the improvement of effectiveness in existing organizations. However, water management needs to be dealt with in an organized manner to benefit the economy. It should involve experts to focus on the problems. The organizations' vision and objectives should move in the same direction. A suggestion was made to out departments related to water management under the Ministry of Natural Resources and Environment. An other suggestion was to set up a Water Board with strong expertise in water to handle the issues effectively, practically, and faster. They should work efficiently with fast mitigation, long-term plans and sustainable outcome.

The main problem is the overlap of authorities. If the Ministry of Water handles water resources and control the use of water, this can complicate the government system and form another redundant agency. It will also involve huge budget, mant new staff, and might not answer the country's needs, and there will be another Cabinet seat for political parties to fight over. To really solve the water management problems, it will be necessary to coordinate all parties involved with water management in the country, to discuss the issues in charting the vision, objectives, and long-term sustainable plan. It also requires concerted efforts from citizens and government staff to be environmentally conscious, considerate, dedicated, and responsible. Thus, the forum seems to support the reorganizing of existing agencies with duties relating to water management under the MNRE, but not establishing a new ministry. In addition, a Water Board should be set up to coordinate with agencies in other ministries whose duties are too complicated to move under the MNRE.

Wastewater Tariff

The background information on this topic is as follows:

"The Bangkok Metropolitan Administration (BMA) is planning to collect wastewater tariff in March 2004 in 13 districts that have access to wastewater treatment plants. The wastewater tariff for a residence is 2 baht per cubic meter, of which BMA will subsidize 1 baht/cubic meter in the first year, and reducing the subsidy every six months by 25 satang. Thus, at the end of the thrid year, each residence will pay a total of 2 baht/cubic meter. Hotels and department stores will pay at the rate of 4 baht/cubic meter, and industries will pay at 8 baht/cubic meter. The 13 districts are Phra Nakhorn, Pomprap Sattruphai, Samphan Thawong, Bang Rak, Yannawa, Sathon, Bang Kholaem, Thung Kru, Rat Burana, Nong Khaem, Phasi Charoen, Bangkae, and parts of Chom Thong. It is expected that the Metropolitan Waterworks Authority will handle the billing of both tap water and wastewater" (translated from Daily News, 26 Sept. 2003).

After conducting the e-forum, the summary is as follows:

Most participants agree that citizens should pay for the tariff. Others think that it should be a shared cost between citizens and government, so that the tariff is affordable. And some think that government has collected enough taxes already, and wastewater treatment should be a basic infrastructure.

If citizens are asked to pay a tariff, the government should first establish a proper, fair, and reasonable tariff system and there should exist a standard system to treat wastewater. Information on plans, policy, treatment technology, efficiency, and effectiveness of the treatment system should be clear and transparent. The tariff scale should be fair and reasonable, according to the technology selected, and able to sustain the operation cost of the treatment system, so the tariff rate should be revised from time to time. Factories releasing wastewater into the environment must be required to have proper pre-treatment facilities on-site, and should be dealt heavy penalties for infringements.

Payers should be categorized according to type of users (large entrepreneurs and factories, private commercialized users, public organizations), amount of water consumed, and pollution load produced. Rather than income factor, an incentive-based rate should be considered. There should be an incentive rate for households consuming less water than the set minimum to be exempted from the tariff. This would also help conserve water. If an incentive rate were used, the tariff should be collected monthly.

Evaluation of E-forum Prototype

In the e-forum, participants can fill out an evaluation form and submit it online. Thirty evaluation responses were analyzed.

Evaluation Results

Concerning the overall view on ease of use, it can be said that the system was fairly easy to use. However, improvements in the design should be made, such as the placing of 'Previous', 'Refresh', and 'Home' links, which should be placed near the top with the use of icons, which would be more attractive. The navigation design to connect the related information was satisfactory overall; however some did not like further links of idea to argument sections, because they preferred to see everything on one page. A search engine will help in finding information in the site.

With regard to learning, the system can be said to be fairly easy to learn. Regarding system feature design, a majority of the respondents agreed that organization of information in this e-forum contributed to effective communication. In system feature design of any e-forum, importance must be given to design layout, use of only cool tone colors, font size, and consistency of design.

Overall, a majority of respondents agreed that website postings is an effective way to conduct a discussion and understand the views of others. Most were comfortable with expressing their ideas. One strikingly high result was that most respondents agreed that the government should conduct an e-forum. Overall, the system proved to be satisfactory.

Conclusion

Citizen Relationship Management (CzRM) is concerned with how the government can become citizen-centric in providing services to its citizen through the use of IT tools. According to the evolution of CzRM, participative democracy involves the highest technology and so must be sophisticated. E-participation can be conducted through an e-forum, which is a text-based, on-line asynchronous communication system through the Internet.

The features of the e-forum website contribute to the success in conducting the c-forum. An important feature of the e-forum is whether to have registration for membership. According to the survey, some people are unwilling to sign up to participate in e-forums, but people will be most motivated to participate in the e-forums if their information is kept secret. Therefore to make participants feel most comfortable and encouraged to express their ideas, the forum should not include a registration form. A search engine is needed in the e-forum, and postings should be labeled or color-coded to show the viewpoints of the writer. The number of participants should be shown for each topic to attract viewers. The system feature design is also important. Importance must be given to user interface, design layout, use of cool tone colors, font size, and consistency in design.

After participating in the e-forum, a majority of the participants were satisfied with the e-forum prototype. It was easy to navigate, and respondents agreed that the organization of information in the e-forum prototype contributed to effective communication. A high quality of discussion was achieved from the e-forum prototype. A moderator, who plays a key role, is needed to monitor the e-forum. The moderator's role is to post/edit issues and summaries, and to delete unsuitable postings. The moderator should delete unsuitable and irrelevant postings and give reasons why such postings were deleted. The moderator should also provide a summary of the forum discussion and post it on the website.

The government is one of the key elements that can make e-forums successful. The government needs to support the use of e-forum and integrate the ideas obtained from citizens in the policy-making process. The government should have a centralized e-forum website, in which various agencies can conduct their forums. The government should design the e-forum to have a time frame to allow sufficient time for the citizens to participate. A schedule should also be available to show the dates when the forums are being held. Important information should also be provided and involve stakeholders, decision makers, and NGOs. The government should adhere to good practice guidelines, so that e-forums will have suitable publicity, responsiveness, rules, inclusion, moderators, privacy, partnership, and training.

CzRM can be conducted through e-forums to promote participative democracy. An e-forum is considered an effective way to start and conduct a discussion. People are often comfortable with expressing their ideas in an e-forum which helps people to understand the topic being discussed and the views of others. The government should promote the use of e-forums as another channel of communication. CzRM through e-forums is a channel for government to foster good governance and to nurture the spirit of e-democracy.

References

Acland, A., 2003. *E-participation and the Future of Democracy.* (accessed on June 17, 2003). http://www.dialoguebydesign.com/open/resources.htm

Backus, M., 2001. *E-governance in Developing Countries.* www.ftpiicd.org/files/research/briefs/brief1.pdf (accessed on May 25, 2003).

Bend, J., Kearns, I., and Stern, B., 2002. *E-participation in Local Government.* http://www.ippr.org.uk/articles/index.php?article=7 (accessed June 18,2003).

Boukis, G., Gorilas, S., and Tambouris, E. *Investigation of Electronic Government.* Accessed on May 15, 2003: http://www.egov-project.org/egovsite/tambouris_panhellenic.pdf

Branston, J., 2001. *Estonia: Experiment in Direct Democracy Launched through the Internet.* www.rferl.org/nca/features/2001/06/27062001112435.asp (accessed on September 27, 2003).

Center for Technology in Government, 1999. *Some Assembly Required: Building a Digital Government for the 21st Century.* (accessed on May 25, 2003). http://www.ctg.albany.edu/resources/abstract/abdgfinalreport.html

Coleman, S., J Gotze. *Bowling Together: Online Public Engagement in Policy Deliberation.* http://bowlingtogether.net/chapter5.html (Accessed September 27, 2003).

Cook, M., Dawes, S., LaVigne, M., Pagano, C., and Pardo, T., 2002. *Making a Case for Local E-Government.* (accessed on May 17, 2003).

http://www.ctg.albany.edu/egov/making_a_case.pdf

Deloitte Research, 2000. *At the Dawn of e-government: The Citizen as Customer.* http://www.deloitte.com (accessed on May 27, 2003).

Division for Public Administration and Development Management, United Nations Department of Economic and Social Affairs. *E-Government Case Studies: e-Democracy.* http://www. unpan1.un.org/intradoc/groups/public/documents/un/unpan008825.pdf (accessed on June 18, 2003).

Evans, C., 2003. *Tech-savvy Estonia founds academy for ex-communist states.* http://www.list.webengr.com/pipermail/picoipo/2003-March/000374.html (accessed on September 27, 2003).

Gordon, T.F., Hagedorn, H., Marker, O., Trenel, M., 2002. *Internet-based Citizen Participation in the City of Esslingen Relevance-Moderation-Software.* www.ais.fraunhofer.de/~maerker/paper/CaseStudyEsslingen.pdf (Accessed on September 27,2003).

Karakaya, R., 2003. *The Use of the Internet for Citizen Participation: Enhancing Democratic Local Governance?* (Accessed on September 27,2003). ww.psa.ac.uk/cps/2003/rabia%20karakaya.pdf,

Marker O., Hagedorn H., Morgenstern B., and Trenel M.. *Integrating Public Knowledge in Decision Making Case Study: Internet Public Hearing in the City of Esslingen.* http://www.buscalegis.ccj.ufsc.br/arquivos/Integrating _public knowledge_into_DMCS.pdf (accessed on June 15, 2003).

Mcdonough, F., 1999. *G8 Government Online County Comments.* (accessed on June 18, 2003). http://www.statskontoret.se/gol-democracy/g7golc.htm

Miles, J.B., 2002. *CRM for Citizens.* (accessed on June 2, 2003).. http://www.cprn.com/jmaxwell/files/wcw_e.PDF

Stahl, G., *Rittel: Deliberating from Perspectives.* (accessed September 26, 2003). http://www.cis.drexel.edu/faculty/gerry/publications/dissertations/computer/ d2.2. html

Xavier M. J., 2002. *Citizen Relationship Management: Concepts,Tools, and Research Opportunities.* (accessed on May 24, 2003). http://www.institutecrm.com/2002proceedings/ICRauthor.htm

E-Commerce, Communities and Government - a Snapshot of the Australian Experience

Andrea Howell[+], Milé Terziovski[*]

[+]Monash University, Australia, [*]The University of Melbourne, Australia
andrea.howell@buseco.monash.edu.au, milet@unimelb.edu.au

Abstract. This paper is based on a research study of 12 local government councils in Australia funded by the Victorian e-Commerce Early Movers Assistance Scheme. (VEEM). Multiple cross-case content analyses were used to identify the underpinning themes in the study sample. It was found that the VEEM scheme was successful in raising awareness of e-Commerce within the community, however there is a wide disparity in local government readiness for e-Commerce and community demand for e-Commerce. In order to accelerate the take-up of e-Commerce practices and technologies within communities, the tripartite relationship between State and Local government and the community is considered critical in diffusing e-Commerce. Specifically, the tripartite relationship should support raising awareness of e-commerce, and encouraging adoption of e-commerce.

Overview

International experience with the information economy indicates that significant benefits fall to early adopters of e-Commerce. In response, the State Government of Victoria (one of six states and two territories in Australia) formulated a strategy - Connecting Victoria - to grow the information and communications technologies (ICT) industry and to share the benefits of these technologies across the community. A central tenet in the 1999 strategy was 'boosting e-Commerce', by 'vigorously promoting e-Commerce'.

P. van den Besselaar et al. (eds.), Communities and Technologies 2005, 341-357.

One of the initiatives from this strategy was the Victorian E-commerce Early Movers (VEEM) scheme. Under the auspices of Multimedia Victoria (MMV), a department within State and Regional Development, this scheme was designed to provide assistance to local municipal councils to accelerate further take-up of e-Commerce practices and technologies to benefit the whole community. In 2000, Victorian councils were eligible to receive $3 from the State, for every $1 they allocated to e-Commerce initiatives. [For non-Australian audiences, a municipal council is a region or precinct which is managed by a body of people elected or appointed to serve as administrators, legislators, or advisors. Designated as "local government" it is the third tier of our government – Federal, State and Local. Each municipal council has responsibility for a range of services provided by Local Government in response to the needs and priorities determined by local communities].

The purpose of the research project was to examine how selected Victorian municipal councils, that received funding under the State Governments' VEEM Scheme, diffused e-commerce within their communities. The primary objective of the research was to determine a model of best practice from a review of the e-commerce initiatives undertaken by these councils, which could be used by councils not funded under this scheme for future strategy setting. The secondary objective was to gain a better understanding of local and state government role in the diffusion of e-Commerce practices and technologies in the wider community.

This paper highlights the strategic and tactical issues facing local government councils when they attempt to diffuse e-commerce initiatives in their communities. It begins with an overview of related concepts including the digital divide, and knowledge communities.

The digital divide

Countries such as the UK, India, Australia and New Zealand have acknowledged the existence of the digital divide. The label is a description of the gap of knowledge between communities with access to information and communication technologies (ICT) as opposed to those with no, or limited access. The gap exists because of several limiting factors, such as geographical, attitudinal and generational (Cullen, 2003).

These factors are particularly relevant to Australia and becoming increasingly important influences in the adoption of ICTs. Australian government policy papers (Department of Communications, Information Technology and Arts, 1999, 2004) and studies (NOIE, 2001) acknowledge that e-commerce is a strategic and competitive imperative for Australian businesses. For example, externally, the internet provides a new stage for business and allows Australian organisations to expand beyond traditional product and market perimeters. Internally, e-commerce has the potential to re-structure organisational processes and functions to allow greater and more efficient utilisation of assets. The internal and external application of e-commerce allows business to strengthen customer and supplier relations which, in turn, facilitates the organisation's transformation of core relations and business processes (Maguire, Terziovski, and Samson, 2000).

International experience with the information economy indicates that early adopters of e-Commerce have reaped significant benefits. The Australian government and society generally recognises the importance of e-commerce adoption. Businesses that deal with governments have had to change the way they interact with government via on-line business dealings through e-Government and e-procurement.

The adoption and diffusion of information technologies amongst Australian SMEs however has been slow (National Office for the Information Economy, 2000). Predominant reasons for resistance relate to the business case for moving online, specifically the cost versus benefit issues; physical access or connectivity to ICTs; content; attitudes, ICT skills and competencies (Cullen, 2003; National Office for the Information Economy, 2000). Sharma and Gupta (2003) suggest disparities with the location and quality of internet infrastructure and the industry structure, business size and location may also contribute to the widening of the digital divide.

Diffusion of ICT

The Victorian Government has been working through a number of initiatives to diffuse information technology through SMEs. This began in 1999 with a vision for growing the information and communications technologies (ICT) industry and for sharing the benefits of these technologies across the community. One of the central tenets in the strategy was 'Boosting e-Commerce', and the government's aim was to 'vigorously promote e-Commerce'. This strategy has since been operationalised through various government initiatives and programs to accelerate further take-up of e-Commerce practices and technologies.

Sharma and Gupta (2003) believe e-commerce diffusion should include the diffusion of internet technologies, telecommunications and the traditional commercial infrastructure. These aspects are considered vital for the ongoing survival of SMEs, and indeed a future measure of the prosperity of a SME maybe the rate of adoption of e-commerce and its integration into their business strategies (National Office for the Information Economy, 2000; Sharma and Gupta, 2003).

Whilst researchers have modelled a variety of diffusion models, none have assessed the tripartite relationship between the levels of government and the community, which is considered critical in diffusing e-Commerce (Hall, 2000). For example, Gibbs, Kaemer and Dedrick's (2003) e-commerce diffusion model examines global, environmental and policy factors. At the national level, national policy is paramount to the diffusion of e-commerce, and includes government promotion initiatives for e-commerce and IT in general. This translates into providing SMEs with technical support, training and funding for IT use (Gibbs et al, 2003) but does not address how this might be operationalised.

The internet diffusion assessment framework of Press, Burkhart, Foster, Goodman, Wolcott and Woodard (1998) is broader in its assessment, focusing on the nation as a unit of analysis and characterising the state of the Internet along six dimensions – pervasiveness, geographic dispersion, sectoral absorption, connectivity infrastructure, organisational infrastructure and sophistication of use. This framework only provides a macro viewpoint of internet diffusion for comparative purposes with other nations, and does not address the role of government, communities and organisations in diffusing telecommunication infrastructure. Similarly, the technology diffusion model of Caselli and Coleman (2001) which focuses on the diffusion of computers around the world, utilises national data such as manufacturing trade openness, size of government, and level of human capital.

Clearly the role of government in diffusing technological infrastructure (e-commerce, internet, or computer) is critical, however evidence from Europe and the UK suggests that if "top down" Government initiatives are not supported by "bottom up" community regeneration programs, there is little likelihood of success (Hall, 2000).   Top down initiatives provide funding and a sense of direction, but are likely to under-perform because they are not sufficiently sensitive to local needs, conditions and infrastructure. As well, government agencies have not been suited to lead information society initiatives because they themselves are laggards in embracing the information society. "Based on empirical evidence, Government organizations have been slow to embrace the web. Therefore, it is argued that the public sector must get better at devolving decision making to local communities because leadership comes from the private sector" (Hall, 2000).

Knowledge communities

ICTs remain important in organising and sharing knowledge (Berawi, 2004). This is because the World Wide Web has transformed geographically dispersed businesses and communities into a global village for information sharing, social interaction and economic exchange (DeFillippi, 2002).

From an organisational viewpoint, knowledge capture and sharing is considered paramount – that is, having the right information at the right time for the right people, in a format that matches the task. Walsh and Ungson (1991) refer to this as organisational memory, or any piece of knowledge that is related to organisational tasks, which is stored and can be bought to bear on present decisions. Management of knowledge – acquisition and dissemination – must be facilitated within the organisation to encourage knowledge sharing and building of the knowledge community. Whilst ICTs provide the infrastructure and environment to support learning, these of themselves may not be sufficient to stimulate effective learning (Barrett, Cappleman, Shoib, and Walsham, 2004). Therefore the knowledge community within the organisation is crucial in forming a supportive "climate" for knowledge sharing.

Whilst there is increasing recognition of the role of communities in knowledge sharing (Wenger and Snyder, 2000), knowledge communities are not limited to organisations but are also evident between people in different organisations coming together across boundaries to learn through sharing knowledge on particular topics (Anand, Glick and Manz, 2002). Therefore both organisational social capital and community social capital can provide leverage for each other, as well as providing a range of socio-economic benefits in different locales. Knowledge diffusion through "strategic communities" – communities or industry clusters that collaborate by disseminating knowledge of technical practices, sharing resources and economizing on set-up and transaction costs – is now recognised as providing significant competitive advantages to those companies and regions that embrace it. Best (2001) describes these as regional communities of innovation and recommends that regionally based companies, educational, and government institutions cooperate in fostering knowledge creation and skills formation.

Methodology

The research study utilised the case study approach and structured interviews to elicit data from twelve participating councils. Councils were asked to fill in a pro-forma questionnaire, and this was supplemented with phone interviews. A case study protocol was developed which addressed procedures, questions, analysis plan and case study reports (Yin, 1994). The procedures related to an initial introductory letter to participating councils from the research team and Multimedia Victoria. This letter sought availability of council officers (for example CEO, VEEM project manager, economic development manager, IT&T manager) and any third party that could enhance the review. First round interviews were organised and participants encouraged to have available sources of information relating to both the VEEM scheme and the Council's IT strategy. Second round interviews were conducted either in person or via telephone, dependent on depth of follow up required and geographic location.

Case study questions related to the VEEM project and its organisational context, e-Commerce strategy formulation, implementation of e-Commerce strategy, and the value of e-Commerce, both operational and business performance.

The case study report and format for analysis was influenced by MMV, and therefore focused primarily on the VEEM project. The report incorporated an

abstract, introduction, and sections on VEEM funding, key processes of the
VEEM project, project completion, and project lessons.

Both the interviews and the case studies provided a longitudinal analysis of the
process of change and the difficulties encountered at each organization in the
formulation and the implementation of its e-Commerce diffusion strategy. An
analysis of the events was documented in terms of what happened, how it
happened, who was involved and the main lessons learned.

Respondents Profile

Thirty-nine Victorian councils were funded under the VEEM project - 18
individual applications and five group applications. Twelve councils were
selected for the research project on the basis of a balance between regional and
metropolitan councils; a combination of group/individual projects; and projects
that covered the range of specified range of categories, such as portal, training, e-
procurement, strategy, GOL, expo, student initiatives, or other initiatives.

Those interviewed included the Chief Executive Officer, Economic
Development Managers, Council Managers and third party suppliers. The range
of job functions of interviewees highlighted both e-commerce expertise and the
best person available. The inclusion of third party suppliers reflected the external
partnerships forged as part of the specific project. Each council and its VEEM
project is briefly outlined [NB The names of the councils have been abbreviated
for ease of reading and to maintain the privacy provisions imposed by MMV]:

1. City of Bt – a regional council (nicknamed Silicon Gully), which has three
    major IT foci: IT2010 Strategy, Televillage and TeleCommunity. VEEM
    funding was to train business people via an e-Commerce Business Planning
    Workshop.
2. City of B - a regional council which also has three major IT foci: a
    Community Telco (a council backed community initiative successfully
    operating since November 1999); a Virtual Electronic Trading Hub
    (VETH), and a learning city vision, based upon education, research and
    development for all the community. The Council, in conjunction with
    support from neighbouring two councils applied for VEEM funding to
    develop a "Community Advantage" E-Charter as the first step in its learning
    city vision.
3. NG Council – a rual council in which local service groups have initiated
    most of the information technology diffusion within the community. VEEM
    funding was used to develop a community portal, analyse and work with 5-
    10 local businesses to develop electronic business plans and transactions,
    conduct one on one awareness and assistance to 120 local businesses, and
    upgrade and enhance Council's web page.

4. City of S – a regional council. In conjunction with support from two neighbouring councils, VEEM funding was approved for the development of a Regional Electronic Facilitation Centre (ETFC). Specifically, the funds would be used to develop and implement a regional business portal, and accelerate the use of information and communication technologies in the region (which is being promoted for its agricultural and horticultural expertise).

5. SH Council – a rural council dedicated to help existing local businesses become more competitive. VEEM funding was for an "On-Line Project" which was divided into two parts: an e-Commerce expo, and development of a regional internet business directory and business profile.

6. City of W – a metropolitan council whose vision is articulated in its multimedia strategy, which is to enhance the level of customer service, provide greater access and business process improvement through the innovative use of multimedia and electronic service delivery. Current technological uses include GPS (Global Positioning System); GIS (Geographic Information System); multimedia, business processing mapping review, and electronic document management. VEEM funding was used to provide e-Commerce training for business proprietors of Non English Speaking Background (NESB), and to develop an e-Commerce supply chain model for the transport and construction sector.

7. City of Wy - a metropolitan council together with its neighbouring shires has formed and continues to support the Western Regional Economic Development Organisation (WREDO). WREDO is a not for profit organisation that seeks to promote the region as the transport and manufacturing hub of Australia, to increase the skill base of the resident youth, and to support local business in the take-up of information technology for promotion and electronic commerce. The City of Wy, together with five neighbouring councils and WREDO applied for VEEM funds to develop a regional portal, and assist with training and e-procurement.

The final draft of each case study was returned to the council for review and approval.

Findings

There were three major findings, each which will be discussed relative to the results from the multi cross-case analysis and flow-on recommendations:

- The tripartite relationship between State and Local Government, and the business/community must be clearly defined, along with responsibilities to sustain momentum of e-commerce diffusion and to develop technology-based knowledge communities.

- The VEEM initiative was successful in raising awareness of e-Commerce in the respective communities however the two important issues both from an organisational and a community viewpoint that councils need to address in order to accelerate the diffusion of e-Commerce practices and technologies are raising awareness and making the business case.
- Technology capabilities – both infrastructure and suppliers - vary in communities and may result in locational or skills-based barriers which need to be addressed.

Tripartite Relationship

Responding councils indicated that they considered continued financial support from the State Government was critically important. According to the interviewees, while the State Government's primary role is to articulate vision and policy, the two drivers for any State government initiatives in promoting e-Commerce should be awareness and skill development. Future e-Commerce initiatives should provide support either to local government as the catalyst for change, or directly to the community.

Many councils acknowledged that without the VEEM funding and indeed ongoing support from the State government, many of the projects would still 'be on the shelf', would not be highly prioritized by council, or would never have got off the ground. However there was also criticism that the State Government was offering too many funding options. This was perceived as creating duplication in funding applications, and had the effect of overwhelming council staff as to how these opportunities could realistically be assessed in terms of meeting local needs. Reviewing, responding to and then operationalising these initiatives required considerable work, and was also dependent on local relevance, and fit with council strategies.

The interviewees placed the role of local government in two categories – leader and facilitator. All councils except one (a rural council) believed local government should be driving the technology push because the uptake of e-Commerce and technology was seen as essential to job creation, sustainable economic development of rural and regional areas, and the stopping of youth leakage.

It is a principal of the State Government to have council provide a leadership role.

We have a strategy that recognises that council has a leadership role in assisting its community become aware of accessing and using IT, especially in rural and country towns (NG Shire Council)

Council is still the heavy driver of e-Commerce and we see this as a community leadership role.

There is a requirement for industry and council based leadership, and if not from industry, then council needs to keep pushing. We've had to work a lot harder than most, because this Shire doesn't have visible industry leadership (City of W).

Whilst philosophically councils agree they play a leading role in economic development of their Shires and economic development has been clearly linked to e-commerce, this has not translated to widespread acceptance at the local government level. Although the merit of having an e-commerce strategy was supported by many local government councils - all managers advised their respective councils had an informal direction or vision for e-Commerce integration - only two councils had formal written IT or multimedia strategies.

These were mainly focused on internal adoption of e-Commerce practices and technologies. Council therefore needs to firstly have a documented e-commerce vision, and secondly needs to demonstrate their own adoption of e-Commerce practices, as an example for the rest of the community. It adds weight to council's push for e-Commerce, if they are seen to be implementing these strategies within their own business practices. This may have an impact on the community uptake of e-Commerce. For example, if councils were promoting e-Commerce but not utilizing it within their own business processes, then the local business community may question the efficacy of e-Commerce practice. This was supported by councils' admission that many businesses displayed a natural reticence to jump on the 'e-Commerce bandwagon' because, amongst other things, there is the perception that council is not adopting e-Commerce.

This reluctance may also reflect council's capacity for change. "Information technology is linked to capacity for change and competitiveness: it is both a response to changing markets and a change agent within the organisation" (Jayne, 1999). When council does not see the need for change (change being the uptake of e-Commerce), then it will do nothing to make change happen. Where a council sees that e-Commerce uptake ties in directly with economic development, a dual e-Commerce focus (internal and external) makes it a stronger contender when competing for resources, investors, and supporters. The NG Shire was the only Council mindful of the change management issues which surfaced during the VEEM project, such as fear of change and the need for ownership. As a result, the CEO implemented a change management program which was primarily aimed at reducing fear, and providing employees with pathways for career development and advancement. Staff were able to incorporate e-Commerce processes within existing job responsibilities.

As part of determining an e-Commerce vision for the shire, Council also needs to assess the role council will play in the context of diffusing e-Commerce technologies and practices within the community. Is council the visionary, catalyst, driver, or facilitator? If the role of council is clearly to govern, then council should be working with the economic development units, and business community to develop catalyst programs and place themselves in the role of facilitators of e-Commerce. However, in some cases, the role needs to be visionary, as the community may not have the breadth or depth of vision to conceive of such things as a Tele-village or an Electronic Trade Facilitation

Centre. Aspects of e-Commerce can then be assessed in terms of the bigger picture for the Shire. For example how does the portal concept fit into a bigger vision for the Shire or region, and will a portal be sustainable in the region or the shire? The research interviews revealed each council was able to describe its role in relation to diffusion of e-Commerce, but when contrasted with the others in the interview set, was quite different in its focus. Two councils viewed themselves as the driver; and another two councils described their role as the catalysts. Other councils saw their role as facilitators in a supporting role, ie. the community and business drove the uptake, and council supported this or the community took action first, but needed council's support to sustain the integration of e-Commerce.

The adoption of the different roles would most likely be informed by the relationship between local government readiness for e-commerce and community demand:

"If you use the surfing analogy, where are we on the wave (and the wave is the demand in the community)? Are we way out in front of them and trying to be the beacon that people are heading towards, where they're saying yes, we want it and we're coming to get it. Or are we lagging behind and the community comes knocking on our door and says we want to pay our rates via a kiosk in the main street. The tension is whether e-Commerce readiness and demand is community led, or the responsibility of council. I think we'd prefer to be a little behind the wave because it is an additional cost in terms of service delivery. We're not necessarily going to save money by going into any of these areas, but we recognise we need to be responding to community demand and we will respond to that so long as the demand is there (City of Wy).

Weaker community demand and support for e-Commerce therefore suggests council may adopt more of a leadership role, whereas stronger community demand and support for e-Commerce may indicate council's role should be more facilitative. Stronger community demand may result in businesses and the broader community take on the responsibility for e-Commerce uptake in the role of initiators and/or partners. Initiators or e-Commerce champions can be individual business owners or centres of influence (businesses such as banks/accountants or community business groups such as Rotary) who are happy to promote awareness of e-Commerce because of their own experience with e-Commerce.

"Champions are required to keep on winding up the awareness campaign. These champions should ideally be in different business sectors to promote the value of e-Commerce (City of B).

Having a champion is the key without a doubt to successful integration of e-Commerce. Champions will come out from the processes but they also need some expertise around them who are equally enthusiastic, and prepared to work hard through these processes and think outside the square (City of S).

"Networking through champions is essential there is no doubt about that, but your champions are busy people and their time is limited. You can't expect to go to them every 2 or 3 years and ask for their involvement. What we've been able to do with our champions is use them in a way that is time limited, for a specific purpose, and project oriented, and once that's finished, we're out of their life" (City of Wy).

Hall (2000) suggested that whenever possible business and community should establish partnerships with local government in e-Commerce uptake and this was supported by the interviewees who stated partnerships presented strong opportunities for showcasing successes and for developing an information society. One group of councils in their search project was able to convince its business champions to become shareholders in the commercialisation of an Electronic Trade Facilitation Centre.

> One single champion becomes a voice in the wilderness over time, enthusing and retaining the interest of the other stakeholders. In this project, the other champions became the stakeholders (City of S).

The research identified the need for a clearly delineated model of diffusion that identifies the role of and relationship between State Government, Local Government and local businesses and communities in diffusing e-commerce. The conceptual framework outlined in Figure 1 attempts to address this gap. The framework suggests that to continually focus on delivering an improved information society, a multi-tiered approach is required.

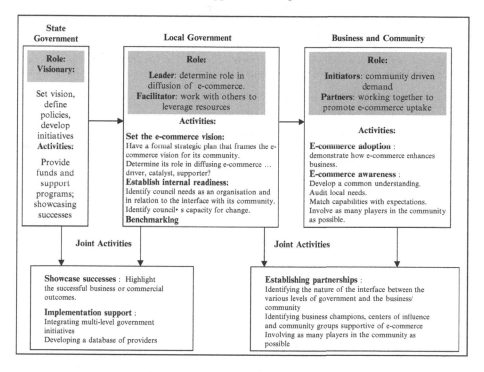

Figure 1. Conceptual framework of the tripartite relationship in diffusing e-commerce within communities

352 A. Howell and M. Terziovski

Organisational and Community Issues

The research project identified two major hurdles facing SMEs and communities: 1) the lack of awareness, understanding and readiness for e-Commerce uptake, and 2) the demonstrable benefits for business.

Members of the community will already have been exposed to e-Commerce in some way, whether this is at the workplace, school, library, doctor's surgery or pharmacy, and of course within the home. However a more targeted approach to develop a common understanding of what e-Commerce is, what it does and how organizations and individuals can benefit from using it, may be the first step in the awareness of e-commerce:

> Within any community it is important to know where the local community is at; if that means starting small, then start small. (SH Council).

> The Expo was designed to start people thinking [about e-Commerce] (SH Council).

> My main role is to assist the local community to accept and grasp the opportunities that IT and T provides. The primary objective of the project has been to push awareness of e-Commerce to local business. We need to work slowly with them. If someone is not sure, for example if Business A doesn't understand and Business B is a bit frightened by the technology, then its very important that a friendly approach is made by our staff and suppliers. The outcomes are more important than trying to finish the project (NG Council)

Raising awareness may also require understanding local needs. In one region, a local community group undertook this survey:

> You need to focus at the community level. For example within our Shire, Rotary undertook a survey of local businesses to determine the needs and discovered there was a need for an Internet Service Provider (NG Shire).

All the research suggests that the use of electronic commerce reduces costs and improves the quality of business-to-business transactions. Most of the council officers and third party suppliers interviewed believe the greatest hurdle for businesses within their communities is being convinced of the business case for the uptake of technology.

Raising awareness may also require understanding local needs. In one region, a local community group undertook this survey:

> You need to focus at the community level. For example within our Shire, Rotary undertook a survey of local businesses to determine the needs and discovered there was a need for an Internet Service Provider (NG Shire).

All the research suggests that the use of electronic commerce reduces costs and improves the quality of business-to-business transactions. Most of the council officers and third party suppliers interviewed believe the greatest hurdle for businesses within their communities is being convinced of the business case for the uptake of technology.

> Full on e-Commerce on the internet is not the savings its cracked up to be – there has to be savings for the business before they'll jump in (SH Shire Council).

The trick is to demonstrate and prove the business proposition to the small business proprietor – without this, which takes a lot of time, many businesses will remain skeptical and unconvinced. E-Commerce awareness is like riding a bike, you've got to get them to do it first! (City of Bt).

The number one criteria for business is that we must be able to demonstrate value for business. E-Commerce has not been high on businesses' priority list because they haven't been given the business value proposition. Building the business case is an issue, but not a difficult one. The emphasis should be to try and convince the SME in the value proposition of doing e-Commerce (City of Bt).

The real issue is not the technology, and not getting it to the region, but getting SMEs to utilise it. The emphasis should be to try and convince the SME in the value proposition of doing e-Commerce. Hopefully the VEEM project addresses all or some of this (City of B).

The issue for those leading uptake of e-commerce is to demonstrate how e-Commerce enhances business. Every business aims to maximize resources in order to make profits. Any demonstration of value to a business will generate some interest. Most often the best advocates for e-Commerce adoption are those that have already incorporated these technologies and practices into their organisation. Therefore the benefit of past experience cannot be over-estimated, and wherever possible should be utilised.

Another regional council brought together thirty local businesses, each with various resources and expertise, to develop an e-charter for the region – a standard set of guidelines to embrace the uptake of e-Commerce. This approach strengthened the e-Commerce knowledge of the community, but more importantly demonstrated the competitive advantage of being a knowledge community:

We sat down with the businesses after doing our sums, and showed them that a significant amount of dollars was being spent outside of the region and not much was being returned to the region. By developing an e-charter, and the virtual electronic trading hub, we could provide an environment where buyers and sellers could first look to local content and thus keep the wealth generated within the region, which means jobs, wealth and a sustainable community development (City of B).

Building the knowledge community results in better understanding, unity within the community, win-win benefits for all, and delivery of tangible and sustainable results. The City of Bt's "Tele-Village" and "Tele-Community" initiatives are based on this principle:

The more players out there delivering this message the better off we'll be. One thing we are finding is that it seems to all be coming together. We've got the banking industry actually pushing the e-Commerce message; we've got other sectors of private industry in terms of portals being put out by the local newspaper, by television and we also have a tourism portal in the area. So the private sector is trying to drive it. The Chamber of Commerce is using it by actually putting out a messaging system in terms of email to all its participants. The Australian Industry Group is also looking at doing something similar. So the recognition is there that this new form of communicating and doing business is appropriate (City of Bt and BD, third party supplier to the VEEM project).

Technology Capabilities

Localities within Australia are widely dispersed and infrastructure development has occurred mainly along the eastern seaboard. Physical access or connectivity to ICTs and the quality of technology infrastructure is therefore reflective of location. This certainly impacted on the two rural councils surveyed, and they saw the issue of infrastructure as a major inhibitor to the uptake of e-Commerce practices and technologies:

......Our town is the furtherest point north which has access to the infrastructure – anything north of this, ie the rest of the municipality is not serviced well. e-Commerce is only as good as the connection. People will get frustrated if they can't get the connection and will resort to traditional methods until there is a consistency of service and delivery (SH Council).

An objective will be to improve the infrastructure to allow small business to develop. By having an IT infrastructure in place means rural and regional business won't have to move to metropolitan Melbourne. However, the quality of the infrastructure here is not good (NG Council).

A second issue is ICT skills and competencies. Councils were keen to match the capabilities already present in the community (the public sector, the private sector, colleges and training centres) with the expectations of the community. One rural council made it a priority to have local service providers. It wanted sustainable momentum (possibly underlined by their relative geographic position) of the project, which could be best delivered by the development of local knowledge and businesses.

Other councils however found local expertise did not match the needs of the project. The City of Wy for example sourced a local provider for their B2B portal, however the provider "fell over", which necessitated sourcing of an outside service provider. To address this issue, councils called for a statewide database of service providers who could assist both local councils and local businesses. Those councils that did not have the expertise internally or within the community could utilise such a database, and this database of service providers might also provide similar benefits for community use. Additionally, councils advised that service providers "did the rounds" with respect to the VEEM projects. The development of a database may have prevented duplication of time and resources for councils when evaluating service providers.

Synthesis

Evidence from overseas countries clearly highlights the importance of e-commerce in the development of a country's social and economic structures. The Australian government, following on from overseas experience has mandated the uptake of e-commerce as a strategic imperative. Whilst both Federal and State governments are actively encouraging the take-up of e-commerce via funding options which have emanated from its strategies, Australian SMEs have demonstrated lower levels of engagement and interest. Rather than appealing to SMEs directly for these reasons, the VEEM project provided funding from State Government to local municipal councils to work with their business communities to increase awareness of e-commerce and adoption of the technology and processes. Based on feedback from the participating councils, this multi-tier approach to the diffusion of e-commerce is the most appropriate. A survey of SME attitudes to this multi-tier approach however may present a different perspective.

Projects funded under the VEEM scheme were disparate and revealed contrasting stages of readiness for e-commerce. The majority of the municipal councils involved in the assessment of VEEM appear to play a major role in driving the uptake of e-commerce. This community focus, rather than reliance on individual businesses, maybe a reflection of the value of group synergy which can facilitate more rapid and widespread interaction.   Working through the community may also dispel some of the negative perceptions associated with top-down initiatives, as the councils have a more intimate understanding of the needs of the community and can encourage horizontal communication and grass roots involvement.

Conclusion

Based on the qualitative analysis in this study we conclude that both council and community readiness for e-commerce are a mitigating factor in the uptake of e-commerce, and should be factored into any model of best practice. However, if council has a leading role in the uptake of e-commerce within the community, this should be limited to a facilitative role once e-commerce champions have been identified. These individuals or community groups can be used to increase awareness of e-commerce, and where necesssary build the business case for the adoption of e-commerce. In turn, this will facilitate a supportive climate for advancement of e-commerce knowledge into the community, and encourage the development of regional communities of innovation. This is exemplified in the communities of at least three of the councils examined under the research project. Ideally, longitudinal qualitative and cross-sectional quantitative research should be conducted with these communities to track the relationship between council and its community, and the social and economic benefits derived from a funded and increased focus on e-commerce diffusion. This approach would enable the development and testing of theoretical models to explain why and how some e-commerce practices work in some situations and not others.

Acknowledgement

The authors wish to thank the anonymous reviewers for their helpful comments which have been incorporated into the final draft of this paper.

References

Anand, V., Glick, W. and Manz, C. (2002) Thriving on the knowledge of outsiders: tapping organisational social capital. Academy of Management Executive 16(1), 87-101.

Barrett, M., Cappleman, S., Shoib, G., and Walsham, G. (2004) Learning in Knowledge Communities: Managing Technology and Context. European Management Journal, 22(1), pp 1-11.

Berawi, M. (2004) Quality revolution: leading the innovation and competitive advantages. International Journal of Quality and Reliability Management, 21(4), pp 425-438.

Best, M. (2001) The New Competitive Advantage: The Renewal of American Industry. Oxford University Press.

Caselli, F. and Coleman, W. (2001) Cross country technology diffusion: the case of computers. The American Economic Review, 91(2), pp 328-335.

Cullen, R. (2003) The digital divide: a global and national call to action. The Electronic Library, 21(3), p 247-257.

DeFillippi, R. (2002) Organizational Models for Collaboration in the New Economy, Human Resource Planning, 25(4), pp 7-18.

Department of Communications, Information Technology and Arts (1999) A Strategic Framework for the Information Economy: Identifying Priorities for Action - December 1998. Commonwealth of Australia Printing Services.

Department of Communications, Information Technology and Arts, (2004) Australia's Strategic Framework for the Information Economy 2004 - 2006: Opportunities and Challenges for the Information Age. Commonwealth of Australia Printing Services.

Gibbs, J., Kraemer, K. and Dedrick, J. (2003) Environment and policy factors shaping e-commerce diffusion: a cross country comparison. Information Scoiety, 19(1), pp 5-18.

Hall, G. (2000) "Social Inclusion in the Information Society", In Standford-Smith, B. and Kidd, P. (Eds) "E-Business: Issues, Applications and Developments", European Commission Conference on e-work and e-Commerce, Madrid, Spain.

Jayne, V. (1999) Six of the Best NZ500 leaders' strategies in fast changing times, NZ Business, 13(7), 10.

Maguire, C., Terziovski, M., and Samson, D. (2000) Reshaping the Organisation Based on E-Commerce Strategy. Unpublished paper, University of Melbourne.

National Office for the Information Economy (2000) "Taking the Plunge, 2000: Sink or Swim – Small Business Attitudes to Electronic Commerce". Commonwealth of Australia Printing Services.

National Office for the Information Economy (2001) "Advancing with E-Commerce". Commonwealth of Australia Printing Services.

Press, L., Burkhart, G., Foster, W., Goodman, S., Wolcott, P., and Woodard, J. (1998) An Internet Diffusion Framework, Communications of the Association for Computing Machinery, 41(10) pp 21-26..

Sharma, S. and Gupta, J. (2003) Soci-Economic Influences of E-Commerce Adoption. Jounrla of Gloabl Information Technology Management, 6(3) pp 3-21.

Walsh, J. and Ungson, G. (1991) Organizational Memory, Academy of Management Review, 16, pp 57-91.

Wenger, E. and Snyder, W. (2000) Communities of Practice: the organizational frontier. Harvard Business Review, Jan-Feb, pp 139-145.

Yin, R. (1994) Case Study Research Design and Methods. Sage Publications, USA.

Collective Action in Electronic Networks of Practice: An Empirical Study of Three Online Social Structures

Fredric Landqvist[+], Robin Teigland[*]

[+]Viktoria Institute, Sweden, [*]Stockholm School of Economics, Sweden
fredric.landqvist@viktoria.se, robin.teigland@hhs.se

Abstract. Electronic networks of practice are computer-mediated social spaces in which individuals working on similar problems self-organize to help each other and share perspectives. Based on previous research positing that the interaction created by network participants produces an online public good of knowledge, the purpose of this empirical paper is to use theories of public goods and collective action to investigate this provision of knowledge. While based on the same technology platform and a similar concept, we examine three cases in different professions: education, healthcare, and tourism by examining how the 1) heterogeneity of the individuals, 2) relational structure of social ties, 3) norms of behavior, 4) affective factors, and 5) sanctions for noncompliance impact the creation of a public good. We find that the most successful effort to create an electronic network of practice was within education and that one contributing factor was the site's ability to leverage existing offline networks of practice to create a relational structure of stronger social ties between members. In summary, these results reveal that taking a unitary view of the underlying collective masks possible heterogeneity along a number of important dimensions and as a result may undermine the likelihood that the public good is created and maintained.

Introduction

Recent advances in information and communication technologies have led to the emergence of online social structures where the primary purpose is knowledge exchange. Known by a variety of names, e.g., virtual, electronic, or online

P. van den Besselaar et al. (eds.), Communities and Technologies 2005, 359-375.
© 2005 *Springer. Printed in the Netherlands.*

communities, the study of these online social structures is critical because they have fundamentally altered our understanding of how and why people share knowledge by removing the barriers of same place and same time communication. Online social structures, such as newsgroups, listservs and bulletin boards, generally comprise an unlimited number of geographically dispersed individuals with diverse organizational, national, and demographic backgrounds who share knowledge by helping each other solve problems, telling stories of personal experiences, and debating issues based on shared interest (Sproull & Faraj, 1995; Wasko & Faraj, 2000). These electronic networks enable individuals to interact around a specific practice, regardless of physical proximity or prior personal acquaintance, thus eliminating the need for people to have met face-to-face in order to communicate. This increases an individual's access to knowledge resources by amassing greater numbers of like-minded individuals through electronic links than previously available in a local community (Teigland 2003).

Although prior researchers have used the term "community" to describe these online structures, we follow Wasko & Teigland (2004) and use the term "electronic network of practice". These researchers define an electronic network of practice as *a self-organizing, open activity system focused on a shared practice that exists through computer-mediated communication.* We feel that the use of the term network rather than community is more appropriate since these online structures are generally characterized by sparsely connected, weak, indirect ties as opposed to the frequent face-to-face interactions and direct personal ties characteristic of a community.

Despite the growing interest in online social structures such as electronic networks of practice, we know surprisingly little about how or why these structures support knowledge exchange (Desanctis & Monge, 1999; Lin, 2001). For instance, an enduring characteristic of these structures is the propensity of individuals to provide their valuable knowledge and insights to strangers (Kollock & Smith, 1996; Rheingold, 1993; Wasko & Faraj, 2000), yet why individuals participate in this activity when there is no obvious benefit to them remains not well understood. Furthermore, the availability of technology to support communication does not necessarily translate into the creation of open discussion forums focused on knowledge exchange. As many organizations have discovered, the creation of an online social space is no guarantee that knowledge sharing will actually take place (Alavi & Leidner, 1999; Orlikowski, 1996).

Thus, the goal of this empirical study is to investigate electronic networks of practice by drawing upon theories of public goods and collective action. Building upon work by Fulk, Flanagin, Kalman, Monge, & Ryan (1996) and Wasko & Teigland (2004), we investigate one fundamental research question: *How do the characteristics of the underlying collective affect the creation and maintenance of a sustainable electronic network of practice?* In order to do so, we investigate three cases built upon the same technical platform and a similar concept in three different professions: tourism, healthcare, and education. The paper then concludes with a discussion and areas for future research.

Theoretical Background

We begin with a discussion of public goods and collective action. Typical examples of public goods include both tangible and intangible goods, such as public parks, lighthouses, and public television, and these goods are generally associated with two characteristics: nonrivalry and nonexcludability. Nonrival goods are those that are not used up or depleted in their consumption (Shmanske, 1991) while nonexcludable goods (Head, 1962) are those that all individuals in a collective may consume regardless of whether they contribute to the production or maintenance of the good. While public goods generally exhibit both nonrival and nonexcludable characteristics, a connection between nonrivalry and nonexcludability does not necessarily exist. A nonrival good can be excludable or non-excludable while a nonexcludable good can be either rival or non-rival (Shmanske, 1991).

Considerable research has provided evidence that public goods are generally subject to underproduction by a collective (Shmanske, 1991). The nonrival nature of a public good allows the good and its benefit to be offered to everyone in the collective, and nonexcludability influences individual decision-making about participation in the production, maintenance, or consumption of the public good. In particular, nonexcludability may result in the tendency to free-ride, i.e., to consume the public good without contributing to its production or maintenance. In fact, the optimal individual decision is to free-ride and consume the public good without contributing anything in return. However, if everyone decided not to contribute, then the public good would not be created and everyone in the collective would be worse off (Teigland & Wasko, 2004).

Applying Collective Action and Public Goods Theories to Electronic Networks of Practice

In the formal language of collective action theory, we suggest then that the participants in an electronic network of practice form the collective. These individuals create a continuous stream of knowledge by posting and responding to messages, and the archive of collective knowledge in the saved messages produced by this interaction exhibits the characteristics of a public good. First, the archive of collective knowledge is nonrival since one individual's use of this knowledge does not deplete the supply or diminish the ability of other individuals to use the knowledge as well. In terms of nonexcludability, when one participant responds to a posting, then all members may benefit even though they did not contribute to the original exchange. Furthermore, the costs of posting a message to the network are the same, regardless of the number of individuals who benefit. Consistent with research on public goods, online social spaces that are created to enhance knowledge exchange often remain empty spaces where no one contributes or some collectives while initially sustained lose participants and then die out over time (Desanctis & Roach, 2002). Based on collective action and public goods theory, researchers would argue that the above occurs because rational individuals act to maximize their own self-interest and as a result do not spend their valuable time contributing to electronic networks of practice.

Prior collective action and public goods research (Wasko & Teigland 2004) has identified five critical areas for understanding the production and maintenance of public goods in electronic networks of practice: 1) heterogeneity of the individuals in the collective, 2) the relational structure of social ties between individuals in the collective, 3) the norms of behavior of the collective, 4) the affective factors of the collective, and 5) the sanctions for noncompliance in the collective. We briefly discuss each of these five critical areas below.

Heterogeneity of the Individuals in the Collective

Researchers have proposed that the more heterogeneous a group is in terms of its interests and resources, the more likely that there is a critical mass or subset of members who have a high enough level of resources and/or interests to produce the public good (Oliver et al., 1985). Prior research has found that individuals who have higher levels of professional expertise and organizational tenure (Constant et al., 1996) and those who lack access to private alternatives such as co-workers or acquaintances (Wasko & Teigland, 2002) are more likely to participate and provide useful advice in electronic networks. Other resources might include time, access to and competency in technology, or position in the particular practice. As for interests, prior research indicates that individual motivations, reputation, organizational/ community affiliation, access to a peer group, access to useful information, enjoyment and learning influence participation in electronic networks (Constant et al., 1996; Lakhani & von Hippel, 2000; Wasko & Faraj, 2000).

Relational Structure of Social Ties

A second area focuses on the attributes of the aggregate network structure of social ties representing the personal relationships that exist between individuals in the collective as a whole. Previous research suggests that electronic networks of practice are characterized by generalized exchange (Fulk et al., 1996) and may have a network structure like a star, where a critical mass of individuals sustain the network by responding to all others in the network as a whole (Wasko & Teigland, 2002). The structure of social ties may also be characterized by the attributes of the network's social ties, e.g., strong, intermediate, or weak (Wellman et al., 1996).

Norms of Collective Behavior

Norms are a key component of collective action (Coleman, 1990; Nahapiet & Ghoshal, 1998; Putnam, 1995a,b) in that they allow collectives to function effectively to produce and maintain public goods by providing a structured set of rules for coordination, as well as setting expectations about acceptable behaviors and actions (Ostrom, 1990). Organizational research suggests that norms of cooperation (Nahapiet & Ghoshal, 1998), reciprocity (Putnam, 1995b), openness and teamwork (Starbuck, 1992), and tolerance of both criticism and failure (Leonard-Barton, 1995) are conducive to knowledge sharing. In electronic networks of practice, prior research suggests that norms develop around the appropriate conduct in the network (Wasko & Faraj, 2000). For instance, in some electronic networks of practice, new participants are expected to review frequently asked questions before posting their questions. Other electronic networks of practice establish various norms around the tone of the exchange, where breaches of "netiquette" result in flaming.

Collective Affective Factors

Researchers suggest that a variety of affective factors, such as trust (McAllister, 1995; Nahapiet & Ghoshal, 1998; Ring & Van de Ven, 1994), influence collective action. Affective factors include obligation to the collective and identification with the collective (Nahapiet & Ghoshal, 1998), affiliation (Leana & Van Buren, 1999), commitment (Mowday et al., 1979), sentiment and ethical legitimation (Reisman, 1990), and organizational citizenship (Organ, 1988). These affective factors support collective action because individuals are more likely to suppress self-interest when there are strong, positive associations between individuals and the collective (Leana & Van Buren, 1999). In online settings, researchers have found that people with a strong sense of identification and attachment are more likely to participate and assist others (Wellman & Gulia, 1997) while individuals posting valuable advice to an intra-organizational electronic network were motivated by a sense of organizational citizenship (Constant et al., 1996). Individuals from electronic networks noted that they participated and helped others due to a moral obligation similar to "been there, done that", to pay back to the network and the profession as a whole (Wasko & Faraj, 2000), and to a sense of identification with the network and with the network's goals (Lakhani & von Hippel, 2000).

Collective Sanctions for Noncompliance

Researchers note that collective action is more likely to occur in collectives that are able to enforce sanctions for noncompliance with collective norms (Olson,

1965; Ostrom, 1990). In order to enforce these sanctions, individual behavior in the collective must be monitored, which consumes time and resources that could be devoted to other activities (Ostrom, 1990). However, Olson contends that in large collectives individuals will prefer to free-ride unless they are restrained and defectors punished for their actions (Olson, 1965). Although active participation in an electronic network of practice is fully visible and easy to monitor, the open, anonymous, and electronic nature of the network makes it difficult to render and enforce significant sanctions against free-riding or other forms of defection.

In summary, collective action research suggests that public goods are more likely to be created and sustained in collectives where there is a heterogeneity of resources and interests, a pattern of social ties that supports exchange, norms to guide collective behavior, strong affective ties between individuals and the collective, and collective sanctions that punish self-interested behavior. We would expect then that the likelihood of creating and maintaining a sustainable electronic network of practice would be dependent upon the ability of the features offered on the network site to support the necessary preconditions for the collective of practitioners.

Research Method and Data Collection

All data from the three business cases have been gathered through interpretive case studies, and one of the researchers has been involved in the development of the described electronic network of practice applications. Table 1 provides an overview of the data collection.

Common Technical Platform and Concept

All three sites used the same technical platform provided by Autonomy, a software vendor in the knowledge management systems arena. This technical solution incorporated features for information retrieval, automatic hyper-linking, intelligent-agents, automatic information classification and taxonomy generation, and lastly dynamic profiling that facilitates the individualization of information services. Autonomy uses advanced pattern-matching techniques together with neural-networks to make concept-agents of either information items (in all forms, structured, semi- and unstructured) or end-user profiling. The profiling feature makes the end-user aware of possible collaboration networks and communities.

All the sites also had similar platforms to encompass different forms of computer-supported collaborative work (CSCW) mainly simple bulletin-board features and document sharing, with either Microsoft or Lotus Notes software. However, there were no listservs or newsgroup applications used. In all cases the principle concept was to use Autonomy as a portal solution, and within this to use the CSCW applications to develop electronic networks of practice. The dynamic end-user profiling thru intelligent agent training and other end-user content related behaviors (searching, posting on bulletin board and reading/browsing) were to help users to find peers with similar interests and with whom the users could collaborate through the CSCW features.

Organization & Site	Interviewee	Data collection
LocusMedicus International Inc. (Healthcare) www.locusmedicus.net	- Founder/owner	- Development of site - Two telephone interviews approx. 30 minutes to 1hour with founder - One 3 hour workshop with founder - Continuous e-mail correspondence with founder - Analysis of project documentation
Swedish Tourism & Travel Council www.turkom.nu	- Infomaster - Project manager - CFO - Stakeholder	- Development of site - Two telephone interviews with infomaster approx. 30 minutes to 1 hour - One 1 hour meeting with infomaster, project manager, and CFO - One 3 hour workshop with infomaster - E-mail correspondence with infomaster - Analysis of project documentation and documented usability reports
The Knowledge Foundation (KKS) (Education) www.kollegiet.com	- Project manager – Stakeholder	- Development of site - Two telephone interviews with project manager approx. 30 minutes to 1hour - One 3 hour workshop with project manager - Continuous e-mail correspondence with project manager and stakeholder - Analysis of project documentation, end-user survey, and web statistics

Table 1. Overview of data collection

Case Studies

LocusMedicus.net (Healthcare)

In 1998 two Swedish medical professionals founded the portal www.locusmedicus.net in order to improve the ability of healthcare professionals to deliver effective care. The primary vision of the site was to cultivate a stronghold for healthcare professionals, be it doctors or nurses, in which LocusMedicus would deliver information services such as a knowledge navigator and decision support in the clinical day-to-day operations. One of the primary driving factors behind the development of LocusMedicus was that patients were becoming increasingly better informed due to their ability to use the Internet to find new clinical findings to their medical problems. A second factor was the exponential increase in available medical information. At the time of LocusMedicus' development, there were more than 6000 medical journals and 100 000 medical information services available on the Internet.

Thus, the principle idea behind LocusMedicus was to provide an information intermediary service that would get healthcare professionals on-line as well as to promote an electronic network of practice by providing collaborative features that would facilitate knowledge sharing between these professionals. LocusMedicus aimed at having a very slim editorial process, primarily by aggregating medical journals and making smart packages of other provider's content. Additionally, the site focused on making the navigation experience as easy as possible through automatic hyperlinks, content categorization, and a personalized information service through the use of intelligent agents. Discussion fora were also created and LocusMedicus personnel were responsible for monitoring the discussions to keep the threads and conversations within a professional and ethical manner.

In order to promote participation, LocusMedicus targeted existing healthcare networks and professional affiliations, and by the end of 1999 there were more than 7000 registered members, primarily doctors and nurses, in Scandinavia. Initially LocusMedicus focused on a closed setting for practitioners only and had very strong identity control mechanisms before individuals could be approved as a worthy LocusMedicus member. One of the main reasons for this was to be able to host a collaborative closed setting where healthcare professionals could speak openly about clinical cases without having "expert-patients" lurking around. First time end-users had the opportunity to browse the content but were restricted from using the "Forum" (collaborative) features. Unfortunately, this strong identity and proven medical educational registration process was later removed based on the idea by the site's management that it would be easier to increase the number of members through open membership and also to get away from an overwhelming administrative task of "checking" every new member.

LocusMedicus managed to allocate well-known experts within the different aspects of the healthcare professional community and had them train intelligent agents (known as "Collectors"). In this manner, it was hoped that the less experienced end-user learn from their more experienced peers and reuse their acknowledged expertise. In contrast to more traditional electronic networks of practice, the use of the intelligent agents was also chosen such that the healthcare experts would only to have to answer the really tricky questions in the "Forum" since the relatively easy questions would then be handled by the underlying trained intelligent agents.

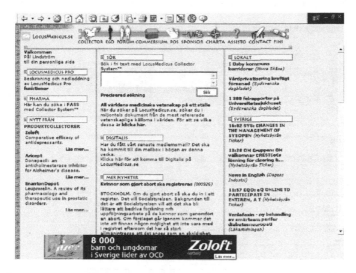

Figure 1. LocusMedicus.net (Personlized startpage, anno 2000)

The strong focus on existing healthcare networks and the involvement of famous well-known experts in the field helped draw the right attention to the use of the site initially. However, LocusMedicus never really managed to become an active and sustainable electronic network of practice and remained an information intermediary portal only. While end-users and engaged well-known experts periodically started new discussions within the CSCW features, these individuals were also searching for peer networks. However, the level of active participants was not sufficient to create an ongoing discussion and knowledge exchange, thus leading to the site's closure.

TurKom.nu (Tourism)

Tourism is a very fragmented and heterogeneous industry in Sweden with more than 20,000 organizations of which almost all are very small, one-man shows or small to medium-sized organizations. The networking within the industry has always been either geographically focused or practice-specific, e.g., the hotel industry. However, in 1999 the Swedish Tourist Authority, the Swedish Tourism & Travel Council, and the Swedish Tourist and Travel Industry Federation together started an inter-organizational development project to increase the effectiveness and efficiency in the tourism industry. This project included the development of the Internet site, www.turkom.nu. The main concept behind TurKom was that the site would provide access to information and knowledge within strategic and important tourism-related areas and that this access would then encourage networking and knowledge sharing among the geographically dispersed Swedish tourism professionals.

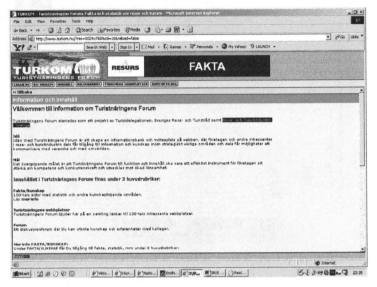

Figure 2. www.turkom.nu

The TurKom project was very influenced by the success story behind LocusMedicus, which basically led to a "copy'n'paste" of the LocusMedicus technical platform as well as the packaging of the different included information services on the site. Since the tourism industry did not have a tradition of refereed "best-practice" in the form of scientific publications such as that of the healthcare profession, TurKom was designed to aggregate a wide variety of information resources with the hope that these would attract the targeted users' attention. Additionally, TurKom included information regarding travel statistics, how to get governmental funding, and how different regional political decisions would affect the tourism industry. Since one of the goals of the site was also to involve the professionals in continuous learning, tourism research sites were also included. Similar to LocusMedicus, users could personally train intelligent agents to search for individual content from the wide variety of information sources; however, the site did not rely upon experts for this training unlike LocusMedicus. It was hoped then that the above features would increase the value offered to users, thus attracting users so that the CSCW features could then be cultivated. During the trials the site development team, however, found it very hard to get the right attention from its targeted users. The complexity in fulfilling all the different information needs of the widely heterogeneous population of tourism professionals led to an extremely heterogeneous information architecture.

Additionally, individuals never took the time to become active participants in the fora launched, thus hindering the development of electronic networks of practice. One reason was that the tourism professionals were not familiar with intelligent agents. As one individual proclaimed in the usability-lab test, "This site is crap, is this an empty void?" He had skipped reading the introduction about how content delivery was based on the end-users training intelligent agents. As a result, he had not personally trained any agents, which made the "personalized start home page" empty with no content at all. Resulting from this is that the end-user then felt that there was no one with whom to discuss in the forum, thus the "forum" feature appeared useless. Another reason relates to the cultural norms of the tourism industry. Individuals in the small organizations were often too busy focusing on performing their day-to-day activities to think about the strategic positioning of their future service offerings. Nor were they used to discussing their problems in open fora. Thus, they never really saw the need to participate in any of the fora. Due to this lack of user activity and collaboration, the TurKom site was closed as of January 1, 2005.

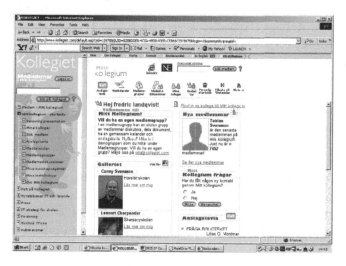

Figure 3. MittKollegiet (the personalized part of the Kollegiet site)

Kollegiet (Education)

The Knowledge Foundation (Stiftelsen för kunskaps & kompetens utveckling, KKS) was established by the Swedish Parliament to help Sweden become more competitive by focusing on research and postgraduate programs, competence development in the education industry, and school development and IT. KKS initiated a project within the focus area of "school development and IT" with the aim of building an electronic network of practice site called Kollegiet ("staff"). The targeted users were teachers and other related professionals in the educational system who were interested in school development. KKS focused on information integration and content provision (as editors), and the content was designed to be of practical use in the day-to-day operations. Additionally, one important task of Kollegiet was to cultivate knowledge sharing among an active network of practitioners with a strong commitment to IT-integrated education and school development, as well as to facilitate the creation of local networks of teachers at the schools. Kollegiet also provided experiences and best-practices within subjects such as ethics and source criticism on the Internet, methods and competencies to accomplish flexible learning processes, internationalization issues, and ideas for how to stimulate children's and youngsters' curiosity within the areas of science and technology.

Kollegiet made a large investment in an editorial process with both an editor and a network of active writers within the main focus areas, encompassing this with the development of a content management system. Kollegiet not only depended on the ideas of information intermediary services aggregating from other free available Internet resources, but Kollegiet also had some extra information services, such as environmental scanning with a subscribed content feed focused on Kollegiet specific issues. This was a very popular way for professionals to stay current with up-coming events and changes in governmental policies dealing with the educational system. The personalization features were covered in a specific part of the site, called "Mitt Kollegium" (My Colleagues), where all features dealing with collaboration and intelligent agents were placed.

To date, Kollegiet is a very active site and has a large (+7000) end-user base registered in MittKollegiet. Moreover, after running this site for more than three years, KKS is now about to unfold more collaborative features for Kollegiet to further facilitate knowledge sharing among its members. However, there is one foreseeable problem in regards to this effort and that is how to get the large end-user base to interact more on a daily basis since the use of Kollegiet is not something that local schools support. The use of Kollegiet is mainly done on a voluntary basis and the interaction is usually performed after work.

Discussion

In summary, while the three cases had the same technical solution and a similar concept for building an electronic network of practice through providing an information service, only one sustainable electronic network of practice resulted, Kollegiet. Below we compare the three cases based on the five critical areas identified: 1) heterogeneity of the individuals in the collective, 2) the relational structure of social ties between individuals in the collective, 3) the norms of behavior of the collective, 4) the affective factors of the collective, and 5) the sanctions for noncompliance in the collective. A summary is presented in table 2.

	LocusMedicus	TurKom	Kollegiet
Attributes of Individuals	Heterogeneous in resources but poor level of technology competency	Very high level of heterogeneity in interests and resources	Heterogeneous in resources, but homogeneous in interests
Relational Structure of Social Ties	Low social ties since the fora never became active	Failed to leverage offline networks of practice	Leveraged strong social ties in offline networks of practice
Norms of Collective Behavior	Collaboration among novices intimidated due to use of intelligent agents trained by experts	Low norms because too diverse user base	Strong norms of collaborating for common good of profession
Collective Affective Factors	Strong sense of identity and high degree of trust	Fear of competition led to decreased level of trust	Strong degree of trust and affiliation
Collective Sanctions for Noncompliance	All discussions monitored and membership initially restricted	Open access, but no monitoring since no active participants	Open access but due to specific and focused content, "intruders" a rare sight
Ability to create sustainable electronic network of practice	Relatively high level of collaboration initially but then failed to sustain this leading to site closure	Poor level of activity and collaboration led to site closure	Successfully sustained electronic network of practice with future developments planned

Table 2. Overview of the three cases

LocusMedicus

In terms of resources and interests, the targeted users of LocusMedicus were quite heterogeneous in terms of professional expertise as indicated by the use of experts to train intelligent agents.   Additionally, individuals within the healthcare profession as in any scientific profession may be characterized by a high degree of interest in reputation and staying current with developments within the field as well as a high level of identity and collective behavior (Van Maanen & Barley, 1984). This may explain the initial interest in the site. However, while there was this initial interest, no critical mass of active collaborators developed. One explanation may be that there was not a sufficient number of users who were competent in using the technology provided by LocusMedicus. Additionally, one reason for the lack of critical mass may be due to the choice to use the experts to train the intelligent agents. This decision may have constrained the development of a critical mass of interested collaborators since it was expected that individuals should use the agents first before asking questions in the fora. This then created the norm that the fora were to be used for expert questions only, perhaps resulting in the situation that more novice individuals may have felt too intimidated to ask questions in these fora. Finally, the decision by the site's management to remove the restricted access through membership may also have changed the nature of the site for its users. Since anyone could enter the fora, the level of trust and thus the affective element of the collective may have been reduced. One interviewee commented on this in the following way, "Maybe when we took away the rigor in membership processing, we also lost some vital trust issues."

TurKom

Individuals within the TurKom's targeted users group could be described as a heterogeneous group in terms of resources, e.g., tenure, expertise, information technology competency, etc. Additionally, since many of those involved in the tourism industry are one-man shows or small operations, they often lacked private alternatives. However, there is some indication that individuals participated in their local offline networks, thus dampening their interest to participate online. This latter factor may have outweighed the former factors in explaining the inability of users within TurKom to create a critical mass. Additionally, as noted above, individuals were more interested in performing their day-to-day activities than discussing strategic or other issues online with others. Finally, their information needs and profiles may have been too diverse, thus leading to the inability of individuals to be able to identify with others online.

Another reason may be inherent in the tourism profession as indicated by one interviewee. She explained that the failure of the TurKom site could be because the Swedish tourism industry does not have a culture of continuous knowledge sharing through knowledge codification, such as documenting best practices or storytelling, other than what occurs during face-to-face meetings at periodic industry conventions. She commented, "The doctors have the knowledge seeking, sharing, networking and continuous learning within their spines, whereas our industry is driven mainly on true entrepreneurship." This spirit of entrepreneurship and an interest in bottom-line profits may have led to a feeling of competition between the members, thus inhibiting members to share knowledge with one another.

Kollegiet

Similar to the other two cases, the members of the Kollegiet were diverse in terms of their resources. However, unlike LocusMedicus, this group displayed a high degree of technology competency, and unlike TurKom, the users were a much more targeted group, i.e., interested in the specific topic of integrating IT in schools. Additionally, this site built upon the already established local networks of education professionals and served as a complement to these, thus leading to stronger ties within the network. Additionally, the teaching profession displays the characteristics of a very strong guild, and the sense of belonging to a practice that is for "the common good" may explain why so many members participated in Kollegiet. Finally, anybody interested in education was welcome to participate in the network, but since the content and discussion were very specific and focused, "intruders" were a rare sight.

Future Research and Concluding Remarks

As of today, Kollegiet is the only active site, thus the future development of Kollegiet and its ability to sustain an electronic network of practice will provide an interesting opportunity to investigate the lifecycle of an electronic network of practice. Future research will focus on end-user interviews, comparing this with the visions shared by the stakeholders in this paper. While our Kollegiet research shows that it is a platform well suited to sustain an electronic network of practice, many end-users still only use it as an information intermediary portal and instead collaborate and network elsewhere. In our future research, we plan to focus more in depth on the relationship between offline and online networks of practice.

In conclusion, these three different cases illustrate the difficulty in transforming an electronic space into a sustainable electronic network of practice in addition to how the underlying characteristics of the collective of practitioners impact this transformation. To build trust and engagement in knowledge creation and sharing among users truly needs an enduring and evolving development process. One interviewee concluded, "If you are able to provide the end-users with an information service that is easy to use and with content that is applicable to their daily practice, they will return on a regular basis. The thing that takes time and effort is to build trust. Without trust there won't be any sustainable networks of practice".

Acknowledgments

We thank the Swedish Council for Working Life and Social Research for sponsoring this research through grant number 004-1268.

References

Alavi, M., and Leidner, D. "Knowledge Management Systems: Issues, Challenges and Benefits," *Communication of the Association for Information Systems* (1) 1999, pp 1-28.Desanctis, G., and Monge, P. "Communication Processes for Virtual Organizations," *Organization Science* (10:6) 1999, pp 693-703.

Coleman, J.S. *Foundations of Social Theory* Belknap Press of Harvard University Press, Cambridge, MA, 1990.

Constant, D., Sproull, L., and Kiesler, S. "The Kindness of Strangers: The Usefulness of Electronic Weak Ties for Technical Advice," *Organization Science* (7:2) 1996, pp 119-135.

374 F. Landqvist and R. Teigland

Desanctis, G., and Roach, M. "Age, Size, and Contribution Dynamics in Online Learning Communities," Academy of Management Conference, Denver, CO, 2002.

Fulk, J., Flanagin, A.J., Kalman, M.E., Monge, P.R., and Ryan, T. "Connective and Communal Public Goods in Interactive Communication Systems," *Communication Theory* (6:1) 1996, pp 60-87.

Head, J.G. "Public Goods and Public Policy," *Public Finance* (17:3) 1962, pp 197-219.

Kollock, P., and Smith, M.A. "Managing the Virtual Commons: Cooperation and Conflict in Computer Communities," in: *Computer-Mediated Communication: Linguistic, Social and Cross Cultural Perspectives,* S. Herring (ed.), John Benjamins, Amsterdam, 1996, pp. 109-128.

Lakhani, K., and von Hippel, E. "How Open Source Software Works: "Free" User-to-User Assistance," The 3rd Intangibles Conference. Knowledge: Management, Measurement and Organization, Stern School of Business, NYU, 2000.

Leana, C.R., and Van Buren, H.J.I. "Organizational Social Capital and Employment Practices," *The Academy Management Review* (24:3) 1999, pp 538-555.

Leonard-Barton, D. *Wellsprings of Knowledge: Building and Sustaining the Sources of Innovation* Harvard Business School Press, Boston, 1995.

Lin, N. *Social Capital* Cambridge University Press, Cambridge, UK, 2001.

McAllister, D. "Affect- and Cognition-Based Trust as Foundations for Interpersonal Cooperation in Organizations," *Academy of Management Journal* (38:1) 1995, pp 24-59.

Mowday, R.T., Steers, R.M., and Porter, L. "The Measurement of Organizational Commitment," *Journal of Vocational Behavior* (14) 1979, pp 224-247.

Nahapiet, J., and Ghoshal, S. "Social Capital, Intellectual Capital, and the Organizational Advantage," *Academy of Management Review* (23:2) 1998, pp 242-266.

Oliver, P.E., Marwell, G., and Teixeira, R. "A Theory of Critical Mass I: Group Heterogeneity, Interdependence and the Production of Collective Goods," *American Journal of Sociology* (91) 1985, pp 522-556.

Olson, M. *The Logic of Collective Action* Harvard University Press, Cambridge, MA, 1965.

Organ, D.E. *Organizational Citizenship Behavior* Lexington Publishers, Lexington, MA, 1988.

Orlikowski, W.J. "Learning from Notes: Organizational Issues in Groupware Implementation," in: *Computerization and Controversy,* R. Kling (ed.), Academic Press, New York, 1996, pp. 173-189.

Ostrom, E. *Governing the Commons: The Evolution of Institutions for Collective Action* Cambridge University Press, Cambridge, 1990.

Putnam, R. "Bowling Alone: America's Declining Social Capital," *Journal of Democracy* (6) 1995a, pp 65-78.

Putnam, R. "Tuning in, Tuning Out: The Strange Disappearance of Social Capital in America," *Political Science and Politics* (December) 1995b, pp 664-683.

Reisman, D. *Theories of Collective Action: Downs, Olson and Hirsch* The Macmillan Press Ltd, Hong Kong, 1990.

Rheingold, H. *The Virtual Community: Homesteading on the Electronic Frontier* Addison Wesley, Reading, MA, 1993.

Ring, P.S., and Van de Ven, A.H. "Developmental Processes of Cooperative Interorganizational Relationships," *Academy of Management Review* (19) 1994, pp 90-118.

Shmanske, S. *Public Goods, Mixed Goods, and Monopolistic Competition* Texas A&M University Press, College Station, 1991.

Sproull, L., and Faraj, S. "Atheism, Sex and Databases: The Net as a Social Technology," in: *Public Access to the Internet*, B.K.J. Keller (ed.), MIT Press, Cambridge, MA, 1995, pp. 62-81.

Starbuck, W.H. "Learning by Knowledge Intensive Firms," *Journal of Management Studies* (29:6) 1992, pp 713-740.

Teigland, R. (2003). *Knowledge Networking: Structure and Performance in Networks of Practice.* Published doctoral dissertation. Stockholm: Stockholm School of Economics.

Van Maanen, J. & Barley, S. R. 1984. Occupational communities: Culture and control in organizations. In B. M. Staw & L. L. Cummings (eds.) *Research in Organizational Behavior*, Vol. 6. Greenwich, CO: JAI Press.

Wasko, M., and Faraj, S. "It Is What One Does: Why People Participate and Help Others in Electronic Communities of Practice," *Journal of Strategic Information Systems* (9:2-3) 2000, pp 155-173.

Wasko, M., and Teigland, R. "The Provision of Online Public Goods: Examining Social Structure in a Network of Practice," *Proceedings of the 23rd Annual International Conference on Information Systems*, Barcelona, Spain, 2002.

Wasko, M.M. & Teigland, R. 2004. Public Goods or Virtual Commons? Applying Theories of Public Goods, Social Dilemmas, and Collective Action to Electronic Networks of Practice. *Journal of Information Technology Theory and Application (JITTA)*. Special Issue on Virtual Communities.

Wellman, B., and Gulia, M. "Net Surfers Don't Ride Alone," in: *Communities in Cyberspace,* P. Kollock and P. Smith (eds.), University of California Press, Berkeley, 1997.

Wellman, B., Salaff, J., Dimitrova, D., Garton, L., Gulia, M., and Haythornthwaite, C. "Computer Networks as Social Networks: Collaborative Work, Telework, and Virtual Community," *Annual Review of Sociology* (22) 1996, pp 213-238.

Bridging among Ethnic Communities by Cross-cultural Communities of Practice

Gunnar Stevens*, Michael Veith*, Volker Wulf*,°

*University of Siegen, Germany °Fraunhofer-FIT, Sankt Augustin, Germany
{stevens, veith, wulf}@fb5.uni-siegen.de

Abstract. The integration of immigrants is a big challenge for western societies. In this paper we describe how to bridge between ethnically defined communities by means of computer-supported project work. Our approach is grounded in socio-cultural theories of learning, especially Community of Practice (CoP). To evaluate our approach, we have built up a computer club in a multi cultural neighbourhood of the city of Bonn. Parents and children of mainly German and Turkish origin work jointly to create multimedia artefacts. These artefacts represent aspects of the neighbourhood's recent history. The paper describes the project and its theoretical background. We also provide empirical findings to evaluate our approach.

Introduction

Germany and other modern western societies are facing the migration from countries with distinctly different socio-cultural backgrounds. Democratically constituted states should encourage social participation of all of their inhabitants, since this is a necessary condition for a sufficient level of integration. The lack of social as well as cultural integration seems to lead to unequal opportunities and lower levels of education which are specifically problematic for migrants of the second and third generation.

Looking at modern western societies, we see integration processes such as of migrants often running into problematical conditions or even failing. In this paper we will focus on the Turkish immigrant community in Germany. Although it exists for more than forty years in Germany, this community is still poorly

P. van den Besselaar et al. (eds.), Communities and Technologies 2005, 377-396.

integrated. When starting with primary school migrant children of the third generation often show, for instance, significant deficits in German language abilities compared to other pupils of the same age. Their language abilities seem to be often even lower than those of their parents who were also brought up in Germany (second generation). Moreover, the social gap between the Turkish immigrant community and the mainstream society seems to be widening recently due to an unequal access to computer infrastructures (digital divide).

In this paper we will present our approach of linking ethnical communities by means of computer-supported project work. In the following we will present some basic concepts dealing with the social integration of migrants and provide some basic facts about the German situation. A survey on computer-based approaches towards social integration comes next. We will then present our concept of the intercultural computer club. Based on socio-cultural theories of learning, we try to establish computer-related Communities of Practice (CoPs) as a bridge between ethnically defined communities. To evaluate our approach, we present empirical findings from the first eight months of the computer club's existence.

Integration Discourse

The scientific and political discourse on the integration of migrants involves concepts which are interpreted differently from person to person, from institution to institution, and from community to community. What do the concepts of acculturation and integration mean, and what is an appropriate level of acculturation and integration? The integration discourse offers a variety of different answers to these questions.

According to Berry (Berry 1984, 1992), acculturation must be seen as a process which begins with the immigration of an individual or a group belonging to a different culture than the dominant one in an existing society. During the process of acculturation immigrants may pass through five possible phases - from pre-contact, contact, conflict, crises, towards an adaptation phase (Roebers, 1997: 17). The crises phase is not obligatory but may emerge if conflicts between the two cultural groups become overwhelming. Depending on the development during the process of acculturation four conceivable levels of adaptation may result: integration, assimilation, separation, and marginalization.

Berry & Kim (1988: 211) state two issues which are decisive factors with regard to attitudes toward different modes of acculturation – namely the maintenance of one's own cultural identity and the maintenance of relationships with other groups. These issues of maintaining socio-cultural values are matters of subjective decisions among immigrants and immigrant groups. If an immigrant can give affirmative answers to both issues, the integration takes place. Therefore, immigrants decide whether they want to be integrated or assimilated. In opposite to Luft (2002), it seems impossible to us to prescribe integration by order.

There are also barriers created by the mainstream society which can hinder integration and may motivate immigrants to separate themselves in autonomous immigrant communities. Integration, in our opinion, is a challenge for both parties as the shortcomings of integration are mostly grounded in behavioural patterns of exclusion and self-isolation. So, the inclusion of all involved communities within a social environment is important for the success of integrative projects. The main challenge for the integrative work is to establish additional identities besides those of the different ethnic communities. These identities could be built on shared practices.

Ethnic Communities and Technology

Global migration seems to confirm the thesis that globalization fostered by latest media- and transportation-technologies diminishes the importance of local places. Therefore, we would end up in a global village. However, migration also stimulates intense discussions whether the integration into local context can be achieved. In particular, the concentration of ethnic minorities in urban neighbourhoods is an interesting phenomenon as it seems that the local context has a strong impact, still today.

Ethnic Communities in Germany

Most large cities in western countries have specific neighbourhoods where primarily ethnic minorities live. In particular in the US the term "inner city" is often used as a synonym for the area where underprivileged classes - mostly ethnic communities - live. In these neighbourhoods the issues of low economical, cultural and social capital are often interrelated.

In quite some German cities, quarters with a primarily Turkish community exist. In these quarters a stabilized and more or less well-working and self-organizing community has been developed over the years. These communities formed their own identity separately from each other (Esser 1996, Unbehaun et al. 1997). Similar phenomena can be found with repatriates of German ancestry emigrating from the territory of the former Soviet Union.

Particularly in areas where autonomous immigrant communities[1] exist, the problem of isolation can become effective and significant. This can lead to the condition that both, parents and children, acquire too little linguistic and intercultural competences to communicate with other communities.

Wedding, a quarter in Berlin with a high degree of foreigners and a high degree of unemployment, is an example for these conditions. In 2001 a study of 20 elementary schools in Wedding showed that only one fourth of the first

---

[1] In German this phenomenon is called "Parallelgesellschaften" meaning 'parallel societies'.

graders could speak sufficiently German. Almost half of the children showed significant deficits. In one day care centre in Wedding 80 % of the children were of non-German origin and 75 % had parents who were unemployed (Naumann, 1998). The linguistic problems seem to correlate with social problems in the quarter. The poverty in linguistic abilities of the children corresponds to their social and economic poverty (Vieth-Entus, 2001). In such a situation it is difficult for immigrants to participate in the cultural and social capital of mainstream society. Hence it will be also difficult to improve their economic situation.

Digital Divide

The digital divide is an issue referring to the socio-economic gap between communities that have access to computers and the Internet and those who do not. In Germany only a few studies exist which investigate how migrants appropriate computers and digital media.

A study conducted for the German Government comes to the conclusion that there is a rather high agreement between children from Turkish and German families regarding their wishes and preferences toward the use of digital media (Granato, 2001). This study does neither consider the aspects of media competence nor those of the media design. It seems that immigrants have less access to new technologies than Germans (Wagner et al. 2002). In order to prevent the digital divide in the Information Society, special support for migrants may be necessary.

There are some initiatives who try to deal with these issues in the German context. The foundation "Digitale Chancen" believes that digital media offer opportunities for integration. Hinkelbein (2004, p. 27) states that the empowerment through the appropriation of new media is an important step for migrants. It will help them to express their needs and to represent themselves to gain more (political) participation.

The effects of digital media on the integration of immigrants are not always considered to be positive. Critics say that global access to media content will increase cultural segregation. For instance, it is argued that the availability of Turkish satellite TV plays a role in the deterioration of the third generation's German language abilities. Aksoy and Robins (2000) criticize such a position as too extreme and argue for a more differentiated analysis. They look upon the increasing consumption of Turkish TV channels rather as a consequence of a failed integration than a reason for the given segregation.

Computer-based Approaches to social Integration

In the following we present some projects which try to integrate migrants by means of digital media. The focus is on projects which try to overcome the digital divide. In general, these issues seem to be still little explored within the scientific discourse, at least in applied computer science. One of the well known approaches in dealing with this issue is the Computer Clubhouses (CCH). This approach has been developed in the specific context of US inner cities. However, it has recently been exported to many other countries and socio-economic conditions. Our work was originally inspired by observing the CCH approach.

Computer Clubhouses

In 1993 a research group of the MIT Media Laboratory opened the first computer club aiming at teenagers from lower social classes and educational backgrounds (inner cities). The pedagogical concept can be seen as an extension to the constructivistic learning paradigm. In constructivism, learning is a process of constructing individual cognitive structures. Papert (1980) extends this idea by stating that these cognitive structures have to be put into practice by constructing artefacts. Thereby a way is found to externalize implicit and tacit knowledge. This is called constructionism (Papert 1980). There have been several approaches to focus on the collective dimension of constructionist activities. For instance, Chapman (2004) argues that the artefacts for learning are put into social context. They are shared and discussed. Other learners are also able to learn from and with these artefacts. In addition, the constructor learns from the others dealing with the artefacts. Shaw (1995) enriches this theory with a socio-cultural aspect. In his perspective constructionist learning is also social learning. Beyond the artefacts, social ties are established during the process of constructionist learning. As a result, the social capital is a part of the underlying concept of the CCH.

Highly innovative ICT is used to stimulate the learning process of the target group. In a long-term perspective, the CCH tries to improve the opportunities of its participants on the labour market (Resnick & Rusk 1996a, Resnick & Rusk 1996b). Hayes et al. (2004) demonstrate the difficulties of bringing this espoused model of the CCH into practice. They also show how it can be in conflict with the actual needs of its members.

While originally strongly influenced by this work, we focused our work rather on strengthening the links between different ethnical communities than on individual and collective learning processes which are stimulated by innovative computer tools. So far, we subordinated the development of innovative tools for learning to the needs for community building.

Projects in the German Context

In the following we present some projects which have been developed with regard to the specific German context. Since these projects are not scientifically evaluated it is difficult to judge their success.

There are several projects which offer specific mentoring for migrants in an internet cafe type of setting. An important aspect of these approaches is the assignment of bilingual volunteers who mentor the computer-based activities of the participants. A goal is to enable self-organized learning experiences. Bilingual teachers offer, for instance, computer courses in German language and only switch if necessary into the mother tongue of the migrants. Multi-cultural project activities are not part of these computer-related activities.

However, we found project-based settings for integration in non-computer-supported settings. "Internationale Gärten" is an interesting integration-project since it asks actors of different ethnical background to share practices. In this project, asylum seekers and local citizens cultivate specific gardens together. The gardening activities were chosen since they seem to be relevant in different cultures (cf. Hinkelbein, 2004).

There are a couple of projects which make use of the increasing amount of channels of mass distribution to provide ethno-specific content to the different migrant communities in Germany. The goal of the project "Seniors: Media – Migration – Integration – Participation" is to develop multimedia material for both an internet platform and broadcasting in a local radio station. It is dedicated to elderly migrants, especially to Turkish women. The production and emission of these materials stimulate the migrant community to discover their cultural identity in a new way and to present their identity to a public audience.

Beyond this project, there exists a variety of different ethno portals in the internet. These portals are often bilingual and offer topics of interest to the different migrant communities. A specific portal tries to integrate parents of foreign children much stronger in the system of public education. These parents get information on educational issues by so called parent letters. A version of these parent letters is addressing Turkish migrant families especially, and these are partially written in Turkish.

While most of these approaches follow the goal of integration, computers and digital media can be used in rather different ways, as well. The Islamic fundamentalist organisation Milli Görus which pursues – according to the German secret service – a segregating and fundamentalist programme is primarily a religious organisation. But it also runs sport studios and computer rooms. In this way, they present an attractive offer to teenagers of Turkish origin.

Conceptual Considerations

When developing our action research approach for the inter-cultural computer club, we were inspired by the theories on Communities of Practice (CoP) (Lave and Wenger 1991; Wenger 1998). In our case, CoPs are an interesting theoretical concept since they relate the experience of shared practice to the process of identity building and knowledge acquisition.

In their work, Lave and Wenger follow socio-cultural learning theories which understand learning as a collective process. The learning process is linked to specific contexts of action. Learning in a CoP is defined by the relationship of *old-timers* and *newcomers* which are inside the community. By means of legitimate peripheral participation, newcomers are confronted with the practice of old-timers which built the core of a CoP. As newcomers interact, work, and communicate with old-timers their experiences increase. This phenomenon shows that learning in a CoP is a process of growing into the community. CoPs are characterized by common conventions, language, tool usage, values, and standards. A CoP is inseparable from issues of (individual and social) identity. Identity is mainly determined by negotiated experience of one's self in terms of participation in a community and the learning process concerning one's membership in a CoP (Wenger 1998, 145).

Following these theoretical considerations, our approach intends to establish a CoP bridging between the rather segregated ethnical communities. We assume that the establishment of a shared practice among members of the ethnical communities would have an impact on the actors' individual and, in a longer term perspective, on the ethnic communities' collective identity.

In collocated but segregated neighbourhoods, a shared practice typically does not exist. Therefore, interventions have to be conceptualized which support the creation of a shared practice between the ethnical communities. Such interventions need to be robust enough to overcome the existing gaps in practices and identities.

Since we do not believe in social determinism, such interventions will rather increase the likelihood of a CoP's emergence than force it into existence (cf. Wenger et al. 2002). To increase the likelihood, these interventions have to be conceptualized with regard to the specific context in a given neighbourhood. Such an intervention has to take two core issues into account (a) the selection of an appropriate domain to establish a shared practice and (b) finding attractors to overcome the gaps between the given ethnical communities.

Local Context

We evaluated our research approach in a project which takes place in the Bonner Altstadt, a neighbourhood of the city of Bonn. The Bonner Altstadt has a population of about 10,000 inhabitants. The social and cultural structure of this district can be characterized as a colourful mixture of different communities[2]. However, the German and the Turkish communities are by far the biggest. Today's situation in the quarter is a result of the post war urban development. In the 60s and 70s, many better-off inhabitants moved away into the suburbs and the

---

[2] A slogan of a local pressure group emphasizes this point clearly by proclaiming "Vielfalt Altstadt" meaning 'diversity in the old town center'.

housing conditions deteriorated. Later on, they were replaced by people searching for new and cheaper accommodation, i.e. mostly immigrants and students. Some statistical data characterize this situation today: The quarter has a high rate of immigrants (22.7% of the population, in comparison to 12.5% in Bonn as total) and a low education rate (35% have just a Hauptschulabschluss[3] and 32% of those in employment are workers). However, the German community consists to a considerable part out of academics, partly former students who stayed in the quarter after their graduation.

The first generation of the Turkish Altstadt community came to Germany as contracted factory labours in the 1960s and early 70s. Most of them emigrated from a rather small rural district in western Turkey. While in the beginning the men came typically by themselves, wives and children followed later on. In the beginning, working in Germany was seen by most of the families as a periodical stay. However, since the 1990s this attitude started to change and the Turkish families bought and restored old houses in the quarter.

In the German context elementary schools are important places where collocated but segregated communities meet. Most kids go to a public elementary school in their local school district. Therefore, schools in multicultural neighbourhoods face considerable challenges in dealing with a differentiated population of pupils.

Our project is conducted in cooperation with Marienschule, an elementary school in the neighbourhood. The school implements the goals, values and methods of the reform pedagogical learning paradigms of Maria Montessori. The focus lies on open and work oriented lessons, e.g. in small groups, workshops, projects, and so on. Each class room is equipped with two or three computers which can be used as resources in the daily work. For more than a decade pupils are taught in classes with mixed age-groups. Beyond the neighbourhood the school has gained reputation for its innovative pedagogies and didactical practice.

The pupils of Marienschule come from very different social and cultural circumstances. About 35% of all pupils are of Turkish origin and come from the rather low educated background of the local community. Moreover, there are a considerable number of additional children with migrant or mixed backgrounds. A considerable portion of the children of German origin comes from middle class families with an academic background.

While innovative in its didactics, Marienschule experiences a couple of serious problems in dealing with their highly differentiated pupils. Offering appropriate education to third generation children of Turkish origin turns out to be a serious challenge for a variety of reasons. A considerable part of these children starts school with little or even without German language abilities. This is particularly surprising since their parents of the second generation often speak much better

---

[3] Hauptschulabschluss is the German equivalent to the certificate of completion of compulsory basic secondary schooling.

German. Moreover, many children of Turkish origin lack parents' support and motivation concerning their school performance. Finally, the children of the Turkish community seem to have little access to digital media. This is not only a question of the availability of computer hardware and software in their homes but also of the level of computer literacy within their families and networks of friends.

Due to these conditions the principal of Marienschule picked up on our ideas and got involved in the project.[4] In the following, we will present the core concepts which we developed for trying to establish a multicultural CoP.

Shared Practice: Computer-Supported Projects

We decided to establish a shared praxis across the ethnical communities by encouraging actors to jointly work on computer-supported projects.

We assumed that dealing with computers and digital media would be attractive for many actors within the different ethnical communities. Observing the school life, we knew that children were rather motivated to use computers and had mostly gained already some experience in dealing with them. This attraction seemed to be rather general across the different communities. We assumed that parents would encourage their children to expand computer related abilities since these qualifications seemed to be socially desired even in the immigrant and non-immigrant communities. We assumed that computer abilities were perceived as being related to professional opportunities and participation in certain aspects of social life.

We needed to find project foci which were interesting to the members of the different communities and provided a base for a multi-cultural dialog. This was a difficult issue since we did not have any experience with regard to appropriate topics. Socio-cultural and ecological issues with an impact on the neighbourhood's daily life were as well discussed as the provision of support for some of the school's recurrent activities. In the course of the last eight months five different projects have been started, some consecutive others in parallel.

One of the projects deals with a multimedia documentation of family histories. Right now, already the third generation of Turkish immigrants lives in the neighbourhood. However, their family histories are only poorly documented if at all.[5] For instance, the experience of the first generation of immigrants who are now in their 60s and 70s are only partly remembered even in their families. These

---

[4] Empirical investigations by Calabrese-Barton (1998) and Nasir (2002) indicate the importance of the pupils' identification with their performance in school settings. Looking at children from minority groups in inner cities in the US, they argue that school performance is often low in case schooling does not play an important role in the self-conception of the children. So schools need to take more care of the pupil's identity and try to adapt their measures accordingly.

[5] For instance, it does not yet exist any museum which documents the history of the post war labour immigration to Germany.

family histories should be presented together with German ones from the same neighbourhood. Such a shared history may support the growth of a joint identity across the different communities.

Supported by computers, the participants in the project get the opportunity to search for historical and social sources within their personal context. Others may learn from the resulting artefacts.

Bridging the Gap: Social Structures and Attractors

We choose the shared practice in a way that it is meaningful and attractive for actors from the different ethnical communities. However, we believed that just offering an infrastructure for a shared practice would not be enough to start the process (cf. Rohde 2004). So we considered appropriate social structures and attractors to support the initiation of the process.

In segregated neighbourhoods there typically exist few social structures on which the establishment of a cross-cultural project can draw on. In the German context elementary schools are one of these structures. In elementary schools children of the different cultural backgrounds meet. Therefore teachers, and specifically the principals of these schools, exercise a cross-cultural impact on the pupils' families. Information distributed by them reaches the pupils' families immediately and is typically taken serious.

To impact identities in the different ethnical communities, we needed to attract parents, as well. The involvement of the parents was important to the school for educational purposes, as well. Since the success of schooling is highly related to the social context of the children, schools and parents need to work together (Lanfranchi et al., 2001). Improving the cooperation with parents, specifically from less educated backgrounds, was a major reason for the elementary school to participate in this project. Thus, we introduced the rule that children may only come to the club if accompanied by at least one adult. By this rule, we drew on the attraction computers have for children to get parents involved in the process. In addition, it is hard for elementary school kids to manage complex projects themselves. So, conceptual support of their parents is needed to realize the envisioned project outcomes. While establishing a project-related practice, we assumed that foreign and German parents would communicate with each other and started impacting their identity.

Methodological Considerations

After a preparation period of 18 months the come_IN computer club was opened officially in March 2004. Since its opening it is running once a week for two hours from 5pm to 7pm. The intended target groups show rather strong interest and active participation in the practice of the club. The successful start of the club is mainly based on the work of volunteers from the neighbourhood (see also section 'Acknowledgements'). Different donations allowed us to buy the initial hardware and software equipment: five computers, two digital cameras, a video camera, and a beamer.

Action Research

The empirical method is based on the concept of action research. We adopted Lewin's cyclic model of action research which includes two basic methodological principles. Firstly, action research is divided into certain sub-tasks which are characterized by specific methodological sub-routines within the researcher's work. Secondly, action research is cyclic, i.e. the sub-routines repeat again and again after running through a full circle of the whole spiral (Holter & Schwartz-Barcott 1993). Following Kemmis & McTaggart (1988: p. 5) three sub-routines or phases are of interest: a) reflection phase, b) planning phase, and c) action and observation phase.

We follow Kemmis' & McTaggert's (1988) concept of participation within action research, i.e. participatory action research (PAR). In the following we will describe how we put this framework into practice. Moreover, we present how we collected and interpreted the empirical data.

The initial reflection phase was strongly oriented on Mills' (2003) framework of action research. First, we explored the research field which included the area of action as well as problems of interest and related social factors (see section 'The Local Context'). Related projects provided us with an overview about existing research practice and results which narrowed the range of possible research questions. Second, we developed and described possible interventions and innovations which were supposed to be put into practice. We cooperated closely with different actors from the neighbourhood, namely the principal of the school, several teachers, some parents and other who became engaged on a volunteer base. Lastly, necessary resources (e.g. room for the project, technical equipment) have been put into consideration. After the installation of the technical equipment the first planning phase was over and the initial action and observation phase could begin.

Empirical Data

Analyzing empirical data by using predefined theories or hypotheses leads to the problem that the uniqueness of the processes cannot be captured. In order to overcome these shortcomings grounded theory develops its concepts based on the data collection, analysis, and theoretical sampling within the field (Dick 2002).

For that reason we employ the methodological ideas of grounded theory in our empirical studies. We collect field notes, conducted additional observations and enrich them by means of semi-structured interviews. By coding these empirical materials, we are able to categorize and structure them. Further memoing (documentation of personal ideas and thoughts which are related to the notes and coding) turned out to be helpful for two reasons: a) ideas did not get lost when they are written down immediately and were helpful in later theoretical sampling, b) memoing offered the opportunity to make subjective assumptions explicit and discuss them related to the data collected.

Two of the authors were strongly involved as action researcher in the emergence of the computer club. The third author joined the project later and mainly focussed on the collection of empirical data by means of semi-structured interviews and participatory observations.

Empirical Findings

Our empirical findings are mainly based on transcripts of club meetings, observations, field notes, and interviews. So far, five semi-structured interviews[6] have been conducted which deepen our understanding of certain phenomena which became obvious in the club. An interview with the principal of the school provided important insights concerning the formal structures within the school and the club.

The participation in the weekly meetings of the computer club fluctuated between 20 to 40 parents and children. Their cultural background was quite heterogeneous. While participants of German and Turkish origin represented the two biggest groups, other nationalities got involved in the club, as well (e.g. Japanese, African).

In the following, we will present selected results which are based on our experience during the first eight months of the computer club's existence.

Importance of existing (formal) Structures

An important factor in realizing our concept was the cooperation with the elementary school. By cooperating with the school, we could draw on its access towards parents and children in the multicultural context. This access is primarily given by the formal structure of schooling institutions regulated by laws, rules, and statutes (see above), and by the special conditions in the Bonner Altstadt.

Beyond these (formal) aspects, a critical factor was the teachers' active support. In particular, the project benefited from the high engagement of the principal of the school. Due to her support, the project was announced in school meetings and letters to parents. This was important, since recommendations and

---

[6] The interviews took between 20 and 45 minutes. They were mainly based on field notes and memos. One exception was the interview with the principal of Marienschule. This interview took about 90 minutes and was supported by a semi-structured interview guideline. This guideline was based on findings from field notes, codings and memos.

advises given by teachers are typically considered seriously by the parents. In particular through the active engagement of the principal, the parents could sense the importance given to the project by the school.

Finally, we took care of a high visibility of the project within the neighbourhood. We had a formal opening event of the computer club at which the mayor of the city of Bonn and a member of the European Parliament were speaking. Later on the computer club was visited by the State Minister of Social Affairs. All of these events were covered by the local newspapers. These events were crowd with people living in the neighbourhood. A participant commented this event: "There was some sort of commotion, when the Madame Minister and the governing mayoress were here at the Marienschule".

We assumed that this kind of publicity increased the attraction of the computer club in bridging the gap between the different ethnical communities.

To understand the motivation of the elementary school, represented by the principal, it makes sense to take a closer look at her biography. Her practical experiences seem to follow a clear policy for her career. The decision to become a teacher, for instance, was strongly influenced by her former habit to help other pupils with their homework. In addition, she used to give coaching to younger schoolfellows. That way, she said, the idea emerged to become a teacher.

Her pedagogical orientation towards the Montessori learning paradigm is motivated by the drastic decrease in the number of pupils the school experienced in the 1980s. To promote her newly introduced concept, she actively advertised it in regional kindergartens. She also got the parents involved in the process of defining the school's new identity. The search for mutual dialogue is one of the main pillars of the success in her school. Her learning process is manifested in school practice and is consequently continued in the computer club. Therefore, she actively supported the concept of mixing different ethnic groups and cross-generational learning as formal conditions within the computer club.

Computer an Attractor for Participation

Our empirical findings indicate that working with computers is an attractor which can draw people to participate in the club. In particular, children use the computer rather playfully and it seems that they have no respect when exploring the computer. They just try out the programmes. This playfully work can be illustrated by a boy, who needed one hour to write a small text with Openoffice. But after doing that he was very proud of mastering this *challenge*: "When he'd written four lines of text, he smiled and got rosy-cheeked" (Comment from Frau Kansy). In addition, occasionally often when parents want to go home, the kids beg and say that they still want to stay "only just a moment".

The role of the parents is interesting. They provide help very readily if a child has a problem. In addition, they are willing to receive help if they are not able to solve a given problem.

But in opposite to the children, they show some sort of respect concerning computers which was also expressed in some of the interviews. This "respectfulness" can lead to a rather passive behaviour, i.e. many parents prefer to watch the club' activities instead of working themselves on the computers. Obviously, German and Turkish parents use the computer club differently. German fathers seem to like the role of being mentors or tutors. But those Germans who do not play the role of tutors act more passively than some of the Turkish parents. Most Turkish adults in the club work rather actively with computers or alternatively participate in a computer-based German language course.

There are some parents in the club who actively use the computers to follow their personal interests and who want to acquire new knowledge purposefully e.g. handling of email programmes, shopping eBay or formatting specific types of documents.

Figure 1: (Left) Turkish son proudly shows his mother his computer skills. (Right) Young girl interview habits of the quarter as a part of the history project (Picture taken from the booklet Come_IN (2004).

Negotiated Experience and Values

In order to initiate the process, we needed to find project foci which were interesting to the members of the different generations and communities and provided a base for a multi cultural dialog. During the first eight months we explored a couple of project foci together with the participants.

The project focus "Bonner Altstadt Geschichten", (Hi-)Stories from the Bonner Altstadt turned out to be rather successful with respect to these goals[7]. The underlying idea of the project is to conserve different narratives from inhabitants of the neighbourhood. On the one hand these narratives give an

---

[7] This project group presents some of the stories in a small booklet which was sold on the Christmas market of the school (Come_IN, 2004)

account of the multicultural character of the neighbourhood during the past decades. On the other hand the project results may help to strengthen a (mainly) German-Turkish identity. We assumed that those who explores the shared past collaboratively will have a common future, manifested in a common identity.

We were able to examine the people's behaviour in large projects. After the introduction of the general theme and a presentation of prototypical realizations of materials, the parents took actively part in the club for the first time. They collected creative ideas concerning the content which was to be included in the neighbourhood's digital history.

When examining the neighbourhood under different perspectives, a process of negotiation emerges. Shared as well as conflicting cultural values get visible. This fact can be illustrated by the following case.

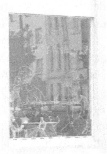

I don't like to passing by this shop. In actual fact it is nice inside the shop/room but the windows are ugly. (I thing that an artist painted the image). I find the picture is ugly, because the painted woman on the window is nude.

Figure 2: A young girl presents one of her ugliest places of the quarter. Text and picture taken from the booklet Come_IN (2004)

As a part of the history project the kids were supposed to take photos of the most beautiful and the ugliest part of the quarter. A young girl of Turkish origin took a photo of an art gallery. The shop window of the gallery was painted with some sketches of figures. Among others, the sketch of a nude woman decorated the window. When describing her photo the girl wrote that she "gets fed up with this, since there are women displayed nude in public". In contrast, others actors felt very differently about the gallery and its window since it enriches the quarter culturally.

This case shows to what extent the perspectives are different concerning certain places in the neighbourhood. We believe that the opportunities of multi media technologies can play an important role in capturing these different perspectives and present them in an adequate manner. Yet, at this stage of the project we have not yet developed explicit strategies how to make use of these artefacts in building on the differences in perspective.

Appropriation of Computers

The empirical data shows that different patterns for the appropriation of computer applications exist. The different appropriation processes are always embedded in social networks structured by individual abilities and friendship ties. We found that, although the club has no formal structure and does not maintain a long-term practice, a grouping into newcomers (novices) and old-timers (experts) takes place. Parents with computer experience – fathers in particular – quickly take the role of mentors.

For example, one father who works for a computer company is typically willing to give advice. He also enriches the club with fresh and innovative ideas. Another example for such phenomena is a German father who comes with his 17 years old daughter to the club where both act as mentors. Their motivation is to "simply do something good within the neighbourhood. The idea [was] good, and doing [would be] much more preferable than moaning". A Turkish father uses to haggle on eBay. He is very proud to demonstrate his practical skills in buying and selling things via the Internet. He also practices that at home, and shows new things he gathered and learnt with his friends. But, he is not interested in taking leadership.

It is also interesting to see that newcomers employ different manners of learning. A comparison between a Japanese and a Turkish mother can illustrate this very well: The Japanese mother is very enthusiastic with the club. She comes very frequently and is eager to learn more about computers. She uses the new competence also for her business (e.g. create leaflets that announce her piano concerts). Talking about her learning progress is mainly the basis for intercultural dialogue. In addition, she motivates other parents to increase their competences as she emphasizes the practical need of using computers.

The Turkish single mother comes also regularly to the club. Her son is very keen to working on computers and is one of the experts among the children. She, in contrast, was very shy at the beginning, had no computer competence and spoke only little German. During their continuous participation she became more and more self-confident, joins the language course and started to work with computers timidly but regularly. Nevertheless, she is not integrated completely since intercultural dialogue, especially among parents, is still rather infrequent.

Another specific aspect of the club is the rather intense cooperation between generations. Parents learn from their children and visa versa. The kids playfully experiment with the software. They also drive the production process of multimedia materials. They often ask adults for advice. The adults either show how to solve a certain problem or ask other mentors to find a solution.

Making use of the high Recognition of Computer Abilities

The computer is an important factor to get the project running (see above). A closer look at the role of computer shows an interesting phenomenon: It is not the actual usefulness of the computer which is important to some of the parents, but the fact that the computer may become useful in the future. Therefore they would like their kids to acquire computer competences. Two interviewed parents interested in the computer club stated that they did not know how to handle a computer, neither did they know what ICT can do for them.

Obviously computer and the ability to deal with them offer a rather high level of social reputation. However, this reputation does not always hold. For example, in case of the German language class, the use of computers had to be stopped since the underlying software could not be applied adequately. Now German classes are exclusively conducted in the classical manner without any computer support. In order to overcome the shortcoming of actual learning applications, typically deeper requirement analyses in multi cultural settings are needed.

Although badly designed standard software is annoying, it is not that bad that we needed to stop our project due to an inadequate technical infrastructure. In particular, we believe that the decisive activities in our project do not happen by means of computer support. These activities which are secondary to the acquisition of computer skills are of primary importance for the establishment of a CoP.

Conclusion

There are many reasons which make integration projects like the one presented above a challenge. Typically, there is neither an existing shared practice nor a common identity on which such projects can be built. Additionally most of the people involved in the project do their work voluntarily and without payment. To create a shared practice and bootstrap an integration process, it is important to choose suitable attractors and formal structures fitting to the particular socio-cultural context.

In our case, the attraction of computers to children was an important factor. Many of them got directly very enthusiastic about the computer club. Moreover, the gentle "grip" the school's principle and other teachers exercised on parents provided formal structures which helped setting up the process. Due to this pressure, some parents felt obliged to participate in the computer club. So the structures of the German public school system and the fact that the different ethnically defined communities lived still in the same neighbourhood helped setting up the integration process.

Duguid (2004) has already pointed out that formal organizational structures such as the division of labour, are highly important for communities of practice.

They shape the space of opportunities for their emergence. Formal social structures such as public schooling may play a similar role in establishing a shared practice and initiating integration processes.

In the course of the project it turned out that the rule which stated that parents must accompany their children to the club became important in an unanticipated way. While originally invented to increase the participation of parents, it soon got a different meaning. This rule provided physical and cultural spaces especially for those women of Turkish origin who were often exclusively bound to their family homes and ethnic community.

There are considerable methodological problems with respect to the evaluation of integration processes. A successful process is difficult to measure, especially when it is ongoing. Actually, we consider the current state of the process as a success. An indicator is the rather high number of actors participating from the side of the German and the Turkish community. The active participation is relatively well measurable. However, it is unclear whether a shared practice or changes in the actor's identities will emerge. Even in case a common practice emerges, its impact on the actors identity is not a given. These changes are much more fundamental and are deeply embedded in a shared practice. Therefore, they are difficult to analyse. Changes in identity are long-term processes which run underneath the behavioural surface and are, therefore, not always obvious. We can just search for individual cases of empirical evidence. An example for such evidence is the appropriation of computers by the Turkish single mother (see above). But it is not for sure, if this is a sustainable process.

The context between the members and their ethnic community is still not evident. It is not clear if people who specially need an enrichment of their cultural and social capital could have been reached. On the contrary we do know only little about how the project reflects to the social net by the participants which makes them a multiplier.

Acknowledgements

Our very special thank goes to Kanan Al-Zubaidi who worked with us on the investigation on the state of the art in Germany and contributed interesting ideas. We would like to thank all the participating families. Special thanks go to the volunteers who generously supported the project with their time and energy. We are indebted to: Ingrid and Klaus Kansy, Norbert Brückner, Barbara Hofmann, Lale Altinay, Astrid Keller-Garbe, Soner Ögükmen, Mojdeh Behaadi, Olav Schüttler, and Peter Schorpfenecker. The Foundation of the Sparkasse of Bonn generously donated the computer equipment. The city of Bonn kindly restored the rooms for the computer club.

References

Aksoy, A. and K. Robins. 2000. "Thinking across spaces. Transnational television from Turkey." European Journal of Cultural Studies 3:343-365.

Berry, J. W. 1984. "Cultural relations in plural societies." Pp. 32-49 in Groups in Contact, edited by N. M. M. Brewer. New York: Academic Press.

— 1992. "Acculturation and adaptation in a new society." International Migration, pp. 69-85.

Berry, J. W. and U. Kim. 1988. "Acculturation and mental health." Pp. 207-236 in Health and cross-cultural psychology: Toward applications. Newbury Park, CA: Sage.

Calabrese Barton, A. 1998. "Teaching Science with Homeless Children: Pedagogy, Representation, and Identity." Journal of Research in Science Teaching 35:379-394.

Chapman, R. 2004. "Pearls of Wisdom: Social Capital Building in Informal Learning Environments." Pp. 301-331 in Social Capital and Information Technology, edited by M. W. Huysman, V. Cambridge: MIT Press.

Come_IN, 2004: "Bunte Altstadtgeschichten, Teil 1", Booklet of the Come_IN presenting parts of the project work, 52 pages, Dezember 2004

Dick, B. 2002. Grounded Theory: a thumbnail sketch. [On line] Available at http://www.scu.edu.au/schools/gcm/ar/arp/grounded.html

Duguid, P. (2004): "The art of knowing – Social and tacit dimensions of knowledge and the limits of communities of practice, in: The Information Society, in press

Esser, H. 1996. "Ethnische Konflikte als Auseinandersetzung um den Wert von kulturellen Kapital." Pp. 64-99 in Die bedrängte Toleranz. Ethnisch-kulturelle Konflikte, religiöse Differenzen und die Gefahren politisierter Gewalt. Frankfurt/M: Suhrkamp.

Granato, M. 2001. "Freizeitgestaltung und Mediennutzung bei Kindern türkischer Herkunft." Presse und Informationsamt der Bundesregierung, Berlin.

Hayes, G. R., K. J. Bevis, and R. A. Amar. 2004. "The Clubhouse Revisited." Georgia Institute of Technology.

Hinkelbein, O. 2004. "Ethnische Minderheiten, neue Medien und die digitale Kluft: Deutschland ein digitales Entwicklungsland?" Bremen, bremer institut für kulturforschung, Universität Bremen.

Holter, I.M. and D. Schwartz - Barcott. 1993. "Action Research: What is it? How has it been used and how can it be used in nursing?" Journal of Advanced Nursing 128:298-304.

Kemmis, S. and R. McTaggert. 1988. The action research planner. Victoria, Australia: Deakin University Press.

Lanfranchi, A. , J. Gruber, and D. Gay. 2001. "Schulerfolg bei Migrationskindern dank transitorischer Räume im Vorschulbereich." in Sammelband des NFP 39 Migration: Seismo Verlag.

Lave, J. and E. Wenger. 1991. Situated Learning: Legitimate Peripheral Participation: Cambridge: Cambridge University Press.

Luft, S. 2002. "Die Dynamik der Desintegration: Zum Stand der Ausländerintegration in deutschen Großstädten." Hanns-Seidel-Stiftung e.V.

Mills, G. E. 2003. Action research: a guide for the teacher researcher. Upper SaddleRiver, NJ:: Pearson Education, Inc.

Nasir, N. 2002. "Identity, goals, and learning: Mathematics in cultural practice." Mathematical Thinking and Learning 4.

Naumann, J. 1998. "Etwas Struktur im großen Chaos." in taz Berlin.

Papert, S. 1980. Mindstorms. New York: Basic Books.

Resnick, M. and N. Rusk. 1996a. "Access is Not Enough." The American Prospect 27:60-68.

—. 1996b. "The Computer Clubhouse: Preparing for Life in a Digital World." IBM Systems Journal 35.

Roebers, C. M. 1997. Migrantenkinder im vereinigten Deutschland. Münster: Waxmann Verlag.

Rohde, Markus 2004. Find what binds. Building social capital in an Iranian NGO community system. In: Huysman, M., Wulf, V. (eds.) 2004: Social Capital and Information Technology, Cambridge: MIT Press, 75-112.

Shaw, A. 1995. "Social constructionism and the inner city." Ph.D. Thesis Thesis, Massachusetts Institute of Technology.

Unbehaun, H., G. Straßburger, and L. Yalcin-Heckmann. 1997. "Die türkischen Kolonien in Bamberg und Colmar - ein deutsch-französischer Vergleich sozialer Netzwerke von Migranten im interkulturellen Kontext." Bamberg: Otto-Friedrich-Universität Bamberg.

Vieth-Entus, S. 2001. "Gravierende Sprachdefizite." in Tagesspiegel.

Wagner, G., R. Pischner, and J. Haisken-DeNew. 2002. "The Changing Digital Divide in Germany." Pp. 164-185 in The Internet in Everyday Life. London: Blackell Publishers Ltd.

Wenger, E. 1998. Communities of Practice. Learning, Meaning and Identity. Cambridge: Cambridge University Press.

Wenger, E., R. McDermott, and W. Snyder. 2002. Cultivating communities of practice: a guide to managing knowledge. Cambridge, MA: Harvard Business School Press.

Supporting Privacy Management via Community Experience and Expertise

Jeremy Goecks, Elizabeth D. Mynatt

Georgia Institute of Technology, USA

{jeremy, mynatt}@cc.gatech.edu

Abstract. We propose a novel approach for supporting privacy management that leverages community experience and expertise via the process of social navigation. Social navigation simplifies the often complex task of managing privacy settings, and systems that employ social navigation can advantageously complement user privacy management processes. We implemented our approach to privacy management in the Acumen system; Acumen uses social navigation to enable individuals to manage their Internet cookies both manually and automatically based on the behavior of others in the community. We present the Acumen system in detail and discuss data obtained from a six-week, preliminary deployment of Acumen. Lastly, we discuss challenges that systems implementing our approach must address if they are to be successful.

Introduction

Privacy has come to the forefront of societal concerns about technology in recent years (Ackerman et al., 1999, FTC, 2000, Harris, 2003, Turow, 2003). The rise of the Internet and ubiquitous computing technologies has made it possible to easily collect, store, aggregate, and share personal information. Such technologies offer many benefits; however, there is significant concern that applications and entities using these technologies (e.g. companies, governments) are marginalizing people's desire for personal privacy. Much can be gained by addressing people's privacy concerns. These technologies and applications are more likely to be fully accepted by and integrated into society if privacy is addressed; in addition,

P. van den Besselaar et al. (eds.), Communities and Technologies 2005, 397-417.

scholars argue that privacy is beneficial to both individuals and society (Westin, 1967, Lessig, 1999).

For the purposes of this paper, we define 'privacy' to be an individual's ability to control when and how he shares his personal information with other people and third parties; when an individual manages his privacy, then, he manages when and how he shares his personal information.

The HCI community has substantially advanced its understanding of privacy management over the past decade. We now understand that privacy management cannot be addressed solely or even largely by a static set of preferences that determine how a user's information can be shared. Rather, privacy management is a fluid, organic process in which users are constantly refining their choices based on any number of contextual facets (Bellotti, 1996, Bellotti and Sellen, 1993, Palen and Dourish, 2003). This is true both for privacy management among peers and also for privacy management between individuals and "third parties," such as corporations and government agencies.

Supporting privacy management, then, is a challenging task for a computational system. In this paper, we propose a novel approach for supporting privacy management that leverages community experience and expertise via social navigation. Social navigation is the process of using other people's behavior to inform one's own behavior (Dieberger et al., 2000). Systems that employ social navigation leverage users' data in aggregate as a form of information or advice to help individuals make decisions. We can consider the users of a social navigation system to be a community; thus, when a community member engages in social navigation, the system provides the member with community data, the aggregate activity data of all community members. Social navigation systems have proven to be successful in many domains (Hill et al., 1992, Resnick et al., 1994, Svensson et al., 2001, Wexelblat and Maes, 1999).

Our approach employs social navigation to support individual privacy management decisions and enable novel privacy management techniques. Social navigation is a promising approach to privacy management for several reasons. Social navigation simplifies the often complex task of managing privacy settings by leveraging people's tacit ability to infer information from others' decisions and use that information as form of advice. Studies have shown that, if advice is available when making a decision, users very often use the advice and make a better decision as a result of using the advice (Harvey and Fisher, 1997, Yaniv, 2004). In addition, social navigation systems offer a technological complement to user privacy management activities; both evolve as user behavior changes, and both are frequently collaborative and situated in other, principal activities.

We have implemented our approach to privacy management in a system that enables users to manage an important facet of their Internet privacy: Internet cookies. Websites use cookies most often to identify users, store preferences, and record users' browsing behavior. While users derive benefits from cookies, the ability of websites' to use cookies to identify and monitor users' activities means that cookies also present a threat to users' privacy.

Internet users are becoming increasingly concerned about their privacy online and about cookies in particular (Ackerman et al., 1999, Harris, 2003, Turow, 2003). Managing cookies on an individual basis is impractical, and existing solutions for managing cookies, such as P3P user agents (Cranor, 2002) and web browsers' tools, are insufficient at times. These tools are not well understood by users, offer little awareness of ongoing cookie activity, and provide inflexible settings that do not adapt to changes in users' needs and attitudes (Friedman et al., 2002, Millett et al., 2001).

The Acumen system employs social navigation to help users manage their cookies. Acumen addresses many problems of existing cookie management solutions and also provides novel methods for managing cookies. Acumen's interface is an Internet Explorer toolbar (Figure 1) that enables users to manage their cookies by leveraging community data. To this end, Acumen collects information about how users are managing their cookies and employs this data for three purposes.

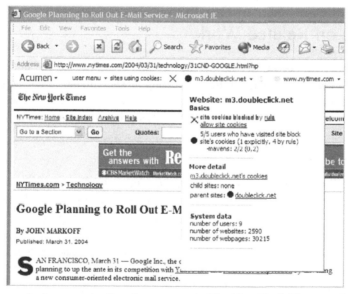

Figure 1. Acumen toolbar for a page on *The New York Times* website.

First, Acumen uses its data to raise users' awareness of cookies, especially those that others have blocked. This information is conveyed via color-coded icons in the toolbar; icons are colored using biased thresholds that accentuate user activity. Second, Acumen makes its data available to help individuals make more informed decisions about whether to block or allow a website's cookies. Third, Acumen enables users to automate cookie management by using simple rules which automatically block cookies that others have blocked.

To address herd behavior (Banerjee, 1992), a common problem in social navigation, Acumen employs data from all users and also from a subset of expert users called *mavens* (Gladwell, 2000). Mavens' data can help deter individuals from blindly following the decisions of others.

Overview

We offer three research contributions in this paper. First, we introduce a novel approach to privacy management that employs social navigation. Second, we demonstrate an application of this approach in Acumen, a system that enables users to manage their Internet cookies. Third, we evaluate Acumen using data from a six week, preliminary deployment of the system. We evaluate how well Acumen helps users manage their cookies and also discuss five challenges that we identified during our design and implementation of Acumen. These challenges are: (1) raising awareness of cookies; (2) understanding decision support; (3) obtaining data coverage; (4) mitigating herd behavior; and (5) addressing a privacy paradox.

Building on Related Work

Previously, we described how privacy management has come to be understood as a dynamic process. Our approach for supporting privacy management builds both on this work and on work in two other areas: (a) social navigation research and (b) research investigating management of Internet privacy and Internet cookies.

Social Navigation

The adage "a crowd draws a crowd" describes one instance of social navigation. When an individual sees a crowd outside an unfamiliar restaurant, she can infer that many people enjoy the food at the restaurant and that the restaurant generally serves good food. Hence, she is more likely to dine at the restaurant than she otherwise would be because the crowd provides information about how much other people like the restaurant. The crowd's behavior, then, is a simple form of data or advice that a bystander can use to make a decision.

In general, social navigation is the activity of using other people's behavior to inform one's own behavior. Social navigation is quite common in everyday life; it has also been demonstrated to be a powerful concept in digital systems (Dieberger et al., 2000). Researchers have built systems that enable users to perform social navigation in numerous domains; these domains include editing and reading documents (Hill et al., 1992), reading newsgroup messages (Resnick et al., 1994), exploring an online food and recipes store (Svensson et al., 2001), and browsing the Internet (Wexelblat and Maes, 1999).

We believe that our approach is the first attempt to explore social navigation as a privacy management solution. Social navigation is a particularly promising approach to privacy management for several reasons. Social navigation is a tacit and natural facet of the decision-making process because people are social beings. People routinely make inferences based on others' behavior and use this information as a form of advice; this advice simplifies and informs what can otherwise be complex decisions (e.g. how fast should I be driving on an unfamiliar road?). Finally, there is substantial evidence that people very often use advice and make better decisions as a result (Harvey and Fisher, 1997, Yaniv, 2004). Social navigation, then, can simplify and improve the often complex decisions that people must make when managing their privacy.

Social navigation systems also offer a technological complement to user privacy management processes. Users' privacy settings evolve to reflect changing needs; changes in how personal information is collected and used or in community norms surrounding use of personal information prompt changes in users' privacy settings (Palen and Dourish, 2003). Social navigation systems evolve as well because user's activities shape the system; thus, the system evolves as users' activities change.

Privacy management is frequently a collaborative process; conventions regarding privacy management develop within communities, and an individual's privacy management decisions are made in the context of these conventions (Bellotti, 1996). Social navigation systems support a similar process. Community conventions are made visible by aggregating community members' data, and an individual's decisions are made in the context of, and often directly using, this aggregated data.

Internet Privacy and Cookies

Internet users have numerous privacy concerns. One of their main concerns is the collection of personal data by third parties; users want the ability to control when, how, and what information they share with third parties. Internet cookies (RFC, 2004) are particularly troublesome in this respect because websites can use cookies to collect and store information about users; sites often use cookies to monitor users' browsing activities. In fact, at least thirty-five percent of websites use cookies to collect such information (FTC, 2000). Managing cookies on an individual or per-request basis is confusing, tedious, and overly invasive for most users. Hence, there is a need for tools that enable users to better manage cookies.

Some online privacy policies describe how a website uses cookies and what data they collect using them. However, online privacy policies are often difficult to locate and understand (Jensen and Potts, 2004). The Platform for Privacy Preferences (P3P) specification enables websites to encode a privacy policy in a machine-readable format; software agents can then interpret and utilize P3P policies (Cranor, 2002).

Much work has been done in an attempt to help users manage their cookies. Both of today's major browsers, Internet Explorer and Mozilla, provide users with the ability to filter out cookies with particular characteristics. Users can block cookies without acceptable privacy policies or cookies from particular websites. However, there are problems and inadequacies with both browsers' cookie management tools. For example, cookie settings are often nested deep inside many menu levels, making them hard to find and modify; also, browsers provide little on-going awareness of cookies and do not enable users to adapt their settings to changes in their needs. Finally, many users do not understand the terminology that is used by browsers (Friedman et al., 2002, Millett et al., 2001). Neither browser uses social navigation to support cookie management.

There have been efforts to develop tools that extend browsers' cookie management capabilities. Cookie Watcher is an awareness tool that displays cookie activity in real-time but does not support cookie management (Friedman et al., 2002). The Privoxy web proxy blocks cookies from websites known to track users' activities via cookies for targeted advertising purposes (Privoxy, 2004). Privoxy provides little awareness to users about cookies; moreover, Privoxy's list of blocked websites is static, and thus it does not support dynamic or flexible cookie management.

Finally, two systems that employ explicit user voting to help users manage other facets of Internet privacy are Cloudmark's SpamNet (Cloudmark, 2004) and the Social Contract Core (SCC) (Kaufman et al., 2002). SpamNet utilizes users' votes to identify and filter spam, and the SCC uses votes to help companies improve their privacy policy or develop separate policies for different groups. Our approach builds on ideas in these systems. While they indirectly support privacy management through user voting, our approach directly leverages community activity data to help individuals manage their privacy.

Acumen

The ACUMEN system (Figure 2) employs a community's activity data to help individuals manage their Internet cookies. Acumen's community is the individuals who use Acumen and thus contribute data to the system via their cookie management activities. Individuals manage cookies at the website level, allowing or blocking cookies from websites. Acumen allows all cookies by default. Acumen's community data consists of the number of individuals who have "visited" a website (i.e. requested a file from the site), the number of such individuals who allow the site's cookies, and the number of individuals who block the site's cookies.

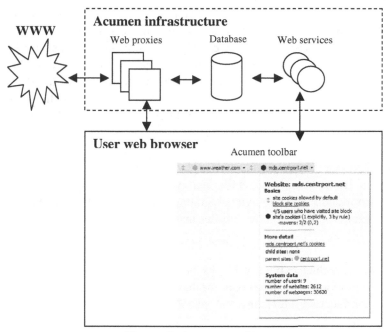

Figure 2. Acumen architecture.

Acumen enables community members to manage their cookies via indirect collaboration through their actions; each individual benefits by leveraging the community's collective knowledge and experiences via social navigation. Acumen enables individuals to leverage its community data in three ways. During their normal web browsing activities, individuals can maintain awareness of the websites using cookies on the webpages that they are visiting and whether other community members generally allow or block cookies from these sites. When making the decision to allow or block a website's cookies, individuals can view the community data for the site in detail and use this information to inform their decision.

Individuals can also employ simple rules that leverage community data to automatically block cookies. Individuals can create rules of the form 'If X% of users have blocked cookies from a website, then automatically block the site's cookies.' Individuals choose a rule's threshold percentage when they create it. The percentage of individuals that block a site's cookies includes both individuals that block cookies explicitly and those that block cookies by rule. Thus, when one individual's rule blocks a site's cookies, it can cause another individual's rule with a higher threshold to block the site's cookies as well, and so on. This chain of rule applications acts like a social epidemic (Gladwell, 2000), and it can propagate the blocking of a site's cookies quite quickly among Acumen's community.

Acumen utilizes community data from all individuals and also from a select subset of individuals called *mavens*. Gladwell defines a maven as a domain expert, someone who has both a deep understanding of a domain and also an intrinsic desire to learn as much as they can about the domain; mavens have been identified in many areas (Gladwell, 2000). Internet privacy mavens almost certainly exist as well; people that read and contribute to the Electronic Privacy Information Center (EPIC) website (www.epic.org) and those that use free cookie management software such as Privoxy are likely mavens. We believe that Acumen is the first computational system that attempts to utilize the concept of mavens.

Acumen leverages mavens' expertise by anonymously identifying and providing data from them. To identify mavens, Acumen computes a 'maven rating' for each individual; an individual's rating is the sum of the square roots of a individual's actions across all the websites that he visited:

$$R_m = \sum_{websites} \sqrt{num\_user\_actions_n}$$

Each time an individual explicitly blocks or allows a site's cookies, Acumen increments the individual's action count for that site.

This function has two interesting features. First, taking the square root of the number of actions decreases the influence of each additional action on a individual's maven rating; for example, the first 4 actions an individual performs on a site will increase his rating by 2, but the subsequent 4 actions that he takes on the site will increase his rating by only 0.82 This feature reflects the fact that people often learn more in early experiences than they do in latter experiences (Fridland et al., 2003); thus, inexperienced individuals' ratings increase more quickly with additional actions than do experienced individuals' ratings.

The second interesting feature of the function concerns the placement of the square root operator. By taking the square root of actions performed for each site rather than the square root of actions performed across all sites, the function balances breadth and depth of individual actions, though breadth is slightly favored.

Acumen labels the individuals with the top 20% of ratings as mavens. It is not clear what percentage of individuals should be labeled as mavens; we are not aware of any estimates about how many mavens are present in a typical domain.

Finally, it is worthwhile to note that we designed Acumen to support privacy management among a small community. Acumen's data is most useful when individuals can effectively infer information from the cookie management activities of Acumen's community, and it is easiest to make effective inferences when Acumen's community members shares norms and practices. Small communities, such as extended workgroups and organizations, often do share norms and practices; thus, members of these communities are very likely to be able to use Acumen's data effectively.

Implementation

Four component types comprise the Acumen system: (1) remote web proxies; (2) a central database; (3) Acumen's toolbar; and (4) web services that act as data intermediaries between the database and the toolbar. The components communicate securely using Secure Sockets Layer (SSL) channels.

All users' web traffic goes through one of Acumen's web proxies. A proxy performs two actions: (1) records the websites that a user has visited and the cookies used by those sites; and (2) blocks cookies from webpage requests and response if a user has explicitly or by rule blocked the site's cookies.

Acumen's database acts as a central repository for all data used by the system. For each website that a user has visited, the database maintains a user-website history; the history contains the cookies that the site uses for the user, whether a user blocks or allows the site's cookies, and, if cookies are blocked, how so.

Acumen's web service acts as the intermediary between its database and its toolbar. When a user visits a webpage, the toolbar obtains data about the page from the service. The service also handles user actions (e.g. blocking a cookie, changing a rule) and updates the database accordingly.

Acumen's web proxies and web services are the performance bottlenecks in the architecture. In order to make these components as responsive as possible, Acumen supports dynamic replication and deployment of the components and uses caches in both components.

Acumen attempts to mitigate privacy concerns by ensuring that user data is anonymous both at the user interface level and at the system level. Acumen's interface enables users to view only aggregated data; users are never able to view another individual's data. Acumen does not record any identifying information about its users beyond a persistent identifier, and it records a user's browsing activities only if she is logged into the system. Finally, Acumen provides a simple interface for users to see what data the system has collected about them; this interface enables a user to exclude some or all of her data from Acumen's community data. Acumen's architecture ensures that the system's complexity is hidden from users. To use Acumen, a user needs only install Acumen's toolbar, set her browser to use Acumen's proxy, and create a pseudonym for persistent identification by Acumen.

Internet Explorer Toolbar

Acumen's toolbar uses a just-in-time approach to provide cookie information. The toolbar lists the websites that are using cookies on the page that a user is currently visiting. Next to each website using cookies are two icons. The icon to the far left of the site name denotes whether the user allows or blocks the site's cookies; a green double arrow indicates that they are allowed, and a red X indicates they are blocked.

The circle icon to the immediate left of the website name denotes Acumen's community data for the site. Recall that Acumen's community data is the number of users who have blocked/allowed a website's cookies. The icon itself has two regions: an inner region and an outer region. The inner region's color denotes data for mavens; the outer region denotes data for the entire community (Figure 3). Regions are colored using a stoplight motif. Green indicates that a great majority of users (90% or more) allow the site's cookies, yellow indicates that most users (75% to 90%) allow the site's cookies, and red indicates that only some users (less than 75%) allow the site's cookies.

The icons serve to alert users to potentially problematic cookies. A user can quickly glance at the toolbar and determine whether there are cookies on a page that others in the community have blocked. A user can also glance at the two icons next to a website name and determine whether her decision about the site's cookies matches others' decisions. A user's decision matches that of others if the icons are the same color; if not, the icons have different colors (Figure 3).

We use non-linear, biased thresholds for the color categories to reflect the often sensitive and conservative nature of privacy management. Even if only a few community members have blocked a site's cookies, this information is reflected in an icon's color and thus communicated to the user. Also, users rarely change default settings (Mackay, 1990); biased thresholds accentuate any deviation in the community data from Acumen's default of allowing cookies.

Clicking on a website's name in the toolbar opens the site's menu (Figure 4). The menu's top section elaborates on the icons next to the site in the toolbar. If cookies are blocked, the menu indicates why; a link is provided to block/allow the site's cookies. Community data is provided numerically, and the number of users who block the site's cookies explicitly and by rule are indicated.

The menu's middle section provides a link to view the cookies that a site uses

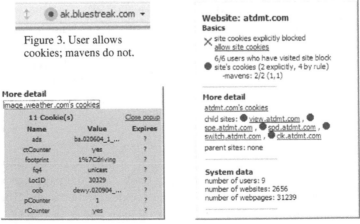

Figure 3. User allows
cookies; mavens do not.

Figure 5. A website's cookies.

Figure 4. Website menu.

Figures 3-5 (ordered clockwise). Screenshots of Acumen's toolbar interface.

(Figure 5) and provides links to menus for child and parent sites. There is an icon next to each child and parent site that denotes the community data for that site. These links enable users to explore Acumen's data via relationships between parent and child sites. For example, a user can easily move to a top-level website (e.g. atdmt.com), view community data for the site, and block all cookies from that site; blocking cookies from a parent site blocks cookies from all its child sites as well.

The menu's lower section provides system information; the number of users, number of websites, and number of documents in Acumen's database are displayed. This information is intended to serve as an incentive for users to utilize Acumen; users are more likely to use Acumen if they know that there is data in the system.

The toolbar's user menu enables users to manage their rules for automatically managing cookies and indicates whether the user is a maven.

Deployment and Evaluation

We deployed Acumen to 9 users for 6 weeks so that we could begin to understand how users would employ Acumen. At the end of the six weeks, Acumen's database contained data for over 2650 websites; users had blocked cookies from 85 websites using Acumen.

All users in our deployment utilize the Internet heavily and as part of their job. Seven users were graduate students; two users were information workers outside the technology industry. Only two users managed their cookies before using Acumen; both were graduate students. The seven other users were familiar with cookies and expressed some concern about them but did not manage them or know their browser's cookie settings. Users employed Acumen on a voluntary basis. We asked users to employ Acumen in the context of their normal browsing activities; we did not ask them to be more proactive in managing cookies than they otherwise would be, though the presence of Acumen's toolbar likely encouraged them to manage cookies more than they would have otherwise.

While the number of users that participated in this deployment is small, it is still constructive to evaluate data obtained from the deployment. Acumen is a novel privacy management system, and this deployment provides needed data that offers insight into how users did and did not use Acumen's features. Evaluation data from this deployment will also inform future iterations of Acumen and stimulate research questions that can be explored in follow up work.

We obtained data about this deployment from informal interviews with users, logging data, and data from Acumen's database. Overall, the data is promising. Users employed many of Acumen's features to manage their cookies, and the data suggests they managed cookies actively and effectively.

We present data from our deployment in the next two sections. In the following section, we address an important but challenging question: are there cookies that users generally agree are "good" and other cookies that users consider to be "bad?" Addressing this question enables us to begin evaluating whether Acumen helped users made good decisions. Then, using data from our deployment, we discuss challenges that we encountered when designing Acumen.

Allowing the "Good," Blocking the "Bad"

One important evaluation criterion for Acumen is the degree to which its community data helps users make high-quality decisions. The question, then, is whether Acumen helps users allow desirable ("good") cookies and block undesirable ("bad") cookies. Before we can evaluate Acumen using this criterion, though, a method or model is needed to label cookies as good or bad; to the best of our knowledge, there is no such model. We first introduce our model for labeling cookies and then apply it to evaluate user decisions in Acumen.

A Model for Labelling Cookies

While there are individual differences in privacy preferences (Ackerman et al., 1999), there is likely to be some agreement among people about which cookies are good and which are bad. The primary obstacle that prevents people from labeling cookies is that they have difficultly operationalizing their privacy preferences. In other words, it is difficult for people to understand how cookies and features of cookies impact their privacy, and thus it is difficult for them to manage their cookies. For example, people may not understand how persistent identification changes when a website uses a long-lived cookie instead of a session cookie or how "third-party" cookies impact their privacy differently than "first-party" cookies.

Compact P3P policies (Cranor, 2002), which are sent by websites in conjunction with cookies, have begun to address these difficulties; however, many technological issues still impede people's ability to determine how cookies impact their privacy. Operationalizing privacy preferences in cookie management is also difficult because feedback is often lacking during management; many websites do not enable people to see how allowing or blocking cookies affects the information that websites collect about them.

We have taken these difficulties into account in our model. We use a simplified objective model, based on one observable and meaningful cookie attribute, to label cookies as good or bad. This attribute is the website from which a cookie originated; a cookie's originating website is available in all cookie management interfaces, including Acumen. By using this attribute to label cookies, we ensure that people can operationalize their privacy preferences within our model and make an educated decision about how to label a cookie.

Our model fuses results from multiple Internet privacy studies (Ackerman et al., 1999, FTC, 2000, Harris, 2003, Turow, 2003). A cookie's host website is remarkably useful information for people. Knowing the host website enables an individual to (a) associate some degree of trust/mistrust in the cookie and (b) infer a rudimentary benefit/cost ratio for using the website's cookies.

Interpreting these two facets as continuously-valued attributes of cookies yields a two-dimensional, four-quadrant model for labeling cookies (Figure 6). The dimensions are (1) the degree of trust in a website/cookie and (2) the benefit/cost ratio of using a website/cookie.

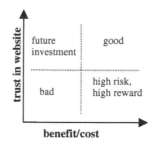

Figure 6. Cookie label model.

The model's dimensions aggregate multiple factors that influence people's privacy preferences. The dimension 'trust in a website' includes a site's reputation, business practices, privacy policies, and data sharing (and selling) policies. The dimension 'benefit/cost ratio' is simpler; people compare the benefits of using a site to its privacy costs. Privacy costs include data necessarily collected by the site so that it can provide benefits, data that is unnecessary but still collected by the site, and uses of collected data (e.g. unwanted email). While people are rarely aware of all data that a website has about them, they often have some knowledge of the data that they have given to or has been collected by a site.

This model is not inclusive or complete, but it is a first attempt to address how people make cookie management decisions given limited knowledge of how cookies and cookies features impact their privacy.

Based on this model, we label cookies that offer a high benefit/cost ratio and are from high trust websites as good; bad cookies are those with a low benefit/cost ratio and are from low trust websites. It is more difficult to label cookies in the other two quadrants. We term cookies that provide a high benefit/cost ratio but are from low trust websites as 'high risk, high reward.' We designate cookies that offer a low benefit/cost ratio but are from trusted websites as 'future investments'; such cookies require that users trust the site to provide benefits in the future given that they are using cookies to collect personal information now.

Evaluating User Decisions

Using this model, we categorized two sets of website cookies: (1) the 85 websites whose cookies were blocked by at least one user; and (2) the 85 most popular websites whose cookies were not blocked by any users. We categorized the websites into one of the four quadrants using information from privacy advocate groups such as Privoxy, EPIC, and the Center for Democracy and Technology (www.cdt.org). Table 1 summarizes these categorizations.

	Allowed cookies	Blocked cookies
Good	34% (29)	3% (3)
Bad	13% (11)	85% (72)
Future investment	28% (24)	2% (2)
High risk, reward	25% (21)	10% (8)

Table 1. Website categorization data.

The data is encouraging. Among websites whose cookies were blocked, most are categorized as bad and only a handful fall into other categories. In contrast, the distribution among websites whose cookies were allowed is broad. Together, good and bad cookies constitute nearly half of all allowed cookies, while future investments and high risk, high reward cookies comprise the other half.

Recall that our goal is to evaluate whether Acumen helps users block bad cookies and allow good cookies. Taken together, this data suggests that it does. Acumen's true positive and true negative rates are an encouraging 91% (29/32) and 87% (72/83), respectively. Acumen false positive rate is only 3%. An interesting result is Acumen's 13% false negative rate; this rate is the number of bad cookies that are allowed by all users. There is no immediate explanation for this rate. It may reflect the fact that users acted conservatively, only blocking cookies they could confidently conclude were bad; alternatively, users may not always be able to recognize bad cookies.

Finally, it is important to note that these results are in aggregate, and Acumen certainly served some users better than others. One prominent Internet privacy study has shown that there are at least nine major factors that influence Internet privacy management (Ackerman et al., 1999). Moreover, the study found that there are three principal classes of users: privacy fundamentalists, privacy pragmatists, and the marginally concerned; each class has demonstrably different privacy needs. Pragmatists, the largest group of users (55%), often make sophisticated privacy judgments that cannot be easily reduced to rules.

We found anecdotal evidence that some users did in fact disagree with our model. One user blocked a "good" website's cookies because she felt that there was no reason for the site to be using cookies. Another user experimented with blocking a "future investment" site's cookies to evaluate how it affected the site's performance; when he found that blocking cookies did not notably degrade the site's performance, he permanent blocked its cookies.

These anecdotes suggest that simply automating cookie management by implementing our model would be insufficient for some users. In particular, Acumen's approach of helping users make informed decisions rather than automating decision making is likely especially useful for pragmatists. Further studies are needed to evaluate how Acumen does and does not support particular types of individual cookie management practices.

Challenges

In this section, we discuss five challenges that we encountered while designing Acumen. The first challenge is universal for privacy management systems, and nearly all privacy management systems must address it. The latter four challenges are unique to our approach, and systems that employ social navigation to support privacy management must address them.

Raising Awareness for an Unknown Problem

Users will not use a privacy management system if they do not perceive a threat to their privacy. Users are largely unaware that cookies can be used to identify them and record their browsing activity, and many Internet cookie management tools go unused as a result (Turow, 2003). Making users aware of the pervasiveness of cookies and the risks that they pose is important if Acumen is to be used.

Acumen raises awareness of cookies by "pushing" information about cookies to the user. Acumen's interface is persistent; it displays all websites using cookies on a webpage and information that details how other community members are managing cookies from these sites. Acumen attempts to draw users' attention to sites that others have blocked cookies from; thus, Acumen attempts to highlight sites that others have deemed a risk to their privacy.

Our data indicates Acumen does raise users' awareness of cookies. Many users commented that they were surprised and somewhat concerned about particular websites that were using cookies. One user was quite surprised when a cookie from the website 'escapefromatlanta.com' appeared on a webpage he was visiting for the first time. This cookie concerned him as it indicated that the website "knew" that he lived in Atlanta even though he had provided no data to the site; thus, another site had likely shared his data with escapefromatlanta.com. After this incident, he became more proactive about managing his cookies.

We were surprised to find that simply presenting community data motivated some users to start managing their cookies. One user commented that since other users were managing their cookies, it was "probably something I should do as well." It did not matter which cookies others were blocking; simply knowing that they were managing their cookies was motivation enough for this user.

Users did take advantage of Acumen's color coding to identify websites from which other users have blocked cookies. Users found Acumen's color scheme useful and not overly distracting. Some users wanted the ability to sort websites based on community data so that sites from which many users have blocked cookies appear first in the toolbar; Acumen currently displays sites in roughly the order that their cookies are found on the page.

Understanding Decision Support

It has been shown that, for simple decisions, people use advice to improve their decision making (Harvey and Fischer, 1997, Yaniv, 2004). Acumen, however, supports privacy management decisions, which are often complex. Understanding when and how Acumen supports individual cookie management is perhaps the most important evaluation criterion for Acumen. Using this criterion, we can ask three questions about Acumen: (1) Did users employ Acumen's community data? (2) If so, how did they employ it when making cookie management decisions? (3) Did users employ Acumen's rules to automate cookie management?

Consider the two initial questions. In our deployment, users, on average, explicitly blocked cookies from 10 websites and automatically blocked cookies from 7 websites. It is not surprising to note that the ratio of cookies explicitly blocked to cookies blocked via rules is higher for mavens than for other users.

Anecdotes obtained from interviews indicate that users employed Acumen's data for different purposes when manually managing cookies. One user stated that, when blocking a website's cookie, he felt like "it was a pat on the back" if others had blocked the site's cookies as well. Thus, this user found a measure of validation for his decision by looking at others' data. Another user said that when she considered making a decision that others disagreed with (e.g. blocking a site's cookies that others had not), she thought more carefully about the decision than she otherwise would have. This user, then, used the data to help her decide which decisions to consider more carefully. There were also users who engaged in herd behavior and blocked a site's cookies because others had.

In addition to these purposes, we expect that there are many more purposes for which users may employ Acumen's data, and more research is needed to identify and understand them. These anecdotes, taken together with our earlier analysis that indicates that users share some agreement of good and bad cookies, suggest that Acumen helped users during the process of decision making and helped them make effective decisions.

There is evidence that users found Acumen's rules for automating cookie management useful. Users created few new rules, yet all users knew about

Acumen's rules and understood how they worked. Acumen automatically created two rules when a user signed up for an account: (1) if 20% or more of all users have blocked cookies from a website, automatically block the site's cookies; and (2) if 10% or more of mavens have blocked cookies from a website, automatically block its cookies.

In our limited deployment, these rules were sufficient for all but the most advanced users. Due to the small number of total users in our deployment, though, there were only two mavens; the small number of mavens did not allow for the latter rule to be meaningful for users. In interviews, most users said that they appreciated the rules as a mechanism for blocking cookies. Users favored using rules to block cookies because they either didn't know which cookies to block or were simply too preoccupied with other tasks to manage their cookies.

Community Data and Coverage

A system that employs community data to support privacy management is most effective when it can provide data about many of the potential decisions a user may face. If the number of potential decisions is too large or many potential decisions are not explored by users (and thus there is no data for these decisions), the system's data is unlikely to provide sufficient coverage over potential decisions and the system is rendered ineffective.

We can evaluate Acumen's data coverage in terms of websites. There are millions of websites, and Acumen will not contain community data for every site. The question, then, is which websites will Acumen likely have data for? And will users notice or be significantly harmed by the data that Acumen is missing? For the purposes of this discussion, we assume that Acumen has community data for a website if two or more uses have visited the site. Thus, any user who visits the site can observe how at least one other person manages the site's cookies.

We can posit answers to the above questions by observing that Acumen's data is tied to user's browsing activities; users will manage only cookies that they encounter while browsing. Hence, Acumen's data coverage mirrors the coverage obtained by users' browsing activities. Traffic among websites on the Internet has been shown to obey a power law distribution (Huberman, 2001). A basic power law distribution for web traffic says that the Nth most popular website receives about 1/N as much traffic as the most popular website. It follows that traffic to the most popular sites is a very, very large proportion of total traffic. Acumen, then, should contain community data for the most popular websites and be exponentially less likely to have data for less popular sites.

Data from Acumen's deployment confirms this hypothesis. The website traffic through Acumen's proxy exhibits a power law distribution (Table 2); traffic to 1.4% of websites accounts for 20% of all traffic, and traffic to 10.1% of sites accounts for 60% of all traffic. Overall, nearly one quarter of websites in Acumen have community data. Among the 20% of websites with the most traffic, however, nearly half have community data, and among the 60% of sites with the most traffic, one-third have data. Table 3 summarizes Acumen's coverage data.

% of Websites	% of Total Traffic
1.4%	20%
2.5%	40%
10.1%	60%
11.2%	80%

Table 2. Acumen's site traffic obeys power law.

% of Websites	% with Com. Data
20%	48%
40%	41%
60%	33%
80%	25%

Table 3. Acumen's attains substantial site coverage.

This data provides preliminary evidence that website coverage can be attained for much of the Internet and for nearly all of the Internet's popular sites. A related question is whether community data is more useful when making cookie management decisions for popular or obscure sites; we plan to explore this question in the future.

Mitigating Herd Behavior

One problem that social navigation systems sometimes experience is herd behavior (Banerjee, 1992). That is, users blindly follow the decisions or behavior of others because that data is available and assumed to be correct. This phenomenon could be especially problematic for Acumen because many users have little experience managing cookies. We attempted to address this problem in Acumen by identifying mavens and presenting community data from them. We hypothesized that mavens' data could offer a more informed–and thus more useful–set of information than could data from the general community.

It was difficult to determine whether mavens' data was useful to the users in our deployment. There were only two mavens during the deployment as the total number of users was small, and many websites did not have data from mavens. When sites did have mavens' data, it was only somewhat useful to users. Some users were skeptical that mavens were more knowledgeable than other users and thus relied on community data from all users rather than on mavens' data.

We speculate that mavens may need to provide credentials in order for users to trust that they are more knowledgeable than others. In addition, more work is needed to investigate how to effectively identify mavens.

Addressing a Privacy Paradox

A paradox arises when employing community data to support privacy management: it is possible to solve one privacy problem while creating another. By collecting and making users' data visible, as Acumen does, it is possible that users' privacy could be compromised.

Recall that Acumen ensures users are anonymous at both the interface level and at the system level. Even with these precautions, many users were mindful that Acumen was recording their activities. Rather than just log out, users sometimes chose to both log out and stop using Acumen's proxy so that they were confident Acumen was not recording their activities. It is unlikely that we can alleviate all users' privacy concerns as long as Acumen employs a central database; one solution is to develop a distributed architecture in which users' data is kept on their personal machine and shared anonymously.

However, there is a tension between the users' anonymity and the usefulness of community data. Community data becomes more useful as the level of anonymity decreases; knowing more about the data's source enables users to better evaluate and employ the data.

Future Work and Concluding Thoughts

We expect to iterate on Acumen's design and deploy Acumen for an extended period of time to an established community. We anticipate that a larger, extended study will enable us to address some of the questions posed in this paper about Acumen's usage and about the challenges discussed above. In addition, deploying Acumen to different communities would enable us to begin to understand how community attributes (e.g. size, purpose, attitudes) affect usage of Acumen.

We are interested in understanding and better supporting the large-scale dynamics that undergird Acumen. Identifying mavens is critical to the success of Acumen, and we plan to further explore methods to identify mavens. Mavens may be best identified by a combination of methods, such as through the recommendation of others, the demonstration of expertise, or via machine learning techniques (e.g. manually identify a few mavens and find others that are similar). Understanding how privacy management norms develop and the role that mavens play in the development process is also an area for future research.

Using social navigation to address privacy management in domains beyond Internet cookies is promising. Cookies are only one area of Internet privacy; other areas include voluntary submission of personal information and adware/spyware. We are interested in developing systems that use social navigation to support privacy management in these areas. We also intend to explore applications of our approach to privacy management problems in ubiquitous computing systems.

Acknowledgments

We thank the Everyday Computing Lab, The Privacy Place, and Sun Microsystems for their support of this research.

References

Ackerman, M., Cranor, L. and Reagle, J. (1999) Privacy in E-Commerce: Examining User Scenarios and Privacy Preferences. Proc. of 1999 ACM Conference on Electronic Commerce, p. 1-8.

Banerjee, A. (1992) A Simple Model of Herd Behavior. Quarterly Journal of Economics 107,3(1992), 797-818.

Bellotti, V. (1996) What You Don't Know Can Hurt You: Privacy in Collaborative Computing. Proc. of the 1996 HCI Conference on People and Computer, 241-261.

Bellotti, V. and Sellen, A. (1993) Design for Privacy in Ubiquitous Computing Environments. Proc. 1993 ECSCW, 77-92.

Cloudmark SpamNet. (2004) http://www.cloudmark.com/products/spamnet/

Cranor, L. F. Web Privacy with P3P. O'Reilly & Associates (2002), Sebastopol, CA.

Dieberger, A., Dourish, P., Hook, K, Resnick, P, Wexelblat, A. (2000) Social Navigation: Techniques for Building more Usable Systems. Interactions 7(6), 36-45.

Federal Trade Commission Report. United States Government (2000) Privacy Online: Fair Information Practices in the Electronic Marketplace: A Federal Trade Commission Report to Congress, May 2000. http://www.ftc.gov/reports/privacy2000/privacy2000.pdf

Fridland, A.J., Reisberg, D., and Gleitman, H. Psychology. W.W. Norton & Company (2003), New York, NY.

Friedman, B., Howe, D., and Felten, E. (2002) Informed Consent in the Mozilla Browser: Implementing Value-Sensitive Design. Proc. of 35th HICSS (2002), Abstract p. 247; CD-ROM for full paper.

Gladwell, M. The Tipping Point: How Little Things Can Make a Big Difference. Back Bay Books (2000), New York, New York.

Harris Inc. Poll #17. (2003) Most People Are "Privacy Pragmatists" Who, While Concerned about Privacy, Will Sometimes Trade It Off for Other Benefits, http://www.harrisinteractive.com/harris_poll/index.asp?PID=365

Harvey, N. and Fischer, I. (1997) Taking Advice: Accepting Help, Improving Judgement, and Sharing Responsibility. Journal of Organizational Behavior and Human Decision Processes, 70(2), p. 117-133.

Hill, W., Hollan, J., Wroblewski, D., McCandless, T. (1992) Edit wear and read wear. Proc. 1992 CHI, 3-9.

Huberman, B. The Laws of the Web: Patterns in the Ecology of Information, MIT Press (2001), Cambridge, MA.

Jensen, C. and Potts, C. (2004) Privacy Policies as Decision-Making Tools: A Usability Evaluation of Online Privacy Notices. Proc. 2004 CHI, 471-478.

Kaufman, J., Edlund, S., Ford, D. and Powers, C. (2002) The Social Contract Core. Proc. of 11th World Wide Web Conference, 210-220.

Lessig, L. Code and other Laws of Cyberspace. Basic Books (1999), New York, NY.

Mackay, W.E. (1990) Users and Customizable Software: A Co-Adaptive Phenomenon. Dissertation, Sloan School of Management. Cambridge, MA, MIT (1990).

Millett, L, Friedman. B., and Felten, E. (2001) Cookies and Web Browser Design: Toward Realizing Informed Consent Online. Proc. 2001 CHI, 46-52.

Palen, L. and Dourish, P. Unpacking "Privacy" for a Networked World. Proc. 2003 CHI, 129-136.

Privoxy web proxy, 2004. http://www.privoxy.org

Request For Comments #2965: HTTP State Management Mechanism, The RFC Archive (2004) http://www.rfc-archive.org/getrfc.php?rfc=2965

Resnick, P., Iacovou, N., Suchak, M., Bergstrom, P., and Riedl, J. (1994) GroupLens: an open architecture for collaborative filtering of netnews. Proc. 1994 CSCW, 175-186.

Svensson, M., Höök, M., Laaksolahti, and J., Waern, (2001) A. Social navigation of food recipes. Proc. 2001 CHI, 341-348.

Turow, J. (2003) Americans and Online Privacy: The System is Broken. Online report; available: http://www.annenbergpublicpolicycenter.org/04_info_society /2003_online_privacy_version_09.pdf

Westin, A, Privacy and Freedom. Atheneum Press (1967), New York, NY.

Wexelblat, A., Maes, P. (1999) Footprints: History-Rich Tools for Information Foraging. Proc. 1999 CHI, 270-277.

Yaniv, I. (2004) "Receiving other people's advice: Influence and benefit." Journal of Organizational Behavior and Human Decision Processes, 93(1), p. 1-13.

Regulation Mechanisms in an Open Social Media Using a Contact Recommender System

L. Vignollet⁺, M. Plu*, J. C. Marty⁺, L. Agosto*

⁺University of Savoie, France, *FranceTelecom R&D, France

Laurence.Vignollet@univ-savoie.fr, michel.plu@rd.francetelecom.com,

Jean-Charles.Marty@univ-savoie.fr, layda.agostofranco@rd.francetelecom.com

Abstract. This paper presents how an information exchange network can be improved by users' collaboration. This social media is based on content recommendation. Instead of using an automated content recommender system, we suggest an alternative approach where the information comes from trusted users. In order to overcome traditional problems of an open social media, we propose some regulation mechanisms. First each user manually controls her/his contacts network. Second we have introduced a contact recommender system to help users to carefully open their closed relationship network. This recommender system selects the recommended relationships in such a way it should optimize some global qualities of the social media. This paper details the algorithms of this recommendation process.

Objectives

Our main goal is to build an information exchange network on the Web, optimized by collaboration. This new service should allow users to better access and discover web resources. The purpose is to provide them with enriching features through the ability to interact and exchange with others. We propose a social media integrating regulation mechanisms in order to decrease information overload, influence of gurus and inefficiency of information spreading. Moreover, users normally have an individual behavior. Those mechanisms are expected to

P. van den Besselaar et al. (eds.), Communities and Technologies 2005, 419-436.

motivate and incite people to exchange information. It results in trustable "web of people" (Plu et al. 2003).

The underlying problematic is similar to other tools like search engines. One of the great challenges of search engines, mainly based on an artificial (computer-based) centralized intelligence, is to be able to select relevant answers according to users' preferences, background, or current activity. In order to face this personalization challenge, many recommender systems have already been proposed and some of them are operational for example inside online bookshops (Resnick and Varian, 1997). Those systems traditionally recommend *contents* to users, trying to match users' interests with contents selected by other users having interests calculated as similar. However, many problems have been identified with such systems using traditional collaborative filtering algorithms (Herlocker et al. 2004), (Resnick and Varian, 1997). We focus our attention on the following ones. First of all, the quality of the information provided depends on the quantity of people using the system: we need a great number of users if we want valuable results. Secondly, the users must be altruistic, as the information centralized by the system has to be annotated. Thirdly, most of the time, these systems rely on a small number of people ("gurus") who provide the relevant information to many other users (Adar and Huberman, 2000). This phenomenon leads to a huge influence of very few people on the nature of information sent to many.

Users prefer recommendation from users

In order to improve recommendation systems, we are developing a complementary approach where:

- **Recommended information is relevant according to user's preferences, background, or current activity**. We take advantage of the synergy of classical collaborative filtering algorithms (Resnick and Varian, 1997) combined with well-known resource classifications.
- **Information is trustable**. The resource relevancy for a given user is also based on the trustworthiness of relationships between users. Indeed, users prefer to trust other users rather than a program to obtain good advice about information resources (Luhmann, 1998).
- **The dependence on "gurus" is reduced**. The relations between users based on the recommendation flow induce a network. Social properties resulting from the analysis of such a network (Waserman and Faust, 1994) guide future recommendations in order to equilibrate the information exchanges.
- **Users control their information exchanges**. They can filter information according to senders and associated metadata.

Our approach is supported by a collaborative system named SoMeOne (Social Media using Opinions through a trust Network) (Agosto et al. 2003). This system offers access to information that has a certain approval, for instance, information coming from appreciated or skilled people in corresponding domains.

One key issue in our system is to motivate users to exchange information. We make the assumptions that this motivation is reinforced by:

- **Recommending users instead of contents**. We suppose users prefer users' advice to impersonal guidance and appreciate having enriching relationships with others.
- **Influencing users to get into touch with others**. In order to receive information from unknown users, a user must be recommended to them according to the quality of the information s/he has already provided.
- **Letting them control their visibility through an open network of people**. A user can control the list of users to whom s/he wants to provide information, and the list of users from whom s/he accepts to receive information. This helps to avoid spamming and to improve trust in the system.
- **Developing the value of information sharing based on users' cooperativeness**. The cost of searching for and producing a piece of information is balanced by the gain of receiving freely other ones induced by having shared this piece of information with others. Of course, "free riders" are supposed to be managed for example by isolating them from the network of cooperative users.
- **Combining personal information management and information sharing functionalities reduces the extra cost of cooperation**. It also let the system grows even without cooperation in order to reach the critical size for cooperation being valuable.

Those assumptions are founded on an analysis of a wide range of literature on cognitive economics and social psychology studies. A review of this abundant literature is outside of the scope of this article but the main publications which inspired our developments are Thibaut, J. W. & Kelley's initial work about groups (Thibaut and Kelly, 1959), P.Bourdieu's work on social capital (Bourdieu, 1986), Turner's work on social identity (Turner, 1982), Luhman's paper about trust (Luhmann, 1988), J.Preece's work on online communities (Preece, 2000).

We detail in the following sections the techniques we have developed to regulate the information exchanges.

Information exchange based on personal taxonomy and distribution lists

The main goal of our SoMEONE system (Agosto et al. 2003) is to help users to exchange recommendations about good contents available through an information network like the WWW or corporate intranet. It is supposed to help people to improve and to optimize their mediated social network, in order to discover and find information resources which are adapted to their needs, taste, background, culture or any other personal features which make humans so different. The way to share personal information in SOMEONE is described as follows (see also Figure 1):

- Each user manages a personal taxonomy, in order to annotate and to index their documents. Each element in that taxonomy is called a topic. In the following, we will call a topic owner the manager of the personal taxonomy in which the topic is included. Since users are free to choose the appropriate name of their topics, the system supports two topics with the same name belonging to two different personal taxonomies. A document could be for instance an email, an image, a video, or a report. In fact, it is anything that can be identified by a URL.

- When displayed, all information associated with a document (also called meta-information) is aggregated. For that, we introduce the concept of review. Reviews are created by associating topic(s) and other information (like a text annotation) on documents.

- The accessibility of reviewed information, and thus the exchange of information between users, depends on the accessibility of topics in the reviews. The accessibility of a topic is defined according to a list managed by the topic owner; this list is called a topic distribution list (TDL for short). It groups the users allowed to access all information having a review with the topic.

- We define a user's contacts as the set of users belonging to the distribution list of at least one of her/his topics. These contacts could be friends, colleagues, family members, or any others.

Information is exchanged between users when they access the system using their personal home page. This page lets the user navigate through all information s/he is allowed to access, and lets him/her create new reviews for personal indexing purposes. However, creating a new review to a document discovered from a received review on that document makes it accessible to all the new users in the TDL of the topics associated to the new review. In consequence, personal indexing is automatically associated to information forwarding. As a result, information in the reviews, including document references, flows through the network of users according to the topic's TDL. We called this information routing process based on the indexing of information, "semantic addressing". This is the basic principle of the "web of people" where information navigates from users to users instead of having users navigating through information (Plu et al. 2003).

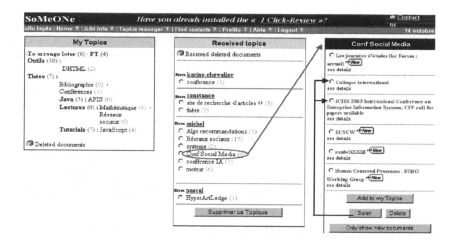

Figure 1. SoMEONE's topic management interface

Recommendation of users instead of content using mediated social networks

Opening closed relationship network

The mains problems of open social media like mailing-list or newsgroup are information overload and spamming. They are avoided with SoMEONE since users can exchange information only if they already know each other. However, in order to open their relationship network, we have developed a contact recommender. It suggests to a user that s/he add some users to the distribution list of some of her/his topics.

For this, the recommender needs first to identify topics which show the similar interests of two users. As many others do, our recommender system uses a collaborative filtering approach (Resnick and Varian, 1997). Our collaborative filtering algorithm is presented in (Plu et al. 2003). It computes similarity between topics of different users, comparing their URLs to classes of URLs existing in recognized classification, like ODP (http://dmoz.org/). When it detects that two topics of different users have similarities, it could propose to each user to add the other to the distribution list of the corresponding topic.

A "socially aware" recommender system

The originality of our work lies in the fact that we complement this approach with the computation of new ranking features based on social network analysis (Wasserman and Faust, 1994). The goal is to filter the recommendations obtained from the collaborative filtering process according to a personal information requirement and users social qualities corresponding to it. We qualify such a recommender as "**socially aware**". More precisely, in order to make contact recommendations, such a system not only takes into account the local profile of the users. It also considers all the existing relationships in the network. By this way, on the one hand, we want to reach individual goals, providing the user with contacts having the similar interests; on the other hand, we want to improve global properties of the social media. This last point is very important since it has been proved in the literature that communication networks having some specific structures (Jin et al. 2001), (Latora and Marchiori, 2003), (Phan, 2003), (Watts and Strigatz, 1998) can improve information spreading or users' cooperativeness.

Using social Network Analysis

In a **social network analysis**, people, groups or organizations that are members of social systems are treated as "sets of nodes" (linked by edges) –forming networks. They represent social structures. Given a set of nodes, there are several strategies for deciding how to collect measurements on the relations among them. Matrices or vectors can be used to represent information, and algebraic computations are done to identify specific patterns of ties among social nodes (Wasserman and Faust, 1994).

Differences in how users are connected can be a key indicator of the efficiency and "complexity" of the global social organization supported by the mediated social network. Individual users may have many or few ties. Individuals may be "sources" of ties, "sinks" (actors that receive ties, but don't send them), or both. The analysis of the relations between users can indicate a degree of "reciprocity" and "transitivity" which can be interpreted, for instance, as important indicators of stability.

The graph structure analysis of a mediated social network can be used for many purposes. It has been largely used in a sub-field of classical information retrieval called biblio-metrics to analyze citations in scientific papers (Garfield, 1972). It has also led to the development of new algorithms for information retrieval algorithms for hypertext like PageRank (Brin and Page, 1998). They are mainly based on the computation of a centrality measure of the nodes in a graph formed by web pages. The assumption is that a link provides some credit to the linked page.

In the next two sections we present the social network we extract from our SoMEONE system, and the social indicators we compute to qualify each nodes.

SoMEONE's social network

The social network we extract from the mediated social network supported by SoMEONE, is a directed graph consisting of a set of nodes with directed edges between pairs of nodes. Nodes are the users' topics and edges are their relations. Those relations between two topics are computed according to reviews being associated within those two topics. Thus, in this social network, there is an edge i from a topic v to a topic u, if the owner of topic u is receiving and taking information associated to topic v. In other words, the owner of topic u is in the distribution list of the topic v and takes at least one review containing the topic v and creates a new review on the same document with her/his topic u. Consequently, the graph representation will show the relation v • u.

The relation v • u indicates the flow of appreciated information through the network. It means that the owner of topic u is receiving and appreciates information from the owner of topic v.

Figure 2 shows a graphical representation of a small example of such a network. In this example, there are six users. Each box shown as a folder represents some of the topics of these users. Each relation v • u between topics is presented by a directed lattice. Reviewed information resources are noted with a lower case letter and a number. A label on a lattice means that a resource has been discovered from a review in the source topic.

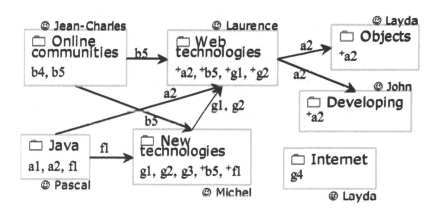

Figure 2. Graphical representation of a network

Having the topics' taxonomy of users, and the distribution list of the topics defined, we are able to extract the social network explained above. We model this directed graph as an adjacent matrix. Each matrix element represents the relationship between two topics. As introduced above, a relationship is established when a user creates new reviews from other reviews received from other users. They thus establish relationships between their topics within the created reviews and the topics of others within the received reviews.

Computing social indicators

In order to filter recommendation the nodes and the relations of the social network described above are qualified with social indicators. Three indicators are computed using the adjacent matrix: fame, coverage, and originality. These computations use indicators which we introduce first.

To take into account the importance of each relation, each vertex is weighted with a measure W(e, f) representing the number of documents received from topic f and then reviewed with a topic e. In other words, W(e, f) is the proportion of documents of topic e coming from topic f: the ones the owner of topic e found relevant. Thus, the range of W(e, f) is [0,1].

We compute a matrix W with each element noted W(e, f), topic e being in the row and topic f in the column of the matrix, for the vertex from f. W(e, f) is computed with the formula:

$$W(e, f) = \frac{Card * (e, f)}{card(e)} \quad \text{or W(e, f) = 0 if card(e)=0} \qquad (1)$$

Card*(e, f) includes all the documents having a review with the topic e and a review with the topic f, the review with topic f being older than the review with topic e; card (e) is the total number of reviews with topic e.

Then, a famous topic is a topic appreciated by users who also have famous topics. Note that famous topics might be considered as expert topics if we first assume that users only appreciate the most expert topics, and second that they know all the topics about the domain of expertise in order to be able to identify the most expert. This indicator is managed as a vector of a value between 0 and 1 for each topic. A value next to 1 (respectively 0) indicates that the topic does (respectively does not) contain the most appreciated references of the corresponding domain.

To compute these values we use a common centrality measure of a topic defined recursively according to the centrality of the topics receiving information from it. Each element F(e) of the fame vector is defined according to the recursive formula:

$$F(e) = \sum_{h \in H} W(h, e) F(e) \qquad (2)$$

For the computation of vector F we use the algorithm named PageRank and used for WWW pages (Brin and Page, 1998). But the matrix used has to reflect a reputation relation ("e is giving reputation to f", f • e). We consider that this relation is the invert of the relation modeled in our matrix W, which reflects the flow of information through the topics (f • e). Indeed, if a user reviews documents received with topic f with his topic e, then topic e is giving reputation (credit) to topic f. That is why we use the weight W(h, e) instead of W(e, h) to compute F(e).

The PageRank algorithm requires that the weights of the adjacent matrix W(e, f) be modified in W*(e, f) in order to have the following needed convergence properties (see (Brin and Page, 1998) for more details). This is partly achieved because the new weights W*(e, f), once normalized, represent the probability for a document being reviewed with topic f of being reviewed with a topic e. Thus, our matrix W corresponds to a stochastic matrix. Following the PageRank algorithm, we also complete the graph with new connections in order to have all nodes connected.

To compute **coverage and originality**, we first define vectors G(e) as the set of all topics g connected to topic e. Second, we define P(e, f) as the proportion of the relation between topic e and f among all the relations with topic e. P(e, f) is computed with the formula:

$$\text{If } f \in G(e): P(e, f) = \frac{W(e, f)}{\sum\limits_{g \in G(e)} W(e, g)} \text{ else } P(e, f) = 0 \tag{3}$$

We define that a topic e covers a topic f if both collect the same type of information from the same sources. In some sense, the coverage indicator identifies topics which are redundant, not only according to their current content but also according to their capacity for aggregating future contents coming from other topics. Explicitly, the coverage between e and f depends on:

- f being connected to e. This means that e is having information from f.
- Topics connected to e being also connected to f. This means that topics sending information to e are also sending it to f.

The evaluation of coverage between topics is computed in a matrix R that computes the redundancy between topics. We compute R(e, f) according to the following formula:

$$R(e, f) = p(e, f) + \sum\limits_{g \in G(e)} p(e, g) p(f, g) \tag{4}$$

Finally we compute the vector O to represent original topics. The originality of a topic is measured according to the novelty of URLs in the topic compared to the URLs received from connected topics. A topic e is original if it contains more URLs discovered by the owner of the topic than received from other topics. It also depends on the number of URLs in the topic. We compute the vector O according to the following formula:

$$O(e) = 1 - \sum\limits_{h \in G(e)} W(e, h) \tag{5}$$

Example

Let's illustrate these calculations with our social network example presented in Figure 2 bringing together six actors, seven topics shown as folders, and reviews noted with a lower case letter and a number.

Before the computation of R, we first have to compute W and P. From (1) we compute W(WT, NT). Then, assuming that b5 were reviewed by WT after being reviewed by NT, we have:

$$\text{W}(WT, NT) = \frac{Card^*(WT, NT)}{card(WT)} = 0.75 \qquad (6)$$

This means that the average of information received by Web-technologies from New-technologies is 0.75, which is high (meaning that their relation is important).

Here are the matrixes P (table I) and W (table II) for our example:

TABLE I

P	NT	WT	Java	OC
NT			0.5	0.5
WT	0.6		0.2	0.2

TABLE II

W	NT	WT	Java	OC
NT			0.2	0.2
WT	0.75		0.25	0.25

With matrix P, we are obtaining the proportion of the relation between WT and NT among all the relations with WT. The value 0.6 indicates an important relation between both topics.

Evaluating famous topics

Let's now compute the fame property. If we follow (2), we will obtain F(WT) =0.095879; F(NT)= 0.080576 for topics WT and NT. This result is interpreted as follows:

- Web-technologies is the most famous topic. We can note (Figure 2) that even if it does not have its own reviews, it has collected different reviews from three topics having a good level of fame. Web-technologies is supplying with its information two other topics, Objects and Developing, which are giving it a kind of credibility or reputation.
- New-technologies is at second level of fame. From Figure 2, we can see that it has collected different reviews from two topics with having a good level of fame but it is supplying only one topic, Web-technologies, with its information! Remember that the computation of F is based on a centrality measure indicating a reputation degree (Brin and Page, 1998). However, its

level of fame being higher than a defined threshold, this topic is kept as a candidate for being recommended.

Evaluating redundant topics

As we explained above, matrix R helps to decide if two topics are redundant to each other. From (4), R(WT, NT) can be computed as:

This value indicates a redundancy between WT and NT, which reveals that WT could be a similar information source to NT; therefore, it is relevant to recommend only one of them. Matrix **R** values are presented as in the following table:

TABLE III

R	Developing	Objects	Internet	NT	WT	Java	OC
Developing		1.0		1.0			
Objects	1.0			1.0			
Internet							
NT					0.2	0.5	0.5
WT				0.8		0.2	0.2
Java							
OC							

The same computation gives R(NT,WT) = 0,2. Note that R(WT,NT) > R(NT,WT) ! This is an important result because it helps the system to decide

$$R(WT, NT) = \left[p(WT, NT) + \left(\begin{array}{l} p(WT, OC)p(NT, OC) + \\ p(WT, Java)p(NT, Java) + \\ p(WT, NT)p(NT, NT) \end{array} \right) \right] = 0.8$$

which topics to recommend according to the user's strategy. We will develop this in a later section.

Evaluating original topics

By applying (5), we obtain the next O vector values:

TABLE IV

Topic	**O(e)**
Internet	1.0
Java	1.0
Online communities	1.0
New technologies	0.6
Web technologies	-0.25
Developing	0.0
Objects	0.0

The results are interpreted as follows:
- Internet is the most original topic. The originality of Internet is evident because it is isolated, because it is not redundant with the others and

because it can bring new information. Java and Online-communities are also original topics because URLs have been reviewed with them before the other topics (see Figure 2).

• However, comparing their places in the vector O, NT is more original than WT. In the next section we describe how we use these social indicators to compute new contact recommendations.

The "socially aware" recommender system

We named SocialRank the algorithm in the socially aware recommender system we have developed.

SocialRank

The SocialRank algorithm uses the computed social indicators to filter contacts which are candidates for recommendations (those owning topics initially computed with the collaborative filtering algorithm). The social indicators effectively used depend on the information strategy chosen by the users.

By using those social indicators as filters, two users with the same interest would not receive the same contact recommendations. Different "social indicators" computed from the social network analysis can be used to choose the contact recommendations in order to influence the way the social network will evolve! Thus, a socially aware recommender system can help to give the social network some interesting global properties depending on the global criteria the designer of a social media wants to optimize. Such interesting properties can be, for instance: a good clustering factor, a small diameter, a good global reciprocity or/and transitivity factor. This could help to decrease the dependence of the system on few "gurus", and to set "free riders" apart. In other words, those indicators are used to regulate the exchanges (Durand and Vignollet, 2003).

We assume that some users will be seeking to be recommended to others. Therefore, by using some specific social indicators in the recommendation process, we think the recommender system can influence the motivation and participation of the users. In other words, if users know the strategy used by the recommender system, we can assume that some users will try to adapt their behavior accordingly to it. To be able to test this idea, we have first implemented the computation of some social indicators and we have implemented some information strategies using these properties in order to select appropriate contact recommendations. In order to let users to select one of the implemented strategies that best fits their needs we have ascribed "names" and descriptions to them. Here are the three we have already implemented and which are experimenting:

- **"Looking for Experts"**. The user only trusts credited experts who filter information for her/him.
- **"Gathering all"**. The user wants to have the widest coverage of a topic, thus gathering as much information as possible.
- **"Going to the sources"**. The user wants to obtain the newest information rapidly, avoiding users who are acting as intermediaries.

We have started with these three strategies but our goal is to look for new ones to improve the existing ones. To avoid the preferential attachment problems (Jin et al. 2001), the "Going to the sources" strategy is selected by default. However, users can change it by editing their personal profile. This choice can be refined for each personal topic.

Applying users' strategies to our example

In our previous example (Figure 2), the URLs of the reviews belong to four ODP categories noted A, B, F, G. For example we note as "a1" a review having a URL referenced in the category A of the ODP directory. A label on a lattice means that a URL has been discovered from a review in the source topic.

In this example, we suppose that the user Layda wants to obtain recommendations about her topic Internet. The CFA similarities computation produces the following recommendations: (Internet → New-technologies) and (Internet → Web-technologies) because these three topics have reviews on URLs referenced in the category G of the ODP category (even if their intersection is empty). A recommendation noted (t1→t2) means that the owner of the topic t2 should be in the distribution list of the topic t1 if it is not already the case.

These initial recommendations are going to be analysed by our SocialRank algorithm. One issue of the analysis is which topic in relation to Layda's topic Internet the system will select, Web-technologies or New-technologies (or both)? R is an important matrix because it helps to decide if two topics are redundant to each other. If so, which of them is more relevant to select according to the user's specific needs? This decision is going to be applied to the topics Web-technologies (noted WT) and New-technologies (noted NT).

Because WT and NT have been identified as redundant, only one will be chosen according to Layda's information strategy. If she has selected:

- **Looking for experts**: this leads to the selection of a topic with the highest fame indicator; the answer of the recommender would be Laurence, WT's owner.
- **Gathering all**: the answer with this strategy is the owner of the topic having the highest value for R, therefore it would be Laurence, WT's owner,

because R(WT,NT) > R(NT,WT) (reinforcing the global approval of WT over NT).

- **Going to the sources**: the selected topic would be NT, because the strategy gives priority to the most original among topics with a sufficient level of expertise. In that case, the recommendation would be Michel.

What happens if Layda does not define an initial strategy? We explained that one of the priorities of our mediated system is avoiding the preferential attachment problem (Jin et al. 2001). Therefore, the default strategy is "Going to the sources", because it should improve the reactivity of the social networks by minimizing intermediaries. Another important situation to encourage is the connection of independent components.

In order to protect users' information privacy, no user can add her/his identifier to the topic access list of any other user's private topics. Thus, recommendations displayed only suggest sending information to new users. In our example, the system will recommend to Layda that she adds Michel owner of NT or Laurence, owner of WT to the distribution list of her topic Internet. But we assume that a user receiving new information will also send back new information. To encourage such reciprocal relationships the recommender also needs to check if the topic Internet satisfies Michel's or Laurence's information strategy for their topic NT or WT. Thus finally the recommender will try to choose the topic that will best satisfy the strategy of the two users involved in the suggested relationship.

Conclusion

Recommendation systems are principally used to reduce information overload and to improve information search and discovery. We propose a new kind of recommendation system, which recommends contacts instead of contents (that what we share with Mc Donald's expertise recommender (McDonald and Ackerman, 1998)). We make the assumptions that users prefer users' advice to impersonal guidance and appreciate having enriching relationships with others. This leads to the "Web of people" (Plu et al. 2003): information navigates from users to users instead of having users navigate through information.

Like many others, our recommender system uses a collaborative filtering approach (Herlocker et al. 2004), (Resnick and Varian, 1997). The value and originality of our work is to complement this approach with the computation of new ranking features based on social network analysis. The goal is to filter the recommendations obtained from the collaborative filtering process according to a particular information requirement and users' social qualities. The use of social network analysis to improve information retrieval in enterprise is also recommended by P. Raghavan in (Raghavan, 2002). However, this paper does not present any recommender system in order to establish exchange relationships between users. Our work was partly inspired by Referral Web (Kautz zt al. 1997) but in our system, the "socially aware" recommender is included in SoMEONE, a personal information management system with information sharing facilities. We have introduced in this recommender the computation of social properties to carefully choose users to be connected to. Moreover, the social network is manually controlled by users and evolves according to users strategy. Those both features are the basis of our proposed regulation mechanism of a social media.

The main contribution of this proposition is to present an improvement to classical recommender systems essentially based on similarity of interests or of topicalities. A "socially aware" recommender system, as we propose in this paper, takes into account other selection factors. Those social factors are sensible to already existing relationships within a whole community and to the specificity of the contributions of each user. The computation of such social factors are defined and illustrated in an example, but of course many others can be defined. We argue that the choice of specific factors for recommending relationships between users can influence the connectivity and efficiency of a computer supported information exchange network.

In order to test our ideas, we have introduced the system in the Intranet of France Telecom R&D and in the portal of the University of Savoie, within the project called "Cartable Electronique" ("Electronic Schoolbag") . We would like to stress the fact that those portals are not an experimental testbed used by an artificial panel of users but ones already used by hundreds of people in their daily work.

The usage of our system in these different contexts should allow us to confirm our initial expectations based on theoretical works (Jin et al. 2001), (Latora and Marchiori, 2003), (Phan, 2003), (Watts and Strogatz, 1998): influencing the topology of the social network by using our "socially aware" contact recommender system improves the global efficiency of the system. Moreover, we also expect to verify that a recommendation process of carefully selected contacts should incite users to produce interesting information and develop collaborative behavior. We will also put particular attention on expected side effects of the use of the system: the motivation for a user to initiate new collaborations.

The analysis methodology of these experiments is described in (Chabert, 2001). But it takes a long time to have users to accept and to effectively use a new tool for their everyday needs. Thus this experimentation is a long time process in order to collect enough significant data.

We now enter a new cycle in the development of SoMEONE guided by the results of the current experimentations. We will also consider specific contexts of use where this social media should be particularly useful. The next section describes our research tracks in a near future.

Perspectives

Although the experiments still going on, first interviews with users state that a user expects:

- a better interface which should decrease cognitive overload; moreover, a non-adapted interface could really interfere with the experimentation results;
- informal communication features to let users express feelings and emotions. This would come up to the expectation of "face to face communication" identified by Dutton (Dutton, 1998);
- a suitable social awareness of the activity:
    - her/his role in her/his relationship network in order to know for example if the information s/he provides is appreciated?;
    - her/his expected/obtained benefits of her/his use of the system in order to improve trust in the value of the system.

We also have to focus our research developments to specific context of use. One environment is definitely enterprise. Intranet companies are getting bigger and bigger as companies grow. In addition, the biggest the company is, the more we find a large diversity of jobs, workers, and cultures. All this diversity hides differences in needs, backgrounds, and sensibilities. To face this diversity, only providing an access to information with some global indexing facilities is not always sufficient. To be efficient, collaborators need to access information relevant to their business and adapted to their personal capabilities and sensibilities. As an example, any industrial researcher knows that s/he will not present her/his work with the same slides to a scientific community or to marketers from a business unit. We believe that this level of adaptation can only come from people networks. These networks are open, flexible and dynamic. They cannot only rely on the enterprise organisation. Collaborators are increasingly working in teams belonging to multiple entities, inside or outside the company. Suppliers, technicians, engineers, marketers, even customers are getting closer relationships in information exchange networks.

For companies in the business of information society, communication is a key issue. In addition, the production of these companies is often based on the production of information and knowledge. The need of such companies is to build valuable social capital, made of the knowledge of their employees and their mutually enriching relationships (Bourdieu, 1986). Here again, SOMEONE is particularly adapted to support and develop these valuable relationships.

Finally, another application domain in enterprise is business intelligence. SOMEONE is a solution for distributing through the company the process of detecting important information and rapidly spreading it to appropriate audience with a validation and commenting process all along the chain that enriches the information.

Acknowledgments

We would like to thank Ghislaine Chabert and Laurence Gagnière for their bibliographic work in psychology and sociology and for the experiments guidance and analysis. We also want to thank Pascal Bellec for his work in developing the system.

References

Agosto L., Plu M., Vignollet L., and Bellec P., 2003 SoMeONe: A cooperative system for personalized information exchange In *ICEIS'03,Volume 4, Kluwer, p. 71-78.*

Adar E. and Huberman B., 2000, Free Riding on Gnutella. First Monday, *5(10). (www.firstmonday.dk).*

Bourdieu P.,1986. The forms of capital. In *J. Richardson (Ed.), Handbook of theory and research for the sociology of education, New York: Greenwood, p. 241-258.*

Brin S. and Page L, 1998, The anatomy of a large-scale hypertextual (Web) search engine. In *The Seventh International World Wide Web Conference.*

Chabert G., 2001, Les usages du cartable électronique® : pour une évaluation des technologies dans l'éducation, p. 280-295, In *Bogue 2001,*

Durand G., Vignollet L., 2003, Améliorer l'engagement dans un collecticiel", In *IHM 2003, Caen, France, November 2003, p. 240, 243*

Dutton W., 1998, Society on the Line: Information Politics in *the Digital Age. Oxford University Press.*

Garfield E., 1972, Citation analysis as a tool In *journal evaluation. Science, 178.*

Herlocker, J. L., Konstan, J. A., Terveen, L. G., and Riedl, J. T., 2004, Evaluating Collaborative Filtering Recommender Systems. In *Proceedings of the ACM Transactions on Information Systems, Vol. 22, No. 1, pp. 5-53.*

Jin E. M., Girvan M. and Newman M. E. J., 2001, The structure of growing social networks, *Phys. Rev. E* 64, 046132.

Kautz H., Selman B., Shah M., 1997, Referral Web: Combining Social Networks and Collaborative Filtering.In *CACM 40(3): p. 63-65.*

Latora V., Marchiori M, 2003, Economic small-world behaviour in weighted networks the *European physical journal ,B 32 p 249-253.*

Luhmann N., 1988, Familiarity, confidence, trust: problems and alternatives. In Gambetta D. (Ed) *Trust: Making and breaking cooperative relations, Oxford, Basil Blackwell, p. 95-107.*

McDonald D. and Ackerman M.S., 1998. Just talk to me: A field study of expertise location. In *Proc. CSCW'98, New York: ACM, , p. 315-324*

Phan D., 2003, "Small Worlds and Phase Transition in Agent Based Models with Binary Choices" in *Muller J.P., Seidel M.M. eds. 4° workshop on Agent-Based Simulation, Montpellier, SCS Publishing House, Erlangen, San Diego.*

Plu M., Agosto L., Bellec P., Van De Velde W. 2003, The Web of People: A dual view on the WWW, In *Proc.of The Twelfth International World Wide Web Conference,   Budapest,   Best   Alternate   Track   Paper (http://www2003.org/cdrom/papers/alternate/P379/P379-PLU.HTM)*.

Preece J., 2000, Online Communities: Designing Usability, Supporting Sociability. *Chichester, UK: John Wiley & Sons, 439 pages*.

Raghavan P., 2002, Social Networks: from the Web to the Enterprise. *IEEE Internet Computing, Jan/Feb 2002, p. 91-94*.

Resnick P., and Varian, 1997, H.R. Recommender Systems. *Commun. ACM 40, 3, p. 56-58*.

Thibaut J. W. & Kelley H.H., 1959, The social psychology of groups. *New York: Wiley*.

Turner J.C., 1982, Towards a cognitive redefinition of the social group, in H. Tajfel (Ed.) *Social identity and intergroup relations, Cambridge; Cambridge University Press*.

Wasserman S. and Faust K., 1994, Social Network Analysis: Methods and Applications. *Cambridge University Press*.

Watts D. J., and Strogatz S. H., 1998, "Collective Dynamics of 'Small-World' Networks.", *Nature 393, 440-442*.

Supporting Communities by Providing Multiple Views

Alessandra Agostini+, Sara Albolino*, Flavio De Paoli*,
Antonietta Grasso#, Elke Hinrichs**

+University of Milano, Italy, *University of Milano – Bicocca, Italy,
#Xerox Research Centre Europe, France, **Fraunhofer FIT, Germany
*agostini@dico.unimi.it, albolino@disco.unimib.it, depaoli@disco.unimib.it,
Antonietta.Grasso@xrce.xerox.com, elke.hinrichs@fit.fraunhofer.de*

Abstract. A number of dimensions are relevant in order to successfully support community life and development. These dimensions include the easiness and broad spectrum of participation, the provision of value in return to the contributions, the visibility of community activity, the support of different levels of membership, the openness to the external world, and the support for evolving phases of the community life. In this paper we present a system that has been designed in order to tackle those dimensions with a particular attention to participation issues. We present first the sources of requirements that have informed the system design and which include the user observation of two companies. Then we present the system, stressing the features of integration with the daily working environment and the provision of multiple situated views, as a means to address the elicited requirements. Finally, we compare our design choices with a broader set of requirements that we have derived from literature.

Introduction

Communities of practice have been widely studied and acknowledged as a major informal organizational structure, pivotal in supporting learning and high adaptation to innovation and change (Lave and Wenger, 1991). Because of this central role, many attempts have been made in recent years in order to foster their creation and people participation, which include the proper design of technology

P. van den Besselaar et al. (eds.), Communities and Technologies 2005, 437-456.
© 2005 *Springer. Printed in the Netherlands.*

in support of them and the deployment of appropriate organizational changes and new processes. These attempts have been however very difficult in several cases, resulting only in a core set of people participating to the community activities and not achieving the broad impact aimed at by the promoting organization. Several reasons could be at the origins of this flop. The first cause, we believe, is due to the top-down approach adopted imposing community structures from the above, instead of aiming at making visible existing activities in the organization areas of expertise and soliciting cross fertilization among areas. This contradicts one of the fundamental attributes of community activity as being spontaneous and bottom-up; asking to participate in them because of management needs, almost certainly ends up in failures because the individual reward is not immediately clear. Community activities flourish in the companies where they do, because people participating in them use them as a place where to give and receive mutual help, a place where to learn and stay up to date with techniques and problems in a certain field. Another issue, related to this one, is that participation has an additional cost with respect the mainstream daily activities, with pressing deadlines and deliverables. When the effort to participate in the community life is too high, e.g. requiring a learning curve of the environment supporting it, or a high time for creating new content, than participation could be less than expected as well.

In this paper we present a system that aims at promoting and supporting participation in communities by making visible the activities going on in the various organizational projects and facilitating participation by providing an integrated working environment where activities both in organizational projects and in communities can be smoothly interleaved. In order to describe our technological proposal, we first describe the set of requirements we have been relying upon. They are based both on existing observational studies of use of community systems and on our own analyses made on two organizations. Then we present how we mapped those requirements into the design and implementation of a system. Finally, we conclude summarizing what we believe are the dimensions where technology design can affect adoption of community support systems.

Determining Community Requirements

The design and implementation of the MILK system, started from a Web based collaborative environment, BSCW (Bentley et al., 1997) that was evaluated as a collaborative platform, on the one hand, already effective to support project based collaboration and, on the other hand, flexible enough to be further extended with features to turn it also into a community support system. Our aim has been to evaluate in which way such a system could be extended in order to be more effective in supporting community activities.

Input to the design of these extensions came from a variety of sources, including ethnographic observation of two organizations and various existing studies of community behaviour and support with technology. In the following sections we report the main issues.

Existing Studies on Community Support

A first study motivating our design analyzed the role of informal communication and the way it articulates in work organizations (Isaacs et al., 1997). In particular, this study reports that there is a category of *spontaneous* communication that happens because two or more people *happen* to encounter each other. These exchanges are among peers, who exchange technical advice, ask support to solve problems and stay up-to-date to interesting results obtained in other projects of their area of expertise. These exchanges are the typical exchanges that happen inside communities of practice, and in the reported study they were made possible by the sharing of a common physical place with its own known rhythms. However, with increased mobility of users and distribution of teams, such a possibility is at risk, because the possibility to cross each other, especially during pause moments of the day, is much less. This led us to identify the first requirement: *Recreate some of the affordances of a common physical place across distributed physical organizational units with a high degree of mobility.* This requirement articulated in recreating the possibility to know about people and some of their activities at the various sites (e.g., who was in the office and who was out, who was currently in the common area) and be aware of their social rhythms, both when in the office and mobile.

A second study informing our set of requirements concerned the use of a community system aimed at circulating relevant competitive information in an IT research environment (Snowdon & Grasso, 2002). This study shows that the potential and actual users could be grouped into three categories: the ones who were actively participating in the system, providing input and getting benefit; the ones who were against sharing information and collaborating inside communities; and, a third category of users who were interested in participating, but to whom the cost of doing it was too high. In particular, this latter category of users reported that the community system was not integrated into their working environment, making necessary learning a new system, and also making an effort to transfer relevant information from one system to the other. This barrier was enough to prevent their participation even if they were willing so and could see potential benefits. This led us to a second requirement: *Decrease the cost of participating in community activities by integrating daily work support systems with community support technology.*

Finally, the same study reported that a reward was expected by community participation in terms of visibility of the own contribution and impact on the community activities, but also on the organizational activities. This was particularly visible in the study, as there were some modalities to introduce contributions, which were not immediately showing where and how they were going to contribute to ongoing community threads of discussions. This was widely reported as a major deficiency even if—in the analyzed system—this was happening only when submitting new content from the public large screens showing community discussions in the social areas; this kind of information was fully visible through the web interface instead. This led us to a third requirement: *Make clearly visible participation in community activities in a pervasive way.*

The above requirements for technology support have also been compared with the set of requirements relevant to support community activities as articulated by Etienne Wenger (2001), which was confirming their centrality, while allowing us to focus on key issues affecting participation.

Qualitative Analysis of Involved Communities

In order to complement our understanding coming from existing studies, we had also the possibility to work with some user organizations of typical knowledge-intensive character. In the following we recall the main issues and outcomes of the user's analysis; for more details see (Albolino et al., 2002).

We engaged ourselves in this study prior to system design, because we are persuaded that the design of socio-technical solutions being able to support and empower knowledge management and working performances within an organization is achievable only by studying people practices. The analysed work practices belong to two different organizations: an Italian consultancy firm and a German software-house. Both companies are part of the new economy context and performing knowledge-intensive activities.

The Italian consultancy firm is active, from more than thirty years, in providing professional services to major enterprises and government agencies in the fields of change management, organization, HR, Knowledge Management and Customer Relationship Management. The firm's approach to consultancy is based on working in partnership with the client to build a "tailor made" solution that lasts in time. Therefore, each project requires a specific, in-depth understanding of the clients' organization and needs, aimed at devising specific solutions to maximize effectiveness and quality of working life. The firm employs around 50 consultants and 9 staff, located in Milan and Rome, and has had 50% newcomers in the last two years, mainly young and just graduated from University.

The German software house has developed a complete Digital Asset Management (DAM) solution under a single roof: software development, MSP – Managed Service Provider, Hotline and support and consulting services. The company has been founded in 1992 and it is in a growing phase. It employs 60 people, located in 3 offices within two sites: Hanover and Hamburg. In comparison with the consultancy company, the software house has a more heterogeneous population of workers. Due to the nature of its business, there are:

technicians that are in charge of developing system functionality; supporting staff people that are responsible for system maintenance and user assistance; and, finally, project managers and sales people both working in direct contact with the clients. The latter are responsible for developing new business while the former are in charge of user requirement analysis and of developing the required solutions.

Even if the two organizations work in very different business areas, they seem to be very similar concerning some working practices and knowledge management issues as it will be clear in the following.

Methodology of study

The analysis of communities and their main knowledge management requirements have been conducted through a combination of ethnographic methods and action learning approach, where the focus is on the observation of the working practices and their analysis lead together with involved workers (Barley, 1996). Our approach has been interactive and aimed to activate user participation on system design as well as to build a mutual understanding among observers and observed workers. The field analysis mainly focused on: the identification of the main knowledge exchanges among people (i.e., identification of knowledge networks among experts in different business sectors) (Holland & Leinhardt, 1979; Wellman, 1988); and, the study of the social usage of the physical space (i.e., relations among knowledge exchange and people location). Moreover, during the case study, representations of typical working scenarios (i.e., scenario-based design analysis (Carrol, 1995)) have been used to support our work.

Typical working practices and knowledge circulation patterns

Both organizations are project based and strongly customer oriented. Every employee usually works on different projects, with different customers located in different sites. According to the fast growing business, people spend more time by the client and less in the office. Thus, all the working activities are characterized by knowledge intensive exchanges in highly mobile contexts. The analysis underlines two main levels of knowledge circulation: inside each project and inside the same area of business.

Knowledge sharing inside project teams is based on personal exchanges by emails or telephone calls, this flow is quite fast and effective. However, *as knowledge produced in each project is exchanged in personal conversations there is no track of it in organizational document management systems, neither of the people who acquired it.* Therefore, usually, *knowledge stays in the projects where it has been generated and people participating in different projects cannot access them.* Since people use to exchange information related to their business activities mostly through emails, the huge number of messages is dramatically increasing and the communication flow becomes very hard to manage. In addition, since servers are not easily accessible from outside the office, people use emails also to exchange working documents (e.g., presentations, new offers, final reports...) and organizational knowledge (e.g., what the company is doing, who is doing what), so *document versioning becomes difficult to manage.*

On the contrary, knowledge circulation within business areas is not very effective; it is mostly based on informal, occasional meetings among people. Unfortunately, people do not meet so often to ensure an effective and complete knowledge sharing. In both organizations people spend a lot of time searching general information and strategic knowledge related to a specific client (e.g., previous projects, contact people, roles, plans, and strategy). It is not only a matter of finding explicit knowledge (Nonaka & Takeuchi, 1995) about that, as documents and formal annotations, but also of knowing who can, among their colleagues, give them the information they need. The analysis reveals that in both organizations usually happen that people work on the development of new methods and tools ignoring that someone else already had work on that. So there is a duplication of efforts to reach the same outcome. *This knowledge is partly present in corporate repositories but it is not linked to daily activities and working practices, so it is not clearly visible to people who need it.* In particular, concerning the consultancy company, the available support for document sharing consists of a mere file system on two servers (one for each site) in which documents are organized hierarchically by client or by project. Project teams are responsible for organizing and managing their own files. Nevertheless, there are not well-established procedures or shared practices for this handling. Thus, *accessing documents is extremely difficult except for people belonging to the project team creating them.* Regarding the software-house company, instead, different systems are in use to support working activities: a document management system as a central repository; a "grass-root" Intranet; various task related systems; a bug-tracking system; internal newsgroups, and MS Exchange Server. All these systems are not integrated and, therefore, also in this case *knowledge is highly fragmented and difficult to access when and where needed.*

According to the project-based activities and to the different physical locations, there are different clusters—based on smaller teams—of people who produce excellence and innovation. These clusters include few people and are focused on specific topics. They can change every time a new project starts or a customer is acquired, or when there is a new service to develop. These networks meet rarely, they mostly communicate through telephone/e-mail to solve a problem or discuss a service development. However, cross-fertilization among different business areas and clusters is not well supported and happens mostly when people move from one project to another or, again, through informal occasional discussions. *There is no track, in the organizational support system, of new knowledge produced within different projects and clusters.*

Typical working day scenarios

To better explain observed working practices, in the following we sketch some typical working day scenarios and main related problems.

Meetings at the customer site. People, above all project managers and consultants, are used to work at the customer site, where they have formal and informal face-to-face meetings to discuss the deployment of projects. Even during business meetings their cellular phones are switched on. Professionals involved in the meeting use remote sources to get fresh inputs to be brought in the discussion; they exchange information and documents with their colleagues in the office through emails and SMSs. Thus, the meeting is not limited to people inside the room. Furthermore, while in a meeting, people are used to monitor other processes to satisfy urgent requests in real time.

Post-meeting communication and circulation of knowledge inside a project. It frequently happens that, after a meeting and while still being at customer site, professionals have a quick conference call with the rest of the project team settled in the office. In this way, the team can use the relevant outcomes of the meeting as soon as possible. Conference participants write down notes on paper and/or on white boards and discuss news about the client. Team members that have not participated to this short conference are individually informed via e-mail – sometimes detailed, sometimes short messages– or by a phone call. Documents in progress are exchanged among team members mostly by e-mail. Only some released documents are stored in the company server. Consequently, *team members cannot have a clear vision of the status of the project*. Therefore, it is likely that some people redo what has already been done or request issues that they will just receive later. *Most of project managers' communications is for putting order in the knowledge shared by the team.*

Moving from one customer to the other: taxi and flight time. When in a mobile situation –the analysis shown– professionals continue working by cellular phone, PDA or laptops. Moving from one customer to the other, knowledge workers have conversations with other team members to receive information about what happened at client site. They also spend time to fix new appointments, update the agenda, look at documents on the laptop, and call customers. Therefore, *professionals need to access and work on the same element or in various related elements in different situations through different media.*

It can also happen to meet colleague while travelling, at the airport for example; in fact, people is used to arrange working meetings within vip rooms to exchange information about projects and company activities. A taxi or a room at the airport can become real offices so as a bar and a restaurant. *These mobile knowledge workers work not in front of their computers. Therefore, traditional PC-centric KM tools are inadequate for their typical working practices. They need enhanced functionalities within their communication tools (mobile telephone, laptop, pda) supporting their strong mobility.*

"Office time". When people work in the office they meet colleagues who work on different projects and business areas. They exchange a lot of knowledge in an informal way, while making photocopy or while having a cup of coffee. These informal discussions represent a key cross-fertilization manner for knowledge sharing. The con is that it is almost the only way in which these organizations exchange knowledge among different project teams. Moreover, knowledge shared within informal meetings is not recorded in any way on the repositories of the company, and therefore it remains private. In addition, since people in both organizations travel a lot, there are few chances for casual encounters and conversations. Therefore, *the conditions for knowledge exchange are strongly reduced.*

The MILK system

In the previous sections we reported on requirements and problems as emerged from existing studies of community support and from our own observations of the work practices of knowledge workers. Combining this large set of requirements we obtained a more precise definition of what features we want to address in the design of the system, both in the form of functional services and in the modes for accessing these services themselves.

We grouped the gathered requirements in four main categories:

(1) Lowering the cost of participation in the system. This objective is particularly important because the lack of integration between the system supporting community activities and the daily working environment can be a barrier sufficient for preventing participation, on the one hand, and effective circulation of knowledge on the other hand.

(2) Addressing the full spectrum of work situations. This objective is related to the observation that work does not happen in a single standardized way at the desktop. Because of the increased mobility of knowledge workers, occasions for getting benefit from community knowledge or for contributing to it can occur in many different settings; restricting the technology to the desktop can imply a reduced participation with respect to the potential one.

(3) Promoting occasions for informal knowledge exchange. This objective derived from the acknowledgement that informal exchange was already happening, especially face-to-face, however mainly in a fortuitous way, with many difficulties in making the exchanges available to other community members as well.

(4) Increasing the visibility of community activities and of personal contributions. This objective is related to providing tangible rewards by community activities, by making visible the efforts and outcomes produced.

The analysis of these objectives, led us to the design of a system that aimed at being very pervasive on the working environment, in order on the one hand to support users in taking benefit from community generated knowledge while performing daily work, and on the other hand to encourage them to contribute to the community exchanges and to have informal communication exchanges. This translated into the definition of a set of services to support daily and community work activities and into a set of *situated views*. The services to support daily and community activities enlarged typical document sharing functionality to both more knowledge focused and people oriented functionality. The content, its semantics, and its relationships are available in the system, but also the support for contacting and communicating with colleagues when needed and in effective way is provided. It is worth to note that the latter services are the basis for the paradigm shift proposed by Kuhlen (2004). The situated views mapped the most typical work situations—being at the desktop, being mobile, and being in a social space—into ways to present the information that was most appropriate in each situation.

While at the desktop, people tend to be very *task oriented* and focused on *content creation*. That is the best moment in which to provide a context to their work, which draws on knowledge coming from similar activities inside the same community of practice, in order to make reuse and exchange of knowledge possible. This is supported by the provision of contextualized links in the *View with Context*. The desktop is also a possible good vehicle for inputting to colleagues inside the same community of practice, which would be better to make visible very promptly. This has been made possible by another desktop view, called *limbo*, which selectively can expose not definitive content a knowledge worker is working on.

While mobile, people tend to have only limited attention capacity and devices with constrained capabilities. Therefore, they cannot afford a fully participation to communitarian exchange. On the contrary, they need very punctual *notification* and *awareness* of relevant news and the ability to contact people accordingly in a precise way. This is supported by views that push information, the *NewsBroker*, or provide quick access to the searched for information, the *KnowledgeBroker* and the *PeopleFinder*.

While in social spaces, people tend to have informal *content sharing* and have more time to browse into community content. Our objective has been to place interactive boards in which the activities going on in the organization, as inferred from DMS logs of use, are automatically published in order to make visible communities activities. Our approach has similarities with the Babble project (Erickson & Kellogg, 2003) that aims as well at dynamic visualizations of community activity; a major difference with the Babble project is related to a visualization design that is aimed at conveying the information on semi-public large boards. In fact, in MILK the boards are posed in semi-public places (e.g., the printer room, the entrance hall, the library) to create attractive information points that can be used to see at a glance what is currently going on inside communities of practice and also inside units of work (business processes, projects, task forces, etc.). The latter information is published for promoting spontaneous communication among professionals sharing the same interests and profile, even if their community is not yet been given a public space, i.e. it is still an emerging community. Additionally, these areas posed in different organizational sites are connected by video and audio links. In this way, we aim at recreating a virtual common space where people have the opportunity to meet as if they were in the same physical space. Views are very specific and organized around channels (i.e., *Thematic, People, News*) that periodically broadcast the information.

The MILK metaphor is providing services through situated views: an integrated solution made of different environments and interfaces, providing information and services using views that are tailored to each of the different work situations. The integrated MILK system infrastructure, to support this metaphor, consists of a heterogeneous distributed multimedia network connecting servers, workstations, mobile devices, interactive and non-interactive screens of various sizes, sensors, etc. It combines wired and wireless communication, including emerging mobile technology, and it has at its heart a common Knowledge Management Engine (KME) which enhances document management services by providing additional knowledge management and communication services to the end user environments: *Office Environment, Social Environment* and *Mobile Access Environment*.

Before describing the various services we introduce the *Knowledge Organization* that has been used to structure the information in the system in a way suitable to the various services building on it; it includes information about people and their activities. The organization of this knowledge is centered on a profiling mechanism that associates comparable knowledge descriptions to objects of different nature. The objective is being able to integrate knowledge associated with objects –*elements* in our terminology– that are documents, people, communities and projects comprehensively, in order to compare and contrast elements of any type for computing various kinds of relationships. It should be stressed that artifacts replace the traditional concept of document. An artifact is a compound object collecting various files, each of them being a different representation of the same conceptual content –e.g., the full-text and slide presentation for a paper. This allows the system providing people the most appropriate representation in accord to the activities they are performing and to the specific situation. Moreover, a single representation can have different file formats (e.g., HTML, pdf, ppt for a presentation) and various versions of any representation may also be available.

On the base of this Knowledge Organization, the MILK KME offers the following services to its client instances:

- *Document Management*: MILK is based on BSCW (Bentley et al., 1997), a web-based groupware system using the notion of shared workspaces. A workspace is a repository for private, shared or public information, accessible to members of a *project team* or of a *community*. Distributed co-authoring of documents is possible by keeping track of versions as well as of the changes made by each author. BSCW provides an Event Scheduler that is used to receive event notifications from KME components, queues the events, and deliver them to other interested components. The BSCW Web interface is replaced in MILK by the situated views and only its API to manage content produced in project or community workspaces is used.
- The *Metadata Management System* (MMS) provides facilities to browse search and retrieves items on the basis of the metadata associated to MILK elements. Metadata are organized by profiles that include significant information to identify and classify elements. The MMS includes a service, which monitors the system activity and automatically updates the profiles of elements. It is based on the extended BSCW event service.
- The *Availability Presence and Awareness Service* presents information about people's activities, reachability and availability in order to help users to interact with each other easily and with minimal disruption. MILK presents information about people to the users as an advice and with a confidence measure leaving the decision on if and how to contact someone to the users themselves.
- The *Mobile Access Service* provides access to the KME services adapted to the characteristics of end-user's mobile devices (data communication protocols, hardware facilities, interface restrictions, etc.). All features are tailored for mobile use and adaptable to device capabilities. For instance, opening a document in the mobile environment may retrieve—depending on the device—the abstract of the document instead of the whole document.

Figure 1 shows the overall architecture of MILK. Boxes represent functional components. Interconnections between boxes depict data flow, mostly bi-directional, in the form of Remote Procedure Calls using the XML-RPC protocol.

Desktop View: the Office Environment

MILK on the desktop, see also (Agostini et al., 2003), helps people to manage information and easily access the right sources for creating new contents. Different views over the contents promote awareness and learning that are specific for the current content creation activity the user is undertaking. Such views are tailored to user profiles and activities. Interaction starts with a simple toolbar (compact mode) keeping active a function of general awareness and information advertising (Figure 2). When users start a work session, by logging to the system, it switches to an expanded mode, which supports—via different interaction mechanisms—browsing, searching for elements, and producing new content.

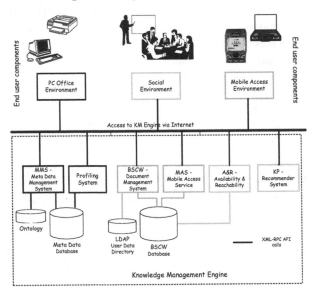

Figure 1. The MILK overall architecture

To facilitate the information discovery, the interaction is centered on the *View with Context* (VwC) panel supplying descriptions of a MILK element (the central panel in Figure 3) along with related elements (the left side panels). The related elements include projects in which the user is involved or on similar topics; documents on subjects that may be of interest to the user; people and communities that share the same interests. The VwC changes the traditional searching approach to information to a more proactive mode in which users receive information that is related to their profile (e.g., expertise, preferences, roles, interests). Just after logging in, the user is supplied by the VwC of his/her personal profile, surrounded by information on elements that are related to that profile. From that presentation the user can navigate the system by setting the focus of the VwC on one of the related elements. Among other things, the VwC facilitates discovering documents without even opening them for verifying the appropriateness, as it is needed in other systems.

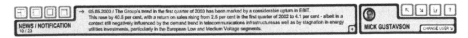

Figure 2. The toolbar in the Office Environment.

Another interaction mode supported by the office environment is through different classifications of elements (the right side panel of Figure 3). Such classifications can be customized according to the needs of the actual organization. The default classification is the ontology hierarchy, which allows the semantic grouping of the content and supports semantic relations among elements. Moreover, the ontology maps the communities of practice managed by the system. In fact, any node of the ontology hierarchy is, potentially, associated with a community since it represents a key expertise for the organization. By simply clicking on a node it is possible to get a VwC centred on the corresponding community. Actually, the ontology is not static; instead it has to be perceived as a live entity evolving in accord to the evolution of communities as well as of various organizational domains of work. We believe that communities, sub-communities and relationships among them are quite naturally modeled upon the ontology hierarchy. For our involved organizations has been developed a second classification supporting a per-project view; in a similar way it is possible to allow further classifications. This classification includes the organizational structure of those companies that associates activities with projects, every project with a client and every client with an industrial sector. It is worth to note that, a project may be related to various communities depending on the addressed topics; and, vice versa, a community has correlations with all those projects working on the specific interest of that community.

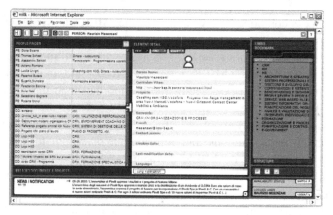

Figure 3. The expanded mode in the Office Environment.

Besides navigation support the office environment offers the opportunity of creating new content by creating new elements. Creating an element means to create a profile and (e.g., for electronic documents) possibly upload a file. Profile creation is supported by the system through the use of the classifications of the right side panel. When a user is filling up a profile form for an element, s/he can include classification information by drug-and-dropping from the ontology, from the organizational structure and from any other classification tree. Moreover, text documents can be automatically processed to extract keywords and key phrases as candidates for content profiling. Such keywords are then compared to ontology entries to actually define the content profile for the document.

As a special feature, MILK permits a user to create a temporary profile of an "under construction" document facilitating the flow of the information in the company and the mutual support. Such profiles are stored in a special personal area named *limbo*. Profiles stored in the limbo are in between (according to the meaning of the word limbo): they are not truly personal documents of a user, but they are not yet fully part of the MILK system. Remembering that documents are composed of two parts, the profile and the text (or picture, or whatever format), they can be in two states: *visible*, which means that the profile is visible and the text is hidden, and *accessible*, which means that both profile and text are accessible. In the former state the profile of the forming documents is shared among the users of the system to promote awareness and trigger useful collaboration processes. It is worth to stress that the View with Context enables others to see the new document and hence users have the opportunity of discovery synergies and possible collaborations. If a document is accessible, besides reading the profile, users can also read the current version of the associated document.

Mobile view: the Mobile Access Environment

The mobile access components give access to the MILK knowledge from various viewpoints. At the user interface, all views are presented in a portal, which directly accesses to the various views. The most recent and most important news are also directly shown in the MILK portal. As already said, in a mobile situation, the "What's new for me" aspect seems more important than the actual access to the content. Therefore, the *NewsBroker* (Figure 4, left) is the primary view. It actively provides awareness about objects, people and their context and helps the user focus on important actions and information or whom to contact next. It pushes active notifications on MILK elements such as documents, links to the Web, appointments, tasks, discussion forums and annotations both in the context of projects and communities a user belong to.

The *PeopleFinder* (Figure 4, center) handles information about people. It provides awareness about: who is active in the system; who is important in a project or for a community; who is available; and, how people can be reached. To facilitate direct communication between users, the PeopleFinder proposes a list of prioritized communication channels for reaching a person, which depends on the availability and reachability profiles.

Mobile devices are typically constrained by their I/O capabilities and available memory, and by network constraints. For these reasons the mobile environment provides only limited document upload and download functionality. The mobile restrictions on I/O, bandwidth, and connectivity also prevent heavily browsing the system knowledge. Nevertheless, it must be possible to browser folders and projects from time to time. Therefore a simple and lightweight browser, the

KnowledgeBrowser (Figure 4, left), is provided. It allows users to navigate folders and check documents and, if necessary and feasible, download documents or their abstracts or redirect documents to other media, e.g. a nearby fax machine.

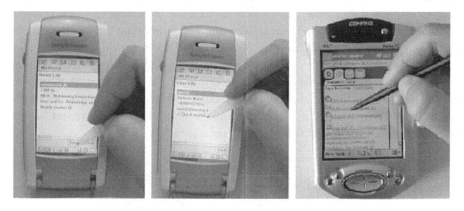

Figure 4. NewsBroker, PeopleFinder, and KnowledgeBrowser views.

Social view: the Social Environment

The way to support the social view has been based on placing interactive boards where the activities going on in the organization—as inferred from DMS logs of use—are automatically published in order to make visible communities activities. The boards are in semi-public places like the printer room, the library, etc. Figure 5 shows one user site installation of MILK, where a leisure area with magazines is augmented with an interactive large screen. Our objective is to create attractive information points that can be used to see at a glance what is currently going on inside communities of practice and also inside units of work (business processes, projects, task forces, etc.). The latter information is published as well in order to promote the spontaneous communication among professionals sharing the same interests and profile, even if their community is not yet been given a public space, i.e. it is still an emerging community. Additionally, these information points are connected by video and audio links. In this way we aim at recreating a virtual common space where people have the opportunity to meet as if they were in the same physical space. The design idea that we had was of an attractive broadcasting space that could support communication whenever needed, e.g., when some information found on the screen triggers the need to know more from the author, or when we want or need to talk to other people who are reading news on the other site.

The public displays, based on what we have defined as a *broadcast* model, work as information pushing devices when nobody is interacting with them, mixing the different channels. As soon as somebody starts interacting with the system it switches to pull mode, and the user gets access to any information s/he needs. The broadcasting mode in the social environment is designed to give both hints of what's going on inside the company to non-interacting onlookers, and to urge them to start interacting with the screen (switching then to pull mode), to go deeper inside the items they find more relevant, or to browse by organizational theme exploring the system content. The alternation between the channels in the broadcasting mode depends on a set of rules based on time of the day and users' activities, controlled and modified by the system administrator to push certain kinds of data and promote specific information to all fellow workers. As mentioned before, information to be broadcast has been clustered in channels. Each channel represents a specific view on the knowledge present in the organization and is relevant for different communities.

Figure 5. One of the site installations

The Thematic channel (Figure 6) is the channel providing information about current units of work, i.e., projects and community forums. It is the channel from where new and interesting information can be accessed, read, bookmarked, and also enriched with comments and personal notes. Moreover, using this channel it is possible to access information across different sites in support of synchronous video contacts. In order to retrieve its content, it monitors the activity in the DMS and prioritizes it for providing only live information. It utilizes some layout rules in order to represent activity parameters:

- Colour: membership of an organizational area of activity.
- Distance from the centre and colour fading: the overall amount of recent activity.
- Size: overall amount of activity.
- Thickness: degree of novelty.
- Shape: to differentiate among projects (circle) and communities (wheel).

The People channel (Figure 7) is the channel providing information about people in the organization, their current location and availability, and the means to contact each person. The channel dynamically updates the information about the current location of the users. The granularity of the information is kept at the level of the different organizational locations or not being in the office. The system integrates functionality from an availability service that can also register at each moment the preferred channels for interactions (e.g., SMS while attending a meeting).

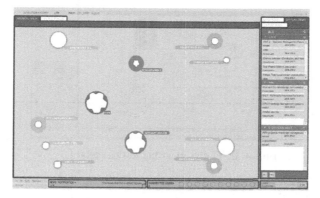

Figure 6. The Thematic channel.

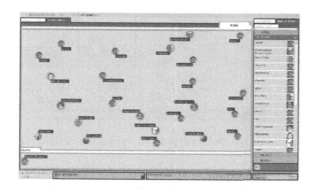

Figure 7. The People channel.

A number of layout rules are used in order to facilitate quick overview:
- Location tabs: each tab represents a site showing the people who have that reference location.
- Colours: identify a location; people currently detected in a location are represented with the colour of the site where they are.
- Guest area: people visiting the site.
- Grey Colour: mobile people.

The News channel (Figure 8) is used to broadcast information that the organisation wants to transmit to everyone on a site or across all sites. The news has its own channel, but is also overlaid to whatever current channel is displayed if no one is interacting with the screen. It is displayed using a style borrowed from newspapers and is meant to attract attention even from afar.

Figure 8. The News channel (overlaid).

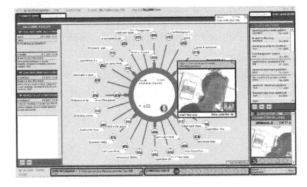

Figure 9. The Video channel (bottom right and overlaid windows).

The Video channel (Figure 9) is a channel devoted to support synchronous communication. It provides the visualization of the connected sites and supports the possibility of unplanned video-audio sessions. It also includes some light support for collaboration, i.e. it is possible to share content on the fly across the various sites in order to support the discussion.

Conclusion

In an already cited report comparing existing systems in support of communities, Wenger (2001) identified a number of dimensions that are relevant in order to successfully support community life and development. These dimensions include the easiness and broad spectrum of participation, the provision of value in return to the contributions, the visibility of community activity, the support of different levels of membership, the openness to the external world, and the support for evolving phases of the community life. If those are compared to the design principles that guided the design of the MILK system, which are the integration of the community support functionality with the daily work environment and the development of situated views mapping different work situations, we can see that the MILK approach provides a contribution to the most relevant of the dimensions identified by Wenger. He acknowledges that the participation in the community life is in competition with all the other activities a member is part of, primarily the work tasks of the ongoing projects. Therefore participation must be easy, in order to reduce possible barriers and lower this tensions in priorities. In MILK we suggest that participation not only must be easy, but also fully integrated with the daily work environment, so to lower not only the learning curve of the community system, but also to smoothly move knowledge from the projects to the communities and vice versa as opportunities for exchange occur. This is also complaint with the other requirements from Wenger of providing a clear value in return to the community participation and activities. MILK also addresses the visibility of community activity, the support of different levels of membership, and the openness to the external world, by enlarging the visibility of communitarian activity to social areas in the organization, where abstract representations of their activities are provided. Finally, regarding the dimensions identified by Wenger, the support for evolution of the community is addressed only in an implicit way by MILK. In fact, the metadata capturing the activities in the system guide the selection of content in some views according to the freshness and likeness of exchange.

Matching our own set of requirements to this set that has been derived by long observation of community life and activities has provided us with a further confirmation that the design approach of MILK is sound. The future work is validating its design and how effectively it affects these dimensions will consist of fieldwork observing its usage in the context of our user organizations. This will be the main task of our future activities related to the MILK system.

Acknowledgments

MILK is a joint research project partly funded by the European Commission (IST 33165). We thank all colleagues from the project consortium for the friendly and fruitful collaboration.

References

Agostini, A., Albolino, S., Boselli, R., De Michelis, G., De Paoli, F., & Dondi, R. (2003): Stimulating Knowledge Discovery and Sharing. In *Proceedings of the ACM Conference GROUP 2003*, Florida, USA, pp. 248-257.

Albolino, S., et al. (2002): MILK Deliverable 1: User Requirements. http://www.milkforum.com/

Barley, S.R. (1996): Technicians in the workplace: Ethnographic evidence for bringing work into organization studies. *Administrative Science Quarterly*, 41(3), pp. 404-441.

Bentley, R., Appelt, W., Busbach, U., Hinrichs, E., Kerr, D., Sikkel, K., Trevor, J., & Woetzel, G. (1997): Basic support for cooperative work on the World Wide Web. *Int. Journal of Human-Computer Studies*, 46(6), pp. 827-846.

Carrol, J.M. (1995): Scenario-Based Design: Envisioning Work and Technology. *System Development*, Carroll, J.M. (ed.).

Erickson, T., & Kellogg, W.A. (2003): Knowledge Communities: Online Environments for Supporting Knowledge Management and its Social Context. *Beyond Knowledge Management: Sharing Expertise*, Ackerman, M.A., Pipek, V. & Wulf, V. (eds.). MIT Press.

Holland, P.W., & Leinhardt, S. (eds.) (1979): *Perspectives on social network research*. Academic Press, New York.

Isaacs, E., Whittaker, S., Frohlich, D., & O'Conaill, B. (1997): Informal Communication re-examined: New functions for video in supporting opportunistic encounters. *Video-Mediated Communication*, Finn, Sellen, & Wilbur, S.B. (eds.), Laurence Erlbaum, New Jersey, pp. 459-485.

Kuhlen, R. (2004): Change of Paradigm in Knowledge Management - Framework for the Collaborative Production and Exchange of Knowledge. *Knowledge Management. An asset for libraries and librarians*, Hobohm, H.C. (ed.), IFLA Publications 108, pp. 21-38.

Lave, J., & Wenger, E. (1991): *Situated learning. Legitimate peripheral participation*. Cambridge University Press, Cambridge.

Nonaka, I., & Takeuchi, H. (1995): *The Knowledge Creating Company*. Oxford University Press, New York.

Snowdon, D., & Grasso, A. (2002): Diffusing Information in Organizational Settings: Learning from Experience. In *Proceedings of the Conference on Computer-Human Interaction (CHI) '02*, ACM Press, pp. 331-338.

Wellman, B. (1988): Networks as Personal Communities. In Wellman & Berkowitz (Eds.) *Social Structures: A Network Approach*. Cambridge University Press, New York, pp. 130-184.

Wenger, E. (2001): *Supporting communities of practice a survey of community-oriented technologies*. Report to the Council of CIOs of the US Federal Government.

Addresses

Alessandra Agostini
University of Milano, DICo
Via Comelico 39, Milano, 20135, Italy
Tel. +39 02 503 16307
Fax. +39 02 503 16373
agostini@dico.unimi.it

Layda Agosto-Franco
France Telecom R&D
2 avenue Pierre Marzin F-22307
Lannion Cedex, France
Tel. +33 2 96 05 94 04
Fax. +33 2 96 05 32 86

Tosin Aiyelokun
Donald Bren School of Information and Computer Sciences,
University of California, Irvine
444 Computer Science Building, Irvine, CA 92697-3425
Tel: +1 (949) 394-0094
Fax: +1(949) 824-1715
oaiyelok@ics.uci.edu

Sara Albolino
University of Milano - Bicocca
Via Bicocca degli Arcimboldi, 8
Milan, 20123, Italy
Tel. +390264487543
Fax. +390264487561
sara.albolino@unimib.it

J.H.Erik Andriessen
Delft University of Technology; Faculty of Technology, Policy and Management
Jaffalaan 5, 2628 BX Delft, the Netherlands
Tel: +31 15 278 3720
Fax: +31 15 278 2950
erika@tbm.tudelft.nl

Flore Barcellini
Eiffel Group INRIA
Domaine de Voluceau, Rocquencourt, BP 105, 78153 Le Chesnay, France
Tel: 33 1 39 63 52 55
Fax: 33 1 39 63 59 95
Flore.Barcellini@inria.fr

Jean-Marie Burkhardt
Université Paris 5 - Laboratoire d'Ergonomie Informatique
45 rue des Saints-Pères, 75270 Paris Cedex 06, France
Tel: 33 1 42 86 21 35
Fax: 33 1 42 96 18 58
Jean-Marie.Burkhardt@univ-paris5.fr

John M. Carroll
School of Information Sciences and Technology, Pennsylvania State University
University Park, Pennsylvania, 16802, USA
Tel: 1.814.863.2476
Fax: .814.865.6426
jmcarroll@psu.edu

Justine Cassell
Northwestern University, Technology and Social Behavior
Frances Searle Building Room 2-148,
2240 Campus Drive, Evanston, IL 60208, USA
Tel. 1-847-491-3534
justine@northwestern.edu

Matthew L. Cooper
Department of Computer Science
Virginia Polytechnic Institute & State University
2160 H Torgersen Hall, Blacksburg, VA 24061, USA
Tel: 1.865.310.7435
Fax: 1.865.966.5844
macooper@vt.edu

Roberto Dandi
Luiss Guido Carli – Scuola di Management
Via O. Tommasini 1, 00162 Roma (Italy)
Tel. +390686506555
Fax. + 390686506547
rdandi@luiss.it

Giorgio De Michelis
University of Milano - Bicocca, DISCo,
Building U7 - Room 468
Via Bicocca degli Arcimboldi 8, 20126 Milano, Italy
Tel: +39 02 6448 7825
Fax: +39 02 6448 7805
gdemich@disco.unimib.it

Flavio De Paoli
University of Milano - Bicocca, DISCo
Via Bicocca degli Arcimboldi 8, Milan, 20123, Italy
Tel: +39 02 6448 7836
Fax: +39 02 6448 7817
sara.albolino@unimib.it

Françoise Détienne
Eiffel Group INRIA,
Domaine de Voluceau, Rocquencourt, BP 105, 78153 Le Chesnay France
Tel: 33 1 39 63 55 22
Fax: 33 1 39 63 59 95
Francoise.Detienne@inria.fr

Vatcharaporn Esichaikul
Asian Institute of Technology, School of Advanced Technologies
Km 42 Phaholyothin Highway, Klong Luang, Pathumthani, 12120, Thailand
Tel: 66-2-5245713
Fax: 66-2-5245721
vatchara@ait.ac.th

Kim Ferriman
Northwestern University, ArticuLab
Frances Searle Building Room 2-154
2240 Campus Drive, Evanston, IL 60208, USA
Tel: 1-847-491-7471
kferriman@northwestern.edu

Jeremy Goecks
GVU Center, Georgia Institute of Technology
85 Fifth Street NW, Atlanta, GA 30332, USA
Tel: +1-404-385-1102
Fax: +1-404-894-3146
jeremy@cc.gatech.edu

Antonietta Grasso
Xerox Research Centre Europe
6, chemin de Maupertuis, Meylan, 38240, France
Tel: +33 (0)4 76 61 50 92
Fax: +33 (0)4 76 61 50 99
Antonietta.Grasso@xrce.xerox.com

Elke Hinrichs
Fraunhofer-FIT, Schloss Birlinghoven
Sankt Augustin 53754, Germany
Tel: +49 2241 14 2442 (Tel)
Fax: +49 2241 14 2084 (fax)
elke.hinrichs@fit.fraunhofer.de

Dr Andrea Howell,
Department of Management, Faculty of Business and Economics
Berwick Campus, Monash University
100 Clyde Road, Berwick, Australia, 3806
Tel: 61 3 99047105;
Fax: 61 3 99047130
andrea.howell@buseco.monash.edu.au

David A. Huffaker
Northwestern University
Media, Technology and Society, Frances Searle Building Room 2-147
2240 Campus Drive, Evanston, IL 60208, USA
Tel: 1-202-550-4559
d-huffaker@northwestern.edu

Eli Hustad
Department of Information Systems, Agder University College
Serviceboks 422, 4604 Kristiansand, Norway
Tel: +47 38141621
Fax: +47 38141061
Email: eli.hustad@hia.no

Philip L. Isenhour
Center for Human Computer Interaction, Virginia Tech
660 McBryde Hall, Blacksburg, VA 24061, USA
Tel: 1 540 2313121
Fax: 1 540 2316075
isenhour@vt.edu

Andrea Kavanaugh
Center for Human Computer Interaction, Department of Computer Science
Virginia Tech.
2160 H Torgersen Hall, Virginia Tech (0295), Blacksburg, VA 24061-0295, USA
Tel: 540 231-1806
Fax: 540 231-6075
kavan@vt.edu

Andrea Kienle
University of Dortmund
August Schmidt Str. 12, 44221 Dortmund, Germany
Tel: +49 231 755 5669
Fax: +49 231 755 2405
andrea.kienle@udo.edu

Valailak Komolrit
Asian Institute of Technology, School of Advanced Technologies
Km 42 Phaholyothin Highway, Klong Luang, Pathumthani, 12120, Thailand
Tel: 66-2-5245713
Fax: 66-2-5245721
vatchara@ait.ac.th

Prof. Dr. Helmut Krcmar
Technische Universität München, Chair for Information Systems
Boltzmannstrasse 3, D 85748 Garching bei München
Tel: +49-89-289-19530
Fax: +49-89-289-19533
krcmar@in.tum.de

Fredric Landqvist
Viktoria Institute
Hörselgången 4, 2nd floor, 417 56 Göteborg, Sweden
Tel: +46 (735) 06 0100
Fax: +46 (31) 772 8963
Email: fredric.landqvist@viktoria.se

Dr. Jan Marco Leimeister
Technische Universität München Wirtschaftsinformatik/ Information Systems
Boltzmannstr. 3, 85748 Garching b. München, Germany
Tel: +49 - 89 - 28 91 95 10
Fax: +49 - 89 - 28 91 95 33
leimeister@in.tum.de

Dr Sonia Liff
IROB, Warwick Business School, Warwick University
Coventry CV4 7AL, UK
Tel: +44-2476-522656
Fax: +44-2476-522646
Sonia.Liff@Warwick.ac.uk

William E. Loges
Department of Sociology, New Media Communications Program,
Oregon State University
218 Oak Creek Building, Corvallis, OR   97331, USA
Tel: 1+541-737-9855
Fax: 1+541-737-2434
bill.loges@oregonstate.edu

Gloria Mark
Department of Informatics, Donald Bren School of Information and Computer
Sciences, University of California, Irvine
444 Computer Science Building, Irvine, CA 92617
Tel: +1 (949) 824-5955
Fax: +1 (949) 824-1715
gmark@ics.uci.edu

Jean-Charles Marty
Laboratoire Systèmes Communicants, Université de Savoie
Campus Scientifique, 73376 Le Bourget du Lac cedex, France
Tel: +33 4 79 75 86 16
Fax: +33 4 79 75 86 90

Caterina Muzzi
Luiss Guido Carli – Scuola di Management
Via O. Tommasini 1, 00162 Roma, Italy
Tel: +390686506781
Fax: + 390686506547
cmuzzi@luiss.it

Elizabeth D. Mynatt
GVU Center, Georgia Institute of Technology
85 Fifth Street NW, Atlanta, GA 30332, USA
Tel: +1-404-385-1102
Fax: +1-404-894-3146
mynatt@cc.gatech.edu

Tadashi Nakano
Donald Bren School of Information and Computer Sciences
University of California, Irvine
444 Computer Science Building, Irvine, CA 92697-3425
Tel: +1 (949) 351-8655
Fax: +1 (949) 824-1715
tnakano@ics.uci.edu

Nail Oztas
Gazi University, IIBF (School of Economic and Administrative Sciences)
Kamu Yonetimi Bolumu (Department of Public Administration)
Ofis 404 (Office 404), Besevler , 06500 Ankara, Turkey
Tel. +90 312 2126859 X1055
Fax. +90 312 213 2036
noztas@gazi.edu.tr

Daniel Pargman
Media Technology Group, Dept. of Computer Science and Numerical Analysis,
Royal Institute of Technology (KTH) 100 44 Stockholm, Sweden
Tel.   +46 8 790 82 80
Fax. +46 791 87 93
pargman@nada.kth.se

Michel Plu
France Telecom R&D
2 avenue Pierre Marzin F-22307, Lannion Cedex, France
Tel: +33 2 96 05 36 98
Fax : +33 2 96 05 32 86
michel.plu@rd.francetelecom.com

Jenny Preece
College of Information Studies, University of Baltimore
4015E Hornbale Building, South Wing
College Park, Maryland, MD 20742, USA
Tel: 301 405 2035/2036
Fax: 301 314 9145
preece@umd.edu

Anabel Quan-Haase
Information and Media Studies/Sociology, Social Science Center,
University of Western Ontario,
London, ON, N6A 5C2 Canada
Tel: 1-519-661-2111 ext. 86952
Fax: 1-519-661-3200
aquan@uwo.ca

Warren Sack
University of California Santa Cruz, Film and Digital Media Department
1156 High Street, Santa Cruz, CA 95064, USA
Tel: 1 831 459-3204
wsack@ucsc.edu

Joseph Schmitz
Department of Communication, Western Illinois University
Memorial Hall 304, 1 University Circle, Macomb, IL, 61455, USA
Tel: 1.309.298.2370
Fax: 1.309.298.2369
js113@wiu.edu

Dong Hee Shin, Ph.D.
School of Information Sciences & Technology, Penn State University at Berks
Reading, PA 19610 USA
Tel: 610 396-6135
Fax: 610 396-6024
dxs75@psu.edu

Carla Simone
Dipartimento di Informatica, Sistemistica e Comunicazione – U7
Universita' di Milano Bicocca
Via Bicocca degli Arcimboldi 8, 20126 Milano, Italy
Tel: +39 02 6448 7821
Fax: +39 02 6448 7805
simone@disco.unimib.it

Jörgen Skågeby
Human Centered Systems Division,, Linköping University
S-58183 Linköping, Sweden
Tel.. +46 13 281965
Fax: +46 13 142231
jorgen.skageby@ida.liu.se

Gunnar Stevens
Institute for Information Systems, University of Siegen
Hölderlinstr 3, Siegen, 57068 Germany
Tel: + 49-271-740-3383,
Fax: + 49-271-740-3384
stevens@fb5.uni-siegen.de

Norman Makoto Su
Department of Informatics, Donald Bren School of Information and Computer
Sciences, University of California, Irvine
444 Computer Science Building, Irvine, CA 92697-3425
Tel: +1 (949) 266-4095
Fax: +1 (949) 824-1715
normsu@ics.uci.edu

Robin Teigland
Center for Competitiveness and Strategy, Stockholm School of Economics
Box 6501, 113 83 Stockholm, Sweden
Tel: +46 (8) 736 9000
Fax: +46 (8) 32 71 85
robin.teigland@hhs.se

Dr Mile Terziovski
Faculty of Economics and Commerce, Level 4, Babel Building,
The University of Melbourne, Parkville, Victoria 3010, Australia
Tel: 61 3 83447868
Fax: 61 3 83443714
milet@unimelb.edu.au

Dona Tversky
Stanford University
43 Pearce Mitchell Place, Stanford, CA 94305, USA
Tel: (650)325-7550
dtversky@stanford.edu

Peter Van den Besselaar
Amsterdam School of Communication Research & Royal Netherlands Academy
of Arts and Sciences
Kloveniersburgwal 45, 1012 CT Amsterdam, The Netherlands
Tel: + 3120 5253984
Fax: + 3120 4650015
p.a.a.vandenbesselaar@uva.nl

Michael Veith
Institute for Information Systems, University of Siegen
Hölderlinstr 3, Siegen, 57068 Germany
Tel +49-271-740-3383,
Fax: +49-271-740-3384
veith@fb5.uni-siegen.de

Murali Venkatesh, Ph.D.
Community & Information Technology Institute (CITI)
4-279 CST School of Information Studies
Syracuse University, Syracuse New York 13244 USA
Tel: 315 443-4477,
Fax: 315 443-5673
mvenkate@syr.edu

Laurence Vignollet
Laboratoire Systèmes Communicants, Université de Savoie
Campus Scientifique, 73376 Le Bourget du Lac Cedex, France
Tel. +33 4 79 75 88 47
Fax. +33 4 79 75 86 90
Laurence.Vignollet@univ-savoie.fr

Yang Wang
Department of Informatics, Donald Bren School of Information and Computer
Sciences, University of California, Irvine
444 Computer Science Building, Irvine, CA 92697-3425
Tel: +1 949 856-0215
Fax: +1 949 824-4056
Yangwang@ics.uci.edu

Christopher Weare
Research Associate Professor
School of Policy, Planning, and Development
University of Southern California
650 Childs Way, Los Angeles, CA 90089-0626, USA
Tel: 1 213-740-4680
Fax: 1 213-740-0001
weare@usc.edu

Martin Wessner
Fraunhofer IPSI
Dolivostrasse 15, Darmstadt, 64293, Germany
Tel: +49 6151 869-954
Fax: +49 6151 869-963
martin.wessner@ipsi.fraunhofer.de

Barry Wellman
NetLab, Centre for Urban & Community Studies, University of Toronto
455 Spadina Avenue, Toronto Canada M5S 2G8
Fax: +1-416-978-7162
wellman@chass.utoronto.ca
http://www.chass.utoronto.ca/~wellman

Volker Wulf
Institute for Information Systems, University of Siegen, Germany
& Fraunhofer FIT, Sankt Augustin, Germany
Hölderlinstr 3, Siegen, 57068 Germany
Tel: +49-271-740-3383,
Fax: +49-271-740-3384
wulf@fb5.uni-siegen.de